Foundations of Physical Education and Sport

13th Edition

Foundations of Physical Education and Sport

13th Edition

Deborah A. Wuest
Ithaca College

Charles A. Bucher

WCB
McGraw-Hill

Boston   Burr Ridge, IL   Dubuque, IA   Madison, WI   New York   San Francisco   St. Louis
Bangkok   Bogatà   Caracas   Lisbon   London   Madrid
Mexico City   Milan   New Delhi   Seoul   Singapore   Sydney   Taipei   Toronto

WCB/McGraw-Hill

A Division of The McGraw·Hill Companies

FOUNDATIONS OF PHYSICAL EDUCATION AND SPORT, THIRTEENTH EDITION

This book is printed on acid-free paper.

1 2 3 4 5 6 7 8 9 0 QPF/QPF 9 3 2 1 0 9 8

ISBN 0–07–092138–5

Publisher: *Edward E. Bartell*
Executive editor: *Vicki Malinee*
Senior developmental editor: *Melissa Martin*
Senior marketing manager: *Pamela S. Cooper*
Project manager: *Renee C. Russian*
Production supervisor: *Laura Fuller*
Designer: *Kiera M. Cunningham*
Senior photo research coordinator: *Lori Hancock*
Supplement coordinator: *Tammy Juran*
Compositor: *ElectraGraphics, Inc.*
Typeface: *10/12 Galliard*
Printer: *Quebecor Printing Book Group/Fairfield, PA*

Three girls/tennis: © *Arthur Tilley/FPG International LLC*
Golf couple: © *Dick Luria/FPG International LLC*
All other cover photos: © *Photodisc*

The credits section for this book begins on page 515 and is considered
an extension of the copyright page.

Library of Congress Cataloging-in-Publication Data

Wuest, Deborah A.
    Foundations of physical education and sport / Deborah A. Wuest,
Charles A. Bucher. — 13th ed.
      p.   cm.
    Includes bibliographical references and index.
    ISBN 0–07–092138–5
    1. Physical education and training.   2. Sports.   3. Physical
education and training—Vocational guidance.   4. Sports—Vocational
guidance.   I. Bucher, Charles Augustus, 1912–   .   II. Title.
GV341.W85   1999
796'.07—dc21   98–37665
                                    CIP

www.mhhe.com

Contents in Brief

Contents

CHAPTER 6   Biomechanical Foundations of Physical Education and Sport   194

CHAPTER 7   Exercise Physiology and Fitness   219

CHAPTER 11   Teaching and Coaching Careers in Physical Education and Sport   387

CHAPTER 12   Fitness- and Health-Related Careers in Physical Education and Sport   425

CHAPTER 13   Sport Careers in Management, Media, Performance, and Other Areas   447

PREFACE

The thirteenth edition of *Foundations of Physical Education and Sport* is designed to provide a comprehensive, contemporary text for introductory and foundations courses in physical education and sport. During the past 25 years the knowledge base of physical education and sport has increased tremendously, both in depth and breadth. The dedication of scholars and increasingly sophisticated research techniques have contributed to this expansion. The growth of this knowledge base is reflected in further development of the specialized areas of study, the subdisciplines of physical education and sport.

Career opportunities have grown dramatically as well. Increased opportunities are available for individuals desiring to teach and coach in nonschool settings, such as community-based programs, senior citizen centers, and corporations. Teachers and coaches increasingly work with people of all abilities and ages. Nonteaching and noncoaching careers have grown in availability, and many prospective physical educators and sport leaders aspire to careers in fitness, exercise science, sport management, athletic training, and sports communication.

This text encourages students from the beginning of their career to contribute to the field of physical education and sport and be active participants in shaping the nature of this dynamic field. Students are challenged to fully develop themselves as professionals and make a commitment to excellence. As young leaders entering the field, they will work collaboratively with other dedicated professionals to address the issues facing us and confront the challenges that lie ahead.

CHANGES IN THE THIRTEENTH EDITION

The thirteenth edition has been revised to reflect the current status of the field as well as emerging developments in physical education and sport. This edition retains a strong emphasis on the foundations of physical education and sport. In addition, the subdisciplines of physical education and sport are rapidly growing, and this edition reflects the latest thinking and research that form the foundations of this dynamic field.

This revision strengthens the previous editions' emphasis on preparing for a career in physical education and sport and recognizing diverse opportunities in the field. It calls on readers to pursue excellence, display a high level of professionalism, and take an active role in resolving problems that confront the field.

This edition of *Foundations of Physical Education and Sport* has been extensively revised to reflect the continuing growth and diversification of the field. Included in this edition is the latest information on the following important topics:

- The landmark document *Physical Activity and Health: A Report of the Surgeon General*
- The Centers for Disease Control and Prevention (CDC) guidelines for schools and communities to promote physically active lifestyles among children and youth
- Influence of physical activity and sport on the lives of girls
- The *Healthy People 2000* midcourse review and the upcoming *Healthy People 2010* document

♦ The National Association for Sport and Physical Education (NASPE) standards for physical education, beginning teachers, and coaches

♦ Understanding changing demographics, working with diverse population groups, and meeting the needs of all people, including those with disabilities

♦ Critical issues confronting physical education and sport, such as creating opportunities for diverse populations and advocacy on behalf of our programs

♦ Technology, including addresses for listservs and Web sites, self-assessment activities based on chapter topics and information available on the Internet

♦ Career preparation, including the development of transferable skills and a four-year timetable for professional preparation

♦ Activism and the importance of professionals addressing inequities in physical activity and sport opportunities

This textbook challenges the reader to play a significant role in shaping the future of our dynamic field.

Organization

The 15 chapters that compose the text have been grouped into four parts. Part One provides the student with an orientation to physical education and sport. Chapter 1 introduces the student to the field of physical education and sport, defines physical education and sport, clarifies terminology that will be used throughout the text, discusses various philosophies, and provides information on how to develop a personal philosophy of physical education and sport. In Chapter 2, the objectives of physical education and sport programs are identified and the assessment of objectives is presented. Chapter 3 examines the role of physical education and sport in society and in education as well as the educational reform, fitness, and wellness movements. Part One concludes with Chapter 4, which presents information about the nature of human movement—the keystone of physical education and sport.

In Part Two, the historical and scientific foundations of physical education and sport are pre-

sented in five chapters. The historical foundations of physical education and sport are covered in Chapter 5. The development of physical education and sport from early cultures to today is traced. The biomechanical, physiological, sociological, and psychological foundations are reviewed in Chapters 6, 7, 8, and 9, respectively. These chapters present students with information about the development of the subdiscipline, questions that are typically addressed by researchers within the field, key concepts, and current areas of study.

Part Three, which consists of four chapters, addresses professional considerations, such as career opportunities within the field, preparation for a career in physical education and sport, and professional responsibilities. Chapter 10 has been expanded to include professional development. The chapter includes material presented in Chapter 14 of the previous edition. The topics of professional responsibilities, leadership development, and professional organizations are now included in Chapter 10. Chapters 11, 12, and 13 offer more in-depth information about specific career opportunities in physical education and sport, including the responsibilities associated with each career, advantages and disadvantages of specific career choices, and specific strategies to enhance professional marketability relative to these chosen careers. Chapter 11 describes teaching and coaching careers and how opportunities for these careers have broadened from the school setting and school-aged population to nonschool settings and to include persons of all abilities and ages. In Chapter 12, the many new employment opportunities in fitness and health-related careers are examined. Careers in sport management, sport communication, performance, and other sport-related careers such as officiating are described as well as information on the growing field of sport entrepreneurship in Chapter 13.

Part Four explores issues and challenges confronting professionals today and looks at the future of physical education and sport. Chapter 14 addresses timely issues in physical education and sport. Five issues are examined: the role of the physical educator in the consumer education movement, the promotion of values, the role of physical education and sport professionals in youth sports, the growing discipline and the debate over its name, and the gap between research and practice. Four of the challenges facing professionals are making quality daily physical education in the schools a reality, conducting effective public relations programs, attaining the health objectives for the year 2000, and promoting lifespan involvement in physical education and sport for all people. The final chapter, Chapter 15, examines the future of physical education and sport. Societal trends are analyzed in light of current developments. To prepare for the future, professionals must be willing to assume the responsibility for the leadership of our field and work to improve the manner in which we provide services to people of all ages.

PEDAGOGICAL FEATURES

To facilitate use by instructors and students, several pedagogical aids have been incorporated into this textbook. These aids include the following:

Instructional Objectives. At the beginning of each chapter the instructional objectives and competencies to be achieved by the student are listed. This identifies for the student the points that will be highlighted in the chapter. Attainment of the objectives indicates the fulfillment of the chapter's intent.

Introductory Paragraphs. A short introduction is provided for each chapter. This serves to provide students with a transition from previously presented material to the material to be presented within the chapter.

Summaries. Each chapter ends with a brief review of the material covered, assisting the student in understanding and retaining the most salient points.

Self-Assessment Tests. Self-assessment tests and activities are presented at the end of each chapter to enable students to check their comprehension of the chapter material.

References. Each chapter provides up-to-date references to allow students to gain further information about the subjects discussed within the chapter.

Suggested Readings. Additional and easily accessible resources from current literature that relate to the chapter topic have been selected and **annotated.** These readings offer students the opportunity to further broaden their knowledge and understanding of various subjects.

Internet Resources. Each chapter begins with a *Getting Connected* feature, which lists Internet sites that provide up-to-date information about relevant topics. The self-assessment exercises have been revised to include activities that draw on these Internet resources.

Photographs. Numerous photographs, many new, have been used throughout the text to enhance the presentation of material and to illustrate key points.

INSTRUCTOR'S MANUAL

The *Instructor's Manual* provides the instructor with additional material to facilitate the use of this text. The *Instructor's Manual* includes the following features for each chapter.

Chapter Overview. The chapter overview presents the salient points covered in the chapter.

Test Items. Subjective test questions and a variety of objective test items are given, including multiple choice, true/false, completion, and matching.

Suggested Activities. Suggested in-class student activities as well as outside assignments are presented.

Case Studies. Case studies in each chapter give students practical opportunities to apply the material presented.

Internet-based Activities. Activities using the Internet, including the resources identified in the *Getting Connected* feature, are provided for small groups and for the class.

Powerpoint Presentations. To assist in presenting key concepts of each chapter, a powerpoint presentation was developed. This can be used to create overheads, to generate slides, and/or to export and post to the World Wide Web.

Foundations of Physical Education and Sport has been written in a style that students find readable and that provides them with important insights into the foundations and the roles of physical education and sport in the world today. Students will find substantial information about the career and professional opportunities that exist for knowledgeable, dedicated, and well-prepared physical educators.

ACKNOWLEDGMENTS

My thanks are gratefully extended to the publisher's reviewers for their insightful comments and critical suggestions, which helped greatly in the revision of this book. They include the following: Karen McNew Thomas, Texas Woman's University; Sharon L. Van Oteghen, University of Memphis; Jim L. Wasem, Eastern Washington University; and Doris L. Watson, University of Utah.

I would like to extend a special recognition to the outstanding professionals at McGraw-Hill, especially my editor, Melissa Martin. Their professional expertise and guidance were invaluable in completing this revision.

I extend most heartfelt thanks to my friends and colleagues, who helped in many ways in the revision of this book. I especially appreciate the help of Sarah Rich for her assistance with photography and editing, and of Vic Mancini for his continued support.

This book is dedicated to my daughter, Meriber Carola DeVida Wuest, who likes "gym" because "you have fun and when you run hard, water comes running down your face." This book is also dedicated to my late-night writing companion, my loyal cat, Abby.

PART ONE

Nature and Scope
of Physical Education
and Sport

Introduction

Part One introduces the reader to the field of physical education and sport. The four chapters in Part One present in a logical manner a definition of physical education and sport and specialized areas within this realm, the influence of various philosophies on physical education and sport programs, the objectives of physical education and sport, the role of physical education and sport in society and in education, and the keystone—movement. Part One provides the foundational information needed to understand the nature and scope of physical education and sport, the role of sport in today's world, and the contribution that persons involved in physical education and sport can make to society. Physical education and sport is a growing and expanding field. The growth of physical education and sport is reflected in the enlargement of the knowledge base and the development of specialized areas of study. The expansion of physical education and sport has created a diversity of career options for professionals in this field.

Meaning and Philosophy of Physical Education and Sport

Instructional Objectives and Competencies to be Achieved:

After reading this chapter the student should be able to—

◆ Discuss the nature of contemporary physical education and sport and show how it has evolved during the past four decades.

◆ Define the following specialized areas of study within the discipline of physical education and sport: sport philosophy, sport history, sport sociology, sport psychology, motor development, motor learning, biomechanics, exercise physiology, sports medicine, sport pedagogy, adapted physical activity, and sport management.

◆ Clarify the relationship between the discipline and the profession of physical education and sport.

◆ Explain the relationship of physical education and sport to allied fields of study.

◆ Discuss key concepts of philosophy and their application to physical education and sport.

◆ Develop a personal philosophy of physical education and sport.

This is one of the most exciting, dynamic periods in the history of physical education and sport. Unfolding before us is the vision of lifespan involvement in physical activity for all people. It is a powerful vision, one that is compelling for professionals who choose to embrace it and extraordinary in its potential to affect the lives of people of all ages.

The scope and focus of physical education and sport have changed tremendously during the past four decades. Traditionally, our programs focused on providing services for children and youth in the school setting. Today our scope is much broader, our settings more diverse, and our influence on participants' lives greater. This greater involvement and changing focus are evident from the descriptions below of participants in our programs.

The crowd cheers as the player dribbles down the court toward the basket. With the score tied and only seconds to go on the clock, the player fakes left, drives around the opponent, and lays the ball up on the rim. Score! The buzzer sounds, ending the game. The crowd

GETTING CONNECTED

Listservs are on-line discussion groups focused on a specific topic area. When you subscribe to a listserv, you receive messages posted by other members of the group and you can post information to the group. Listservs provide a wonderful opportunity to exchange ideas, discuss problems, and explore solutions with professionals worldwide.

To subscribe, send an e-mail message to the **Listserv host address.** Leave the subject line blank. In the body of the message include the subscription request (usually the word "subscribe"), the **List name,** and your name. By return mail you will receive a confirmation message with specific information on how to post to the group, set a digest option (consolidate e-mail messages into one post), and unsubscribe. For example, if you wanted to subscribe to the athletic training listserv, you would send an e-mail message as follows, where Listserv@listserv.net is the host name, athtrn-L is the list name, and Dana Smith is your name. *Important! Leave the subject line blank.*

```
To:      listserv@listserv.net
Cc:
Attachment:
Subject:
----------------- Message Text -----------------
subscribe athtrn-L Dana Smith
```

Focus of List	Listserv Host Address *Send e-mail message to subscribe to this address*	Message & List Name *Include the list name in the message text*
Athletic Training	listserv@listserv.net	subscribe athtrn-L FirstName LastName
Biomechanics	listserv@listserv.net	subscribe biomch-L FirstName LastName
Fitness	listserv@listserv.net	subscribe fit-L FirstName LastName
International Sport & Physical Education	listserv@listserv.net	subscribe iscpes FirstName LastName
Sport History	listserv@listserv.net	subscribe sporthist FirstName LastName
Sport Injuries	listserv@listserv.net	subscribe sptsinj-L FirstName LastName
Sport Law	listserv@listserv.net	subscribe sportlaw FirstName LastName
Sport Management	listserv@listserv.net	subscribe sportmgt FirstName LastName
Sports Medicine	mailbase@mailbase.ac.uk	join sport-med FirstName LastName
Sport Sociology	listserv@listserv.net	subscribe sportsoc FirstName LastName
Sport Psychology	listserv@listserv.net	subscribe sportpsy FirstName LastName
Sport for Persons with Disabilities	listserv@listserv.net	subscribe D-sport FirstName LastName
Sport Science	majordomo@stonebow.otago.ac.nz	subscribe SPORTSCI FirstName LastName
Physical Education Teaching K–12	http://pe.central.vt.edu	Follow prompts to subscribe
Physical Education Teaching PE-TALK	http://www.sportime.com/pe-talk/	Follow prompts to subscribe

cheers, acknowledging the great performance of both teams, as the women walk off the court. Sports are not just for boys and men anymore!

Giving one final push, he raises his arms in triumph as he leans toward the finish line of the Boston Marathon—the first wheelchair racer to finish. Working closely with the athletic trainer after his shoulder surgery had brought him back to his pre-injury competitive level. The hard training was really worth it. Few things are more satisfying than winning a hard-fought race.

She practices her somersaults and then works on the balance beam. When the music begins, she joins her group at the mat. As the instructor presents different movement challenges, she responds eagerly, enjoying the chance to be creative and try new things. After the lesson is completed, the toddler runs across the gym to her mother. Although it is expensive, her mother thinks the Kidnastics preschool program is a wonderful contribution to her daughter's development.

He hustles out of the locker room, looking forward to his workout. Following warm-ups, he completes his weight-training program. After cooling down, he changes clothes and goes back to his office to finish the project that is due tomorrow. He makes a note on his desk calendar to attend the nutrition seminar tomorrow offered by the fitness center staff. The comprehensive employee fitness program is a great company benefit.

She mounts the medal stand—she has won the silver medal for the 100-meter freestyle swimming event at the state games. Not bad for a 76-year-old grandmother, she thinks to herself as her grandchildren and teammates cheer! This is the healthiest she has felt in years, and she enjoys the new friends she has made in the program.

They work carefully, using the skinfold calipers to take each other's measurements at selected sites on their bodies. After entering the measurements into the computer, the data analysis program produces a profile of their body composition. In another area of the gym, their peers engage in step aerobics, using heart-rate monitors to keep track of their work intensity. In the weight area, students work on their individualized training programs. High school physical education is changing!

The patient stands quietly as the electrodes are attached. The cardiac rehabilitation specialist checks his heart rate on the ECG monitor. He is nervous about starting to exercise so soon after his heart attack. After the specialist reassures him that everything looks fine, he begins his warm-up exercises. The other members of the group, all post-heart attack patients themselves, make him feel welcome with their positive comments and enthusiasm as they exercise beside him. He begins to feel better already.

Getting the family to eat dinner together is difficult. Someone is always rushing off to practice. Tonight it is Mom's turn to hurry off to volleyball practice at the school gymnasium. An active participant in the community sports program, Mom plays soccer in the fall and volleyball in the winter. She looks forward to learning to play golf in the spring; the instructors appreciate the enthusiasm of the adults who want to learn new sports to enjoy in their leisure time.

• • •

Welcome to contemporary physical education and sport. Yes, this is physical education and sport today! Dramatic changes in the field have occurred within the past four decades. Traditionally, physical education and sport programs focused on providing services to school-aged populations in the school setting. Today, physical education and sport has expanded to include persons of all ages and abilities. Programs are offered in many different venues and encompass the school, community, worksite, home, hospitals and clinics, and private or commercial enterprises. Involvement in carefully designed programs can enhance the health and quality of life of the participants.

Athletic opportunities for girls and women have increased since Title IX was passed in 1972.

Instructional opportunities have expanded to community centers. Parents guided by an aquatic specialist help their young children learn to swim.

Since the 1960s the knowledge base of physical education and sport has grown rapidly. The growth of the discipline of physical education and sport has led to the development of specialized areas of study. A myriad of career opportunities has emerged for professionals in the field. The traditional career of teaching and coaching has expanded to new settings. Careers in athletic training, cardiac rehabilitation, fitness, sport management, and sport media, just to name a few, are now popular.

A professional entering the field needs a sound philosophy of physical education and sport. Philosophy guides one's actions, improves professional practice, and assists in explaining the value and contributions of physical education and sport to individuals' lives and society. Traditional philosophies include idealism, realism, pragmatism, naturalism, and existentialism. Modern educational philosophy, with its emphasis on the development of the whole person, has influenced the field of physical education and sport. The development of a well-conceived philosophy of physical education and sport is an important task for every professional in the field.

This chapter introduces the study of physical education and sport. Physical education and sport is defined, the expanding dimensions of the field are explored, and its relationship to the allied fields of health, recreation, and dance is discussed. The importance of a philosophy is emphasized, various philosophies are reviewed, and guidelines for the development of a professional philosophy are presented.

INTRODUCTION TO THE STUDY OF PHYSICAL EDUCATION AND SPORT

The proliferation of physical education and sport programs during the last four decades has been remarkable. Our programs have expanded from the traditional school setting to community, home, worksite, commercial, and medical settings. School-community partnerships bring sport instruction and fitness programs to adults in the community and offer increased opportunities for youth involvement. Community recreation programs offer a great variety of instruction and sport activities for people of all ages and abilities. Personal trainers work with clients in their homes. Adults seeking the convenience of working out at home boosted the sales of home exercise equipment to $2.6 billion a year.[1] Corporations offer

employees comprehensive health promotion programs, encompassing fitness classes, cardiac rehabilitation, nutritional counseling, smoking cessation, and occupational safety. Fitness and health
clubs enroll millions of members who take advantage of aerobic dance classes, resistance training,
and life-enrichment classes such as yoga. Tennis,
golf, gymnastics, and karate clubs offer instruction
to customers, both young and old. Movement
programs span the ages, involving everyone from
preschoolers to adults to the aged at senior citizen
centers. Hospitals sponsor cardiac rehabilitation
programs and increasingly offer fitness programs
to community members. Sports medicine clinics
treat injured sport and fitness participants. Walkers
move briskly through the neighborhood, intent
on meeting the daily requirement of including 30
minutes of moderate physical activity in their lives.
Joggers, bikers, skaters, and swimmers join the
millions who have made daily physical activity an
integral part of their lives.

People of all ages are seeking out sport opportunities in many different settings. Youth sports
involve more than 25 million children a year. Millions participate in interscholastic and intercollegiate athletics. Sport events such as the New York
State Empire State Games, A.A.U. Basketball, Senior Games, the Boston Marathon, and master's
swimming competitions involve millions of adults
in sport competitions. Community recreational
leagues for basketball, softball, soccer, and volleyball provide increased opportunities for participation. Sports such as the Super Bowl, the Olympics,
the World Cup, and the National Collegiate Athletic Association basketball tournament capture
the enthusiasm of millions of spectators. Girls and
women are participating in sports and physical activities in record numbers.

School physical education programs focus on
promotion of lifespan involvement in physical activity. Students learn the skills, understandings,
and attitudes that will enable them to participate
in various physical activities throughout their lives.
Elementary school physical education programs
focus on helping children attain competency in
the fundamental motor skills (e.g., throwing and
catching) and movement concepts (e.g., balance)

that form the foundation for later development
of specialized games, sport, fitness, and dance activities (see Chapter 4). As children progress
through school, skill and fitness development is
accompanied by an increased knowledge and understanding of physical activity. High schools offer
students the opportunity to choose from several
different activities for their physical education program. Some instruction may take place in the
community, increasing the range of activities that
can be offered to students and encouraging students to use the community facilities during their
leisure time. Courses in anatomy, exercise physiology, and athletic training may be included in the
curriculum, further developing students' understanding and appreciation of physical activity. Intramural competitions afford students of all skill
levels the opportunity to compete against their
classmates. Interscholastic athletics offer highly
skilled boys and girls the chance to compete
against students from other schools.

At the collegiate level, young adults enroll in
courses in martial arts or tennis, work out at fitness centers, join aerobic dance classes, and take
part in recreational sports programs. Intercollegiate athletic programs for men and women continue to expand, involving more participants and
attracting greater interest from the public.

Several factors have contributed to this unprecedented involvement in physical activity and sport.
The growing societal emphasis on wellness encouraged greater involvement in physical activity
and increased interest in well-being. Eating right,
being active, managing stress, maintaining healthy
relationships, and reducing health risk factors are
among the basic tenets of wellness. Wellness
stresses personal responsibility for one's health and
active involvement in achieving and maintaining
an optimal state of well-being.

Our public health goals emphasize health promotion and disease prevention, rather than remediation of disease. This public health policy recognizes that many diseases can be prevented by
individuals' taking a proactive approach to their
health, that is, adopting lifestyles and making decisions that enhance their well-being and reduce risk
factors for disease. The 1979 report *Healthy Peo-*

People of all ages enjoy athletic competition.

ple[2] and the 1980 report *Promoting Health/Preventing Disease: Objectives for the Nation*[3] established broad national health goals and specific objectives to achieve them. Exercise and fitness was identified as one of 15 priority areas in which changes in the habits of people would have a positive influence on their health and, subsequently, the health of the nation. The publication of *Healthy People 2000*[4] in 1990 and the 1996 publication of *Physical Activity and Health: A Report of the Surgeon General*[5] presented overwhelming evidence on the role of physical activity in preventing disease and its health benefits. The primary thrust of the *Physical Activity and Health* report is that persons of all ages can greatly improve their health and quality of life by developing a lifelong habit of including moderate amounts of physical activity in their daily lives. Further, increased health benefits can be gained with increases in the intensity and duration of activity.[5] Collectively, these national health reports substantiate the need for well-trained physical educators and sport leaders to provide quality programs to serve individuals of all ages and needs.

Although an unprecedented number of people are involved in physical activity and it is common knowledge that physical activity is beneficial, more than 60% of adults are not regularly active, and 25% of adults are not active at all.[5] Socioeconomic status, race, gender, and age influence physical activity patterns. Many of those who are inactive are economically disadvantaged, minorities, women, older adults, and individuals with disabilities.[5] Their limited opportunities for physical activity adversely affect their health, lifespan, and quality of life. As professionals, we must make a greater commitment to reach out to these groups and involve them in our programs.

Helping individuals develop a belief that physical activity is beneficial to them should begin at an early age. School physical education programs are the primary avenue for achieving an active lifestyle. Their potential to contribute to health goals is enormous, and, in some schools, physical education is regarded as an integral component of a comprehensive school health program. These programs, which reach millions of children and youth, can help them develop skills, understandings, and habits for a healthy lifestyle. Health policy reports call for daily, high-quality physical education for all students K–12.[3,4] Unfortunately, the number of children participating in daily physical education is declining. Daily participation in physical education by high school students decreased from 42% in 1991 to 25% in 1995.[5] Physical education programs in the school have been criticized for declining student fitness levels, for failure to teach sport skills for lifetime participation, and for poor quality. These criticisms are serious and must be addressed by professionals. School physical education programs also face constraints due to budgetary problems; austerity budgets frequently lead to reduction in physical education and sport offerings. Additionally, as schools respond to pressure for educational reform by restructuring the curriculum to devote more time to academics, the time allocated to physical education is decreased.

The expansion of physical education and sport programs to new settings and an effort to serve people of all ages have created a wide array of career opportunities for persons interested in this exciting field. Employment opportunities range from the traditional career in teaching and coaching to activity-related careers in community and commercial facilities. "Nontraditional" careers in cardiac rehabilitation, athletic training, fitness, worksite health promotion, sport marketing, sport management, and sport communication are growing in popularity.

The scientific basis of physical education and sport has expanded dramatically since the 1960s. Academicians involved in research activities enlarged our body of knowledge, the theoretical framework of the field. As our scope of knowledge broadened, specialized areas of study such as exercise physiology, sport sociology, and sport psychology emerged. Colleges and universities developed new programs to prepare professionals for careers in these specialized fields of study, such as fitness and cardiac rehabilitation and sport management.

The expansion of the knowledge base of physical education and sport has strengthened our foundation for professional practice. As a professional, no matter what your career aspirations, you must be highly knowledgeable about our field and aware of its tremendous worth and substance. As you mature as a professional, it is hoped that you will achieve a greater understanding and appreciation of the role of physical education and sport in our changing society and the potential we have to positively affect the health and lives of all people.

As you begin your professional career, remember that your future is in your hands. In 1983, as pressure for educational reform mounted, the National Commission on Excellence in Education released a report entitled *A Nation at Risk: The Imperative for Education Reform*.[6] The report decried the rising tide of mediocrity in the nation's schools. The poor quality of education threatened the strength of our nation. Although the report was directed at public education, the writers' advice to students is particularly applicable to persons beginning their studies within our important field. The writers stated that it is the student's responsibility to put forth a "first-rate effort." They continue:

You forfeit your chance for life at the fullest when you withhold your best effort in learning. When you give only the minimum to learning, you receive only the minimum in return . . . in the end it is your work that determines how much and how well you learn.[6]

Dedicate yourself to excellence at the onset of your career. Make a commitment to service and to providing opportunities for all people—regardless of socioeconomic status, race, gender, age, or ability—to participate in lifespan physical activity.

Physical Education and Sport Defined

Historically, physical education programs focused on teaching children and youths in the school setting. The expansion of physical education beyond its traditional realm to nonschool settings and people of all ages requires a more inclusive definition to encompass the diversity of programs and the wide range of goals achieved by participants.

Siedentop asserts that "there is probably less agreement today on the basic meaning of physical education than there has been at any time in our professional history."[7] However, he states that the mostly widely accepted meaning for physical education is based on the developmental model.[7] This model is based on the belief that all school subjects, including physical education, should contribute to the development of the whole child. Carefully structured physical activity is recognized as a means through which educational goals can be achieved.

Ziegler, in discussing the increasingly specialized and diverse nature of the field, argues that "developmental physical activity—that is, some sort of planned physical activity in sport, exercise and related expressive movement"[8]—is our common focus. As professionals, we are working to promote "developmental physical activity for people of all ages,"[8] abilities, and needs. Ziegler states "we have a 'womb to tomb' responsibility for the developmental physical activity for all citizens throughout their lives."[8]

To encompass the rapidly changing and ever-expanding scope of the field, *physical education* is defined as an educational process that uses physical activity as a means to help individuals acquire skills, fitness, knowledge, and attitudes that contribute to their optimal development and well-being. In this definition, the term *education* is broadly defined as the ongoing process of learning that occurs throughout our lifespan. This definition recognizes that education, just like physical

An adult with a mental disability learns basic movement concepts with the guidance of his teacher.

education, can and does take place in a variety of settings and is not limited to a specific age group. Home schooling, continuing education through professional organizations, in-service education, distance learning, adult education, and preschools are just some of the expanded settings for education. Teachers today may be described by various labels such as "instructors," "leaders," or "facilitators." Today's students are people of all ages, spanning the range from the very young attending a preschool to the elderly taking courses at a university.

Physical education uses physical activity to enhance the development of the whole person. Physical education includes the acquisition and refinement of motor skills, the development and maintenance of fitness for optimal health and well-being, the attainment of knowledge about physical activities and exercise, and the fostering of positive attitudes conducive to lifelong learning and life-span participation. Physical education is concerned with the promotion of active lifestyles for people of all ages and abilities. A physical education program under qualified leadership enriches participants' lives.

To more fully understand physical education, its relationship to play, games, and sport must be examined. Physical education, play, games, and sport are different entities, although they may share some common elements. *Play* refers to activities engaged in freely for amusement. Play is spontaneous, and the act of playing is rewarding in itself. Play emphasizes the joy of participation. Derived from play, *games* are contests in which the outcome is determined by strategy, skill, or chance.[7] *Sports* are organized, competitive physical activities governed by rules. Rules standardize the competition and conditions so that individuals can compete fairly. Sports provide meaningful opportunities to demonstrate one's competence and to challenge one's limits. Competition can occur against an opponent or oneself. Sports can also be viewed as games that emphasize physical involvement and where strategy and skill play a significant role in the determination of the outcome.[7] People engage in sports for enjoyment, personal satisfaction,

Children with disabilities must have access to sport competition.

and the opportunity to attain victory or obtain rewards. When sport is highly developed, governing bodies regulate sport and oversee its management. At this level, coaches play a significant part, athletes are highly skilled, specially trained officials ensure the fairness of the competition, records are kept, events are promoted through the media, and spectators assume an important role. Derived from

sport, *athletics* are highly organized, competitive sports engaged in by skillful participants.

Sport occupies a prominent position in our culture. Sport is tremendous in its scope. Sport participants number in the millions. Participants' involvement encompasses recreational to professional levels. Participants vary in age, ranging from the very young to the aged. Their involvement ex-

Sport competition in which highly skilled people participate is called athletics.

tends from youth sports to master's competitions. Interscholastic, intercollegiate, and professional athletics involve millions more participants. Spectating is a popular leisure pastime, attracting millions. Media coverage of sport is extensive, drawing millions of viewers and readers. Expenditures for sports-related activities and sports equipment exceed $60 billion annually.[1] As sport has grown, so have opportunities for individuals who want to work in sports-related areas. Athletic trainers, sport managers, sports promoters, equipment developers, sports sales personnel, strength and conditioning specialists, sport psychologists, coaches, and officials are just some of the many professionals involved in the sport enterprise.

Since the early 1970s, there has been an enormous interest in the scholarly study of sport. Its significant role in our society, its massive impact on our culture, and its far-reaching involvement of millions as participants and spectators has drawn the attention of scholars. Scholars have studied the philosophical, sociological, and psychological dimensions of the sport experience.

The realm of physical education and sport today embraces many different programs, diverse settings, and people of all ages. This recent growth of physical education and sport has been accompanied by an increased interest in its scholarly study. This research has led to the development of specialized areas of knowledge. The subsequent increase in the breadth and depth of knowledge provides a foundation for professional practice. The expansion of physical education and sport has led to a tremendous growth of career opportunities for enthusiastic and committed professionals.

Physical Education and Sport: The Field

Corbin[10] defines a field as a "combination of a well-established discipline and one or more professions that deliver a social service" and are "focused on common goals." Disciplinarians engage in research and scholarly endeavors to advance this knowledge base. This knowledge serves as a foundation for the professionals who deliver services to people.[10] Professionals use this knowledge and their skills to design and deliver programs to meet the unique and changing needs of the people they serve. The relationship of the academic discipline to the profession is shown Figure 1-1. As we continue to grow and become increasingly specialized, we must keep sight of our common focus on physical activity. Both the professional and disciplinary dimensions of our field enrich our understanding and ability to promote lifespan involvement in regular physical activity for all people.

The profession

Physical education and sport can be described with reference to its status as a profession. A *profession* is an occupation requiring specialized training in an intellectual field of study that is dedicated to the betterment of society through service to others. Professionals provide services to others

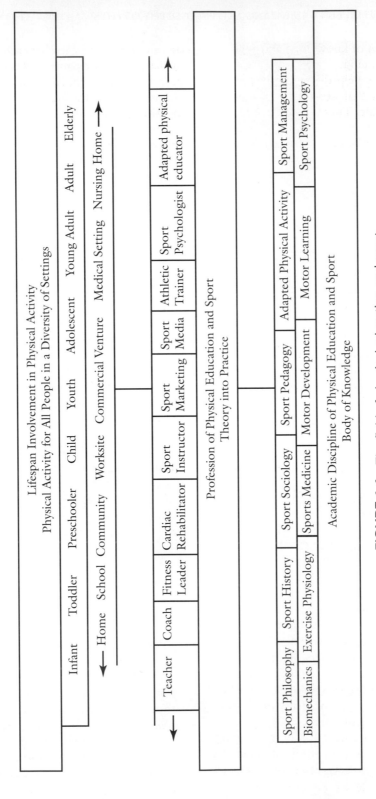

FIGURE 1-1 The field of physical education and sport.

through the application of knowledge and skills to improve people's well-being.

Several characteristics help distinguish a profession from occupations that are not a profession, such as a trade or a craft. These characteristics include:

- ◆ an organized and continually expanding body of knowledge that forms the theoretical foundation for practice.
- ◆ educational preparation that includes an extensive course of study focusing on the acquisition of knowledge, development of specialized skills, and attainment of needed competencies.
- ◆ criteria for entry into the profession, which can include participation in an accredited program, a certification process, or licensing procedures.
- ◆ formal associations and opportunities for communication among the membership.
- ◆ established opportunities for continued development and enhancement of professional knowledge and skills.
- ◆ a professional code of ethics to govern its membership and provide guidelines for service.
- ◆ recognition by society for its valuable contribution to the welfare of its citizens.
- ◆ dedication to helping others and serving people.

Physical educators and sport leaders possess a bachelor's degree and increasingly pursue advanced study via graduate programs in the field. Their professional preparation programs include extensive study in the theoretical aspects of the field, skill development, and often practical experiences that allow them to apply their knowledge and use their skills under the guidance of qualified professionals. Graduates need to fulfill certain requirements to receive their degree. Additional requirements and certifications may be necessary to engage in professional practice.

Many professional organizations offer the opportunity for members to exchange ideas, become aware of new research, and enhance their skills through participation in workshops and clinics. These associations provide a means for communication among their members through conferences, journals, and newsletters. The Internet allows for a rapid exchange of information and communication with professionals worldwide (see Getting Connected). Codes of ethics guide professionals as they engage in their work with people.

Today there is increased recognition by society of the valuable contribution professionals in our field make to the lives of others. Our commitment to promoting lifespan physical activity for all members of society benefits the health of the nation. The expansion of physical education and sport programs to different settings and the involvement of people of all ages in our programs offers professionals increased opportunities to serve others and enhance their well-being.

Traditionally, physical education has been considered part of the teaching profession. Today, our professional emphasis continues to grow as our programs expand to teaching or activity-related careers in nonschool settings, health- and fitness-related careers, and sport-related careers. The emergence of new professional opportunities in our field has created a need for highly qualified professionals, who possess a high level of skill, an appreciation and understanding of the needs of an increasingly diverse population, and a sound grasp of the knowledge of the field.

The academic discipline

Since the mid-1960s there has been a phenomenal surge in the scientific study of physical education, which advanced its status as an academic discipline. Henry[11] defines an *academic discipline* as

an organized body of knowledge collectively embraced in a formal course of learning. The acquisition of such knowledge is assumed to be an adequate and worthy objective as such, without any demonstration or requirement of practical application. The content is theoretical and scholarly as distinguished from technical and professional.

An academic discipline has a focus, a conceptual framework that provides structure for the field, a unique scope in comparison to other fields, and distinct scholarly methods and modes of inquiry leading to the advancement of knowledge and deeper understanding. This body of knowledge is worthy of study for its own sake and does not need to have any immediate application to professional practice. Traditional academic disciplines include biology, psychology, philosophy, history, and mathematics.

The seminal point in the development of the discipline movement occurred in 1964 when Franklin Henry called for the "organization and study of the academic discipline herein called physical education."[11] His clarion call came at a time when forces in society were exerting pressure for educational reform, improved educational standards, and greater academic rigor in the preparation of teachers. Then, physical education teacher preparation programs focused on the application of knowledge and endured criticism for their lack of academic rigor, emphasis on the learning of job-related skills, and their focus on performance courses, such as Basketball Fundamentals.[7]

Henry's call for an academic discipline stimulated greater scholarly activity by academicians at colleges and universities. Developing technologies, theoretical knowledge, and methods of scientific inquiry from other disciplines were directed to the study of physical education and increasingly to

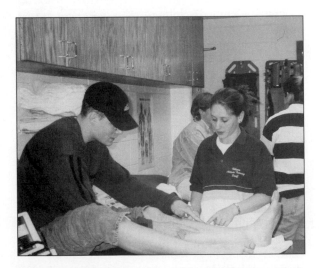

One of an athletic trainer's responsibilities is to evaluate athletes' injuries.

sport. The discipline of psychology, for example, provided the foundation for the development of motor learning and the sport psychology. Sociology laid the groundwork for the growth of sport sociology. The proliferation of research and generation of scholarship led to the development of specialized areas of study, commonly called *subdisciplines*.

Subdisciplines of physical education and sport

The discipline of physical education and sport consists of 12 subdisciplines. The cross-disciplinary nature of physical education and sport is evident from the names of the subdisciplines. Theories, principles, scientific methods, and modes of inquiry from many other academic disciplines were used by researchers and scholars in the development of these specialized areas of study. Knowledge and research methods from the "hard sciences" of biology, chemistry, physics, anatomy, physiology, and mathematics strongly influenced the development of the subdisciplines of exercise physiology and sport biomechanics. Psychology, sociology, history, and philosophy, often called the "social sciences," formed the foundation for the development of sport psychology, motor development, motor learning, sport sociology, sport history, and sport philosophy. The rehabilitation sciences, particularly physical therapy, exerted an important influence on the development of sports medicine and adapted physical activity. Educational research significantly affected the development of sport pedagogy. In the subdiscipline of sport management, the influence of management, law, communication, and marketing is evident.

The growth of the subdisciplines broadens the scope of our field. Equally important, the interdependence between these growing areas offers us valuable knowledge and greater insight as we move towards the accomplishment of our goals. The 12 subdisciplines of physical education and sport are briefly described below.

Exercise physiology is the study of the effects of various physical demands, particularly exercise, on the structure and function of the body. The exercise physiologist is concerned with both short-term (acute) and long-term (chronic) adaptations of the various systems of the body to exercise. The effects of different exercise programs on the muscular and cardiovascular system, the immune system, and the health status of different population groups such as children and the aged are just some areas of study within the field. Clinical exercise testing, design of rehabilitation programs for post-cardiac patients, and planning of exercise programs to prevent cardiovascular disease are among the responsibilities of exercise physiologists. (See Chapter 7.)

Sports medicine is concerned with the prevention, treatment, and rehabilitation of sports-related injuries. Athletic trainers' responsibilities are broader than just administering treatment to the injured athlete on the playing field. From the standpoint of prevention, the athletic trainer works with the coach to design conditioning pro-grams for various phases of the season, to correctly fit protective equipment, and to promote the welfare of the athlete, such as counseling the athlete about proper nutrition. With respect to treatment and rehabilitation, the athletic trainer assesses injuries when they occur, administers first aid, works collaboratively with the physician to design a rehabilitation program, provides treatment, and oversees the athlete's rehabilitation. (See Chapter 12.)

Sport biomechanics applies the methods of physics and mechanics to the study of human motion and the motion of sport objects (e.g., baseball or javelin). Biomechanists study the effect of various forces and laws (i.e., Newton's Laws of Motion) on the body and sport objects. The musculoskeletal system and the production of force, leverage, and stability are examined with respect to human movement and sport object motion (e.g., spinning across the circle to throw a discus).

Biomechanics focuses on the mechanical aspects of an athlete's motion to improve his or her performance.

Analysis of movements with respect to efficiency and effectiveness are used to help individuals improve their performance. (See Chapter 6.)

Sport philosophy is a field of study that focuses on examining the nature of reality and values. It also embraces the study of how knowledge and logic are gained. Sport philosophers study the beliefs and values of participants in sport. Moral issues and conduct are the focus of ethics. Philosophy, as a search for truth, helps us attain a deeper understanding of the sport experience. Our philosophy influences our thoughts, actions, and decisions both in our personal and professional lives. (See Chapter 1.)

Sport history is the critical examination of the past, with a focus on events, people, and trends that influenced the development and direction of the field. History is concerned with the who, what, when, where, how and why of sport.[9] These facts when placed in the social context of the time help us better understand the present and gain insight regarding the future. (See Chapter 5.)

Sport psychology uses principles and scientific methods from psychology to study human behavior in sport. Sports psychologists help athletes improve their "mental game," that is, develop and effectively apply skills and strategies that will enhance their performance. Achievement motivation, regulation of anxiety, self-confidence, rehabilitation adherence, cohesion, and leadership are among the topics studied by sport psychologists.

Sport psychologists help athletes achieve optimal levels of performance.

Recently, sport psychology and exercise psychology have become more closely aligned. Exercise psychology is concerned with exercise addiction, adherence, and other psychological issues affecting the well-being of people who are physically active. (See Chapter 9.)

Motor development studies the factors that influence the development of abilities essential to movement. The motor development specialist uses longitudinal studies, that is, studies that take place over a span of many years, to analyze the interaction of genetic and environmental factors that affect an individual's ability to perform motor skills throughout their lifespan. The role of early movement experiences, heredity, and maturation on children's development of motor skills is an important focus of study. Professionals use theories of development to design appropriate movement experiences for people of all ages and abilities. (See Chapter 9.)

Motor learning is the study of changes in motor behavior that are primarily the result of practice and experience. The effect of the content, frequency, and timing of feedback on skill learning is a critical area of study. Motor learning is concerned with the stages an individual progresses through in moving from a beginner to a highly skilled performer. The most effective conditions for practicing skills, the use of reinforcement to enhance learning, and how to use information from the environment to modify performance are investigated by motor learning specialists. (See Chapter 9.)

Sport sociology is the study of the role of sport in society, its impact on participants in sport, and the relationship between sport and other societal institutions. Sport sociologists examine the influence of gender, race, and socioeconomic status on participation in sports and, more recently, physical activity. Drug abuse by athletes, aggression and violence, the effect of the media on sport, and player-coach relationships interest sport sociologists. The experience of the millions of children involved in youth sport has also drawn the attention of sport sociologists. (See Chapter 8.)

Sport pedagogy can be defined broadly to include the study of teaching and learning in school

Sport pedagogy studies how coaches provide an effective learning environment. Coach Pat Summitt instructs players at the University of Tennessee during a time out.

and nonschool settings. Sport pedagogy studies how physical educators and sport leaders provide an effective learning environment, achieve desired learning goals, and assess program outcomes. It seeks to determine the characteristics and skills possessed by effective teachers and coaches and how these influence student/athlete activity and student/athlete learning. The curriculum, its goals, its organization, and how it is implemented are studied. The preparation of teachers is a major focus of this area. (See Chapter 11.)

Adapted physical activity is concerned with the preparation of teachers and sport leaders to provide programs and services for individuals with disabilities. Specialists modify activities and sport to enable people with different abilities to partici-

pate. By federal law, adapted physical educators have a role in designing an individualized educational plan for students with disabilities so that they can participate to the fullest extent they are able in school physical education. Advocacy to secure services and leadership to create more opportunities in physical education and sport are important aspects of this field. (See Chapter 11.)

Sport management encompasses the many managerial aspects of sport. These include personnel management, budgeting, facility management, and programming. Other aspects of sport management are law, policy development, fundraising, and media relations. Knowledge from this area can be used by professionals in many different aspects of the sport enterprise, including interscholastic and

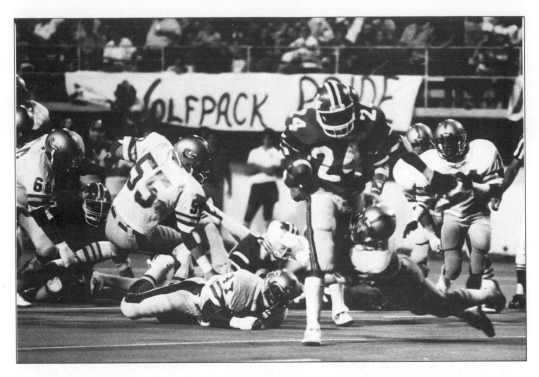

Sport sociology is concerned with the social behavior of people in sport situations, such as these football players at the University of Nevada–Las Vegas.

intercollegiate sports, professional sports, fitness and health clubs, community sport and recreation programs, and sporting goods sales. (See Chapter 13.)

Specialization and unification

The emergence of subdisciplines led to specialization by both the academicians and practitioners in the field. The creation of new professional societies and scholarly journals provided a forum for professional dialogue, the dissemination of scientific findings, and the sharing of scholarly work. At colleges and universities, curricular changes were implemented as new courses were developed and, eventually, new undergraduate majors were added, such as those in sport studies, athletic training, and fitness and cardiac rehabilitation. These new career options attracted an increasing number of students, and the number of graduates of these programs soon exceeded the number of graduates

from the traditional teaching program. The graduates of these nonteaching programs often prefer to describe their occupation with reference to their specialized areas of study. Thus, these professionals refer to themselves as athletic trainers, exercise scientists, and sport managers rather than physical educators. The new graduate programs offered at the master's and doctoral levels, such as those in exercise physiology, sport pedagogy, and sport psychology, reflect the increasingly sophisticated, complex nature of the discipline.

As the discipline movement has continued to expand over the decades, the body of knowledge has grown tremendously. As specialization increases, it is important not to lose sight of the whole breadth of the field. Even though specialized areas have developed significant knowledge bases, they are not mutually exclusive. There is an overlap in content, ideas, and areas of inquiry, as we are based on a common focus, which has been increasingly defined as physical activity. McNeill defines as the basic focus of our field "our connection and commitment to the health and well-being of all people".[12]

Table 1-1 shows how physical educators and fitness leaders can use knowledge from each of the subdisciplines to enhance the effectiveness of their programs. In this era of continued growth of the whole field and increased specialization within the field, we should strive to make connections between the subdisciplines. Charles advises that when we eschew boundaries that define the subdisciplines, we can give isolated factors greater meaning by placing them in the perspective of the larger field.[13] Lumpkin suggests that as a field "we should commit to common goals, different roles, and a cross-disciplinary body of knowledge."[14] We must understand the significant contribution of each of these scholarly fields and the important role each of us play in achieving the goal of life-span participation in physical activity for people of all ages. It is equally important to remember that as professionals working with people, we are dealing with the whole person—their mind and body in the context of society. We must be sensitive to society's changing needs and capitalize on them as an opportunity for growth. Charles states that "we must recognize and capitalize on indicators of cultural change that point toward a future society that places a premium on health and well-being and that values personal fulfillment through physical activity."[13] If we can do this, we can achieve our fullest potential as a significant force in society.

TABLE 1-1

Subdisciplines of Physical Education and Sport— Application to Fitness Instruction and Program Leadership

Subdiscipline	Questions to Be Answered
Biomechanics	What are the correct techniques for weight training? How can I evaluate a participant's gait?
Exercise Physiology	What is the frequency, duration, and intensity of exercise to yield health benefits? How long will it be before participants will achieve a significant difference in their health status?
Sports Medicine	What exercises will prevent injury? How should exercise be modified for hot, humid weather?
Motor Development	What are the developmental needs of the participants? How can the program be designed to meet these needs?
Motor Learning	What are the best practice conditions for learning a skill? How does the frequency of feedback and praise influence participation?
Sport Philosophy	What is my role as a fitness leader in involving participants in the program? What is the responsibility of the participants in this program?
Sport Psychology	What are the best strategies to help program participants adhere to or continue their involvement in the program?
Sport Sociology	What are societal factors that influence the activity choices of the program participants? What are the societal forces that influence their participation?
Sport Pedagogy	What are characteristics of effective teachers? What are guidelines for most effectively presenting instruction?
Adapted Physical Activity	How can the program be modified to meet individual needs? . . . to accommodate individuals with disabilities?
Sport Management	What is the best way to promote the program? How can I bring about a change in policy?

A New Name for the Field

As the discipline movement grew in the decades following Henry's 1964 call for its development, academicians in higher education engaged in what has become a protracted debate about the proper title for the field. Some scholars expressed concern that the traditional name of *physical education* was too narrow and did not clearly convey the rapidly growing academic nature of the field. It failed to reflect the expanding scholarly interest in sport that had, over the decades, emerged as a legitimate area of study.[9] Moreover, the name was too closely linked to the traditional profession of teaching in the schools that had evolved from being the primary profession of our field to being one of many professions. However, other scholars favored the retention of the traditional title *physical education*. Instead of changing the title, they advocated changing the image of the field to more accurately reflect its evolving nature, expanded scope, and changing focus. In short, physical education was experiencing an "identity crisis."

Scholars have engaged in extended discussions to define the field's focus. They sought a new title for the field that would reflect both our disciplinary and professional aspects. As scholars debated, departments of physical education in higher education began changing their names to reflect their expanding mission and changing direction. Starting in the 1960s, some physical education departments in colleges and universities began changing their name to *kinesiology*. Kinesiology is defined as the study of human movement. Proponents of this name believed it reflected the growing scholarly attention to the many facets of human movement. In 1989, after years of debate, the prestigious American Academy of Physical Education voted to change its name to the American Academy of Kinesiology and Physical Education and recommended *kinesiology* as the title of the discipline. Those who opposed this title expressed concern about the lack of recognition of the name by the public. Accomplishing our mission is difficult if people do not know what we stand for and recognize the value of what we do.

Exercise science, sometimes in conjunction with *sport science,* became a popular term used by departments in the 1990s. Exercise science defines the broader emphasis of the field and, in terms of name recognition, is easy for the public to understand. Sport, although perceived as too narrow to represent the whole of the field, does capture the growing focus of the field's scholarly endeavors.

Physical education and sport is also a popular title for the field. Ziegler reported that in 1994 it was the most common title used worldwide.[8] By linking physical education with sport, it clearly identifies sport as a vital, but not sole, concern of the field. This designation retains the traditional term *physical education* that is familiar to the public. It includes the term sport which has emerged as a prominent area of scholarly study.

Today, there is a growing consensus that physical activity is our central focus. There is still no common agreement as to the title of the field. Ziegler, in 1997, addressed this continuing dilemma by noting that "the situation has now ballooned into a whirling vortex of more than 150 names in the United States" for departments in higher education. He calls for resolution of the issue, the recognition of developmental physical activity as the focus, and the closer alignment of the "professional and scholarly dimensions of our work."[8] It is time, Ziegler states, "to take bold, positive steps to present a much sharper, more precise image to those who use our services (e.g., students, clients)."[8]

ALLIED FIELDS

Health, recreation, and dance are frequently referred to as allied fields of physical education and sport. These fields share many purposes with physical education and sport, namely the development of the total individual and concern for quality of life. However, the content of the subject matter of the allied fields and the methods used to accomplish their goals may vary from the subject matter and methods of physical education and sport. The title of the largest professional organization, the American Alliance for Health, Physical Education, Recreation and Dance (AAHPERD), reflects the close and important relationship between these fields. AAHPERD's membership consists of professionals in physical education, sport, athletics, health, safety, recreation and leisure, and dance.

Health

Health education concerns itself with the total well-being of the individual, encompassing physical, mental, social, emotional, and spiritual health. Three areas within health education are health instruction, the provision of health services, and environmental health.

Teaching the basics of healthful living is the focus of health instruction. Health instruction is targeted at individuals of all ages, ranging from preschoolers to the elderly, and is delivered through a diversity of agencies—including educational institutions at all levels, public health services, and private programs. Health instruction can encompass many areas, including disease prevention, mental health, nutrition, physical fitness, stress management, and dealing with abuse of drugs and alcohol.

Delivery of health services is the second area of health education. These services are concerned with developing and maintaining a satisfactory level of health for all people. Health services are provided at educational institutions at all grade levels and are more frequently becoming an integral part of employee health services offered by corporations. Services may include routine eye examinations, cholesterol and blood pressure monitoring, and cancer screening.

Environmental health is the third area included within health education. Its primary concern is the development of healthful and safe environments. Standards have been developed to ensure that individuals within an environment are not needlessly exposed to hazards such as toxic chemicals or infectious materials.

Americans are becoming increasingly conscious of the instrumental role physical activity plays in one's quality of life. Data supporting the health benefits of participation in appropriate physical activity on a regular basis continue to mount. Accrued benefits of regular physical activity include

Corporate fitness programs are becoming increasingly popular. Tenneco employees participate in step aerobics classes offered as part of their health and fitness program.

the prevention of coronary heart disease, hypertension, noninsulin-dependent diabetes mellitus, osteoporosis, obesity, and mental health problems.[5] Other benefits may include the reduction of the incidence of stroke and the maintenance of the functional independence of the elderly.[5] Additionally, it has been found that, on average, individuals who are physically active outlive individuals who are physically inactive.[5] The strong role regular and appropriate physical activity plays in the health and well-being of individuals further confirms the allied nature of health and physical education and sport.

Recreation

Another area allied with physical education and sport is recreation. Recreation is generally thought of as self-chosen activities that provide a means of revitalizing and refreshing one's body and spirit. The spectrum of activities ranges from active to passive and from group to individual in nature. Recreation is important for individuals of all ages. Through recreation, individuals can learn to use their leisure time constructively in ways that are personally fulfilling.

Physical activity contributes to health and fitness throughout life. Bicycling is an excellent activity for young and old alike.

Like physical education and sport, recreation is experiencing a period of rapid growth and expansion. The number and types of available activities have increased, the settings in which programs are offered have become more diverse, and the number and range of populations served have expanded. Concern for the environment has also led to calls for resource management by national and local authorities to preserve the environment while providing for the careful expansion of outdoor recreational facilities.

Recreational opportunities abound. Schools, communities, and businesses offer a wide range of activities to meet the fitness and leisure needs of individuals. Worksite fitness programs, industrial sport leagues, commercial fitness programs, competitive recreational leagues, instructional clinics, and open facilities for drop-in recreation are increasing in number. During nonschool hours, school facilities are the site for various recreational offerings for people of all ages. Many individuals and families pursue recreational activities independently as well.

Therapeutic recreation focuses on providing a broad range of services for individuals of all ages who have disabilities. Through a diversity of interventions, the individual's quality of life is enhanced, the development of leisure skills is encouraged, and the integration of the individual into community recreational opportunities and life is emphasized.

Recreation, like physical education and sport, can contribute to the quality of an individual's life. It provides opportunities for individuals to engage in freely chosen activities during their leisure time.

Dance

The third allied area is dance. Dance is a popular activity of people of all ages and is both a physical activity and a performing art that gives participants an opportunity for aesthetic expression through movement.

People dance for a variety of reasons. Dance is used to communicate ideas and feelings and is considered a creative art form. As with all of the arts, dance should be an integral part of the

educational experience. As a form of recreation, dance provides opportunities for enjoyment, self-expression, and relaxation. Dance also can be used as a form of therapy, providing opportunities for individuals to express their thoughts and feelings. It provides a means to cope with the various stresses placed on individuals. Dance is increasingly used as a means to develop fitness.

There are many forms of dance that are enjoyed by individuals—including ballet, ballroom, folk, clog, modern, square, and tap. Cultural heritage is reflected in and passed on through dance activities.

Within the past two decades, aerobic dance has grown in popularity. Aerobic dance provides participants with an opportunity to develop fitness and experience the fun and enjoyment of working out to music.

Health, recreation, and dance are allied fields to physical education and sport. The overall focus of these fields of endeavor is the development of the total individual and the enhancement of each person's quality of life. Attainment of these aims involves health promotion, pursuit of worthy leisure-time activities, and creative expression through dance. These experiences, coupled with the movement activities that compose the realm of physical education and sport, offer the potential to enhance the lives of people of all ages. Fulfillment of this potential will depend on the quality of leadership provided by professionals in health, recreation and leisure, dance, physical education, and sport.

TERMINOLOGY

These terms are used frequently in this textbook and may be helpful in understanding the material presented.

Physical Activity, Exercise, and Physical Fitness

Physical activity is any bodily movement produced by the contraction of the skeletal muscles that increases energy expenditure above the baseline level.[5] Physical activity can be described in terms of its duration, intensity, type, and purpose. Some examples of physical activity are daily living tasks, occupational tasks, leisure activities, sports and exercise.

Exercise is physical activity that is planned, structured, and repetitive and has as its purpose the improvement or maintenance of physical fitness.[15]

Physical fitness is the capacity of people to perform physical activities. It has been described as the ability to carry out daily tasks with vigor and without undue fatigue, and with sufficient energy to engage in leisure-time pursuits, to meet unforeseen emergencies, and the vitality to perform at one's fullest capacity.[5] Physical fitness can be described in terms of its relationship to health and to performance.

Health-related fitness is concerned with the development and maintenance of fitness components that can enhance health and well-being. Health-related fitness is important to all persons throughout life. The components of health-related fitness are cardiorespiratory endurance, muscular strength, muscular endurance, flexibility, and body composition. (See the box below.)

Performance-related fitness is concerned with the development and maintenance of those fitness components that can enhance performance in physical activities such as sport. The components of performance-related fitness include agility, balance, coordination, power, reaction time, and speed.

COMPONENTS OF FITNESS

Health-related Fitness Components	Performance–related Fitness Components
Body composition	Agility
Cardiovascular endurance	Balance
Flexibility	Coordination
Muscular endurance	Power
Muscular strength	Reaction time
	Speed

Health, Wellness, and Holistic Health

Health is the general well-being of the individual and comprises several different dimensions: physical health, mental health, social health, emotional health, and spiritual health. Traditionally, health was defined as the absence of disease. Thus, by definition, if an individual was not sick, he or she was well. Today, however, health is defined in terms of the achievement of an optimal state of being or wellness.

Wellness, a state of optimal well-being, stresses the importance of the individual taking an active role in achieving a healthy lifestyle. Today, the primary causes of death and disease in our society are related to lifestyle choices. By choosing to smoke, be sedentary, or eat a high-fat diet, an individual increases his or her risk for disease. Wellness emphasizes making healthy choices to reduce disease risk factors and promote health. Attaining a high degree of wellness is achieved through proper nutrition, regular and appropriate physical activity, adequate rest and relaxation, effective stress management, adherence to sound safety practices, and elimination of controllable risk factors such as smoking, excessive consumption of alcohol, or drug abuse.

Holistic health is closely aligned with wellness. The basic tenet of holistic health is that an individual's health is affected by most aspects of an individual's life. Physical, psychological, emotional, social, spiritual, environmental, and genetic factors all interact to influence an individual's state of health.

• • •

PHILOSOPHY

For some people the term *philosophy* conjures up visions of an individual sitting in the ivory towers of a university pondering seemingly unanswerable questions. Or it may call up the image of an individual sitting atop a rock next to the bank of a stream, looking at the water rippling by and contemplating the meaning of life. Perhaps you think of philosophy as too abstract in nature to have practical value. Maybe it would help you to appreciate the worth of philosophy if it was defined simply as a set of beliefs that guides one's actions and gives direction to one's life.

Philosophy, from the Greek word *philosophia*, means love of wisdom.[16] *Philosophy* can be defined as the pursuit of the truth, through the systematic investigation of reality, knowledge, meanings, and values. Philosophy is important for those who aspire to a career in the field. It provides direction; it enables the use of knowledge and skills in the most effective manner. A well-formulated philosophy promotes the development and clarification of beliefs and values, which serve as a foundation for one's behavior. Philosophy aids in decision-making; morals and values guide our conduct not only in our professional capacity but also in our daily living.

What Is Philosophy?

The essence of any discipline can be appreciated only by a thorough consideration of philosophy in general and the philosophies of the particular field being investigated. Philosophy is a field of inquiry that attempts to help individuals evaluate, in a satisfying and meaningful manner, their relationships to the universe. Philosophy helps people evaluate themselves and their world by giving them a basis to deal with the problems of life and death, good and evil, freedom and restraint, beauty and ugliness.

Aristotle said that philosophy is the grouping of the knowledge of the universals. Dictionary definitions report that it is the love of wisdom and the science that investigates the facts and principles of reality and of human nature and conduct. Philosophy helps individuals answer problems that confront them and the world through critical thinking and reflective appraisal of experiences. Philosophy offers an explanation of life and the principles that guide human lives.

Questions that reflect the concerns of philosophers include the following:

- ◆ What is the role of human beings on this earth?
- ◆ What are the origin and nature of the universe?
- ◆ What constitutes good and evil, right and wrong?
- ◆ What constitutes truth?
- ◆ Is there a God?
- ◆ Do human beings have souls, that is, some essence that exists yet cannot be seen?
- ◆ What is the function of education in society?
- ◆ What relationship exists between mind and matter?

Philosophy is conventionally divided into four domains or branches of study, providing a framework for examination of philosophical concerns. Each branch contributes to our understanding, and offers us greater insight in our search for wisdom.

Branches of Philosophy

Philosophy's branches of study are generally divided into four domains: metaphysics, epistemology, axiology, and logic. *Metaphysics* seeks to address the ultimate nature of reality, that is, what is real and exists. Speculative in its approach, metaphysics may be used to understand the relationship between mind and body or the essential meaning of sport. *Epistemology* is the branch of philosophy concerned with examining the nature of knowledge. It uses critical, analytical methods to examine the structure of knowledge, its origin, and limits. This approach can help us in defining the nature of the discipline (i.e., body of knowledge) of physical education and sport. *Logic* focuses on the examination of ideas in an orderly and systematic way. Logic uses a critical approach to study how ideas relate to each other, and applies sound and reasoned judgment to decision making. Logic can help members of our field design sound research approaches or organize facts to document the contribution of physical activity to well-being. *Axiology* examines the nature of values. Two extensions of axiology are ethics and aesthetics. *Ethics* is concerned with issues of right and wrong, responsibility, and standards of conduct. Speculative in nature, ethics examines moral values.

Moral reasoning helps people determine what is the right thing to do in a given situation or circumstance. The development of character, nature of fair play, and issues of justice are just a few of the ethical concerns of physical education and sport. *Aesthetics* is the study of the nature of beauty and art. The beauty of skilled movement and artistic expression through dance enable us to see movement as an art form.

These branches represent different aspects of philosophy. In developing a comprehensive philosophy for a discipline, such as physical education and sport, each of these areas is addressed. See the box below for a definition of each branch of philosophy, a typical question posed, and an example of a question that might be asked concerning physical education and sport.

Why Have a Philosophy?

In today's changing society a sound philosophy of life and physical education and sport is necessary for the professional to be effective. Professionals must ask themselves the following important questions:

♦ What has value in today's society?
♦ What is relevant to the needs of people today?

Physical educators and sport leaders also may find a philosophy helpful in addressing more specific questions confronting them. For example:

♦ Should youth sport programs mandate equal playing time for all participants?
♦ Should intercollegiate athletes be required to maintain a certain grade-point average to participate?

BRANCHES OF PHILOSOPHY

Branch	Focus	General Questions	Questions Relating to Physical Education and Sport
Metaphysics	Nature of Reality	What is the meaning of existence? What is real?	What experiences in a physical education program will better enable the individual to meet the challenges of the real world?
Epistemology	Nature of knowledge and methods of obtaining knowledge	What is true?	What is the validity of the knowledge pertaining to physical activity and its influence on the development of the individual?
Logic	Systematic and orderly reasoning	What is the method of reasoning that will lead to the truth?	What process should a researcher use to determine the value of physical education to program participants?
Axiology	Aims and values of society	How do we determine what has value, and on what criteria is this judgment based?	What is the value of physical education programs to the individual?
Ethics	Issues of conduct, right and wrong	What is the highest standard of behavior each person should strive to attain?	How can sport be utilized to develop ethics?
Aesthetics	Nature of beauty and art	What is beauty?	Why are skilled performers' movements beautiful to view?

♦ Should athletic trainers be required to report illegal drug use by an athlete?

♦ Should the coach, athletic trainer, or athlete make the final determination if an injured athlete can play?

♦ Should employees be required to participate in a corporate fitness program?

♦ Should certification be required of all health/fitness club employees?

♦ Should individuals who have tested HIV positive be allowed to participate in physical education classes and on athletic teams?

♦ Should the media scrutinize the private lives of professional athletes?

♦ Should physical educators be role models and "practice what they preach"?

A philosophy of physical education and sport can help physical educators and sport leaders resolve these and other questions and concerns confronting them. A philosophy of physical education and sport serves several functions. Philosophy guides physical educators and sport leaders in determining the goals, objectives, content, and manner of conduct of physical education and sport programs. A sound and well-reasoned philosophy helps them to better evaluate physical education and sport programs and practices. A philosophy of physical education and sport helps guide one's actions and offers direction for one's efforts. A well-defined philosophy of physical education and sport will help in interpreting those values important in society so that programs can be established to help meet these needs.

General Philosophies

The five philosophies most often examined in relationship to education are idealism, realism, pragmatism, naturalism, and existentialism. These philosophies have influenced the goals, objectives, educational content, methodology, and values associated with education as well as the roles and responsibilities of teachers and students in the education process. Given physical education's historic association with education, these philosophies have affected the nature and conduct of the physical education program as well. An overview of

CENTRAL BELIEFS UNDERLYING TRADITIONAL PHILOSOPHIES	
Idealism	The mind interprets events and creates reality; truth and values are absolute and universally shared.
Realism	The physical world is the real world and it is governed by nature; science reveals the truth.
Pragmatism	Reality is determined by an individual's life experiences; the individual learns the truth through experiences.
Naturalism	Reality and life are governed by the laws of nature; the individual is more important than society.
Existentialism	Reality is based on human existence; individual experiences determine what is true.

these philosophies is provided as well as how they influence the conduct of physical education and sport programs and the roles and responsibilities of teachers and students.

Idealism

As a philosophy, idealism emphasizes the mind as central to understanding. Idealism encompasses such general concepts as: The mind is the focus of the person's being. All reality comes from the mind. In the scheme of the universe, people are more important than nature because nature is interpreted by the mind. Values and ideals exist independently of individuals and are universal and absolute; they never change. An individual exercises free will in choosing between right and wrong. Reasoning and intuition help individuals arrive at the truth.

When these general principles of idealism are applied to educational thinking, they result in such concepts as: Education develops the personality and character, particularly the moral and spiritual values, of the individual. Acquisition of knowledge and the development of the mind is of primary importance. Education is a process that originates within the self. Thus, the student is responsible for his or her own motivation and learning. The curriculum is centered around ideals. The student is a creative being who is guided by the teacher.

When the general principles of idealism are applied to the area of physical education and sport, they result in such concepts as: Physical education and sport involve more than the "physical." Even though the mind and body are to be developed as one, in reality idealism emphasizes the development of the mind and thought processes. Physical fitness and activities are valued for their contribution to the development of one's personality. Ideals are emphasized in the physical education and sport program. The teacher is a role model for the students, particularly in terms of character and values. Self-development is emphasized.

Realism

The physical world is the central focus of the philosophy of realism. Realism deals with such concepts as: The physical world of nature is the real world. All physical events that occur in the universe are the result of the laws of nature; nature is in control. The truth can best be determined through the scientific method. People's senses and experiences also help them to understand nature. The mind and the body have a close, harmonious relationship.

When the general principles of realism are applied to education, they result in such concepts as: Education develops one's reasoning power and ability to apply the scientific method to interpret the real things in life; this is essential for lifelong learning. The educational process is scientifically based. The teaching process and curriculum should be based on scientific principles and provide for orderly learning. Evaluation should be objective and standardized.

When these general principles are applied to the area of physical education and sport, they result in such concepts as: Education is for life. Physical education and sport should focus on the develop-

ment of the total person. Physical education and sport is valuable because of its contribution to health. A healthy person can lead a fuller life and be more productive. Programs are based on scientific knowledge and an orderly progression. Drills are used extensively, and learning is evaluated objectively.

Pragmatism

According to the philosophy of pragmatism, experiences—not ideals or realities—are the means to achieving the truth. Pragmatism deals with such concepts as: Truth is based on one's experiences. Because individuals experience different circumstances and situations, reality changes in pragmatism. Success is the only criterion of the value and truth of a theory. Truth is situational; whatever works in a given situation is correct at that time. Values are relative and are derived from one's experiences. Social responsibility is important; individuals are an integral part of a larger society.

When the general principles of pragmatism are applied to education, they result in such concepts as: The individual learns through experience. Problem solving is the primary educational method and is a necessary skill for coping with an everchanging world. Individual differences are considered; education is child-centered. Education is for social efficiency, with the emphasis on becoming a productive member of society. Development of the total individual is important.

When the general principles of pragmatism are applied to the area of physical education and sport, they result in such concepts as: The curriculum should be based on the needs and interests of the students. The curriculum should be varied to provide a diversity of experiences for learning. Learning is accomplished through the problem-solving method. Social outcomes from participation in the program are important. The teacher serves as a guide.

Naturalism

A belief that life is governed by the laws of nature is central to the philosophy of naturalism. Naturalism includes such general concepts as: Any reality that exists is found only within the physical

Philosophy influences athletes' attitudes towards winning and helps them interpret the meaning of success.

realm of nature. Nature itself is the source of value. The individual is more important than society, but society is necessary to prevent chaos.

When the beliefs of naturalism are applied to educational thinking, they result in such concepts as: Education must satisfy the inborn needs of the individual. Education is guided by the individual's physical, cognitive, and affective development. The teacher has an understanding of the laws of nature and serves as a guide in the educational process. Students must be self-directed. Students learn through inductive reasoning. The development of both the mind and the body are important.

When the principles of naturalism are applied to the area of physical education and sport, they result in such concepts as: Physical activity is important for the development of the total person; it provides a medium for the development of physical, mental, social, emotional, and moral skills. Teachers pace instruction according to the individual's needs. Students are self-directed. Individualized learning through self-activity leads to the attainment of individual goals. Highly competitive performance between individuals is discouraged; competition against oneself is encouraged, however. Play is an important part of the educational process. Noncompetitive activities and outdoor pursuits provide beneficial opportunities for individual growth.

Existentialism

Reality is determined by individual experiences, according to the existentialist philosophy. Existentialism deals with such concepts as: Human existence is the only true reality. Individuals must accept responsibility for themselves and the choices they make. An individual's experiences and choices are unique, affecting their perception of reality. Individuals must determine their own systems of values and follow them, but they also must accept the consequences of their actions. Individuals are more important than society; however, they must acknowledge their societal responsibility.

When the general principles of existentialism are applied to educational thinking, they result in such concepts as: Education is an individual process. The curriculum presents to students a variety of activities from which they choose activities suited to their needs. The teacher serves as a stimulator in the educational process.

When the general principles of existentialism are applied to the area of physical education and sport, they result in such concepts as: Each student is free to choose from a variety of activities within the curriculum. Individual activities provide opportunities for students to develop self-awareness and self-responsibility. The teacher serves as a counselor, promoting reflective thinking while allowing students to make choices and deal responsibly with the consequences of those choices.

These philosophical schools of thought influenced education, including physical education. Most schools today follow a modern educational philosophy that is based on much of what was advocated by John Dewey, leader of the progressive education movement.

Modern Educational Philosophy

Today's educational philosophy reflects several influences. Dewey's ideas were influential in shaping American education. Humanism, a philosophy that grew popular in the 1960s and 1970s, also altered the focus of American education.

Dewey's ideas of *progressive education* reflect a pragmatic orientation. Progressives believed that education was the avenue to improve the social conditions of society. This child-centered approach to learning emphasized children taking an active role in their learning, as opposed to being passive recipients of knowledge conveyed to them by the teacher.[8] Dewey's approach of "learning by doing" significantly changed the nature of American education. Furthermore, Dewey believed in the unity of the mind and the body. Educational activities were viewed as contributing to the development of the total person, not just the mind. The tenets of progressive education lent support to the inclusion of physical education in the school curriculum. Physical activity developed the physical as well as contributing to the intellectual and social goals of education. This philosophy of education through the physical was to become one of the most important influences on twentieth-century physical education.[8]

A *humanistic philosophy* emphasizes the development of the full potential of each individual. Personal growth, self-actualization, and the development of values are central tenets of this philosophy. Treating students as individuals, valuing the dignity of each person, enhancing self-esteem, fostering personal and social development, and promoting self-responsibility were hallmarks of this approach. Within the realm of physical education and sport, humanism encouraged teachers to place a greater emphasis on meeting individual needs and evoked recognition that one type of physical education program is not suited to all individuals. The feelings, needs, goals, capabilities, and limitations of individuals should carefully be considered in conducting programs. Although the popularity of this approach to education has decreased, the influence of humanism on professional practice can be readily discerned, both within and outside of the educational setting. For example, in corporate fitness programs, programs are designed to meet the needs of individual clients, assumption of responsibility for one's own health and fitness is stressed, and a holistic approach to health is emphasized.

Philosophy of Physical Education and Sport

One question philosophers have examined is the relationship between the mind and the body. Is the mind a separate entity from the body? Or, are the mind and body as one, a unified, interdependent organism? The answer holds a great significance for physical education and sport.

What is the primary goal of physical education programs in our schools? Should we emphasize the development of physical fitness and motor skills? This certainly is our unique contribution to the education of the child. A program conducted from this philosophical perspective, *education of the physical,* would stress the development of total fitness and acquisition of motor skills. Programs in the nineteenth century reflected this approach with their emphasis on physical training. Students engaging in these programs developed the necessary strength and vigor to be productive, worthy contributing members of society. This philosophical approach reflects the belief that the mind and body are separate.[8]

The *education through the physical* approach reflects unity of the mind and the body. According to Siedentop, it is one of the most dominant forces in contemporary physical education.[8] From this philosophical viewpoint, physical activity is seen as the medium for the development of the total person. Participation in physical education not only develops the body but contributes to the attainment of the intellectual and social goals of education. Physical education's contribution to the development of the total individual and the goals of education helped solidify physical education's position in the educational curriculum.

Eclectic Approach to Philosophy

One common approach to philosophy is the eclectic approach. The major philosophies that have influenced education and physical education and sport practices have been reviewed in previous sections. Many people find it difficult to believe in

Some sports, such as the martial arts, emphasize the development of the mind and spirit as well as the body.

all the tenets associated with a particular philosophy. Thus in an effort to develop a philosophy that they can believe in, they have combined a variety of concepts and tenets from different philosophical schools into a set of compatible beliefs. The combining of the beliefs from various philosophical schools is called *eclecticism*. While this combination of beliefs resembles no single philosophical school, these beliefs, when woven thoughtfully together, provide a sound philosophy for the individual.

YOUR PHILOSOPHY OF PHYSICAL EDUCATION AND SPORT

A philosophy of physical education and sport is essential for all physical educators and sport leaders. Traditionally, philosophy as it applies to physical education and sport programs in schools and colleges has been emphasized; however, the implications are clear for programs outside the schools.

A philosophy of physical education and sport also must be applicable to these diverse programs. For example, the importance of physical education and sport is now stressed for all segments of the population, including industrial employees, the elderly, youths, and the public in general. Physical educators who serve as leaders, administrators, and instructors for these groups should also be concerned with developing a sound philosophy of physical education and sport. Most of the concepts of a philosophy for programs in schools and colleges are applicable to programs that exist outside the educational realm. A philosophy of physical education and sport for both school and non-school programs should be humanistic in its approach, commit to meeting the unique needs of participants, have a sound scientific basis, and understand the role of physical activity in enhancing the quality of life for people.

What is your philosophy of physical education and sport? Development of a philosophy is a difficult task but one that is necessary as you proceed toward your goal of becoming a physical educator and sport leader. Perhaps the place to start is with your personal philosophy.

What is your philosophy of life? What are the values by which you lead your life? Maybe your philosophy of life is succinctly captured by one of these often heard adages:

- ◆ "Do unto others as you would have them do unto you."
- ◆ "The end justifies the means."
- ◆ "Look out for number one."
- ◆ "Honesty is the best policy."
- ◆ "Things work out for the best."
- ◆ "Keep you nose to the grindstone, your shoulder to the wheel."
- ◆ "Be the best you can be."

These adages are only a few examples of the beliefs that guide some individuals' lives. If your philosophy of life is not represented by the above statements, can you capture its essence in a single, noteworthy expression? How is your philosophy represented by the manner in which you lead your life? Are your actions congruent with your beliefs?

Many readers of this textbook have participated in athletics at some level, be it youth, interscholastic, or intercollegiate. Critically reflect back on this experience. What was your coach's philosophy? How did that philosophy translate into the conduct of practices and games? Is your coach's philosophy reflected in one of the statements below?

◆ "Winning is everything."
◆ "Play hard, play fair."
◆ "No pain, no gain."
◆ "Win at all costs."

How did your coach's philosophy contribute to your experience and the value you derived from participation?

As you continue you education and pursue a career in your chosen area, it is important that you have a philosophy to guide your actions and efforts. During your undergraduate professional preparation, you will be encouraged in your classes to develop your own philosophy, to think logically and analytically about your beliefs. The following guidelines are presented to help you in your endeavors to determine, define, and articulate your philosophy of physical education and sport.

1. **Review your past experiences in physical education and sport.** Examine them critically. What were some of your most outstanding experiences in this field? What were some of your most disheartening ones? Why? Is there a physical educator that you particularly admire, one that served as a role model for you and even prompted your entry into this field? If so, what was his or her philosophy?

2. **Read about the different philosophies.** What theories are compatible with your beliefs? What theories are at odds with them? How do these theories translate into practice? What are the characteristics of programs conducted from this philosophical perspective?

3. **Review the philosophies of the leaders in physical education and sport.** Determine the philosophies of leaders in the field. Then determine which of their beliefs are compatible with yours and which are not compatible.

4. **Take advantage of opportunities you have during your professional preparation to talk to various professors about their philosophies.** What beliefs are evident in their teaching? Critically examine your experiences during your professional preparation. Ask why things are as they are. Speculate on how things could be changed. Talk with practitioners in the career you are seeking to enter and determine the beliefs that guide their actions.

5. **Express your philosophy.** Undoubtedly during your preparations you will be asked to write and discuss your philosophy several times. Take advantage of these opportunities for expression to clarify your thinking and more closely examine your beliefs. You may wish to save your papers so that you can look back and see how your philosophy has evolved during your education.

Developing a personal philosophy is a difficult task and some would say a never-ending process. Your philosophy will likely change and mature during your experiences in the field. Try to be open to the various experiences in your life, reflect upon them, learn from them, and view your life as an ongoing process of change and growth.

SUMMARY

Contemporary physical education and sport is a rapidly changing, dynamic field. Physical education is defined as an educational process that uses physical activity as a means to help individuals acquire skills, fitness, knowledge, and attitudes that contribute to their optimal development and well-being. Education is the ongoing process of learning that occurs throughout our lifespan. Education, just like contemporary physical education, takes place in a multiplicity of settings and reaches out to involve individuals of all ages. Sport is a highly organized, competitive physical activity governed by rules where the outcome is largely determined by skill and strategy. Rules standardize the competition and conditions so that individuals can compete fairly.

The field of physical education and sport includes both disciplinary and professional dimensions. The discipline is the body of knowledge of the field. Scholars and researchers engage in activities designed to provide greater scientific understanding and insight. The professional dimension of the field focuses on providing services to people of all ages in many different settings. Professionals use the body of knowledge and specialized skills to meet the unique needs of people and help them improve their health and quality of life. The growth of knowledge in physical education led to specialized areas of study, such as sport psychology, sport sociology, sport pedagogy, sport philosophy, sport biomechanics, exercise physiology, motor development, motor learning, adapted physical activity, sport history, and sport manage-

ment. Each practitioner should be knowledgeable about these specialized areas of study as well as appreciate their interrelatedness and their contribution to the discipline as a whole.

Philosophy is critical to our endeavors. The major branches of philosophy include metaphysics, epistemology, axiology, ethics, aesthetics, and logic. Philosophies such as idealism, realism, pragmatism, naturalism, and existentialism have influenced the nature and practice of education and physical education and sport programs. As the twentieth century has progressed, the philosophy of education through the physical has significantly influenced physical education and sport programs.

Each professional should develop his or her own philosophy. One's philosophy influences the objectives or outcomes sought from one's programs and the methods by which these objectives are attained. The objectives of physical education and sport are discussed in the next chapter.

SELF-ASSESSMENT TESTS

These tests are designed to help you determine if you have mastered the materials and competencies presented in this chapter.

1. Without consulting your text, describe the 12 subdisciplines of physical education and sport. Discuss how these areas are interrelated. Use examples to illustrate why it is important to be knowledgable about the various specialized areas within the discipline.

2. Compare the characteristics of physical education and sport programs, in either the school or nonschool setting, guided by each of the following philosophies: idealism, realism, pragmatism, naturalism, and existentialism.

3. Attempt to write your philosophy of physical education and sport. Try to follow the suggestions for the development of a philosophy. Reflect on your experiences, review various philosophies, and take time to talk with some of your professors about their philosophy.

4. The Getting Connected box on page 3 lists e-mail discussion groups for physical education and sport. Subscribe to one of these groups. Discuss the benefits the Internet offers to professionals in the field.

REFERENCES

1. Sporting Goods Manufacturers Association: The sports and recreation industry exceeds $60 billion, Press Release, May 26, 1997.

2. US Department of Health, Education, and Welfare: Healthy people: the Surgeon General's report on health promotion and disease prevention, Washington, D.C., 1979, US Government Printing Office.

3. US Department of Health and Human Services: Promoting health/preventing disease: objectives for the nation, Washington, D.C., 1980, US Government Printing Office.

4. US Department of Health and Human Services: Healthy people 2000: national health promotion and disease prevention objectives, Washington, DC, 1990, US Government Printing Office.

5. US Department of Health and Human Services: Physical activity and health. A report of the Surgeon General, Atlanta, Ga., 1996, US Department of Health and Human Services, Centers for Disease Control and Prevention, National Center for Chronic Disease Prevention and Health Promotion.

6. National Commission on Excellence in Education: A nation at risk: the imperative for reform. A report to the nation and the Secretary of Education, US Department of Education, Washington, D.C., 1983, US Government Printing Office.

7. Siedentop D: Introduction to physical education, fitness, and sport, ed 3, Mountain View, Calif., 1998, Mayfield.

8. Ziegler EF: From one image to a sharper one! Physical Educator 54(2):72–77, 1997.

9. Freeman WH: Physical education and sport in a changing society, ed 5, Boston, Mass., 1997, Allyn and Bacon.

10. Corbin C: The field of physical education—common goals, not common roles, JOPERD 64(1):79, 84–87, 1993.

11. Henry F: Physical education: an academic discipline, Journal of Health, Physical Education, and Recreation 37(7):32–33, 1964.

12. Charles JM: Scholarship reconceptualized: the connectedness of kinesiology, Quest 48:152–164, 1996.

13. McNeill AW: Reflections on scholarship reconsidered, Quest 48:140–151, 1996.

14. Lumpkin A: Physical education and sport: a contemporary introduction, ed 4, Dubuque, Iowa, 1998, McGraw-Hill.

15. Casperson CJ, Powell KE, and Christenson GM: Physical activity, exercise, and physical fitness: definitions and distinctions for health-related research, Public Health Reports 100: 126–131, 1985.

16. Mechikoff RA and Estes SG: A history and philosophy of sport and physical education, Dubuque, IA, 1998, McGraw-Hill.

SUGGESTED READING

Bain, LL: Mindfulness and subjective knowledge, Quest 47:238–253, 1995.

The importance of subjective experience as a form of knowledge is analyzed in relation to its impact on research and professional practice.

Charles JM: Scholarship reconceptualized: the connectedness of kinesiology, Quest 48:152–164, 1996.

The connectedness between the subdisciplines, the connection of kinesiology to society, and professional challenges are discussed.

Corbin CB: The field of physical education— common goals, not common roles, JOPERD 64(1):79, 1993.

Discusses why physical education should be a field, encompassing both the discipline and profession.

Locke LF: Dr. Lewin's little liver patties: A parable about encouraging healthy lifestyles, Quest 48:422–431, 1996.

A thoughtful examination of strategies for promoting healthy lifestyles and creating change.

Lumpkin A, Stoll SK, and Beller, JM: Sports ethics: applications for fair play, St. Louis, Mo., 1994, Times Mirror Mosby.

Moral reasoning provides the foundation for a discussion of ethics in relation to violence, ergogenic aids, commercial sport, and equity issues in sports.

McNeill AW: Reflections on scholarship reconsidered, Quest 48:140–151, 1996.

The importance of valuing teaching as one form of scholarship is discussed.

Mechikoff RA and Estes SG: A history and philosophy of sport and physical education, Dubuque, Iowa, 1998, McGraw-Hill.

The authors trace the development of physical education and sport, including the Olympics, from ancient civilizations to modern times.

Shepard RJ: Habitual physical activity and the quality of life, Quest 48:354–365, 1996.

People may be more motivated to engage in habitual physical activity if the benefits of enhanced quality of life and increased years of active life are emphasized rather than solely focusing on the extension of life.

Siedentop D and Locke L: Making a difference for physical education: what professors and practitioners must build together, JOPERD, 68(4):25–33, 1997.

The authors advocate for collaboration between school teachers and teacher educators as a means to improve our school programs.

US Department of Health and Human Services: Physical activity and health. A report of the Surgeon General, Atlanta, Ga., 1996, US Department of Health and Human Services, Centers for Disease Control and Prevention, National Center for Chronic Disease Prevention and Health Promotion.

This noteworthy document reviews the historical background, responses to exercise and physical activity, relationship of physical activity to health, patterns and trends, and recommendations.

Ziegler, EF: From one image to a sharper one! Physical Educator 54(2):72–77, 1997.

Ziegler calls for bold steps in resolving the dilemma of the name for the field and the competencies required by its members.

Objectives for Education and Field of Physical Education and Sport

Instructional Objectives and Competencies to be Achieved:

After reading this chapter the student should be able to—

- Describe the goals of education in our society.
- Discuss the goals and objectives of physical education and sport.
- Identify the characteristics of a physically educated person.
- Explain what is meant by the cognitive, affective, and psychomotor domains of behavior and how education contributes to development within these domains.
- Articulate the contributions of physical education and sport to education.
- Describe the purposes and the importance of assessment in physical education and sport.

Contemporary American education is challenged to prepare individuals with a wide range of abilities and from diverse socioeconomic, racial, ethnic, and cultural backgrounds to function effectively in today's and tomorrow's world. Because physical education and sport is part of the total educational curriculum, its goals are closely aligned with those of education. Both education and physical education and sport contribute to the development of the whole person.

Today, more than 50 million children and youths are enrolled in our nation's elementary and secondary schools. More than 15 million students are enrolled in higher education. School-based physical education and sport programs offer stu-

dents the opportunity to work toward achieving the goals and objectives of education through an active learning process. Furthermore, school-based physical education and sport programs offer our profession the greatest opportunity to reach children from diverse backgrounds and help them gain the skills, knowledge, and habits for lifetime participation in regular physical activity.

Contemporary physical education and sport programs have expanded beyond the school and operate in a variety of settings. Millions of participants of all ages engage in physical education and sport programs. As professionals, we must define the goals and objectives of our programs based on the context in which we work, whether it is in a

GETTING CONNECTED

NASPE's National Standards for Physical Education contains information about purpose, background, content standards, and assessment techniques.
>   Site: http://www.aahperd.org/naspe/stdspe.html

National Center for Educational Statistics site includes access to current education statistics and publications on the status of American education.
>   Site: http://nces.ed.gov/indihome.asp

corporate fitness center, cardiac rehabilitation program, or a community sports program. Furthermore, we must be sensitive to the needs of the population with whom we are working. Their needs, personal goals, and past experiences in physical education and sport are of utmost importance in designing relevant and meaningful programs. Clearly defined goals and objectives are essential in physical education and sport if the potential of our field to foster optimal human development, to enhance health and well-being, and to enrich the quality of life is to be fulfilled.

If your career aspirations lie outside the educational arena, remember that learning is a process that can take place in many different settings. As a major societal institution, the nation's schools exert a profound influence on all members of society. Thus, all physical education and sport professionals may find it helpful to understand the goals and objectives of education and the contribution of physical education and sport to their attainment. Education and school-based physical education and sport programs form the foundation for future learning. Today's students are tomorrow's adults. Physical education and sport programs in the school influence adults' participation patterns and their lifestyle habits.

ROLE OF EDUCATION IN SOCIETY

Education contributes to the development, advancement, and perpetuation of the nation's cul-

ture. The desirable aspects of society are preserved and maintained through transmission of these values to youth. Education gives individuals the knowledge and the skills to function effectively, act responsibly, and contribute to society. Through education, individuals have the opportunity to acquire critical thinking skills and to contribute to purposeful societal change.

Educational institutions play a primary role in developing society's human resources. Schools, colleges, and universities are clearly the most powerful and effective institutions that society has to

People of all ages enjoy golf, an increasingly popular leisure-time activity.

impart the intellectual skills, knowledge, understanding, and appreciation needed by its citizens to make wise decisions and good judgments, and to logically analyze problems and work toward their resolution. Directly or indirectly, educational institutions are the chief agents of society's progress, whether it is progress concerned with arts, technology, social conscience, or other areas essential to a nation's growth. Education must prepare individuals to meet the challenges of society. Therefore, our educational system should concern itself with the well-being of students in their preparation for a productive and meaningful life in which their individual potential is realized and in which freedom will be assured.

Education is concerned with preparing the individual for a meaningful, self-directed existence. To achieve this outcome, young people must have an understanding of (1) the nature of self and others and a capacity for continuing self-development and for relating to others, (2) the contemporary social scene and the values and skills necessary for effective participation, (3) their cultural heritage and the ability to evaluate it, (4) the role of communication and skill in communicating, (5) the world of nature and the ability to adapt to it, and (6) the role of aesthetic forms in human living and the capacity for self-expression through them.

What Is Meant by the Terms *Goals* and *Objectives?*

Before discussing the goals and objectives of education and physical education and sport, defining these terms may be helpful. *Goals* are statements of purposes, intents, and aims that reflect desired accomplishments. Goals are expressed as general statements and are very broad in their direction. They state long-term outcomes to be achieved by participants in the program. A goal of contemporary education is to help all students acquire the necessary knowledge and competencies to engage in lifelong learning. A goal of contemporary physical education and sport is to help people acquire the necessary knowledge, skills, and appreciations to participate in physical activity throughout their lifespan.

Objectives are derived from goals. Objectives describe learning, specifically what individuals should know, do, or feel as a result of instruction. Objectives are more specific than goals. They are short-term statements of specific outcomes that build cumulatively to reach a goal. Objectives can be stated in many different ways and vary in their degree of specificity. They can be stated with reference to general behavior or with reference to specific outcomes. For example, one goal of *Healthy People 2000* is to increase life expectancy.[1] A general objective that will contribute to this goal is to increase the number of people who engage in exercise to achieve cardiorespiratory fitness.

When an outcome approach is used, objectives describe the behavior the individual will demonstrate when the desired outcome is achieved. Melograno[2] recommends linking outcomes to content goals to enhance the meaningfulness of the objectives to program participants. Using this approach, an objective has four components:

♦ The **goal component** relates the learning objective to the content goal.
♦ The **performance or behavioral activity** describes the specific behavior or action to be achieved by the participant.
♦ The **criterion standard** specifies in measurable terms the minimum level of success to be achieved.
♦ The **condition** describes the situation under which learning will take place. Conditions for learning may vary and reflect the needs of individual participants.

Thus, an objective for an executive participating in a corporate fitness program or for a student enrolled in a physical education program may be written as follows:

To improve cardiorespiratory endurance (goal component), the participant will run a mile (performance component) in 10% less time (criterion component) than at the beginning of the 4-week physical fitness program (condition component).[2]

Well-constructed objectives can take on many different forms and can differ in the number of components. Most importantly, whatever the format, objectives should describe the behavior the

EXAMPLES OF PHYSICAL EDUCATION AND SPORT OBJECTIVES

Regardless of the setting in which they are conducted, all physical education and sport programs should have objectives that are clearly defined and relevant to the needs and interests of the participants. Can you identify the program associated with these objectives? Are these objectives for students in a secondary school physical education program, employees in a corporate fitness program, clients enrolled in a commercial fitness club, or adults involved in a community fitness and recreation program?

Physical Fitness Development Objective

◆ The participant will complete a 20-minute aerobic dance routine designed to improve cardiovascular fitness.

Motor Skill Development Objective

◆ The participant will demonstrate the proper technique in executing the tennis forehand.

Cognitive Development Objective

◆ The participant will be able to explain the scoring system used in golf.

Affective Development Objective

◆ The participant will demonstrate an appreciation for the contribution of exercise to his or her life by participating in an unsupervised program of vigorous physical activity three times a week.

individual will demonstrate when the desired outcome is achieved. When objectives are stated in terms that are measurable, they provide a means to assess the individual's progress toward the achievement of the goal. (See the box above.)

Objectives may be derived for different areas of learning, that is, intellectual development, physical development, or social-emotional development. Objectives guide the development of assessment procedures and instructional experiences. They help professionals focus their efforts on the subject content that is most important for participants to learn.

Quality programs have a clearly defined mission and well-articulated goals. Objectives relate to the goals and are relevant to society's and participants' needs, experiences, and interests. Instruction is designed to help participants achieve the desired objectives and, ultimately, attain stated goals. Ongoing assessment yields meaningful information about participants' progress toward achievement of the goal.

Goals of Education: Historical Development

The needs of society and those of the individual have influenced the goals of education. Justification for inclusion of subjects in the curriculum of the school is based on their potential to contribute to the attainment of educational goals and to the total development of the individual.

Over the years, many national commissions and noted authorities have set forth many purposes and goals for education. In 1918, a committee of the National Education Association stated the "Seven Cardinal Principles of Education": health, command of fundamental processes, vocation, citizenship, worthy home membership, worthy use of leisure time, and ethical character.[3] In 1938, the Educational Policies Commission consolidated the Seven Cardinal Principles into four comprehensive aims: self-realization, human relationship, economic efficiency, and civic responsibility.[4] In 1944, these aims were expanded into the ten "imperative needs of youth"[5]; among them were good health and physical fitness and good use of leisure time. Over twenty years later, in 1966, a commission of the American Association of School Administrators identified nine imperatives of education, which included making the best use of leisure time. In 1978, the "Seven New Cardinal Principles of Education" were advanced in an effort to make the original principles more relevant to the changing world. These principles were enhancement of personal competence and development, skilled decision making, promotion of civic interest and participation, global concern for humankind,

EDUCATIONAL GOALS FOR THE YEAR 2000

◆ All children will start school ready to learn.
◆ High school graduation rates will be at least 90%.
◆ Students will leave grades 4, 8, and 12 having demonstrated competency in challenging subject matter, including English, mathematics, science, history, and geography; students will be prepared for responsible citizenship, future learning, and productive employment.
◆ U.S. students will be first in the world in math and science.
◆ All adults will be skilled and possess the knowledge and skills necessary to compete in the global economy and uphold the rights and responsibilities of citizenship.
◆ Every school will be free of drugs and violence and offer a safe, disciplined environment conducive to learning.
◆ Teachers will have access to programs for continued development of their professional skills.
◆ Schools will promote partnerships that will increase parental involvement in promoting the social, emotional, and academic growth of their children.

From: United States Department of Education: *The Goals 2000: educate America act—launching a new era in education,* Washington, D.C., 1994, US Government Printing Office.

fostering family cohesiveness, development of moral responsibility and ethical action, and respect for nature and the environment.[7]

In 1994 President Clinton signed into law the *Goals 2000: Educate America Act.* This act set into effect the National Education Goals for the year 2000. These goals provide a clear direction and focus for educational efforts for the future. (See the box above.)

Goals 2000: Education for the Future

Goals 2000 encompasses eight areas: (1) ensuring readiness to learn, (2) improvement of gradua-

tion rates, (3) attainment of competency in five core subjects, (4) achievement of international prominence in math and science, (5) promotion of literacy in adults, (6) establishment of a positive, safe learning environment, (7) provision of greater opportunities for professional development for teachers, and (8) creation of partnerships by schools to promote parental involvement in education.[8]

Readiness to learn focuses on the importance of all children starting school with the necessary basic skills and knowledge to serve as the foundation for a lifetime of learning. Achievement of this goal requires that greater attention be directed to the needs of preschool children. In particular, we must address the inequalities that adversely affect students' readiness to learn. Many young children who are socially and economically disadvantaged lack access to opportunities that promote readiness, such as quality preschool programs or adequate nutrition. Other children may have disabilities that affect their ability to learn. National education authorities have identified several objectives central to achieving this goal. These include providing access to quality preschool programs for children who are disadvantaged and disabled, focusing on the role of the parent as the child's first teacher, and ensuring children arrive at school healthy. Learning readiness must be nurtured throughout the children's school years.

Improvement of graduation rates from the current 71% to the targeted level of 90% requires a multifaceted approach.[9] It involves preventing dropouts from occurring in the first place and reaching out to those who have withdrawn to enroll them in a degree or degree equivalency program. Additional efforts must be targeted at preventing dropouts among children of color, who are overrepresented in the dropout rate.

A diversity of social and environmental factors contribute to the student's potential for dropout. Low self-esteem and perceptions that school does not provide an avenue for personal success are part of the problem. Lack of a strong family structure places children at risk for dropping out. To improve the graduation rate, schools need to offer opportunities for success in meaningful areas, nurture the self-concept of learners, develop a strong network of support that addresses students' needs, and foster within its students the motivation to work toward relevant goals.

Competency in core subjects emphasizes attainment of proficiencies in five core subjects: English, mathematics, science, history, and geography. Learning must include acquisition of competencies for lifelong learning and for employment in a competitive global economy. Although not identified as core subjects, this goal calls for all students to have access to health education and physical education to ensure that they are healthy and fit. This goal also promotes the development of good citizenship, values, and appreciation for cultural diversity.

World leadership in math and science achievement aims to have U.S. students be first in the world in mathematics and science. For the United States to be the best in this area requires strengthening the mathematics and science components of the educational curriculum, especially courses offered in the early school years. Courses must become more challenging, and more stringent standards need to be established to assess students' performance in these areas. Achievement of these higher standards will enable students as adults to live, work, and compete effectively in a global economy.

Adult literacy advocates that all adults should be literate. An educated workforce contributes to enhanced economic success. Yet, many adults today do not have basic literacy skills. More than 42 million Americans, 22% of the population, cannot read; 50 million, 27% of the population, read at or below the fifth-grade reading level.[10] A disproportionate number of these adults are minorities. Opportunities for lifelong learning should be developed so that all adults have the opportunity to get a degree or its equivalent. Furthermore, provision must be made to ensure that adults can receive additional education and training throughout their lifetime, so that they may continue to meet the changing job needs of the twenty-first century.

Adults must also have opportunities to acquire the skills necessary for responsible citizenship. These include the ability to evaluate information

and engage in decision making and problem solving. They must have the opportunities to exercise their rights as citizens of the nation.

A safe and positive learning environment that is conducive to achievement is necessary for all students. Today, reports of violence in schools abound. The incidence of drug use by students and the selling of drugs within the school itself have raised considerable alarm. Other social issues that affect students' lives and their ability to learn include the disintegration of the family unit and resulting lack of support for children, and health-related issues such as AIDS and teen pregnancy. If our educational goals are to be achieved, schools must be involved as part of a comprehensive approach to address these societal problems.

The professional development of teachers is crucial to the achievement of our education goals. Teachers must have access to programs that allow them to acquire the skills and knowledge to instruct effectively and prepare students for the next century. Greater opportunities for training allow teachers to learn about new technologies, acquire competencies in new instructional techniques to teach learners of all abilities, develop new curricula to achieve the national standards, and gain skill in using assessment techniques to monitor students' progress.

The goal of *parental involvement* charges schools to promote partnerships with parents. Parents are actively encouraged to become involved in the education of their children. This goal recognizes the importance of parents as their children's teachers, not only in the early years but throughout their educational career. Parents and teachers are to work collaboratively to promote the academic and social development of the child. Besides eliciting parental support, schools are encouraged to forge partnerships within their local communities to accomplish educational goals.

The educational goals for the year 2000 reflect an emphasis on attainment of competencies that will allow students to participate effectively as adults in our workforce and that will enable the United States to be competitive in the global economy. The goals stress providing students and adults with the skills and knowledge necessary for

Each individual's level of development should be considered in planning activities.

lifelong learning. Preparing individuals for responsible citizenship and to function as contributing members of society are valued outcomes of the educational process.

As we move closer to the twenty-first century, improvement in education and progress toward achievement of *Goals 2000* can be seen. For example, strides are being made in mathematics and science education. In 1997, the results of the Third International Mathematics and Science Study revealed that American fourth-graders were "near the very top in science achievement in the world."[11] They also exceeded the international average in mathematics.[11] Students in the higher grades, however, did not score as well. The President emphasized the need to continue our efforts in the lower levels and heighten our efforts in the later grades.

In 1997, President Clinton's *Call to Action for American Education in the 21st Century* set forth ten goals. These include:

◆ the development of rigorous national standards with periodic testing to make sure children are achieving.

◆ making sure there is a talented and dedicated teacher in every classroom.

◆ expansion of preschool programs and greater efforts to involve parents in their children's education.

◆ increased use of technology to enable students to achieve at higher levels.

◆ ensuring our schools are safe, disciplined, and drug free and instill American values.

◆ increased educational accountability.

◆ opening the doors of college to those who qualify, making the 13th and 14th years of education as universal as high school.[12]

Further efforts must be focused on addressing inequities in the schools, such as programs to reduce the dropout rate and improve the achievement of disadvantaged youth. Students from racial and ethnic minority backgrounds and low-income families are at greater risk for poor school outcomes. In 1998, the *Hispanic Dropout Project* revealed the Hispanic dropout rate to be 30%.[13] This was 2.5 times the rate for blacks and 3.5 times the rate for white students.[13] Of even greater concern, Hispanics make up 56% of all

U.S. immigrants; however, they make up nearly 90% of all immigrant dropouts.[13] If this continues, many adults in United States' soon-to-be largest minority group will be underprepared for employment and engaging in civic life.[13] As we move into the twenty-first century, professionals must take an active role in addressing these inequities and ensuring equal educational opportunities for all students.

Physical Education and the Goals of Education

Physical education can contribute to the goals of education in many significant ways. First, physical education makes a unique contribution to the development of the total person. It is the only area of the school curriculum that promotes the development of motor skills and fitness. No other curricular area contributes to development in the psychomotor domain.

Second, a quality physical education program enhances the health and well-being of its students. Students who are healthy can learn more effectively, have more energy to expend on educational tasks, and possess a greater vigor and vitality not only for learning but for daily living. Since one primary goal of education is to prepare students to be productive members of society, attention must be given to the health and welfare of the individual. Adults who are healthy can work more efficiently and effectively. Participation in regular physical activity enhances one's overall health. The physical education program can give students the skills, knowledge, and attitudes that will result in a lifetime of participation in physical activity, thus contributing to good health in adulthood and increased productivity.

Third, physical education can contribute to learning readiness. The first of the goals for the year 2000 states that all children should enter school ready to learn. Movement experiences are critical to learning readiness. Movement is the means by which infants explore their environment, develop their senses, and lay the foundation for future learning in all domains. As infants move from crawling to walking, they enlarge their world and become engaged in the exciting process of discovery. Their language skills expand as they learn to describe what they encounter in their environment, and their cognitive skills grow as they investigate their world. Through movement and play, young children become independent as they explore, gain confidence as they accomplish new feats, and acquire social skills as they interact with others. Additionally, movement stimulates growth and development and enhances the child's health.

Parents, as the child's first teachers, need to provide a vast array of diversified movement experiences for their children during this preschool period to promote school readiness. As the number of preschool and preprimary programs grow, it is envisioned that they will include some type of physical education program. In the twenty-first century, preschool and preprimary education programs will be increasingly associated with the public schools. Thus, it appears that physical educators will have an increasing role in promoting readiness. Furthermore, once children enter school, the contribution of physical education to learning readiness is not diminished.

Fourth, physical education can be an important part of an integrated educational curriculum. Traditionally, schools have organized subject matter into discrete areas—mathematics, science, health, English, physical education, and so on. It was assumed that students, on their own, could integrate what they had learned into a meaningful whole and see the interrelatedness among various areas.

Today we see a greater emphasis on multidisciplinary learning, with the integration of subject content across the curriculum. Integration provides opportunities for students to see new relationships, to transfer what they have learned from one setting to the next, and to reinforce learning in various ways. Physical education offers some exciting possibilities as part of a multidisciplinary approach to learning. The content from physical education can be transferred across the curriculum, and content from other curriculum areas can be integrated into physical education. For example, physical education can provide a laboratory for students to use the information they learned in physics about the laws of motion, forces, levers, and mechanics.[14] Through various movement experiences, they can see how concepts from physics

High-quality education and sport programs, such as master's swim teams, benefit participants physically, mentally, emotionally, and socially.

apply to their lives and affect their daily living, including their movements. Learning experiences focusing on fitness provide opportunities for students to study biochemical changes associated with exercise, reinforce what they have learned about anatomy and physiology, use their mathematical skills to calculate energy expenditure and evaluate fitness results, and support what they have learned in health class about the importance of good nutrition. A multidisciplinary approach to learning helps students understand how the various subjects are interrelated in the real world.

Quality physical education and sport programs contribute to students' physical, intellectual, and social-emotional development. However, whether the potential of physical education and sport to contribute to educational outcomes is fulfilled depends heavily on teachers' commitment to conducting quality programs, and the support they receive for their work from within the school system and from their community.

GOALS OF PHYSICAL EDUCATION AND SPORT

Physical education and sport has as its primary goal the improvement of the well-being and quality of life of individuals who participate in our pro-

grams. We can accomplish this by socializing individuals into the role of participants who will make a long-term commitment to participation in enjoyable and meaningful physical activity and sport experiences. Our main purpose is to provide people with the skills, knowledge, and attitudes to participate in regular physical activity throughout their lifespan.

Participation in high-quality programs contributes to the development of the whole person. The development of the whole person—that is, "education through the physical"—has been the dominant philosophy influencing the goals and objectives of physical education and sport programs in the twentieth century. Involvement in high-quality physical education and sport programs benefits people physically, mentally, emotionally, and socially. The commonly acknowledged objectives of our field reflect this commitment to the development of the whole person.

Historical Development of the Objectives of Physical Education and Sport

Throughout the years, many leaders in the field have articulated the goals and objectives of physical education and sport. When we trace the historical development of the goals and objectives of the field, we see a shift from emphasizing education *of* the physical to a focus on education *through* the physical; that is, the focus has shifted from exercising the body to enhancing the development of the whole person. In the twentieth century, the developmental model, education through the physical, has emerged as the dominant focus.[15]

The developmental model began to take shape in the late nineteenth and early twentieth century. A leading physical educator of that time, Thomas Wood, in 1883, stressed that physical education should contribute to the complete education of the individual. In the 1880s, Dudley A. Sargent, the Director of Physical Education of the Hemenway Gymnasium at Harvard University, cited hygienic, educative, recreative, and remedial objectives to be achieved by participants in his program. In 1910, Clark Hetherington, the acknowledged "father of modern physical education," viewed physical education's contribution to the educational process as encompassing organic education, psychomotor education, intellectual education, and character education. These objectives of the "new" physical education greatly influenced the nature and conduct of programs in the nation's schools. Most of the objectives set forth by leaders of physical education and sport today can be encompassed within the four areas originally defined by Hetherington.

Over a half century later, in 1964, Charles Bucher,[16] identified four developmental objectives for physical education. These objectives were physical (organic) development, motor and movement development, mental development, and social development. Achievement of the outcomes associated with each of these objectives contributes to the development of "well-rounded individuals who will become worthy members of society."

The American Alliance for Health, Physical Education, Recreation and Dance (AAHPERD), one of our largest professional organizations, and its forerunners have taken a leadership role in delineating the goals, purposes, and objectives for physical education. In 1934, the American Physical Education Association's (APEA) Committee on Objectives listed physical fitness, mental health and efficiency, social-moral character, emotional expression and control, and appreciation as desired objectives. In 1950, the American Association for Health, Physical Education and Recreation (AAHPER) stated these objectives for physical education: (1) to develop and to maintain maximum physical efficiency, (2) to develop useful skills, (3) to conduct oneself in socially useful ways, and (4) to enjoy wholesome recreation.

In 1965, the American Association for Health, Physical Education and Recreation (AAHPER) in a document entitled *This Is Physical Education* stated five major objectives:

1. To help children move in a skillful and effective manner in all the selected activities in which they engage in the physical education program, and also in those situations that they will experience during their lifetime.

2. To develop an understanding and appreciation of movement in children and youth so that their lives will become more meaningful, purposive, and productive.

3. To develop an understanding and appreciation of certain scientific principles concerned with movement that relate to such factors as time, space, force, and mass-energy relationships.

4. To develop through the medium of games and sports better interpersonal relationships.

5. To develop the various organic systems of the body so that they will respond in a healthful way to the increased demands placed on them.[17]

These objectives stressed the role of physical education in preparing students for lifetime involvement in physical activity. Besides the development of fitness and movement skills, intellectual, social, and emotional development were emphasized.

The 1971 Physical Education Public Information (PEPI) project of AAHPER sought to inform the public, educators, policy makers, and funding agencies about the goals and values of physical education. PEPI defined a "physically educated" person as possessing knowledge and skill concerning his or her body and how it functions.[18] Further emphasized was the significant contribution physical education can make to the education and lives of students, both as youths and adults. Among the values highlighted are the following:

- ◆ Physical education is health insurance.
- ◆ Physical education contributes to academic achievement.
- ◆ Physical education provides skills and experiences that can last a lifetime.
- ◆ Physical education helps in developing a positive self-image and the ability to compete and cooperate with others.

As you review the goals and objectives of physical education in Table 2-1, some commonalities can be seen, although the wording of the objectives varies. The prominent emphasis is on the development of the whole person, not just the body. The goals and objectives of physical education are encompassed within four primary areas: fitness development, skill development, knowledge, and social-emotional development. The contribution of physical education to the preparation for life as a contributing member of society is also a highly regarded outcome.

TABLE 2-1

Goals and Objectives of Physical Education: The Last One Hundred Years

Late 1800s	1910	1934	1950	1964	1965	1971	1990
Sargent	Hetherington	APEA*	AAHPER**	Bucher	AAHPER**	AAHPER**	AAHPERD***
Hygienic	Organic education	Physical fitness	Develop and maintain maximum physical efficiency	Physical development	Skillful and effective movement	Health insurance	Skills to perform a variety of physical activities
Educative	Psychomotor education	Mental health and efficiency	Develop useful skills	Motor and movement development	Development of organic systems of the body	Contributes to academic achievement	Physical fitness
Recreative	Intellectual education	Social-moral character	Conduct oneself in socially useful ways	Mental development	Understanding and appreciation of movement	Skills and experiences to last a lifetime	Regular participation in physical activity
Remedial	Character education	Emotional expression and control	Enjoy wholesome recreation	Social development	Understanding and appreciation of scientific principles related to movement	Positive self-image	Knows benefits and implications of involvement in physical activity
		Appreciation			Development of inter-personal relationships	Ability to compete and cooperate with others	Values physical activity and its contribution to a physically active lifestyle

* American Physical Education Association.
** American Association for Health, Physical Education and Recreation.
*** American Alliance for Health, Physical Education, Recreation and Dance.

Educational athletics—that is, sports associated with educational institutions—have justified their inclusion within the school by stressing their contribution to the total development of the individual. Professionals commonly cite similar developmental objectives for sports programs. The potential of sports to prepare individuals for life and worthy citizenship is an often-expressed benefit of participation.

Although the leaders have disagreed on the number of objectives and their wording, the objectives of physical education and sport can be encompassed within four main groups: physical fitness development, motor skill development, cognitive development, and affective development. All physical educators, whatever the setting in which they work, should be concerned with fostering the development of these objectives. However, emphasis given to each objective will vary according to the goals of the programs and the needs of the participants.

Contemporary Goals and Objectives for Physical Education

What are the characteristics of a physically educated person? What outcomes should be achieved by students as a result of participation in physical education? To address these questions, in 1986 the National Association for Sport and Physical Education, an association of AAHPERD, appointed an Outcomes Committee to answer the question, "What should students know and be able to do?" The Outcomes Project defined a physically educated person as one who

- ◆ Has learned the skills necessary to perform a variety of physical activities.
- ◆ Is physically fit.
- ◆ Does participate regularly in physical activity.
- ◆ Knows the implications of and the benefits from involvement in physical activities.
- ◆ Values physical activity and its contribution to a healthful lifestyle.[19]

In 1990, this definition was expanded to 20 specific outcomes, which are shown in the box on page 48. Sample benchmarks for selected grade levels offered teachers guidelines to determine students' progress. As you review these outcomes, reflect upon the extent to which your school physical education program accomplished the goal of physically educating their students.

In 1992 NASPE formed a Standards and Assessment Task Force and gave it a twofold charge. First, the task force was to develop content standards based on the outcomes that clearly identified consensus statements about what students should achieve as a result of participation in a quality physical education program. Second, once the content standards had been developed, the task force would focus their efforts on developing teacher-friendly assessment guidelines to allow ongoing evaluation of student progress while facilitating the inclusion of assessment into the instructional process. These content standards and assessment guidelines would expand and complement the physical education outcomes document.

The work of the task force reflected one of the primary focuses of the national education reform movements—the clarification of important goals and establishment of national content standards for each area of the school curriculum. The development of national content standards for physical education parallels the development of national standards for each of the other areas of the school curriculum.

The task force document, *Moving into the Future: National Standards for Physical Education: A Guide to Content and Assessment*,[20] identifies the content standards for physical education. These are shown in the box on page 49.

The assessment guidelines give teachers various benchmarks or performance outcomes. This helps teachers determine "how good is good enough." Specific criteria and assessment techniques aid teachers in evaluating student achievement and integrating assessment into the teaching/learning process. Guidelines are given for grades kindergarten, 2, 4, 6, 8, 10, and 12. The box on page 50 shows a sample of a content standard and related benchmarks for the fourth grade.

NASPE's outcomes and standards initiatives were developed through a consensus-building process that involved physical education professionals working at all levels throughout the United States. Developed to answer the question "What

CHARACTERISTICS OF THE PHYSICALLY EDUCATED PERSON

A physically educated person:

HAS learned skills necessary to perform a variety of physical activities

◆ Moves using concepts of body awareness, space awareness, effort, and relationships

◆ Demonstrates competence in a variety of manipulative, locomotor, and nonlocomotor skills

◆ Demonstrates competence in combinations of manipulative, locomotor, and nonlocomotor skills performed individually and with others

◆ Demonstrates competence in many different forms of physical activity

◆ Demonstrates proficiency in a few forms of physical activity

◆ Has learned how to learn new skills

IS physically fit

◆ Assesses, achieves, and maintains physical fitness

◆ Designs safe personal fitness programs in accordance with principles of training and conditioning

DOES participate regularly in physical activity

◆ Participates in health-enhancing physical activity at least three times a week

◆ Selects and regularly participates in lifetime physical activities

KNOWS the implications of and the benefits from involvement in physical activities

◆ Identifies the benefits, costs, and obligations associated with regular participation in physical activity

◆ Recognizes the risk and safety factors associated with regular participation in physical activity

◆ Applies concepts and principles to the development of motor skills

◆ Understands that wellness involves more than being physically fit

◆ Knows the rules, strategies, and appropriate behaviors for selected physical activities

◆ Recognizes that participation in physical activity can lead to multicultural and international understanding

◆ Understands that physical activity provides the opportunity for enjoyment, self-expression, and communication

VALUES physical activity and its contributions to a healthful lifestyle

◆ Appreciates the relationships with others that result from participation in physical activity

◆ Respects the role that regular physical activity plays in the pursuit of lifelong health and well-being

◆ Cherishes the feelings that result from regular participation in physical activity

Reprinted by permission of National Association for Sport and Physical Education, Physical Education Outcomes Committee: *Definition of the physically educated person; outcomes of quality physical education programs,* Reston, Va., 1990, AAHPERD.

do children need to know and be able to do to prepare for their futures?" the NASPE outcomes and standards offer a clear direction for physical education programs throughout the country.

Though developed in reference to school physical education, these significant goals and objectives are relevant to physical activity and sport programs in nonschool settings serving people of all ages. As Zeigler[21] stated:

The profession has a responsibility to function and serve through the entire lives of people, not just when they are children and young people in schools and colleges. This means we should serve both boys and girls and men and women of all ages who are "special," "normal," and "accelerated."

This can be carried out throughout the lifespan by both public and private agencies, as well as by families and individuals in their own ways. To assume lifetime responsibility would permit us to enlarge the scope—the breadth and the depth—of our profession's outlook.

NASPE's initiatives offer professionals in both school and nonschool settings a common concep-

CONTENT STANDARDS IN PHYSICAL EDUCATION

A physically educated person:

- ◆ Demonstrates competency in many movement forms and proficiency in a few movement forms.
- ◆ Applies movement concepts and principles to the learning and development of motor skills.
- ◆ Exhibits a physically active lifestyle.
- ◆ Achieves and maintains a health-enhancing level of physical fitness.
- ◆ Demonstrates responsible personal and social behavior in physical activity settings.
- ◆ Demonstrates understanding and respect for differences among people in physical activity settings.
- ◆ Understands that physical activity provides opportunities for enjoyment, challenge, self-expression, and social interaction.

National Association for Sport and Physical Education, *Moving into the future: national standards for physical education*, 1995. Reprinted with permission from the National Association for Sport and Physical Education (NASPE), 1900 Association Drive, Reston, VA 20191-1599.

tual framework to guide their endeavors. This framework clearly identifies goals and outcomes associated with quality programs. Professionals in all settings can incorporate the assessment benchmarks, points of emphasis, criteria, and suggested assessment techniques into their programs. The assessment guidelines provide both a means to evaluate their participants' achievements and, at the same time, enrich learning by incorporating assessment strategies into the instructional process.

The past one hundred years have seen the emergence of a consensus about the primary objectives of physical education and, more recently, the characteristics of a physically educated person. Both in the traditional school and nonschool settings, quality physical education and sport programs can contribute to the development of the whole person. The four primary objectives of physical education and, by extension, sport—physical fitness, motor skill development, cognitive development, and social-emotional development—and the goals and outcomes characteristic of a physically educated person relate to the three domains of learning. The three learning domains—cognitive, affective, and psychomotor—help us understand the needs of participants and the skills and abilities to be acquired. In education as well as within the field of physical education and sport, achievement of goals and objectives have traditionally been described with reference to learning in the three domains, as will be discussed in the next section.

LEARNING IN THE THREE DOMAINS

Objectives for learning can be classified into three domains or areas of behavior: cognitive (thinking), affective (feeling), and psychomotor (doing). The cognitive domain is concerned with the acquisition of knowledge and its application. The affective domain includes the promotion of values, the fostering of social skills, and enhancement of emotional development. The psychomotor domain involves the development of motor skills and physical fitness.

It is critical that professionals consider all three domains when planning learning experiences to meet individuals' needs. Separation of behaviors into domains does simplify the formulation of objectives. It enables us to more readily take into account individuals' level of development in each domain as we design and conduct activities. However, these domains are interrelated and, as professionals, we must keep this at the forefront of our minds as we work with people in our programs.

Physical education and sport can contribute to learning in each of the three domains. In the school setting, physical education and sport, like other subjects in the educational curriculum, supports cognitive and affective development. However, it places the greatest emphasis on the psychomotor domain. The extent to which physical education and sport contributes to cognitive and affective development depends heavily on the

SAMPLE CONTENT STANDARDS AND BENCHMARKS FOR ACHIEVEMENT FOR A FOURTH-GRADE CHILD

Content Standard: Achieves and maintains a health-enhancing level of physical fitness.

By the fourth grade, students will begin to match different types of physical activity with underlying physical fitness components and should participate in moderate to vigorous physical activities in a variety of settings. Students should begin to be able to interpret the results and understand the significance of information provided by formal measures of physical fitness. Fitness testing may be introduced at this level. Meeting the criterion health standards prescribed by Fitnessgram is available.

The emphasis for the fourth-grade student will be to:

◆ Identify several activities related to each component of physical fitness.
◆ Associate results of fitness testing to personal health status and ability to perform various activities.
◆ Meet the health-related fitness standards as defined by the Fitnessgram.

Sample benchmarks:

1. Engages in appropriate activity that results in the development of muscular strength.
2. Maintains continuous aerobic activity for a specified time and/or activity.
3. Supports, lifts, and controls body weight in a variety of activities.

4. Regularly participates in physical activity for the purpose of improving physical fitness.

Assessment examples:

1. Student project.
   Have the students collect pictures of people participating in physical activities and identify those activities that contribute to each component of health-related fitness.

   Criteria for Assessment
   a. Provides a minimum of two examples for each fitness component.
   b. Associates activity with the appropriate component of fitness.
2. Student project.
   Students are asked to select an exercise intended to achieve a personal fitness-related goal. Practice the exercise regularly over the course of several weeks (specify the exact length of time). Have the student record the results of each exercise session and graph the progress.

   Criteria for Assessment
   a. Correctly identifies a personal goal that needs work.
   b. Records progress towards goal on a regular basis.
   c. Shows consistent improvement over time.
   d. Meets their own goal at the end of the month.

National Association for Sport and Physical Education, *Moving into the future: national standards for physical education,* 1995. Reprinted with permission from the National Association for Sport and Physical Education (NASPE), 1900 Association Drive, Reston, VA 20191-1599.

degree to which this development is emphasized within the physical education and sport program.

Physical education and sport's unique contribution to the educational curriculum is in the psychomotor domain. Development in this domain encompasses the objectives of motor skill development and physical fitness. While the psychomotor domain is our primary focus, there are many ways that we can accomplish our goals in this area while enhancing development in the other two domains.

Education is a process of learning that can take place in many different settings. In programs conducted outside the school setting, physical education and sport contributes to the cognitive, affective, and psychomotor development of program participants. These programs involve people of all ages, in a diversity of settings, and with many different goals. As we continue to expand our programs, we must actively seek to extend the opportunity for participation to all people, regardless of sex, race, ethnic and cultural background, and socioeconomic status.

Taxonomies

Taxonomies serve as a guide for professionals in planning for learning outcomes and achievement of the desired goals. A taxonomy organizes educational objectives in a hierarchy using developmental theories as a basis for formulating objectives. Objectives are ordered progressively from low to high. Behaviors at one level serve as the foundation and prerequisite for behaviors at a higher level. Stated more simply, lower-order objectives serve as stepping stones to the attainment of higher levels of achievement.

Taxonomies have been developed for each domain. Although these taxonomies are often described with reference to education and the school setting, they offer guidelines for professionals in all fields who work with people to enhance learning and promote human development. Quality physical education and sport programs contribute to development in each domain.

Cognitive Domain

The cognitive domain is concerned with the acquisition of knowledge and the development of intellectual skills. Bloom and his colleagues developed a taxonomy of educational objectives for this domain in the 1950s.[22] These objectives reflect an increase in complexity at each level of development. Learning facts is the initial objective, and from this grows understanding and application of concepts, critical analysis, synthesis, and evaluation. The box to the right presents the objectives for the cognitive domain.

Development of knowledge and understanding is an important objective for physical education and sport programs in all settings. Physical education and sport is concerned with educating individuals about the many dimensions of human movement, including the knowledge within this discipline.

Physical education and sport contributes to knowledge of the human body, exercise, disease,

THE COGNITIVE DOMAIN

Category	Description
1. Knowledge	Memory; ability to recall; bringing to mind appropriate information; represents lowest level of learning outcomes in cognitive domain
2. Comprehension	To grasp the meaning of material; understanding without perceiving implications; interpret; translate; estimate; predict; one step beyond memory; represents lowest level of understanding
3. Application	Ability to use learned information in new situations; can apply rules, methods, and concepts; higher level of understanding
4. Analysis	To break down material into its component parts; organization and relationships between parts made clear; identifying; selecting; inferring; higher intellectual level
5. Synthesis	To put parts together to form a new whole; produce new patterns, routines, or structures; creative behaviors stressed
6. Evaluation	Judge value of ideas, concepts, based on definitive criteria or standards; highest learning outcome because it contains elements of all other categories and judgments based on specific criteria

and health. In the school setting, physical education is the sole area of the curriculum that teaches students about human movement and explores its many dimensions. Through the physical education program, individuals can gain a greater understanding of the various organ systems of the body (e.g., cardiorespiratory system), how they function, and how they can best be maintained. The

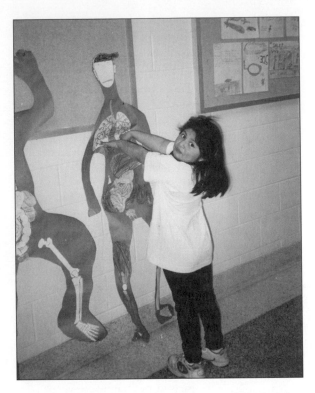

Physical education can help children understand the human body. This 8-year-old is pointing to the lungs, which she says "help you live and get air to run hard."

relationship between exercise and physical activity, disease, and health is an important one for students to comprehend. Students who apply this knowledge to their own lives can enhance their health and reduce their chances for disease, enabling them to lead happier and more productive lives. In other settings, such as wellness clinics in hospitals or worksite health promotion programs, professionals who help adults learn how incorporating physical activity into their daily lives can help them lead longer, healthier lives.

The learning of physical activities involves various cognitive processes. Learners must understand the techniques of the skill being taught and then be able to translate this information into an appropriate, coordinated movement. Related principles and concepts of movement should also be taught so that individuals can move more effectively. For example, children should know that a throw is more effective when one steps in the direction of the throw and follows through toward the intended target. Moreover, successful performance in many sport activities requires modifying movements to meet the demands of a changing situation (e.g., applying backspin to the tennis ball to catch one's opponent off-guard). This requires individuals to learn from their experiences which modifications of a skill lead to success. Cognitively, individuals must analyze their performance, synthesize the information, and apply it to the new situation.

Professionals in all settings need to place more emphasis on the scientific principles and concepts underlying the performance of various activities. Physical activities are not performed in a vacuum. As such, instructors should continually provide appropriate knowledge and information for participants and encourage them to question what they are doing. "Why should I exercise regularly? How will this exercise contribute to the rehabilitation of my knee? Why is warming up before exercising important? How can I get more distance for my golf drive? What can I do to throw the ball farther? Why is it important to play by the rules?" Participants should be provided with more opportunities to think, to apply problem-solving skills to physical education and sport situations, and to experience situations that allow for creativity and individual expression.

Teachers can also use fitness activities to stimulate cognitive development. Students can self-analyze their fitness levels, identify areas of improvement, apply their knowledge to design an individualized exercise program, and evaluate their progress regularly, adjusting their program as needed. These cognitive skills of analysis, identification, application, and evaluation contribute to the educational goal of preparing students to be lifelong learners. These activities also give students skills to modify their fitness programs during their adult lives as their needs change, a critical feature of lifespan involvement.

Technology is increasingly being used to enhance the teaching of concepts of physical activity. For example, a physical education teacher at the

Agassiz Middle School, Fargo, North Dakota, uses heart-rate monitors to help students understand important concepts related to physical activity.[23] Students learn about the Fitness Education Pyramid, which graphically depicts the different types of health benefits associated with varying levels of activity intensity. The heart-rate monitors give students vivid feedback about the effects of activity on their hearts and enable them to monitor their efforts as they participate. This feedback enhances the students' understanding of important fitness concepts.

Instructors of physical education and sport should structure the learning experience so that participants acquire a knowledge of technique, rules, and strategies. Also, proper etiquette should be addressed during instruction. Safety principles must be emphasized so that the well-being of individuals is not compromised during their participation. For example, for their own safety, runners must be aware of precautions to be taken when exercising in conditions of high heat and humidity.

Physical education and sport contributes to our understanding of sport, a major institution in our society and in many other cultures throughout the world. Sport affects a country's economy, politics, government, and educational system. Sport dominates the newspapers, magazines, radio, and television. Millions of people of all ages are involved as participants in sport, and millions more enjoy sport as spectators. Since sport is a part of our culture and others throughout the world, it should be understood from a sociological and psychological perspective. Of course, a body of sport knowledge also exists concerning such things as rules, strategy, safety measures, terminology, and etiquette.

Physical education and sport can help people become wise consumers of goods and services that influence their health and fitness. The health and fitness industry is a multibillion dollar industry. Unfortunately, it is an area in which goods and services of doubtful value find a ready market. Advertisements in popular magazines promise a quick weight loss or a rapid shape up. Infomercials promoting exercise equipment and nutritional supplements capture the attention of thousands of peo-

Children at Agassiz Middle School, in Fargo, North Dakota, learn about the Fitness Pyramid.

ple. Professionals can help participants in their programs learn how to evaluate such pronouncements critically and be wise consumers in the burgeoning marketplace.

Physical education can contribute to cognitive development in many significant ways. Like other curricular areas, it can promote the development of critical thinking skills, and it can provide exciting opportunities for multidisciplinary study. Uniquely, physical education is the one area of the curriculum where students can obtain knowledge about human movement, fitness, and sport to serve as a foundation for a lifetime of participation.

Affective Domain

Many factors influence individuals' learning, including their feelings about themselves, the learning experience, and the subject. Recognizing this, Krathwohl and his associates developed the taxonomy for the affective domain.[24] This taxonomy reflects the development of values, appreciations, attitudes, and character. As individuals progress through the levels within this domain, they move from a concern about themselves to a value

THE AFFECTIVE DOMAIN

Category	Description
1. Receiving	Sensitivity to the existence of certain events, stimuli; awareness; willingness to receive or attend to phenomena
2. Responding	Actively attending to stimuli; reacts to situation beyond mere perception; overt response
3. Valuing	Stimuli or phenomena assigned worth; learner places a value on events; characteristics of a belief or an attitude; appreciation
4. Organizing	Internalizes values and organizes them into a system; determines interrelationship among values; arranges values in hierarchical form; compares, relates, synthesizes values
5. Characterizing by a value or complex	Acts in accordance with internalized values; behavior consistent with accepted values and becomes a part personality; highest level of affective domain

structure that embraces concern for others. At the highest level, their internalized values directly influence their choices and actions. Affective development also encompasses the social and emotional development. The objectives of the affective domain are shown in the box above.

Quality physical education and sport programs conducted by qualified leaders can enrich development in the affective domain. These desirable outcomes should not be left to chance, but actively sought through carefully planned approaches designed to promote growth in this area.

All people have certain basic social needs. These include a feeling of belonging, recognition, self-respect, and love. Fulfillment of these needs contributes to social development. Physical education and sport programs can help participants meet many of these social needs. For example, elderly participants who join an exercise program typically benefit not only physically but socially, deriving pleasure from meeting with their group regularly and forming new friendships. Such interactions help to diminish the feelings of isolation experienced by many elderly who live alone.

Social development is further encouraged by opportunities to interact with program participants. For example, in school physical education programs, students have more opportunities to interact with one another and work together than in any other area of the educational curriculum. Interscholastic sport programs have long extolled their value in promoting learning that teaches athletes how to work together as part of a team, compete fairly, accept responsibility, and respect the rights of others.

Promotion of a positive self-concept is an important outcome of this domain. Individuals need to develop feelings of self-worth and self-respect. One way that physical education and sport activities can contribute to these feelings is to provide opportunities for individuals to develop competence in physical skills and to challenge themselves to attain new levels of achievement and realistic goals. Experiences should be structured to allow for meaningful success for all involved. Individuals who perceive themselves as competent and have confidence in themselves as movers are more likely to seek involvement in physical activities.

Helping young people develop a healthy self-esteem is important. Drug and alcohol abuse and a myriad of other social problems have been linked to low self-esteem. Programs that empower participants through opportunities for leadership, promotion of competence, and development of improved self-image through establishing and maintaining a high level of fitness enhance the self-esteem of participants.

The development of positive attitudes and appreciation for the contributions that engaging in regular physical activity makes to lifelong health and well-being are outcomes that professionals in the field are increasingly emphasizing. Knowledge of the benefits of physical activity and the development of the skills to participate in various activities are not, in and of themselves, sufficient to promote lifespan involvement. If we are to achieve our goal of promoting regular physical activity, we must instill participants with the motivation to lead a healthy, active lifestyle. Our programs should help participants appreciate the contribution that physical activity can make to their health, performance, and rewarding use of leisure time.

Professionals should be concerned with helping individuals clarify and think through their value judgments. We must move beyond the lower-order objective of creating an interest in physical activity. Helping participants achieve the higher-order objective of internalizing values should be our focus. At this level, values directly influence what individuals choose to do and how they behave. Thus, we must help individuals develop values that will lead to a physically active lifestyle. Additionally, we must give attention to developing their decision-making and self-management skills, which will help them in translating their values into action.

Decision-making skills and self-management skills are particularly important for achieving wellness. Many lifestyle choices that individuals make have the potential to influence their health. Decisions that individuals make about eating, exercising, managing stress, and using leisure time can have a positive or negative impact on their health. Helping individuals clarify their values and make decisions congruent with their beliefs can enhance their quality of life.

Physical education can promote social responsibility, an important component of good citizenship. Hellison[25] developed a model to promote responsibility that has been successfully used with at-risk students. This model emphasizes personal growth through self-control, involvement, goal setting, and assisting others. Success, personal awareness, problem solving, and self-reflection are also incorporated within this model. This approach and other thoughtfully designed instructional experiences can do much to promote the development of socially acceptable values.

Professionals must also give careful thought to the influence of their own behaviors, values, and actions on their program participants. How important is it for professionals to practice what they preach? Professionals who aspire to promote affective development must carefully weigh this question. As leaders, they serve as models for participants. Consideration for the needs and feelings of others, respect for each individual, and enthusiasm for physical activity are some behaviors physical educators should exhibit if they want to promote the same behaviors within their participants.

Physical education and sport also provides a venue to develop ethics and morals. In physical education classes and sport experiences, students and athletes have the opportunity to respond to codes of conduct, to decide what is right or wrong, and to make choices that have moral implications. Professionals can promote further development in this area by having students and athletes reflect on their decisions and behavior. Students can also be asked to assume officiating responsibilities in games or to make their own calls (e.g., calling one's own fouls in a game or calling the ball in or out in a tennis match). Discussion of students' and athletes' behaviors following these situations can help participants further clarify their values.

Physical education and sport has long been extolled as a means through which character development can occur. However, character development can be either positive or negative in nature. As Docheff points out, "The outcome of character development is determined by a number of factors—that is, the character of those that support and drive the endeavor, including coaches, teachers, administrators, parents. . . ."[26] Professionals can exert a great influence on character development. However, as professionals, "we must take personal responsibility for the development of good character in others by the demonstration of good character in ourselves." Gough suggests that the most significant character-building challenge is "often more a matter of doing the good, than a matter of knowing the good, more a matter of having the strength of character to do that right thing than a matter of analyzing and resolving complicated moral dilemmas. . . ."[27] Helping individuals develop the habit of "doing good" is critical to our character-building endeavors.

Physical education contributes to an appreciation of beauty. An educated person should develop admiration and respect for beauty. The human body is a thing of beauty if it has been properly

Fostering concern for others is one affective development objective of physical education and sport.

developed. The ancient Greeks stressed the "body beautiful" and did their exercises and athletic contests in the nude to display the fine contours of their bodies. Physical activity is one key to a beautiful body. Also, a beauty of movement is developed through physical activity. When a person moves, whether it is to perform an everyday task or a sport skill, their movements can have a degree of elegance and beauty. For example, when a person picks up an object from the floor, it can be done with a great deal of skill and grace, or it can be done awkwardly. Included in the performance of such acts as catching a football, making a basketball goal, executing a high jump, completing a two-and-one-half somersault dive, or performing a complex dance, can be rhythm, grace, poise, and ease of movement that are beauty in action. Such beauty comes only with practice and perfection.

Physical education and sport fosters development in the affective domain. The enhancement of self-esteem, promotion of social responsibility, clarification of values, development of attitudes, and appreciation of beauty are just some contributions that physical education and sport can make to the development of the whole person.

Psychomotor Domain

Developed by Harrow, the taxonomy of objectives in the psychomotor domain shows a progression of development that provides the foundation for programs of physical activities.[28] The lower-order objectives focus on the acquisition of basic movements and perceptual abilities. The higher-order objectives emphasize the development of fitness and highly skilled movements, as well as increased creativity in the use of these movements. Objectives of the psychomotor domain are shown in the box on page 57.

Development of fitness is also included within this domain. Corbin presents a taxonomy that

THE PSYCHOMOTOR DOMAIN

Category	Description
1. Reflex movements	Actions elicited without conscious volition in response to some stimuli; flexing, extending, stretching, postural adjustments; provides base for movement behavior
2. Basic fundamental movements	Inherent movement patterns based on combinations of reflex movements; patterns provide starting point for improvement of perceptual and physical abilities; basis for complex skilled movement
3. Perceptual abilities	Interpretation of stimuli from various modalities so adjustments can be made; includes auditory, visual, tactile, kinesthetic, coordinated perceptual abilities
4. Physical abilities	Characteristics that, when developed to a high degree, provide learner with a sound, efficiently functioning body; organic vigor essential to development of highly skilled movement; endurance, strength, agility, flexibility
5. Skilled movements	Degree of efficiency in performing a complex movement task; consists of a vertical and horizontal continuum, based on inherent movement patterns
6. Nondiscursive communication	Movement expressions that are part of a movement repertoire; movement interpretations that include any efficiently performed skilled movement; movement patterns designed to communicate a message to the viewer; ranges from facial expressions through sophisticated choreographies

moves in progression from exercising to achieving fitness and then to establishing personal exercise habits.[29] The higher-order objectives focus on learning how to evaluate one's own fitness level and resolve fitness problems.

The psychomotor domain is the main focus of our field. Psychomotor development of the individual is our primary contribution to the educational curriculum. Although physical education can contribute in many meaningful ways to development in the other domains, psychomotor development in the schools is the unique responsibility of the physical educator. Psychomotor development is concerned with two of the primary objectives of physical education: motor skill development and physical fitness development.

Motor skill development

The development of motor skills is sometimes referred to as the development of neuromuscular or psychomotor skills because effective movement depends on the harmonious working together of the muscular and nervous systems. The acquisition and refinement of motor skills essential for everyday activities like posture and lifting and for movement in a variety of physical activities, such as dance, sports, aquatics, or outdoor pursuits, are important outcomes of motor skill development. The development of motor skills focuses on helping individuals learn how to move effectively to accomplish specific goals efficiently, that is, with as little expenditure of energy as possible.

Motor skill development is a sequential process that occurs throughout one's lifespan. Infants possess reflexive, involuntary movements that are replaced with voluntary movements as they mature. Fundamental movements, such as running and throwing, begin to develop in early childhood around the time the child can walk independently. These fundamental motor skills progress through various stages, leading to the mature form of the skill. As children progress through these stages, they exhibit a greater degree of proficiency in their movements, enhanced control and precision of response, and improved coordination.

Fundamental movements form the basis for the development of specialized motor and sport skills

Development of motor skills is one objective of elementary physical education programs.

in the later childhood years. Fundamental movements such as running, kicking, trapping, and dodging now can be applied to a sport such as soccer. Movements such as running, striking, and sliding can be incorporated into a game of tennis. In these situations, increased demands are placed on the individual with respect to form, speed, accuracy, and complexity of skill performance. If we are to achieve our goal of lifespan participation in physical activity, careful attention must be paid to the development of each individual's motor skills. As our programs expand to meet the needs of people of all ages, from preschoolers to the elderly, we must be prepared to promote the acquisition and refinement of motor skills in diverse populations.

The development of individuals' motor skills to their fullest potential requires that individuals have the opportunity to be involved in structured movement experiences that are appropriate to their development level. These experiences should provide meaningful instruction, offer sufficient opportunity for skill practice, and encourage effort and continued practice outside the structured setting. Physical educators who work with young

children play a critical role in achieving our goal of promoting lifelong participation. It is important that children acquire competency in the basic, fundamental motor skills so that they can adapt these skills to the more stringent demands of sports and other physical activities such as dance and recreational pursuits. Individuals who lack the prerequisite skills will have trouble meeting these demands. Learning experiences that provide for success while developing skill proficiency increase the probability that students will incorporate physical activity into their lifestyle.

Physical education is the only area within the school that helps students in developing their motor skills. Through a progressive curriculum, students move from competency in the basic movements to the performance of skilled movements, including sport skills. They are provided with opportunities to learn how to modify these movements to meet changing situational demands and unique personal needs. They also have the opportunity to explore movement as a medium for communication, as a vehicle for creativity, and as a means to understand other cultures. Though many current physical education curriculums are emphasizing fitness promotion, the development of motor skills should not be neglected. This is essential for lifespan participation. The likelihood of individuals engaging in physical activity regularly increases if they have the skills to participate successfully in activities that are enjoyable and personally satisfying.

School physical education programs should offer a balanced variety of activities that allow young people to develop competency in lifetime activities that are personally meaningful and enjoyable. A balance should exist in any physical education program among team, dual, and individual (lifetime) sports. Team sports such as basketball and soccer provide an opportunity for students to develop skills and to enjoy working and competing together as a team. However, in many school physical education programs, team sports dominate the curriculum at the expense of various individual and dual sports, like tennis, swimming, badminton, and golf. In such cases the students are deprived of the opportunity to develop skills in activities that they can participate in throughout their adult lives. Only through a balanced program of team, dual, and individual sports is it possible to develop well-rounded individuals.

In adulthood, an individual's participation in sports and recreational activities is influenced by a number of factors. Past exposure, interests, abilities, enjoyment, motivation, opportunity, time, and financial considerations are just a few factors that influence the nature and level of adults' participation. If one primary purpose of physical education and sport is to promote a physically active lifestyle that will contribute to the optimal development and health of the individual, we must provide individuals of all ages with the necessary motor skills to do so. The skills individuals acquire will help determine how they spend their leisure time as well as what path they will choose to develop fitness. For example, a person who excels in swimming may spend much of his or her leisure time engaged in related activities, or choose to follow a fitness program based on swimming. If an individual excels in tennis, he or she may frequent the courts.

Physical education and sport professionals working outside the school setting with adults face special challenges in teaching motor skills. Adults may want to learn a new sport, yet lack proficiency in the prerequisite fundamental movement skills. They may, for example, exhibit poorly developed running or throwing skills. Professionals working with these adults must use instructional strategies to help them master the fundamental movements while incorporating instruction about the sport skills into the lesson to challenge the adults.

Physical education also contributes to the goal of promoting worthy use of leisure time. Sports, aquatics, and dance give individuals enjoyable activities for use during their free time. They offer a pleasurable means to relax after work and are popular recreational pursuits on the weekends. Development of motor skills for participation in sport and recreational activities is important for people of all ages, including those individuals with disabilities. Physical education and sport professionals in all settings must be prepared to teach individuals with a diversity of needs and to modify activities and instructional strategies to be appropriate to the abilities of the individuals with whom they are working. Challenging activities that lead to skill development and meaningful participation are essential to providing a positive learning experience for all individuals, including those with special needs.

Physical fitness development

The evidence supporting the contribution of physical activity and health-related fitness to the well-being and quality of life is overwhelming. Development and maintenance of physical fitness has long been heralded as one of the most important outcomes of school physical education programs. Fitness promotion is the focus of many nonschool physical education and sport programs as well.

Educational institutions are charged with preparing individuals to be productive members of society. An individual's health status directly affects his or her ability to lead a productive life. Thus, promotion of fitness as well as the skills and knowledge to maintain it throughout one's lifetime are important contributions of physical education to educational goals.

A progressive, systematic approach to the development of physical fitness should be used. First and foremost, the program should consider the needs of the individual. Based on these needs, the program should be designed to accomplish the desired outcomes. Careful attention should be given to helping individuals identify and develop proficiency in activities that are enjoyable and meaningful to them while contributing to the attainment of fitness. This will encourage individuals to make these activities an integral part of their lifestyle.

If we are to accomplish our objectives related to physical fitness, a multifaceted approach is needed. Obviously, we must teach exercises and activities that promote fitness. However, this is not enough. Through our programs, individuals must acquire the knowledge to design and modify their fitness program to meet their changing needs. Moreover, our programs must instill within each individual the desire to make fitness a lifelong pursuit, enjoyment of physical activity, and appreciation of the value of leading a healthy, active lifestyle.

Contemporary physical education and sport supports the development of physical fitness and physically active lifestyles for people of all ages. Unfortunately, the majority of our nation's people are not involved in physical activity on a regular basis and, thus, do not realize the concomitant health benefits. Minorities, people who are economically disadvantaged, women, older adults, and persons with disabilities are disproportionately inactive. As a field, we must increase our efforts to reach out and involve people from these populations in our programs.

Quality physical education and sport programs can contribute significantly to the education of the individual and to the goals of education. They enhance learning and development in all three domains: cognitive, affective, and psychomotor. For professionals working in settings outside the school, an understanding of the behavioral domains, taxonomies, and objectives helps them to more effectively structure their programs to achieve desired outcomes. Physical education and sport professionals in all settings must also assess the progress of their participants in achieving the desired outcomes. Assessment should be an integral part of all physical education and sport programs.

ASSESSMENT OF LEARNING

How do professionals determine whether the participants in their physical education and sport programs have achieved the stated objectives? How do we diagnose the needs of the individuals engaged in our programs? What is the best way to monitor participants' rate of progress? How do participants know when they have accomplished their goals? How can we motivate people to persist in their endeavors? What changes can we make in our programs to be more effective? How can we show the worth of our programs in this era of accountability? How can we, as professionals, enhance our own abilities to meet the needs of participants in our programs? Assessment enables us to answer these and many other important questions.

Improving fitness is an important goal of many worksite health promotion programs, such as the one offered at the Taking Care Center, in Hartford, Connecticut.

Assessment is a critical component of quality physical education and sport programs. Assessment should be a dynamic, ongoing process integrated into programs and viewed as an essential, crucial element of any program, be it conducted in a school or nonschool setting. The development of quality physical education and sport programs requires establishing clear goals, assessing participants' needs, setting specific objectives, planning learning experiences, providing effective instruction, and evaluating the outcomes.

Assessment can yield important information about participants' progress, program quality, instructional practices, and the effectiveness of professionals. Evaluation encourages accountability: participants are accountable for their performance, and physical education and sport leaders are accountable for participants' achievement. Today, more than ever, demonstrating the worth and value of our programs is critical. Assessment is central to this purpose because it provides meaningful information about learning and achievement related to goals, objectives, and outcomes in the affective, cognitive, and psychomotor domains.

The NASPE content standards for physical education clearly identifies what a physically educated person should "know and be able to do." Assessment answers the question of whether participants' achievements are "good enough." Assessment links the content standards to the instructional process and to the participants' achievements. Assessment is a continual endeavor, one that is essential to the learning process.

Assessment Defined

Assessment is a process used to gather information about the participant's achievement and to make decisions and judgments based on that evidence for many purposes. Measurement and evaluation are closely related processes. *Measurement* is the process of gathering information or collecting data. *Evaluation* is the process of interpreting the information or data. Assessment is more encompassing in its scope than evaluation, including data collection, interpretation, and decision making.

NASPE identifies "the primary goal of assessment as the enhancement of learning, rather than documentation of learning."[20] Assessment has a broader purpose than the assignment of a grade to denote progress. As a critical component of any program, assessment helps professionals make decisions and conduct programs that are in the best interests of the participants.

Assessment will be used in its broadest sense in this discussion to encompass a variety of measurement, evaluation, and assessment techniques that have as their primary purpose the gathering and interpretation of information to make decisions that will enhance the outcomes achieved and the experiences of participants in physical education and sport programs.

Purposes of Assessment

There are many purposes for assessment. As an integral component of a quality physical education and sport program, assessment, when used correctly, can contribute in many ways to the achievement of learning and enhancement of development in the cognitive, affective, and psychomotor domains. The main purposes of assessment include diagnosis, placement, monitoring of progress, determination of achievement, motivation, program improvement, and teacher effectiveness.

Diagnosis is one of the most important uses of assessment. Diagnostic procedures can be used to identify individuals' strengths and weaknesses, levels of abilities, and developmental status in the various domains. When working with children with disabilities, the adapted physical activity specialist may use the Denver Developmental Screening Test to identify motor, language, and personal-social skills of the children. A sport psychologist working with an intercollegiate athletic team to improve its performance uses several paper-and-pencil tests to find out athletes' satisfaction, perception of team climate, attentional styles, and leadership roles. Additional knowledge gleaned from interviews of the athletes and coaches and from personal observation of the team during practice and games helps the sport psychologist identify factors limiting the team's achievement.

Prescription uses diagnostic information to design programs to meet identified needs. A cardiac rehabilitation specialist uses the results of an exercise stress test to prescribe an exercise program for the postcardiac patient. A personal trainer reviews the various assessments of a client's fitness levels, nutritional status, and lifestyle habits and then designs an individualized wellness program for the client. Working with the athlete's physician, an athletic trainer plans a program of exercise to restore the full range of motion to the athlete who is recovering from a rotator cuff injury.

Classification or placement of individuals into groups based on their abilities is another purpose of assessment. For children with disabilities, assessment influences their educational placement and the type of services they receive. Sport activity instructors commonly assign people to ability groups for instruction, believing that same ability grouping facilitates learning.

Determination of achievement is one of the primary purposes of assessment. Physical education and sport involves purposeful activity directed toward the attainment of certain goals. Have the program participants achieved the stated objectives? Does the senior citizen know how to modify his walking program as he increases in fitness? Are the children in a youth sport program mastering the basic skills of soccer? Do the physical fitness test results reveal that the student has achieved a satisfactory level of health-related fitness? Does the running log of a participant in the community fitness program reveal a commitment to exercising on a regular basis? Without assessment, how would we know whether our participants have achieved the desired objectives? Assessment can provide an indicator of achievement at the end of a program. When assessment is done at both the beginning and the end of the program, improvement can be seen. Incorporation of various assessment techniques throughout the program allows for the tracking of participants' progress.

Assessment can enhance the motivation of participants, encouraging them to improve further. Learning experiences that provide for frequent self-testing and incremental successes allow the sixth-grade students to see that their volleyball skills are improving and that hard work yields results. An athlete is motivated to continue to rehabilitate her knee when she sees that the weight that she can lift with her injured leg increases each week. An employee in a corporate fitness program is motivated to continue to exercise each day at 6:00 A.M. when he sees a decrease in his time to complete a mile and perceives himself as having more energy to meet the demands of the day. Assessment is also motivating to professionals when they see that the time and effort they have invested in their programs have benefitted the program's participants.

Assessment affects participants in varied ways. Assessment influences participants' perceptions of themselves as learners and, more specifically, their perceptions of their competence as movers. It can enhance their confidence in their abilities and create positive attitudes toward participation. Participants can use assessment to focus their learning on relevant tasks, to guide their expenditure of time, to consolidate their learning, and to develop learning strategies for the future.

Another purpose of assessment is program evaluation. Assessment can provide evidence of the effectiveness of the program. Corporate fitness directors can document the progress and concomitant health gains made by employees enrolled in the program. This lets the employer know if the program is beneficial to the employees and whether the investment in the program has yielded cost savings. This more global approach can also be used to improve the program. From this perspective, items such as program content, progression of instructional experiences, administration and organization, facilities and equipment, and time allocation are addressed as part of the overall program assessment. This enables professionals to make improvements in their programs to heighten their effectiveness.

Physical educators and sport leaders who care deeply about their professional endeavors reflect upon all the information gathered via the assessment process to improve their own effectiveness. They might ask themselves, "Are there any changes that I can make in my presentation? Is the order of the instructional tasks the best sequence

Essential for Good Health—A Physically Active Lifestyle

Child's Name _____   Class _____

I CAN   Physical Education Report
5th 6 week period 1998-99
Grade 4

We are learning how to learn. Your child has rated his/her ability level in the space next to each skill.
If my rating is different from your child's rating you will see my rating in GREEN *Please ask your child "what do these letters you wrote mean?" Hopefully you will get a thoughtful answer like "I put L for learning because I can do that some of the time, but not all of the time." If my rating is different you may also want to ask why s/he thinks they are different. There may be a good reason. Encourage you child to think about what s/he needs to work on and celebrate new skills. Thanks, Dolly Lambdin, Physical Education Teacher*

> **B** = Beginning – I can do it once in a while
> **L** = Learning – I can do it most of the time – but I have to really think about it
> **M** = Mastered – I can always do it – It is easy for me.
> **P** = Problems – I have problems with this.

In physical education we learn to move our bodies and objects with skill and confidence.

Basketball
__ I can dribble with one hand at a time without looking at the ball.
__ I can dribble (without stopping and dribbling again) when someone is guarding me.

__ I can do three kinds of basketball passes.
  They are _____, _____ , and _____
__ I can pivot when not dribbling the ball.

__ When I shoot I start with the ball in front of my forehead.
__ When I shoot I remember to follow through with a wave.

__ I know when to guard my partner.
__ I know how to guard my partner.

We encourage and support each other and make class a good place to learn.

__ I listen during instructions.   __ I move safely.
__ I follow the directions.   __ I work well with any partner.
__ I do **quality work**.   __ I help make fair teams.
                                          __ I like to play basketball.

Thanks for reading this 5th report card. Have your child return this slip for a "playdough" treat.
  Child's Name _____   Parent's Signature _____
Walk, jog, bike, EXERCISE with you children!!! Enjoy a healthy lifestyle.

FIGURE 2-1 Sample physical education report card that includes both self-assessment and teacher assessment.

to enhance participants' development? Do I need to give participants more guidance? These and other questions can help professionals enhance their effectiveness and, thus, influence the outcomes of the participants in their programs.

Types of Assessment

There are many considerations in the assessment process. One must decide what type of measures to use, the quality of the measurement, when the measures will be used, and how the results will be interpreted. First and foremost, however, the assessment should be related to the objectives of the program. There should be congruence between the assessment procedures and the objectives of the program.

There exist many measures to assess learning in the three domains. Professionals must carefully evaluate these measures. Do they possess *validity*? That is, does the test measure what it is supposed to measure? Is it *reliable*? Does the test produce consistent results? Does the measure possess *objectivity*? That is, does the participant receive the same score or rating no matter who is administering the assessment? These are criteria for selection of measures to evaluate performance. Administrative feasibility—in terms of time, cost and equipment—is an important consideration.

Assessment may take place at many different points throughout the program. *Formative assessment* refers to gathering and evaluating data about participants' progress throughout the program. This mode of assessment contributes to learning by providing meaningful feedback to both the participant and the professional. Formative assessment helps professionals make adaptations, modifications, and corrections to better serve participants and address their needs. Participants benefit from the feedback regarding their performance and the greater focus on specific objectives. Formative assessment—that is, continual assessment of participants' progress—enhances learning. A fitness professional uses formative assessment to help adults set realistic fitness goals and achieve them. The professional provides periodic testing, uses the test results to pinpoint specific areas of need,

and modifies the training program to address these needs, thus facilitating achievement.

Summative assessment occurs at the conclusion of the program. In the school setting, a grade may be assigned at the end of an instructional unit. Summative assessment enables a professional to determine an individual's status after a period of time. For example, in a corporate fitness program, an evaluation at the end of a 6-month fitness program gives participants information about their fitness status—cardiorespiratory endurance, heart rate, body composition, and weight.

Assessment can focus on the product or the process. *Product assessment* focuses on the end result of the performance and is usually expressed in quantitative terms. In the psychomotor domain, this outcome is usually a numerical, objective measure, such as a score in golf or time to run a mile. *Process assessment* refers to the quality of the performance or its form and is usually described in qualitative terms. In the psychomotor domain, this assessment usually relies on the professional's critical observation and, sometimes, the comparison of performance against stated criteria. For example, an individual's tennis forehand is judged against certain criteria to find out whether the objective has been met.

Assessment can use either norm-referenced or criterion-referenced standards. *Norm-referenced* tests compare an individual's performance against established standards for a population group with similar characteristics. For example, a student's score on a fitness test is compared with students of the same age and sex. *Criterion-referenced* tests compare an individual's performance against a predetermined standard of performance, not against other individuals. It determines the individual's degree of competence. An individual who has achieved the criterion standard is considered to have mastered the task. For example, the AAHPERD Physical Best standard for the 1-mile walk/run for 12-year-old boys is 11 minutes. If a boy completes the test in 10:30 seconds, he has met the standard and would be judged as possessing a satisfactory level of cardiorespiratory fitness.

There are many different avenues that professionals can use to assess the outcomes achieved by participants in their programs. The ability of as-

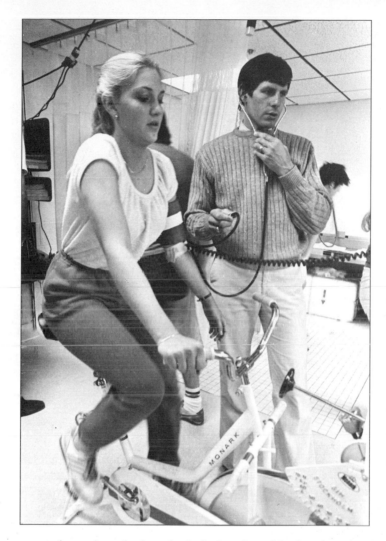

It is important to determine whether physical education objectives have been met. This woman is being tested at the Dow Health and Physical Education Center, Hope College, Michigan.

sessment procedures to enhance learning by connecting assessment to instruction and to enrich the experience of program participants makes it critical that assessment is included as an integral part of physical education and sport programs.

Traditional and "Alternative" Assessment

The past decade has been marked by a heightened societal interest in assessment and educa-

tional reform supporting the establishment of rigorous standards. Calls for accountability and for improved instructional effectiveness have contributed to the increased emphasis on assessment. On the other hand, this greater emphasis on assessment comes at a time when there is growing dissatisfaction with traditional assessment techniques.[30] In physical education programs in the schools, traditional assessment techniques, such as multiple-choice knowledge tests, psychosocial

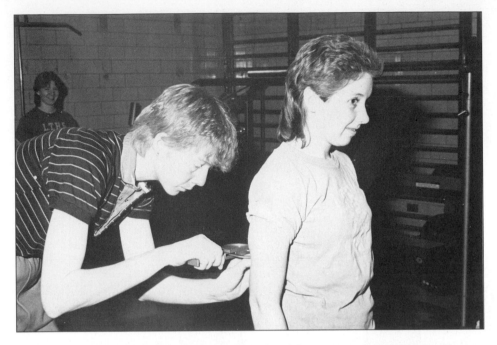

Skinfold measurement is part of the health-related fitness test administered at Lyons Township High School, in LaGrange, Illinois.

inventories, and standardized sport skills and physical fitness tests, were perceived as too specific, too narrowly focused, and, all to often, too artificial in nature.[30] Moreover, some physical educators expressed concern that these traditional approaches failed to measure important outcomes of interest to teachers and students.[30] "Alternative assessment" addresses these concerns.

Alternative assessment methods, proponents believe, "facilitate teaching, enhance learning, and result in greater achievement."[30] *Alternative assessment* emphasizes *performance-based outcomes* requiring that participants demonstrate important skills and competencies. Alternative assessment approaches may be perceived as more informal in nature than the traditional assessment approaches. Yet, they convey powerful information about participants' achievement of program objectives. A score sheet detailing a youth's serving percentage in a tennis game or a completed checklist evaluating a kindergartner's use of critical elements when

throwing overhand helps professionals find out these participants' level of achievement and where more work needs to be done. A fitness specialist reviewing with a member his running diary, which contains a record of his training—distance run, time, heart rate, feelings, perceived exertion, and days worked out—can determine the extent of the member's commitment to exercise and progress toward personal fitness goals. A careful review of a high schooler's portfolio of self-reflections, peer evaluations of skill performance, self-testing activities, journal chronicling participation in fitness activities outside the school setting, and other materials, in conjunction with the teacher's critical reflection about the student's participation in classes, enables the teacher to make a judgement about the high schooler's achievement of the stated objectives.

Authentic assessment requires that the assessment take place in a realistic situation as opposed to an artificial, contrived setting often associated

The sit-and-reach test is part of the health-related fitness test administered at Lyons Township High School, in LaGrange, Illinois.

with traditional assessment approaches.[31,32] Assessment tasks closely approximate what would happen in an actual setting. With traditional assessment, a student's tennis ground strokes are assessed by hitting balls tossed by a partner under prescribed test conditions. An authentic assessment approach assesses the student's ability to use the ground strokes in a game situation; a scoring rubric (rating scale) guides the assessment process.

Alternative approaches to assessment have been used by physical education and sport leaders for many years and are applicable to many physical education and sport programs in a diversity of settings. Thoughtfully established criteria related to outcomes, skilled observation and critical analysis, and informed judgments by professionals can yield meaningful and relevant information about the achievements of participants.

Both traditional and alternative assessment techniques can be used to assess learning in the cognitive, affective, and psychomotor domains. As a dynamic process, assessment continually yields information about participants' progress toward achievement of objectives. The increasing integration of both assessment and technology in our programs can enhance the rate of participants' progress and facilitate achievement of objectives.

The Role of Technology in Assessment

Technology is increasingly influencing the assessment processes. Microcomputers can be helpful in maintaining records of test results or keeping a log of participants' involvement in the program.

One example of computerized record keeping is the Cooper's Institute for Aerobics Prudential Fitnessgram. The Fitnessgram is used in many schools throughout the nation to provide students and their parents with information about the individual's fitness profile. The program measures the health-related components of fitness—cardiorespiratory endurance, muscle strength and endurance, flexibility, and body composition. The Fitnessgram test items and a sample of the Fitnessgram can be seen in Figures 2-2 and 2-3. The Fitnessgram provides a computerized report on the fitness status of each student. The profile is constructed from the individual's performance on the test items. When necessary, exercise recommendations are made, based on the test performance of the individual. The Fitnessgram also makes it easy for teachers, parents, and students to compare their performance on the current test to performances on previous tests. This makes it easy to note where improvements have been made and identifies fitness areas that require attention. The Fitnessgram helps teachers keep track of their students' fitness level and determine whether the stated program objectives are being achieved.

Corporate fitness centers also use microcomputers in their fitness programs. A computerized check-in system records employee participation. After exercising, employees use the computer to record the type of exercise they performed, the duration of the exercise period, and their weight. A record of each employee's progress toward his or her goals is easily maintained. This information is helpful to program managers in charting facility usage, calculating the benefits of the programs, and documenting program effectiveness.

Heart-rate monitors are valuable tools for teaching children and adults about fitness in both school and nonschool settings. These monitors, worn on the wrist, track heart rate and provide positive reinforcement to the wearers as they work to achieve their goals. They provide physical education teachers and sport leaders with valuable information that they can use to modify their teaching methods. A printout of the exercise session provides a permanent record of participants' work.

The impact of computer technology has been felt throughout the field of physical education and sport. Exercise physiologists use computers to regulate equipment during highly complex tests of cardiovascular function and to analyze the voluminous amounts of data generated. Athletic trainers assess the extent of an injury, carry out a course of treatment, and monitor the rehabilitation process. Computerized equipment, such as the Cybex, offers both the injured athlete and the athletic trainer continuous feedback on their weight-training efforts during rehabilitation. Biomechanists use special computer programs to analyze motions and force production. Sport sociologists and sport psychologists use computers to conduct sophisticated data analysis. Fitness professionals rely on computers for record keeping. Club members punch in their personal code on a computer console next to each piece of exercise equipment. As a digital display shows weight lifted and repetitions performed, the computer keeps track as well, providing the member and the professional with a continuous record of the member's progress.

SUMMARY

Today American education faces the challenge of preparing individuals with a wide range of abilities and from diverse backgrounds to function effectively in today's and tomorrow's world. Physical education, as an integral part of the school curriculum, can play a significant role in this endeavor.

Because education is a major societal institution and school physical education and sport programs serve millions of children and youth, an understanding of education's goals and objectives is important for all professionals in our field. Goals are broad statements of aims that reflect desired accomplishments. Objectives are more specific statements of outcomes that build progressively to the achievement of goals. *Goals 2000* identifies American educational goals for the next century. These include readiness to learn, improvement of graduation rates, increased competency in core subjects, international prominence in math and science, improvement of adult literacy, creation of a safe

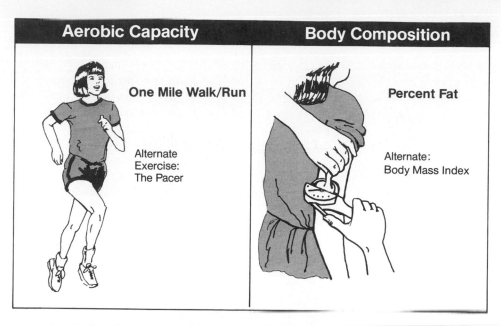

Aerobic Capacity

One Mile Walk/Run

Alternate
Exercise:
The Pacer

Body Composition

Percent Fat

Alternate:
Body Mass Index

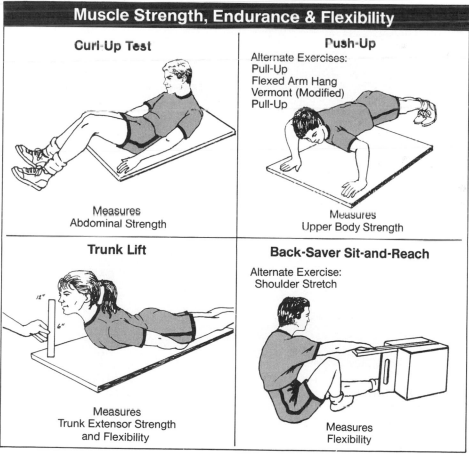

Muscle Strength, Endurance & Flexibility

Curl-Up Test

Measures
Abdominal Strength

Push-Up

Alternate Exercises:
Pull-Up
Flexed Arm Hang
Vermont (Modified)
Pull-Up

Measures
Upper Body Strength

Trunk Lift

12"
6"

Measures
Trunk Extensor Strength
and Flexibility

Back-Saver Sit-and-Reach

Alternate Exercise:
Shoulder Stretch

Measures
Flexibility

FIGURE 2-2 Test items for the Fitnessgram.

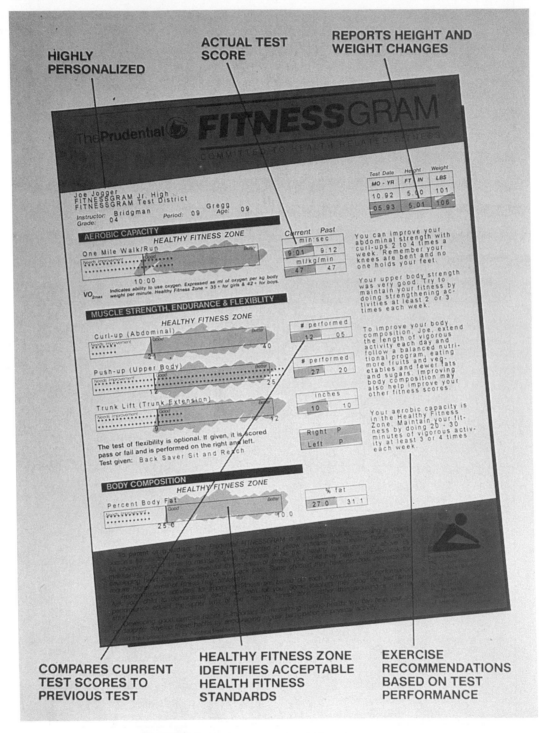

FIGURE 2-3 An example of the Fitnessgram.

learning environment, professional development for teachers, and school-parent partnerships. Physical education and sport programs in the school can help achieve these goals by enhancing school readiness, contributing to the health and vitality of students, facilitating an integrated approach to learning, and promoting lifelong learning.

The goals of physical education and sport have historically been defined for school-aged populations. Today, our programs embrace a wide range of ages and settings. Physical education and sport in the twentieth century has emphasized the development of the whole person through participation in quality physical education and sport programs. The objectives of physical education and sport encompass four areas: fitness development, skill development, knowledge, and social-emotional development.

The past decade has seen professional efforts devoted to identifying the qualities of a physically educated person. According to NASPE, a physically educated person has learned skills to perform a variety of physical activities, is physically fit, participates regularly in physical activities, knows the benefits of involvement in physical activity, and values the contribution of physical activity to a healthy lifestyle. NASPE developed content standards for physical education and guidelines for assessment. These standards and guidelines offer professionals in all settings a valuable framework to guide their efforts.

Human behavior is often described with reference to three domains: cognitive, affective, and psychomotor domains. Taxonomies organize the objectives associated with each domain into hierarchies. These taxonomies guide professionals in designing programs to meet the needs of their participants. Physical education and sport contributes in many ways to learning in these three domains.

Assessment of learning is critical in physical education and sport. Assessment is a continual process that serves many purposes. These include diagnosis, prescription, classification, determination of achievement, documentation of progress, enhancement of motivation, program improvement, and professional development. There are many types of assessment methods for professionals to utilize. The past decade has been marked by educational reform, including pressure for accountability, establishment of standards, and emphasis on assessment. On the other hand, there is a growing dissatisfaction with traditional assessment measures. Alternative assessment is growing in popularity. Alternative assessment emphasizes performance-based outcomes and uses assessment techniques that require the participants to demonstrate important skills and competencies. Authentic assessment promotes the value of assessing outcomes in realistic, as opposed to contrived, settings.

Technology is increasingly influencing the assessment process. Computers have been used for record keeping, regulation of testing equipment, and data analysis. Professionals in all settings have found technology to be of great value in their endeavors.

The next chapter will discuss the role of physical education and sport in our society, as well as the educational reform movement and its impact on physical education and sport.

SELF-ASSESSMENT TESTS

These tests are designed to help you determine if you have mastered the material and competencies presented in this chapter.

1. Provide specific examples of how physical education and sport, both in the school and non-school setting, can contribute to attaining each of the *Goals 2000*. How did *Goals 2000* influence your high school curriculum? What impact did it have on physical education and sport programs in your school district?

2. Using the information provided in Getting Connected, access the NASPE web site and read

the National Standards for Physical Education. Review carefully the background, purpose, standards list, and sample assessment. Discuss how these standards could be applied in a community fitness program for adults or in a high school physical education program.

3. Review carefully the characteristics of a physically educated person and the outcome statements. Then compare your knowledge, skills, and attitudes to the desired outcomes. Are you physically educated?

4. Reflect on your experiences in youth, interscholastic, and intercollegiate sport. How did these experiences contribute to your development in the cognitive, affective, and psychomotor domains? What changes could have been made in the conduct of the programs to further enhance development?

REFERENCES

1. US Department of Health and Human Services: Healthy people 2000: national health promotion and disease prevention objectives, Washington, D.C., 1990, US Government Printing Office.

2. Melograno VJ: Designing the physical education curriculum, ed 3, Champaign, Ill., 1996, Human Kinetics.

3. Commission on reorganization of secondary education: Cardinal principles of secondary education, Washington, D.C., 1918, US Government Printing Office.

4. Educational policies commission: The purposes of education in an American democracy, Washington, D.C., 1938, National Education Association.

5. Educational policies commission: Education for all American youth, Washington, D.C., 1944, National Education Association.

6. Association of School Administrators: Imperatives in education, Washington, D.C., 1966, Association of School Administrators.

7. Gross RE: Seven new cardinal principles, Phi Delta Kappan 60:291–293, 1978.

8. US Department of Education: The goals 2000—launching a new era in education, Washington, D.C., 1994, US Government Printing Office.

9. Children's Defense Fund: Children 1990: a report card, briefing book, and action primer, Washington, D.C., 1990, Children's Defense Fund.

10. National Center for Educational Statistics: Adult literacy in America, Washington, D.C., 1996, US Department of Education.

11. US Department of Education: Americans beat international averages in science and math, Washington, D.C., Community Update, 49:6, 1997.

12. US Department of Education: US Mayors support President Clinton's call for action for American education, Washington, D.C., Community Update, 49:5, 1997.

13. US Department of Education: Hispanic dropout project, Washington, D.C., 1998, US Department of Education.

14. Sadler WC, Tentinger LG, and Wiedow GA: American 2000: implications for physical education, Physical Educator 50:77–86, 1993.

15. Siedentop D: Introduction to physical education, fitness, and sport, ed 3, Mountain View, Calif., 1998, Mayfield.

16. Bucher CA: Foundations of physical education, ed 4, St. Louis, 1964, Mosby.

17. American Association for Health, Physical Education, and Recreation: This is physical education, Washington, D.C., 1965, American Association for Health, Physical Education, and Recreation.

18. Biles F: PEPI—The physical education public information project, Journal of Health, Physical Education, and Recreation 41(7):53–55, 1971.

19. National Association for Sport and Physical Education: Definition of a physically educated person: outcomes of quality physical education programs, Reston, Va., 1990, AAHPERD.

20. National Association for Sport and Physical Education: Moving into the future national standards for physical education: a guide to content and assessment, St. Louis, 1995, Mosby.

21. Ziegler E: The professional's relationship to fitness for people of all ages, Journal of Physical Education, Recreation and Dance 56(1):15, 1985.

22. Bloom BS, editor: Taxonomy of educational objectives: the classification of education goals, handbook I: cognitive domain, New York, 1956, David McKay.

23. Strand B, Mauch L, and Terbizan D: The fitness education pyramid—Integrating the concepts with the technology, JOPERD 68(6):19–27, 1997.

24. Krathwohl DR, Bloom BS, and Masia BB: Taxonomy of educational objectives, handbook II: the affective domain, New York, 1964, David McKay.

25. Hellison D: Teaching personal and social responsibility in physical education. In S Silverman and C Ennis, editors, Student learning in physical education: applying research to enhance instruction, Champaign, Ill., 1996, Human Kinetics.

26. Docheff D: Character in sport and physical education—summation, JOPERD 69(2):24, 1998.

27. Gough RW: Character development—A practical strategy for emphasizing character development in sport and physical education, JOPERD 69(2):18–20, 23, 1998.

28. Harrow A: A taxonomy of the psychomotor domain, New York, 1964, David McKay.

29. Corbin CB: Becoming physically educated in the elementary school, Philadelphia, 1976, Lea & Febiger.

30. Hensley LD: Alternative assessment for physical education, JOPERD 68(7):19–24, 1997.

31. Lund J: Authentic assessment: its development and applications, JOPERD 68(7):25–28, 40, 1997.

32. Melograno VJ: Integrating assessment into physical education teaching, JOPERD: 68(7): 34–37, 1997.

SUGGESTED READINGS

Docheff D, editor: Character in sport and physical education, JOPERD 68(9), 1997.

A five-part feature on character development, this includes information on the history of character education, physical education's impact on character development, sports' effect on character, measurement, and practical strategies for character development in physical education and sport.

Martens R, editor: Technology in kinesiology and physical education, Quest 49(3), 1997.

This special issue of Quest is devoted to technology and its application to the study of physical activity.

National Association for Sport and Physical Education: Moving into the future national standards for physical education: A guide to content and assessment, St. Louis, 1995, Mosby.

National content standards, standards, sample benchmarks, and assessment samples provide practitioners with a framework for their work.

Tomme PM and Wendt JC: Affective teaching: psycho-social aspects of physical education, Journal of Physical Education, Recreation, and Dance 64(8):66–69, 1993.

Provides illustrations of how cooperative activities can lead to psychosocial development, including promotion of honesty, respect, concern, and self-discipline.

Zhu W: Alternative assessment: what, why, how, JOPERD 68(7), Feature, 1997.

A series of articles covering alternative assessment for physical education, authentic assessment, using portfolios, integrating assessment into teaching, and quality control in alternative assessment.

CHAPTER 3

Role of Physical Education and Sport in Society and in Education

Instructional Objectives and Competencies to be Achieved:

After reading this chapter the student should be able to—

• Understand the changing demographics of the United States and their implications for physical education and sport.

• Interpret to colleagues and to the public the role of physical education and sport in the promotion of health and the attainment of wellness.

• Discuss the fitness movement and the implications of the movement for physical education and sport.

• Discuss the current educational reform movement and its implications for physical education programs.

Societal trends influence the role of physical education and sport in our society. One significant trend is the changing demographics of our population. Our society is more culturally diverse than at any other time in its history. Researchers indicate that this diversity will become even greater as we move into the twenty-first century. As professionals committed to enriching the lives of all people, we must, as DeSensi states, increase our "consciousness and appreciation of differences associated with heritage, characteristics, and values of people."[1]

Two other societal trends that hold implications for physical education and sport are the wellness movement and the fitness and physical activity movement. The wellness movement emphasizes the individual's responsibility to make informed choices that will lead to an optimal state of health. Disease prevention and health promotion are the cornerstones of this movement. The fitness and physical activity movement reflects the enthusiasm of individuals to engage in exercise, sports, and physical activity on a regular basis. There is substantial evidence to support the value of leading a physically active lifestyle across the lifespan.

Another significant trend is the educational reform movement. During the past two decades, calls to redesign, revitalize, and strengthen the educational system have increased. The nature of the educational reforms implemented could have far-reaching consequences for the conduct of physical education and sport programs in our schools.

GETTING CONNECTED

Physical Activity and Health: A Report of the Surgeon General contains a wealth of information about physical activity and health, including the most recent studies of physical activity patterns of youth and adults.
Site: http://www.cdc.gov/nccdphp/sgr/sgr.html

Centers for Disease Control and Prevention presents information on a variety of health status indicators, including news, health information, and data and statistics. This site also provides access to *Morbidity and Morality Weekly Report.*
Site: http://www.cdc.gov/

Physical Activity and Health Network offers links to research on physical activity and health, fitness, nutrition, and other related topics.
Site: http://www.pitt.edu/~pahnet/

United States Department of Education site provides current news and information about educational initiatives, including *Goals 2000.*
Site: http://www.ed.gov/

Participation in daily physical education has declined during this decade. Furthermore, physical activity among children declines during adolescence. School-based programs offer us a great opportunity to address inequities in participation in physical activity and to encourage continued involvement in physical activity.

CHANGING DEMOGRAPHICS

As we enter the twenty-first century, population changes will influence physical education and sport programs. For one, we are living longer.[2] In 1996, life expectancy reached an all-time high of 76.1 years, up from 75.8 years in 1995. The gender gap in life expectancy narrowed from 6.4 years in 1995 to 6 years in 1996, with females living longer than males. The difference in life expectancy between Caucasians and African-American populations narrowed from 6.9 to 6.5 years, with Caucasians living longer than African Americans.

Our population is becoming older.[3] In 1997, people 65 years of age and older composed 12.7% of our population. This percentage will rise to

18.5% in 2025. The number of people 85 years and older is projected to increase from 3.8 million in 1996 to more than 7 million in 2025. It is estimated that minority populations will represent 25% of the older population in 2030, up from 13% recorded in 1990.

The number of individuals with disabilities continues to grow.[4] In 1995, about 54 million Americans, 1 in every 5, reported some level of disability. Twenty-six million Americans, 1 in every 10, described their disability as severe. About 70% of Americans 80 years and older have a disability, and more than 50% of them have a severe disability. In 1992, there were only 49 million people with disabilities, and 24 million people with severe disabilities.

As a society, we are become more culturally diverse.[4] By the year 2000, it is projected that 71.6% of the population will be non-Hispanic Caucasians, 12.2% non-Hispanic African Americans, 4.1% Asians/Pacific Islanders, and 0.7% American Indians/Alaskan natives. People of Hispanic origin are expected to compose 11.1% of the population. By 2005, Hispanic Americans are expected to

Participation in appropriate exercise can help elderly people increase their cardiovascular endurance and flexibility.

outnumber African Americans. It is projected that by 2050, the Hispanic or Latino population will constitute 25% of the U.S. population.

Changes will be seen in the school-aged population. Hispanic children will outnumber African-American children by 1998.[5] In 2050 it is projected that Hispanic children will compose 31% of all children, compared to 43% and 16% for Caucasians and African Americans, respectively.

Immigrants will increase our diversity.[6] According to projections by the U.S. Immigration and Naturalization Service, during the 1990s the United States will have received the largest number of immigrants in our nation's history—10 million people. There are several school districts in the United States where more than 100 languages are spoken.

There are many changes in the structure of our families.[4] The proportion of children living in single-parent families has more than doubled since 1970. In 1994, nearly 60% of African-American children lived in single-parent families, compared to 29% for Hispanics and 19% for Caucasians. Children in single-parent families, compared to the traditional two-parent family, are twice as likely to drop out of school, be suspended from school, and to have emotional problems. Twenty-five percent of single-parent families live below the poverty level.

Socioeconomic status exerts a significant influence on health status and school outcomes. In 1996, 36.5% of Americans fell below the poverty level, which was defined as $16,036 for a family of four.[4] Caucasians made up more than 66% of

Americans living below the poverty level. Hispanics compose 23.8% of the poor, and African Americans 25.8% of the poor. Minorities are disproportionately represented among the poor; for instance, 70% of youths in communities of color live in extreme poverty. One in every 4 children under the age of 6 lives in poverty at this critical juncture in their development. Nearly 1 in every 5 of the elderly population lives below or near poverty level. Poverty is associated with poor health outcomes for all ages, including higher rates of mortality. Children and youths of low socioeconomic status are at greater risk for poor school outcomes compared to their peers who enjoy a higher standard of living.

As we reflect on these societal changes, we must ask ourselves how we can better provide opportunities for participation in physical activity. How can we involve a greater number of older individuals in our programs? How can we design programs that are sensitive to the values and needs of different cultures? How do we reach underserved populations, and what is our commitment to do so?

These changing demographics require physical educators and sport leaders to reflect carefully on their view of cultural diversity and their commitment to providing opportunities for lifelong involvement in physical activity for all people. DeSensi defines cultural diversity as the "differences associated with gender, race, national origin, ethnicity, social class, religion, age, and ability/disability, but it can also be extended to include difference in personality, sexual orientation, veteran status, physical appearance, marital status, and parental status."[1] Physical education and sport professionals need to adopt a multicultural approach to their work if they are to meet the needs of participants in their program. This involves appreciation of differences, valuing the uniqueness of individuals, and commitment to working to redress inequities in opportunities.

WELLNESS MOVEMENT

The twentieth century has seen a gradual, epidemiologic transition from infectious to chronic disease as the leading causes of death. In 1900,

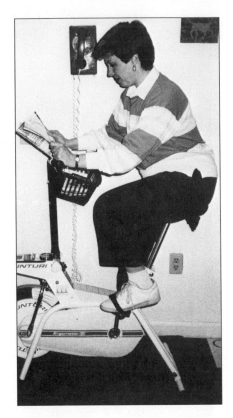

Sales of home exercise equipment continue to increase. Various types of equipment are available that allow people to work out at their convenience in their own homes.

the leading causes of death were influenza, pneumonia, tuberculosis, and gastrointestinal problems (e.g., diarrhea). Life expectancy was 47.3 years. Half a century later, in 1950, there was a phenomenal rise in life expectancy to 68 years.[7] The development of antibiotics, the availability of vaccines, and improvements in housing, sanitation, food and water supplies, and diet were instrumental in achieving this dramatic gain. In 1995, the leading causes of death were chronic diseases, specifically heart disease, cancer, and stroke. These causes accounted for 62% of all deaths.[2] In 1996, life expectancy reached the all-time high of 76.1 years.[2]

As this shift occurred, evidence accumulated regarding the role behavioral risk factors play in disease and early mortality. Health risk factors such as smoking, inactivity, high-fat diet, obesity, and stress influence the occurrence of chronic disease. For example, individuals who lead a sedentary lifestyle are almost at twice the risk for coronary heart disease, the number one cause of death in the United States, as those individuals who are physically active.[8] In 1994 the Centers for Disease Control and Prevention estimated that 47% of premature deaths could have been prevented by changes in individuals' behaviors and another 17% through reduction of environmental risks.[9] In contrast, only an estimated 11% of premature deaths could have been prevented through improvements in access to medical treatment.[9] As can be seen, significant reduction of these controllable risk factors can lead to remarkable improvement in the health of the individual as well as the health of the nation.

During the twentieth century, our view of health has also changed. Traditionally the public viewed good health as freedom from disease. If an individual was not ill, he or she was considered healthy. This perspective has changed during the twentieth century. While it is generally agreed that not being ill is one part of being healthy, health can also be defined in terms of being well. According to the World Health Organization (WHO), health is a "state of complete physical, mental, and social well-being and not merely the absence of disease and infirmity."[10] Health, then, is not solely concerned with one's physical state; it extends beyond concern with the body to include emotional and social well-being.

In the later part of the twentieth century, the holistic approach to health has grown in popularity. The holistic approach is an even broader approach to health than presented in the WHO definition. Besides encompassing the physical, mental, and social dimensions of health, holistic health also incorporates the intellectual and spiritual dimensions of well-being. Holistic health focuses on the whole person. Individuals who are healthy, according to the holistic definition of health, are said to have achieved a high level of wellness.

Wellness is a state of optimal health and well-being. It is living life to the fullest and maximizing one's potential as a whole person. Wellness incorporates five different components: physical wellness, emotional wellness, social wellness, intellectual wellness, and spiritual wellness. Physical wellness encompasses physical fitness and proper nutrition. Emotional wellness focuses on emotional stability and managing stress effectively. Social wellness emphasizes the development of interpersonal skills and healthy, fulfilling relationships. Intellectual wellness is characterized by sound decision-making skills, intellectual growth, and values. Spiritual wellness takes on different meanings according to the beliefs of the individual.

Wellness emphasizes individuals taking personal responsibility for their health and leading a lifestyle that enhances their well-being. However, while focusing on individual responsibility, it is important to recognize that a multitude of forces—environmental, genetic, societal, and personal—interact to affect one's well-being. Living conditions, heredity, and societal conditions such as poverty and discrimination also exert a significant influence on one's health and well-being.

Americans today are taking a more active role in protecting and enhancing their health. There is a growing realization that our health and our quality of life are significantly influenced by the manner in which we live our lives. Many lifestyle choices we make, whether to smoke tobacco or to exercise on a regular basis, influence our potential for health, function, and well-being both on a daily basis and across our lifespan. This realization is accompanied by a greater understanding of the important role of personal responsibility—that is, informed and responsible behavior—in achieving good health, both on a personal and national level.

During the past two decades societal interest in promoting health and preventing disease has increased. The accumulation of evidence supporting the fact that changes in behaviors could reduce individuals' risk of disease, increase their span of healthy life, and improve their quality of life has stimulated the growth of health promotion and disease prevention initiatives. National health reports, *Healthy People*,[11] *Objectives for the Nation*,[12] and *Healthy People 2000*[8] emphasized that further improvements in the health of Americans

Community fitness trails are popular with residents.

depended not only on advances in health care and increased health care expenditures but also on a national commitment to disease prevention and health promotion.

The latest report, *Healthy People 2000*,[8] sought to significantly improve the nation's health through a comprehensive emphasis on disease prevention and health promotion. Three broad goals for improving the health of the nation were identified. The goals to be accomplished by the year 2000 are:

◆ increase the span of healthy life.
◆ reduce disparities in health among population groups.
◆ achieve access to preventive services for all Americans.[16]

Healthy People 2000 objectives emphasize the principle that efforts to increase life expectancy must be accompanied by efforts to increase health throughout life. The focus is on health efforts that will lead to a full range of functional capacity throughout the lifespan, from infancy through old age.

Healthy People 2000 stressed the need to address disparities in health if the nation's overall health profile was to be improved. Efforts need to be directed at making substantial improvements in health in population groups disadvantaged economically, educationally, and politically and are at highest risk for premature death, disability, and disease. For example, life expectancy at birth for Caucasian males is 73.8 years, while for African-American males it is 66.1 years.[2] Infant mortality is twice as high for African-American babies as for Caucasian babies.[2] Estimates of disabilities among different groups reveal inequities in health. The rate of disability is 6.6% for Hispanics, 9.3% for Caucasians, 11.2% for African Americans, 13.4% for Native Americans, and 18.9% for low-income populations.[8] These few striking examples speak strongly to the need to address the health needs of racial and ethnic populations and those individuals who are economically disadvantaged.

Achieving access to health care and preventive services is an important factor in accomplishing our national health goals. Barriers to care such as lack of monies, inadequate health insurance, limited hours of service availability, and cultural constraints must be removed. Families, schools, work sites, and community members are all important opportunities for prevention. Attainment of our national health goals relies on greater access and use of preventive services.

These goals set the health agenda for the nation. To realize these outcomes, 298 specific objectives were developed and organized into 22 priority areas. These priorities relate to health promotion, health protection, preventive services, and surveillance (see the box below). Full achievement of the goals and objectives requires the integration of personal health care with public health care. "The vision of healthy people in healthy communities moves beyond what happens in physicians' offices, clinics, and hospitals—beyond the traditional medical care system—to the neighborhoods, schools, workplaces, and families in which people live their daily lives. These are the environments in which a large portion of prevention occurs."[7]

The *Healthy People 2000* report recognizes the increasing evidence supporting the health benefits of regular physical activity. Engaging in physical activity on a regular basis increases life expectancy, helps older adults maintain functional independence, and enhances the quality of life. Physical activity can help prevent and assist in the management of a number of diseases and conditions, including coronary heart disease, hypertension, and diabetes. In particular, the potential of physical activity to reduce the risk of coronary heart disease, the leading cause of morbidity and mortality in this country, was noted. Leading a sedentary lifestyle almost doubles an individual's risk for coronary heart disease. Physical inactivity also contributes to other risk factors for coronary heart disease, such as obesity and hypertension. Objectives for physical activity and fitness are shown in the box on pages 82 to 83.

In 1995, *The Health of the Nation: A Midcourse Review* was released by the Public Health Service. The report noted the following:

♦ Better dietary and exercise patterns can contribute significantly to reducing heart disease, stroke, diabetes, and cancer, and could prevent 300,000 deaths.

♦ The financial burden of heart disease and stroke is $135 billion a year.

♦ Since 1990, life expectancy has increased by 1 year.

♦ Healthy life years are estimated to be 85% of the life expectancy. Fifteen percent of the life years are estimated be unhealthy, with major limitations of life activities, such as self-care, recreation, and work. Because activity limitations increase with age, it is important to reduce disability and to increase the health and independence of older adults. Years of healthy life have declined.

♦ Disparities in health, both in morbidity and mortality, and the use of health services between Caucasians and minorities continue to be substantial.

♦ Progress has occurred in reducing heart disease and stroke rates for adults.[7]

HEALTHY PEOPLE 2000 PRIORITY AREAS

Health Promotion
Physical Activity and Fitness
Nutrition
Tobacco
Alcohol and Other Drugs
Family Planning
Mental Health and Mental Disorders
Violent and Abusive Behavior
Educational and Community-based Programs

Health Protection
Unintentional Injuries
Occupational Safety and Health
Environmental Health
Food and Drug Safety
Oral Health

Preventive Services
Maternal and Infant Health
Heart Disease and Stroke
Cancer
Diabetes and Chronic Disabling Conditions
HIV Infection
Sexually Transmitted Diseases
Immunizations and Infectious Diseases
Clinical Preventive Services

Surveillance and Data Systems
Surveillance and Data Systems

HEALTHY PEOPLE 2000: PHYSICAL ACTIVITY AND FITNESS OBJECTIVES

	Objective	**Baseline (Year)**
1.1	Reduce coronary heart disease deaths to no more than 100 per 100,000 people.	135/100,000 (1987)
1.2	Reduce prevalence of overweight to less than 20% among people age 20 and older and to less than 15% among adolescents aged 12–19.	26% for people 20 years or older; 15% for youths ages 12–19 (1976)
1.3	Increase to at least 30% the proportion of people age 6 and older who engage regularly, preferably daily, in light to moderate physical activity at least 30 minutes per day.	22% for people age 18 or older who were active 5 or more times/week (1985)
1.4	Increase to at least 20% the proportion of people age 18 or older and to at least 75% the proportion of children and adolescents age 6–17 who engage in vigorous physical activity that promotes the development and maintenance of cardio-respiratory fitness 3 or more days per week for 20 or more minutes per occasion.	22% for people age 12 and older (1985); 66% for youth ages 10–17 (1984)
1.5	Reduce to no more than 15% the proportion of people age 6 or older who engage in no leisure-time physical activity.	24% for people age 18 or older (1985)
1.6	Increase to at least 40% the proportion of people age 6 or older who regularly perform physical activities that enhance and maintain muscular strength, muscular endurance, and flexibility.	No baseline data
1.7	Increase to at least 50% the proportion of overweight people age 12 or older who have adopted sound dietary practices combined with regular physical activity to attain an appropriate body weight.	30% of females and 25% of males age 18 and older (1985)
1.8	Increase to at least 50% the proportion of children and adolescents in 1st–12th grade who participate in daily school physical education.	36% (1984–1986)
1.9	Increase to at least 50% the proportion of school physical education class time that students spend being physically active, preferably engaged in lifetime physical activities.	27% (1983)
1.10	Increase the proportion of work sites offering employer-sponsored physical activity programs as follows:	(1985)

Work Site Size	2000 Target	
50–99 employees	20%	14%
100–248 employees	35%	23%
250–749 employees	50%	32%
≥ 750 employees	80%	54%

1.11	Increase community availability and accessibility and fitness facilities as follows:		(1986)
	Facility	2000 Target	
	Hiking, biking, and fitness trail miles	1 per 10,000 people	1 per 71,000
	Public swimming pools	1 per 25,000 people	1 per 53,000
	Acres of parks and recreation open spaces	4 per 1,000 people	1.8 per 1,000 people
1.12	Increase to at least 50% the proportion of primary care providers who routinely assess and counsel their parents regarding the frequency, duration, type, and intensity of each patient's physical activity practices.		30% (1988)

Public Health Service, US Department of Health and Human Services: *Promoting health/preventing disease: year 2000 objectives for the nation*, US Government Printing Office, 1990.

The report revealed that more than two-thirds of the overall objectives for which data were available were moving toward their targets. Progress toward the achievement of the physical activity objectives, expressed as the percentage of attainment, is shown in Figure 3-1. As can be seen from Objective 1.1, progress has been made toward reducing deaths from coronary heart disease. Deaths from heart disease declined 4%. Objectives 1.2 and 1.7 show a movement away from the target percentage. The prevalence of obesity continues to rise among adults and children. The third National Health and Nutrition Examination Survey (NHANES III)[13] revealed that nearly 15% of children and youth are overweight. One in every 3 adults is overweight.

Some progress was made in promoting involvement in physical activity. Objectives 1.3 and 1.4, which refer to the regular participation in vigorous and moderate physical activity, show modest improvement. Objective 1.5 shows no change in the sedentary lifestyles of adults. However, improvements were seen in specific population groups. The percentage of adults reporting no leisure-time activities dropped from 43% to 29% for adults over 65 and from 35% to 30% for people with disabilities. The involvement of individuals with low income remained the same, at 32%. Objective 1.6 shows a small increase in the number of people who engage in activities to improve muscular strength.

Schools are the primary setting to reach over 51 million children and adolescents. Unfortunately, as can be seen from Objectives 1.8 and 1.9, participation in daily physical education and access to quality physical education decreased significantly. On the other hand, worksite fitness programs, Objective 1.10, show a dramatic increase for all sizes of employers. No data were available at the time to track the growth of community facilities or counseling on physical activity by primary-care providers.

Data released in 1998 provided information about Objective 1.12. Few doctors counsel people about how to prevent heart disease. Doctors discussed physical activity during 19% of the visits, diet during 23%, weight loss during 10%, and referred patients to smoking cessation programs during 41% of the visits.[14] Doctors perceived themselves as not having much influence on their patients' behavior. For instance, even though 59% of primary-care physicians acknowledged the importance of physical activity, only 24% believed they could influence patients to change their sedentary behavior.[14]

Health promotion and disease prevention have the potential to significantly constrain the enormous and growing cost of health care in this country. In 1996, health care spending increased by 4.4%, the lowest rate in 37 years.[15] However, at the time, national health care expenditures for the first time exceeded $1 trillion. National health

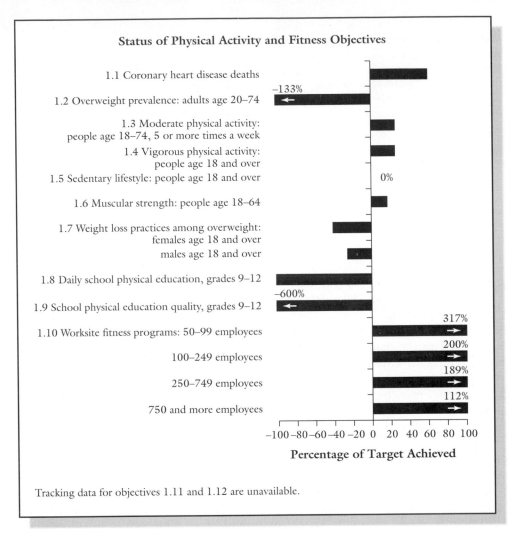

FIGURE 3-1 The Healthy People 2000 Midcourse Review showed mixed results in achieving the nation's physical activity and fitness objectives. The data were reported by the President's Council on Physical Activity and Fitness.

care expenditures were $1.04 trillion, 13.6% of the gross national product (GNP).[15] Costs continue to rise at an astronomical rate and are projected to hit $1.9 trillion by the year 2000 unless there is significant reform of our health care system.

U.S. businesses are concerned about spiraling health care costs. If our current system of health care continues, it is estimated that business will pay $512 billion for health care by the year 2000.

Poor employee health is costly. Illness and premature death cost American industry billions of dollars a year. Poor health and fitness contribute to decreased productivity and increased absenteeism. Premiums for medical insurance continue to rise. Growing health care costs and the realization of the benefits to be gained through physical fitness have led many corporations to establish health promotion and fitness programs for their employees.

Corporations have found that such programs make economic sense. Benefit/cost ratios compare the benefits achieved to the cost of conducting programs. Benefit/cost ratios for worksite health promotion programs range from 1.15 to 5.52; that is, for every $1 invested, between $1.15 and $5.52 was saved.[16] Businesses have become increasingly aware of the short- and long-term benefits of employee health and fitness programs (i.e., greater productivity and reduced medical expenditures). It appears that preventive measures may be cheaper in the long run than curative ones.

Individuals are also responding to the wellness movement. People are making changes in their lifestyle to enhance their well-being. During the past decade there has been a steady decline in the number of adults who smoke cigarettes. Individuals are becoming more conscientious about their eating habits and making modifications where necessary, such as decreasing sodium and fat in their diet. Some individuals are incorporating physical activity into their lifestyle on a regular basis. In short, individuals are becoming increasingly aware that the manner in which they live and the personal choices they make can have a significant impact on their health and quality of life.

What Are the Implications of the Wellness Movement for Physical Education and Sport?

What role should physical education and sport take in promoting health and achieving national public health goals? The public health focus on health promotion and disease prevention presents a tremendous opportunity for physical education and sport professionals to increase their contributions to the health and welfare of all people. As you review the *Healthy People 2000* goals and the specific objectives for physical activity, ask yourself the following questions:

◆ How can physical education and sport contribute to the realization of these objectives and the goal of optimal health and well-being for all segments of the population?
◆ What are the implications of these objectives for the structure and content of physical edu-

cation and sport programs in all settings and for a diversity of populations?
◆ What are the implications for the manner in which we deliver services? How can we expand our services to reach underserved populations?
◆ What are the implications for job opportunities in the field?

The potential of physical education and sport to contribute to the national health objectives for physical activity and fitness is tremendous. Physical education and sport programs in both school and nonschool settings provide an avenue for people of all ages to be active and to learn the skills, knowledge, and values conducive to leading a physically active lifestyle.

School physical education programs have a critical role to play in achieving the national health goals. If the health of the nation is to be improved, effective use must be made of school health and physical education programs. The schools provide an efficient means to reach over 51 million students a year. The school offers us the best vehicle to address disparities in opportunities associated with socioeconomics status. As professionals, we must be strong, passionate spokespersons on behalf of physical education and sport. The decline in the number of children participating in daily physical education must be reversed. Quality programs are critical to this effort. The inclusion of physical education as an integral component of a comprehensive school health program is another approach to increase physical education programs. During these impressionable years, much can be done by schools and parents working together to lay the groundwork for healthy living as an adult.

School physical education programs should provide the foundation for participation in physical activities throughout one's lifespan. Physical education programs for young children should focus on attainment of proficiency in fundamental skills and movement concepts. In the upper-elementary grades and middle-school years, students should be exposed to a variety of activities in the areas of sports, dance, aquatics, and outdoor pursuits. This exposure allows students to identify activities that

Jumping rope is a popular means of developing and maintaining cardiorespiratory endurance.

are enjoyable and satisfying to them. In high school, students should have the opportunity to develop competency in several activities that are personally meaningful. Fitness promotion is important. Teachers must provide a sequence of experiences that will give students a knowledge base of physical education and sport so that they can learn how to direct their own exercise programs, modify physical activities to suit their changing needs, and wisely select activities to participate in during their leisure time. Physical educators must also remember it is important to offer experiences that are challenging, meaningful, and personally satisfying to participants and are conducive to developing motivation for continued participation throughout life. The entire physical education

program should be seen as developmental in nature, offering a series of planned learning experiences that focus on development of fitness, motor skills, knowledge, and values that will lead to life-span participation.

The school setting also offers a means to reach adults. Over 5 million adults are employed by the schools, both in instructional and noninstructional positions.[17] More schools are offering worksite health promotion programs, similar to those found in corporations, to their employees. These programs often encompass fitness promotion, skill development, and health education.

The use of the school as a community center has not reached its full potential. Although more schools are opening their doors to the community during evening hours, on the weekend, and during the summer, many schools remain unused and others underutilized. The use of the school as a community center would enable us to reach adults and offer a diversity of programs to meet their needs. Moreover, adult school-based programs offer a means to bring physical activity and sport experiences to adults who lack the financial resources to join a fitness club or do not have a program at their work site. They provide an avenue to reach all people within the community. Programs can be designed to focus on the needs of people of all ages, ranging from young adults to the elderly, at a minimal cost. Other programs can be started that foster family participation, emphasizing children and parents participating in activities together.

The growing number of older Americans makes it important to have physical education and sport programs to meet their many needs. Their needs are quite diverse. Millions of older Americans participate in sports. Other older Americans can benefit from physical activity programs that help them maintain the necessary health and vitality to live independently for as long as possible. In this manner, physical education and sport can increase the number of years of healthy life as well as make life more satisfying.

Worksite health promotion programs have grown tremendously. Many worksite programs have increased their scope of offerings from just a fitness program to include an array of different ac-

Daily, quality physical education is an educational basic.

tivities. Programs vary but may include fitness programs, recreation activities, and health promotion programs such as cancer and hypertension screening, nutritional counseling, and smoking cessation. Another change is that businesses have moved from viewing these programs as the perks of upper management to making these programs available to employees at all levels. This growth of programs has led to an increase in career opportunities in this sector.

Commercial fitness clubs and community agency programs, such as those at the YMCA, are growing. Additionally, they have expanded the populations served. While these programs were initially targeted towards adults, they are now reaching out to the elderly and preschool children. These programs provide instruction in skills, encourage the development of fitness, offer education, and strive to promote regular participation.

Physical educators can also contribute to the attainment of public health goals by contributing, directly or indirectly, to the achievement of objectives in the other *Healthy People 2000* priority areas. For example, physical education class provides a ready means to discuss how the use of tobacco, excessive alcohol consumption, and drug abuse are deterrents to fitness, thereby contributing to the objectives in three priority areas. Physical educators can reinforce nutritional concepts and provide opportunities for students to explore the impact of nutrition on performance. Teaching stress reduction techniques, such as progressive relaxation, or sharing with students how physical activity can help alleviate stress, or how fitness can serve as a stress buffer, can contribute to attaining the objectives for mental health.

In addition to contributing to the priority areas associated with health promotion, physical educators

These college students at the University of Nevada–Las Vegas are learning yoga, which may help them to manage stress.

can also promote health protection and preventive services. For example, by teaching swimming and water safety skills to all students, schools can help reduce the number of drownings, an objective related to the priority area of unintentional injuries. Physical activity can reduce risk for heart disease and stroke, another priority area.

If physical educators conduct quality programs and offer leadership that promotes the development of self-esteem, the potential of physical education to advance other priority areas grows. Low self-esteem has been associated with a multitude of health risk behaviors, such as drug abuse, teen pregnancy, and alcohol use. Thus, fostering positive self-esteem in students can be beneficial to their health in many ways.

As the United States becomes more diverse, the challenge of addressing disparities in health status and access to opportunities will become greater. Greater efforts must be made to reach racial and ethnic minorities, people with disabilities, and people with low incomes. As Siedentop states,

professionals should understand inequities that may limit access to opportunities to participate in activity based on "irrelevant attributes such as race, gender, age, handicapping condition, or socioeconomic status. Individuals should value fair access to participation so much that they are willing to work at local, regional, and national levels to make that activity more available to more people."[18]

If we are to improve the health of the nation, a greater emphasis needs to be placed on school-community partnerships. Both the resources of the school and the community need to be used if the objectives for the year 2000 are to be achieved. If physical educators are to take on a public health role, they must be willing to work as part of a comprehensive team dedicated to the improvement of the nation's health status. Physical educators must realize that physical activity is only a part of the means to achieving optimal health. Nutritionists, health educators, medical personnel, and others have a critical role to play in the wellness movement. It is important that all professionals work cooperatively to achieve the realization of the nation's health goals and the attainment of optimal well-being for each individual.

Healthy People 2010 is scheduled to be released in 2000. An extension of *Healthy People 2000*, *Healthy People 2010* will emphasize two overarching goals: increasing the years of healthy life, and eliminating health disparities between different population groups.[19] Four enabling goals have been identified at this time:

◆ promote healthy behaviors
◆ protect health
◆ assure access to quality health care
◆ strengthen community prevention.

Physical activity and fitness is one of 20 priority areas and currently includes 12 specific objectives related to physical activity and fitness. *Healthy People 2010* will offer a framework to guide the efforts of professionals as we move into the next century committed to health for all.

PHYSICAL ACTIVITY AND FITNESS MOVEMENT

Enthusiasm for exercise and fitness is at an unprecedented level in the United States today, with millions of people spending countless hours and billions of dollars on exercise and sport. The fitness movement, which began as a trend in 1970s, has nearly three decades later grown to be an enduring feature of our society. Men and women of all ages are participating in fitness and sport activities to an extent not witnessed before in this country. It appears that being physically active is for many children and adults an ingrained part of American life.

However, when data about participation in fitness activities are closely examined, the widespread extent of the physical activity and fitness in American society is not supported. Available data show that many children and adults are leading sedentary lives.

In 1996, *Physical Activity and Health: The Surgeon General's Report*[20] was released. This landmark document convincingly set forth the

---

THE BENEFITS OF REGULAR PHYSICAL ACTIVITY

Regular physical activity improves health in the following ways:
◆ Reduces the risk of dying prematurely.
◆ Reduces the risk of dying from heart disease.
◆ Reduces the risk of developing diabetes.
◆ Reduces the risk of developing high blood pressure.
◆ Helps reduce blood pressure in people who already have high blood pressure.
◆ Reduces the risk of developing colon cancer.
◆ Reduces feelings of depression and anxiety.
◆ Helps control weight.
◆ Helps build and maintain healthy bones, muscles, and joints.
◆ Helps older adults become stronger and better able to move about without falling.
◆ Promotes psychological well-being.

US Department of Health and Human Services: *Physical activity and health: a report of the Surgeon General*, Atlanta, Ga., US Department of Health and Human Services, Centers for Disease Control and Prevention, National Center for Chronic Disease Prevention and Health Promotion, 1996.

---

contribution physical activity can make to the health and lives of all people. The contribution of physical activity to health is shown in the box above.

Several key messages are presented in this document. These include:

◆ People of all ages can benefit from physical activity.
◆ People can improve their health by engaging in a moderate amount of physical activity on a regular basis.
◆ Greater health benefits can be achieved by increasing the amount of physical activity, through changing the duration, frequency, or intensity of effort.

Moderate physical activity is defined as physical activity that results in an energy expenditure of

150 calories a day or 1,000 calories per week. Walking for 30 minutes, swimming laps for 20 minutes, or wheeling oneself in a wheelchair for 30–40 minutes will satisfy the requirement for moderate physical activity. Physical activity can be accumulated throughout the day by doing intermittent activities such as walking 3 times a day for 10 minutes or gardening.

The recommendation to include moderate physical activity as part of one's daily schedule represents an effort to broaden the scope of physical activity recommendations. Traditionally, an exercise period of 20 minutes at an intensity of 60% to 85% maximum heart rate performed 3 or more times per week was the recommended standard for promoting health fitness and preventing disease. In 1995, the American College of Sports Medicine and the Center for Disease Control and Prevention, in an effort to encourage greater involvement in physical activity, emphasized participation in moderate physical activity on most days of the week. It is hoped that with additional opportunities to engage in beneficial physical activity, more people will participate. While participation in some cases is not of sufficient intensity to develop cardiovascular fitness, being physically active does yield health benefits.

The Surgeon General's report stresses that physical inactivity is a national problem. If offers a serious challenge for reducing the burden of unnecessary illness and premature death. It is estimated that poor diet and lack of activity together account for at least 300,000 deaths per year. Lifestyle factors, such as lack of physical activity, diet, and tobacco use, account for more than 50% of premature death and disability.[7]

The emphasis on moderate physical activity and the focus on integration of physical activity into one's lifestyle offers additional opportunities for sedentary individuals to improve their health through participation in physical activities that are enjoyable, personally meaningful, and fit more easily into their daily schedules. Healthy lifestyle patterns, including regular physical activity, should be developed when people are young. These lifestyle patterns can then be carried into adulthood, reducing the risk of disease. People who regularly participate in moderate amounts of physical activity can live longer, healthier lives.

Fitness and Physical Activity of Children and Youth

The fitness status of the nation's children and youth has been a cause for public concern in these past two decades. Fitness levels of children and youth were found to be discouragingly low.[21,22] One popular newsmagazine, *Time,* awarded the fitness status of our nation's children a grade of "F for flabby."[23]

Two comprehensive studies of children's and youths' fitness undertaken in the mid-1980s substantiate the need for concern.[21,22] These studies were conducted by the U.S. Department of Health and Human Services Office for Disease Prevention and Health Promotion in cooperation with other interested agencies, including AAHPERD. These studies emphasized health-related fitness, and test items were selected to assess the participant's current health status and potential resistance to disease. The test items included the following:

Distance runs to provide a general indicator of cardiovascular capacity; maintenance of a high capacity may reduce the individual's susceptibility to cardiovascular disease.

Determination of percent of body fat by skinfold measures from selected sites. A large percent of body fat indicates vulnerability to a host of degenerative diseases including hypertension, heart disease, and diabetes.

Assessment of lower back flexibility and abdominal strength, which are important in preventing lower back or other musculoskeletal problems, through the individual's performance on the sit-and-reach test and the sit-up test.

Chin-ups or modified pull-ups to measure upper body strength. An adequate level of upper body strength is needed to perform various functional tasks associated with daily living without risk of injury.

The 1985 National Children and Youth Fitness Study I (NCYFS I),[21] was designed to elicit information about the health and fitness of youths aged 10 to 17 (grades 5 through 12) as well as information about their physical activity habits. A total of

Since physical activity patterns are formed in childhood, children must be encouraged to spend less time watching TV and more time being active. Computer time should be limited as well.

8,800 boys and girls completed the five-item fitness test (bent-knee sit-ups, chin-ups, 1-mile walk/run, sit-and-reach, and skinfold thickness) and a self-report questionnaire on physical activities to assess health-related fitness. The results revealed much cause for concern: Compared with children tested in 1960, there was a significant increase in percent body fat, indicating the nation's youths had become fatter. Another concern was the poor performance of the youths on the cardiorespiratory measure—the 1-mile walk/run. Examination of the average score revealed that many children completed the distance at a slow jog, with girls taking more time to complete the distance than boys.

According to NCYFS I, only slightly more than one-third of the students (36.3%) participated in daily school physical education programs, and only about half the youths participated in appropriate physical activity essential for maintenance of an adequate level of cardiorespiratory function. The data revealed that secondary school physical education programs tended to focus more on competitive and team sport activities rather than on life-time and individual skills and activities that can be used by adults for participation throughout life. Furthermore, more than 80% of the physical activity of students was performed outside of the school physical education classes, primarily in community programs.[21]

The NCYFS II[22] examined the fitness levels and physical activity habits of 4,678 children aged 6 to 9 (grades 1 through 4). Fitness levels were measured using five test items similar to those utilized in the first study. Parents completed a questionnaire describing their own and the child's activity patterns, and information about the school physical education program was obtained directly from the teachers.

The results, released in 1987, raised concerns similar to those voiced about the findings of the NCYFS I. Compared with results of fitness tests conducted 20 or more years ago, children today have a higher percentage of body fat. The tests also showed that neither the cardiorespiratory capacity nor the upper body strength of the typical child is well developed.

NCYFS II revealed that nearly all children were enrolled in a physical education program of some kind and that 36.4% of the children had daily physical education. In the early grades, the physical education program focused largely on movement experiences and development of fundamental skills. However, by grades 3 and 4, a shift toward competitive team sports was noted, an emphasis that persisted throughout the high school years. Nearly all children engaged in at least one physical activity through a community program.

Examination of the data on parents also revealed cause for concern: Only 30% participated in vigorous physical activity sufficient to realize maximum health benefits, and 50% of the parents reported that they never engage in vigorous exercise. Children who watched a greater amount of television as compared with their peers also tended to have lower physical activity levels and lower levels of participation in organized sports and community activities.

The health and fitness of children were found to be influenced by several factors. In terms of cardiorespiratory capacity, children who performed well on the distance run participated in more community-based activity, watched less television, were rated more physically active by their parents and their teachers, received more of their physical education instruction from a physical education specialist, and had greater opportunities to participate in periodic fitness testing than their peers who scored lower on this measure. These children were also leaner in terms of body composition. Equally noteworthy, the parents of leaner children were physically active and exercised more frequently with their children. The findings of the NCYFS I and II provide a wealth of information about the fitness status of our nation's children and youth. Concerns about the poor fitness status of this population appear to be well founded.

To determine the extent to which the *Healthy People 2000* objectives for physical activity and fitness were being met, several national surveys were conducted in the 1990s. The 1992 National Health Interview Survey-Youth Risk Behavior Survey (NHIS-YRBS) gathered information on the physical activity of over 10,000 youths aged 12–21 years.[24] The survey identified participation in various activities by youths during the previous 7 days. The findings revealed:

♦ Overall, 13.7% of the youths were inactive, and inactivity was higher among females than males (15.3% vs. 12.1%).

♦ Overall, 53.7% of the youths participated in activities that made them sweat and breathe hard 3 or more days (vigorous physical activity).

♦ Overall, 45.6% of the students participated in strengthening or toning activities.

♦ Overall, 48% of the students engaged in stretching activities at least 3 days of the week.

♦ With respect to light or moderate physical activity, 26.4% of the youths reported having biked or walked for 30 minutes or more on at least 5 of the 7 days. Males participated more than females (29.1% vs. 23.7%).

People who participate in physical education programs often learn sports that they will enjoy for a lifetime. These students at Concord High School, in Connecticut, are receiving instruction in golf.

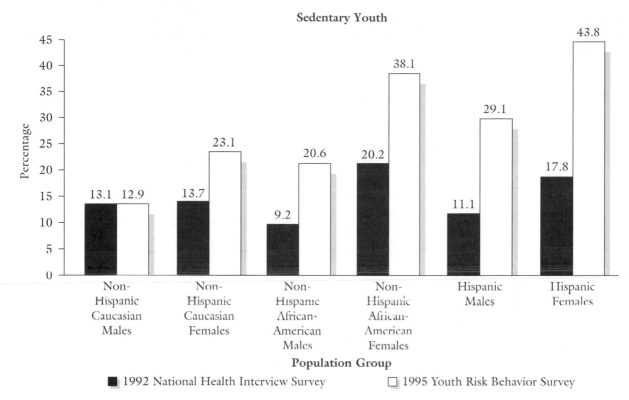

FIGURE 3-2   Percentages of sedentary youth of various population groups.

Generally, activity decreased with age, and inactivity or sedentary living increased with age. Caucasians generally had higher participation rates than African Americans and Hispanics, and males higher rates than females (see Figure 3-2).

NHIS-YRBS also recorded youth participation in seven selected activities: aerobics or dancing; baseball, softball, or Frisbee; basketball, football, or soccer; house cleaning or yard work; running, jogging, or swimming; skating, skiing, or skateboarding; and tennis, racquetball, or squash. Males were more likely to participate in all activities than females except for aerobics or dancing and housekeeping or yardwork. For most activities, participation decreased with age.

In 1995 the Centers for Disease Control and Prevention conducted the Youth Risk Behavior Survey (YRBS), which sampled 10,645 students in grades 9–12. The findings relative to physical activity offer us insight into youths' physical activity patterns and their school physical education experiences. The findings report the students' activity patterns for 7 days preceding the survey.[25]

◆ Overall, 10.4% of students were inactive, and inactivity was higher among females than males (13.8% vs. 7.3%).

◆ Overall, 63.7% of the students reported that they engaged in vigorous activity 3 or more days. Vigorous physical activity was more common among males than females (74.4% vs. 52.1%).

◆ Overall, 50.3% of the students participated in strengthening activities. Male students' involvement was greater than that of female students (59.1% vs. 41.4%).

◆ Overall, 53% of the students engaged in stretching activities. Male students participated more than that of female students (55.5% vs. 50.4%).

◆ With respect to light or moderate physical activity, 21.1% of the students reported having biked or walked for 30 minutes or more on at least 5 of the 7 days. Males and females participated at similar levels.

In general, Caucasian students were more active than their African American and Hispanic peers. Activity decreased as students' grade in school increased. The YRBS also provides data on enrollment, daily participation, and activity time in physical education. In 1995, 59.6% of the students were enrolled in physical education. Little variability was seen in enrollment by sex or race/ethnicity, but enrollment decreased by grade. Only 25.4% of high school students, 1 in every 4, participated in daily physical education. For both male and female students, participation in daily physical education decreased as the students' grade in school increased (see Figure 3-3). Participation was highest in grade 9 and progressively decreased to its lowest level in grade 12. It was also noted that participation in daily physical education decreased from 41.6% in 1991 to 25.4% in 1995. During physical education class, 69.7% of the students were physically active for 20 minutes or more, which is about half the class period. Males were more active during class than female students (74.8% vs. 63.7%), and Caucasian students more active than African-American students (71.3% vs. 59%).

Data were also gathered on students' participation in sports. Student participation on sports teams organized by the school was 50.9%. More males participated in school sports than females (57.8% vs. 42.4%). Caucasian students participated more often than Hispanic students (53.9% vs. 37.8%). Participation on sports teams run by organizations besides the school was greater for male students than for female students (46.4% vs. 26.8%). Caucasian students participated more than Hispanic students (39.1% vs. 32.0%).

As can be seen, much work needs to be done to improve the fitness status of the nation's youth and encourage a more active lifestyle. The 1996 Surgeon General's report on *Physical Activity and Health*[20] reached the following conclusions about the physical activity patterns of our nation's adolescents and young adults:

1. Only about one-half of young people ages 12–21 regularly participate in vigorous physical activity. One-fourth engage in no vigorous physical activity.

2. Approximately one-fourth of young people engage in light to moderate physical activity, that is, walking or biking, nearly every day.

3. About 14% of young people are inactive, reporting no vigorous or no light to moderate activity. The prevalence of inactivity is higher among females than males and among African-American females than Caucasian females.

4. Males are more likely than females to engage in strengthening activities, light to moderate activities (biking and walking), and vigorous physical activity.

5. Participation in physical activity declines markedly as age or grade in school increases.

6. About 80% of 9th grade students are enrolled in physical education. This figure declines strikingly during the next years in high school. By 12th grade, only about 40% of the students are enrolled in physical education.

7. From 1991 to 1995, the number of students enrolled in daily physical education decreased from 42% to 25%.

8. Within physical education class, the number of students who reported being active for at least 20 minutes a class period declined from 81% to 70% during the first half of the 1990s.

9. Among students who attended daily physical education, only 19% report being active for 20 minutes or more.

Lack of participation among youth is a serious problem. During this important period between childhood and adulthood, adult habits begin to emerge. If we are to become a healthier nation, the decline in physical activity during this critical time period must be addressed. Moreover, special efforts must be made to reach out to population groups that have low physical activity participation rates, such as minorities and females.

During the 1990s, several assessments were made of children's and youths' fitness status and

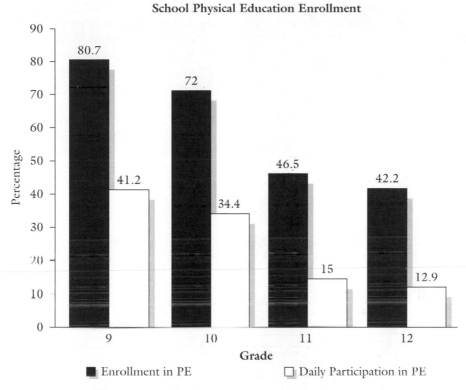

FIGURE 3-3   Enrollment in physical education programs and participation in daily physical education by high school students.

physical activity patterns. Policy makers, teachers, parents, and community members need to collaborate to enhance the fitness status and physical activity of children and youth. This is particularly important in light of the increased evidence supporting the relationship between childhood health fitness and adult degenerative diseases. Heart disease does begin in childhood. Children whose percent of body fat is too high and whose patterns of inactivity contribute to low levels of cardiorespiratory function tend to maintain these risk factors as they age, placing them at increased risk for degenerative disease.

Fitness and Physical Activity of Adults

It is difficult to secure information about the fitness status of adults. For children and youth,

the schools provide a convenient venue to complete fitness testing. No similar venue exists for the adult population. However, information is available on the physical activity patterns of adults. This information is typically gathered through large-scale surveys, which often span several decades.

The physical activity patterns of adults reveal a need to get more adults involved in physical activity on a regular basis. Studies conducted in late 1980s showed that only 10–20% of adults exercise with sufficient frequency, intensity, and duration (i.e., exercise involving large muscles in dynamic movement for a minimum of 20 minutes, 3 or more days per week at an intensity of 60% or greater of cardiorespiratory capacity) to develop and maintain adequate levels of health-related fitness.[11,26,27] Forty percent of the adult population

Fitness is important for all people. This visually impaired woman is being trained at a local fitness center.

engages in moderate physical activities sufficiently often to realize some health benefits.[11,26,27] The remainder of the population is inactive or sedentary.

The research also showed that participation in fitness activities is influenced by such factors as age, sex, race, education, economic level, occupation, community setting, and geographic location.[11,28] The prevalence of physical activity decreases with age, is higher among men than women, and is greater among Caucasians than minorities. High school and college graduates, middle- and upper-middle-income people, and professional persons tend to participate more. Higher participation rates are also noted for individuals who live in suburban settings and those who live in the western part of the United States.

The National Health Interview Survey (NHIS), the Behavioral Risk Factor Surveillance System (BRFSS), and the National Health and Nutrition Examination Survey (NHANES III), conducted in the 1980s and 1990s, revealed information about the physical activity patterns of adults. These studies are summarized in *Physical Activity and Health: A Report of the Surgeon General.*[20] The following conclusions can be drawn about the physical activity patterns of adults:

1. Approximately 15% of adults engage regularly (3 times per week for at least 20 minutes) in vigorous physical activity.
2. About 22% of adults engage regularly (5 days a week for at least 30 minutes) in sustained physical activity of any intensity.
3. Approximately 25% of adults report participating in no physical activity during their leisure time.
4. Individuals with disabilities were less likely to engage in vigorous (27.2%) or regular moderate (9.6%) physical activity than were people without disabilities (37.4% and 14.2%, respectively). People with disabilities were inactive more than adults without disabilities (32% vs. 27%).
5. Physical activity is more prevalent among males than females, among Caucasians than African Americans and Hispanics, among younger adults than older adults, and among the more affluent than the less affluent.
6. Physical activity appears to decline with age. However, it seems to increase during the senior years.
7. Among all ages and sexes, the most popular physical activity is walking, with a participation rate of 44%. Other popular activities, in terms of participation, are gardening or yard work, stretching exercises, weight lifting, jogging or running, aerobics, riding a bicycle or exercise bicycle, stair climbing, and swimming for exercise.

Although it is disheartening that 1 in 4 adults leads a sedentary lifestyle, there is reason for optimism. A 1997 survey by the Sporting Goods

Manufacturers Association revealed that sport participation by adults 55 years and older has risen tremendously from 1992 to 1996.[29] The number of adults exercising to music for 100 or more days a year rose by 257%, from 274,000 in 1992 to 884,000 in 1996. Adults who used treadmills for more than 100 days a year increased by 170.3%, from 828,000 in 1992 to over 2.2 million in 1996. Seniors engaging in weight training rose from 351,000 to 876,000, an increase of 150% in the 4-year period. The number of golfers doubled, rising to over 2.4 million. Fitness walking rose over 25%; participation increased from 5.1 million to 6.8 million.

Although people are not as physically active as it may first appear, nor the fitness movement as pervasive as it seems, the number of participants is growing each year. Expenditures for sport and exercise equipment can indicate the degree of interest. In 1997, the Sporting Goods Manufacturers Association reported that expenditures reached an all-time high. It is estimated that Americans spend $17.2 billion a year on sports clothing and $9.5 billion a year on athletic shoes.[30] Sales of home exercise equipment have skyrocketed, from $723 million in 1982 to over $2.6 billion in recent years.[30] Home exercise equipment has become more expensive and more sophisticated. Stationary bicycles, treadmills, cross-country ski machines, rowers, stair machines, and weight systems are popular. More equipment incorporates heart-rate monitoring electronics and workout computers to give users increasingly sophisticated feedback about their efforts. Sales of diet books and exercise videos continue to rise. It is important to note, however, that buying apparel, shoes, and exercise equipment does not guarantee that they will be used by their owners on a regular basis.

Corporate fitness and commercial health clubs have attracted a record number of participants. The number of participants in athletic and recreational programs in the schools and communities has increased as well during recent years. An increasing number of communities have fitness and bicycling trails, which have proven to be popular with community residents.

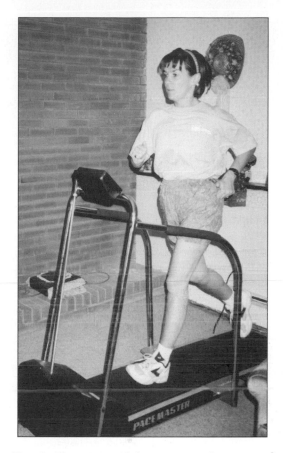

Treadmills are one of the most popular types of home exercise equipment.

What Are the Implications of the Fitness Movement for Physical Education and Sport?

Although many Americans of all ages are not exercising vigorously with sufficient frequency, intensity, and duration to maintain an adequate level of health-related fitness, an increasing number of people are making a commitment to incorporate physical activity into their lifestyle (see the box on p. 98). Furthermore, the increased documentation of the positive relationship between adequate levels of health-related fitness and wellness offers strong support for physical education and sport programs. It also emphasizes the need for fitness programs to reach all ages of our society,

FITNESS STATUS OF THE NATION

Adults

◆ More than 60% of adults do not achieve the recommended amount of regular physical activity.

◆ Approximately 15% of U.S. adults engage regularly (3 times a week for at least 20 minutes) in vigorous physical activity during leisure time.

◆ Approximately 22% of adults engage regularly (5 times a week for at least 30 minutes) in sustained physical activity of any intensity during leisure time.

◆ Twenty-five percent of all adults do not engage in any leisure-time physical activity.

◆ Inactivity increases with age and is more common among women than men, among blacks and Hispanics than Caucasians, among older than younger adults, among the less affluent than the more affluent, and among the people with disabilities than people without disabilities.

Adolescents and Young Adults

◆ Nearly half of young people age 12–21 are not vigorously active on a regular basis.

◆ About 14% are inactive.

◆ Physical activity declines dramatically with age during adolescence.

◆ Female adolescents are much less physically active than male adolescents.

High School Students

◆ The prevalence of inactivity was 10.4%; inactivity was higher among females than males (13.8% vs. 7.3%), among non-Hispanic African Americans than Hispanics and non-Hispanic Caucasians

(15.3% vs. 11.3% vs. 9.3%). Inactivity increased as grade in school increased.

◆ Over 60% (63.7%) of students participated in vigorous physical activity. Participation was higher among male than female students (74.4% vs. 52.1%), among non-Hispanic Caucasians than Hispanics and non-Hispanic African Americans (67% vs. 57.3% vs. 53.2%). Activity decreased as grade in school increased.

◆ Over 20% (21.1%) engaged in moderate physical activity. Males and females participated at similar rates (21.6% vs. 20.5%). Participation was higher among non-Hispanic Caucasians than among Hispanics and non-Hispanic African Americans (18.3% vs. 26.8% vs. 27.0%). Activity decreased as grade in school increased.

◆ Enrollment in physical education was 59.6%. Enrollment decreased as grade in school increased.

◆ Illinois is the only state that mandates daily physical education for students K–12. Forty-six states have varying requirements. Colorado, Mississippi, and South Dakota have no requirements for physical education.

◆ In high school, enrollment in daily physical education classes dropped from 41.6% in 1991 to 25.4% in 1995. Daily physical education declined as the grade in school increased.

◆ Only 19% of all high school students are physically active for 20 minutes or more in physical education classes every day during the school week.

US Department of Health and Human Services. *Physical activity and health: A report of the Surgeon General.* Atlanta, Ga., US Department of Health and Human Services, Centers for Disease Control and Prevention, National Center for Chronic Disease Prevention and Health Promotion, 1996. National Association for Sport and Physical Education, Shape of the Nation, Reston, Va., National Association for Sport and Physical Education, 1997.

regardless of sex, race, educational level, occupation, economic status, and community setting. As professionals, we must capitalize on the interest in fitness and its contribution to health to promote and secure funding for our programs.

Professionals must also become leaders in the fitness movement and exert a significant influence on its direction. Corbin[31] pointed out that medical doctors, self-appointed experts, and movie stars are at the vanguard of the fitness movement. Many of these people lack the qualifications, training, and expertise to direct this movement. Additionally, the proliferation of products and programs related to exercise and fitness has raised some concern about their validity. Corbin states that professionals have the necessary knowledge and skill and must take over the leadership responsibilities within the movement. This viewpoint is further supported by the prestigious American Academy of Kinesiology and Physical Education. The Academy urged professionals to be "active in the consumer education movement related to physical activities."[32] Specifically, professionals should educate the public to be wise consumers of exercise products and programs; they should serve as a resource to which the public can turn for help and guidance. Additionally, professionals should provide the participants in their programs with the knowledge and skills to solve their own exercise and physical activity problems and to evaluate their own fitness needs.

As Corbin states, in assuming the burden of leadership, we must practice what we preach. Professionals should be role models and should reflect a commitment to a healthy lifestyle, with physical activity as an integral component of that lifestyle. Failure to practice what we preach damages our credibility.

NCYFS I and II findings relative to the physical fitness levels of the nation's youth show an urgent need for the fitness movement to reach the children and youth of our nation. Schools should emphasize lifelong fitness, and this education should begin early in life. School-based programs must teach students the skills for lifetime participation and foster an appreciation for the value of fitness and physical activity in maintaining an optimal state of well-being. Fitness education should also be extended to parents. Parents' role in shaping their children's physical activity habits should be recognized, and professionals should involve them in creating positive physical activity patterns. Because much of children's and youths' physical activity takes place outside of the school setting, school and community physical activity programs should be closely coordinated so that the maximum benefits are derived from participation. The Centers for Disease Control and Prevention (CDC) has developed guidelines for school and community programs to promote physical activity among the nation's youth.[33] These guidelines, shown in the box on page 100, make it clear that promoting lifelong physical activity requires a co-

ordinated effort between the home, school, and community. Moreover, it emphasizes the inclusion of physical education as part of a comprehensive school-wide approach to promote well-being.

Many adults, when questioned about reasons for lack of participation in physical activity, cite lack of time. With the new recommendations on physical activity, more options are provided to incorporate physical activity into daily life. Furthermore, as the number of worksite programs continues to grow, greater opportunities for involvement will be available. Convenience is a factor that influences whether or not people will work out. On-site opportunities with flexible hours will make it more convenient for adults to incorporate physical activity into their daily routine. Some corporations are also rewarding individuals who work out by reducing their out-of-pocket costs for insurance. The growth in sales of home exercise equipment is also a positive sign that people are meeting their need to exercise by placing equipment in their homes. Some adults have hired personal trainers to guide their home exercise programs.

There must be increased efforts to reach out to underserved populations. This is true for both children and adults. As can clearly be seen from the NCYFS I and II, the family is an important role model for physical activity involvement. However, an increasing number of children in single parent families, many of whom are at risk for poor school outcomes, may not have the parental support for involvement. Collingwood states that physical fitness programs for at-risk youths require strong leadership, role modeling, and a focused, structured effort to achieve the desired outcomes.[34] Besides fitness promotion, structured physical fitness programs can affect many risk factors associated with the problems of at-risk youth. Properly designed and led by committed leaders, programs can increase well-being, enhance self-esteem, and teach important life skills such as goal-setting, planning, and values development.[34]

Socioeconomic status is a significant influence on participation in physical activity. Individuals who come from affluent backgrounds have greater involvement than those from less affluent circumstances. They have more disposable income they

CDC YOUTH PHYSICAL ACTIVITY RECOMMENDATIONS

1. Establish policies that promote enjoyable, life-long physical activity
   ◆ Require daily, comprehensive physical education K–12
   ◆ Require comprehensive health education K–12
   ◆ Commit adequate resources for physical activity instruction and programs
   ◆ Hire qualified specialists in each area
   ◆ Require that physical activity programs meet the needs and interests of all students
2. Provide physical and social environments that encourage physical activity
   ◆ Provide access to safe spaces/facilities in school and community
   ◆ Strive to prevent physical activity-related injuries and illness
   ◆ Provide time in the school day for unstructured physical activity
   ◆ Offer worksite health promotion programs for the school faculty and staff
3. Implement planned, sequential physical education curricula that encourage students to develop the knowledge, attitudes, motor skills, and confidence needed to adopt physically active lifestyles
   ◆ National standards form the framework for the curriculum
   ◆ Incorporate active learning strategies and emphasize enjoyable participation
   ◆ Develop students' positive attitudes toward, mastery of motor skills for, and confidence in participating in physical activity
   ◆ Foster participation in enjoyable physical activity in school, community, and home
4. Implement planned, sequential health education curricula that encourage students to develop the knowledge, attitudes, and behavioral skills needed to adopt physical activity lifestyles
   ◆ National standards form the framework for the curriculum
   ◆ Promote collaboration among physical education, health education, classroom teachers, and specialists for physical activity instruction

◆ Develop students' mastery of behavioral skills and acquisition of positive attitudes needed to adopt and maintain a physically active lifestyle
5. Offer extracurricular physical activity programs that meet all students' needs and interests
   ◆ Provide a diversity of developmentally appropriate physical activity programs for all students
   ◆ Link students to community physical activity programs, and use community resources to support extracurricular physical activity program
6. Involve parents/guardians in physical activity instruction and extracurricular physical activity programs, and encourage them to support their children's participation in enjoyable physical activity
   ◆ Encourage parents to advocate for high-quality physical activity instruction and programs for their children
   ◆ Encourage parents to support their children's participation in appropriate, enjoyable physical activity
   ◆ Encourage parents to replace their children's sedentary activities with physically active ones
   ◆ Motivate parents to be role models for physical activity and to incorporate physical activities into family activities
7. Provide physical education, health education, recreation, and health-care and other important professionals with training that imparts the knowledge and skills needed to effectively promote physical activity among youths
   ◆ Through higher education institutions, provide preservice training for education, recreation, and health-care and other professionals
   ◆ Instruct educators how to deliver physical education that provides a significant percentage of each student's weekly physical activity
   ◆ Teach active learning strategies needed to develop knowledge about, attitudes toward, skills in, and confidence in physical activity

- ◆ Create supportive environments that enable youths to enjoy physical activity instruction and programs
- ◆ Teach volunteers who coach sport and recreation programs for youths how to provide quality experiences
8. Health services must regularly assess physical activity among youths, reinforce physical activity among active youths, counsel inactive youths and refer them to physical activity programs, and advocate for physical activity instruction and programs for youth

9. Provide a range of developmentally appropriate, noncompetitive community sport and recreation programs that are attractive to youths
10. Evaluate school and community physical activity instruction, programs, and facilities on a regular basis
- ◆ Conduct process evaluations to determine how policies, programs, and training are implemented
- ◆ Conduct outcome evaluations to measure students' achievements of knowledge, motor skills, and adoption of healthy behaviors

Centers for Disease Control and Prevention: *Guidelines for school and community programs to promote physical activity among young people, 1997,* US Public Health Service, US Department of Health and Human Services, Washington, D.C.

can use to support their involvement in fitness and sports. Children, youths, and adults from lower economic strata have fewer resources available. Their limited resources—money, energy, and time—must be spent on securing the necessities of life: food, shelter, clothing, safety, and medical care. There is little left for the less crucial activities of life, such as exercise and sports. Even access to physical activity programs that are affordable may be difficult for those living in low-income neighborhoods. The relatively poor health of people in lower socioeconomic groups may also limit their participation. Harris notes that these obstacles to physical activity are "outward manifestations of the relative lack of power that accompanies low socioeconomic status."[35] Compared to those who are wealthier, those who are poor have less control over their lives, encounter greater stress, receive less social support from others, and must deal with the realization that they are deprived. "In general, they encounter serious barriers to an immediate access to a high quality of life, to chances of attaining such a life in the future . . . and have little power to bring about changes that might improve the situation."[35] As professionals, we must understand these inequities, the powerful feelings they evoke, and the type of strategies that can be effectively employed to change this situation.

Within the past two decades, there has been an enormous growth of private sector industries re-lated to sport and fitness, such as gymnastics clubs and fitness clubs. These industries have provided greater opportunities for participation for those able to afford the fees. Siedentop notes that this growth exacerbates a problem, the "increasingly strong relationship between wealth and opportunity in sport, fitness, and physical education."[36] Historically, the most widely available opportunities for participation have been in the public sector in schools, community recreation programs such as youth soccer, and public facilities such as parks and swimming pools. As the shift toward private opportunities continues, efforts must be directed at expanding public sector opportunities and making them available to people of all socioeconomic classes. Offering low-cost programs and reduced fees for those unable to pay will allow individuals from low-income groups to participate. However, reducing fees may not be sufficient. For example, one city pool lowered its fees for children but found it did little to increase the number of participants from lower-income families. When the city offered free bus transportation to the pool, participation increased in record numbers. Not only must opportunities be provided, but steps must be taken to ensure that people can access these opportunities. Even in the public sector, fees may limit participation. For example, some school systems faced with budget shortfalls charge athletes a fee to participate in interscholastic sports. This "pay-to-play" approach could lead to the exclusion of students unable to afford the participation fees.

A concerted effort by professionals must be made to reach all segments of the adult population and to give them the necessary skills, knowledge, and attitudes to develop and maintain adequate levels of health-related fitness. We must sustain participation by that small segment of society, the individuals who exercise vigorously enough to maintain an adequate level of health-related fitness. We must encourage the people who engage in moderate physical activity to upgrade the intensity of their efforts to achieve the full benefits of appropriate vigorous exercise. Finally, we must reach out to those individuals who exercise irregularly, if at all, and help them to begin to incorporate physical activity into their lives. Accomplishment of these goals requires committed, qualified professionals and a diversity of programs conducted in a variety of settings and targeted to all segments of the population.

EDUCATIONAL REFORM

The 1970s and 1980s were marked by calls for the reform of America's schools. These calls were prompted by several factors, including the public's desire for accountability, the poor reading and writing performance of students, the reduction of academic standards for high school graduation, the relaxation of requirements for college entrance, and the loss of professional status by teachers. The growing social disorder and problems within the school environment, such as student drug abuse, also contributed to the public's dissatisfaction. Concern was also raised by the significant differences in performance between Caucasian and minority students and between the affluent and the poor.

The 1983 report, *A Nation at Risk,* issued by the National Commission on Excellence in Education, headed by then Secretary of Education Terrell Bell, captured the public's attention with its bold declaration that "the educational foundations of our society are presently being eroded by a rising tide of mediocrity that threatens our very future as a Nation and a people."[37] America's preeminent position in commerce, industry, science, and technological innovation was being challenged and overtaken by countries throughout the world. Our educational system was faulted for failing to develop in the country's youth the skills necessary to compete within the world marketplace. The report stressed that individuals who do not possess the necessary skills, literacy, and training will be disadvantaged economically and disenfranchised from a chance to participate fully in our society.

A Nation at Risk, The Paideia Proposal: An Educational Manifesto,[38] *High School: A Report on Secondary Education in America,*[39] and other reports of this time called for reform of the educational system. Viewing these reports collectively, some generalizations about the changes needed to strengthen our educational system can be made. First, the reports called for improvement of student learning. They recommended greater emphasis on the basic subjects. The poor quality of students' reading and writing, and their performance on standardized achievement tests, showed a need to improve skills in these basic areas. Science, mathematics, computer literacy, and foreign language instruction also must be stressed. Elimination of the "frills" in the curriculum would provide greater time to develop students' skills in these areas. Besides spending more time on the basics, use of competency tests and tougher graduation requirements were recommended.

Second, the reports called for the improvement of teaching and suggested that the professional status of teachers be strengthened by (1) giving teachers greater access to opportunities for meaningful continuing education, (2) providing more competitive salaries, (3) creating opportunities for advancement and increased responsibility for decision making, (4) requiring more stringent entrance requirements for teacher preparation programs, and (5) changing the content and format of teacher preparation. Competency testing to ensure that teachers had mastered the content they were teaching and basic pedagogical skills was also suggested.

Third, changes were recommended in the organization of the schools and their funding. To provide more time for instruction, lengthening of the school day and year was suggested. Formation of school and industry partnerships and strengthening of community and school alliances were recommended to improve learning opportunities for students. It was also recognized that greater financial support was needed to make reform a reality, including the directing of financial resources to economically disadvantaged school districts.

Fourth, schools must prepare students to be lifelong learners. The basics are viewed as providing a foundation for learning. Since we live in an information age, students must be taught how to seek information, process information, and communicate information in an articulate, accurate, and meaningful manner.

The report *The Condition of Education 1994*[40] outlined the educational advances of students in the decade since the publication of *A Nation at Risk*. Since the cries for educational reform in the early 1980s, all 50 states have, to varying degrees, implemented changes. School systems have been significantly revamped in approximately 12 states, high school graduation requirements have been raised in 42 states, and 47 states have mandated student testing standards. A greater proportion of students are completing the recommended core curriculum in English, science, social studies, mathematics, and computer science. More high school students are taking advanced placement examinations. Mathematics and science achievement has increased. A greater number of students are attending college after they graduate from high school. Fewer students are dropping out of high school between 10th and 12th grade; the dropout rate decreased from 11% in 1980 to 6% in 1990. However, an increasing number of younger students are dropping out; 7% of the students dropped out before the 10th grade. The most commonly given reason was that they did not like school. One-third of the females who dropped out gave pregnancy as a reason for leaving.

Getting a quality education has always been seen as one of the best ways to improve one's life, particularly for those who are socially or economically disadvantaged. Many minorities are at an educational disadvantage for several reasons, including lower level of parental education, greater likelihood of living with a single parent, fewer community resources, attending a disadvantaged school that is less conducive to learning, and greater likelihood of living in poverty. Minorities have made gains since the advent of *A Nation at Risk,* but they still lag behind their Caucasian peers with respect to educational access, attainment, and achievement.

Females have made important advances in education, narrowing the gender gap in educational attainment. Females read and write better than males, although they perform worse than males in science and mathematics. Females are more likely to go to college immediately after high school. Teacher salaries have risen, and the teacher work force is more experienced. While there is recognition that some improvements have been made, much more needs to be accomplished to improve American education.

As we move toward the twenty-first century, calls for strengthening the American school system continue. As previously discussed, the 1994 *Goals 2000: Educate America Act*[41] established national education goals for the year 2000. These goals emphasize a more challenging curriculum and higher academic standards, improvement of the learning environment within the school, better professional development of teachers, greater parental and community involvement in the schools, and increased attention to lifelong learning. It stresses that if educational reform is to succeed, attention must be given to addressing some of the societal problems that influence the educational process.

Our country is becoming increasingly diverse. Children from a variety of family situations, economic circumstances, and cultural backgrounds present a challenge to an educational system charged with providing equal opportunities for all students. Compared with Caucasians and students from high-income families, students from racial and ethnic minority backgrounds and low family incomes are at higher risk for poor school outcomes, such as repeating a grade, requiring special educational services, and being suspended and dropping out of school.[42] Problems of alcohol abuse, illicit drug use, AIDS, sexual experimentation, and pregnancy are seen all too frequently among today's students. Minority students suffer disproportionately from these problems. Disintegration of the family unit, growing poverty, and an increasing number of single-parent families are judged as contributing to these problems.[43] These problems, and many others affecting the nation's students and their ability to learn, make school reform a herculean task.

What Are the Implications of the Educational Reform Movement for Physical Education?

Despite the potential of physical education to contribute in many significant ways to the educational goals, is the future of physical education itself at risk? How will physical education programs be affected by the reform movement? The focus of the reform movement on the "basics" of education could alter the future of physical education in the schools. What is the status of physical education? Is it a "frill" or a "basic"?

Many advocates of educational reform regard physical education as a "frill" or a nonessential subject. In some educational reports, physical education was not even deemed worthy of mention; other reports relegated physical education to the status of a personal service or ancillary course. In essence, physical education is viewed by some as a subject that cannot be justified for inclusion in the new educational curriculum. As the curriculum is reorganized to provide increased time for math, science, and other core subjects, time allotted to "nonessential" subjects in the curriculum, such as physical education or art, is likely to be reduced.

Advocates of daily quality physical education have frequently encountered arguments that time "wasted" on physical education could be used to improve academic performance. Shephard, in a review of physical education and academic performance, offers a different perspective:

Daily programs of physical education should not be introduced with the expectation that they will lead to major gains in academic performance. However, available

All three learning domains should be considered in planning instruction to meet each child's needs as a thinking, feeling, and moving human being.

data suggest that the rate of academic learning per unit of class time is enhanced in physically active students, so that lack of curricular time is not a valid reason for denying children a daily program of quality physical education.[44]

Furthermore, the importance of developing positive health habits early in the child's development cannot be overlooked.

Some proponents of educational reform support the role of physical education in the education process. When the *Nation at Risk* report was released in 1983, then Secretary of Education, Terrell Bell, supported the recommendation that schools focus their efforts on teaching students the "basics." However, he also acknowledged that "there must be room in the curriculum for physical education and athletics. . . ."[45] The Carnegie Commission report *High School* stated: "clearly no knowledge is more crucial than knowledge about health. Without it, no other life goal can be successfully achieved."[39] A course in lifetime fitness was recommended for all students. These reports recognize the valuable contribution physical education can make to students' education and lives.

Strong support for the inclusion of physical education in the school curriculum is offered by the four national health reports: *Healthy People*,[10] *Objectives for the Nation*,[11] *Healthy People 2000*,[8] and *Physical Activity and Health*.[20] These reports clearly identify the important contribution of physical activity to health and the important role of school physical education programs in promoting healthy lifestyles. Although the *Healthy People 2000* objectives identify areas where school physical education programs can be improved, the report does make a strong case for the contribution of physical education to the overall health goals. It supports daily physical education programs for students in all grades.

School physical education programs provide the means to reach more than 50 million students at a very important time in their lives. Developing positive health habits at an early age is important in sustaining a physically active lifestyle as an adult. Moreover, the school physical education program provides one of the greatest means of reaching disadvantaged population groups. The schools have a critical role to play in promoting the health of the nation. New, stronger partnerships are being forged between families, schools, and communities to improve the health of all people.

Is physical education a basic? The best strategy, it seems, for physical educators to follow in promoting physical education as a basic is to set forth clearly and articulately how and why physical education is an integral part of the educational program of every educational institution. In response to the educational reform reports, Osness,[46] past president of AAHPERD, stated that it is essential that the public, legislators, and other decision makers be accurately informed about the contribution of physical education to the educational process.

One positive step in the recognition of the contributions of physical education to education was the passing of a resolution by the U.S. Senate and the House of Representatives in 1987 encouraging state and local governments to provide quality, daily physical education programs for all students in kindergarten through 12th grade. The resolution, shown in the box on page 106, noted that

physical education enhanced the following educational objectives:

◆ academic performance
◆ mental alertness
◆ readiness to learn
◆ enthusiasm for learning
◆ self-esteem
◆ interpersonal relationships
◆ responsible behavior
◆ independence
◆ overall health
◆ skillful movement
◆ physical fitness
◆ active lifestyle
◆ constructive use of leisure time

It was noted in the resolution that the Surgeon General of the United States had recommended increasing the number of school physical education programs focusing on health-related fitness. Furthermore, the resolution cited the Secretary of Education as recognizing the mandate of elementary schools to give their students the

Learning tennis skills is one way in which people with disabilities can participate in recreational activities.

CONGRESSIONAL PHYSICAL EDUCATION RESOLUTIONS

To encourage state and local governments and local educational agencies to provide quality daily physical education programs for all children from kindergarten through grade 12.

Whereas physical education is essential to the physical development of the growing child;

Whereas physical education helps improve the overall health of children by increasing cardiovascular endurance, muscular strength and power, flexibility, weight regulation, improved bone development, improved posture, skillful moving, increased mental alertness, active lifestyle habits, and constructive use of leisure time;

Whereas physical education helps improve the mental alertness, academic performance, readiness to learn, and enthusiasm for learning of children;

Whereas physical education helps improve self-esteem, interpersonal relationships, responsible behavior, and independence of children;

Whereas children who participate in quality daily physical education programs tend to be more healthy and physically fit;

Whereas physically fit adults have significantly reduced risk factors for heart attacks and strokes;

Whereas the Surgeon General, in *Objectives for the Nation*, recommends increasing the number of school-mandated physical education programs that focus on health-related physical fitness;

Whereas the Secretary of Education, in *First Lessons—A Report on Elementary Education in America*, recognized that elementary schools have a special mandate to provide elementary school children with knowledge, habits, and attitudes that will equip the children for a fit and healthy life; and

Whereas a quality daily physical education program for all children from kindergarten through grade 12 is an essential part of a comprehensive education: now, therefore, be it

Resolved by the Senate (the House of Representatives concurring), that Congress encourages state and local government and local educational agencies to provide quality daily physical education programs for all children from kindergarten through grade 12.

---

knowledge, skills, and attitudes that will enable children to lead a fit and healthy life. The resolution acknowledged that physical education is an essential part of a comprehensive curriculum for all students. Thus, the Congress encouraged state and local governments to provide quality daily physical education programs for all school-aged children. However, while this sounds encouraging, the responsibility for education resides with state and local governments. Although 47 states, up from 42 in 1987, now mandate physical education, professionals are facing intense pressure to defend their programs in this time of economic restraint.[47] Only one state, Illinois, requires daily physical education for kindergarten through 12th grade. Furthermore, the majority of high school students enroll in physical education for only one year between 9th and 12th grades.

Professionals are under increased pressure to defend their programs. It seems ironic that at a time when we know more than ever about the significant relationship between physical activity and health, we are under greater pressure to defend our programs. Never at a time in our history have we had greater support from the government in its public health endeavors or more sweeping endorsements of our worth, ranging from the American Medical Association to the National Education Association. A strong national effort by professionals is needed to capitalize on this support to increase the time requirement for physical education in the nation's schools and to make quality, daily physical education a reality for all students.

SUMMARY

The role of physical education and sport in our society is influenced by societal trends. One significant trend is the changing demographics of our population. Our society is more culturally diverse than at any point in its history, and the diversity will increase as we move into the twenty-first century. We are living longer. Our society is becoming older; the number of people 65 years of age and older will increase from 12.7% of the population in 1997 to 18.5% in 2025. The number of people with disabilities continues to grow. The structure of the family is changing. Nearly 1 in every 3 Americans lives in poverty; poverty is associated with poor health and school outcomes. As physical educators and sport leaders, we must be committed to providing opportunities for lifelong involvement in physical activity for all people. If we are to accomplish this goal, we must adopt a multicultural approach to our work. This approach requires an appreciation of differences, valuing the uniqueness of individuals, and commitment to addressing inequities in opportunities.

The wellness movement and physical activity and fitness movement also hold several implications for physical education and sport. The wellness movement emphasized health promotion and disease prevention through lifestyle modification and individual responsibility for one's own health. Physical activity and fitness are integral parts of a healthy lifestyle. The evidence supporting the contribution of physical activity to health continues to mount. *Healthy People 2000* and *Physical Activity and Health: A Report of the Surgeon General* document the significant role physical activity plays in promoting well-being. Within the past few decades there has been a tremendous surge of interest in physical activity and fitness. However, when participation patterns are examined, 1 in every 4 children and adults leads a sedentary lifestyle. Professionals need to increase their efforts to involve people in physical activity. The wellness and and physical activity and fitness movements offer strong support for the development of nonschool physical education and sport programs to reach people of all ages.

The educational reform movement received its impetus from a series of reports decrying the status of education in America's schools and identifying specific areas for reform. The reports call for a greater emphasis on the "new basics" of English, science, social studies, math, and computer science. Lifelong learning was stressed. These reports disagreed on the status of physical education as an educational basic. Thus it is up to physical educators to make a strong case for physical education as a basic, before physical education is eliminated from the educational curriculum. The emphasis on lifelong learning supports the need for physical education and sport programs for individuals of all ages.

Regardless of the setting and the population served, movement is the keystone of physical education and sport. The nature of movement is discussed in the next chapter.

SELF ASSESSMENT TESTS

These tests are designed to help you determine if you have mastered the material and competencies presented in this chapter.

1. You have been invited to speak to a community group on the role of physical activity in the promotion of health and attainment of wellness. Prepare a short speech reflecting the contribution of physical education and sport to a healthy lifestyle. Use the information provided in the Getting Connected box to locate current information about the value of physical activity.

2. For each of the *Healthy People 2000* objectives for physical activity and fitness, provide specific examples of how school and nonschool physical

education and sport programs can help in their attainment.

3. As can be seen from the information on changing demographics, our society is becoming more diverse. What specific steps can physical education and sport take to reach underserved populations? What is your personal commitment to diversity?

4. The school board of your hometown is considering a proposal to decrease the time allocated to physical education in the school curriculum. Specifically, the board is considering a proposal to eliminate daily physical education for K–12. Students would then take physical education 3 days a week until 10th grade, at which time it would become an elective. Under the new policy, students who participate in interscholastic athletics and marching band would be excused from physical education during the season. As a professional, what arguments would you make against this resolution? What arguments would you offer in support of this resolution? What would be your position as a parent of a child in this school?

REFERENCES

1. DeSensi JT: Understanding multiculturalism and valuing diversity: a theoretical perspective, Quest 47:34–43, 1995.

2. Centers for Disease Control and Prevention: 1996 vital statistics of the United States, Washington, D.C., 1997, US Government Printing Office.

3. US Administration on Aging and American Association of Retired Persons: A profile of older Americans, 1997, Washington, D.C., 1997, US Government Printing Office.

4. US Bureau of the Census: Statistical abstracts of the United States 1997, ed 117, Washington D.C., 1997, US Government Printing Office.

5. Del Pinal J and Singer A: Generations of diversity: Latinos in the United States, Population Bulletin 52(3):2–47, 1997.

6. Hamilton L: Immigration, Congressional Daily Record, 143(93), E1337, June 27, 1997.

7. Department of Health and Human Services: The health of the nation: highlights of the healthy people 2000 goals 1995 report on progress, Washington, D.C., 1996, US Government Printing Office.

8. US Public Health Service, US Department of Health and Human Services: Healthy people 2000: national health promotion and disease prevention objectives, Washington, D.C., 1996, US Government Printing Office.

9. Centers for Disease Control: Ten leading causes of death in the United States. Atlanta: Ga., 1980. Updated 1994.

10. World Health Organization: Constitution of the World Health Organization, Chronicle of the World Health Organization, 1:29–43, 1947.

11. US Department of Health, Education, and Welfare: Healthy people: the Surgeon General's report on health promotion and disease prevention, Washington, D.C., 1979, US Government Printing Office.

12. US Public Health Service, US Department of Health and Human Services: Promoting health/preventing disease: objectives for the nation, Washington, D.C., 1980, US Government Printing Office.

13. Centers for Disease Control and Prevention and National Center for Health Statistics: National health and nutrition examination survey 1988–1994, Atlanta, Ga., 1997, US Department of Health and Human Services.

14. Centers for Disease Control and Prevention: Missed opportunities in preventive counseling for cardiovascular disease—United States, 1995, Morbidity and Mortality Weekly Report 47(5), 1998.

15. Health Care Financing Administration: Health care spending rise at a record low, Press Release, January 13, 1998, Washington, D.C.

16. President's Council on Physical Fitness and Sports: Economic benefits of physical activity, The President's Council on Physical Fitness and Sports Physical Activity and Fitness Research Digest 2(7), 1966.

17. US Department of Education: Office of Educational Research and Improvement. National Center for Educational Statistics, Washington, D.C., 1989, US Government Printing Office.

18. Siedentop D: Valuing the physically active life: contemporary and future directions, Quest 48:266–274, 1996.

19. US Department of Health and Human Services: Issues brief: development of healthy people 2010, Washington, D.C. (http://odphp.osophs.dhhs.gov/pubs/hp2000).

20. US Department of Health and Human Services: Physical activity and health: a report of the Surgeon General, Atlanta, Ga. 1996, US Department of Health and Human Services, Centers for Disease Control and Prevention, National Center for Chronic Disease Prevention and Health Promotion, and The President's Council on Physical Fitness and Sports.

21. Ross JG and Gilbert CG: The national children and youth study: a summary of the findings, Journal of Physical Education, Recreation, and Dance 56(1):45–50, 1985.

22. Ross JG and Pate RR: The national children and youth fitness study II, Journal of Physical Education, Recreation, and Dance 58(9):51–56, 1987.

23. Putting on the Ritz at the Y, Time, p 65, July 21, 1986.

24. US Department of Health and Human Services: National health interview survey—youth risk behavior survey, Washington, D.C., 1992, US Department of Health and Human Services.

25. Centers for Disease Control and Prevention: 1995 youth risk behavior surveillance system, At-lanta, Ga. (http://www.cdc.gov/nccdphp/dash/yrbs/suph.htm).

26. Blair S, Kohl H, and Powell K: Physical activity, physical fitness, exercise, and the public's health, The Academy Papers 20:53–69, 1987.

27. Montoye H: How active are modern populations? The Academy Papers 21:34–45, 1988.

28. Lupton CH III, Ostrove NM, and Bozzo RM: Participation in leisure time activities: a comparison of existing data, Journal of Physical Education, Recreation, and Dance 55(9):19–23, 1984.

29. Sporting Goods Manufacturers Association: The senior sports revolution, Press Release, November 3, 1997, Sporting Goods Manufacturers Association.

30. Sporting Goods Manufacturers Association: The sports and recreation industry exceeds $60 billion, Press Release, May 26, 1997, Sporting Goods Manufacturers Association.

31. Corbin CB: Is the fitness bandwagon passing us by? Journal of Physical Education, Recreation and Dance 55(9):17, 1984.

32. Park RJ: Three major issues: the academy takes a stand, Journal of Physical Education, Recreation, and Dance 54(1):52–53, 1983.

33. Centers for Disease Control and Prevention: Guidelines for school and community programs to promote lifelong physical activity among young people, Atlanta, Ga. 1997, Centers for Disease Control and Prevention, Public Health Service, US Department of Health and Human Services.

34. Collingwood TR: Providing physical fitness programs to at-risk youth, Quest 49:67–88, 1997.

35. Harris, JC: Enhancing quality of life in low-income neighborhoods: Developing equity oriented individuals, Quest 48:366–377, 1996.

36. Siedentop D: Introduction to physical education, fitness, and sport, ed 3, Mountain View, Calif., 1998, Mayfield.

37. Gardner D: A nation at risk: the imperative for educational reform, Washington, D.C., 1983, US Government Printing Office.

38. Adler M: The Paideia proposal: an educational manifesto, New York, 1982, Macmillan.

39. Boyer E: High school: a report on secondary education in America, New York, 1983, Harper & Row.

40. US Department of Education: The condition of education 1994, Washington, D.C., 1995, US Government Printing Office.

41. US Department of Education: The goals 2000: educate america act—launching a new era in education, Washington, D.C., 1994, US Government Printing Office.

42. US Department of Education: The condition of education 1996, Washington, D.C., 1997, US Government Printing Office.

43. Lawson HA: School reform, families, and health in the emergent national agenda for economic and social improvement: implications, Quest 45:289–307, 1993.

44. Shepard RI: Curricular physical activity and academic performance, Pediatric Exercise Science 9:117–126, 1997.

45. Bell T: American education at a crossroads, Phi Delta Kappa 65(8):531–534, 1984.

46. National Association for Sport and Physical Education: Shape of the nation 1993, Reston, Va., 1993, American Alliance for Health, Physical Education, Recreation and Dance.

47. National Association for Sport and Physical Education: Shape of the nation 1997, Reston, Va., 1997, American Alliance for Health, Physical Education, Recreation and Dance.

SUGGESTED READINGS

Kanters MA and Montelpare WJ, editors: Enabling healthy lives through leisure, Journal of Physical Education, Recreation, and Dance 65(4):25–48, 1994.

A series of articles on the contribution of leisure-time activities to health promotion.

Lawson HA: School reform, families, and health in the emergent national agenda for economic and social improvement: implications, Quest 45:289–307, 1993.

Discusses the interaction among schools, families, and health care institutions and agencies and implications for physical education in the future.

Martinek TJ, editor: Serving underserved youth through physical activity, Quest, 49, 1997.

The entire issue focuses on underserved youths and includes articles about the conditions in which underserved youth live, youth resiliency, role of

the subdisciplines in meeting youth's needs, and examples of programs.

Shepard RJ: Curricular physical activity and academic performance, Pediatric Exercise Science 9:117–126, 1997.

Discusses the impact of quality, daily physical education on young children's academic performance and the development of an evidenced-based public policy for school boards.

Siedentop D: Valuing the physically active life: contemporary and future directions, Quest 48:266–274, 1996.

The importance of the social context in promoting physical activity and the need to strengthen our programs and infrastructure to meet the needs of the population.

US Department of Health and Human Services: Physical activity and health: a report of the Surgeon General, Atlanta, Ga., 1996, US Department of Health and Human Services, Centers for Disease Control and Prevention, National Center for Chronic Disease Prevention and Health Promotion, and The President's Council on Physical Fitness and Sports.

This report is a comprehensive reference for all physical education and sport professionals, covering research on physical activity and health, historical development, physical activity patterns of different population groups, and promotion of involvement.

Movement: The Keystone of Physical Education and Sport

Instructional Objectives and Competencies to be Achieved:

After reading this chapter the student should be able to—

- Explain why movement is the keystone of physical education and sport.
- Discuss and provide examples of the four movement concepts of body awareness, space awareness, qualities of movement, and relationships.
- Define and give examples of fundamental locomotor, nonlocomotor, and manipulative skills.
- Show the relationship between movement concepts, fundamental movement skills, and specialized game, sport skills, dance, and fitness activities.
- Provide suggestions on how to help individuals learn movement concepts and fundamental movement skills.

Movement is the central concern of physical education and sport professionals. As professionals, our primary goal is to help people of all ages lead a healthy, physically active lifestyle. We strive to help human beings to move efficiently, to increase the quality of their performance, to enhance their level of fitness, to gain an understanding of movement, and to appreciate the contribution of physical activity to their life. Movement is the foundation of a physically active lifestyle. An individual's movement is influenced by biomechanical, physiological, psychological, and sociological factors. Since movement is the keystone of physical educa-

tion and sport, it is important that professionals in this field understand some of its dimensions.

To work effectively with individuals in their programs, professionals must be knowledgeable about movement concepts and fundamental movement skills. Movement concepts are knowledge and understandings of movements that allow individuals to adapt and modify their movements to achieve specific movement goals. Movement concepts include body awareness, spatial awareness, qualities of movements, and relationships. Fundamental movement skills, such as running and throwing, are the foundation for the development of more

GETTING CONNECTED

CyberActive contains information about motor skill development, including activities for children with special needs. The Activity Database has lesson plan ideas for the development of motor and sport skills.
> Site: http://www.tc.umn.edu/nlhome/g032/arnt0008/kara/

Human Kinetics InfoKinetics Physical Activity Links offers links to over 70 different physical activities. Incorporated within these activity links is information about the history of the activity, skill development, and additional resources. (Go to the *Human Kinetics* home page, click on InfoKinetics, then click on Physical Activity Links, then click on the physical activity of your choice.)
> Site: http://www.humankinetics.com/

PE Central provides lesson plans focusing on the development of many different skills. It is a growing resource for professionals in physical education.
> Site: http://pe.central.vt.edu/

Sports Media contains physical education lesson plans, sports links, and coaching links.
> Site: http://www.ping.be/sportsmedia/

complex and specialized skills used in games, sports, dance, and fitness activities and in work and life situations in which human beings are in motion.

As a profession, we have committed ourselves to involving people across the lifespan in healthy, physical activity. We can increase the number of people involved in physical activity by providing them with instructional experiences that develop competence in skills and confidence in their ability to move effectively. Ideally, this should occur in early childhood, in the elementary school, where instruction should focus on developing skillful movers who enjoy being physically active and have the confidence to try new activities. As these students mature, they can understand and apply these movement fundamentals to more advanced sport, dance, and fitness activities.

Developing proficiency in motor skills is critical to lifespan participation. Children who develop proficiency in skills are more likely to use these skills throughout life. Children who don't possess adequate skills are often excluded from play and

games with their more skillful peers and may experience frustration and failure when learning more complex sport skills. The lack of adequate fundamental skills, perceived incompetence as a mover, and frustration contribute to lack of participation in physical activities as an adult. Giving children opportunities to develop skill proficiency, an understanding of movement concepts, and confidence to participate enjoyably in many activities is essential to promoting lifespan involvement.

Many methods can be used to help individuals learn about movement. One approach that can be used to help children develop an understanding of movement concepts and attain proficiency in fundamental movement skills is movement education. Movement education uses a series of movement challenges and problem-solving situations to help individuals explore the body's movement capabilities and apply movement concepts to different skills and changing environmental circumstances. Instructional programs that are developmentally appropriate are sensitive to the needs of the learners, promote the development of competence that

Playgrounds provide opportunities for children to explore how their bodies can move.

leads to confidence in their abilities as movers, and encourage learners to participate in physical activity regularly.

GENERAL FACTORS THAT AFFECT MOVEMENT

Human movement involves most of the systems of the body, such as the skeletal system (e.g., skeletal levers), the nervous system (e.g., nerve impulses to the muscles), the muscular system (e.g., muscular contractions for force), and the cardiovascular system (e.g., heart's response to exertion or exercise). All movement is governed by certain mechanical principles. An understanding of the forces that act on the human body as it moves is essential if people are to engage in creative and meaningful movement. Knowledge of the biomechanical principles of movement is important for professionals if they are going to teach movement skills effectively (see Chapter 6).

Physiological factors affect the learner's movement. Physical fitness is one factor that affects

movement. Physical fitness qualities such as cardiovascular endurance, muscular strength and endurance, and flexibility can positively or negatively influence an individual's movement. For example, poor muscular development hinders the generation of force, reducing the effectiveness of the movement (e.g., distance thrown). A high level of flexibility allows a greater range of motion when executing skills, enhancing performance (e.g., gymnastics). Further, physically fit learners can practice for longer periods before becoming fatigued (see Chapter 7).

Psychological factors influence an individual's movement and performance. Phenomena such as fear, anxiety, and self-confidence can alter movement. An adult who fears the water may have trouble learning to swim. A child who is anxious about performing in front of his classmates experiences clumsiness and appears uncoordinated. A young adult who is confident of abilities as a mover seeks out new activities to try and enjoys the challenge of learning new skills (see Chapter 9).

Sociological factors impact an individual's movement. Membership in a group can influence participation. For example, children who come from families who regularly participate in sports and value such participation are more physically active. Gender roles—that is, what it means to be masculine and feminine in our society—influence learners' participation in physical activity. Economics can impact children's opportunities to participate in movement activities. As the number of private, preschool movement programs grows and community and private sports programs for young children increase, we will see greater disparities in the skills of children entering elementary school. Children from economically advantaged backgrounds may be better skilled than their peers because of the increased opportunities available to them to develop their motor skills. Elementary

physical educators must act to address these children's needs before the disparities in motor skills widen further (Chapter 8).

MOVEMENT FUNDAMENTALS

Movement concepts and fundamental movement skills—that is, *movement fundamentals*—form the foundation for movement learning (see Figure 4-1). Ideally, this foundation should be solidly developed in childhood, during the elementary school years. From this foundation the child develops more complex and specialized sport skills, dance, and fitness activities. Movement fundamentals are the basis for lifetime participation in physical activity.

Movement concepts are knowledge about movement that can be applied to modify and

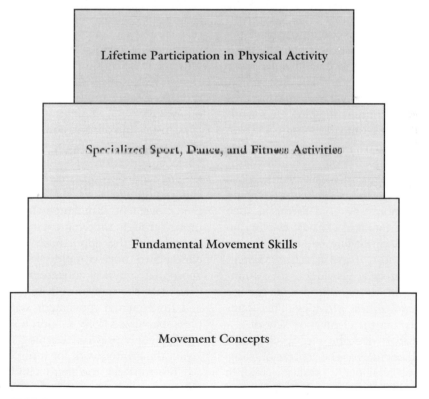

FIGURE 4-1   Building a foundation for lifetime participation in physical activity.

enrich the performance of motor skills. Learners who understand body awareness concepts can bat a ball effectively by correctly sequencing their actions, can use their body to communicate feelings in expressive dance, and can apply the concept of tension and relaxation to Tai Chi. A wheelchair athlete creating a passing lane in basketball, a 60-year-old moving through the full range of motion performing flexibility exercises, and a young child zigzagging across the playground to escape being tagged are all using spatial concepts to modify their movements to fit their needs, the task, and the situation. The runner accelerating as she rounds the corner in track, the gymnast with her explosive tumbling moving effortlessly from one skill to the next, the young child cradling the ball, absorbing the force as he catches it so it does not pop out of his hands, are all using concepts pertaining to qualities of movement to enhance their performance. The tennis doubles team uses relationship concepts to constantly adjust their positions on the court, as does the blind skier who shadows his guide as they traverse down the slope. Understanding movement concepts helps individuals of all ages use their movement skills more effectively.

Fundamental skills include basic skills such as throwing, catching, running, jumping and landing, pushing and pulling, and dribbling. Softball, basketball, rowing, and soccer are just some sports that use these basic skills in a more complex fashion. The fundamental skills of striking with an object, dodging, turning and sliding, and leaping find expression in more advanced forms in such activities as hitting a tennis backhand, evading an opponent in lacrosse, propelling oneself across the circle in the discus, and sparring in karate. Mastery of these fundamental skills provides a solid foundation for learning more specialized skills for use in sports, dance, and fitness activities. This foundation should be laid in the elementary school.

Several professionals describe the development of movement fundamentals as the process of learning the movement alphabet.[1,2] Just as children must learn individual letters before they read words, and understand words before they can comprehend sentences, children must learn the movement alphabet. The movement alphabet consists of movement concepts and fundamental movement skills. Once learned, the movement alphabet, like letters, can be combined and used in many different ways (i.e., like words), and structured (i.e., like sentences) according to the task. If children have the important concepts and possess the necessary skills, their chances increase for success at more complex activities. As Graham, Holt/Hale, and Parker[1] state, "If children learn to throw and catch, for example, their chances of playing and enjoying a sport such as softball or basketball increase, because they have a reasonable chance to succeed at that sport." Competence in movement fundamentals builds self-confidence, and this contributes to children's willingness to try new sports and activities. Thus, if lifetime activity is our goal, individuals must develop the necessary knowledge and skills to participate.

What is the relationship of movement concepts to fundamental movement skills? Buschner[2] describes movement skills as action words or verbs (e.g., the first grader will *run*). He conceptualizes movement concepts as adverbs that modify the movement skills (e.g., the first grader will run in a *zigzag* pathway). Children use movement concepts to modify movement sequences, depending on the task.

Learning movement concepts and fundamental movement skills should be the focus of elementary physical education. Through progressively challenging and appropriately designed experiences, children should have the opportunity to master the movement fundamentals. As the children move through the elementary school years, they should have the opportunity to apply movement concepts to more complex skills. Developmentally appropriate physical education programs help children make the transition from movement concepts and fundamental movement skills to more complex, specialized skills. Children should be encouraged to apply previous learning to new situations, laying the groundwork for future learning.

Unfortunately, too many children emerge from elementary school without an understanding of movement concepts or the ability to perform fundamental movement skills correctly. There are several reasons that children are unskilled. Frequently, children are taught sports and dance before they have learned the necessary skills and movement concepts. One consequence of this teaching approach is that they are frustrated when placed in game situations and experience failure too frequently because they do not have the necessary skills. Because of the decrease in time allocated for elementary physical education in the school and the lack of elementary physical education specialists, children don't have sufficient time or leadership to develop the prerequisite fundamentals. These children are disadvantaged as they progress throughout school. Physical educators and sport leaders working with older children and adults need to address these deficiencies as part of assisting individuals to be active throughout the lifespan.

MOVEMENTS CONCEPTS

Movement concepts must be understood by both physical education and sport professionals and their students (regardless of age) for there to be a meaningful understanding of basic movement. These concepts are derived from Rudolph Laban's[3] four components of movement: (1) *body awareness* (What can the body do?), (2) *spatial awareness* (Where does the body move?), (3) *qualities of movement* (How does the body move?), and (4) *relationships* (With whom or what does the body move?). (See Fig. 4-2).

Children typically study movement concepts through student-centered learning experiences. These experiences typically involve the teacher designing questions or movement challenges[4] that enable the students to explore the various dimensions of each movement concept. As students develop, emphasis shifts from understanding the concept to creative application of the concept utilizing many different movement skills in a variety of situations.

In this section are presented selected movement concepts pertaining to the major categories of body awareness, spatial awareness, qualities of movement, and relationships. Objectives for the study of each area are listed. Examples of movement

MOVEMENT CONCEPTS	
Concept	**Description**
Body Awareness	What can the body do?
Space Awareness	Where does the body move?
Qualities of Movement	How does the body move?
Relationships	With whom or what does the body move?

challenges and questions to explore various movement concepts are noted.[1,2,4] The boxes on pages 123, 126, 129, and 130 list movement concepts and verbal cues associated with each concept.

Body Awareness

Concepts pertaining to body awareness emphasize understanding of what the body does during movement. Body awareness encompasses being able to name and identify the movements of body parts, to demonstrate the many different ways the body and specific body parts can move, and to make different shapes of the body. Body awareness includes an understanding of the use of the body to communicate and an awareness of tension and relaxation.

Objectives related to body awareness include
1. To name and locate body parts of oneself and others.
2. To demonstrate the various shapes and positions the body can make.
3. To understand how various body parts function and the movements they can make.
4. To use the body to express feelings and ideas.
5. To distinguish between muscle tension and relaxation and to understand their role in movement.

Identification and location of body parts

Activities related to this movement concept focus on helping children learn the names and

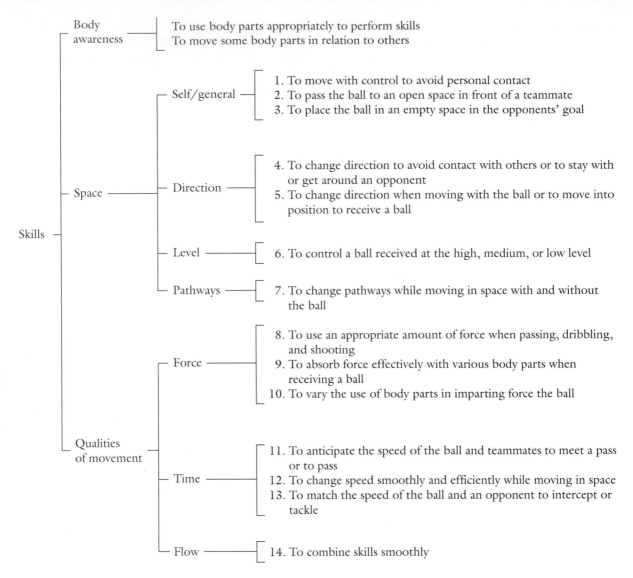

FIGURE 4-2 Application of movement concepts to soccer.

locations of their body parts. Children enter elementary school, which increasingly includes pre-kindergarten, with some knowledge of the names of some body parts. Teachers should assess what children know and build upon this knowledge. Being able to name the body parts used in movements enriches the children's understanding of the range of movements of the body. Further, it enables them to utilize cues from the teacher more effectively (e.g., in learning the overhand throw, a child can be cued to "lead with the elbow"). This concept forms the foundation for learning more about the body and its capabilities. For example, some teachers have their students learn new information about the body each week. Their students, as they progress through school, learn about the different body parts, bones, and muscles and their actions.

Examples of activities, movement challenges, and questions related to this concept follow and are presented as a teacher would present them to his/her students:

- ♦ As I call out the name of the body part, can you move it?
- ♦ Can you balance a beanbag on your head? ear? hip? knee? and so on. Can you balance the beanbag on five different body parts? Name those body parts.
- ♦ Can you touch your elbow to your knee? your hand to your shoulder? your chin to your chest? Can you name two parts to touch together?
- ♦ Working with a partner, take turns calling out the names of a body part and then gently touching those body parts together.
- ♦ Given a large piece of paper, place the paper on the floor. Lie down on the paper and have your partner trace an outline of your body. Once both of you have completed your tracings, label each body part.
- ♦ What body parts make up the leg? Can you move each one as you name them? Begin at the toes and move up the leg; can you name each of the small parts of the leg in order?

Body shapes and positions

Awareness of various body shapes and the ability to vary the position of the body based on the task is important to effective movement. For example, in springboard diving, when performing a $2\frac{1}{2}$ tuck somersault, the diver takes off with the body in a stretch position, moves quickly into a tuck position, and finishes the dive by straightening out the body while entering the water. Skillful divers can improve their chances for success by modifying the tuck position to alter their spin; pulling the tuck tighter speeds up the spin, while loosening the tuck a bit slows down the rate of spin.

The body can make many shapes, such as curved and straight, narrow and wide, stretched or curled, symmetrical and asymmetrical. Children need to understand why certain shapes can be

Students play a game that helps them identify parts of their bodies.

beneficial in a movement and other shapes can hinder a movement. Additionally, children need to be able to vary the shape of the body depending on the task. Examples of activities, movement challenges, and questions related to this concept are listed below and are presented as a teacher would present them to his/her students:

- ♦ Show children picture of athletes performing different skills: for example, Michael Jordan dunking the ball, Shannon Miller tumbling, Tiger Woods driving off the tee, Rebecca Lobo guarding an opponent, and so on. Ask children to describe the shape of the athlete's body. Is it stretched, curled, twisted, wide or narrow?
- ♦ Can you use your body to make a letter of the alphabet? Can you use your body to spell a word? Working with a partner, how many letters of the alphabet can you make?
- ♦ Working in your own space, can you make a shape that is wide? Can you change it to a shape that is narrow? Explore other shapes and changing from one to another. Try moving from one shape to another as quickly as you can; now try moving as slowly as you can.

◆ Explore symmetrical and asymmetrical shapes. In a symmetrical shape both sides of the body are performing the same movement, and in an asymmetrical shape, each side of the body is different.

Body movements

Body parts can move in many different ways. Flexion (bending), extension (straightening), rotation (turning), abduction (movement away from the median axis, or apart), and adduction (movement toward the median axis, or together) are just some of the movements that can be made. As children explore the movements of their body and its parts, they gain an understanding of how body parts can be used efficiently to perform movements. Further development of this concept includes understanding the role that joints play in movement and recognizing that different joints produce different types of movements.

Examples of activities, movement challenges, and questions related to this concept are listed below and are presented as a teacher would present them to his/her students:

◆ Starting at your toes, bend one body part, then straighten it. Then try another. Bending a body part is called flexion; straightening a body part is called extension. Vary how much you bend and flex each part. Try changing the speed of your movements as you flex and extend different body parts. Jump as high as you can. What body parts are flexed and what body parts are extended? Jump several times, varying the hardness and softness of your landing. What body parts are used in landing and what are their actions?

◆ Working with a partner, start at the head and move down the body. Try to make three different movements with each body part. Now, take turns being leaders. First match your partner's movements; then mirror your partner's movements. Describe the movements of three different body parts. Can you think of a sport skill that uses these movements?

◆ Working with beanbags, how can you use different body parts to move them? With your partner, take turns throwing the beanbag at the target on the wall. What body parts are involved in throwing? What movements do they make? Move further and further back each time you throw. How do the movements of the body parts change?

Body as a communicator

The body is a medium for communication. Through the actions of the body we express feelings and ideas. Facial expressions, gestures, body posture, and movements help convey our emotions and interpret our thoughts. Dance is one of the most common outlets for creative expression and the use of the body as a means of communication. However, the use of the body for communication is not limited to dance. There are many other situations where an individual's ability to use the body as a means of communication is useful. For example, a basketball player uses a head fake to get around an opponent; the head action communicates to the opponent that the player is intending to move one way. The guard responds to that communication (message) and commits to that direction; the player then moves around the guard toward the basket.

Examples of activities, movement challenges, and questions related to this concept are listed below and are presented as a teacher would present them to his/her students:

◆ Pretend you are your favorite animal. Without making a sound, show us how your animal would move through its habitat. How does it look for food? What does it look like when it is sleeping? Show us how the animal would look at play.

◆ Working with a partner, take turns acting out different emotions while your partner tries to guess what feelings you are sharing. Try using your posture, body movements, gestures, and facial expressions to show your feelings. Now try using only facial gestures to share your feelings, then only posture, and so on. Explore the communication of such emotions and events as happy, sad, love, confidence, anger, surprise, winning, losing, good and bad sportsmanship, and so on.

◆ Facing your partner, try to move past the partner to reach the line at the end of the

Dance offers opportunities for creative expression and teaches children how to use their bodies to communicate.

gym. Use body language to fool your partner into thinking you will go to one side while you go to the other. Explore different ways of tricking your partner so you can get past. Which ways worked best? Move to another partner and try the same activity. Which ways worked best with this partner? Are they the same ways that were successful with the first partner?

♦ Working with a partner, act out your favorite story. When you are done, have your partner tell you the story. Did your partner understand what you were trying to share? Which parts of the story did your partner understand? Which parts of the story were different than what you had intended to "say"?

Awareness of muscle tension and relaxation

The ability to distinguish between tension and relaxation is important to skillful movement. As individuals move, some muscles tense and others relax. Appropriate tension and relaxation in the muscles contributes to coordinated, efficient movement. The ability to control muscle tension through conscious relaxation is a skill that can be used throughout one's lifetime to reduce stress and contribute to well-being.

Examples of activities, movement challenges, and questions related to this concept are listed below and are presented as a teacher would present them to his/her students:

♦ As each body part is called out, tense it and then relax it. Now, try tensing the body part slowly and relaxing it to the count of 10. Make a fist. Where do you feel the muscle tension in your arm? Keeping your fist, bend your arm at the elbow. What muscles are tense now? Now, make your arm as limp as it can be, just like a floppy, wet noodle. What is the difference between tension and relaxation?

◆ Balance on different body parts. Try to balance so that only one body part is touching the floor. Which body parts are tense? Which are relaxed? Try to balance on two, three, and four different body parts. Notice which muscles are tense and which are relaxed.

◆ Lying on your back on a mat, close your eyes, and slowly take several deep breaths. Imagine the breath going in your body, through your lungs, and down to your toes. As you exhale, imagine all your muscle tension flowing up and out from your body. See yourself floating on a cloud and becoming more and more relaxed. Breathe slowly, allowing yourself to relax more fully. How do your muscles feel when they are relaxed? What other sensations do you notice in your body? When you are ready, open your eyes, tense your muscles a little bit, and slowly stand up.

Body awareness concepts help children learn about their body and its movements. An understanding of the different actions of body parts, different shapes and positions that the body can assume, muscle tension and relaxation, and the ability of the body to communicate enhance the individual's movement potential.

Spatial Awareness

All movement takes place in space. An understanding of the different aspects of space is essential if individuals are to move effectively and safely. Spatial awareness concepts help individuals understand where the body can move and move successfully in a variety of activities. Concepts pertaining to spatial awareness include location in space (self and general space), direction, levels, pathways, and range of movement.

Objectives related to spatial awareness include

1. To recognize one's self- or personal space and to respect the self-space of others.
2. To move within the boundaries of general space safely, taking into consideration the movements of others and modifying one's movement as necessary to avoid touching and collisions.

A child's earliest learning is motor in nature and forms the foundation for subsequent learning.

3. To understand different levels of movement in space and be able to move smoothly from one level to the next.
4. To recognize the different directions in which the body can move and to change directions.
5. To travel through different pathways and to recognize the different pathways (trajectories) that objects travel in space.
6. To express movement through different ranges and adjust the range of movements according to the task and situation.

Self-space

Self-space or personal space is the area immediately surrounding a person, including the area that can be reached by extending parts of the body (e.g., reaching the arms out wide, straddling the legs). Each person has a self-space. This self-space moves with us as we move throughout an area, like being inside of a bubble. Understanding of

DIMENSIONS OF BODY AWARENESS AND CUES FOR LEARNING

Dimension	Cues for Learning
Names and locates body parts	Head, foot, knee, elbow, shoulder, hand, leg, arm, hip, waist
Awareness of body shapes	Curved and straight, narrow and wide, symmetrical and asymmetrical, straight or extended
Awareness of movements of the body	Flexion and extension, rotation, supination, pronation, adduction and abduction
Use of the body in communication	Communication of feelings, ideas, and interpretations through body posture, gestures, and movements
Awareness of muscle tension and relaxation	Tension and relaxation, tense and relaxed

self-space includes respecting the self-space of others and realizing that working with objects, such as racquets, increases the self-space needed. Further development of this concept includes understanding the relationship between self-space and general space—that is, the boundaries that define an area.

Examples of activities, movement challenges, and questions related to this concept are listed below and are presented as a teacher would present them to his/her students:

◆ Scatter within the boundaries of the gymnasium. Find a space where you can work without touching anyone. Explore the boundaries of your self-space by reaching out as far as you can with your arms and legs—stretch as high and as wide as you can. Twist and turn as you try to touch all parts of your self-space. Now make your self-space as narrow as possible. Can you make it smaller?

◆ Share with your partner the dimensions of your self-space. Move with your partner in the general space. When you are asked to stop, "freeze." Then check and make sure that your partner's self-space and yours do not overlap. Continue to move in different ways in general space, stopping on signal and checking to make sure that you are respecting each other's self-space.

◆ With your ball, try some different activities within your self-space. How does the ball change the size of your self-space? Being careful not to collide with anyone, move through general space bouncing your ball. Try to keep your ball in control as you move so that it stays within your own self-space.

General space

General space is the total area within which an individual or individuals can move. It is defined by boundaries, such as lines, walls, or cones. Within this area, children need to be able to move with control and safety, avoiding collisions. Children also need to learn to use all available space and to vary movements in general space in relation to others, the changing size of general space, and objects. In situations such as games and sport settings, the ability to move effectively in general space may include such skills as passing a ball to an open space in front of a teammate or moving to close off a passing lane to an opponent.

Examples of activities, movement challenges, and questions related to this concept are listed below and are presented as a teacher would present them to his/her students:

◆ Let's explore the boundaries of our general space by visiting many different areas of our general space. As you move to different locations, try to stay as far away as you can from other people. Check around you, and as you see open spaces, try to move toward them. When you hear the signal to "freeze," stop and make sure that your self-space is not touching anyone else's space. Once we can move successfully slowly, we will try harder challenges such as moving faster and in a smaller space.

♦ Explore different sizes and shapes of general space. Cones define different general spaces such as a circle, rectangle, triangle and square. Vary the sizes of these shapes. Move within these shapes and vary your movements within these shapes (e.g., galloping, skipping, walking slowly, running). How did your movements change with different shapes? Different sizes? Different ways of moving?

♦ In a general space defined by cones, work in small groups of four or five, moving the ball back and forth between members of your group. Remember to control the ball and to try different movements. Increase the size of your general space by picking up the cone and stepping back two steps. Continue to move the ball back and forth, perhaps rolling it or bouncing it. Increase the size of your general space again by another two steps. Move the ball back and forth again. Now, reduce the size of your general space and make it smaller. Move the cones two steps closer to the center. Pass the ball to others in your group. Make the space even smaller. What did you have to do to pass the ball to others as the space became larger? Smaller? What movements worked best?

Directions

Individuals can move in many different directions. These include forward and backward, up and down, and sideways (left and right). The individual's direction in space is relative to his or her body's orientation in space. Thus, directions depend on the way the individual is facing. Changing directions while moving, moving in a variety of different ways in each direction (e.g., backpedaling quickly down a basketball court), and performing skills and moving with others while varying directions are embraced within this concept.

Examples of activities, movement challenges, and questions related to this concept are listed below and are presented as a teacher would present them to his/her students:

♦ Let's start out all facing me. Now, begin to travel carefully through general space, changing the direction you are moving on

my signal. Next, when you hear the signal to change, change to the direction that I ask you and choose a different movement to travel.

♦ With your partner, explore different directions. Take turns being the leader and challenging your partner to move in different directions. First, have your partner move different body parts in different directions (move your right arm forward, stretch your left foot sideways as far as it can go, point your chin up). Once you have both taken several turns, try moving in different directions as your partner calls them out. Vary your movements as well when you move. Be careful not to let your self-space touch another person's. What did you do to help change direction quickly?

♦ Pretend you are a character in a computer game. Move along the lines on the floor, changing direction and movements each time you come to a new line. Now, have your partner chase you along the lines, trying to tag you. Both of you must change directions and movements at the intersection of the lines. After you are tagged, switch roles.

Levels

Levels refer to horizontal areas in space, described in relationship to the standing body. High level is the area above the shoulders. Low level is the area below the hips. Middle level is the area between the hips and the shoulders. Levels describe where the body and its parts are positioned and can move. For example, when a child is running, the feet move at a low level, the arms may be held at a medium level, and the head is at a high level. The body and its parts can change levels, and children can handle objects at different levels. For example, raising the arms above the shoulders places them at a high level. Jumping moves more of the body into a high level. Catching a rolling ball occurs at a low level; if a thrown ball is caught at the waist, it is caught at a middle level. This concept also emphasizes the ability to change levels.

Examples of activities, movement challenges, and questions related to this concept are listed below and are presented as a teacher would present them to his/her students:

- As you travel in general space, move up and down as you move to all areas. Can you change direction as you move, still moving up and down through different levels? Can you move your arms into the low level while traveling? A high level? Can you move one or both feet into different levels? Can you travel with all of your body parts at one level?
- Working with your balloon, can you keep it at a high level? Can you let the balloon sink to a low level before you hit it? Try using different body parts at different levels to keep your balloon up in the air. Try changing your own level as you hit the balloon.
- With a partner, find different ways that you can pass your nerf ball to your partner at the low, medium, and high levels. What are some different ways you can catch the ball at each level?

Pathways

A pathway is the line of movement from one point to another, either on the ground or in the air. It can refer to a person or an object. For example, if we were to look down from above at a child moving in different patterns in general space and trace the child's movement, the tracing would reveal the pathway that the child took from one point to another. Another example would be a basketball coach's diagram of players' pathways or movements for a certain play. A flight of a ball could be described as an arc or a rainbow. Pathways can be straight, curved, or angular (i.e., zigzag). The ability to move in different pathways, alone or with others or an object, is important in moving effectively.

Examples of activities, movement challenges, and questions related to this concept are listed below and are presented as a teacher would present them to his/her students:

- Several pathways have been marked on the floor with tape. The pathways are curved (such as a circle and figure eight), straight, zigzag, and combined such as a squiggle. Travel along the different pathways, using different movements.

- Here is a map or a pathway for you to follow to move from one side of the room to the other. Look carefully at this map as you follow this path to the other side. Now, take the path back to your starting point. Let's see if you can make up your own map. Using this paper and pencil, start at this side of the room and draw an interesting pathway that will help you move to a spot underneath the basketball hoop at the other side. Try out your pathway. Now, switch pathways with your partner. Which pathway got you to the other side of the room most quickly and why?
- Toss the ball to yourself. Toss it up in the air at different heights. What kind of pathway does the ball make in the air? Toss the ball to your partner. Toss the ball back and forth, with each of you stepping back two steps each time. How does the pathway of the ball change? What if there were a tall tree between you and your partner and you had to throw the ball over the tree? What would the pathway look like? What if you wanted to toss the ball to your partner at a low level—what would the pathway look like then?

Range

Range of movements concerns the extension of the body into self-space. It also incorporates the relationship of the body parts to one another or to objects. Range can be described using such terms as large and small, near and far, big and little, and wide and narrow. Examples of activities, movement challenges, and questions related to this concept are listed below and are presented as a teacher would present them to his/her students:

- In your self-space, make the smallest shape you can. Try to make your shape so small that you are almost "invisible." Slowly open up and expand, making the largest shape you can. Now, pretend that you are a flower bud. As you grow and feel the warmth of the sunlight, gradually open up and blossom. As the sun slowly sets, close yourself slowly back up for the night.

◆ In your self-space, try to bring two body parts together until they touch. After you touch them together, slowly move them as far apart as possible. For example, slowly move so that your head and toes are touching. What type of shape did you need to make? Move your head and toes as far apart as you can. How did your shape change? Try several different combinations.

◆ Stand facing your partner. As your partner performs a movement, you copy it but change the range of the movements. If your partner's movements are small and narrow, your movements should be the same, but large and wide.

Qualities of Movement

As persons move, they vary their movements by altering the body's balance and adjusting the time or speed of the movement, the force used, and the flow of the movements. These adjustments allow persons to modify their performance according to the demands of the situation. An understanding of these factors and their effects on movement contribute to efficient movement in a diversity of situations. Mechanical principles underlie the application of these concepts.

Objectives related to qualities of movement include

1. To understand the nature of static and dynamic balance and the role of balance in movement.
2. To differentiate among speeds and to increase or decrease the speed of movement.
3. To distinguish between different levels of force and to create and modify one's force to meet the demands of the task.
4. To combine movements smoothly and to perform movements within a restricted time or space.

Balance

Balance refers to the stability of the body. When the body is balanced, a person's center of gravity is over the base of support. Changes in an individual's base of support alter the stability of the body.

DIMENSIONS OF SPATIAL AWARENESS AND CUES FOR LEARNING

Dimension	Cues for Learning
Self-space	Recognition of personal space and personal space of others, boundaries and changing dimensions of self-space, movement in self-space
General space	Movement in general space with respect for others, responding to changing boundaries
Directions	Forward, backward, sideways, left and right, up and down
Levels	Low, middle, high
Pathways	Straight, curved, zigzag
Range	Big and little, wide and narrow, large and small, near and far

The larger the base of the support, the more stable the body. Balance is also affected by the movement of body parts and by the use of an object (e.g., a tennis racquet). To maintain balance, movements on one side of the body need to be compensated with movements on the other side (e.g., a tennis player stroking a ball uses the free arm for balance). An understanding of both dynamic balance and static balance is important. Dynamic balance refers to being on-balance when moving, using various locomotor skills, starting, and stopping. It also includes maintaining a balanced state while performing activities, such as throwing or jumping. Static balance means maintaining a desired shape while stationary, such as holding a pose in gymnastics.

Examples of activities, movement challenges, and questions related to this concept are listed below and are presented as a teacher would present them to his/her students:

◆ See how many ways you can balance with four body parts on the floor. Change the four parts you are using. How large a base of

Through individual exploration, this child will have experiences that help him understand the concept of balance.

support can you make? How small a base can you make? Now try to balance with three (two, one) body parts. How large a base can you make? How small? How does this affect your base of support? What positions enable you to balance most easily? Why?

◆ As you run carefully through general space, stop when you hear the signal. Each time you stop, try a different stopping position. Try different positions of your feet, your body, and your arms. In which position were you the most balanced? Why?

◆ Pick a line on the floor to be your own personal balance beam. Try moving in different ways (walking, sliding) across your balance beam and in different directions (backward,

sideways). As you travel across your beam, move through different levels and explore different ranges of movement. Now that you can travel across your beam successfully, travel across the beam stopping part of the way across, create an interesting shape—that is, a pose—and hold it for a count of 5. Continue your travel and stop again, assuming another shape. How did you keep your balance when you were moving? How did the speed, type of movement, and level affect your balance? How did you keep your balance when you were holding your shape?

Time

Time refers to the speed or pace of movement. Movements vary on a continuum from slow to fast. Successful movement requires that the person adjust the speed of the movements to the requirement of the task. At times, it may be necessary to accelerate, increasing the speed of movement, and decelerate, decreasing the speed of movement. This change in speed occurs in many situations, such as a runner in touch football slowing down to allow blockers to set up, and then speeding up to outrun the opponents. A child may accelerate to outrun a tagger. Runners pace themselves over a 5-kilometer course to be in an advantageous position and to use their energy efficiently. In addition to moving with varying speeds, learning to control the speed of movements is an important aspect of this concept.

Examples of activities, movement challenges, and questions related to this concept are listed below and are presented as a teacher would present them to his/her students:

◆ As you move through general space, be careful to respect each other's self-space. Move from one side of the gym to the other as quickly as you can. Now, can you start out very slowly and accelerate to your fastest speed by the time you reach the other side? Try another way of traveling across the space. How did you increase your speed? What happened to your movements as you slowed down?

◆ As you travel through general space, listen carefully to the beat of the drum. Move with the beat of the drum, changing your pace as the drum changes. When the drum stops, freeze in a balanced position. What changes do you make in your movements to do them slowly? What happens when you move quickly?

◆ Develop a sequence of 5 movements that includes traveling, freezing, two different shapes, and one change of level. Practice this sequence several times. When you are ready, show your partner the sequence 3 times: first at "normal" speed, second at a fast pace, and third in slow motion. How did your movements change as you changed speed?

Force

The energy required to move an object is termed force. Force is initiated through muscular contraction. The amount of force can vary on a continuum from strong to weak. Learning how to generate an appropriate amount of force, absorb force, and control the direction of force are included within this concept. Youths playing soccer learn to kick the ball with the correct amount of force to get it to their teammates and to keep it within bounds. They also learn that dribbling successfully requires a light application of force. Catching a ball safely and successfully requires the child to absorb the force and "give with the catch." In baseball, skillful batters bunting the ball control the amount of force and its direction, carefully laying down the bunt along the base path.

Examples of activities, movement challenges, and questions related to this concept are listed below and are presented as a teacher would present them to his/her students:

◆ Here on the mat are marked different distances, some very close to you and others farther away. With your partner, take turns jumping. Jump in many different ways. Change the distance you jump. How did you change the force required to jump each distance? What changes did you make in your body movements as you jumped further?

◆ Each person has three balls of different weights and sizes. Working with your partner, practice throwing to one another, throwing with just enough force so that your partner can catch the ball easily. As you throw, change balls and increase the distance. What changes did you make in your movements as you threw heavier balls? threw a greater distance? How did your catching change?

◆ As you travel through general space, strive to move forcefully. Try a number of different movements and vary the way in which your body parts are used. When you hear the signal to stop, show me a shape that looks strong. Now, let's travel through space moving as lightly as we can. Explore different ways to move. When you hear the signal to stop, show me a shape that looks light. How did your movements change from moving strongly to moving lightly?

Flow

Flow is the ability to smoothly join together different movements. It refers to the continuity of movement, the ease with which one movement flows or leads to the next. A smooth flowing movement requires the control of various forces so that there is a proper transition between the movements. Flow can be described as bound or free. Bound flow occurs when the movement is momentarily stopped, such as in a floor exercise routine. At several points during the routine, the performer may move into a balanced pose, such as a cartwheel into a handstand, and then continue the movement. Free flow describes movements that are controlled or continued to completion. They are often very hard to interrupt, such as stopping a leap in midair. An understanding of flow allows persons to achieve coordinated movements.

Examples of activities, movement challenges, and questions related to this concept are listed below and are presented as a teacher would present them to his/her students:

◆ Can you travel quickly across this mat, stop in a balanced position, hold for 3 seconds, and continue moving? Try different shapes and levels as well as altering your speed and changing directions. What adjustments did you need to make to stop in a balanced position?

◆ Now you are going to create your own sequence of movements. In creating your sequence, include a balance on 3 body parts, a change of direction, and a change of level. When you have practiced your sequence, demonstrate your sequence to your partner.

◆ As you travel through general space, change your movements, levels, speed, and direction. However, keep moving continuously, from one movement to the next, as long as the movement continues. How do you adjust your body to move from one movement to the next?

Relationships

The concept of relationship embraces an understanding of the position of body parts relative to one another, the position of the individual with respect to other individuals or a group, the relationship of the body to others, and the relationship of the body to objects. Children benefit from understanding that their body parts can be wide or narrow, near or far from each other, symmetrical or asymmetrical. Different body parts can be used to lead movements and to support the body. Body parts can move in unison, opposition, or sequence. As persons move with others through space, they can lead, follow, or be alongside. As individuals work on movement challenges together, they can match or mirror their partner's movements. In a group, people may be near or far away from each other, in front or behind, or meeting and parting. Their movements may be made in unison or contrast with each other. When working with objects, such as a racquet or a bat, the body may be close to the object. When navigating an obstacle course, children enjoy the opportunity to go under, around, through, over, on, and off various obstacles.

Objectives related to qualities of movement include

1. To understand the relationship of body parts to one another and the body.
2. To move effectively relative to other individuals and within a group.
3. To understand the relationship between the body and its parts to objects.

Examples of activities, movement challenges, and questions related to this concept are listed below and are presented as a teacher would present them to his/her students:

◆ As we move through general space, we are going to explore using different body parts to lead the movement. Try moving leading with your foot, then leading with your elbow, then your head. How did your movements change as the leading part changed?

◆ Facing your partner, try to match his or her actions as you meet and part at different levels, using different ranges, shapes, and levels. Explore symmetrical and asymmetrical movements. After you take turns being the leader, try to mirror your partner's actions. How did different movements affect your balance?

DIMENSIONS OF QUALITIES OF MOVEMENT AND CUES FOR LEARNING

Dimension	Cues for Learning
Balance	Static and dynamic, losing and regaining, on- and off-balance, balancing objects and balancing with others
Time	Slow and fast, accelerating and decelerating, pacing, rhythm
Force	Creating and absorbing force, varying force, light and heavy, weak and strong
Flow	Free or bound, smooth, continuous, controlled, restrained

An understanding of movement concepts aids in performing sport skills, such as those used in playing soccer.

DIMENSIONS OF RELATIONSHIPS AND CUES FOR LEARNING

Dimension	Cues for Learning
Relationship of body parts to each other	Near and far, meeting and parting, above and beneath, match-
Relationship of individual to a partner or group	ing and mirroring, ahead and behind, leading and follow-
Relationship of body to an object	ing, inside and outside, over and under, around and through; unison, sequence, opposition

that emphasize exploration and creativity by children. These experiences should be challenging, provide opportunities for meaningful successes, and instill in children confidence in their abilities as movers. They should be developmentally appropriate, progressing in difficulty according to the accomplishments of each child.

SELECTED FUNDAMENTAL MOVEMENTS

Fundamental movement skills encompass a broad range of skills that form the foundation for successful participation in games, sports, dance, and fitness activities. These skills can be categorized into locomotor, nonlocomotor, and manipulative skills. Locomotor skills are those in which the body moves through space, and include running, jumping, and sliding. Nonlocomotor skills, or axial movements, are typically done from a relatively stationary position, using a stable base of support. Generally performed in place, nonlocomotor skills include bending, stretching, pushing, and stretching. Manipulative skills are skills used in handling objects; throwing, catching, striking, and kicking are examples of manipulative skills.

♦ As you move through the obstacle course, carefully read the directions. This obstacle course challenges you to leap over hurdles, crawl through a tunnel, go underneath a bar, jump on and off a box, lead your partner, and follow. Once you and your partner complete the obstacle course, think how you can modify it to make it even more challenging.

• • •

The movement concepts of body awareness, spatial awareness, qualities of movement, and relationships help modify our movements, enhancing our ability to move with greater efficiency, success, and understanding. When helping children learn movement concepts, understanding of the concepts should initially be emphasized. This can be achieved by providing a diversity of experiences

Fundamental movement skills are combined to create the specialized movement necessary in many activities. For example, the softball throw requires a combination of sliding (locomotor skill) and throwing (manipulative skills) and twisting (nonlocomotor skill). Other specialized sport skills require more complex combinations of movements.

The learning of fundamental skills progresses through several stages. With proper instruction, guidance, and opportunity, individuals progress from the initial stages of the skill to the mature form of the skill. The rate of progress varies with the individual. When sufficient time or instruction is not provided, individuals may not attain the mature form of the skill. This lack of development may hinder their participation in activities in the future.

The next section contains a brief analysis of selected locomotor, nonlocomotor, and manipulative movement skills. As children learn the skills, they should also acquire knowledge of the critical elements important to skill performance. This knowledge increases children's understanding of the technique and forms the foundation for future learning.

Locomotor Movements

The following locomotor movement skills are discussed: walking, running, jumping (for distance and height), hopping, leaping, skipping, sliding, and galloping. These are the skills most commonly used by elementary schoolchildren. Opportunities for students to explore and use these skills by themselves and in combination with nonlocomotor movements should create a sufficient foundation for more complex movement skills.

Walking

Walking involves the transfer of weight from one foot to the other while moving. The weight of the body is transferred in a forward direction from the heel to the ball of the foot and then to the toes. The feet should move parallel to each other, with the toes pointing straight ahead. One foot is in contact with the ground always; this is the

FUNDAMENTAL MOVEMENT SKILLS		
Locomotor Skills	**Nonlocomotor Skills**	**Manipulative Skills**
Walk	Bend and stretch	Throw
Run	Twist and turn	Catch
Jump and land	Push and pull	Strike an object
Hop	Swing and sway	Dribble
Leap		Kick
Slide		Volley
Gallop		
Skip		
Dodge		

support foot. The body is erect, with the head up. The arm action is coordinated with leg action; the opposite arm and leg move in the same direction. These movements should be rhythmical and natural.

Running

Running is similar to walking in several ways. However, some critical differences exist. In running, the speed of the movement is faster. The length of the stride is longer, the flexion and extension of the legs are greater, and there is a momentary period of flight where the body is not supported at all. The body leans slightly forward to place the center of gravity above the front foot in the stride. The arms swing forward and back, opposing the legs, and contribute power to the movement.

Jumping

Jumping varies according to the goal of the task. Jumping for distance and jumping for height are common skills. The standing long jump, for example, is done by bending the knees and lowering the upper body into a crouched position. As the body rocks back on the feet, the arms are brought down and beyond the hips. At takeoff,

Physical education and sport offers participants a variety of challenges. This young woman is striving to achieve her best effort in the broad jump.

the forward and upward swing of the arms is coordinated with the powerful extension of both the feet and legs. The body is propelled forward as if reaching for an object in front of the body. The knees bend in midair so that the feet do not touch the ground prematurely. The landing is on the feet, with the knees bending to absorb the impact, and the body falling forward.

Hopping

Hopping involves forcefully pushing off the ground from one foot, a brief suspension in the air, and landing on the same foot. The push-off from the ground is made from the toes and the ball of the foot (supporting foot), with the knee of the opposite foot bent and the foot off the ground (nonsupporting foot). The arms are thrust upward to aid in body lift. The landing is on the toes, ball, and heel of the foot in that order. The knee is bent slightly to help absorb the shock of the landing. To aid in balance, the arms and nonsupporting foot are used. Hopping should be practiced with both feet.

Leaping

Similar to the run, a leap is a long step forward to cover distance or to go over an obstacle. It is an exaggerated running step, with the stride longer and the body projected higher in the air. In the leap, the toes of the takeoff foot leave the floor last, and the landing is on the ball of the opposite foot. The arms should be extended upward and forward to give added lift to the body during the leap. Often the legs are extended in the air. Before the execution of the leap, usually a short run is taken to gain momentum for the leap itself.

Skipping

A skip is a combination of a step and a hop, with feet alternating after each step-hop. A long step is taken on one foot, followed by a hop on the same foot, and then a step with the opposite foot, again followed by a hop. Balance is aided by swinging the arms in opposition to the legs.

Sliding

A slide is a sideways movement in which the weight of the body is shifted in the direction of the slide. In a slide to the right, the right foot steps sideways (leading foot); then the left foot (trailing foot) is quickly drawn close to the right foot. Weight is shifted from the lead foot to the trailing foot. The same foot continues to lead in sliding movements. The body maintains an upright posture and the arms are used for balance. The legs should not be crossed. The slide should be practiced in both directions.

Galloping

Galloping is similar to sliding, but the movement is performed in a forward direction. One foot leads in the forward direction (leading foot). After a step by the leading foot, the rear or trailing foot is brought quickly forward and close to the lead foot. The stepping leg is always the lead leg. Opportunities to lead with the right foot and with the left foot should be included in practicing the gallop.

Nonlocomotor Movements

Nonlocomotor movements are generally performed using a stable base of support. The nonlocomotor movement skills discussed are bending, stretching, twisting, turning, pushing, pulling, and swinging. Generally, they are performed in place and can be done from a variety of body positions (e.g., standing or sitting). They can also be combined with locomotor movements.

Bending and stretching

Bending is a movement occurring at the joints of the body in which body parts are brought closer together. For example, by bending the body at the hips to touch the toes, a person is decreasing the angle between the upper and lower body at the hip joint. This is called flexion. Bending movements may be in several directions: for example, forward, backward, sideways, or in a circular motion. The range of bending movements is determined by the type of joint at which the movement occurs. Ball-and-socket joints permit the greatest movement. Hip joints and shoulder joints are examples of ball-and-socket joints. Hinge joints permit only backward and forward movements. The knee joint is a hinge joint.

A stretch is an extension or hyperextension at the joints of the body. Stretching is the opposite of bending. Most movements require complete extension only where the body parts adjacent to the joints are at a straight angle (180°). However, in movements such as the wrist cock before a throw, hyperextension is needed to give added impetus to the throw.

Bending and stretching are necessary to maintain flexibility—the full range of movement about a joint. Bending and stretching are common to most of the activities of daily life, and they are very important to physical education activities. Teachers should provide daily activities in which these skills can be practiced and refined.

Twisting and turning

Twisting is a rotation of the body or a body part around its axis while maintaining a fixed base of support. Twisting movements can take place at the neck, shoulders, spine, hips, ankles, and wrist. The body can be in different positions: for example, standing or lying down. As in bending and stretching movements, the range of a twisting movement is determined by the type of joint.

Turning generally refers to a rotation of the body around in space. When the body is turned,

Bending movements are often used in gymnastic activities.

Rowing requires both pushing and pulling as teammates synchronize their actions to move as one.

the base of support is shifted from one position to another. Jumping up and landing facing the opposite direction and pivoting are examples of turns. A twisting action is typically used to initiate a turn. Turns should be practiced in both directions, left and right or clockwise and counterclockwise.

Pushing and pulling

Pushing is a forceful action directed toward increasing the distance between the body and an object. A push can be used to move an object away from the body or the body away from an object. Pushing an opponent away in a wrestling match or a box across the floor are two examples of pushing. The effectiveness of a push can be enhanced by properly positioning the body. A forward stride position enlarges the body's base of support, and bending the knees lowers the center of gravity and increases the body's stability. Proper body alignment is important in preventing back injuries.

Pulling is a forceful action designed to decrease the distance between the body and an object. A pull brings the body and the object closer together. As in pushing, widening the base of support and lowering the center of gravity increases effectiveness. In a tug-of-war, participants widen their base of support and "dig their heels in" as they try to pull their opponents across the dividing line. Partner resistance exercises and rowing use both pushing and pulling. Steady, controlled movements are recommended for both pulling and pushing.

Swinging

A swing is a circular or pendular movement of a body part or of the entire body around a stationary center point. The center point may be a joint, such as the shoulder in swinging the arm, or an outside axis, such as the swing on a high bar. When the force necessary to hold a body stationary is released, the force of gravity will cause that body part to swing. In most body movements, the force of muscular contractions is necessary to maintain body swing. Swinging movements should be continuous, rhythmical, and free flowing.

Manipulative Skills

Manipulative skills involve the propulsion and control of objects. The body is used to generate force to an object and to absorb force when receiving or controlling an object. The manipulative skills of throwing, catching, kicking, and striking are briefly described.

Throwing

Throwing an object may involve the use of the underhand, sidearm, or overhand pattern. Since the overhand throwing pattern is most frequently employed by children and adults, this movement will be described.

When throwing, the ball is held in the fingers of the throwing hand. As the throwing action is initiated, the ball is brought back and the body rotates so the opposite side is toward the target. Weight is transferred back to the foot on the same side as the throwing hand. The arm is bent at the elbow, and the elbow leads slightly as the arm is brought forward for the throw. As the arm accelerates, a step forward onto the opposite foot is taken and the hips rotate forward. The arm quickly extends, the wrist snaps, and the ball is released. The arm follows in the direction of the throw, coming down and across the body.

Catching

Catching involves the use of hands to stop and gain control of an object. As the object approaches, the individual makes a judgment about where it can be intercepted and moves to a location directly in line with the object, placing the hands in a position for effective reception. The eyes follow the flight of the object, and both hands reach out toward it. The object is grasped by the hands and pulled in by the arms and hands toward the body to absorb the object's force.

Kicking

Kicking is imparting force to an object by the foot and the leg. The kicking of a stationary object is the foundation for the kicking of a moving object and for punting.

In kicking, the supporting foot is placed alongside the object. The kicking leg, knee bent, moving freely from the hip, swings through an arc toward the object. As the foot contacts the object, the knee is extended, and the body leans back for balance. The kicking leg follows through, continuing its movement toward the direction of the flight of the object. The arms, relaxed, move in opposition to the legs. The eyes focus on the object throughout the kick.

Striking

Striking involves using a body part (e.g., hand) or an implement (e.g., paddle, racquet, bat) to apply force to a stationary or moving object. The length, size, and weight of the implement as well as characteristics of the object being struck influence the nature of the movement pattern. Kicking, described earlier, is also considered a striking task.

For the striking action typically seen in batting, the body is positioned perpendicular to the line of flight of the oncoming ball. The feet are placed in a forward-backward stride position, approximately shoulder-width apart. The trunk is rotated back, the weight is shifted to the rear foot, and a backswing is taken. The flight of the ball is followed by the eyes until just before making contact. Body weight is shifted onto the forward foot in the direction of the intended flight of the ball. With the hips leading, the hips and trunk are rotated in the same direction as the weight shift. Arms move forward into contact, and the follow-through action occurs in the direction of the line of flight.

● ● ●

Fundamental motor skills are the foundation for the development of specialized game, sport, dance, and fitness activities. These skills are the building blocks for the future. Acquisition of skills for lifetime participation begins with the mastery of these fundamental movement skills. All children, the skilled and the unskilled, need sufficient opportunities and a variety of experiences to master these important movement basics.

Movement is the central focus of physical education and sport. Professionals working in a diversity of settings need to be familiar with movement concepts and skills. Professionals have an obligation to become familiar with the science of movement if they are to help individuals move efficiently and understand the "why" and "how" of movement.

Fundamental skills are the foundation for developing specialized sport skills. Can you identify other fundamental skills used in softball?

TEACHING MOVEMENT FUNDAMENTALS

Movement concepts and fundamental motor skills are usually taught in elementary school physical education. Many preschool programs, both public and private, offer movement programs for very young children. Whatever the setting, programs to develop movement fundamentals should focus on the "how" and "why" of movement. Through these programs, children learn to move effectively and acquire an understanding of movement concepts that enables them to vary, modify, and enhance their movements in diverse situations.

Several approaches can be used to help children learn movement concepts and fundamental movement skills. Movement education and the developmental approach allow children to learn about their body and its capacity for movement through a progressive sequence of experiences. Children acquire fundamental movement skills through frequent opportunities for practice. Satisfaction and enjoyment derived from effort and meaningful achievements enrich the children's learning.

Movement Education

Movement education uses a problem-solving approach to help children develop body awareness and use their bodies in an effective manner unique to their own physical resources. Movement education strives to make the individual aware of the movement of the entire body and to become intellectually as well as physically involved. The challenge set by a problem in movement is first perceived by the intellect and then solved by the body moving through space, reacting to any obstacles within that space and to the limitations and existing restrictions. Learning accrues as the individual accepts and attempts to solve more difficult problems. Inherent in this process is the concept of individual differences. Many ways to solve a stated problem may exist, and one chooses the method that best suits one's abilities and capacities. Individual development is the basic premise of movement education.

Movement education can be traced back to the 1940s and the theories of Rudolf Laban, an Austrian dancer who established the Laban Art of Movement Centre in England. Laban stressed that the body is the instrument through and by which

people move and that each individual is en-
dowed with certain natural kinds of movement.[6]
Laban believed strongly in exploratory movement and in a spontaneous quality in movement.[6]
He was opposed to the traditional rigid set of
exercises that composed physical education programs. He believed these prescribed exercises
constrained creativity and self-expression. Laban
was a movement analyst, and his classification system forms the framework of the movement concepts. He believed that people not only could
learn to move efficiently and effectively, but also
could develop a strong kinesthetic awareness of
movement.

During World War II, England revised its entire educational structure and restated its philosophy of education. Physical education had once
been little more than formal gymnastics, but
now freedom of bodily movement, creativity,
and expression were emphasized. Laban's principles were freely employed. Through the years
they have been expanded and broadened into
the concept of movement education as it is known
today.

In movement education, the program is based
on problem solving. The teacher sets the problem
and then guides, assists, and suggests but in no
way dictates a solution. The teacher uses a series of
skillful questions to pose movement challenges for
the children to solve. There is no teacher demonstration and thus no imitation, leaving children to
establish their own patterns of movement, set their
own tempo, and make wise use of space.

Within the last 40 years, movement education
programs have developed in the United States,
based on the English programs. These programs
are typically incorporated into elementary physical
education programs and preschool programs.
Over the years, the growth of movement education programs has encouraged the use of more
child-centered approaches in physical education. It
led to a greater focus on cognitive aspects of
movement—that is, an understanding of factors
that influence movement—in physical education
programs. Movement education promoted the development of motor skills using problem-solving

experiences that were sensitive to the individual
needs of children.

Developmental Approach

In 1992, COPEC, or the Council on Physical Education for Children, released a document entitled
"Developmentally Appropriate Physical Education
Practices for Children."[5] This offers physical education teachers guidelines for curriculum development and for making choices about teaching
strategies. Appropriate and inappropriate practices
are described for many components of the physical
education programs. The description for the development of movement concepts and motor skills
is presented in the box below.

MOVEMENT CONCEPTS AND BASIC SKILLS

Appropriate Practice

Participants are provided with frequent and
meaningful age-appropriate practice opportunities that enable individuals to develop a
functional understanding of movement concepts (body awareness, space awareness, effort,
and relationships), and build confidence in
their ability to perform a variety of motor
skills (locomotor, nonlocomotor, and manipulative).

Inappropriate Practice

Individuals participate in a limited number of
activities where the opportunity for them to
develop basic concepts and motor skills is
restricted.

From: Developmentally appropriate physical education
practices for children, Council on Physical Education
for Children, National Association for Sport and
Physical Education, American Alliance for Health,
Physical Education, Recreation, and Dance, 1992.

The developmental approach emphasizes educational experiences that are based on the cognitive, psychomotor, and affective needs of children. Child-centered, the developmental approach stresses the progressive sequencing of experiences to encourage the optimal development of each child. Instruction is designed to be appropriate and congruent with the needs of the children being taught. Many different teaching strategies are employed to aid children in acquiring the necessary knowledge and skills to be skillful, confident movers. Teacher explanations, demonstrations, and questioning are used appropriately. With the guidance of the teacher, students may work together or independently toward the attainment of lesson goals. Active participation in learning experiences is emphasized. Children are challenged to grow and develop in a safe learning environment. Individual differences are respected. Experiences that foster a positive self-concept, promote the value of physical activity, and encourage regular participation contribute to the goal of incorporating physical activity into one's life. Assessment and evaluation of student progress is integral to this approach.

Suggestions for Teaching Movement Fundamentals

Both the development of fundamental movement skills and movement concepts should be emphasized in the elementary-school physical education program. The process for learning movement fundamentals and movement concepts differs. When teaching movement concepts, the teacher emphasizes the process of moving, creativity, and variation. Fundamental skills are incorporated into lessons on movement concepts, but understanding of the concept is stressed, as opposed to emphasizing skill development.

In contrast, fundamental skill development initially focuses primarily on the acquisition of correct technique. Appropriate progressions and plentiful practice help children learn and achieve greater proficiency (see the box on p. 137). As students become increasingly skilled, they are involved in instructional experiences that allow them to apply their understanding of movement concepts to modify their movements and adapt them to different tasks and situations.

Elementary-school physical education specialists offer general guidelines for the teaching of movement fundamentals.[1,2,4,7,8] These guidelines include providing a safe environment, focusing on the needs of the child, offering frequent and meaningful practice opportunities, progressively sequencing content from simple to complex, and holding children accountable for their actions.

Provision of a safe learning environment

Teachers must provide for both the physical and psychological safety of their students. As for the physical environment, the area should be free of hazards that may cause harm to students. Adequate practice space should be available. Equipment should be appropriate for the ability of the child, and children should be instructed in its proper use. Enforcement of class rules that emphasize safety helps ensure the well-being of students.

Attention should also be directed toward the development of a class climate or atmosphere where children feel psychologically safe. Respect for others, appreciation for individual differences, and valuing of effort contribute to a warm, nurturing class climate. In this climate, children feel free to try new activities, explore and create, and challenge themselves to achieve. Learning is viewed as a collaborative effort between the teacher and students; students are also encouraged to work cooperatively with each other to achieve desired learning outcomes.

Child-centered instruction

Instruction should be appropriate to the developmental needs of the students. Teachers need to be sensitive to individual differences and knowledgeable about the physical, mental, and social abilities and needs of the students. Activities are adapted to the children's developmental stages. Children's previous learning, their background, and interests are important considerations in designing learning experiences.

Movement education encourages children to explore the various positions of their bodies in space.

Child centered instruction focuses on the active involvement of students in the learning process. Students are invited to have some degree of decision making in the learning process. For example, students can choose one task from among several variations to complete; they can choose the one that best fits their ability. Students are encouraged to develop their own ideas, creativity is valued, and contributions are welcomed. Teachers are concerned with the development of the whole child. Teachers also structure learning to promote self-responsibility and self-direction.

Practice opportunities

Numerous practice opportunities facilitate learning. Ample practice gives children the chance to develop their movement fundamentals. Practice opportunities should be appropriate to the skill, offer variety within each lesson, and be purposeful. As children develop proficiency in the skill, opportunities to refine the skills are introduced. As mastery increases, students apply their skills and understandings to new situations.

Well-organized and planned practices maximize student time-on-task—that is, the time students are engaged in learning. Teacher monitoring and active guidance help maximize student involvement. Plentiful opportunities for children to be successful contribute to student motivation. Success is achieved through effort and hard work. Teacher and peer encouragement promote persistence and continued effort.

Progression

Careful sequencing of learning experiences contributes to success. Learning experiences should be sequenced from simple to complex. Carefully structured variations on a task enrich children's movement repertoire. Opportunities to perform skills under different environmental conditions broaden children's skills. Increments in tasks are carefully arranged to challenge children to achieve. Meaningful challenges promote growth and reaching beyond current levels of performance. Teachers recognize that students learn at different rates and use a range of progressions to accommodate individual differences.

Accountability

Assessment and evaluation of student learning is important. Assessment helps teachers measure students' progress. Students' abilities can be quickly measured at the beginning of a unit of instruction. Knowing the entry level of the students, the teacher can closely tailor instruction to the current abilities of the students, rather than design instruction based on where they should be.[7] When the unit of instruction is completed, students' abilities can again be assessed. Student progress is then determined by comparing the assessments. Students also benefit from receiving feedback on their progress. It reinforces their efforts and helps shape their perceptions of their movement abilities.

Assessment helps teachers find out whether program goals and objectives have been attained. Teachers can determine their own effectiveness by evaluating the extent of student progress. Significant student progress indicates teacher effectiveness. If student progress is not significant, teachers can use this information to explore different teaching strategies and/or restructure instructional experiences to foster greater achievement.

Students must also be held accountable for their learning. Teachers who foster a work ethic, value effort, and carefully monitor student achievement help children become self-directed learners. Involving students in the assessment process through self-testing activities or through peer assessment helps students develop analytical skills. Accountability and self-assessment help students become lifelong learners.

LEARNING ACROSS THE LIFESPAN

Instruction in movement concepts and skills is not limited to children. Adults benefit from instruction as well. This instruction takes place in a diversity of settings. Some professionals working in corporate fitness settings offer instruction in movement skills to their clients. For example, corporations offer programs to help their employees learn how to lift objects and move objects (push and pull) correctly. These programs reduce employee injury and increase job efficiency. Athletic trainers helping a softball player rehabilitate from a shoulder injury may observe the athlete's overhand throws to ensure that they are performed correctly and do not subject the shoulder to undue strain because of poor movement mechanics. An understanding of movement fundamentals aids the athletic trainer in this task. When necessary, basic movements are retaught. Fitness professionals working in rehabilitation programs may spend time ensuring that their clients are running properly, or work with the elderly on exercises to enhance balance. Sport instructors begin their teaching by evaluating the participants' movements. Just like children, adults benefit from experiences that promote the understanding of movement concepts. This allows them to modify their movements according to different situations, and enhances movement effectiveness.

Youths, adults, and older individuals who lack fundamental movement skills may find that their success with specialized sport skills and fitness activities is limited. How can this limitation be addressed? For youths, the secondary school physical education program offers a chance to develop their skills further and to correct inefficient ones. Changing inefficient skills requires considerable practice and commitment. Secondary-school physical education teachers must be willing to work with these students to improve the movement basics, rather than ignore the problem and move on to more advanced and complex skills. If these actions are not corrected, students may not achieve their potential as movers. For adults and the aged, the expansion of physical education instructional programs to community settings offers the opportunity to learn the skills they are lacking and to replace incorrect actions with correct movement patterns. These programs should be appropriate to the developmental level of the individual and provide a progressive sequence of learning experiences designed to meet individual needs. Programs that focus on the acquisition of movement fundamentals set the stage for a lifetime of participation.

SUMMARY

Movement is the keystone of physical education and sport. Human movement may be affected by a variety of factors, including biomechanical, physiological, psychological, and sociological factors. Understanding of the basic concepts of movement—body awareness, spatial awareness, qualities of movement, and relationships—is essential for physical educators and their students. Physical educators must also be concerned about individuals' development of fundamental skills (locomotor, nonlocomotor, and manipulative skills), for they form the foundation for participation in a variety of activities throughout life.

Several different approaches can be used to teach movement fundamentals. Movement education, a system based on the theories of Laban, explores the science of movement and helps people of all ages move more effectively. Another approach, the developmental approach, emphasizes learning experiences based on the unique developmental needs of children. These experiences are progressively sequenced and instructionally appropriate to the needs of children.

Education about movement takes place across the lifespan. Although movement fundamentals are taught primarily to children, the increase in lifespan participation offers new opportunities for movement development. Teaching opportunities with adults focus on remediating incorrect actions, providing opportunities to learn new skills, and promoting a greater understanding of movement. If lifespan participation is our goal, people must have the basic skills and knowledge to move effectively and enjoyably.

SELF-ASSESSMENT TESTS

These tests are designed to help you determine if you have mastered the material and competencies presented in this chapter.

1. You have been asked by a local recreational group to give a presentation on the subject of "Movement: The Keystone of Physical Education and Sport." Prepare in writing your presentation.

2. Analyze the movement concepts associated with the performance of the following skills:
    Hitting a baseball
    Playing tackle in a football game
    Running 100 meters
    Performing a free-exercise routine in gymnastics

3. Select five sport skills, each from a different sport. List the locomotor, nonlocomotor, and manipulative skills necessary for performing each sport skill.

4. Getting Connected Activities:
    a. Access the *CyberActive*, *PE Central*, or *Sports Media* site. Locate a lesson plan for the development of movement concepts and/or fundamental movement skills. Try teaching the lesson to your classmates.
    b. Access *Human Kinetics InfoKinetics Physical Activity Links*. Select one sport. Using the information provided by the various links, identify several skills involved in the sport. Then describe the fundamental movement skills and movement concepts used in the sport.

REFERENCES

1. Graham G, Holt/Hale S, and Parker M: Children moving: a reflective approach to teaching physical education, Mountain View, Calif., 1998, Mayfield.

2. Buschner CA: Teaching children movement concepts and skills: becoming a master teacher, Champaign, Ill., 1994, Human Kinetics.

3. Laban R: Modern educational dance, London, 1948, MacDonald and Evans.

4. Nichols BA: Moving and learning: the elementary school physical education experience, St. Louis, 1994, Mosby.

5. American Alliance for Health, Physical Education, Recreation, and Dance: Developmentally appropriate physical education practices for children, Reston, Va., 1992, AAHPERD.

6. Laban R: The mastery of movement, London, 1960, MacDonald and Evans.

7. Gallahue DL: Developmental physical education for today's children, Dubuque, Iowa, 1996, Brown & Benchmark.

8. Sanders SW: Designing preschool movement programs, Champaign, Ill., 1992, Human Kinetics.

SUGGESTED READINGS

American Alliance for Health, Physical Education, Recreation, and Dance: Developmentally appropriate physical education practices for children, Reston, Va., 1992, AAHPERD.
　　Presents guidelines for appropriate physical education programs for young children.

Buschner CA: Teaching children movement concepts and skills: becoming a master teacher, Champaign, Ill., 1994, Human Kinetics.
　　Ideas to incorporate movement concepts and skills into programs and learning experiences.

Gallahue DL: Developmental physical education for today's children, Dubuque, Iowa, 1996, Brown & Benchmark.
　　Offers an overview of developmental physical education, curriculum development, teaching, skill themes, and activities.

Graham G, Holt/Hale S, and Parker M: Children moving: a reflective approach to teaching physical education, Mountain View, Calif., 1998, Mayfield.
　　Teaching skills, movement concept development, and learning experiences to develop skill themes are presented.

Hammett CT: Movement activities for early childhood, Champaign, Ill., 1992, Human Kinetics.
　　Presents an array of activities for preschoolers organized about the development of movement concepts and fundamental motor skills.

Jensen MA: Composing and guiding creative movement, JOPERD 54(3):85–87, 1983.
　　Offers guidance in the use of creative movement experiences with elementary school children. Diagrams describing the basic movement actions and their variations and a table listing descriptive vocabulary for movement exploration enhance the author's presentation.

Kruger H and Kruger JM: Movement education in physical education: a guide to teaching and planning, Dubuque, Iowa, 1981, Wm. C. Brown Publishers.
　　Presents a comprehensive overview of movement education as well as specific guidelines for teaching and planning lessons.

National Association of Physical Education for College Women and National Association of Physical Education for College Men: The language of movement, *Quest*, Monograph 23, Jan. 1975.

This entire issue of *Quest* is devoted to movement. Thematic areas include the meanings of movement, symbols of movement, forms of movement, and expression of movement.

McClenaghan BA and Gallahue DL: Fundamental movement: a developmental and remedial approach, Philadelphia, 1978, W.B. Saunders.

Presents fundamental movement skills as well as activities to promote their development and improve their performance. Excellent diagrams of the fundamental skills and their stages of development enhance the usefulness of this text.

Nichols BA: Moving and learning: the elementary school physical education experience, St. Louis, 1994, Mosby.

Combining the philosophies of movement education and motor skills development, this text serves as an excellent resource for teaching elementary physical education.

Sanders SW: Designing preschool movement programs, Champaign, Ill., 1992, Human Kinetics.

Offers suggestions on designing curriculum and teaching; lists activities for teaching movement concepts and fundamental skills.

PART TWO

Foundations of Physical Education and Sport

Introduction

In Part One the term physical education and sport was defined and its philosophy and objectives discussed, as was the role of movement. Part Two builds on that knowledge by discussing the foundations of physical education and sport. Trained physical education and sport professionals should understand the foundations of their field. Part Two begins with a discussion of the historical foundations of physical education and sport, in Chapter 5. Chapters 6, 7, 8, and 9 present the biomechanical, physiological, sociological, and psychological bases from which physical education and sport derives its principles and concepts. These areas of study are the major sciences or subdisciplines of physical education and sport—namely, exercise physiology, motor learning, sport psychology, sport sociology, and biomechanics. A mastery of the principles and concepts discussed in these chapters will show the professional what knowledge is needed to plan and conduct meaningful programs in physical education and sport.

Historical Foundations of Physical Education and Sport

Instructional Objectives and Competencies to be Achieved:

After reading this chapter the student should be able to—

♦ Trace the history of physical education and sport from earliest times to the present.

♦ Explain the contributions of the Athenian Greeks to physical education and sport.

♦ Explain why asceticism, scholasticism, and puritanism were deterrents to physical education and sport's progress.

♦ Identify events that served as catalysts for physical education and sport's growth.

♦ Identify some of the outstanding leaders in physical education and sport over the course of history and the contributions each made to the field.

♦ Discuss recent developments in physical education and sport.

♦ Draw implications from the discussion of history of principles that will guide the professional future of physical education and sport. Project future developments for physical education and sport based on recent trends.

Today's beliefs and experiences of physical education and sport professionals are influenced by the history of this field of endeavor. This history is the source of physical education and sport's identity. In a sense, little basis exists for this professional field, except its past. The experiences of yesteryear help guide professionals' endeavors today. The only professional maturity is that which is built on the events of days and years gone by.

The nature of physical education and sport in the United States today has been influenced by the contributions of many different cultures. The influence exerted by U.S. leaders was also profound. By knowing the accomplishments of leaders in the past, today's professionals can attempt to build on those accomplishments. One qualification exists—professionals must use only that from the past which is true, significant, and

GETTING CONNECTED

Hickok's Sport History site offers information about the history of specific sport, organized via an index from A to Y.

   Site: http://www.ultranet.com/~rhickok/sprtindx.shtml

Paralympic Games offers information about this elite competition for athletes with physical disabilities.

   Site: http://www.uscpaa.org/cppara.htm

United States Olympic Committee site offers information about all aspects of the Olympics.

   Site: http://www.usoc.org/

applicable to the present and the future. This chapter provides an overview of the history of physical education and sport from ancient times to recent developments. Much can be learned about physical education and sport from a critical analysis of its history.

WHAT LESSONS CAN BE LEARNED FROM HISTORY?

What can be learned about physical education and sport from studying its history? Many of today's activities have forerunners. For example, the first recorded Olympics date back to 776 B.C. in ancient Greece. Yoga and karate, activities of current interest, date back to ancient Oriental societies. Studying the past will help the professional to understand the present better.

In Chapters 1 and 2 the influence of various philosophies—idealism, realism, naturalism, pragmatism, existentialism, and humanism—on physical education and sport objectives and programs was discussed. The influence of the various philosophical schools of thought on physical education throughout history will be evident. Traditionally the objectives of physical education have been categorized as either promoting **"education of the physical"** or **"education through the physical."** Education *of* the physical focused on the development of the body as an end in itself; that is, precedence was given to the development of the body

and physical skills rather than outcomes that could be accomplished through physical activities. Education *through* the physical emphasized the acquisition of physical skills and bodily development as well as attainment of other educational outcomes, such as affective, social, and intellectual objectives, through physical activity. This approach utilizes carefully selected physical activities as a medium through which various desirable objectives can be achieved. The emphasis on these two approaches may be discerned throughout the history of physical education and sport.

It is interesting to note the various purposes for which physical education and sport has existed in the lives of people of different countries and cultures. From the earliest times until the present, either directly or indirectly, physical activity has played a part in the lives of all people. Sometimes this activity has been motivated by a factor such as the necessity for earning a livelihood, whereas in other instances, it has resulted from a desire to live a fuller life. Furthermore, it is clear that the objectives of physical education and sport have changed over the course of history, so that at the present time they are directed at the better development of human beings, not only physically but psychologically and socially. These changing concepts of physical education and sport have come about as a result of many years of experience and study in regard to the value of participating in physical activity under qualified leadership.

Women's basketball at Smith College, Northampton, Massachusetts, 1904.

Members of primitive societies did not think of physical education as people do today. No organized physical education program was found in primitive society or in the cultures of the ancient Oriental nations. In regard to better physical development, primitive people did not need to set aside a period during the day when they could participate in various forms of activity since being active was part of their daily regimen. Well-developed bodies and sound organic systems were commonplace among primitive people. Their physical activity consisted of hunting and searching for food, erecting shelters, and protecting themselves from the hostile environment.

History has shown that certain tendencies in human beings have been responsible for their formal and informal participation in physical activity. Some of the more important of these have been the search for food to satisfy hunger, the desire for protection against enemies, innate drives for mating and propagation, the urge to manipulate brain and brawn, fear of the strange and unknown, and the need to associate with others. Hunting, fishing,

dancing, warfare, and play evolved as a result of these general tendencies, explaining to some extent why primitive people and all persons in general have been likely to engage in motor activities whether they wanted to or not. Whether these activities should be characterized as work or play depends on the motive behind the participation in the activity. Work is characterized by need and necessity and is more or less compulsory. On the other hand, play is spontaneous, internally driven, and utilized for fun and relaxation.

Civilization has brought the need for an organized physical education and sport program. As a result of labor-saving devices, sedentary pursuits, and security, the need has arisen for some type of planned program whereby individuals may realize the physical benefits that were once a part of a person's daily routine, as well as many sociological, psychological, and intellectual benefits. Therefore, it is interesting to examine certain ancient cultures to determine the part that physical education and sport played in the lives of their people. Through an understanding of the history of physical education and sport, a person is better able to understand and interpret the field today.

PHYSICAL EDUCATION AND SPORT IN ANCIENT NATIONS

As you read about the development of physical education and sport in ancient nations, it may be helpful to reflect upon the following questions for each nation and time period:

- ◆ What was the primary purpose of physical activity, physical education, and sport in society during this time period? Was it for the purpose of survival, health benefits, religious reasons, nationalist reasons, military preparedness, contribution to education, recreational pursuits, or for some other reason?
- ◆ Did the objectives emphasize education of the physical or education through the physical?
- ◆ Who were the significant leaders and how did they contribute to the development of physical education and sport? What were the significant contributions of the time period to the field?
- ◆ What events served to promote the growth of physical education and sport in society? What events served as a deterrent to its development?
- ◆ What parallels and similarities may be discerned between the events of the time period and today?

China

Ancient China followed a policy of isolation. This country did not care to associate with the rest of the world but instead desired to live unto itself. At first the topography of the land provided China with the necessary natural protection against invaders. Where the Himalaya Mountains no longer served this purpose, the Great Wall was built; when the Wall became obsolete, laws were passed to keep foreigners out of the country.

The fact that the ancient Chinese lived an isolated existence was detrimental in many ways to a belief in physical education. Because China did not fear aggression, it lacked the military motivating

factor of being physically strong. Furthermore, the teaching of the people of ancient China was mainly concerned with memorizing the works of Confucius. Ancestor worship was also an important part of their religious life. Individuality was suppressed, and all persons were destined to live a rigid and stereotyped existence. In a country that espoused such beliefs, little room was made for organized physical education. Physical activity meant stressing the importance of the body and individual freedom of expression, which were contrary to the teachings of this ancient culture.

Certain evidence exists of participation in physical education and sport activities in China despite the emphasis on intellectual excellence and the influence of Taoism, Confucianism, and Buddhism, which stressed the studious, quiet, and contemplative life. In many Chinese classics, discussions abound of how sons of rich families engaged in music, dancing, and archery. Wrestling, jujitsu, boxing, ts' u chu (football), polo, tug-of-war, water games, ch'ui wan (similar to golf), shuttlecock, and flying kites were also popular. Thus the more favored classes engaged in play, but it seems the masses had little opportunity for participation in formal physical activities.

It is interesting to note that the Chinese thought that certain diseases were caused by inactivity. As a result, history discloses that the

Senior citizens who are residents of an independent living community practice Tai Chi.

Cong Fu gymnastics were developed in 2698 B.C. These were medical gymnastics intended to keep the body in good organic condition. It was believed that illnesses were caused by internal stoppages and by malfunctioning of organs. Therefore, if certain kneeling, bending, lying, and standing exercises could be performed, together with certain types of respiratory training, the illness could be alleviated.

India

In many ways, ancient India is similar to ancient China. Indian people lived an existence that was very religious in nature. Two of the major religions were Hinduism and Buddhism. Hinduism stressed that the human soul passed through several reincarnations before being united with Brahma, the supreme goal. The quickest and most certain way to attain this goal was to refrain from catering to the body and enjoying worldly things. The person who desired to be holy ignored the physical needs of the body and concentrated solely on spiritual needs. It can readily be seen that physical activity had little place in the culture of these religious people.

Buddhism emphasized that right living and thinking, including self-denial, will help the individual's soul reach Nirvana, a divine state. However, Buddha's prohibitions of games, amusements, and exercises in ancient India did not totally prevent participation in such activities. Evidence is available about pastimes such as dice, throwing balls, plowing contests, tumbling, chariot races, marbles, riding elephants and horses, swordsmanship, foot races, wrestling, boxing, and dancing. Yoga, an activity common in India and involving exercises in posture and regulated breathing, was popular. This disciplining of mind and body required the instruction of experts, and a person fully trained in this activity followed a routine involving 84 different postures.

Ancient Near East

The civilizations of ancient Egypt, Assyria, Babylonia, Syria, Palestine, and Persia mark a turning point in the history of physical education and sport. Whereas the culture of China and India stressed religious and intellectual matters, these countries were not restricted by a static society and religious ritual. On the contrary, they believed in living a full life, including, all types of physical activity. It is in these countries that physical education and sport also received an impetus from the military, who saw in it an opportunity to build stronger and more powerful armies.

Egyptian youths were reared in a manner involving much physical activity. As young boys they were instructed in the use of various weapons of war, such as bow and arrow, battleaxe, mace, lance, and shield. They were required to participate in exercises and activities designed to make the body supple, strong, and capable of great endurance and stamina. These activities included marching, running, jumping, wrestling, pirouetting, and leaping. Before their military training started, they had numerous opportunities to engage in many sports and gymnastic exercises. They also found great enjoyment in hunting and fishing expeditions.

In the countries between the Tigris and Euphrates rivers, great stress was placed on physical activities, especially among the upper classes. Whereas the lower social strata of the population found few opportunities for recreation and sport, the upper classes indulged themselves in these pastimes at regular intervals. Horsemanship, use of bow and arrow, water activities, and training in physical exercises were considered as important as instruction that was more intellectual in nature.

Persia is a good example of a state that had as its main objective the building of an empire through military aggression. A strong Persian army meant a healthy and physically fit army. Under King Cyrus the Great, the imperialistic dreams of Persia were realized. At the end of his rule in 529 B.C. the Persian Empire encompassed the area that is referred to today as the Near East. The success of King Cyrus' campaigns was largely the result of the moral and physical conditioning of his soldiers. At the age of 6 years the state required all boys to leave their homes for training, which consisted of events such as running, slinging, shooting a bow, throwing a javelin, riding, hunting, and marching. The soldier had to be able to travel without much food and clothing and was compelled to endure all sorts of hardship.

Where the military emphasis existed, physical education and sport was aimed at imperialistic ends. Strength, endurance, stamina, agility, and other physical characteristics were not developed so that the individual could live a full, vigorous, and more interesting life but, instead, so that the state could utilize these physical attributes in achieving its own national militaristic aims.

PHYSICAL EDUCATION AND SPORT IN GREECE

Physical education as well as sport experienced a "golden age" in ancient Greece. The Greeks strove for physical perfection, and this objective affected all phases of their life. It influenced the political and educational systems, sculpture and painting, and the thinking and writings of that day. It was a unifying force in Greek life, playing a major part in national festivals and helping to build strong military establishments. No country in history has held physical education or sport in such high esteem as did ancient Greece.

Evidence exists of physical education and sport activities being popular in Cretan culture as early as 2500 B.C. Archeological investigations at Mycenae and other centers of Aegean civilization have unearthed buildings, pottery, and other artifacts that point to the importance placed on physical education and sport in this ancient culture. Literature, such as Homer's *Iliad* and *Odyssey,* is another source of this information. Lion hunting, deer hunting, bull grappling, boxing, wrestling, dancing, and swimming are commonly referred to by historians who have written about these ancient civilizations.

Physical education was a vital part of the education of every Greek boy. Gymnastics and music were considered the two most important subjects—music for the spirit, and gymnastics for the body. "Exercise for the body and music for the soul" was a common pronouncement. Gymnastics, it was believed, contributed to courage,

discipline, and physical well-being. Furthermore, gymnastics stressed a sense of fair play, development of the individual's aesthetic values, amateurism, and the utilitarian values inherent in the activity. Professionalism was frowned on. Individuals ran, wrestled, jumped, danced, or threw the javelin not for reward but for what it would do for their bodies. Beauty of physique was stressed, and boys and men participated in the nude, which motivated development of the "body beautiful."

Because of the topography of the land and for various political reasons, Greece was composed of several city-states, each exercising its own sovereignty and existing as a separate entity. Each waged war and conducted all its affairs separately from the other city states. This situation influenced not only the political aspects of each city-state but also the objectives of physical education and sport within each state. Sparta and Athens exemplify two such city-states.

In Sparta, a city state in the Peloponnesus district of Greece, the main objective of physical

This Greek vase, called an *amphora,* was found in eastern Greece and dates to about 550 to 525 B.C.

education and sport was to contribute to a strong and powerful army. The individual in Sparta existed for the state. Each person was subservient to the state and was required to help defend it against all enemies. Women, as well as men, were required to be in good physical condition. It was believed that healthy and strong mothers would bear healthy and strong sons. Spartan women may have begun their physical conditioning as early as 7 years of age and continued gymnastics in public until they were married. Newborn infants, if found to be defective or weak, were left on Mount Taygetus to die. Thomas Woody, an educational historian, points out that mothers bathed babies in wine to test their bodies and to temper them for future ordeals. A boy was allowed to stay at home only for the first six years of his life. After this he was required to stay in the public barracks and entered the agoge, a system of public, compulsory training, in which he underwent an extremely vigorous and rigid training schedule. If he failed in this ordeal, he was deprived of all future honors. A major part of this training consisted of physical activities such as wrestling, jumping, running, throwing the javelin and discus, marching, horseback riding, and hunting. This Spartan conditioning program developed a strong army that was second to none.

Athens, a city-state in eastern Greece, was the antithesis of Sparta. Here the democratic way of life flourished and had a great bearing on the objectives of physical education and sport. Athens did not control and regulate the individual's life as rigidly as Sparta. In Athens the people enjoyed the freedom that is characteristic of a truly democratic government. Although the military emphasis was not as strong in Athens as in Sparta, the emphasis on physical education and sport was just as great or greater. Athenians engaged in physical activity to develop their bodies, for aesthetic value, and to live a fuller and more vigorous life. An ideal of Athenian education was to achieve a proper balance in moral, mental, physical, and aesthetic development. To the Hellenes, each person was a whole and was only as strong as his or her weakest part.

Gymnastics for the youth were practiced in the palaestra, a building that provided rooms for various physical activities, for oiling and sanding of bodies, and an open space for activities such as jumping and wrestling.

Some of the more noted palaestras were those of Taureas, Timeas, and Siburtios. The *paidotribe,* or proprietor of the palaestra, was similar to a present-day physical educator. He taught many activities, understood how certain exercises should be adapted to various physical conditions, knew how to develop strength and endurance, and was an individual who could be trusted with children in the important task of making youthful bodies serve their minds. As a boy approached manhood, he left the palaestra and attended the gymnasium.

Gymnasiums became the physical, social, and intellectual centers of Greece. Although the first use was for physical activity, men such as Plato, Aristotle, and Antisthenes were responsible for making gymnasiums such as the Academy, Lyceum, and Kynosarges outstanding intellectual centers as well. Youths usually entered the gymnasium at about 14 to 16 years of age. Here special sports and exercises received the main attention under expert instruction. Although activities that had been engaged in at the palaestra were continued, other sports such as riding, driving, racing, and hunting were added. Instruction in the gymnasium was given by a paidotribe and also a *gymnast*. The paidotribe had charge of the general physical training program, whereas the gymnast was a specialist responsible for training youth in gymnastic contests. The chief official at the gymnasium, in overall charge of the entire program, was called a *gymnasiarch*. In keeping with the close association between physical education and sport and religion, each gymnasium recognized a particular deity. For example, the Academy recognized Athena; the Lyceum, Apollo; and the Kynosarges, Hercules.

The national festivals were the most important events in the lives of the Greeks and were also important in laying the foundation for the modern Olympic games. These national festivals were in honor of some hero or deity and consisted of feasting, dancing, singing, and events involving physical prowess. Although many of these national festivals were conducted in all parts of Greece, four of them were of special importance and attracted national attention. The first and most famous was the Olympia festival in honor of Zeus, the supreme god, which was held in the western Peloponnesus district. The second was the Pythia festival in honor of Apollo, the god of light and truth, held at Delphi, which was located north of the Corinthian Gulf. The third was the Nemea festival in honor of Zeus, held at Argolis near Cleonae. The fourth was the Isthmia festival in honor of Poseidon, the god of the sea, held on the isthmus of Corinth. Athletic events were the main attraction and drawing force at each festival. People came from all over Greece to see the games. The stadium at Olympia provided standing space for approximately 40,000 spectators.

During the time the games were held, a truce was declared by all the city-states in Greece, and it was believed that if this truce was broken, the guilty would be visited by the wrath of the gods. By the middle of the fifth century this truce probably lasted for 3 months.

A rigid set of requirements had to be met before anyone could participate as a contestant in the games. For example, the contestant had to be in training for 10 months; he had to be a free man, not a slave; he had to have a perfect physique and be of good character; he could not have a criminal record; he had to compete in accordance with the rules. The contestants, as well as their fathers, brothers, and trainers, had to swear to an oath that they would not use illegal tactics to win. Once enrolled for a contest, the athlete had to compete. Physical unfitness was not a good excuse. Events included foot racing, throwing the javelin, throwing the discus, wrestling, broad jumping, weight throwing, boxing, and horse racing. The victors were presented with a wreath of olive branches. However, when the victors returned to their homes, they were accorded special privileges, receiving monetary rewards, feted at banquets, and honored in triumphal processions. Furthermore, they had many privileges bestowed on them by their home city-states. To be crowned a victor in an Olympic event was to receive the highest honor that could be bestowed in Greece. The Olympic games were first held in 776 B.C. and continued every fourth year thereafter until abolished by the Romans in A.D. 394. However, they have since been resumed and today are held every 4 years in a different country.

Physical education and sport in ancient Greece will always be viewed with pride by members of this field. The high ideals that motivated the various gymnastic events are objectives that all persons should try to emulate.

PHYSICAL EDUCATION AND SPORT IN ROME

About 700 B.C., another Indo-European people was migrating to Italy and settling in the central and southern parts of this country. One of these wandering tribes settled near the Tiber River, a settlement that later became known as Rome. The Romans were to have a decided effect not only on the objectives of physical education and sport in their own state but also on those of the Greek world, which they conquered.

The Romans, through their great leaders and well-disciplined army, extended their influence throughout most of the Mediterranean area and all of Europe. This success on the battlefield brought influences into Roman life that affected Roman ideals. The Romans were not truly interested in the cultural aspects of life, although often some of the finer aspects of Hellenic culture were taken on as a means of show. Particularly during the latter days of the Roman Empire, wealth became the objective of most citizens, and vulgar displays became the essence of wealth. Luxury, corruption, extravagance, and vice became commonplace.

In respect to physical education and sport, the average Roman believed that exercise was for health and military purposes. He did not see the value of play as an enjoyable pastime. During the period of conquest when Rome was following its strong imperialistic policy and before the time of professional troops, citizens between the ages of 17 and 60 years were liable for military service. Consequently, during this period of Roman history army life was important, and physical activity was considered essential to be in good physical shape and ready to serve the state at a moment's notice. Soldiers followed a rigid training schedule that consisted of activities such as marching, running, jumping, swimming, and throwing the javelin and discus. However, during the last century of the Republic, mercenary troops were used, with the result that the objectives of physical training were not considered as important for the average Roman.

After the conquest of Greece, Greek gymnastics were introduced to the Romans, but they were never well received. The Romans lacked the drive for clean competition. They did not believe in developing the "body beautiful." They did not like nakedness of performers; they preferred to be spectators rather than participants; they preferred professionalism to amateurism.

Athletic sports were not conducted on the same high level as in ancient Athenian Greece. The Romans wanted something exciting, bloody, ghastly, and sensational. At the chariot races and gladiatorial combats, excitement ran high. Men were pitted against wild animals or against one another and fought until death to satisfy the spectators' cravings for excitement and brutality. Frequently large groups of men fought each other in mortal battle in front of thousands of pleased spectators.

The rewards and incomes of some individuals who engaged in the chariot races were enormous. Diocles of Spain retired at 42 years of age, having won 1,462 of 4,257 races and rewards totaling approximately $2 million. Other famous contestants were Thallus, Crescens, and Scorpus.*

---

*At the site where the inhabitants of Rome once yelled with delight at the skill and daring of their favorite charioteers and gladiators, Romans of today are applauding the exploits of soccer players, who have replaced the chariot drivers and slaves in public estimation.

The Circus Maximus, the oldest and greatest of the Roman circuses, was situated at the foot of the Palatine Hill and dated back to the last king of Rome, Tarquinius the Younger (534 to 510 B.C.). It reached its greatest splendor in imperial times and seated as many as 200,000 persons. It reached its final form under Trajan (A.D. 53 to 117). The Roman Municipal Council decided that this unusual site should be transformed into a sports center.

The thermae and the Campus Martius in Rome took the place of the gymnasium in Greece. The thermae were the public baths, where provision was also made for exercise, and the Campus Martius was an exercise ground on the outskirts of the city. Most of the exercise was recreational in nature.

PHYSICAL EDUCATION AND SPORT DURING THE DARK AGES

The fall of the Roman Empire in the west about A.D. 476 resulted in a period of history that is generally referred to as the Dark Ages. This period, however, was anything but dark in respect to the physical rejuvenation brought about by the Teutonic barbarians overrunning the Roman Empire.

Before considering the Dark Ages it is interesting for the student of physical education and sport to note a cause of the fall of Rome that brought on this new period in history. Historians list many causes for the breakdown of the Roman Empire, but the most outstanding one was the physical and moral decay of the Roman people. The type of life the Romans led, characterized by the dissolution of marriage and family through divorce, "bloodsport" games, and suicide, caused a decrease in population. Extravagance, doles, slave labor, and misuse of public funds caused moral depravity and economic ruin; luxurious living, vice, and excesses caused poor health and physical deterioration. The lesson is borne out in Rome, as it has been in many civilizations that have fallen along the way, that for a nation to remain strong and endure, it must be physically and morally fit.

As a morally and physically weak Roman Empire crumbled, physically strong Teutonic barbarians overran the lands that once were the pride of the Empire. The Visigoths overran Spain, the Vandals—North Africa, the Franks and Burgundians—Gaul, the Angles and Saxons—Britain, and the Ostrogoths—Italy. These invasions brought about the greatest decline in literature and learning known to history. The so-called cultural aspects of living were disregarded.

Despite all the setbacks to learning, public works, and government associated with the invasions that resulted in this period being named the "Dark Ages," the entire world still received physical benefits. The Teutonic barbarians were a nomadic people who lived out-of-doors on simple fare. They were mainly concerned with a life characterized by hunting, caring for their cattle and sheep, and participating in vigorous outdoor sport and warfare. Such a regimen built strong and physically fit bodies.

Asceticism and Scholasticism

Although the Teutonic invasions of the Dark Ages supported the value of physical activity, two other movements during approximately this same period in history worked to its disadvantage—asceticism and scholasticism.

Out of pagan and immoral Rome, Christianity and asceticism grew and thrived. Certain individuals in ancient Rome became incensed with the immorality and worldliness that existed in Roman society. They believed in "rendering unto Caesar the things that are Caesar's and unto God the things that are God's." They would not worship the Roman gods, attend the baths, or visit the games. They did not believe in worldly pleasures and catered to the spirit and not to the body. They believed that this life should be used as a means of preparing for the next world. They thought that physical activities were foolish pursuits because they were designed to improve the body. The body was evil and should be tortured rather than improved. They preached that the mind and body were distinct and separate entities and that one had no bearing on the other. The Christian emperor Theodosius abolished the Olympic games in A.D. 394 because he considered them to be pagan.

The spread of Christianity resulted in the rise of asceticism. This was the belief that evil exists in the body, and therefore it should be subordinated to the spirit, which is pure. Worldly pursuits are evil, and individuals should spend their time by being alone and meditating. The body is possessed of the devil and should be tortured. Some individuals wore hair shirts, walked on hot coals, sat on thorns, carried chains around their legs, and exposed themselves to the elements so that they might bring their worldly body under better control. For many, such practices led to poor health and shattered nervous systems.

As Christianity spread, monasteries were built where Christians could isolate themselves from the world and its evils. Later, schools were attached to these monasteries, but early Christianity would not allow physical education to be a part of the curriculum. The medieval university also frowned on physical education and sport.

Another influence that has had a major impact on the history of physical education and sport is scholasticism—the belief that facts are the most essential items in education. The key to a successful life is knowing the facts and developing one's mental and intellectual powers. Scholasticism deemphasized the physical. This movement developed among the scholars and universities of the Middle Ages.

PHYSICAL EDUCATION AND SPORT DURING THE AGE OF FEUDALISM

As a result of the decentralization of government during the period of the Dark Ages, the period of feudalism came into being between the ninth and fourteenth centuries.

The feudalistic period appeared because people needed protection, and since strong monarchs and governments that could supply this protection were rare, the people turned to noblemen and others, who built castles, had large land holdings, and made themselves strong. Feudalism was a system of land tenure based on allegiance and service to the nobleman or lord. The lord who owned the land, called a *fief*, let it out to a subordinate who was called his *vassal*. In return for the use of this land the vassal owed his allegiance and certain obligations to his lord. The largest part of the population, however, was made up of *serfs*, who worked the land but shared little in the profits. They were bound to the land, and as it was transferred from vassal to vassal, they were also transferred.

Two careers were open to sons of noblemen during feudalistic times. They might enter training for the church and become members of the clergy, or they might become knights. If they decided in favor of the church, they pursued an education that was religious and academic in nature; if they decided in favor of chivalry, they pursued an education that was physical, social, and military in nature. To the average boy, chivalry had much more appeal than the church.

The training that a boy experienced in becoming a knight was long and thorough. Physical training played a major role during this period. At the age of 7 years a boy was usually sent to the castle of a nobleman for training and preparation for knighthood. First, he was known as a page, and his instructor and teacher was usually one of the women in the lord's castle. During his tenure as a page, a boy learned court etiquette, waited on tables, ran errands, and helped with household tasks. During the rest of the time he participated in various forms of physical activity that would serve him well as a knight and strengthen him for the arduous years ahead. He practiced for events such as boxing, running, fencing, jumping, and swimming.

At the age of 14 years the boy became a squire and was assigned to a knight. His studies included keeping the knight's weapons in good condition, caring for his horses, helping him with his armor, attending to his injuries, and guarding his prisoners. During the time the boy was a squire, more and more emphasis was placed on physical training. He was continually required to engage in vigorous sport and exercises such as hunting, scaling walls, shooting with bow and arrow, running, climbing, swordsmanship, and horsemanship.

If the squire proved his fitness, he became a knight at 21 years of age. The ceremony was solemn and memorable. The prospective knight took a bath of purification, dressed in white, and spent an entire night in meditation and prayer. In the morning the lord placed his sword on the knight's shoulder, a ceremony known as the accolade; this marked the conferring of knighthood.

Jousts and tournaments, two special events in which all knights engaged several times during their lives, were tests of their fitness. These special events served both as amusement and as training for battle. In the jousts two knights attempted to unseat one another from their horses with blows from lances and by skill in horsemanship. Many knights participated in tournaments, programs designed to exhibit the skill and showmanship gained during their long period of training. They were lined up as two teams at each end of the lists, as the grounds were called, and on a signal they attempted to unseat the members of the opposing team. This meleé continued until one team was declared the victor. Many knights wore their lady's colors on their armor and attempted with all their strength and skill to up-hold her honor. During these tournaments death often resulted for participants. In these exhibitions a knight had the opportunity to display his personal bravery, skill, prowess, strength, and courage.

PHYSICAL EDUCATION AND SPORT DURING THE RENAISSANCE

The transitional period in history between the medieval period and the beginning of modern times, the fourteenth to the sixteenth centuries, was known as the age of the Renaissance and was a time of great progress for humankind.

During the medieval period conformity was emphasized. Individuality was a lost concept, and interest in the hereafter was so prevalent that people did not enjoy the present. The Renaissance caused a change in this way of life. There was a revival or rebirth of learning, a belief in the dignity of human beings, a renewed spirit of nationalism, an increase of trade among countries, and a period of exploration. Scientific research was used to solve problems; books were printed and thus made available to more people; renewed interest was shown in the classics. This period is associated with Petrarch, Boccaccio, Michelangelo, Erasmus, da Vinci, da Gama, Columbus, Galileo, and Harvey.

The Renaissance period also had an impact on physical education and sport. With more attention being placed on enjoyment of the present and the development of the body, asceticism lost its hold on the masses. During the Renaissance the theory that the body and the soul were inseparable, that they were indivisible, and that one was necessary for the optimum functioning of the other became more popular. It was believed that learning could be promoted through good physical health. A person needed rest and recreation from study and work. The body needed to be developed for purposes of health and for preparation for warfare.

Some outstanding leaders during the Renaissance who were responsible for spreading these beliefs concerning physical education and sport are discussed briefly.

Vittorino da Feltra (1378 to 1446) taught in the court schools of northern Italy and was believed to be one of the first teachers to combine physical and mental training in a school situation. He incorporated daily exercises in the curriculum, which included dancing, riding, fencing, swimming, wrestling, running, jumping, archery, hunting, and fishing. His objectives emphasized that physical education was good for disciplining the body, for preparation for war, and for rest and recreation, and that good physical condition helped children learn other subject matter much better.

Martin Luther (1483 to 1546), the leader of the Protestant Reformation, did not preach asceticism as a means of salvation. He saw physical education as a means of obtaining elasticity of the body, a medium for promoting health, and a substitute for vice and evil pursuits such as gambling and drinking during leisure hours.

John Milton (1608 to 1674), the English poet, expressed his views on physical education in his *Tractate on Education*. In this treatise he discussed how physical education helps in body development, is a means of recreation, and is good preparation for warfare.

John Locke (1632 to 1704), famous English philosopher and a student of medicine, supported physical education in a work entitled *Some Thoughts Concerning Education*. His objectives could be summarized as a means of meeting health emergencies involving hardships and fatigue and as a means of having a vigorous body at one's command.

Michel de Montaigne (1533 to 1592), a French essayist, stressed that physical education was necessary for both body and soul and that it was impossible to divide an individual into two such components, since they are indivisible to the individual being trained.

Jean Jacques Rousseau (1712 to 1778), a French writer, in his book *Emile* points out that in an ideal education, physical education would contribute to the objectives of health and a vigorous body. He stressed that an individual's mind and body are an indivisible entity and that both are bound together.

The Renaissance period helped to interpret the worth of physical education to the public in general. It also demonstrated how a society that promotes the dignity and freedom of the individual and recognizes the value of human life will also highly respect the development and maintenance of the human body. The belief that physical education is necessary for health, preparation for warfare, and as a means of developing the body became prevalent.

PHYSICAL EDUCATION AND SPORT IN EUROPE

A study of the various individuals and countries that influenced physical education and sport during the modern European period shows what each contributed to the growth and advancement of this field.

Germany

Physical education and sport in Germany during the modern European period is associated with names such as Basedow, Guts Muths, Jahn, and Spiess.

Johann Bernhard Basedow (1723 to 1790) was born in Hamburg and early in life went to Denmark as a teacher, where he witnessed physical education in practice as part of a combined physical and mental training program. After gaining a wealth of experience in Denmark, he went back to Germany and decided to spend all his time reforming educational methods. In 1774 he was able to realize his objective of establishing a school at Dessau that he called the Philanthropinum. In this model school, physical education played an important part in the daily program of all students. The activities included dancing, fencing, riding, running, jumping, wrestling, swimming, skating, and marching. This was the first school in modern Europe that admitted children from all classes of society and that offered a program in which physical education was a part of the curriculum. Basedow's innovation greatly influenced the growth of physical education in Germany and in the rest of the world.

Johann Christoph Friedrich Guts Muths (1759 to 1839) was influential in the field of physical education through his association with the Schnepfenthal Educational Institute, which had been founded by Christian Gotthilf Salzmann (1744 to 1811). Guts Muths succeeded Christian Carl Andre as the instructor of physical education at this institution and remained on the staff for 50 years. His beliefs and practices in physical education were recorded for history in various books, two of which are of special importance—*Gymnastics for the Young* and *Games*. These books provide illustrations of various exercises and pieces of apparatus, arguments in favor of physical education, and discussions of the relation of physical education to educational institutions. Because of his outstanding contributions, Guts Muths is often referred to as one of the founders of modern physical education in Germany.

Friedrich Ludwig Jahn (1778 to 1852) is a name associated with the Turnverein, an association of gymnasts that has been in evidence ever since its inception by Jahn. Jahn's incentive for inaugurating the Turnverein movement was love of his country. It was during his lifetime that Napoleon overran Germany and caused it to be divided into several independent German states. Jahn made it his life's work and ambition to help bring about an independent Germany free from foreign control. He believed that he could best help in this movement by molding German youth into strong and hardy citizens who would be capable of throwing off this foreign yoke.

To help in the achievement of his objective, Jahn accepted a teaching position in Plamann's Boys' School. In this position he worked regularly with the boys in various outdoor activities. He set up an exercise ground outside the city called the

Drawing of a *turnplatz*, a German exercise ground that included equipment for jumping, vaulting, balancing, climbing, and running.

Hasenheide. Before long Jahn had erected various pieces of apparatus, including equipment for jumping, vaulting, balancing, climbing, and running. The program grew in popularity; soon hundreds of boys were visiting the exercise ground, or turnplatz, regularly, and more apparatuses were added.

Jahn's system of gymnastics was recognized throughout Germany, and in many cities Turnvereins were formed, using as a guide the instructions that Jahn incorporated in his book *Die Deutsche Turnkunst*. When Jahn died, his work continued, and turner societies became more numerous. In 1870 there were 1,500 turner societies, in 1880 there were 2,200, in 1890 there were 4,000, in 1900 there were 7,200, and in 1920 there were 10,000. Turnvereins are still in existence in many parts of the world.

Adolph Spiess (1810 to 1858) was the founder of school gymnastics in Germany, and more than any other individual in German history he helped to make physical education a part of school life. Spiess was proficient in physical education activities himself and was well informed as to the theories of such men as Guts Muths and Jahn. His own theory was that the school should be interested in the total growth of the child—mental, emotional, physical, and social. Physical education

Associations of gymnasts called *Turnverein societies* were still popular in the 1920s. At left, a society member practices his skills on an apparatus in the turnplatz. At right, members of the Durlach Turnverein are shown.

should receive the same consideration as the important academic subjects such as mathematics and language. It should be required of all students, with the possible exception of those whom a physician would excuse. An indoor as well as an outdoor program should be provided. Elementary schoolchildren should have a minimum of 1 hour of the school day devoted to physical education activities, which should be taught by the regular classroom teacher. The upper grades should have a progressively smaller amount, which should be conducted by specialists who were educators first but who were also experts in the physical education field. The physical education program should be progressive, starting with simple exercises and progressing to the more difficult ones. Girls as well as boys need an adapted program of physical activity. Exercises combined with music offer an opportunity for freer individual expression. Marching exercises aid in class organization, discipline, and posture development. Formalism should not be practiced to the exclusion of games, dancing, and sports.

Sweden

The name of *Per Henrik Ling* (1776 to 1839) is associated with the rise of physical education to a place of importance in Sweden. The Lingiad, held at Stockholm, in which representatives of many nations of the world participate, is a tribute to this great man.

Ling's greatest contribution is that he strove to make physical education a science. Formerly physical education had been conducted mainly on the premise that people believed it was good for the human body because it increased musculature; contributed to strength, stamina, endurance, and agility; and left one exhilarated. However, many claims for physical education had never been proved scientifically. Ling approached the field with the mind of a scientist. Utilizing the sciences of anatomy and physiology, he examined the body to determine what was inherent in physical activity to enable the body to function in a nearly optimum capacity. His aims were directed at determining such things as the effect of exercise on the heart, musculature, and the various organic systems of the body. He believed that through such a scientific approach he would be able to better understand the human body and its needs and to select and apply physical activity intelligently.

Ling is noted for establishing the Royal Central Institute of Gymnastics at Stockholm, where teachers of physical education received their preparation in one of three categories—educational gymnastics, military gymnastics, or medical gymnastics.

Ling believed that physical education was necessary for weak and strong persons, that exercise must be prescribed on the basis of individual differences, that the mind and body must function harmoniously together, and that teachers of physical education must have a foundational knowledge of the effects of exercise on the human body.

In 1839 *Lars Gabriel Branting* (1799 to 1881) became the director of the Royal Central Institute of Gymnastics after the death of Ling. Branting devoted most of his time to the area of medical gymnastics. His teachings were based on the premise that activity causes changes not only in the muscular system of the body but also in the nervous and circulatory systems. Branting's successor was *Gustaf Nyblaeus* (1816 to 1902), who specialized in military gymnastics. It was during his tenure that women were first included in the school.

The incorporation of physical education programs in the Swedish schools did not materialize as rapidly as many leaders in the field had hoped. As a result of the teachings of Ling and other leaders, a law was passed in 1820 requiring a physical education course on the secondary level. More progress was made in education as the values of physical education in relation to the growth and development of children became apparent in Sweden. *Hjalmar Fredrik Ling* (1820 to 1886) is due most of the credit for the organization of educational gymnastics in Sweden. He was largely responsible for physical education becoming an essential subject for both boys and girls in all schools and on all institutional levels.

Denmark

Denmark has been one of the leading European countries in the promotion of physical education. *Franz Nachtegall* (1777 to 1847) was largely responsible for the early interest in this field. He played a significant role in introducing physical education into the public schools of Denmark and in preparing teachers of this subject.

Franz Nachtegall had been interested in various forms of physical activity since childhood and had achieved some degree of skill in vaulting and fencing. He began early in life to teach gymnastics, first to students who visited his home and then in 1799 in a private outdoor gymnasium, the first to be devoted entirely to physical training. In 1804 Nachtegall became the first director of a Training School for Teachers of Gymnastics in the Army. The need for instructors in public schools and in teachers' colleges was great, so graduates readily found employment. In 1809 the secondary schools and in 1814 the elementary schools were requested to provide a program of physical education with qualified instructors. Shortly thereafter Nachtegall received the appointment of Director of Gymnastics for all Denmark.

Nachtegall's death in 1847 did not stop the expansion of physical education and sport throughout Denmark. Some of the important advances since his death have been the organization of Danish Rifle Clubs, or gymnastic societies, the introduction of the Ling system of gymnastics, complete civilian supervision and control of programs of physical education as opposed to military supervision and control, greater provision for teacher education, government aid, the incorporation of sport and games into the program, and the work of *Niels Bukh* (1880 to 1950).

One of the innovations in the field of physical education and sport has been the "primitive gymnastics" of Niels Bukh. Patterned to some extent after the work of Ling, primitive gymnastics attempted to build the perfect physique through a series of exercises performed without cessation of movement. Bukh's routine included exercises for arms, legs, abdomen, neck, back, and the various joints. In 1925 he toured the United States with some of his students, demonstrating primitive gymnastics.

Great Britain

Great Britain is known as the home of outdoor sports, and that country's contribution to this field has influenced physical education and sport throughout the world. When other European countries were using the Ling, Jahn, and Guts Muths systems of gymnastics, England was using a program of organized games and sport.

Athletic sports are a feature of English life. As early as the time of Henry II, English youth were wrestling, throwing, riding, fishing, hunting, swimming, rowing, skating, shooting with the bow and arrow, and participating in various other sports. The games of hockey and quoits, for example, were played in England as early as the fifteenth century, tennis as early as 1300, golf as early as 1600, and cricket as early as 1700. Football (soccer) is one of the oldest of English national sports.

In addition to outdoor sports, England's chief contribution to physical education and sport has been through the work of *Archibald Maclaren* (1820 to 1884). Maclaren enjoyed participating in many kinds of sport at an early age, especially fencing and gymnastics. He also studied medicine and was eager to make physical training a science. In 1858 he opened a private gymnasium where he was able to experiment. In 1860 Maclaren was designated to devise a system of physical education for the British Army. As a result of this appointment he incorporated his recommendations into a treatise entitled *A Military System of Gymnastic Exercises for the Use of Instructors*. This system was adopted by the military.

Maclaren contributed several other books to the physical education field, including *National Systems of Bodily Exercise, A System of Fencing, Training in Theory and Practice*, and *A System of Physical Education*. In his works he points out that the objectives of physical education should take into consideration that health is more important than strength; that the antidote for tension, weariness, nervousness, and hard work is physical action; that recreative exercise as found in games and sport is not enough in itself for growing boys and girls; that physical exercise is essential to optimum growth and development; that physical training and mental training are inseparable; that mind and body represent a "oneness" in human beings and sustain and support each other; that exercises must be progressive in nature; that exercises should be adapted to an individual's fitness; and that physical education should be an essential part of any school curriculum.

One of the major contributions of England to physical education and sport has been movement education, which is discussed at length in Chapter 4.

● ● ●

Germany, Sweden, Denmark, and Great Britain led Europe in the promotion of physical education and sport. As a rule, other European countries imported the various systems of Jahn, Guts Muths, and Ling. Persons from other countries also contributed much to the field of physical education and sport and should be mentioned. From Switzerland, Clias did a great deal to advance the field of physical education and sport, as did Pestalozzi with his educational theories, and Dalcroze with his system of eurythmics. Colonel Amoros from France inaugurated a system of gymnastics, and Baron Pierre de Coubertin was instrumental in reviving the Olympic games in 1896 at Athens. Johann Happel from Belgium was an outstanding physical educator and was director of a normal school of gymnastics. Dr. Tyrs from Czechoslovakia organized the first gymnastic society in his country.

PHYSICAL EDUCATION AND SPORT IN THE UNITED STATES

Physical education and sport in the United States has experienced a period of great expansion from the colonial period. At that time there was little regard for any planned program of activity—in contrast to today, when programs are required in the public schools of most states and where physical education and sport is becoming a respected profession.

Colonial Period (1607 to 1783)

During the colonial period, conditions were not conducive to organized physical education and sport programs. The majority of the population lived an agrarian existence and thought that they received enough physical exercise working on the farms. Also, during this period few leisure hours could be devoted to recreational activities. In certain sections of the country, such as New England, religious beliefs were contrary to participation in play. The Puritans, especially, denounced play as the work of the devil. Participation in games was believed to be just cause for eternal damnation. Pleasures and recreation were banned. Stern discipline, austerity, and frugality were thought to be the secrets to eternal life and blessedness.

People of some sections of the nation, however, brought the knowledge and desire for various types of sport with them from their native countries. The Dutch in New York liked to engage in sports such as skating, coasting, hunting, and fishing. However, the outstanding favorite was bowling. In Virginia, many kinds of sports were popular, such as running, boxing, wrestling, horse racing, cockfights, fox hunts, and later, cricket and football.

During the colonial period little attention was given to any form of physical activity in the schools. The emphasis was on the three Rs at the elementary level and the classics at the secondary level. Teachers were ill-prepared in the methodology of teaching. Furthermore, at the secondary level students were prepared mainly for college, and it was thought that physical activity was a waste of time in such preparation.

National Period (1784 to 1861)

During the national period (the period from the American Revolution to the Civil War) in the history of the United States, physical education and sport began to assume an important place in society. The academies, as many of the secondary schools were called, provided terminal education for students; instead of preparing for college, they prepared for living. These educational institutions utilized games and sports as after-school activity. However, they had not reached the point at which they thought its value should occupy a place in the daily school schedule. They encouraged participation during after-school hours on the premise that it promoted a healthy change from the mental phases of school life.

The United States Military Academy was founded in 1802, and physical training held an important place in its program of activities. Throughout its history the academy has maintained such a program.

It was during the national period that German gymnastics were introduced to the United States. In 1823 Charles Beck introduced Jahn's ideas at the Round Hill School in Northampton, Massachusetts, and Charles Follen introduced them at Harvard University in Boston. Both Beck and Follen were turners and proficient in the execution of German gymnastics. Their attempt to introduce German gymnastics into the United States, however, was not successful at this time. A few years later they were introduced with more success in German settlements located in cities such as Kansas City, Cincinnati, St. Louis, and Davenport. Turnverein associations were organized, and gymnastics were accepted with considerable enthusiasm by the residents of German extraction. The majority of Americans, however, thought that a formal type of gymnastic program was not suitable for their purposes.

The Turnverein organizations spread, and by 1852, 22 societies were in the North. The oldest Turnverein in the United States, which still flourishes today, is the Cincinnati Turnverein, founded November 21, 1848. The Philadelphia Turnverein, one of the strongest societies today, was founded May 15, 1849. A national organization of Turnvereins, now known as the American Turnerbund, was established in 1850 and held its first national turnfest in Philadelphia in 1851. Societies from New York, Boston, Cincinnati, Brooklyn, Utica, Philadelphia, and Newark were represented. In 1851, 1,672 turners were active in the

United States. At the outbreak of the Civil War approximately 150 Turnverein societies and 10,000 turners were in the United States. After the Civil War these organizations continued to grow and exercised considerable influence on the expanding physical education profession. The Turnverein organizations were responsible for the establishment of the Normal College of the American Gymnastic Union. Many outstanding physical education leaders graduated from this school.

Notable advances in physical education and sport were made before the Civil War. In 1828 a planned program of physical education, composed mainly of calisthenics performed to music, was incorporated by Catherine E. Beecher in the Hartford Female Seminary in Connecticut, a famous institution of higher learning for women and girls. The introduction of the Swedish Movement Cure in America, the construction of gymnasiums in many large cities, the formation of gymnastic and athletic clubs by many leading institutions of higher learning, and the invention of baseball were all important events in the progress of physical education and sport in America during this period.

Civil War Period until 1900

Many outstanding leaders and new ideas influenced physical education and sport in the United States in the period from the Civil War to 1900.

After the Civil War, Turnverein societies were established for both boys and girls. The members of these associations gave support to various phases of physical education and sport and especially encouraged the program in the public schools. The objectives of the turners were notable. They disapproved of too much stress being placed on winning games and professionalism. They believed that the main objectives should be to promote physical welfare and to provide social and moral training. They opposed military training as a substitute for physical education in the schools and supported the playground movement.

In 1852 Catherine Beecher founded the American Women's Educational Association. From 1859 to the early 1870s Dr. George Barker Winship gained considerable publicity by emphasizing

gymnastics as a means of building strength and large muscles.

In 1860 Dr. Dio Lewis devised and introduced a new system of gymnastics in Boston. As opposed to Winship, Lewis was not concerned with building muscles and strength. He was more interested in the weak and feeble persons in society. He aimed at developing agility, grace of movement, flexibility, and improving general health and posture. He also stressed that teachers should be well prepared, and in 1861 he established a normal school of physical education in Boston for training teachers. Lewis opposed military training in schools. He thought that sports alone would not provide an adequate program and that gymnastics should also be included. Through lectures and written articles Lewis became a leading authority on gymnastics used in the schools and the public in general. He is noted for advancing physical education to a respected position in United States society. Several leading educators, after hearing Lewis, set up planned physical education programs in their school systems.

In the 1880s the Swedish Movement Cure was made popular by Hartvig Nissen, head of the Swedish Health Institute in Washington. This system was based on the Ling or Swedish gymnastics, well known in Europe and recognized in the United States for inherent medical values. Also in the 1880s Mrs. Hemenway and Amy Morris Homans added their contributions to physical education. They stimulated the growth of Swedish gymnastics; founded a normal school for teachers at Framingham, Massachusetts; offered courses of instruction in Swedish gymnastics to schoolteachers; and influenced the establishment of the Boston Normal School of Gymnastics.

In the 1890s the Delsarte System of Physical Culture was introduced by Francois Delsarte. It was based on the belief that by contributing to poise, grace, beauty, and health certain physical exercises were conducive to better dramatics and better singing.

During this period American sport began to achieve some degree of popularity. Tennis was introduced in 1874, and in 1880 the United States Lawn Tennis Association was organized. Golf was

Wand drills were an important part of physical education program activities in the 1890s.

played in the United States in the late 1880s, and in 1894 the United States Golfing Association was formed. Bowling had been popular since the time of the early Dutch settlers in New York, but it was not until 1895 that the American Bowling Congress was organized. Basketball, one of the few sports originating in the United States, was invented by James Naismith in 1891. Some other sports that became popular during this period were wrestling, boxing, volleyball, skating, skiing, lacrosse, handball, archery, track, soccer, squash, football, and swimming. In 1879 the National Association of Amateur Athletics of America was developed, from which the American Athletic Union was later formed.

The AAU has played an instrumental role in the participation of the United States in the Olympic Games. In 1896, the Olympic Games were revived in Athens, Greece. Baron Pierre de Coubertin worked for several years to reestablish the games. A pedagogist, he was attracted to the idea of using sport as a means to develop pride and honor among the youth of France. His efforts to use athletic competition to develop character were not well received.

During a visit to the United States, he met with Princeton history professor William Sloane, who shared with him information about the ancient Olympic Games. An idealist, Coubertin saw that the Olympics could embody the ideals to which he

ascribed: amateurism, fair play, good competition, promotion of good will, and fostering of understanding among athletes of the world.

Upon returning to France in 1892, he proposed the reestablishing of the Olympic Games to the governing athletic organization. His proposal was not endorsed. Coubertin persisted and continued to work toward his goal. At an international meeting of amateur athletic associations in Paris in 1894, Coubertin was successful in establishing the modern Olympics and nurtured its growth as the first president of the newly created International Olympic Committee.

The first modern Olympics were held in Athens in 1896. A small delegation of American athletes, organized by Professor Sloane, participated in the Athens Olympics. Participation was limited to males and to 28 events in four sports: track and field, gymnastics, target shooting, and fencing. From the first modern Olympiad in 1896, the Olympics grew in scope and popularity to become the event that it is today.

Physical education has played a large part in the Young Men's Christian Association (YMCA), an organization that is worldwide in scope and that is devoted to developing Christian character and better living standards. Robert J. Roberts was an outstanding authority in physical education for the YMCA in the late 1800s. In 1885 an International Training School of the YMCA was founded at

Staff and students of the first physical education class at the Chautauqua School in New York in 1886.

Springfield, Massachusetts. Roberts became an instructor there, as did Luther Gulick, who later became Director of Physical Training for the New York City Public Schools. After Gulick left Springfield, Dr. McCurdy became head of the physical education and sport department.

The first Young Women's Christian Association (YWCA) was founded in Boston in 1866 by Mrs. Henry Durant. This organization is similar to the YMCA and has a broad physical education and sport program for its members.

Physical education and sport made major advances in colleges and universities with the construction of gymnasiums and the development of departments in this area. Two of the leaders in physical education during the last half of the nineteenth century were Dr. Dudley Allen Sargent, who was in charge of physical education at Harvard University, and Dr. Edward Hitchcock, who was head of the physical education department at Amherst College. Sargent is known for his work in teacher preparation, remedial equipment, exercise devices, college organization and administration, anthropometric measurement, experimentation, physical diagnosis as a basis for activity, and scientific research. Some of the schools that constructed gymnasiums were Harvard, Yale, Princeton, Bowdoin, Oberlin, Wesleyan, Williams, Dartmouth, Mt. Holyoke, Vassar, Beloit, University of Wisconsin, University of California, Smith, and Vanderbilt.

Intercollegiate athletics grew during this time period. With the first intercollegiate meet in the form of a crew race between Harvard and Yale in 1852, intercollegiate sports began to play a prominent role on college campuses. Williams and Amherst played the first intercollegiate baseball game in 1859, and Rutgers and Princeton the first football game in 1869. Other intercollegiate contests soon followed in tennis, swimming, basketball, squash, and soccer. Although mostly males participated in athletics, opportunities were available for women. For example, in 1896, the first intercollegiate women's basketball game was held, with teams from the University of California and Stanford University competing.

Initially, intercollegiate athletics were organized and directed primarily by the students. Athletics were viewed by school administrators and faculty as extracurricular activities because they were not perceived as central to the educational mission of the university. However, as athletics grew in

Dr. Rich's Institute for Physical Education.

popularity and prominence, problems and abuses became more frequent. Faculty raised concern about student-athletes' academic performance, eligibility, commercialization, payment of athletes, and overemphasis on athletics at the expense of academics.

To address these and related concerns and to control its future growth, faculty and administrators became involved in the governance of athletics. Faculty athletic committees were formed on campus. Harvard University was the first to establish a committee in 1892. The next step in assumption of faculty control was the development of university associations to govern athletics. In 1895, the Intercollegiate Conference of Faculty Representatives was formed. Comprising faculty representatives from seven Midwestern institutions, they established eligibility requirements for students pertaining to enrollment and academic performance, imposed limits on athletic financial aid, and developed guidelines for the employment and retention of coaches. This conference, which

later became the Big Ten, was the forerunner of other conferences established throughout the country to govern intercollegiate athletics and to define its role in university life.

Organized physical education programs as part of the curriculum began to appear early in the 1850s in elementary and secondary schools. Boston was one of the first communities to take the step under the direction of Superintendent of Schools Nathan Bishop; St. Louis and Cincinnati followed soon afterward. During the next two decades physical education was made part of the school program in only a few instances. However, in the 1880s the drive in this direction was renewed, and the result was that physical education directors were appointed in many larger cities, and many more communities recognized the need for planned programs in their educational systems.

In 1885 in Brooklyn the American Association for the Advancement of Physical Education was organized, with Edward Hitchcock as the first president and Dudley Sargent, Edward Thwing, and Miss H. C. Putnam as vice-presidents. William G. Anderson was elected secretary and J. D. Andrews, treasurer. This association later became the American Physical Education Association and until recently was known as the American Association for Health, Physical Education, and Recreation (AAHPER). It is now known as the American Alliance for Health, Physical Education, Recreation, and Dance (AAHPERD).

A struggle among the Swedish, German, and other systems of gymnastics developed in the 1890s. Advocates of each system did their best to spread the merits of their particular program and attempted to have them incorporated as part of school systems. In 1890 Baron Nils Posse introduced the Swedish system in the Boston schools, where it proved popular, and it was later adopted throughout the schools of Massachusetts. The Swedish system had more popularity in the East, and the German system was more prevalent in the Middle West. A survey in the 1890s indicates not only the prevalence of the various systems of gymnastics but also the prevalence of physical education programs in general throughout the country. It was reported after a study of 272 cities that 83 had a director of physical education for their school systems; 81 had no director, but teachers were responsible for giving exercises to the students; and in 108 cities the teachers could decide for themselves whether exercises should be a part of their daily school programs. A report on the dates the physical education programs were established in the schools surveyed showed that 10% were established before 1887, 7% from 1887 to 1888, 29% from 1889 to 1890, and 54% from 1891 to 1892. In respect to the system of gymnastics used, the report showed 41% used the German type of gymnastics, 29% Swedish, 12% Delsartian, and 18% eclectic. Only 11 cities had equipped gymnasiums. It was not long, however, before expansion occurred in gymnasiums, equipment, trained teachers, and interest in physical education. In 1892 Ohio was the first state to pass a law requiring physical education in the public schools. Other states followed, and by 1925, 33 states had a physical education law.

Early Twentieth Century

A survey by the North American Gymnastic Union of physical education programs in 52 cities showed that gymnastic programs averaged 15 minutes daily in the elementary schools and two periods weekly in the secondary schools. Cities that were surveyed showed 323 gymnasiums in existence and many more under construction.

Extensive interscholastic programs also existed. A survey of 290 high schools in 1907 showed that 28% of the students engaged in one or more types of sport.

The controversy over interscholastic athletics for girls was pronounced, with people such as *Jessie Bancroft* and *Elizabeth Burchenal* stressing the importance of intramural games rather than interscholastic competition for girls.

A majority of colleges and universities had departments of physical education, and most institutions of higher learning provided some program of gymnastics for their students.

A survey by *Thomas D. Storey* in 1908 gave information concerning leadership in physical education. It showed that of the institutions surveyed, 41% of the directors of physical education possessed medical degrees, 3% of the directors held doctor of philosophy degrees, and the remaining possessed bachelor's degrees.

Intercollegiate athletics were brought under more rigid academic control as abuses mounted. Intramural athletics gained in prominence as the emphasis on athletics for all gained momentum.

Names that should be mentioned in any discussion of the history of physical education and sport during the early part of the twentieth century include the following:

Thomas Dennison Wood made an outstanding contribution to the field of physical education. He attended Oberlin College, was the first director of the physical education department at Stanford University, and later became associated with Teachers College, Columbia University. He believed more emphasis should be placed on games and game skills and introduced his new program under the name "Natural Gymnastics."

Ina Getings, a student at the University of Nebraska, pole vaulting in 1905.

Clark Hetherington was influenced by his close association with Thomas D. Wood, who chose Hetherington as his assistant when he was at Stanford. Hetherington's contributions resulted in a clearer understanding of children's play activities in terms of survival and continued participation. This was also true of athletics and athletic skills. Hetherington became head of the physical education department at New York University and, with his successor *Jay B. Nash,* was responsible for its becoming one of the leading teacher training schools in the nation.

Robert Tait McKenzie, a physical educator, surgeon-scientist, and artist-sculptor, served distinguished periods at McGill University and the University of Pennsylvania. He was known for his contribution to sculpture, for his dedication to helping physically underdeveloped and atypical individuals overcome their deficiencies, and for his writing of books such as *Exercise in Education and Medicine,* published in 1910.

Jessie H. Bancroft, a woman pioneer in the field of physical education, taught at Davenport, Iowa; Hunter College; and Brooklyn and New York City public schools. She greatly influenced the development of physical education as a responsibility of homeroom teachers in elementary schools. She also contributed much to the field of posture and body mechanics and was the first living member of the AAHPER to receive the Gulick Award for distinguished service to the profession. She was well-known for her book *Games for the Playground, Home, School, and Gymnasium.*

Delphine Hanna, an outstanding woman leader of physical education, developed a department of physical education at Oberlin College, which sent outstanding graduates all over the country. She was instrumental in motivating not only many female leaders but also men such as Thomas Wood, Luther Gulick, and Fred Leonard to follow illustrious careers in physical education.

Playday at the John Muir School in 1924.

James H. McCurdy studied at the Training School of Christian Workers at Springfield Medical School of New York University, Harvard Medical School, Springfield College, and Clark University. He was closely associated with Springfield College, where he provided leadership in the field of physical education. He published *The Physiology of Exercise* and was editor of the *American Physical Education Review*.

Luther Gulick, born in Honolulu, was director of physical education at Springfield College, principal of Pratt High School in Brooklyn, Director of Physical Education for Greater New York City public schools, and president of the American Physical Education Association. He taught philosophy of play at New York University, helped found and was the first president of the Playground Association of America (later to become the National Recreation Association), was associated with the Russell Sage Foundation as director of recreation, and was president of Camp Fire Girls, Inc.

The playground movement had a rapid period of growth after the first sand garden was set up in 1885 in Boston. In 1888 New York passed a law that provided for a study of places where children might play out-of-doors. The name *Jacob A. Riis* symbolized the playground movement in New York. In Chicago a playground was managed by Hull House. In 1906 the Playground and Recreation Association of America was established to promote the development of rural and urban playgrounds, with Dr. Gulick as president.

In the field of physical education, higher standards for teacher education were established and better trained leaders were produced. The two-year normal school became a thing of the past, with four years of preparation being required. The trend in professional preparation required students to receive a broad general education, a knowledge of child growth and development and the psychology of learning, and specialized training in physical education.

Sports, athletics, and team games became more important in the early twentieth century, with broad and extensive programs being established in schools, recreational organizations, and other agencies. The National Collegiate Athletic Association (NCAA), the National Association of

Women playing field hockey at Smith College, in Northampton, Massachusetts, in 1904.

Intercollegiate Athletics (NAIA), and other leagues, organizations, and associations were formed to keep a watchful eye on competitive sport.

During the early twentieth century a new physical education started to evolve. By means of a scientific basis it attempted to discover the physical needs of individuals and the part that a planned physical education program can play in meeting these needs. This new physical education recognized that education is a "doing" process and that the individual learns best by doing. It stressed leadership, in which exercises and activities are not a matter of mere physical routine but, instead, are meaningful and significant to the participant. A varied program of activities was stressed that included the fundamental skills of running, jumping, climbing, carrying, throwing, and leaping; camping activities; self-testing activities; organized games; dancing and rhythmical activities; dual and individual sports; and team games. This new physical education stressed the need for more research and investigation into what type of program best serves the needs of children and adults. It stressed the need for a wider use of measurement and evaluation techniques to determine how well objectives are being achieved. Finally, it provided a program that

better served to adapt individuals to the democratic way of life.

World War I (1916 to 1919)

World War I started in 1914, and the United States' entry in 1918 had a critical impact on the nation and education. The Selective Service Act of 1917 called to service all men between the ages of 18 and 25 years. Health statistics gleaned from Selective Service examinations aroused considerable interest in the nation's health.

Social forces were also at work during this period. The emancipation of women was furthered by passage of the Nineteenth Amendment. Women also began to show interest in sport and physical education, as well as in other fields formerly considered to be "off limits."

During World War I many physical educators provided leadership for physical conditioning programs for the armed forces and also for the people on the home front. Dudley Sargent, Luther Gulick, Thomas Storey, and R. Tait McKenzie contributed their services to the armed forces. The Commission on Training Camp Activities of the War Department was created, and Raymond

1851

1866

1910

1920

1927

*yesterday
today
tomorrow . . .
the right costume
for gymnasium,
pool & dance*

Early physical education attire for American women.

Fosdick was named the head of this program. Joseph E. Raycroft of Princeton University and Walter Camp, the creator of "All-Americans," were named to head the athletic divisions of the Army and the Navy, respectively. Women physical educators were also active in conditioning programs in communities and industries at home.

When the war ended, the public had an opportunity to study the medical examiner's report for the men who had been called to military duty. One-third of the men were found physically unfit for armed service and many more were physically inept. Also, a survey by the National Council on Education in 1918 showed that children in the elementary and secondary schools of the nation were woefully subpar physically. The result was the passing of much legislation in the various states to upgrade physical education programs in the schools.

Golden Twenties (1920 to 1929)

The period between 1920 and 1929 showed the way for a "new" physical education advocated by such leaders as Hetherington, Wood, Nash, and Williams. The move away from the formal gymnastic systems of Europe was well received. The temperament of the times seemed to emphasize a less formal program. More games, sports, and free play were the order of the day.

The belief that physical education had greater worth than building strength and other physical qualities, as incorporated in the thinking of the new physical education, aroused much discussion. Franklin Bobbit, a University of Chicago educator, commented: "There appears to be a feeling among physical educationists that the physical side of man's nature is lower than the social or mental, and that . . . they, too, must aim primarily at those more exalted, nonphysical things of mental and social type." Clark Hetherington believed that physical education had different functions in a democratic society than in Europe, where some of the gymnastic systems prevailed. Jesse Feiring Williams stressed the importance of physical education in general education.

Thomas D. Wood, Rosalind Cassidy, and Jesse Feiring Williams published their book *The New*

Tennis at the turn of the century at Smith College, in Northampton, Massachusetts.

Physical Education in 1927; it stressed the biological, psychological, and sociological foundations of physical education.

Another development during this period was the emphasis on measurement in physical education, by such persons as David K. Brace and Frederick Rand Rogers, as a means of grouping students, measuring achievement, and motivating performance.

Programs of physical education and sports continued to expand in schools and colleges. The elementary school program of physical education stressed mainly formal activities. The secondary school program also felt the influence of the formalists. In addition, periodic lectures on hygiene were provided. Interscholastic athletics continued to grow in popularity, with the need being felt to institute controls. The National Federation of

High School Athletic Associations was established in 1923. At the college level a study by George L. Meylan reported in 1921 that of 230 institutions surveyed, 199 had departments of physical education presided over by administrative heads and an average of four staff members per institution. Many of the staff members had professional rank. More than three-fourths of the institutions required physical education for their students, with the most general requirement being 2 years. The 1920s also saw a boom in the area of stadium construction.

Many problems arose in regard to college athletics. As a result, the Carnegie Foundation provided a grant in 1923 for a study of intercollegiate athletics in certain institutions in the South by a Committee of the Association of Colleges and Secondary Schools. Later a study of athletic

American physical education leaders William G. Anderson and Amy Morris Homans.

practices in American colleges and universities was conducted. The report of this study was published in 1929 under the title *American College Athletics*. The report denounced athletics as being professional rather than amateur in nature and as a means of public entertainment and commercialization. Problems such as recruiting and subsidizing athletes also were exposed.

During this period the intramural athletic programs increased in colleges and universities. Women's programs experienced an increase in the number of staff, hours required for student participation, activities offered, and physical education buildings in use.

Depression Years (1930 to 1939)

The 1929 stock market crash ushered in the Great Depression, which affected education. Unemployment and poverty reigned. Health and physical education had a difficult time surviving in many communities.

During the period of economic depression in the United States, many gains achieved by physical education in the schools of the nation were lost. Budgets were cut back, and programs in many cases were either dropped or downgraded. Between 1932 and 1934 an estimated 40% of the physical education programs were dropped completely. Legislative moves were made in several states such as Illinois and California to do away with the physical education requirement.

Another development during the depression years was that the physical educator became more involved in recreation programs in the agencies and projects concerned with unemployed persons. These later programs were being subsidized with special government assistance. The national association, recognizing the increased interest in recreation, voted to change its title to include the word *recreation*—the American Association for Health, Physical Education, and Recreation.

The trend in physical education programs was away from the formal-type approach to an informal games-sports approach. Also, what constitutes an acceptable program of physical education at various school and college levels was outlined by William R. LaPorte of the University of Southern California in his publication *The Physical Education Curriculum—a National Program,* published in 1937.

Interscholastic athletic programs continued to grow and in some situations dominated physical education programs and created many educational problems. The collegiate athletic program received a temporary setback from the Carnegie Report but then started to grow again. The National Association of Intercollegiate Basketball was established in 1940 for the purpose of providing an association for the smaller colleges. It later changed its name to National Association of Intercollegiate Athletics in 1952. In 1937 representatives of the Junior Colleges of California met for the purpose of forming the National Junior College Athletic Association.

Intramural athletics continued to grow in colleges and universities. Women's athletic associations also increased in number. The principles that guided such programs were established largely during the early years by the National Section of Women's Athletics.

Mid-Twentieth Century (1940 to 1970)

Physical education made progress in the middle of the twentieth century.

Impact of World War II

The country was jolted from depression by World War II. Physical education received an impetus as physical training programs were established under Gene Tunney in the Navy, Hank Greenburg in the Air Force, and sports leaders in other branches of the armed forces. Schools and colleges were urged to help develop physical fitness in the youth of the nation. A return to more formalized conditioning programs resulted.

The need for a national program of physical fitness was evident as a result of Selective Service examinations and other indications that young people were not in sound physical condition. Several steps were taken in this direction. President Franklin Roosevelt appointed John B. Kelly of Philadelphia National Director of Physical Training. In 1941 Mayor Fiorello LaGuardia of New York City was appointed by President Roosevelt as Director of Civilian Defense in Charge of Physical Fitness, and a National Advisory Board was established. William L. Hughes of the national association was appointed chairman. In 1942 a Division of Physical Fitness was established in the Office of Defense, Health, and Welfare Services. In 1943 John B. Kelly was appointed chairman of a Committee of Physical Fitness within the Office of the Administrator, Federal Security Agency.

The war years had their impact on programs of physical education in the nation's schools and colleges. In many instances elementary school physical education classes met daily, and secondary and college classes also increased in number. The program of activities took on a more formal nature with the purpose of physically conditioning the children and youth of the United States for the national emergency that existed. Girls and women, as well as boys and men, were exposed to these programs.

The Physical Fitness Movement

In December 1953 an article was published in the *Journal of Health, Physical Education, and Recreation* entitled "Muscular Fitness and Health." The article reported the results of the Kraus-Weber Minimal Muscular Fitness tests given to European and American children. Nearly 60% of the American children had failed, compared with only 9% of the European children. The fitness test primarily measured flexibility and abdominal strength. Nevertheless, the deplorable condition of the American youth was cause for concern.

James B. Kelly of Philadelphia and Senator James Duff of Pennsylvania alerted the President of the United States to the information discussed in this article. In July 1955 President Eisenhower gathered a group of prominent sports figures in Washington, D.C., to explore the fitness problem. Later he called a Youth Fitness Conference at the Naval Academy in Annapolis. At the conclusion of the conference President Eisenhower issued an executive order establishing a President's Council on Youth Fitness and appointed Dr. Shane MacCarthy as executive director. After this a President's Citizens Advisory Committee on Fitness of American Youth was appointed.

As a result of President Eisenhower's decrees fitness became a national topic for consideration. Several states established their own committees on physical fitness. The YMCA, Amateur Athletic Union (AAU), and other organizations put forth special efforts to promote fitness. Several business concerns became involved. *Sports Illustrated* magazine devoted regular features to fitness. The National Research Council of the AAHPER authorized physical fitness testing of American children. The College Physical Education Association for Men published a special report entitled "Fit for College." Operation Fitness USA was inaugurated by the AAHPER to promote fitness, leadership, public relations, and research. The project established motivational devices such as certificates of recognition, achievement awards, and emblems for students at various levels of achievement.

When John F. Kennedy became President of the United States, he appointed Charles "Bud" Wilkinson to head his council on youth fitness. The name was changed to the President's Council on Physical Fitness. The council introduced its "Blue Book" with suggestions for school-centered programs. Later, the council's name was again changed to its current name, the President's Council on Physical Fitness and Sports.

Professional preparation

The war and postwar teacher shortage represented a critical problem for the nation. During the war 200,000 teachers left jobs, and 100,000 emergency certificates were issued. Many of those who left did not return, and inadequately trained replacements were hired. The critical shortage forced administrators to discard their standards in selecting teachers.

Professional preparation programs increased in number during this period, with over 600 colleges and universities participating in such programs. Some of the larger institutions developed separate professional programs for health, physical education, and recreation personnel, whereas many smaller institutions were concerned with only physical education.

Athletics

Four significant developments occurred in athletics during the mid-twentieth century. Renewed interest was shown in girls' and women's sport, intramurals, lifetime sports, and sport programs for boys and girls below the high school age.

Girls' and women's sports. In 1962 the Division for Girls' and Women's Sports (DGWS) and the Division of Men's Athletics of the AAHPER held their first joint conference so that the views of both men and women in the profession could be expressed. Two years later the first National Institute on Girls' Sports was held to promote sports for girls and women. In 1965 a study conference met to discuss and develop guidelines needed in the areas of competition for girls and women. Other steps taken to promote girls' and women's sports included the development of a liaison with Olympic Games officials as a part of the Olympic development movement, the publication of guidelines for girls and women in competitive sports by the DGWS, and the exploration of the social changes in society that had implications for sport programs for women. All these steps represented a new departure toward providing greater opportunities for girls and women to engage in competitive sports at both the high school and college levels.

Intramurals. As sport became increasingly popular at various educational levels, interest was renewed in providing sport competition for all students, not just for the skilled elite. A meeting that helped to spur this movement was held in 1956, when the National Conference on Intramural Sports for College Men and Women met in Washington, D.C. Its purpose was to consider intramural programs for college men and women, to formulate principles, to recommend administrative procedures relating to current and future programs, and to provide greater opportunity for more young men and women to participate in healthful recreational activities. The intramural movement continued to grow, with leadership being provided by the National Intramural Association.

Lifetime sports. An emphasis was placed on sports that can be played during a person's entire lifetime. Giving leadership to this movement was the establishment of the Lifetime Sports Foundation in 1965. Its purpose was to promote fitness and lifetime sports and to give assistance to groups engaged in these areas. This same year the AAHPER approved the Lifetime Sports Education Project, an adjunct of the Lifetime Sports Foundation. School and college physical education programs reflected the influence of such projects, with greater emphasis being given to teaching activities such as bowling, tennis, golf, and badminton.

Sport programs for boys and girls below the high school level. Considerable controversy was generated during this period concerning sports for children below the high school level. In 1953 a National Conference on Program Planning in Games and Sports for Boys and Girls of Elementary School Age was held in Washington, D.C. It was the first time that organizations representing medicine, education, recreation, and other organizations serving the child had ever met with leaders of organizations who promote highly organized competitive activities for children. Two recommendations to come out of this conference were (1) that programs of games and sport should be based on the developmental level of children and that no contact sports should be allowed for children under 12 years of age and (2) that competition is inherent in the growth and development of the child and will be harmful or beneficial depending on a variety of factors.

International developments

International meetings of leaders of health, physical education, and recreation from various parts of the world were initiated in the mid-twentieth century. Furthermore, the Peace Corps recruited many physical educators to work in selected countries of the world.

World seminars in physical education were held, such as the one in Helsinki in 1952. The first International Congress in Physical Education was held in the United States in 1953 and considered such topics as recreation, sport, correctives, dance, and tests and measurements.

In 1958 at the annual meeting of the World Confederation of Organizations of the Teaching Profession (WCOTP), a committee was appointed to make plans for a World Federation of National and International Associations of Health Education, Physical Education, and Recreation. The purpose was to provide a way in which to unite representatives from all associations of these fields in a worldwide organization. The following year the WCOTP established the International Council of Health, Physical Education, and Recreation (ICHPER).

Programs for individuals with disabilities

In the mid-twentieth century physical educators realized that their field of specialization could make a contribution to students with special needs, including individuals who are mentally impaired, physically disabled, and/or culturally disadvantaged. One event that accented this movement was a grant from the Joseph P. Kennedy, Jr., Foundation in 1965, which enabled the AAHPER to establish the Project on Recreation and Fitness for the Mentally Retarded for the purposes of research, program development, and leadership training.

Since its inception in 1968, the Special Olympics has provided competitive sport opportunities for individuals who are mentally impaired.

Adapted physical education programs received increasing attention, with special programs being included in professional preparation institutions to provide leadership for this area. Furthermore, governmental grants of funds enabled greater emphasis to be placed on this particular area of the physical education program.

Research

The need for research in physical education assumed greater importance in the eyes of physical educators than it had heretofore. The Research

Council of the AAHPER was established in 1952 as a section under the General Division. Its functions and purposes included promoting research along strategic lines, developing long-range plans, preparing the disseminating materials to aid research workers in the field, and synthesizing research materials in areas related to the professional fields.

Research became increasingly specialized. Studies were conducted in areas such as exercise physiology, motor learning, sociology of sport, and pedagogy.

Facilities and equipment

With the growth of physical education programs and the construction of new facilities to accommodate these programs, meetings, research, and interest were generated regarding facilities and equipment for physical education.

In 1947 a grant was made by the Athletic Institute to help sponsor a National Facilities Conference at Jackson's Mill, West Virginia. Fifty-four outstanding education, park, and recreation leaders met with architects, engineers, and city planners to prepare a guide for planning facilities for health, physical education, and recreation programs. Facilities conferences have been held periodically in various parts of the United States since 1947.

The Council on Equipment and Supplies of the AAHPER was formed in 1954. Its purpose was to allow manufacturers, distributors, buyers, and consumers of materials used in the areas of health education, physical education, and recreation to work together on problems of mutual concern.

The great amount of monies expended for facilities and equipment in physical education, including sports programs, has been responsible for continued interest in this area so that these monies may be expended in the most beneficial manner.

SIGNIFICANT RECENT DEVELOPMENTS (1970 TO PRESENT)

Physical education and sport currently is in one of its most exciting eras. So many changes have occurred since 1970 that capturing them all in such a limited space is difficult. They include the disciplinary movement, the quest for identity, the emergence of the subdisciplines, new directions in professional preparation, and increased career opportunities in this dynamic field. The national emphasis on disease prevention and health promotion and increasing evidence of the positive relationship between physical activity and health have stimulated participation by people of all ages and created new opportunities within the realm of physical education and sport. Sport participation at all levels and within all segments of the population has exploded. Legislation has increased opportunities for girls and women in sports and for people with disabilities. The Olympics have experienced a period of growth, withstood the politicization of the Games, and emerged as a commercial venture of huge proportions. Technology has contributed in many ways to the continued growth of physical education and sport.

The Discipline of Physical Education and Sport

The disciplinary movement is generally acknowledged to have begun with Franklin Henry's 1964 clarion call for the study of the academic discipline of physical education.[1] It was, however, during the 1970s, and continuing to this date, that the body of knowledge composing the discipline of physical education and sport grew most rapidly. Expanded and rigorous research efforts by dedicated academicians, coupled with improvements in technology, have contributed to the quality and quantity of knowledge. Specialized areas of study or subdisciplines such as exercise physiology, motor learning, and sport psychology have emerged. (See Chapter 1.) There has been considerable discussion of what should be the primary focus of our field. In the late 1990s, there was a growing consensus that physical activity is the central focus of our field.

The disciplinary movement that has been evolving since the 1970s led to considerable debate about the best name for our field of endeavor (see Chapter 1). The traditional name of *physical education* was perceived by some as too narrow and as failing to convey the expanding scholarly interest in sport. In 1989 the prestigious American Academy of Physical Education voted to change its name to the American Academy of Kinesiology and Physical Education and recommended *kinesiology* as the title of the discipline. Other popular names were *physical education and sport, exercise science,* and *exercise and sport science.* In 1994, Ziegler reported that *physical education and sport* was the most widely used title for the field worldwide.[2] As the disciplinary movement continued to grow in the 1970s and 1980s, departments of physical education in colleges and universities were changing their name in an effort to convey more accurately the nature of their work. In 1997, in the United States, there were more than 150 different names for departments in higher education.[3]

The growth of the discipline influenced professional preparation programs at colleges and universities. New courses were developed to embrace the knowledge within the subdisciplines. At the undergraduate level, these courses were initially incorporated into teacher preparation programs. Graduate programs were further developed to offer study within those areas of specialization. Beginning in the late 1970s, an increasing number of undergraduate programs offered their students the opportunity to specialize. To this end, undergraduate programs in specialized areas such as exercise science, sport studies, or sport management were developed. The broadening of professional preparation programs within physical education and sport to encompass specialized areas of study has allowed students to prepare for a diversity of career opportunities within this expanding field.

In the late 1960s and early 1970s, the proliferation of research and the desire to share findings with colleagues helped stimulate the formation of specialized scholarly organizations. For example, the North American Society for the Psychology of Sport and Physical Activity was founded in 1967 and the Philosophic Society for the Study of Sport was begun in 1972. Interest in research grew markedly, and in 1980 the *Research Quarterly* was renamed the *Research Quarterly for Exercise and Sport.* Today there exist many professional

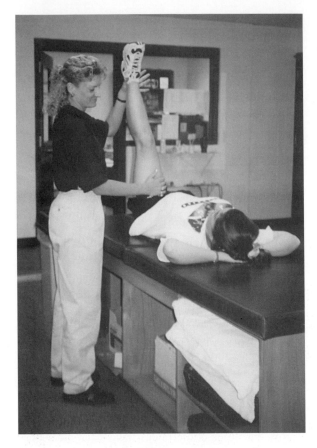

New professional preparation programs train students for nontraditional careers, such as athletic training.

organizations and journals focusing on specialized fields of study within physical education and sport, providing a plethora of outlets for the dissemination of research findings through presentations at conferences and through professional journals.

The scope of physical education and sport widened considerably in the 1970s, and it appears that it will continue to do so throughout the 1990s and into the twenty-first century. Physical education and sport programs have expanded from serving school- and college-age populations to serving people of all ages—from preschoolers to the elderly. Expansion of programs from the traditional school setting to nonschool settings such as community centers and corporate fitness centers has occurred at an increasing rate. There has also been a growing shift to private sector physical education and sport programs. These programs, part of the health-enhancement and leisure-services industry, have created a diversity of career opportunities for well-prepared individuals. Certification programs for professionals began to increase in number. The American College of Sports Medicine (ACSM), the National Athletic Trainers Association (NATA), National Strength and Conditioning Association (NSCA), and Aerobics and Fitness Association of America (AFAA) offer certification programs for professionals. (Professional preparation programs and career opportunities are discussed in Part Three.)

One milestone in this period was the celebration in 1985 by the American Alliance for Health, Physical Education, Recreation, and Dance (AAHPERD) of the one hundredth anniversary of its founding as the American Association for the Advancement of Physical Education.

Preventive Medicine: Disease Prevention and Health Promotion

One of the most significant changes in society during these past decades is the increased emphasis on disease prevention and health promotion. As disease prevention and health promotion initiatives grew, greater attention was directed at helping individuals improve their health by incorporating health-enhancing behaviors into their lifestyle. At this time there was an emerging consensus of epidemiologists, experts in exercise science, and health professionals, as well as a growing body of evidence, that supported the contribution of physical activity to health and well-being. Three national health reports—*Healthy People* (1979)[4], *Objectives for the Nation* (1980)[5], and *Healthy People 2000* (1990)[6]—clearly identified the contribution that physical activity could make to well-being. The establishment of specific physical activity objectives to be achieved by the nation clearly delineated a greater public health role for physical education and sport. These reports established specific objectives to be accomplished by physical education and sport, the attainment of which would

lead to the improvement of the health of the nation. Among these objectives were promoting a greater national participation in physical activity, increasing the number of schools offering daily physical education, expanding community recreation programs, and establishing worksite health promotion programs.

In 1996, the landmark report *Physical Activity and Health: A Report of the Surgeon General*[7] affirmed the contribution of physical activity to the attainment and maintenance of health. This report on physical activity and health emphasized that all Americans can substantially improve their health and quality of life by including moderate amounts of physical activity in their daily lives. It is a national call to action to improve the health of the nation and offers a tremendous challenge to all members of our field.

School Physical Education

Public health initiatives since 1970 have emphasized the critical role that school physical education programs can play in helping children acquire the skills, knowledge, and habits to be active throughout their lives. The emphasis on lifetime sports has continued, with activities such as orienteering, cross-country skiing, and golf part of the school curriculum. Movement education, with its emphasis on exploring skillful movement, understanding and application of knowledge of human movement, and the joy and significance of movements has been an important influence on elementary-school physical education programs (see Chapter 4). The child-centered developmental approach has influenced content, teaching methods, and assessment techniques.

Many different curriculum frameworks have emerged since the 1970s. Some have emphasized fitness, including both fitness development and understanding of the underlying fitness concepts. Other models, such as adventure or sports education, bring a different focus to school physical education. Adventure education models capitalize on the interest in outdoor pursuits, such as backpacking, high-ropes course, or challenge initiatives in which members of a group have to work together to solve a task, such as getting everyone over a 12-foot-high wall. The sport education model involves all students, not just the elite athletes, in the sport experience. This model recognizes that within the playful competition of sport, educational values can be achieved by all students. In contrast to the traditional physical education program, students are divided into teams that practice together throughout the sport season (traditional unit) and participate in formal competition that ends in a culminating event. Students assume the role of the coach, referee, and administrator.[8]

These decades have been marked by efforts to promote physical education and advocacy on behalf of daily quality physical education in the schools. In 1971, the *Physical Education Public Information Project* (PEPI) was begun to inform the public, educators, and policy makers about the value of physical education. PEPI emphasized that "physical education is health insurance."[9] In 1986, the National Association of Physical Education and Sport (NASPE), an association of AAHPERD, defined the characteristics of a "physically educated person" (see Chapter 2).[10] In 1992, NASPE developed national content standards for physical education. This was followed by the development of assessment guidelines. In 1995, the NASPE published *Moving into the Future: National Standards for Physical Education: A Guide to Content and Assessment*.[11] This document offered physical educators for the first time a national framework to guide their efforts.

In 1987 Congress passed a resolution urging individual states to mandate high-quality, daily physical education programs for all school-aged children. Organizations supporting the resolution included the National Education Association, American Heart Association, American Medical Association, National Association of Elementary School Principals, Association for Supervision and Curriculum Development, American School Health Association, and the American Alliance for Health, Physical Education, Recreation, and Dance.

In 1987 AAHPERD released the results of its study of state physical education requirements.

Entitled *The Shape of the Nation: A Survey of State Physical Education Requirements,*[12] the study reported that 40% of children aged 5 to 8 exhibit coronary risk factors such as obesity, elevated blood pressure, high levels of cholesterol, and inactivity. As many as half of the children are not exercising sufficiently to develop adequate cardiorespiratory endurance. Furthermore, one-third of school-aged boys and one-half of school-aged girls cannot run a mile in less than 10 minutes. The lack of quality daily physical education programs contributes to the poor fitness status of our country's youths. The survey found that only one state, Illinois, requires all students from kindergarten through grade 12 to take physical education every day; 8 states have no physical education requirements for schools.

In 1995, the Youth Risk Behavior Surveillance System (YRBSS) survey found 59.6% of students in grades 9 to 12 were enrolled in physical education.[13] Enrollment in daily physical education declined between 1991 and 1995, decreasing from 41.6% to 25.4%.[13] Daily physical education decreased as grade in school increased.[13]

In 1997, a follow-up survey, *The Shape of the Nation 1997,*[14] revealed that the number of states mandating physical education had increased from 42 in 1987 to 47. Ten years after the original survey, Illinois was still the only state to require daily physical education for all students, K–12. Three states have no state-wide mandates relating to physical education instruction; individual school districts in these states establish the requirements. However, it was noted that physical educators were experiencing tremendous pressure to justify their programs due to fiscal constraints.

As we move into the twenty-first century, greater efforts must be directed at promoting physical education as an educational basic, an integral part of the school curriculum for children and youth in all grades.

Physical Fitness and Participation in Physical Activity

The fitness movement began as a trend in the 1970s and has continued to expand. People are

Sales of sports equipment have increased dramatically in the last decade, creating many new career opportunities in sports retailing.

engaging in activities such as jogging, walking, weight training, and aerobic dance to an extent never before witnessed. For example, the Sporting Goods Manufacturers Association reported that in 1996 2.2 million adults over the age of 55 used treadmills for more than 100 days a year.[15] Nearly 7 million adults walked for fitness.[15] Sales of home exercise equipment grew from $723 million in 1982 to over $2.6 billion in 1996.[16] Although it appears that we have become an active nation, studies report that 25% of adults engage in no physical activity during their leisure time.[7]

There has been a shift in emphasis from performance-related to health-related fitness, and, most recently, a shift to an emphasis on incorporating moderate-intensity physical activity into one's daily life. In the 1970s and 1980s, as the emphasis on disease prevention and health promotion grew, the contribution of fitness to health was emphasized. Physical inactivity was recognized as a major health problem. To improve health it was recommended that people engage in fitness activities on a regular basis. In terms of cardiovascular fitness, this required engaging in vigorous physical activity 3 to 5 times a week, at 60–90% of the age-adjusted maximum heart rate, for at least 20 minutes a session. During this time, the emphasis in fitness development and testing in the schools shifted from performance-related fitness to health-related fitness. In 1980 AAHPERD inaugurated the Health-Related Physical Fitness Test.[17] The test was designed to measure the physical fitness components associated with health. The test battery included a distance run to assess cardiorespiratory endurance, skinfold measurements to determine body composition, one-minute sit-ups to measure neuromuscular function of the lower trunk and abdominal strength and endurance, and the sit-and-reach test to determine lower back and hamstring flexibility.

In 1985, the National Children and Youth Fitness Study (NCYFS I), the first nationwide assessment of youth fitness in nearly a decade, revealed that only one-third of youth aged 10 to 17 participated in appropriate physical activity essential for the maintenance of cardiorespiratory endurance.[18] In 1987, the National Children and Youth Fitness Study II (NCYFS II) results for children aged 5 to 9 revealed a low level of cardiorespiratory endurance within this population.[19] For both children and youth, percentage of body fat was greater than in their counterparts of the 1960s. NCYFS I and II raised the concern that current school physical education programs may be inadequate to promote lifetime fitness.

A new fitness test and educational program entitled Physical Best[20] was introduced by AAHPERD in 1988 to replace the Health-Related Physical Fitness Test. Physical Best emphasizes the cognitive, affective, and psychomotor dimensions of fitness. The fitness test battery assesses five components of fitness—cardiovascular endurance, body composition, flexibility, and upper body and abdominal strength and endurance—with the use of a distance run, skinfold measurements, sit-and-reach test, pull-ups, and sit-ups, respectively. The educational program helps teachers to help students attain desirable fitness habits through individualized goal-setting, motivation techniques, and encouragement of participation in physical activities outside the school setting. In 1994, AAHPERD and the Cooper Institute for Aerobic Research (CIAR) announced an agreement to collaborate on youth fitness testing. AAHPERD agreed to adopt the CIAR's Prudential Fitnessgram system for testing and assessment of youth fitness. CIAR agreed to adopt AAHPERD's Physical Best educational materials that promote healthy lifestyles for all children and youth. It is hoped that this partnership will help teachers across the country to improve the fitness levels of all school children.

Although no national study of fitness has been conducted since the NYCFS I and II, there is recent information about the participation patterns of children and youth. The 1992 National Health Interview Survey-Youth Risk Behavior Survey (NHIS-YRBS)[21] and 1995 YRBSS[14] provided information on the physical activity patterns of youth ages 12–21 and high school students (see Chapter 3). The NHIS-YRBS reported that 53.7% of the youths engaged in vigorous physical activity and 26.4% engaged in moderate physical activity, walking or bicycling, 30 minutes or more during 5 of the 7 days preceding the survey. No participation in physical activity was reported by 13.7% of the youth. The 1995 YRBSS found that 63.7% of the students participated in vigorous physical activity, and 21.1% of the students engaged in moderate physical activity, walking or bicycling, for at least 30 minutes or more during 5 of the 7 days preceding the survey. No participation in physical activity was reported by 10.4% of the youth.

Evidence on the health benefits of physical activity continued to mount during this time. It was found that health-related benefits could be obtained at more moderate levels of activity intensity than previously realized. In 1995, the Center for Disease Control and Prevention (CDC) and the American College of Sports Medicine (ACSM) recommended that all adults should accumulate 30 or more minutes of moderate-intensity activity on most, preferably all, days of the week.[7] The National Institute of Health (NIH) Consensus Development Conference State on Physical Activity and Cardiovascular Health recommended that all population groups, including children and youth, accumulate at least 30 minutes per day of moderate-intensity physical activity.[7] These new recommendations by the CDC, ACSM, and NIH also emphasized that greater benefits would accrue by engaging in moderate-intensity activities for a greater period of time or participating in more vigorous physical activity.[7]

The Growth of Sports

Participation in sports has experienced phenomenal growth at all levels since the 1970s. Participation by children and youth involved in organized sport activities outside the school setting, under the guidance of public or private agencies, has grown tremendously. It is estimated that children and youth sports involve more than 25 million children, 3 million adult volunteer coaches, and 500,000 paid coaches, working primarily in private sports clubs with elite performers. Among the most popular programs are soccer, baseball, softball, and swimming. Children and youth are also enrolling in record numbers in commercial sport organizations, such as gymnastics and tennis clubs.

Participation in interscholastic sports has grown from 3,960,932 boys and girls in 1971 to 6,178,268 in 1996–1997.[22] More than 50% of students had played on a sports team in a given year. There is an increased trend toward specialization at an early age in a specific sport. A youth may play on the school soccer team in the fall, participate in a recreational league indoor soccer in the winter, play spring soccer, and then attend soccer camp in the summer. Some school districts, facing budgetary difficulties, have instituted "pay-to-play" plans where athletes are charged fees to participate. Considerable concern has been raised that these fees will limit participation and disproportionately affect students from lower socioeconomic groups. The National Federation of State High School Associations opposes this practice, stating that sports have educational value and therefore students should have access to them as part of their educational experience.

At the collegiate level, participation in sports has increased as well. The National Collegiate Athletic Association (NCAA) reported that during the 1989–1990 academic year, 266,268 collegians participated in intercollegiate athletics; in 1996–1997 participation was 331,282.[23] Nearly another 100,000 students participated in sports at colleges that are members of the National Association of Intercollegiate Athletes (NAIA)[24] and at community colleges that are governed by National Junior College Athletic Association (NJCAA)[25]. Moreover, during this time, sport has emerged as "big business" in NCAA Division I schools. Media revenues for televising football and basketball games and tournaments have reached millions of dollars. For example, the major NCAA Division I-A football schools shared more than $100 million in revenue for the bowl games.

Participation in recreational leagues by adults has increased enormously as well. "Over-55" basketball leagues and softball leagues have been added as part of the popular adult leagues in many communities. Many different kinds of sporting interests are accommodated in these recreational programs. Adult soccer and volleyball leagues have increased in popularity. Road races attract thousands of participants. Amateur competitions draw millions of more competitors of all ages. Master's programs in swimming and track and field, the National Senior Games, the national Olympic Festival, and state games, such as the New York Empire State Games, engage people of all ages in various levels of competition in a multitude of sports.

Professional sports have also increased during this time. Since the 1970s, expansion has resulted in the addition of many professional hockey, football, and baseball teams. Salaries of professionals have increased dramatically; multimillion dollar contracts have become increasingly common. Professional opportunities for women have increased as well. In 1996, two women's professional basketball leagues were organized. The eight-team American Basketball League began its 40-game schedule on October 18, 1996; the Columbus Quest captured the first championship. The Women's National Basketball Association, backed by the National Basketball Association, began its inaugural season on June 21, 1997. To avoid direct competition with the NBA season, the league played its 28-game schedule in the summer. The Houston Comets captured the first championship. The number of women participating in professional sports, such as the Ladies Professional Golf Association (LPGA), has grown tremendously. Male and female athletes in both tennis and golf can now compete for prizes worth millions of dollars.

Girls and Women in Sport

Participation by girls and women in sports began to grow rapidly in the 1970s and continues.

Cynthia Cooper, Women's National Basketball League MVP, drives for the basket. In the late 1990s, opportunities for women to participate in professional sports increased.

The changing attitudes toward women in society was one factor that promoted the growth of participation. Participation was also greatly enhanced by the passage of Title IX of the Educational Amendments Act of 1972. In essence, Title IX states, "No person in the United States shall on the basis of sex be excluded from participation in, be denied the benefits of, or be subjected to discrimination under any education program or activity receiving Federal financial assistance." This legislation has had wide-ranging effects on physical education and athletic programs in the United States.

One major reason Title IX came into existence was to ensure that girls and women receive the same rights as boys and men. Testimony before congressional committees prior to the enactment of this legislation showed that girls and women were being discriminated against in many educational programs, including physical education and athletics. While Title IX applies to all types of educational programs, probably the most dramatically affected have been sport and physical education programs. Girls' and women's athletic programs, in particular, have grown rapidly in only a few short years. In the early 1970s comparatively few varsity interscholastic and intercollegiate teams were for girls and women. However, because of the federal regulation banning sex discrimination, girls' and women's sport teams have come into their own and are flourishing throughout the nation.

Participation in sports by girls and women has risen dramatically since the enactment of Title IX. According to the National Federation of State High School Associations, during 1971, the year before Title IX legislation, 3,366,000 boys and 294,000 girls competed in interscholastic sports in the United States. In 1996–1997 the Federation reported that 3,706,225 boys and 2,472,043 girls took part in interscholastic sports. Participation by women at the intercollegiate level also showed substantial increases. For example, according to the NCAA, 32,000 women competed in intercollegiate sports in 1972, whereas in 1996–1997 the NCAA reported that 129,285 women competed (These figures include only NCAA-sponsored championship sports; thus the number of participants is greater than reported here.)

Title IX mandated certain provisions for physical education and athletic programs. With respect to physical education, no discrimination could occur in program offerings, quality of teachers, and availability and quality of facilities and equipment. Physical education classes must be organized on a coeducational basis. However, classes may be separated by sex for contact sports such as wrestling, basketball, and football. Also, within classes, students may be grouped by ability or another basis, except sex, although such groupings may result in single-sex or predominately single-sex groupings.

Title IX also resulted in changes in the conduct of athletic programs. Separate teams for men and women or a coeducational team must be provided in schools and colleges. For example, if only one team is organized in a particular school for a sport such as swimming, then students of both sexes must be permitted to try out for this team. Both sexes in educational institutions must be provided with equal opportunities for the following: equipment and supplies, use of facilities for practice and games, medical and training services, coaching and academic tutoring, travel allowances, housing and dining facilities, compensation of coaches, financial assistance, and publicity. Equal aggregate expenditures are not required; however, equal opportunities for men and women are mandated.

There have also been changes since 1972 in the governance of women's intercollegiate sports. The Association of Intercollegiate Athletics for Women (AIAW), founded in 1972, initially was the governing body for women's intercollegiate sports. The AIAW established policies and procedures governing competition and conducted national championships for women's intercollegiate sports. In 1980–81, 960 institutions were members and 99,000 women participated in AIAW events; the AIAW conducted 39 national championships encompassing 17 sports. The NCAA used its vast financial resources to entice teams to leave the AIAW; over a period of time, this led to the demise of the AIAW. In 1982 the NCAA and the NAIA (National Association of Intercollegiate Athletics) assumed the governance of intercollegiate sports for women at all NCAA and NAIA institutions.

Throughout its history many challenges to Title IX have been heard by the courts. In 1984 the United States Supreme Court in a 6 to 3 decision ruled in the *Grove City College v. Bell* case that Title IX should be regarded as program specific. In essence, this narrow interpretation of Title IX held that only programs directly receiving federal aid were required to comply with Title IX, not the institution as a whole. Before this ruling, Title IX was interpreted broadly; that is, institutions receiving any federal funds were required to comply with Title IX in all institution activities. Since athletic programs typically receive little, if any, direct federal funding, the threat of losing funding for noncompliance and nonsupport of women's athletics is without substance. While some institutions remained deeply committed to women's athletics, the fear existed that some institutions, without the threat of noncompliance, would allow women's athletics to stagnate or even to become victims of budgetary cutbacks.

In 1988 the Civil Rights Restoration Act superseded the 1984 United States Supreme Court ruling. Once again, Title IX was interpreted broadly and its applicability to athletics was reinstated. In 1991, the Office of Civil Rights announced that investigation of Title IX athletic complaints would be one of the office's priorities.

Title IX has led to dramatic changes in the conduct of physical education and athletic programs and to significant increases in participation by girls and women within these programs. However, the impact of Title IX has been limited by several factors, including gender biases, limited budgets, inadequate facilities, lack of qualified leadership (i.e., coaches), and resistance to change. Although equal opportunity is mandated by law and great strides have occurred within the last decades, much still needs to be accomplished within both physical education and athletic programs to achieve equity.

Programs for Individuals with Disabilities

In recent years many judicial decisions and legislative acts have supported the rights of students with disabilities to have the same educational opportunities as other students. These mandates have resulted in significant changes in the conduct of physical education programs and athletic programs for individuals with disabilities. The rights of persons with disabilities in programs for which schools and other sponsoring organizations receive federal funds were guaranteed by Section 504 of the Rehabilitation Act of 1973 (P.L. 93-112). This law provided for access to all school programs, including physical education and athletics.

The most widely known and important law related to education for people with disabilities is P.L. 94-142, or the Education of All Handicapped Children Act of 1975. This law provided for a free and appropriate education for children 3 to 21 years of age. Section 121a.307 of the regulations stated that physical education services, specially designed if necessary, were to be made available to every disabled child. All educational services are to be provided for disabled students in the least restrictive environment. In essence, this means that a disabled child is placed in a special class or mainstreamed into a regular class or moved between the two environments as dictated by his or her abilities and capabilities. Furthermore, the school assumes the responsibility of providing the necessary adjunct services to ensure that students with disabilities perform to their optimum capacity, whether they are integrated into a regular program or left in a special class. Each child with disabilities must have an individualized educational plan or IEP.

In 1986 the Education for All Handicapped Children Amendments of 1986 (P.L. 99-457) was passed and implementation began in 1990. This law mandated that educational services to individuals with special needs from 0 to 2 years of age be provided and that services for 3 to 5 year olds be expanded. Special educational services, including physical education, are required. Preschool physical education programs will need to be expanded to accommodate the diverse needs of these individuals and to fulfill the mandate of the law.

In 1990, P.L. 101-476, the Individuals with Disabilities Education Act (IDEA) was passed. Among its mandates was a requirement that all references to "handicapped children" be changed

The Special Olympics provides a variety of athletic opportunities for people who are mentally impaired.

to "children with disabilities." It mandated that transitional services be provided to students as early as 14 and no later than 16 years of age. Transitional services are a coordinated set of activities designed to help students with disabilities make the transition from the school to post-school life in the community. It emphasizes creating linkages between the school and private and public services within the community. For example, if fitness de-

velopment was part of the IEP, then linkages need to be created between the school and local fitness programs. IDEA also provides more opportunities for children with disabilities to receive assistive technologies to improve their abilities. For example, students can get racing wheelchairs or other specialized equipment that would enhance their ability to participate. Children with disabilities must have the opportunity to participate in extracurricular activities and services, such as athletics, intramurals, and the art club.

IDEA stated that physical education and sport must be available to every child who is receiving a free and appropriate education. Each student with a disability must be afforded the opportunity to participate in a regular physical education program with children who do not have a disability unless the child is enrolled full-time in a separate facility or needs a specially designed physical education program. The philosophy, known as inclusion, is based on the rights of children with disabilities, regardless of severity, to attend their home schools and participate in the regular educational setting rather than be isolated from their peers in special programs. An alternative approach is the use of the least restrictive environment. The least restrictive environment places a child in the educational setting that is most appropriate for his or her abilities and developmental level. The environment can range from full inclusion in the regular setting to special programs in a self-contained setting. Regardless of the approach, it is important that children with disabilities have individualized programs that are appropriate for their developmental levels and that optimize their potential.

Federal legislation directed toward improving conditions of persons with disabilities and meeting their educational needs has caused many changes. Schools are now required to provide physical education, intramurals, recreational programs, and athletic programs for students with disabilities. Adapted physical education programs have expanded. Teachers have had to learn different strategies to enhance the learning opportunities for students with disabilities participating in regular physical education classes. Facilities have to be altered and modified to meet the needs of the disabled. It is hoped that the commitment to improve the educational opportunities and to meet the educational needs of individuals with disabilities will continue in the years ahead. A greater emphasis also must be placed on meeting the activity needs of individuals with disabilities by developing expanded opportunities for participation in the community setting.

In 1990, a landmark law, the Americans with Disabilities Act (ADA) (P.L. 101-336) was passed. This law seeks to end discrimination against individuals of all ages with disabilities and to remove barriers to their integration into the economic and social mainstream of American life. Five areas are addressed by the law: employment, public accommodations, public services, transportation, and telecommunications. The effects of this law are far-reaching. For example, the ADA mandates that all facilities, including recreational and sport facilities, must provide equal access and equal services to individuals with disabilities. This law opens playgrounds, swimming pools, gymnasiums, and health spas, for example, to individuals with disabilities, increasing their opportunities to participate in fitness and sport activities. In 1998, professional golfer Casey Martin sued the Professional Golfers Association under the ADA for the right to ride a motorized cart in competition. Martin has Klippel-Trebauney-Weber syndrome, a painful ailment that affects the circulation in his lower right leg and limits his ability to walk the golf course. It was ruled that the PGA Tour must accommodate Martin.

Since the 1970s the number of individuals with disabilities participating in competitive sports has increased. The Amateur Sports Act of 1978 (P.L. 95-606) charged the United States Olympic Committee to encourage provisions for sporting opportunities for the disabled, specifically to expand participation by individuals with disabilities in programs of athletic competition for able-bodied individuals. This charge served as the impetus for the formation of the Committee on Sports for the Disabled in 1983. The committee is to promote participation in sport by individuals with disabilities and to support amateur sports programs for athletes with disabilities. Participation in national and international competitions and games by athletes with specific disabilities continues to rise. Competitions include the Paralympics, the Special Olympics, World Games for the Deaf, and the World Wheelchair Games, to name just a few. Competition at the state and local level, such as Connecticut's Nutmeg Games for the Disabled, continues to grow. It is likely that this trend will continue as all segments of our society find participation in sport to be a meaningful and satisfying experience.

Olympics

In 1996, the Centennial Olympic Games were held in Atlanta, Georgia. In the 100 years since their rebirth in 1896, the Olympics have evolved into an event of global magnitude. In the 1896 Olympics held in Athens, 311 athletes from 11 nations competed. In Atlanta, 10,750 athletes from 197 nations competed.

The modern Olympic Games, organized originally with the idealistic goal of fostering understanding among the people of the world, has become an instrument for political goals. Ideological differences have exerted a profound influence on the conduct of the Games. The 1972 Munich Olympics were marked by terrorism. Eight armed Arab guerrillas entered the Olympic Village complex occupied by the Israelis; a day later eleven Israelis, five terrorists, and one German policeman were dead. Millions of people around the world mourned the slain athletes. After a memorial ceremony, the Munich Olympics continued.

Social and political issues led to boycotts at the 1976 Olympics in Montreal over the issue of representation of China and the issue of apartheid. The United States led a boycott of the 1980 Olympics in Moscow in protest of the Soviet Union's invasion of Afghanistan. The Soviet Union, in turn, led a boycott of the 1984 Olympics in Los Angeles, claiming that the United States failed to adhere to the Olympic ideals. The 1988 Olympics in Seoul Korea saw the Americans and Soviets competing in the XXIVth Olympiad. The International Olympic Committee took a strong position against drug "doping." Canadian sprinter Ben Johnson tested positive for steroid use after winning the 100 meters, and American Carl Lewis was then awarded the goal medal.

Several monumental events in the early 1990s had a significant impact on the world and the Olympics. The collapse of the Berlin Wall that had separated East Germany from West Germany and the collapse of the Soviet Union contributed to the end of the Cold War and a decrease in East-West tensions. In 1992, the Germans competed in Barcelona as a unified team and athletes from the former Soviet Union competed as part of the Commonwealth of Independent States. South Africa competed for the first time in decades, and the Baltic States participated as independent countries for the first time since World War II. As more countries began to be more open about paying their athletes for their performances, the issue of amateurism became a moot point. Professional athletes began to participate in the Games in increased numbers. Public attention was focused on the United States basketball "Dream Team," largely comprised of professionals such as Michael Jordan, David Robinson, and Larry Bird. Growing commercialism and concern about the use of drugs continued.

In the 1996 Centennial Olympic Games in Atlanta, a record number of athletes, nearly 11,000, from a record number of nations, 197, made the Games a memorable event. The athletes participated in 271 events. The event was broadcasted to an estimated 3.5 billion people. NBC paid the International Olympic Committee $456 million dollars for the broadcast rights; compare this to the $394,000 paid by CBS to telecast the 1960 Games in Rome. Rights to the 2000 Olympic Games in Sydney and the 2002 Winter Games in Salt Lake City, Utah, were purchased by NBC for $1.27 billion. Commercialization extended further than broadcast rights. To be an official corporate sponsor of the Games costs each of the selected companies $40 million.

The Winter Games also flourished during this time and mirrored the changes seen in the Summer Games. In the early 1990s, the International Olympic Committee voted to stagger the Winter and Summer Games in a 2-year rotation instead of a 4-year rotation. This started with the 1994 Winter Games in Lillihammer, Norway. It was believed that, given the high degree of public interest in the Olympics, the public would embrace this change. There would also be an economic benefit to the International Olympic Committee if the games were held every 2 years rather than every 4.

Participation by women has increased during these past decades. Women's softball in 1996 and women's ice hockey in 1998 are just two of the new sports added to the Games. In 1998, following the Winter Games in Nagano, Japan, the International Olympic Committee stated that no new events would be added to the competition unless a comparable event could be added for women.

"Nontraditional" sports have been added to the Olympic Games. Beach volleyball, mogul skiing, and snowboarding are just a few of the new sports included in the Olympics.

The Paralympics is an international Olympic competition for persons with disabilities. In the early 1990s, the International Olympic Committee mandated that the Paralympics would be the responsibility of the same country that hosted the Olympic Games. The same venues would be used, and the Paralympics would take place immediately following the closing of the Olympic Games. In 1996, the Paralympics in Atlanta involved over 4,000 athletes representing 127 nations. Over the 10 day competition, the athletes competed in 17 sports. More than 1,000 coaches, 1,500 officials, and 15,000 volunteers were involved in the Paralympics.

In recent years the Olympics have been used as a means to further political ideologies. The line between amateurism and professionalism has disappeared. Commercialization has reached new heights and continues to grow. The Olympics have become an embedded component of our global culture.

Technology

Scientific and technological advances have had a tremendous impact on physical education and sport during this time. Computer technology and increasingly sophisticated research equipment have enabled researchers to enlarge our knowledge base. Technology has created new equipment that has led to record-breaking achievements for elite athletes and enhanced performance for people of all skill levels. The fiberglass pole led to new heights in the pole vault. The recent 1998 Nagano Winter Olympics served as a showcase for the advent of clap skates, which shaved seconds off speedskating records. Graphite tennis rackets and golf clubs improved the games of people of all skill abilities. Many types of artificial playing surfaces have been manufactured since the inception of artificial grass surfaces. Synthetic surfaces are replacing wooden gymnasium floors, cinder tracks, and various types of surfaces on tennis courts. Enclosed facilities and stadiums have become increasingly common, and many of these buildings feature dome-shaped and air-supported structures. Solar collection devices are starting to be used in buildings to reduce heating costs.

Computer analysis of diet, strength and endurance training, and workout performance enables athletes to fine tune their training to better achieve their goals. Observers can gather data on teaching behaviors via laptop computers and generate an instant profile of teachers' and students' behaviors. Teachers and students enter data from fitness tests directly into the computer to yield an almost immediate analysis of their fitness status as well as specific recommendations for improvement. Heart-rate monitors provide students in physical education classes, athletes working out, participants in aerobic dance classes, and adults jogging on the roads with immediate feedback about the intensity of their training.

Swimmers at the Olympic Training Center in Colorado Springs are videotaped while racing in a swimming treadmill called a flume. The coaches analyze the swimmers' strokes and then show the videotape to the athletes and discusses their technique with them. In many sports, computer simulation allows one to compare an athlete's performance against the model of the ideal performance. Changes then can be made in the athlete's performance to increase efficiency and effectiveness. Virtual reality is beginning to be used to enhance sport performance.

These Paralympic athletes, who are amputees, await the start of the sit-volleyball competition at the 1996 Paralympic Games in Atlanta.

As technology continues to develop, researchers and practitioners in all areas of physical education and sport must be prepared to take advantage of these gains. Some of these advances will open up new avenues of research. Practitioners in all subdisciplines will find also that these technological developments will assist participants in their programs to more readily attain their goals.

SUMMARY

History provides the foundation for the discipline of physical education and sport. Many of our physical education and sport programs and activities today have been shaped by our heritage. Studying history also provides one with an appreciation for other cultures and the role of physical education and sport in these societies.

An adage states that "history tends to repeat itself." Recurring themes are apparent throughout the history of physical education and sport. For example, wars frequently served as the impetus for societies to intensify their physical education program or to justify its existence. Physical fitness was promoted among the populace to prepare for these war efforts.

However, obviously not all history repeats itself. Changes are apparent too. The impact of different philosophies on the content and structure of physical education and sport programs and changes in the nature and the importance of objectives can be discerned throughout the years. It is important to be aware of the events that served as catalysts and deterrents to the growth of physical education and sport.

The recent history of physical education and sport reveals many changes. Since the 1970s, the growth of the discipline, the emphasis on disease prevention and health promotion, changes in school physical education, the fitness movement and emphasis on physical activity, and the phenomenal growth of sports have contributed greatly to our field. By understanding the history of physical education and sport, a professional can better understand the nature of the field, appreciate the significant developments of today, and project trends for the future.

SELF-ASSESSMENT TESTS

These tests are designed to help you determine if you have mastered the materials and competencies presented in this chapter.

1   Reflect on the history of physical education and sport and then prepare a graph that traces its history from ancient times to recent times. Identify the high and low points of physical education and sport in the graph, and supply a rationale for your analysis.

2. Describe events and philosophies that served as catalysts for the growth of physical education and sport, and events and philosophies that served as deterrents to the growth of physical education and sport throughout history.

3. Using the information provided in the Getting Connected box, explore the history of the Olympic Games or other sports.

4. Project future developments for physical education and sport based on historical events, including events from both early and recent times.

REFERENCES

1. Henry F: Physical education: an academic discipline, Journal of Health, Physical Education, and Recreation 37(7):32–33, 1964.

2. Ziegler EF: Physical education and kinesiology in North America: professional and scholarly foundations, Champaign, Ill., 1994, Stipes.

3. Ziegler EF: From one image to a sharper one! Physical Educator 54(2):72–77, 1997.

4. US Department of Health, Education, and Welfare: Healthy people: the Surgeon General's report on health promotion and disease prevention, Washington, D.C., 1979, US Government Printing Office.

5. US Public Health Service, US Department of Health and Human Services: Promoting health/ preventing disease: objectives for the nation, Washington, D.C., 1980, US Government Printing Office.

6. US Public Health Service, US Department of Health and Human Services: Healthy people 2000: national health promotion and disease prevention objectives, Washington, D.C., 1990, US Government Printing Office.

7. US Department of Health and Human Services: Physical activity and health: a report of the Surgeon General, Atlanta, Ga., 1996, US Department of Health and Human Services, Centers for

Disease Control and Prevention, National Center for Chronic Disease Prevention and Health Promotion, and The President's Council on Physical Fitness and Sports.

8. Siedentop D, Mann C, and Taggart A: Physical education: teaching and curriculum strategies for grades 5–12, Palo Alto, Calif., 1986, Mayfield.

9. Biles F: The physical education public information project, *Journal of Health, Physical Education, and Recreation* 41(7):53–55, 1971.

10. National Association for Sport and Physical Education: Definition of a physically educated person: outcomes of quality physical education programs, Reston, Va., 1990, AAHPERD.

11. National Association for Sport and Physical Education: Moving into the future: national standards for physical education: a guide to content and assessment, St. Louis, Mo, 1995, Mosby.

12. National Association for Sport and Physical Education: Shape of the nation 1993, Reston, Va., 1993, American Alliance for Health, Physical Education, Recreation and Dance.

13. Centers for Disease Control and Prevention: 1995 youth risk behavior surveillance system, Atlanta, Ga. (http://www.cdc.gov/nccdphp/dash/yrbs/suph.htm).

14. National Association for Sport and Physical Education: Shape of the nation 1997, Reston, Va., 1997, American Alliance for Health, Physical Education, Recreation and Dance.

15. Sporting Goods Manufacturers Association: The Senior sports revolution, Press Release, November 3, 1997, Sporting Goods Manufacturers Association.

16. Sporting Goods Manufacturers Association: The sports and recreation industry exceeds $60 billion, Press Release, May 26, 1997, Sporting Goods Manufacturers Association.

17. American Alliance for Health, Physical Education, Recreation, and Dance: Health-related fitness test, Reston, Va., 1980, AAHPERD.

18. Ross JG and Gilbert CG: The national children and youth study: a summary of the findings, JOPERD 56(1):45–50, 1985.

19. Ross JG and Pate RR: The national children and youth fitness study II, JOPERD 58(9):51–56, 1987.

20. American Alliance for Health, Physical Education, Recreation, and Dance: Physical best, Reston, Va., 1988, AAHPERD.

21. US Department of Health and Human Services: National health interview survey-youth risk behavior survey, Washington, D.C., 1992, US Department of Health and Human Services.

22. National Federation of State High School Associations, January 1998, Personal communication.

23. National Collegiate Athletic Association, January 1998, Personal communication.

24. National Junior College Athletic Association, January 1998, Personal communication.

25. National Association of Intercollegiate Athletes, January 1998, Personal communication.

SUGGESTED READINGS

Cordts H, editor: Physical education, recreation and dance—an international view, JOPERD 58(9):18–49, 1987.

These fourteen articles provide an overview of physical education programs in other nations, specifically Nigeria, the former Soviet Union, New Guinea, China, Denmark, Federal Republic of Germany, and Bahrain, and offer cross-cultural perspectives.

Davenport J, editor: The normal schools: exploring our heritage, JOPERD 65(3):25–56, 1994.

A series of eight articles that describe the normal schools of the 1800s, which provided professional education for individuals seeking to enter the field.

Gerber EW: Innovators and institutions in physical education, Philadelphia, 1972, Lea & Febiger.

The contributions of outstanding leaders and institutions in American and European physical education are described in this comprehensive text.

Massengale JD and Swanson RA, editors: The history of exercise and sport science, Champaign, Ill., 1997, Human Kinetics.

This books presents in depth the historical development of the exercise and sport sciences, including sport pedagogy, adapted physical activity, sport sociology, sport history, philosophy of sport, motor behavior, sport and exercise psychology, biomechanics, and exercise physiology.

Mechikoff R and Estes S: A history and philosophy of sport and physical education, ed 2, Dubuque, Iowa, 1988, McGraw-Hill.

Provides an overview of significant philosophies and traces the development of sport and physical education from the time of the ancient Greeks to the present day, including the history of the modern Olympics.

Polidoro JR and Simri U: The Games of 676 B.C.: A visit to the centenary of the ancient Olympic games, JOPERD 67(5):41 45.

A interesting and insightful review of the nature and events of the Olympic Games during 676 B.C.

Remley ML, editor: Women in the Olympics: challenge and change, JOPERD 67(5):25–40, 1996.

These four articles provide a perspective on women in the Olympics. The articles include the involvement of women on the International Olympic Committee, the psychological issues and concerns of elite women athletes, the use of biomechanics to enhance performance, and gains in women's participation at the Games.

Wiggins, DK, editor: Sport in America: from wicked amusement to national obsession, Champaign, Ill., 1996, Human Kinetics.

This series of essays focus on the evolution of American sport, including the relationship between urbanization and sport, the participation in sport by different racial and ethnic groups, and the influence of consumerism on sport.

CHAPTER 6

Biomechanical Foundations of Physical Education and Sport

Instructional Objectives and Competencies to be Achieved:

After reading this chapter the student should be able to—

- Define the term biomechanics and indicate its relationship to kinesiology.
- Identify the value of biomechanics for the physical education and sport professional.
- Understand some of the terminology associated with the subdiscipline of biomechanics.
- Explain the meaning of mechanical principles and concepts that relate to stability, motion, leverage, and force. Illustrate the application of these principles to physical skills and sport techniques.
- Describe some of the techniques used to analyze motion.

Understanding the factors that govern human movement is essential for physical education and sport professionals. Throughout history individuals have been interested in optimizing their physical performance. During prehistoric times, when survival depended on physical skills, individuals sought to improve their physical prowess to stay alive. Today physical abilities are not as essential to survival. However, the interest in physical fitness and physical activities is at an all-time high in our society, and individuals are interested in enhancing their physical skills.

Physical educators and sport leaders are concerned with helping individuals to learn how to move efficiently and effectively. In elementary physical education classes, the teacher is concerned with helping students learn fundamental motor skills such as throwing and running, which provide a foundation for learning more advanced sport skills. In competitive athletics, where the difference between winning and losing may be one hundredth of a second or a fraction of a centimeter, a coach may use scientific methods such as high-speed photography and computer simulation to fine-tune an athlete's form. The weekend golfer, seeking to break par, requests the assistance of the golf pro to eliminate a troublesome slice from his or her swing. The golf pro may then

GETTING CONNECTED

Biomechanics Magazine specializes in lower extremity movement. The current issue, back issues, and special issues are located at this site.

> Site: http://www.biomech.com/

Biomechanics World Wide is a large site with links to a broad range of topics, including biomechanic journals, research, societies, and career opportunities.

> Site: http://www.pcr.ualberta.ca/biomechanics/

Exploratory Activities in the Health Sciences for children includes many activities that use principles from biomechanics.

> Site: http://www.exploratorium.edu/sports/index.html

videotape the golfer's performance to determine the source of error and to illustrate to the golfer the needed changes. The athletic trainer rehabilitating an athlete recovering from shoulder surgery uses knowledge of the range of motion of this joint to help develop an effective rehabilitation program. The adapted physical educator analyzes the gait of a child with cerebral palsy in order to prescribe physical activities to improve it. The exercise instructor closely monitors a client working on a Nautilus machine to ensure the exercise is being performed properly through the range of motion. These examples show how physical education and sport professionals use the scientific knowledge of human motion from the realms of kinesiology and biomechanics to help individuals move efficiently and effectively.

BIOMECHANICS AND KINESIOLOGY

The study of human movement is the focus of kinesiology and biomechanics. *Kinesiology* is the scientific study of human motion. The term kinesiology is derived from the Greek *kinesi,* meaning motion. The field of kinesiology is concerned with the anatomical and physiological elements that carry out movements—specifically bones, tissues, muscles, and nerves. To understand human motion fully, one needs an understanding of body movement, or kinesiology.

Kinesiology focuses on the anatomical and musculoskeletal analysis of human movement. It involves the study of the skeletal framework, the structure of muscles and their functions, the action of the joints, and the neuromuscular basis of movement. Kinesiology helps us appreciate the intricacies and wonder of human motion. Luttgens and Hamilton[1] write,

> One who gives it any thought whatever cannot help being impressed not only by the beauty of human motion but also by its apparently infinite possibilities, its meaningfulness, its orderliness, its adaptability to the surrounding environment. Nothing is haphazard; nothing is left to chance. Every study that participates in the movement of the body does so according to physical and physiological principles.

Kinesiology helps us see human motion through new eyes and gain a greater appreciation for human movement.

Students of physical education and sport study kinesiology in order to learn how to improve performance by analyzing the movements of the body and applying the principles of movement to their work. Luttgens and Hamilton[1] identify three important purposes for the study of kinesiology by students in the field of physical education and sport. Professionals in the field of physical education and sport can use their knowledge of kinesiology to help the people with whom they work perform with optimum safety, effectiveness, and efficiency. Safety is of paramount concern for all physical education and sport professionals. We design and conduct movement experiences for participants in our programs so that participants avoid doing harm to their body. Professionals and participants work together to set goals for effective performance. Typically, the effectiveness of a performance is judged by success or failure in meeting those goals. Our programs should be designed to enable our participants to achieve their goals. Professionals and participants strive to achieve their stated goals as efficiently as possible—that is, with the least expenditure of effort. Thus, according to Luttgens and Hamilton, safety, effectiveness, and efficiency are the underlying aims of using kinesiology in physical education and sport.[1]

Kinesiology helps prepare physical education and sport professionals to teach fundamental motor skills and specialized sport skills to people of all ages, as a means of optimizing performance. Kinesiology offers professionals a background from which to evaluate exercises and activities and how they effect the body. Physical education and sport professionals involved in rehabilitation, such as athletic trainers, and professionals working with individuals with disabilities, use their knowledge of kinesiology to help restore lost function and/or assist individuals to adapt their movements to maximize their potential.

It should be noted that the term kinesiology is often used in a broad sense to mean the study of human movement from the perspective of both the arts and sciences. Today, kinesiology is used as a broad umbrella term to encompass the entire discipline of what has traditionally been called physical education.

Biomechanics, as a subdiscipline of physical education and sport, focuses on the application of the scientific principles of mechanical physics to understand movements and actions of human bodies and sport implements (e.g., a tennis racquet). The term biomechanics can be better understood by examining the derivation of the word. *Bio* is from

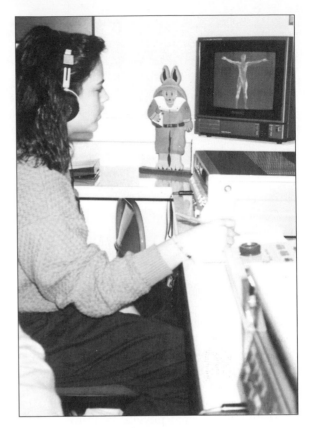

Kinesiology is concerned with the anatomical basis of movement. This student is using a self-paced instructional module to review anatomy.

Greek and refers to life or living things and *mechanics* refers to the field of Newtonian physics and the forces that act on bodies in motion. Biomechanists study how various forces affect human motion and how movements can be improved.

Kinesiology and biomechanics are integrally related. An understanding of how the body moves, including the function and actions of the joints, muscles, and bony structure, is essential to the understanding of biomechanics. In order to effectively study the influences of forces on motion—biomechanics—one must be knowledgeable about the actions of the joints and the muscles that cause these forces; this is the realm of kinesiology. Both kinesiology and biomechanics are fundamental to understanding human movement and to helping individuals attain their fullest potential.

Growth and Use of Biomechanics

The principles of biomechanics can be applied in many fields of study including biology, physiology, engineering, aerospace engineering, physical and occupational therapy, and medicine. Some physical education practitioners who would utilize this specialty include athletic trainers, coaches, teachers, and exercise physiologists. Until recently specialization in the study of biomechanics in the United States has been very limited, whereas in other countries this has long been a popular and accepted field of study. For example, Israel, England, Switzerland, Germany, and Russia have had curriculums for physical education biomechanists for some time. Russia has many specialists in biomechanics and uses this field of study in a manner that has practical application to specific kinds of sport such as volleyball and track and field. In the United States until recently the emphasis has been on theory. In the last two decades the emphasis has changed to reflect a more practical approach.

For example, at the 1996 Olympic Games in Atlanta, biomechanists studied the performance of athletes in 10 sports, including track and field, tennis, softball, and gymnastics. High-speed cameras, capable of up to 200 frames per second, recorded the athletes' movements. The cameras shot athletes from two or more angles, allowing a detailed portrait of the athletes in motion. Specialized software translated the films into computerized images and data. Computerized human figures allow the athletes' movements to be viewed with great precision in three dimensions. Statistical analyses yielded further insights. Working together, biomechanists and coaches can determine what adjustments can be made in the movements of elite athletes to improve their future performances. Even tiny improvements can be the difference between a silver and a gold medal, between personal glory and defeat. Biomechanical analyses are also helpful in reducing injuries and increasing safety.

In recent years several international conferences have been held on the subject of biomechanics, thus affording the opportunity for the mutual exchange of research findings and ideas. These meetings have been attended by a variety of specialists including physiologists, engineers, biomechanists, computer specialists, and rehabilitation experts. In the 1970s the International Society of Biomechanics and the American Society of Biomechanics were created, thus helping to ensure a further exchange of ideas in the future. The Kinesiology Academy of the National Association for Sport and Physical Education, a subdivision of AAHPERD, also provides a forum for the discussion of both biomechanics and kinesiology. The expansion of the knowledge and growth of interest in the field of sport biomechanists led to the formation of the International Society of Biomechanics in Sport in 1982.

The Olympic Training Centers

The U.S. Olympic Committee (USOC) operates Olympic Training Centers (OTC) in Colorado Springs, Colorado, Lake Placid, New York, and Chula Vista, California. There is also an Olympic Education Center in Marquette, Michigan, at Northern Michigan University. More than 25,000 athletes utilize these centers each year to prepare for competition. The USOC provides athletes with free room and board, use of the training facilities, sports medicine care, and sport science testing and analysis. At the OTC in Colorado Springs, the new Sports Medicine and Sport Science building offers athletes and coaches access to state-of-the-art care and technology. The sports medicine area includes rehabilitation training areas, vision clinic, and nutrition lab. The sport science center includes labs for strength and power testing, biomechanics, and psychology. Sport scientists, including biomechanists, work with athletes and coaches to improve performances.

Sport Scientist: A Day in the Life profiles Jeff Broker, a sport biomechanist in the Sport Science and Technology division at the OTC in Colorado Springs.[2] Broker works on the development of biomechanics programs for cycling, rowing,

The U.S. Olympic Training Center in Colorado Springs, Colorado.

archery, ski jumping, and weight lifting. Distance running, canoe/kayak, volleyball, and water polo have also been among his responsibilities. In working on these projects, he is involved in testing athletes at the camp, data analysis, computer simulation, library research, and writing. For the weight-lifting project, he and his support staff are studying the forces, motion, and detailed mechanics of different Olympic lifts. Related studies are exploring the use of power lifting as a strength and conditioning activity for power-oriented events such as sprinting, jumping, wrestling, and judo. He is also working on projects to expedite the measurement of aerodynamic forces in such sports as cycling, luge, ski jumping, speed skating, downhill skiing, and bobsled. The design of an instrumented rowing ergometer to help rowers train more effectively is assisted by reviewing the on-water data collected by the Rowing Data Acquisition System (RDAS). This data will also be used by

the head coach of the U.S. Men's Team to refine the team's technique as it enters the final phase of preparation for the Olympics. These and a multitude of ongoing projects create a very full day for this sport biomechanist. For qualified students interested in biomechanics and other sport sciences, there are internships available at the OTC.

Reasons for Studying Biomechanics

The emergence of biomechanics as a viable subdiscipline of physical education and sport is now recognized. As a result of reading this chapter, prospective professionals will have a better understanding of the parameters of this field of study and will recognize the value it has for them in future careers. In some cases perhaps it will motivate further study and specialization in this field of endeavor.

Many professionals can profit from the study of biomechanics. To be effective teachers and masters of their trade, physical educators and sport professionals should have an understanding of the principles of biomechanics. Knowledge of biomechanics will provide the professional with a better understanding of the human body and the various internal and external forces that affect human movement, as well as the forces that act on object motion. This in turn will enable professionals to be better instructors and coaches of the many physical activities and skills within physical education and sport.

Coaches who want to be expert in their field need a sound foundation in the area of biomechanics. Biomechanics offers important scientific knowledge that can improve performance, and the best coaches are taking advantage of this knowledge. Coaches of athletes today who are involved in many areas of high school, college, and Olympic sport find competition very intense. Therefore, coaches of athletes who wish to excel must use all the knowledge and the best techniques available. Biomechanics can be used to improve sport techniques and equipment, thus enhancing athletes' performance while assuring their safety.

Biomechanics is often at the forefront of changes in technique and technology. In the late 1960s and early 1970s, our understanding of swimming changed and new techniques emerged as elite coaches and biomechanists worked together. Coach James Counsilman, author of *The Science of Swimming,* worked with biomechanists to study the forces involved in propulsion in swimming.[3] In 1971, Brown and Counsilman filmed swimmers wearing lights on their hands as they swam in a darkened pool. This allowed the pattern of the swimmers' hands and feet to be identified and their actions carefully studied. It was found that the traditional technique of the arm pull based on drag forces for propulsion was not as efficient as an arm pull technique that created lift forces.[4] Counsilman's continued work in this area, along with that of other coaches and researchers, soon revolutionized the sport of swimming.

Innovations by athletes have also advanced biomechanics research. Athletes have created new techniques that have led to higher levels of performance in, for example, high jumping and tennis. Until the late 1960s, high jumpers approached the bar from an angle, thrust an arm and a leg up and over, then executed a kick, and the body "rolled" over the bar. In 1968 high-jumper Dick Fosbury, utilizing his unorthodox flop style of jumping, won the Gold Medal at the Olympic Games in Mexico. The "Fosbury Flop" style of jumping used a curved approach to the bar, with the jumper going over backward in a twisting lay-back of the body. Within 10 years, the traditional, long-used roll style of jumping was replaced by the flop style and records soared to new heights. As a young tennis player, Chris Evert used a two-handed backhand drive to return the ball over the net. Now it is common to see players use this stroke, which gives greater control and speed than the traditional one-handed backhand stroke.

Some other professionals within the field of physical education and sport who use the principles of biomechanics to improve an individual's movements and skill performance are adapted physical educators, athletic trainers, and exercise leaders. Knowledge of kinesiology and biomechanics helps these professionals design and conduct programs to enhance individual movement skills.

There are many specialized areas of study within biomechanics. Developmental biomechanics focuses on studying movement patterns and how they change across the lifespan, from infancy to old age and with people with disabilities. Especially with the aged, an understanding of the biomechanical principles involved in activities of daily living, such as walking, climbing stairs, lifting, and carrying, is important in designing activities to enable individuals to remain independent and able to care for their needs.

The biomechanics of exercise is another specialized area of study. Exercise should be based on both physiological and biomechanical principles. An understanding of the biomechanics of exercise can help maximize the benefits of exercise and reduce the chances of injury. Physical educators and sport leaders can use biomechanical principles of exercise to make sure individuals are performing the exercise correctly and achieving maximum benefits.

Rehabilitation biomechanics is applied to the study of the movement patterns of people who are injured or who have a disability. This helps professionals understand how the injury or disability has altered the "normal" movement pattern of individuals. This information is then used to design programs to help individuals move optimally within their constraints and to restore normal function when possible.

Equipment design is a growing area of biomechanics. Changes in equipment can lead to dramatic increases in performance. The speedskating event at the 1998 Nagano Olympics served as a showcase for new technology: the clap skate. The Dutch-invented clap skate, with its hinged blade, redefined record times. With conventional skates, the skater uses the quadriceps, not the calf muscles, and pushes through the back side of the skate. The clap skates use a hinge-and-spring mechanism to attach the front of the skate boot to the blade. The heel is not attached to the blade; thus when the foot is raised above the ice, the blade snaps back to the heel, making the characteristic clapping noise. The clap skate allows the skater to use his/her calf muscles, making the push more powerful. The blade also remains on the ice for a longer time, allowing for a longer stride and greater speed. Speedskaters also wore tight skin suits with tight hoods to reduce drag. On their heads and legs they wore silicone strips, costing only $2.50, to reduce further the effects of drag and thereby increase their speed.

Biomechanists working in the area of equipment design have also contributed to great changes in sport techniques, higher levels of performance, reduction of injury, and increased safety. The design of running shoes has changed radically since the early 1970s. More cushioning, greater attention given to injury prevention, establishment of greater variety of sizes, and designs to fit specific purposes (e.g., running, cross training, basketball, court shoes, etc.) are reflected in athletes shoes today. Athletic shoes are designed today to accommodate users' special needs, such as pronation, and to enhance comfort and performance. Greater attention has also been given to the needs of women. The sport goods industry, since the mid-1980s, is building equipment, such as skis or running shoes, specifically for women as opposed to simply manufacturing a scaled-down version of the men's models. An understanding of the way the body works, knowledge of the demands of the sport, and the ability to apply biomechanical principles is important in equipment design.

The application of biomechanical principles is not limited to the realm of physical education and sport. Biomechanists working in industry use this information to ensure safe working conditions and efficient performance from the workers. In medicine, knowledge from biomechanics can be used by orthopedists to evaluate how pathological conditions affect movement or to assess the suitability of prosthetic devices for patients. As the field of biomechanics continues to expand, its contribution to our understanding of human movement will become even more significant.

Major Areas of Study

Biomechanics is concerned with two major areas of study. The first area is biological in nature as implied in the term biomechanics. Motion or movement involves biological aspects of the human body, including the skeletal and muscular systems. For example, movement occurs as a result of such things as force applied to bones, contraction of muscles, and bones acting as levers. Bones, muscles, and nerves work together in producing motion. It is not possible to understand motor skill development without first knowing about biological aspects underlying human movement such as joint action, anatomical structures, and muscular forces.

The second major area of study in biomechanics relates to mechanics. This area of study is important because it utilizes the laws and principles of Newtonian physics and applies them to human motion and movement. Biomechanics is also concerned with object motion. The study of mechanics includes *statics,* or the study of factors relating to nonmoving systems or those characterized by steady motion (e.g., the center of gravity in positions of balance). It also includes *dynamics,* or the study of mechanical factors that relate to systems in motion. In turn, dynamics can involve a *kinematic* or *kinetic* approach. Kinematics is concerned with the study of time and space factors in motion such as velocity and acceleration, whereas kinetics is involved with forces such as gravity and muscles that act on a system.

Research in biomechanics is concerned with studying movement and factors that influence performance. The kinds of questions that may be studied are listed below:

- How do running motions change as children develop?
- How do forces summate to produce maximum power in the tennis serve?
- What are the movement patterns of world-class hurdlers?
- How can athletic shoes be designed to reduce injuries on artificial turf?
- What is the wrist action of elite wheelchair marathon athletes?
- What is the optimal design of the javelin?
- What are the critical performance elements of throwing? Of various fundamental motor skills? Of various sport skills? What are the common errors associated with the performance of these skills and how can they best be remediated? How do the mechanics of these fundamental motor skills change with age?
- Which techniques are best for increasing the range of motion after reconstructive surgery of the shoulder?
- What is the best body position for swimming the butterfly stroke?
- Is a specific brand of rowing ergometer safe to use? Can individuals of all fitness levels effectively use this piece of fitness equipment? Are the benefits claimed by the manufacturer for its use accurate?

These are only a few of the questions that can be addressed through biomechanical research

techniques. In answering these questions, researchers measure such factors as joint angles and muscle activity, force production, and linear and angular acceleration. The next section presents selected biomechanical terms.

SELECTED BIOMECHANICAL TERMS RELATING TO HUMAN MOTION

The field of biomechanics has a specialized scientific vocabulary that describes the relationship between force and motion. As previously defined, kinematics is concerned with understanding the spatial and temporal characteristics of human movement, that is, the direction of the motion and the time involved in executing the motion. Important terms related to kinematics include *velocity, acceleration, angular velocity, angular acceleration,* and *linear* and *angular motions.* Kinetics is concerned with the forces that cause, modify, or inhibit motion. Terms related to kinetics are *mass, force, pressure, gravity, friction, work, power, energy,* and *torque.*

Velocity refers to the speed and direction of a body and involves the change of position of a body per unit of time. Because bodies in motion are continually changing position, the degree to which the body's position changes within a definite time span is measured to determine its velocity. For example, the velocity of a baseball from the time it leaves the pitcher's hand to the time it arrives in the catcher's glove can be measured in this manner.

Acceleration refers to the change in velocity involving speed or direction of a moving body. An individual playing basketball, for example, can add positive acceleration when dribbling toward the basket on a fast break, or the player can change pace and slow down (decelerate) to permit another player to screen for him or her.

Angular velocity is the angle that is rotated in a given unit of time. *Angular acceleration* refers to the change of angular velocity for a unit of time. For example, when a bowling ball is rolled down a lane, its angular velocity can be computed mathematically in terms of revolutions per second. The angular acceleration, on the other hand, occurs after the bowling ball is released and the ball actually starts rolling, instead of sliding, which occurs immediately on release.

The relationship between *linear* and *angular motions* of body parts should be understood. Northrip, Logan, and McKinney[5] cite the following examples: (1) a throwing motion involves angular velocity of the wrist joint, which helps to determine throwing speed; (2) kicking a football involves the angular velocity of the kicker's ankle joint, which helps to determine kicking performance. The final linear velocity that results in both cases is achieved as the sum of many angular motions at the body joints. Because most body movements are rotational movements at the body's joints, to achieve the best results in skill performance it is necessary to integrate linear and angular motions.

Mass is the amount of matter possessed by an object. Mass is a measure of the object's inertia, that is, the resistance of the object to efforts made to move it and, once the object has begun to move, resistance to changing its motion. The mass of an object influences the amount of force needed to produce acceleration. The greater the mass, the larger the force needed. For example, in track and field a larger force would be needed to

produce an acceleration of a 16-pound shot than a 12-pound shot.

Force is any action that changes or tends to change the motion of an object. Forces have both a magnitude (i.e., size) and a direction. Forces on the body can occur internally, such as when a muscle contracts and exerts forces on the bone to which it is attached. External forces such as gravity also can act on the body.

Pressure refers to the ratio of force to the area over which the force is applied. For example, 16-ounce boxing gloves will distribute a given force over a larger surface area than 12-ounce boxing gloves, thus reducing pressure. In this case, distributing the pressure will ensure less chance of injury from blows when the 16-ounce gloves are used.

Gravity is a natural force that pulls all objects toward the center of the earth. An important feature of gravitational pull is that it always occurs through the center of weight or mass of an object. In the human body, the center of weight is known as the *center of gravity*. The center of gravity is the point at which all of the body's mass seems to be located and the point about which an object would balance. The center of gravity is constantly changing during movement. It can be either within or outside the body, depending on the shape of the body. It always shifts in the direction of movement or the additional weight. When human beings stand erect with their hands at their sides, the center of gravity is located at the level of the hips. Athletes can use their knowledge about the center of gravity to better their skills. For example, the basketball player during a jump ball swings both arms forward and upward to assist in gaining height. Once in the air, the player allows one arm to drop to his or her side and strives to get maximum reach with the other arm. By dropping one arm to the side the player can reach farther beyond the center of gravity than with two arms overhead.

Friction is a force that occurs when surfaces come in contact and results from the sliding of one surface on the other. Friction can have negative or positive results. For example, it can lead to

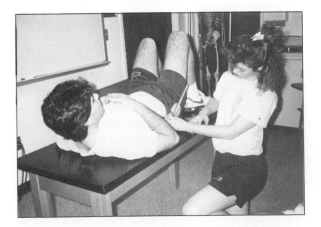

Students use goniometry to measure joint angles.

loss of motion and thus, under certain circumstances, produce negative results. On the other hand, it has positive results in the sport of baseball when pine tar or a glove is used to increase the friction between the hands and the bat and thus ensure better control of the bat.

Work refers to the force that is applied to a body through a distance and in the direction of the force. An individual who bench presses 240 pounds through 2 feet is doing work. The direction of the motion is the same as the direction of the force, and therefore the total amount of work is figured by multiplying 240 pounds by 2 feet, which equals 480 foot-pounds of work for each repetition.

Power is the amount of work accomplished in one unit of time. For example, a person performs a certain task, such as running, and exerts a certain amount of horsepower to perform the task in a given amount of time. In order to exert twice as much horsepower, the runner would have to perform the same task and accomplish the same amount of work (i.e., run the same distance) in half the amount of time.

Energy relates to the capacity of a body to perform work. Two types of energy used in biomechanics are (1) kinetic energy, the energy a body has because it is moving (such as a skier whose weight and velocity determine kinetic energy); and (2) potential energy, the energy that accrues as a result of the position that a body occupies relative to the earth's surface. The weight of the body and its height above the surface are used to determine potential energy. For example, a diver at the peak of a dive has the capacity to do work because of his or her position relative to the earth's surface. When he or she falls toward the water, the weight of the body does work equal to its magnitude times the distance the body moves in the direction of force.

Torque represents a twisting, turning, or rotary force related to the production of angular acceleration and is contrasted with the force necessary to produce linear acceleration. Torque can also be produced as a result of the rotation of a body or body part. For example, supination and pronation of the radioulnar joint can produce torque. The production of torque is essential in gymnastics because of the many movements required in routines that use apparatus such as the high bar, parallel bars, uneven parallel bars, and rings.

MECHANICAL PRINCIPLES AND CONCEPTS RELATED TO MOVEMENT

Movements are governed by mechanical principles. Biomechanists use these principles in the analysis of movement. To illustrate, some mechanical principles, selected principles and concepts relating to stability, motion, leverage, and force are presented in this section.

Stability

Stability is an important factor in all movement skills. It is related to equilibrium and balance. When all the forces acting on the body are counterbalanced by equal and opposite forces so that the sum of the forces equals zero, equilibrium is maintained. A state of equilibrium occurs when the body's center of gravity is over its base of support and the line of gravity (a line drawn from the center of the gravity to the center of the earth) falls within the base. The base of support of the body is the area outlined when all the points in contact with the ground are connected. The greater the body surface in contact with the ground, the larger the base of support. Thus, a sitting position has a larger base of support than a standing position. A stance that places four points of the body in contact with the ground, rather than just two points as in standing, typically increases the base of support.

Stability is the body's ability to return to a position of equilibrium after it has been displaced. The greater the body's stability, the more difficult it is to affect its equilibrium.

Static equilibrium is when the center of gravity is in a stable position (e.g., when one is sitting or performing a handstand in gymnastics). Dynamic equilibrium is a state in which the center of gravity is in motion (e.g., when one is running or performing a cartwheel in gymnastics). In sport and movement terminology, stability is often referred to as balance. The body's ability to maintain stability or balance is governed by three primary principles.

Principle

The lower the center of gravity is to the base of support, the greater the stability. When performing activities that require stability, individuals should lower their center of gravity. In running, for example, individuals can stop more efficiently and quickly if they bend their knees, thereby lowering the center of gravity, and place their feet in a forward stride position. Other examples include a wrestler taking a semi-crouched position and the football lineman assuming a three-point stance.

Principle

The nearer the center of gravity is to center of the base of support, the more stable the body. When the center of gravity extends beyond the boundaries of the base of support, balance is lost. Keeping the body's weight centered over the base of support helps promote stability. However, in activities where the objective is to move quickly in one direction, shifting the weight in the direction of the movement can aid performance. For example, in starting a sprint race, the runners will lean forward to get out of the starting blocks quickly.

Some activities such as walking on a balance beam require a small base of support. It is very easy to lose one's balance in these types of activities. When balance is lost while performing on the balance beam, the arm or leg on the opposite side from which the person is leaning is raised to shift the center of gravity back toward the base of support.

Principle

Stability can be increased by widening the base of support. Widening the base of support helps achieve greater stability. When standing, for example, spreading the feet in the direction of

movement adds stability. For activities where a stance is required, using both hands and feet will create the widest base.

To increase stability in situations when receiving or applying force, the direction of the force must be considered. When receiving either a fast-moving object or a heavy force, widen the base of support in the direction from which the force is coming. When applying a force, widen the base in the direction from which the force is to be applied.

Motion

Motion implies movement, which consists of destroying or upsetting the equilibrium of the body. A force is required to start a body in motion, to slow it down, to stop it, to change the direction of its motion, or to make it move faster. Everything that moves is governed by the laws of motion formulated by Sir Isaac Newton. These laws describe how things move and make it possible to predict the motion of an object.

Newton's first law

The law of inertia states that a body at rest will remain at rest and a body in motion will remain in motion at the same speed and in the same direction unless acted on by some outside force.

For a movement to occur a force must act on a body sufficiently to overcome that object's inertia. If the applied force is less than the resistance offered by the object, motion will not occur.

Concepts
1. Once an object is in motion it will take less force to maintain its speed and direction (i.e., momentum). For example, it takes an individual more effort to start pedaling a bicycle to get it underway than it does to maintain speed once the bicycle is moving.
2. The heavier the object and the faster it is moving, the more the force that is required to overcome its moving inertia or to absorb its momentum. In football an opponent will have to exert more force to stop a massive, fast-moving lineman than he would to stop the lighter weight and slower-moving quarterback.

Newton's second law

The law of acceleration states that a change in velocity (acceleration) of an object is directly proportional to the force producing it and inversely proportional to its mass.

If two unequal forces are applied to objects of equal mass, the object that has the greater force applied will move faster. Conversely, if two equal forces are applied to objects of different masses, the lighter mass will travel at the faster speed.

For example, in shot putting the athlete who is stronger and thus able to expend more force will toss the 12-pound shot farther than an athlete who possesses less strength. Also, an athlete will find more force is needed to propel a 16-pound shot than a 12-pound shot.

Concepts

1. The heavier the object, the more force needed to speed it up (positive acceleration) or slow it down (negative acceleration).
2. An increase in speed is proportional to the amount of force that is applied; the greater the amount of force that is imparted to an object, the greater the speed with which that object will travel.
3. Momentum is a measure of both speed and mass. If the same amount of force is exerted for the same length of time on two bodies of different mass, greater acceleration will be produced in the lighter or less massive object. If the two objectives are propelled at the same speed, the heavier object will have greater momentum once inertia is overcome and will exert a greater force than the lighter object on something that it contacts.

Newton's third law

The law of action and reaction states that for every action there is an equal and opposite reaction.

Bouncing on a trampoline or springing from a diving board are examples of the law of action and reaction. The more force one exerts on the downward bounce, the higher the bounce or spring into the air. The thrust against the water in swimming is another example of an equal and opposite reaction—the water pushes the swimmer forward with a force equal to the force exerted by the swimmer on the backward thrust of the strokes.

Concept. Whenever one object moves, another object moves too and in the opposite direction. When you push something, it pushes back; when you pull on something, it pulls back.

Linear and Rotary Motion

Motion is linear or rotary. The human body usually employs a combination of both. The rotary action of the legs to propel the body in a linear direction is an example.

Linear motion

Linear motion refers to movement in a straight line and from one point to another. In running, for example, the body should be kept on a straight line from start to finish. Also the feet and arm movements should be back and forth in straight lines rather than from side to side across the body.

Rotary motion

Rotary motion consists of movement of a body about a center of rotation, called the *axis*. In most human movements rotary motion is converted into linear motion. Rotary motion is increased when the radius of rotation is shortened. Conversely, rotary motion is decreased when the radius of the moving body is increased. Examples include tucking the head when performing tumbling stunts to increase the rotation of the body and holding the arms out when executing a turn on the toes on ice to slow the body.

Leverage

Efficient body movement is made possible through a system of levers. A lever is a mechanical device used to produce a turning motion about a fixed point, called an *axis*. A lever consists of a fulcrum (the center or axis of rotation), a force arm (the distance from the fulcrum to the point of application of force), and a weight or resistance arm (the distance from the fulcrum to the weight on which the force is acting). The bones of the body act as levers, the joints act as the fulcrums, and the

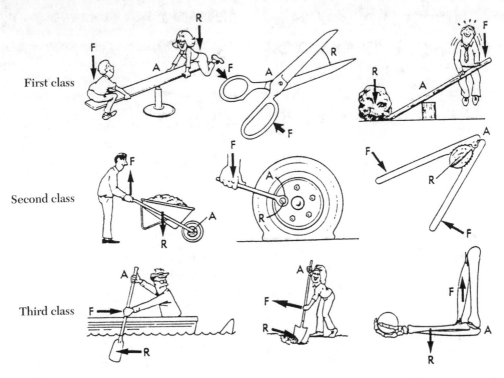

FIGURE 6-1   First-, second-, and third-class levers (A = axis, F = force, R = resistance).

force to move the bone or lever about the joint or fulcrum is produced by the contraction of the muscles.

Three types of levers are determined by the relationship of the fulcrum (axis), the weight, and the point of application of force. In a *first-class lever* the fulcrum is located between the weight and point of application of force. In a *second-class lever* the weight is between the fulcrum and the force. In a *third-class lever* the force is between the fulcrum and the weight. (See Fig. 6-1 above.)

Levers enable one to gain a mechanical advantage by producing either strength or speed. First-class levers may produce both strength and speed, unless the fulcrum is in the middle of the force and weight, which produces a balanced condition. Second-class levers produce force, and third-class levers favor speed. The movements of the body are produced mostly through third-class levers. In third-class levers, the point of application of the force (produced by the muscles), is located

between the fulcrum (the joint), and the resistance (the object to be moved).

The length of the force arm is the key to producing either force or speed. If great force is desired, the force arm should be as long as possible. If great speed is desired, the force arm should be shortened. The internal levers of the body cannot be controlled in regard to the length of the force arm. However, when using implements such as bats and racquets, long force arms would be created by holding the implement near the end, thereby producing greater force. If a person was interested in greater speed to swing a bat, he or she would "choke up" on the bat to reduce the force arm. When using an implement to produce greater force or speed, the size and the length of the implement must match the strength of the person who is handling the implement.

Concepts
1. Levers are used to gain a mechanical advantage by either producing speed or force.

2. Greater speed is produced by lengthening the resistance arm, and greater force is produced by lengthening the force arm.

Force

Force is the effect that one body has on another. It is invisible, but it is always present when motion occurs. It should be pointed out, however, that there can be force without motion. An example of a force in which no motion is evident is the push against a wall by a person. The wall does not move, although great force might be exerted. Another example occurs when two arm wrestlers are pushing against each other with equal force and their arms remain relatively motionless.

Teachers should be aware of the principles relating to the production, application, and absorption of force when they teach movement activities.

Production of force

Body force is produced by the actions of muscles. The stronger the muscles, the more force the body is capable of producing. However, the force of the muscle group or groups must be applied in the same direction and in proper sequence to realize the greatest force. In the high jump, for example, the body should be lowered on the last step before the jump. This lowering of the body will enable the jumper to contract the muscles of the thigh, which are the strongest of the body. The upward movement of the arms will give added force to the jump when coordinated with the upward push of the legs. It should be remembered that the principles of stability and the laws of motion must be observed in the performance of the high jump if the greatest height is to be attained.

Force also must be generated to propel objects. The same principles apply as mentioned above. In the swing of a softball bat the application of force is possible because of the production of force by different muscle groups in a coordinated manner. For maximum force the body should be rotated at the hips, shoulders, arms, and hands in a sequential order. The summation of these forces will produce the greatest momentum. A follow-through is necessary both to avoid jerky movements and to reduce the possibility of injury to the muscles or tendons.

Application of force

The force of an object is most effective when it is applied in the direction that the object is to travel. Many activities in sport involve the projection of the body or another type of object into the air. To project an object or the body forward most efficiently, the force should be applied through the center of the weight of the object and in a forward direction. To move the body upward, the body must be straight and all the force must be directed upward through the center of the body. The example of the high jump will illustrate this principle. Force from the legs must be applied through the center of the body if the greatest force is to be applied to the jump. Some of the force will be dissipated if the jumper leans to one side when pushing off from the ground.

In throwing an object the following three main factors are of concern: (1) the speed of the throw, (2) the distance of the throw, and (3) the direction that the object will travel.

The *speed* of the throw depends on the speed of the hand at the moment of release of the object. The speed of the arm can be increased by lengthening it to its fullest, rotating the body, shifting the weight properly, and taking a step in the direction of the throw. These movements must be done in a continuous motion to maintain momentum. If an implement such as a bat or paddle is used, it becomes an extension of the arm. Therefore the same principle applies. The implement should be held as close to the handle end as possible to create a long movement arm. This will enable the person to apply more force.

The *distance* of the throw will be affected by the pull of gravity and air resistance. The distance that an object will travel, therefore, will depend on the angle of release in addition to the force imparted to the throw. The pull of gravity and air resistance will affect objects thrown less if they are released at an angle of approximately 45 degrees. This represents a compromise between releasing an object

A dynamometer is used to measure strength.

at a large angle and having it remain in the air but not go very far because of wind resistance and releasing the object at a smaller angle where the pull of gravity will keep it from traveling very far.

The *direction* or accuracy of the throw depends on the point of release of the object. The release must be a point in the arc of the arm at which the object is tangent to the target. To better achieve the desired angle of release, the throwing arm should be moved in a flatter arc at the time of release. In making the overhand throw in softball, for example, the hand should travel in the straightest line possible toward the target, both on the backswing and the follow-through.

In addition to gravity and air resistance, the flight of thrown and batted objects is also affected by the spin of the object. The object will travel in the direction of the spin.

Absorption of force

Many instances occur when persons must receive or absorb force. Examples include absorbing the force of a thrown object, as in catching a football or softball; landing after a jump; and heading a soccer ball. The impact of the force should be gradually reduced, and it should be spread over as large an area as possible. Therefore when catching a ball, the arms should be extended to meet the ball. On contact, the hand and arms should "give" with the catch. When landing from a jump, the person should bend the hips, knees, and ankles to gradually reduce the kinetic energy of the jump, thereby reducing the momentum. The feet must also be spread slightly to create a large area of impact (base).

Concepts

1. The more muscles that are used, the greater the force that is produced (provided, of course, that they are the same sized muscles).

2. The more elasticity or stretch a muscle is capable of, the more force it can supply. Each working muscle should be stretched fully to produce the greatest force.

3. When objects are moved, the weight of the objects should be pushed or pulled through the center and in the direction that they are to be moved.

4. When heavy objects are moved or thrown, the force of the muscles should be used in a sequential manner. For example, the order in throwing should be trunk rotation, shoulder, upper arm, lower arm, hand, and fingers.

5. When body parts (arms and legs) or implements such as bats and paddles are used, they should be extended completely when making contact with an object to be propelled. This creates a long movement arm, thereby creating the greatest force; the implements should be gripped at the end.

6. When receiving or absorbing the force of a thrown object (as in catching a ball), a fall, or a kick, the largest possible area should be used to absorb the force. For example, the

student should use two hands to catch a hard-thrown ball; more area will be available to absorb the force of the ball.

7. The absorption of force should be spread out as long as possible by recoiling or "giving" at the joints involved in the movement.

• • •

To analyze an individual's motor performance, physical education and sport professionals need to be cognizant of the principles governing movement. Selected principles pertaining to stability, motion, leverage, and force were discussed in this section. Professionals are also concerned about such concepts as friction, aerodynamics, hydrodynamics, and ball spin and rebound in the evaluation of performance. An understanding of both biomechanics and kinesiology provides the professional with a foundation for understanding and analyzing human movement.

BIOMECHANICAL ANALYSIS

Various instruments and techniques are used by biomechanists to study and analyze motion. During the past 15 years improvements in instrumentation coupled with advances in computers and microchip technology have greatly assisted biomechanists in their endeavors. Additionally, the development of better and more creative methods of using these instruments has greatly enhanced the understanding of human movement and the ability to improve performance.[6] These tools include computers, anthropometry, timing devices, cinematography, videography, electrogoniometry, electromyography, dynamography, and telemetry. These tools, as well as visual observation, can be used to perform quantitative and qualitative analysis of human movement.

Instruments

Computers have become increasingly important in biomechanical research. Biomechanical analysis requires dealing with prodigious amounts of data. The use of the computer in dealing with such data

has become a necessity. Additionally, much of the instrumentation used in biomechanical research is linked to a computer. Much of the analysis of information can be performed on-line so that the results can be available almost instantly.

Computers can also be used to simulate movements. *Simulation* requires the use of mathematical formulas to develop models of a specific movement. Then, this computer model can be used to assist biomechanists in determining the effects of certain modifications in the movement or certain variables on performance. For example, simulation can address such questions as what is the effect of altering the takeoff position of a dive on the subsequent performance? Or, how does air resistance affect a skier's performance? This approach helps researchers determine how a performance can be improved. Comparisons of the optimal or ideal performance and an individual's actual performance are enhanced through the use of computer technology. The computer is used to generate graphic representations of the ideal performance and the actual performance. The drawing of the actual performance is compiled from analysis of the films of the performer. These graphic representations of the ideal performance and an individual's actual performance can then be compared. This helps to detect errors and identify strategies to improve performance. Computers offer biomechanists tremendous assistance in understanding human movements.

Cinematography is one of the basic tools employed in biomechanical research. Sophisticated movie cameras are used to film an individual's performance. These cameras film at thousands of frames per second (the old home movie cameras operate at 16 to 24 frames per second). These high speed cameras capture details of movements that may escape the unaided eye of the professional observing the performer's movements. As a result of cinematography, it is possible to film movement and capture such things as the speed, angle, range, and sequence of moving segments. Cinematography provides a permanent record that can be studied after the movement action takes place. Slow-motion and stop-action techniques aid in the study of the performance. From the film, graphic representations of the movement can be developed, either through hand drawing or through computer analysis. Completion of mathematical calculations based on information provided from the films is an essential part of movement analysis. This process is greatly speeded and simplified through the use of computers.

Stroboscopy is a photographic technique that also is used for the study of movement. This technique allows filming to take place against a darkened background, with light being flashed onto the subject being filmed. The total movement is recorded on a single frame of film as a sequence of images. For example, with this technique it is possible to take a picture of the total forehand stroke in tennis, which shows the path of the various body segments in the total execution of the stroke. This facilitates the analysis of the individual's movements. Using this technique, one person's execution of a movement skill (e.g., the forehand tennis stroke or the wrist action used) can be compared with that of another person or the ideal performance.

Videography is the use of video systems to record an individual's performance. Video systems consist of a video camera, recorder, and a playback unit. Unlike cinematography, video systems are relatively inexpensive, easy to use, and readily available to practitioners. The ability to directly play back what has been recorded allows for immediate viewing by the analyst and prompt feedback to the performer. Videography systems can be interfaced with computers to provide movement analysis. This is one of the most inexpensive high technology systems for the analysis of movement. Advances in technology have led to better quality cameras as well as sophisticated playback capabilities that yield greater clarity of still and stop-action images.

Anthropometry is concerned with the measurement of the human body. The length, width, diameter, circumference (girth), and surface area of the body and its segments are measured. Correct identification of anatomical landmarks is crucial to obtaining accurate measurements. Information about the structure of the human body is used to calculate the forces acting on the joints of the body and the forces produced by movement. Information about the structure of an individual's body is important in developing computer models of performance.

Timing devices or chronoscopes are used to record speeds of body movements and its parts. Some types of timing devices are stop watches, digital timers, counters, switch mats, photoelectric cells, and real-time computer clocks. The chronoscope is started at a preselected point in time, typically the initiation of a movement, and then stopped at a preselected time, such as the completion of a movement. The speed of movement is then calculated. Radar guns can also be used to provide instantaneous information about speed.

Electrogoniometry is a technique that can be used to provide information about the angles of the joint as part of a total motion pattern. Another term for an electrogoniometer is an elgon. A goniometer (see Chapter 7 for information about the use of goniometers to measure flexibility) is used in conjunction with an electrical device called a *potentiometer* to measure the degrees of movement at a joint. This information can be transferred directly to a computer, recording paper, or oscilloscope. For example, this instrument would permit the study of the knee-joint action when a particular skill, such as walking or running, is executed. It can also measure range of motion, angular velocity, and acceleration. Electrogoniometry may be particularly useful when combined with electromyography.

Electromyography (EMG) is used to measure the electrical activity produced by a muscle or muscle group. When properly processed, this measurement serves as an approximate indicator of the amount of force being developed by a muscle. This provides a means to observe the involvement of a particular muscle or muscle group in a movement. Surface electrodes are placed over the muscle or muscle group or fine wire electrodes are inserted into the muscle to be observed. Electrical impulses from muscle activity are then processed, recorded, and displayed on an oscilloscope, recording paper, or computer. EMG can be used to record the muscle activity associated with

Computers, video cameras, and other types of equipment are used to measure and evaluate human movement.

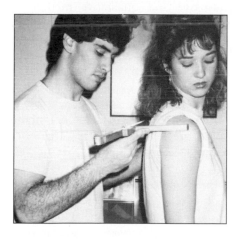

Anthropometry is the measurement of the human body. Various devices are used to provide information about the body and its segments.

a particular performance; when done during various periods of time, a record of progress can be made. Certain rhythms of muscle activity are associated with a performance. An athlete who is not performing well or is in a slump may display a different EMG rhythm than normal. This information can be used to assist the athlete to correct errors and regain the desired form. EMG is often used in conjunction with electrogoniometry. Researchers may also make recordings of brain wave activity using the electroencephalograph (EEG) concurrently with EMG activity; this provides the researcher with information on how the brain influences motor activity (this is studied within the realm of motor control).

Dynamography is a technique used to measure the forces produced during a movement. When measuring strength, particularly static strength, spring devices and cable tensiometers are used. Strain gauges are devices that are also used to measure strength. They have been incorporated into equipment such as athletic footwear insoles, bicycle pedals, and uneven parallel bars to measure the force produced by the performers using this equipment. Another device that is used to measure force is the force platform. Force platforms can be built into the floor to measure forces such as those associated with a foot striking the floor during walking. They can also be designed to

Light-emitting diodes facilitate the tracking and analysis of movements.

measure force production by athletes during sprint starts, pole vaulting, and gymnastics.

Telemetry involves the wireless recording of various aspects of movement. Telemetry systems consist of specialized electrodes that are attached to the individual and a transmitter that sends the information to the receiver that records it. Telemetry systems can be used to transmit information about heart rate or joint angles (electrogoniometry) during a performance. A distinct advantage of this technique is that it permits movement data to be recorded without encumbering the performer with wires and other equipment that can hinder performance.

Advances in computers and instrumentation as well as the manner in which they are used have contributed much to the understanding of human movement. For example, the intersection of biomechanics and biofeedback has stimulated the development of new devices to improve sport. Biofeedback is the provision of information about a physiological parameter, such as muscle tension, to an individual. The individual then uses this information to modify his or her response. The Swing Trainer and the Cycle Trainer developed by Innovative Sports Training can be used in rehabilitation or as an aid to improve performance. The Swing Trainer provides complete real-time, 3-D golf swing analysis and biofeedback training (Fig. 6-2). Using sensors that easily attach to the body, the swing trainer captures the full range of the golf swing and provides precise information on all aspects of the golf swing. Audio and visual biofeedback ensures optimal body positioning. When the individual is out of position, a tone alerts the individual, and a video displays the proper position. The Cycle Trainer works in a similar fashion. The Cycle Trainer measures critical orthopedic angles, body positions, pulse, and power output during cycling.

Analysis

Quantitative and qualitative methods can be used to analyze human movement. *Quantitative analysis* uses many of the techniques described previously to provide specific numerical information about the movement being studied. Specific information, for example, about the joint angles during movement, the force generated, and the speed of movement is provided. Quantitative analysis is used predominantly in research efforts and is increasingly incorporated as part of the overall training program of elite athletes to help them optimize their performance (e.g., biomechanists work with elite athletes at the U.S. Olympic Training Center at Colorado Springs, Colorado).

Qualitative analysis also provides important information about the movement being studied. Qualitative analysis relies most commonly on visual evaluation of the movement. The movement can be described in such terms as successful or unsuccessful or performed with difficulty or with ease. An individual's performance also can be compared with another individual's performance or against a standardized model. Videography, which can be used for quantitative analysis, can also be used effectively for qualitative analysis.

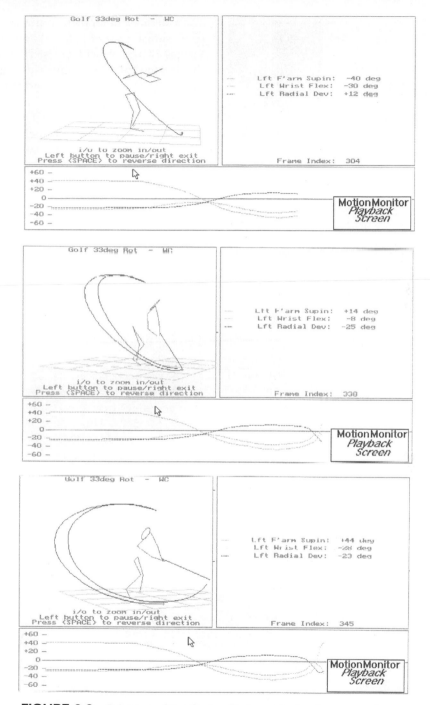

FIGURE 6-2   Printout of the Swing Trainer playback screen, showing three forearm and wrist angles for monitoring.

The Swing Trainer, developed by Innovative Sports Training, provides real-time, 3-D golf swing analysis.

Instead of using the videotape to calculate various kinematic and kinetic measures, the videotape of an individual's movement can be studied to identify performance errors and to determine effective corrections.

Qualitative analysis is most commonly used by practitioners. It offers practitioners who may not have access to sophisticated equipment nor have the background to employ advanced techniques a method to effectively analyze an individual's movements. Biomechanical analysis can be used by athletic trainers in designing a rehabilitation program, by physical educators for conducting an evaluation of fundamental motor skills, and by exercise leaders in ensuring that clients perform each exercise correctly.

Teachers and coaches can use biomechanical analysis to improve students' and athletes' performance of sport skills. Additionally, teachers and coaches are often faced with the task of evaluating several performers of diverse skill levels in a short period of time. The use of videotape and slow-motion/stop-action playback can be useful to the practitioner in assessing an individual's performance. Videotape equipment has become increasingly available in school and community settings.

If videotape equipment is not available, then the professional must rely directly on his or her observations of the individual's performance. Whether the professional is using videotape or directly observing the individual's performance, the professional should keep in mind relevant biomechanical principles, have a mental image of the ideal performance of the skill being observed, and thoroughly understand the nature of the skill being performed. As an observer, the professional should be objective and proceed in a systematic fashion.

Adrian and Cooper[7] and Brown[8] offer several suggestions to physical education and sport professionals using visual evaluation techniques to assess skill performance. These suggestions, which can be incorporated into the practitioners' observation plan, are listed below:

◆ Observe the skill from a correct vantage point. Being in the correct position is essential to observe the critical components of the skill. When possible, view the skill from at least two perspectives.

◆ Observe the individual perform the skill several times before offering suggestions for improvement. This will permit the identification of consistent performance problems that may not be evident during a single performance attempt.

◆ Use the whole-part-whole method for the observation. After observing the total movement, focus on the movement of the body parts (e.g., legs, trunk). Observe the sequencing and timing of these parts. Observe the range of motion and look for unnecessary or extraneous movements. Then, again observe the whole body and focus on the coordination and sequencing of the movements of various body parts with respect to each other.

◆ If the performer is using an implement such as a racquet, or imparting force to another object such as throwing a discus or kicking a ball, it is also important to focus on the action of the implement.

◆ The overall effectiveness of the movement should be evaluated.

◆ A performance checklist can be used to guide the observation and to ensure that critical performance elements are viewed and not overlooked.

Once the observation is completed, practitioners should identify the errors in performance and give the performer accurate and relevant feedback about his or her performance. (See Chapter 9 for a discussion of feedback.)

The analysis of movement requires practice and an understanding of the biomechanical principles as well as kinesiology. Both kinesiology and biomechanics offer practitioners valuable information to help them understand human movement and improve the performance of the individuals with whom they work.

The Future

Technology will continue to drive the advancement of knowledge. Adrian and Cooper state, "With today's sophisticated technology, we have been able to learn more about human movement in the past ten years than in any previous decade."[7] To answer the questions of the next decade, Adrian and Cooper assert that "we must use basic concepts about what is known to pose the questions of the future and create more effective, safe, and rewarding human movement."[7]

Adrian and Cooper state that mathematical modeling of the anatomical characteristics of individuals coupled with computer simulation techniques enables biomechanists to make predictions of performance as well as to develop new and advanced performance techniques. Expertise in mathematics, anatomy, physiology, physics, and computers is necessary to take advantage of these approaches. Data collected via the tools of cinematography, videography, dynamography, electrogoniometry, electromyography, and accelerometry form the foundation for modeling and are entered into the computer where the data are analyzed using various software packages. Simulations allow movements to be varied with respect to speed, timing, range of motion, and environment. Through simulations these changes in movement variables can be explored and determinations can

be made about the optimization of performance and its safety. Computer-assisted drawing and design programs can expedite the design of equipment.

Advances in the analysis of human movement continue to be made at a rapid pace. The increased availability of technology at a decreased cost will make sophisticated analyses readily available to teachers, coaches, athletic trainers, athletes, fitness participants, and practitioners. The use of multidisciplinary teams, composed of sport scientists from the various subdisciplines, will facilitate the integration of data from multiple sources, enhancing our comprehension and enabling physical education and sport professionals to work more effectively with students, athletes, and individuals of all ages seeking to move more efficiently and effectively. The integration of biomechanics with motor development can increase our understanding of movement across the lifespan and enable us to more readily design solutions to remediate problems and safely advance the motor performance of people of all ages and abilities.

Expert profiling and simulations advance the frontier of knowledge and lead to improvements in performance. The United States Olympic Committee Sports Science and Technology Committee has funded several projects, including simulations of bobsled runs and modeling and simulation of paddles and oar blades for rowing and canoeing.

World-wide databases make data available to interested researchers throughout the world. These databases allow for diagnosis of movement problems, profiling, and collaborative research ventures.

The World Wide Web offers a wealth of information to individuals interested in biomechanics. For example, one site—*Biomechanics World Wide* (see Getting Connected box)—offers links to profiles of different biomechanists, laboratories worldwide, and even a place to trade or sell equipment. Specialized areas of study are represented, including gait and locomotion, sport and exercise biomechanics, muscle, motor control, computer simulations, ergonomics, orthopedics, prosthetics, and biomedical engineering. Also included on the site is information on biomechanics societies, career opportunities, and professional journals. This site and other related sites offer access to current information and a venue to share ideas and stimulate collaborative endeavors as we move into the future.

SUMMARY

Understanding the factors that govern human movement is essential for physical education and sport professionals. Physical education and sport professionals are concerned with helping individuals optimize their movements. To accomplish this task they need to thoroughly understand the mechanical principles that regulate movement. The analysis of human movement and sport object movement using the principles of physics and mechanics is called biomechanics. In recent years the study of biomechanics has grown tremendously in the United States and is commonly recognized as a subdiscipline of physical education and sport. Additionally, in the United States a greater emphasis has been placed on practical applications as opposed to theoretical research.

Biomechanics is concerned with two major areas of study. The first area focuses on the anatomical aspects of movements while the second area concerns itself with the mechanical aspects of movement. Needless to say, these areas are closely related. Biomechanists have a specialized scientific vocabulary to describe their area of study. The terms *power, acceleration, velocity, mass, pressure, friction, work, energy, angular velocity* and *acceleration, torque,* and *gravity* are defined in this chapter. Selected biomechanical principles and concepts pertaining to stability, motion, leverage, and force are explained and illustrated.

Within the last 15 years improvements in instrumentation and its application have been numerous, which has greatly expanded the knowledge base. While the practitioner may not have access to much of the specialized equipment used by the biomechanist researcher, the practitioner can use available equipment such as videotape equipment or direct observation to analyze performance. Understanding the principles of biomechanics is essential in improving individuals' performance.

SELF-ASSESSMENT TESTS

These tests are designed to help you determine if you have mastered the materials and competencies presented in this chapter.

1. Write an essay of 250 words on the worth of biomechanical knowledge to the practitioner in physical education and sport. Write the essay from the perspective of a practitioner in a career that you are considering for the future, that is, teacher, coach, athletic trainer, exercise physiologist, or sports broadcaster.

2. Explain and illustrate the meaning of each of the following terms: power, acceleration, velocity, mass, pressure, friction, work, energy, torque, and center of gravity.

3. Using a sport with which you are familiar, illustrate principles and concepts relating to stability, motion, leverage, and force.

4. Using the information provided in the Getting Connected box, access *Biomechanics Magazine.* Select an article of interest and write a short summary of the article and its application to your future career.

5. Using the information provided in the Getting Connected box, access *Exploratory Activities in Health Sciences.* Find one activity that is of interest to you and write a short description of that activity to present to the class.

REFERENCES

1. Luttgens K and Hamilton N: Kinesiology, ed 9, Dubuque, Iowa, 1997, Brown & Benchmark.

2. Miner R: Sport scientist: a day in the life, Olympic Coach 6(2):10–13, 1996.

3. Counsilman JE: The science of swimming, Englewood Cliffs, N.J., 1968, Prentice Hall.

4. Brown RM and Counsilman JE: The role of lift in propelling swimmers. In J Cooper, editor, Biomechanics, Chicago, 1971, The Athletic Institute.

5. Northrip JW, Logan GA, and McKinney W: Introduction to biomechanical analysis of sport, ed 2, Dubuque, Iowa, 1979, William C. Brown.

6. Atwater AE: Kinesiology/biomechanics: perspectives and trends, Research Quarterly for Exercise and Sport 51:193-218, 1980.

7. Adrian MJ and Cooper JM: The biomechanics of human movement, Dubuque, Iowa, 1987, Benchmark Press.

8. Brown EW: Visual evaluation techniques for skill analysis, Journal of Physical Education, Recreation, and Dance 53(1):21-26, 1982.

SUGGESTED READINGS

Abendroth-Smith J, Kras J, and Strand B: Get aboard the B-BOAT (Biomechanically based observation and analysis for teachers), JOPERD 67(8):20–23, 1996.
  Practical strategies that teachers and other practitioners can use for biomechanical analysis.

Adrian M and Cooper J: Biomechanics of human movement, ed 2, Dubuque, Iowa, 1997, Brown & Benchmark.
  Basic biomechanical principles are explained, tools for movement analysis presented, and application of principles to development across the lifespan, exercise, sport, rehabilitation, occupational settings, and the arts described.

Carr G: Mechanics of sports: a practitioner's guide, Champaign, Ill., 1997, Human Kinetics.
  A practical approach to the analysis of mechanical concepts underlying sport performance is presented. This text provides the reader with information to guide the observation, analysis, and correction of sport techniques.

Gregor RJ, Broker JP, and Ryan M: Performance feedback and new advances in biomechanics. In RW Christina and HM Eckert, editors, Enhancing human performance in sport: new concepts and development, American Academy of Physical Education Papers No. 25:19–32, Champaign, Ill., 1992, Human Kinetics.
  Future trends and directions for research and practical applications are discussed.

Hay JG: The biomechanics of sports techniques, ed 4, Englewood Cliffs, N.J., 1995, Prentice Hall.
  Sport specific analysis and a discussion of techniques are presented for a multitude of sports.

Hay J: Reaction to performance feedback: advances in biomechanics. In RW Christina and HM Eckert, editors, Enhancing human performance in sport: new concepts and development, American Academy of Physical Education Papers No. 25: 33–37, Champaign, Ill., 1992, Human Kinetics.
  Addresses issues and presents challenges regarding future developments and directions for the field of sport biomechanics.

James R and Dufek JS: Movement observation: what to watch and why, Strategies 7(2):17–19, 1993.
  Practical guide to qualitative performance evaluation.

Knudson D: Biomechanics of the basketball jump shot—six key teaching points, JOPERD 64(2): 67–73, 1993.

Illustrates how biomechanical research can be effectively translated into teaching practice.

Kreighbaum EF and Smith MA, editors. Sports and fitness equipment design, Champaign, Ill., 1996, Human Kinetics.

Provides information about various factors that are taken into consideration during the design of equipment.

Luttgens K and Hamilton N: Kinesiology, ed 9, Dubuque, Iowa, 1997, Brown & Benchmark.

This text includes information on kinesiology, biomechanics, and application of principles and concepts to motor skills, including activities of daily living, fitness, and sport.

Miner R: Sport scientist: a day in the life, Olympic Coach 6(2):10–13, 1996.

Provides an overview of the responsibilities of a sport biomechanist during a day at the USOC Olympic Training Center in Colorado Springs.

Exercise Physiology and Fitness

Instructional Objectives and Competencies to be Achieved:

After reading this chapter the student should be able to—

♦ Define exercise physiology and understand the importance of exercise physiology to the practitioner.

♦ Understand concepts of health and motor-performance fitness.

♦ Understand and appreciate the role of exercise in achieving physical fitness.

♦ Explain the principles and guidelines for designing fitness programs.

♦ Use the FITT formula to design a fitness program.

♦ Identify and discuss contributors and deterrents to fitness.

Exercise physiology is the study of the body's responses and its adaptation to the stress of exercise. Exercise physiologists are concerned with investigating both the immediate (acute) and the long-term (chronic) effects of exercise on all aspects of body functioning. These effects include the responses of the muscular system, the action of the nervous system during physical activity, the adjustments of the respiratory system, and the dynamics of the cardiovascular system. Improving the body's response to exercise also is an important area of study. The effects of exercise are examined at different levels, ranging from the subcellular level to the systemic level. Describing and explaining the myriad of functional changes caused by exercise sessions of variable frequency, duration, and intensity is one major area of study for exercise physiologists.

The field of exercise physiology offers professionals a strong foundation of knowledge about the effects of exercise on the body. Professionals, whether teachers in a school or nonschool setting, coaches, fitness leaders employed in a commercial club, or exercise physiologists working in a corporate fitness setting or a hospital, must understand the body's responses to exercise. Knowledge of the principles governing different types of training programs and the guidelines to be followed in constructing an exercise prescription enables professionals to design programs to meet each individual's physical activity needs and goals.

Exercise physiology has become increasingly sophisticated. New research procedures and measurement techniques coupled with advances in equipment, computer technology, and other related disciplines such as biochemistry have

GETTING CONNECTED

Fitness Link—All the News that's Fit includes fitness information and links to other fitness sites on the Web, including nutrition, alternative healing, and body building.

      Site: http://www.fitnesslink.com/

Stretching and Flexibility contains an array of information on stretching and flexibility, including the physiology of stretching, different types of stretches, range of motion, and safety precautions.

      Site: http://www.cs.huji.ac.il/papers/rma/stretching_toc.html

PHYS Calculators allows individuals to calculate target heart rate, calories used for various activities, nutritional needs, body mass index, ideal weight, body fat percentage, and health risks.

      Site: http://www.phys.com/c_tools/02calculator/frm/uber_intro.html

contributed to rapid expansion of the knowledge base. While fitness and the elite performer long have been a key concern of the exercise physiologist, interest in recent years has encompassed virtually all aspects of human performance and people of all skill abilities and of all ages, from the very young to the elderly, including individuals with disabilities.

EXERCISE PHYSIOLOGY: AN OVERVIEW

Exercise physiology is one of the most rapidly growing fields of specialization in physical education and sport. Exercise physiology is the study of the effects of exercise on the body. Specifically, exercise physiology is concerned with the body's responses and adaptations to exercise, ranging from the system level to the subcellular level. These modifications can be short term, that is, lasting only for the duration of the activity, or long term, present as long as the activity is continued on a regular basis. Knowledge of exercise physiology is essential for professionals in physical education and sport.

As a subdiscipline, exercise physiology is one of the largest and most popular areas of study within the realm of physical education and sport. It has one of the richest traditions; interest in the effects of exercise on the body can be traced to ancient times. Today the depth and breadth of knowledge in exercise physiology is growing rapidly because of the proliferation of research, which is facilitated by increasingly sophisticated technology and by the widespread interest of professionals in this field.

Scope and Status of Exercise Physiology

Exercise physiology encompasses a broad range of topics. Examples of some areas of study are listed below:

◆ Effects of various exercise programs on the systems of the body, including circulatory, respiratory, nervous, skeletal, muscle, and endocrine systems.

◆ Relationship of energy metabolism to performance.

◆ Effectiveness of various training programs in promoting gains in specific components of fitness (e.g., effects of Nautilus training on strength).

◆ Effects of various environmental factors such as temperature, humidity, altitude, pollutants, and different environments (e.g., space or undersea) on physiological responses to exercise and performance.

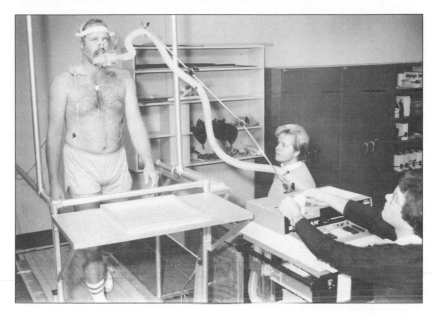

Exercise physiologists use sophisticated laboratory equipment to study the effects of exercise on various body systems.

- Effects of individual differences such as age, sex, initial level of fitness, or disability on fitness development and performance.
- Identification of factors that limit performance.
- Effectiveness of various rehabilitation programs on the recovery of injured athletes, on diseased individuals, and on individuals with disabilities.
- Effects of ergogenic aids such as drugs or music on performance.
- Health and therapeutic benefits to be accrued from engaging in appropriate levels of physical activity.
- Effects of nutrition on performance.

Exercise physiologists can work in many different settings. They can be involved in conducting research in a laboratory setting, teaching exercise science courses at a college or university, or engaged in a variety of clinical activities, such as guiding an elite athlete through a graded exercise test on a treadmill, directing a cardiac rehabilitation program at a hospital, or administering a worksite health promotion program.

Historically, performance and fitness are the two areas of research that have dominated exercise physiology. Much attention has been directed by researchers to the area of cardiovascular exercise physiology, which examines how oxygen is used by the cardiovascular system during exercise. Researchers have also focused a great deal of effort on the study of exercise metabolism, investigating the metabolic responses to exercise and training conducted under a variety of conditions.

In recent years, cardiac rehabilitation and exercise biochemistry are two areas that have become increasingly popular as major fields of study. *Cardiac rehabilitation* focuses on the assessment of cardiovascular functioning and on the determination of the effectiveness of various exercise programs in preventing cardiovascular disease and rehabilitating individuals suffering from the disease. *Exercise biochemistry* involves examination of the effects of exercise at the cellular level, specifically within the muscle cell. Two emerging areas of study within exercise physiology are exercise epidemiology and pediatric exercise science. *Exercise epidemiology* focuses on studying the relationship between physical activity and mortality. The increasing public health role for professionals in physical education and sport requires that we have a greater understanding of the relationship between physical activity, morbidity, and mortality. *Pediatric exercise science* encompasses the scientific study of the response of the body to exercise during childhood, including the effects of growth and maturation and differences in response between children and adults.

The application of knowledge from the realm of exercise physiology appears to focus predominantly on studying the effects of physical activity and exercise on the body. Two primary areas of application can be discerned: first, the enhancement of fitness, promotion of health, and prevention of disease; and second, the improvement and refinement of motor performance, especially in sport. The principles of exercise physiology can be used to improve and maintain both health-related fitness and motor skill-related fitness. As in the other subdisciplines of physical education and sport, there is a growing emphasis on research and application across the lifespan, from the very young to the aged.

Knowledge of and skills associated with exercise physiology are used in many different ways by professionals in physical education and sport. Physical education teachers help children set and attain fitness goals, both in physical education class and through participation in physical activity outside the school. Coaches typically use training guidelines to help their athletes achieve the high levels of fitness essential for performance in specific sports. Cardiac rehabilitation specialists work in hospitals, clinics, work sites, or community settings, enhancing the fitness of post-heart attack patients, performing fitness evaluations, and leading preventive programs. Fitness professionals in private clubs, community programs, and corporate settings design, conduct, and evaluate fitness programs for people of all ages. Strength-training specialists work with professional and intercollegiate athletes and in rehabilitation. Athletic trainers develop preventive programs and rehabilitation programs for injured athletes.

The current tremendous interest in health, fitness, and physical activity by the public and the expansion of the knowledge base of this field also have enhanced professional opportunities. An increasing number of young people are undertaking undergraduate and graduate study in exercise physiology and preparing to pursue careers in adult fitness, cardiac rehabilitation, and strength development. (Career opportunities in these areas are discussed in Chapter 12.)

Physical Fitness

Physical fitness is one area of study within exercise physiology. *Physical fitness* is the ability of the body's systems to function efficiently and effectively. Individuals who are physically fit have the ability to "carry out daily tasks with vigor and alertness, without undue fatigue, and with ample energy to enjoy leisure-time pursuits and to meet unforeseen emergencies."[1]

Contemporary professionals commonly view physical fitness as a quality comprising eleven different components, each with specific requirements for its development and maintenance. Fitness components typically are classified into two categories: those pertaining to health and those pertaining to motor-skill performance. The terms health fitness and motor-performance fitness are currently used when discussing these two areas.[2] Box 7-1 identifies and defines the health and motor-performance components.

Health fitness is important for all individuals throughout their lifespan. The achievement and maintenance of those qualities necessary for an individual to function efficiently and to enhance his or her health through the prevention and remediation of disease are the central focus of health fitness. An increasing body of research supports the contribution of regular, appropriate physical activity to health and quality of life.

Motor-performance fitness emphasizes the development of those qualities that enhance the performance of physical activities such as sport. Whereas health fitness is concerned with living better, motor-performance fitness is concerned with performing sport-related skills better and more efficiently. Moreover, motor-performance fitness is specific to the sport or activity in which the

DEFINITIONS OF PHYSICAL FITNESS COMPONENTS

Fitness Component	Definition
Health-fitness components	
Body composition	Amount of body fat relative to fat-free content expressed as a percentage
Cardiorespiratory endurance	Maximum functional capacity of the cardiorespiratory system to sustain work or physical activity involving large muscle groups over an extended period
Flexibility	Range of movement possible at a joint or joints
Muscular endurance	Ability of a muscle or muscle group to repeat muscular contractions against a force or to sustain a contraction over time
Muscular strength	Maximum amount of force that can be exerted by a muscle or muscle group against a resistance during a single contraction
Motor-performance fitness components	
Agility	Ability to change direction rapidly with control
Balance	Ability to maintain equilibrium while stationary or moving
Coordination	Ability to execute movements smoothly and efficiently
Power	Ability to produce force at a fast speed; a combination of strength and speed usually applied during a short period
Reaction time	Time elapsed between the administration of a stimulus and the body's response to the stimulus
Speed	Ability to move the body quickly

individual engages. Different degrees of motor-performance fitness components are needed, depending on the specific motor activity. For example, the degree of power, agility, and speed needed by a football player is different from that required by a tennis player, though both individuals need these qualities to perform at an optimal level.

Fitness, be it health-related or motor-skill related, must be viewed in relation to an individual's characteristics (e.g., age, health status, occupation, preferences), needs, goals, and the tasks that must be performed. All individuals possess certain levels of each of the health and motor-performance fitness components. The extent to which each quality is developed depends on the individual. A weekend tennis player needs a different level of physical fitness than a competitive wheelchair marathoner; 70-year-old grandparents require a different level of fitness than the 10-year-old grandchild. Professionals charged with the responsibility of designing and conducting fitness

programs should ask the program participants, "Fitness for what?" Does the participant desire physical fitness that will contribute to general health or to outstanding performance in a particular sport? All people should seek to achieve and maintain an optimal level of physical fitness with respect to their individual needs.

Proper development and maintenance of physical fitness require the application of knowledge from the realm of exercise physiology. Because exercise physiology is concerned with both the body's immediate and long-term responses to exercise, the development and conduct of fitness programs to meet an individual's specific fitness needs should be guided by knowledge from this field. Elite athletes preparing for competition, healthy adults wanting to work out on a regular basis, patients recovering from heart disease, youth sport athletes training for competition, injured participants rehabilitating from injury, elderly citizens aspiring to live independent lives, and individuals with disabilities who are striving to meet the challenges of life can all benefit from participation in a well-designed physical fitness program based on the principles of exercise physiology.

Physical Activity, Physical Fitness, and Health

Research on the effects of physical activity and fitness on the health status of the individual is a major area of research in exercise physiology today. A major threat to the health and well-being of Americans is chronic diseases, many of which can be categorized as hypokinetic diseases. *Hypokinetic diseases* are caused by insufficient physical activity, often in conjunction with inappropriate dietary practices. Coronary heart disease, hypertension, osteoporosis, noninsulin-dependent diabetes, chronic back pain, and obesity are examples of hypokinetic diseases.

Research increasingly supports the fact that lack of physical activity can adversely affect one's health. Individuals who lead a sedentary, that is, physically inactive, life, have increased risk of morbidity and mortality from a number of chronic diseases.[1,3,4,5] One striking example is the relationship between physical activity and coronary heart disease, the leading cause of death in the United States. Individuals who are inactive have almost twice the risk of coronary health disease as those who are active.[1,5] The degree of risk is similar to those better known risk factors of cigarette smoking, hypertension, and obesity. Moreover, because physical inactivity is the greatest single risk factor for coronary heart disease, reduction of this risk factor can positively influence the health of the nation.[5]

Dose-response debate

There has been an ongoing debate about the amount of physical activity necessary to achieve health benefits. This *dose-response debate* has centered on questions such as these: "What kind of activity should be performed? For how long, at what intensity, and how often should physical activity be performed to realize health benefits?"

Appropriate, sustained vigorous exercise promotes health fitness and leads to the achievement of desirable health outcomes, reduction in risk for disease, and increased longevity.[3] The 1996 document *Physical Activity and Health: A Report of the Surgeon General* showcased the growing body of scientific evidence that regularly engaging in moderate physical activity, below the threshold to promote physical fitness, can also lead to substantial health gains. Individuals who engage in moderate-intensity exercise (e.g., walking, taking the stairs) for at least 30 minutes a day for most, or preferably all, days of the week can improve their health and decrease their risk for disease.[1] Additional health benefits can be derived from increasing the time engaged in moderate-intensity physical activity or by participating in more vigorous physical activity associated with health fitness. Even very sedentary individuals who begin an appropriate physical activity program in middle age can achieve health benefits. It is never too late to be active!

Health benefits

The relationship between physical activity, physical fitness, and health gives professionals in physical education and sport the opportunity to make a significant contribution to the health of the nation. Professionals can help people of all ages in a diversity of settings incorporate physical activity into their lives and improve their health. Furthermore, professionals can help people achieve greater health benefits by encouraging them to increase their activity to a sufficient level to develop health fitness.

Enhanced cardiovascular function is one health benefit of physical activity. This helps reduce the risk of heart disease. Benefits accrued include a more efficient level of cardiovascular function, stronger heart muscles, lower heart rate, reduced blood pressure, increased oxygen-carrying capacity of the blood, and improved coronary and peripheral circulation. Resistance to atherosclerosis is improved as desirable serum cholesterol levels are maintained; low-density lipids are reduced and protective high-density lipids are increased. Thus, the risk of a heart attack is lessened, and the chances of surviving a heart attack are increased. Physical activity can also help reduce other risk factors associated with cardiovascular disease such as obesity and hypertension.

Physical activity can help maintain a desirable body composition. Excessive body fat is hazardous to one's health and it can shorten one's life. Elevated serum cholesterol levels, diabetes, hypertension, gallbladder disease, cardiovascular disease, osteoarthritis of the weight-bearing joints, and some types of cancer are all associated with being overweight. Research has shown that among persons whose weight exceeds normal by only 15% to 25%, death rates increase by approximately 30%.[6] Additionally, many adults and children who are obese experience psychological stress and self-concept problems. Being physically active on a regular basis helps maintain a healthy body composition by using excess calories and by preventing the addition of undesirable weight, thus reducing susceptibility to disease. Because overweight children often become overweight adults, and because

the tendency to be overweight increases with age, it is important that proper activity habits as well as balanced nutritional practices are acquired early in life. Physical activity also can contribute to improved physical appearance and self-image.

Muscular strength, muscular endurance, and flexibility also are important to good health. Millions of Americans suffer from problems with low-back pain. Many of these problems can be attributed to muscular weakness and imbalance, which in turn can be attributed to inactivity or participation in inappropriate activities. Millions of elderly and disabled individuals may have trouble performing tasks of daily living because of insufficient development of these fitness components. Regular and appropriate physical activity can help these individuals achieve functional independence. Reduced risk of muscle and joint injury is also a positive outcome of regular and appropriate activity.

The value of physical activity is not limited only to the body; it also contributes to sound mental

Employees of the Kimberly-Clark Corporation participate in an aerobic dance class.

health. It may help alleviate mental illness and reduce susceptibility to depression and anxiety. Being active can help individuals withstand and manage stress more effectively. Many people find exercising provides a release from tensions. Exercise makes a person feel better. Those who exercise often comment about this directly: "I feel more alive," "I have more energy," "I'm not as tired in the evening," "I can do a lot more with my life."

Regular participation in physical activity can contribute to the development of a positive self-concept and greater self-esteem. It enhances self-confidence, emotional stability, assertiveness, independence, and self-control.

Socialization is another benefit of participation in exercise and physical activities. Sports, recreational activities, and exercise groups offer opportunities to fulfill the desire to belong to a group as well as the desire for recognition. These are important psychosocial needs.

Besides enhancing health, health fitness can contribute to increased work efficiency. Individuals who are fit have more energy, which contributes to greater productivity and efficiency of both physical and mental tasks. More energy is available for recreational activities and leisure-time pursuits. Fit individuals can also better withstand fatigue. Physical exercise can improve one's sleeping patterns.

Health fitness can improve overall general motor performance. Physical activities associated with daily living as well as sport skills can be performed more efficiently by individuals who are fit. Additionally, fit individuals recover more quickly from vigorous exercise and work than do unfit individuals. Physical activity enhances one's appearance and posture through the development of proper muscle tone, greater flexibility, and an enhanced sense of well-being.

Regular exercise can help mitigate the debilitating effects of old age. Generally, after age 30, physical qualities such as coordination and muscular endurance tend to diminish.[8,9] This degenerative process can be slowed by engaging in regular physical activity. To be most effective in mitigating the effects of aging, the integration of regular physical activity into one's lifestyle should begin early in life. Individuals who remain active and physically fit throughout their life will retain a more desirable level of cardiovascular health, muscular strength, muscular endurance, and body composition.

Individuals who exercise regularly are likely to engage in other positive forms of health-promoting behavior. Because they do not want to negate the benefits accrued from exercise, they may also strive to eat properly, get sufficient rest and relaxation, and manage the stress in their lives. Personal health and well-being becomes an important personal priority.

Regular and appropriate physical activity has many benefits. However, to realize these benefits, a person must be active all year. To function properly and at a high level, the human organism needs exercise as an essential ingredient on a regular basis, just as it demands nutritious food every day. Being active throughout one's life is essential for continued good health.

FITNESS DEVELOPMENT

In order to plan a fitness program, physical education and sport professionals must have a knowledge of how energy is produced for physical activity. Understanding the energy demands helps in structuring the fitness program to achieve desired results. Principles of fitness training offer guidance for program planning. In developing fitness programs, the frequency, intensity, time, and type of physical activity must be specified.

Energy Production for Physical Activity

Energy is necessary for the performance of physical activity, whether it is physical activity associated with the activities of daily living, moderate-intensity activity to improve health, exercise to improve fitness, participation in sports for recreation, or involvement in highly competitive athletics. Muscles must produce energy to move. Metabolism is the sum of all chemical reactions in the body, including energy production and energy utilization.

Energy for muscular contraction is produced from the breakdown of food we eat; food serves as a fuel source for the body. Protein, carbohydrates, and fat nutrients from food are broken down via a series of processes to three main molecules—amino acids, glucose, and fatty acids. These molecules, in turn, are delivered via the bloodstream to the cells. In the cells, through a series of chemical reactions, *adenosine triphosphate*, or *ATP*, is created. ATP is used as energy to perform muscular activity.

There are two major ways that energy, specifically ATP, is generated for activity: the anaerobic system and the aerobic system. *Anaerobic* means without oxygen; *aerobic* means with oxygen. The type of task performed, specifically the duration of the activity and its intensity (or the rate at which energy is expended), determines which energy system will contribute the majority of the energy required.

The anaerobic system provides energy for tasks that demand a high rate of energy expenditure for a short period—for example, the 100-yard dash, 50-yard freestyle swim sprint, or shot put—or in events where power—that is, quick, explosive movements—is necessary, such as in gymnastics or football.[7] This system produces energy quickly to meet immediate demands. It uses ATP and other necessary molecules for the chemical reactions that are stored in the muscle cells. When these small stores of ATP are used up, the body then uses stored glycogen as an energy source. Glycogen is broken down to glucose, which is then metabolized within the muscle cells to generate ATP for muscle contraction. Because body fuels can be metabolized to produce small amounts of ATP for energy without the use of oxygen, this is referred to as anaerobic metabolism. However, the amount of work that can be performed anaerobically is limited. The anaerobic system can support high-intensity exercise for only about 1 minute. One product of anaerobic energy production is lactic acid, which accumulates in the muscles and contributes to fatigue.

When exercise continues for a prolonged time, the aerobic system provides the energy for physical activity. Physical activities requiring a lower rate of energy expenditure over a longer time, such as jogging 5 miles, cross-country skiing 10 kilometers, or engaging in a basketball game, use aerobic metabolism to supply the energy.[7] In performing aerobic activities a constant supply of oxygen is required by the muscles performing the work. Oxygen is used as part of a more complex process to generate ATP from carbohydrates and fats. The aerobic system is tremendously efficient at extracting ATP from the food nutrient molecules and without producing fatiguing by-products such as lactic acid.

In many activities, these systems function simultaneously. For example, many physical activities that would be considered aerobic in nature, such as basketball, soccer, racquet ball, or long-distance races, include an anaerobic component. These activities require periodic bursts of vigorous activity. Sprinting up the court for a long pass, accelerating past an opponent to an open space, and sprinting toward the finish line are examples when a burst of speed or power is needed.

The relative contribution of each of these energy systems will depend on the intensity of the exercise and its duration. (See Table 7-1.) For intense efforts lasting approximately 1 minute or less, the anaerobic system supplies the required energy. As the activity becomes less intense and the duration longer, the aerobic system predominates.

The anaerobic and aerobic systems of the body can be improved through training. Anaerobic training typically involves alternating high-intensity activity with rest periods of varying lengths; the number of repetitions in this cycle depends on the goal of the training. Anaerobic training increases the ability to do anaerobic work, tolerance for lactic acid, and muscle size. In contrast, aerobic training generally involves exercising at a lower intensity for a longer amount of time. Aerobic training improves the capacity of the body to transport and use oxygen, to generate ATP aerobically, and to utilize carbohydrates and stored fats for energy production. Aerobic training improves the function of the cardiovascular system. Understanding the different energy systems is important in developing, implementing, and evaluating training programs to improve fitness.

TABLE 7-1		
Energy Systems Used		
Energy System	**Length of Time**	**Type of Activity**
Anaerobic	6–60 seconds	Any type of sprinting event (running, swimming cycling) Short-duration, explosive activities
Combined systems	1–3 minutes	Medium-distance activities ($1/2$ to 1 mile run); intermittent sports activities
Aerobic	More than 3 minutes	Long-distance events (running 5 miles, swimming 1,500 meters); long-duration intermittent sport activities

From Prentice W: Fitness for college and life, ed 5, St. Louis, 1997, Mosby.

Principles of Fitness Training

Knowledge from the field of exercise physiology offers guidelines for professionals to use when planning and conducting programs to improve fitness. These principles should be followed whether the exercise program is being designed by an elementary physical educator to improve students' health fitness, by a coach to improve athletes' performance, by an exercise leader to enhance adults' fitness, or by an exercise specialist as part of a patient's cardiac rehabilitation program. Several physiological and behavioral factors must be taken into account if the sought-after benefits— improvement and maintenance of fitness—are to be realized.

1. **Principle of overload.** Overload is essential if fitness gains are to be realized. Simply, the principle of overload states that for improvements in fitness to occur, one must perform more than one's normal amount of exercise. For example, if improvement in muscular strength is wanted, the muscles must be exercised with more intensity than normal. Once the desired level of fitness has been reached, individuals must continue to train at a level that will maintain the desired level.

2. **Principle of specificity.** The kinds of physiological changes that occur because of training are related to the type of training employed. Training programs should be designed with specific goals in mind. Therefore, it is imperative that professionals understand the demands of the sport or requirements for physical activity so that a specific training program can be designed. For example, to realize the maximum gains in cardiorespiratory endurance, activities and programs should be designed specifically to achieve this aim.

3. **The individual's initial level of fitness must be considered.** An individual embarking on an exercise program should obtain approval from a physician. Following approval, the individual's present level of fitness should be assessed by qualified professionals. The individual's current fitness status should be taken into consideration in designing the exercise program. Those who have a relatively low level of fitness or lead a sedentary lifestyle should start their exercise program at a lower level of intensity than individuals who have a relatively high level of fitness.

4. **Progression should be followed in planning a program.** The use of progression is critical if a fitness program is to be effective. Progression depends on the individual. Using the initial level of fitness as a starting point, exercises being performed should increase as an individual becomes adjusted to the exercise program. This can be done by increasing the frequency, duration, or intensity of the exercise. Progression should be

steady, and progress carefully monitored so that the individual is challenged by the exercise program but not overwhelmed.

5. **Individual differences must be taken into account.** The individual's needs and objectives must be taken into account when planning an exercise program. Factors that may influence the individual's performance warrant attention as well. The nature of the individual's work, diet, and lifestyle should be considered when designing an exercise program. The amount of stress an individual is currently experiencing also may significantly affect his or her performance.

6. **The elements of a training program should include a warm-up, the workout, and a cool-down.** Warm-up and cool-down activities are important. Warm up activities of at least 5 to 10 minutes in duration should precede the vigorous part of the exercise session. Warm-up activities can help prevent injury and prepare the body for the strenuous activities that are part of the exercise program. Following the workout, a cool-down period of 5 to 10 minutes is recommended to allow the body to begin returning to its normal state. Individuals with low levels of fitness or individuals who are middle-aged and older should take more time to warm up and cool-down. Stretching exercises and low-level aerobic activity are suggested for warm-up and cool-down.

7. **Safety is paramount.** Safety of the individual should be a primary concern. Before starting an exercise program, individuals should have a thorough medical screening. This is particularly critical when special conditions exist, such as beginning an exercise program after a long period of inactivity or for rehabilitation after an illness (e.g., heart attack). Individuals engaged in physical activities involving body contact or other hazards should be strongly cautioned to use essential protective equipment, especially for the head, neck, eyes, and teeth (e.g., individuals playing racquetball should be required to use eye guards). Individuals should be warned of proper precautions to take when exercising in special weather conditions such as intense heat, high humidity, or extreme cold. Finally, individuals should learn how to monitor carefully their responses to exercise and to report any unusual occurrences (e.g., excessive breathlessness) to the professional conducting the program or to a physician.

8. **Behavioral factors should be considered in developing and implementing a fitness program.** Consideration must be given to motivating individuals to adhere to their fitness programs and to incorporate their program into their daily living. Essentially, how can physical education and sport professionals facilitate adherence by individuals to the exercise program that has been so carefully designed? How can individuals be motivated to work so that their optimal level of fitness can be realized?

Pollock and Blair[8] suggest that professionals need to establish lines of communication with each participant. Communication can be enhanced by treating each person as an individual and by nonjudgmental acceptance of his or her exercise habits. Second, professionals need to help each individual assume responsibility for his or her own behavior. The individual should be held accountable for following the exercise program. Next, the professional and the individual, working cooperatively, should set goals that are personally meaningful, as well as realistic and attainable. Both short-term and long-term goals should be set. Short-term goals lead incrementally to the achievement of the long-term goal. For example, an individual may choose to embark on an exercise program because he or she wants to complete a 10-kilometer road race; this is a long-term goal. The short-term goal initially may be to exercise 3 times a week for 30 minutes at a moderate level of intensity. Gradually, the individual would increase the time exercising, the level of intensity, and the number of days per week until the long-term goal is achieved.

Professionals can also facilitate adherence to the exercise program by having the participant maintain records of his or her performance. Record keeping helps the individual focus on the task at hand and provides a means for documenting progress toward goals. Positive reinforcement from the professional as well as friends may help the individual continue the exercise program. However, the best motivation is internal. Finally, professionals can enhance individuals' adherence to exercise by being good role models. Professionals should practice what they preach. They should exemplify a healthy, active lifestyle.

Physical educators and sport leaders must be aware of physiological principles when designing an exercise program. The principles of overload and specificity must be followed. Consideration also must be given to individual differences. Behavioral strategies such as goal setting and positive reinforcement can facilitate exercise adherence. Physical educators should also realize the importance of being a good role model for a healthy lifestyle.

Planning a Fitness Program

To achieve and maintain fitness, individuals must exercise on a regular basis. They must exercise sufficiently to cross the threshold of training; to achieve optimal results, they must exercise within the fitness target zone. When professionals prescribe an exercise program for an individual, they must specify the frequency, intensity, time, and type of exercise. These variables are used in constructing an exercise prescription or program for an individual.

Each fitness component has a specific threshold of training that must be achieved. The *threshold of training* is the minimum level of exercise needed to achieve desired benefits.[9] The *target zone* begins at the threshold of training and defines the upper limits of training.[9] To achieve fitness benefits, individuals must exercise with sufficient intensity, duration, and frequency to stay within the target zone. Exercise beyond the upper limit may be counterproductive. The target zone defines the optimal level of exercise.

Frequency refers to the number of exercise sessions per week—for example, 3 to 5 times per week. Achieving and maintaining health fitness requires that the individual exercise on a regular basis.

Intensity is the degree of effort or exertion put forth by the individual during exercise. It is how hard a person works. For example, the intensity of effort put forth by a runner can be described as 80% of his or her maximum effort, and the effort put forth during strength training can be described as weight lifted—for example, 80 lb. Intensity is often viewed as the most important of the exercise variables.

Time is the duration or the length of the activity. Time is how long an exercise must be performed to be effective. Time is frequently expressed in units of time, such as 40 minutes of exercise.

Type is the mode of exercise being performed. Since fitness development is specific, different types of activities build different components of fitness. Activities such as jogging, rowing, bicycling, stretching, and weight training are types of exercise that can be used to realize specific fitness gains. The selection of the type of exercise should be guided by the fitness goal to be achieved.

Many adults exercise with sufficient intensity, duration, and frequency to realize health benefits.

The acronym *FITT* can be used to help remember these prescriptive variables. These exercise variables are interrelated and can be manipulated to produce an exercise program appropriate to an individual's needs and to the outcomes wanted. For example, cardiovascular improvement can be realized by jogging (type) at 70% effort (intensity) for 40 minutes (time) 5 times a week (frequency) or at 85% intensity for 20 minutes 4 times a week. Individuals who are just starting a program to improve their fitness may be more successful if they exercise at a lower intensity for a longer session. Individuals who are obese may find it beneficial to exercise for shorter periods (duration) but more often during the week (frequency).

The interactive nature of the exercise components allows for the design of exercise programs to meet unique needs. Individualization is very important. Personal characteristics such as fitness status, medical status, and age must be considered when prescribing exercise. Individuals who have lower initial fitness levels require a lower level of intensity when beginning a program than individuals who are fit. Medical conditions, such as heart disease, diabetes, and asthma, must be taken into account when designing an exercise program. Appropriate modifications must be made so that the individual can participate safely. Individuals beginning an exercise program at middle age or older may need to start at a lower intensity. It is important to note that gender is not a limiting factor; men and women respond equally to training.

The participant's fitness needs and goals also must be considered when planning an exercise program. The program must be designed to provide opportunities for the development of the fitness quality the participant desires to improve. Selected activities should be specific to the goal. For example, if the participant's goal is to improve stamina or cardiorespiratory endurance, the activities selected should stimulate the circulatory and respiratory systems (e.g., running or swimming) and the exercise components manipulated to allow the participant to achieve this goal.

Enjoyment is another critical factor in the selection of the type of exercise. Adherence to the training program is enhanced when the participant enjoys the prescribed exercise. Activities should allow participants to achieve the desired fitness goals while maintaining interest and enjoyment. Individuals who find an activity enjoyable will be more likely to continue the exercise long enough to realize desired fitness improvements and to incorporate exercise into their lifestyle to maintain these improvements.

Equally important in planning an exercise program is the provision of experiences that will promote the development of the cognitive and affective outcomes essential for lifetime fitness. Achievement of a desirable level of fitness is a significant concern, but attention also must be directed to educating participants about the principles of designing a personal exercise program, assessing their own fitness, and resolving personal fitness problems. Development of a knowledgeable, independent fitness and health consumer—an individual who can achieve and maintain fitness for a lifetime—is an important priority. People need to take charge of their own lives and assume personal responsibility for their level of fitness.

HEALTH FITNESS COMPONENTS

The components of health fitness include cardiorespiratory endurance, body composition, muscular strength and endurance, and flexibility. In this section, each fitness component is defined, its relationship to health delineated, methods to improve the fitness component discussed, and techniques to measure the component identified.

Cardiorespiratory Endurance

Cardiorespiratory endurance is the body's ability to deliver oxygen effectively to the working muscles so that an individual can perform physical activity. Efficient functioning of the cardiovascular system (i.e., heart and blood vessels) and the respiratory system (i.e., lungs) is essential for the distribution of oxygen and nutrients and removal of wastes from the body.

The performance of sustained vigorous physical activities is influenced by the efficiency of the cardiorespiratory system. The more efficient the system, the greater the amount of physical activity an individual can perform before fatigue and exhaustion occur. Performance diminishes greatly when sufficient oxygen cannot be provided by the cardiorespiratory system to the working muscles.

Cardiorespiratory endurance is regarded as the most important component of health fitness. Because of the benefits derived from improved cardiorespiratory function—such as the potential for reducing the risk of cardiovascular disease, improving work capacity, and providing greater resistance to fatigue—this component, if properly developed, can make a major contribution to an individual's health.

Health fitness can help prevent hypokinetic disease. Hypokinetic diseases are caused by insufficient physical activity. Persons who have hypokinetic diseases frequently experience loss of flexibility, cardiovascular degeneration, bone and muscle weakness, and bladder and bowel malfunctions. One risk factor that contributes to premature susceptibility to heart disease and stroke is lack of physical activity. Moreover, it is believed that hypertension and obesity, which are also risk factors associated with heart disease, can be helped by participation in regular physical activity.

Cardiorespiratory endurance is concerned with the aerobic efficiency of the body. Aerobic efficiency is the body's ability to supply fuel and oxygen to the muscles. One of the major factors influencing aerobic efficiency is the capacity of the heart to pump blood. A well-conditioned heart is able to exert greater force with each heartbeat; consequently, a larger volume of blood is pumped through the arteries and throughout the body.

Another important factor in cardiorespiratory endurance is the efficiency of the lungs. The amount of oxygen that can be supplied to working muscles is a limiting factor in performance. Oxygen is required to produce the energy needed for activity. Food is metabolized to provide needed fuel, and oxygen is essential for this process. Air is inhaled; oxygen from the air is transported to the heart and is then carried from the heart to the organs needing oxygen. From the organs the blood carrying carbon dioxide is returned to the heart and finally to the lungs, where it is exhaled.

When demands for oxygen increase, such as during strenuous exercise, the body's ability to take in and provide oxygen to the working muscles is an important determinant of the amount of work that can be performed. The greater the body's ability to take in and deliver oxygen, the longer a person can exercise before fatigue and exhaustion occur. Thus individuals who have well-developed circulatory and respiratory systems can deliver more oxygen and therefore can exercise for a longer period.

Many benefits have been attributed to aerobic exercise. Aerobic exercise is activity that can be sustained for an extended period without building an oxygen debt in the muscles. Bicycling, jogging, skipping rope, rowing, walking, cross-country skiing, and swimming are some examples of aerobic activities.

The benefits of aerobic exercise include the ability to use more oxygen during strenuous exercise, a lower heart rate at work, the production of less lactic acid, and greater endurance. Aerobic exercise improves the efficiency of the heart and reduces blood pressure.

Cardiorespiratory endurance is important for the performance of many sport activities. In sport activities that require an individual to perform for an extended period, such as a 500-yard swim or a soccer game, cardiorespiratory endurance can have a profound impact on performance.

Individuals who have trained and developed a high level of cardiorespiratory endurance can work at a higher level of intensity without fatigue than individuals who are unfit. Additionally, fit individuals can perform more work before reaching exhaustion. Furthermore, following exercise, fit individuals recover faster than unfit individuals.

Cardiorespiratory fitness can be improved and maintained through a well-planned program of exercise. Physical activity of an appropriate intensity, duration, frequency, and type can enhance cardiorespiratory fitness.

Intensity. To develop cardiorespiratory fitness, physical activities must be of sufficient intensity. During exercise, heart rate changes in proportion to the energy requirements of the task. As the

Participants in the Annual Marine Corps Marathon must have a high level of physical fitness.

energy requirements increase, there is a corresponding increase in heart rate. Thus heart rate can be used to monitor the intensity of exercise. The box on page 234 shows how to measure heart rate. Because heart rate slows within 1 minute following exercise, it is often recommended that the pulse be monitored for 10 seconds and then multiplied by 6 (or monitored for 6 seconds and multiplied by 10) to determine beats per minute. To obtain an accurate reading, the heart rate should be monitored within 15 seconds of the cessation of exercise.

Exercising at a proper intensity is essential for a safe and effective workout. Intensity can be controlled by speeding or slowing the pace of the exercise. To realize training benefits, the intensity of the exercise must be regulated so that the heart rate is elevated to a predetermined level and maintained within a certain range. This level is called the threshold of training and the range called the target heart rate zone.

There are several methods to calculate the threshold of training and the lower and upper limits of the target heart rate zone. One method that is easy to use is the maximal heart rate (MHR). The maximum heart rate is estimated to be 220 beats per minute (bpm). Maximal heart rate is related to age. As individuals get older, the maximum heart rate decreases. Thus, for any given age of an individual, maximal heart rate can be estimated by taking the maximum heart rate, which is 220 bpm, and subtracting the individual's age. The threshold of training would be 60% of the maximal heart rate. The lower and upper limits of the target heart rate zone are between 60% and 90% of the maximal heart rate. Those who are beginning an exercise program who possess an extremely low level of fitness, or who have limitations can benefit from starting at a lower level of intensity, such as 50% of their maximal heart rate.

The box on page 234 and Figure 7-1 show how to calculate the threshold of training and the target heart rate zone. Individuals should select an intensity that takes into account their current level of fitness and their fitness goals. Intensity can be progressively increased as conditions warrant.

MEASURING YOUR HEART RATE

You can determine your heart rate by counting the frequency with which your heart contracts in a period of time and converting this to the standard measure in beats per minute. Make sure you press just firmly enough to feel the pulse. If you press too hard it may interfere with the rhythm.

You can detect your pulse by placing a finger or fingers on your lower arm near the base of the thumb.

Your pulse can also be easily detected over the carotid artery in the front of the neck.

DETERMINING YOUR TARGET ZONE HEART RATE

Maximal Heart Rate (MHR)

Maximal Heart Rate (MHR) = 220 bpm* – age
Threshold target HR/lower limit of target zone = MHR bpm × 60%
Upper limit of target zone = MHR bpm × 90%

Target zone = 60%–90% MHR

* bpm = beats per minute

MHR Calculations for a 20-Year-Old

MRH = 220 bpm – 20 = 200 bpm
Threshold HR/lower limit of target zone = 200 bpm × 60% = 120 bpm
Upper limit of target zone = 200 bpm × 90% = 180 bpm
Target zone = 120–180 bpm

Time. It is generally accepted that minimal improvement requires at least 20 minutes of sustained activity of sufficient intensity to maintain the heart rate within its target zone.

It is important to remember that the intensity and duration of the activity are critical to achieving and maintaining fitness. Generally, as the intensity of the activity increases, its duration decreases; conversely, as intensity decreases, the duration of the activity increases. Typically, for development of health-related cardiorespiratory endurance, lower intensities and longer durations are recommended. It is important to remember, however, that both the intensity and the duration of the activity must meet minimum requirements for fitness development to occur.

Frequency. Three exercise sessions per week are necessary to realize minimal improvement in cardiovascular fitness. Many individuals choose to work out more often. It is important to remember,

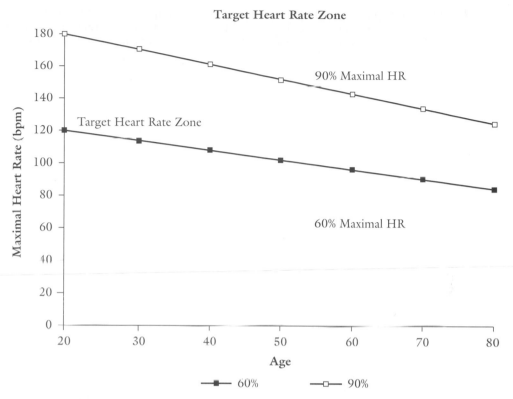

FIGURE 7-1   Target heart rate zone for adults 20 to 80 years old.

however, that the body must have time to recover from the effects of exercise. Many persons build this recovery time into their exercise program by exercising only every other day. Although daily workouts are not required to develop health fitness, many other individuals choose to work out on a daily basis. To allow the body to recover, they often follow a strenuous workout day with a less strenuous recovery day.

Type. Aerobic activities should be used to develop cardiorespiratory endurance. Basically, aerobic activities are those in which a sufficient amount of oxygen is available to meet the body's demands. During the performance of these activities, the heart rate is maintained at an elevated level for an extended period. These activities typically involve vigorous and repetitive whole body or large muscle movements that are sustained for an extended period. Popular aerobic activities

Students at Agassiz Middle School, in Fargo, North Dakota, use heart rate monitors to measure the intensity of their efforts.

include jogging, running, walking, swimming, cycling, rowing, aerobic dance, and cross-country skiing. Because these activities are somewhat continuous in nature, the intensity of the workload can be easily regulated by controlling the pace. Intermittent activities such as racquetball, basketball, and tennis involve various intensities of effort during the course of the activity. Thus it is more difficult to regulate the degree of effort expended during these activities. However, these activities can contribute to the improvement of cardiorespiratory endurance if they are of sufficient intensity.

In summary, to develop and maintain cardiorespiratory fitness, it is recommended that the individual exercise 3 to 5 times a week, with an intensity sufficient to elevate and sustain the heart rate in the target zone for at least 20 minutes. Exercise should involve aerobic activities that are continuous, vigorous, and, also important, enjoyable to the individual. Once a desirable level of cardiovascular fitness has been achieved, regular appropriate exercise is necessary to maintain it. Individuals who stop exercising tend to lose their fitness gains within 5 to 10 weeks. Achieving and maintaining a high level of this critical fitness component requires a long-term commitment and the incorporation of exercise into one's lifestyle.

Cardiorespiratory fitness can be measured. The best method to determine the level of cardiovascular functioning is to measure maximum oxygen consumption. The more oxygen the body is able to deliver and use, the more work the body is able to perform before becoming fatigued. Maximum oxygen consumption is the greatest rate at which the oxygen is processed and used by the body.

Measurement of maximum oxygen consumption requires a sophisticated laboratory setting and well-trained personnel to monitor carefully the performance of the individual during the test. This testing is usually done on an individual basis. Following prescribed test protocols, the individual exercises on a treadmill or bicycle ergometer and breathes through a specially designed mouthpiece. Various physiological and metabolic parameters are monitored, such as heart rate, respiration rate, and rate of oxygen consumption. The exercise task is made progressively more difficult until no further increase in oxygen consumption is noted; this point is considered to be the maximum oxygen intake for the task. Although this test yields highly accurate information, it is expensive, time consuming, and requires sophisticated equipment and highly trained personnel.

There are a variety of other methods that can be used to provide a good estimate of cardiorespiratory endurance. These tests measure the maximum amount of work that can be performed over a specified period. The most commonly used tests are the 12-minute or the 9-minute run/walk, the

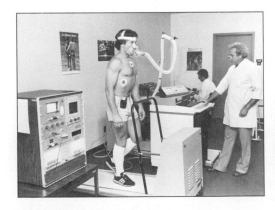

A treadmill or bicycle ergometer can be used to determine maximum oxygen consumption.

timed $1^{1}/_{2}$- or 1-mile run/walk, and the Harvard step test. These tests are most often used in school and community fitness programs. When these tests are properly conducted, results can be used to accurately estimate maximum oxygen consumption and provide an indicator of cardiorespiratory fitness.

Body Composition

Body composition is a description of the body in terms of muscle, bone, fat, and other elements. With respect to health fitness, it refers to the percentage of body weight composed of fat as compared with fat-free or lean tissue. Having a high percentage of body fat is a serious deterrent to fitness and health.

Height and weight tables traditionally have been used to determine desirable body weight. Individuals whose body weight exceeds set standards for their sex, age, and physical stature by 10% to 20% are considered overweight.[7,10] Persons overweight by 20% of their optimum weight are obese, and those who are overweight by more than 50% of their optimum weight are considered morbidly obese or superobese.[7]

It should be noted that being overweight can be attributed to having an excess of either fatty tissue or lean tissue. For example, certain athletes such as football players could be classified as overweight. However, when their body composition is examined, the excess weight is attributable to muscular development and their overall percentage of body fat is quite low (e.g., a professional football player can weigh 250 pounds or more, yet have only 12% body fat or less). The important consideration with respect to health fitness, therefore, is not weight but proportion of fat. The average percentage of body fat is 18% for men and 23% for women. With respect to health fitness, the desirable level of body fat for men is 12% or less and for women, 18% or less. The percentage of body fat should not be less than 3% in men and 12% in women (the higher percentage for women is necessary for protection of the reproductive organs).[7,10] Extremely low percentages of body fat are hazardous to one's health. It is highly important

that professionals and the public realize that a certain amount of adipose tissue or fat is essential for the body to function. Body fat also serves to protect internal organs. *The goal of fitness programs is not the elimination of body fat but helping individuals attain the desirable levels of body fat.*

A high percentage of body fat is associated with numerous health problems. Obesity contributes to an increased incidence of cardiovascular disease and is also associated with other cardiovascular risk factors, including hypertension. An increased incidence of diabetes, elevated serum blood cholesterol levels, respiratory problems, muscle and joint problems, low back pain, and certain psychological problems are also found among individuals with a high percentage of body fat. Mortality is higher at a younger age, and life expectancy is decreased for chronically obese individuals.

The problem of obesity is widespread. It is estimated that more than 50% of the adult population and about 40% of the school-aged population in the United States is overweight. Moreover, overweight children typically grow up to be overweight adults.

Determination of the cause of obesity is important. In most cases obesity can be attributed to overeating and a lack of physical activity. In a few cases, however, obesity can be the result of disease. When dealing with obesity, particularly individuals who are superobese, it is important that a physician be consulted. A physical examination and careful monitoring of eating and exercise habits are helpful in determining the cause of the problem. A qualified physician can offer guidance in designing and implementing a sound fitness program to deal with the problem of obesity.

Body composition is primarily influenced by nutrition and physical activity. Although body composition is genetically related to body type, the nature and amount of food consumed and the extent of participation in physical activity exert a profound influence on body composition. Poor nutritional practices contribute to an unfavorable body composition. Eating more calories than needed and consumption of a high-fat diet lead to high percentages of body fat. Caloric consumption should be consistent with caloric expenditure. Dietary guidelines suggest that individuals reduce their consumption of fat. The average American derives 49% of his or her calories from fat, compared with the recommended 25%. Sedentary individuals have lower levels of caloric expenditure. Leading a physically active lifestyle can contribute to a favorable body composition.

Energy balance is important to achieving a favorable body composition. The relationship between food intake and energy expenditure is critical. This relationship is often referred to as energy or caloric balance:

Energy or caloric balance	=	Number of calories taken into the body as food	−	Number of calories expended

Energy is expended through three processes: (1) basal metabolism or maintenance of essential life functions; (2) work, which is any activity requiring more energy than sleeping and includes exercise; and (3) excretion of body wastes.

A neutral balance occurs when the caloric intake is equal to the caloric expenditure. Under these circumstances, body weight is maintained. When a positive balance exists, that is, when more calories are consumed than expended, the excess is stored as fat and body weight increases. A negative balance occurs when more calories are expended than consumed; this results in weight loss. Weight control requires maintaining the appropriate energy or caloric balance. Individuals must be careful about food intake and conscious of energy expenditures. Caloric tables are useful in monitoring the number of calories consumed. Energy expenditure tables are helpful in monitoring energy expended. These tables provide information about the calories expended both during the performance of daily living tasks such as house cleaning and during participation in physical activities such as bicycling.

Body composition can be improved. Individuals who have an unhealthy percentage of body fat can reduce it by modifying their lifestyle. Fat loss can be accomplished by several means: (1) consuming fewer calories through dieting, (2) increasing caloric expenditure by increasing the amount of exercise, and (3) combining a moderate decrease in caloric consumption with a moderate increase in exercise or caloric expenditure.

Experts recommend that fat loss be accomplished through a combination of diet and exercise. For example, if caloric intake is reduced by 200 to 300 calories per day and caloric expenditures are increased by 200 to 300 calories a day, approximately 3,500 calories—1 pound of fat—will be lost over the course of a week. Adoption of sound nutritional practices in conjunction with regular, appropriate exercise will help most individuals achieve a desirable body composition.

Exercise increasingly is being recognized as a critical component of fat loss. Often those desiring to lose fat focus on counting the number of calories consumed and neglect the exercise component. Exercise can aid in fat loss in several ways: (1) it can increase caloric expenditures (a 180-lb. person walking 4 miles in an hour will expend approximately 400 calories); (2) it can suppress appetite and thereby contribute to reduction in caloric intake; (3) it can increase the metabolic rate for some time after vigorous exercise, thereby permitting extra calories to be burned; and (4) it can contribute to health fitness. Also, because sedentary living contributes to poor body composition, incorporation of regular appropriate exercise into one's lifestyle helps to successfully manage one's body composition.

Attention to the composition of one's diet is important in attaining a healthy level of body fat. Increasingly, nutritionists are encouraging individuals to pay close attention to the fat calories they consume. Eating a low-fat diet is an effective way to manage one's percentage of body fat. A low-fat diet also reduces the risk of heart disease and cancer. Adults who are at a healthy weight and want to prevent cancer should follow a diet that provides 20% to 30% of the calories from fat. Individuals who have a high percentage of body fat and/or have heart disease should derive 10% to 20% of their calories from fat.

Individuals who try to follow a low-fat diet are typically encouraged to monitor the percentage of fat in the foods they consume and to choose foods that have less than 30% of the calories from fat.

Another way to keep track of fat consumption is to count the number of grams of fat eaten each day and to keep the total number of fat grams at or below the desired level. To calculate the number of fat grams per day, use the following formula:

$$\frac{\text{Number of calories needed} \times \text{desired percentage of calories from fat}}{9 \text{ (number of calories in a fat gram)}} = \text{fat grams}$$

So, if you need 2,000 calories per day and you want to eat a diet that has 20% of the calories from fat, your calculations would reveal that you should consume 44.4 grams or less of fat per day:

$$\frac{2,000 \text{ calories} \times 20\%}{9} = 44.4 \text{ grams of fat per day}$$

Careful attention to dietary practices and physical activity habits are important in attaining a healthy body composition.

Note that individuals who desire to gain weight should focus on increasing lean body mass (muscle) rather than body fat. This can be accomplished by following a sound muscle training program in conjunction with an appropriate increase in caloric intake to realize a gain of 1 to 2 pounds per week. Failure to incorporate a muscle training program as part of the total program will result in excess calories being converted to fat. Thus, even though the weight gain is achieved, the percentage of body fat may be less than optimal. Therefore, a weight-gaining program should combine a reasonable increase in caloric intake and a well-planned muscle training program to achieve an optimal body composition.

Sound practices should be followed in losing fat. Experts suggest the following guidelines regarding fat loss:

1. Prolonged fasting and diets that severely restrict calories are medically dangerous. These programs result in loss of large amounts of water, electrolytes, minerals, glycogen stores, and other fat-free tissue, with a minimal amount of fat loss.
2. Moderate caloric restriction is desirable, such as consuming 500 calories less than the usual daily intake. It is important that the minimum caloric intake not go below 1,200 calories per day for a woman and 1,400 calories per day for a man and that sound nutritional practices are followed.
3. Appropriate regular exercise of the large muscles assists in the maintenance of fat-free tissue, including muscle mass and bone density, and results in the loss of weight, primarily in the form of fat.
4. A sound program should be comprehensive in nature. It should include a nutritionally sound, low-fat diet with mild caloric restriction, regular and appropriate exercise to increase caloric expenditure, and behavior modification. Weight loss should not exceed 2 pounds per week.
5. Maintenance of proper weight and desirable body composition requires a lifetime commitment to proper eating habits and regular physical activity.

A word of caution: Some individuals become obsessed with weight loss, dieting, and exercise. This obsession can, in conjunction with a host of other factors, contribute to the development of an eating disorder. Two common eating disorders are anorexia nervosa and bulimia.

Anorexia nervosa is a disease in which a person develops a psychological aversion to food, resulting in a pathologic weight loss. Bulimia involves recurrent episodes of binge eating and subsequent purging by self-induced vomiting, use of laxatives, and/or excessive exercising. Both disorders have a higher prevalence among young women, although men do suffer from these conditions as well. These disorders pose a severe threat to health and require professional treatment. For more information about these eating disorders, see the box on page 240.

Body composition can be measured. Several methods can be used to determine the percentage of body fat. One of the most accurate methods is hydrostatic weighing. This involves weighing an individual on land and then in an underwater tank. Body density is then determined, and this information is used to calculate the percentage of lean body weight and body fat. This technique is used most often in exercise physiology laboratories

SIGNS AND SYMPTOMS OF EATING DISORDERS

Anorexia Nervosa

◆ Intense fear of fatness, which does not diminish as weight loss progresses
◆ Altered perception of body image ("feeling fat" when emaciated)
◆ Weight loss of 15% or more below minimal normal body weight for height
◆ Absence of sexual desire. In females, three or more missed menstrual periods.
◆ Obsessional focus on losing increasing amounts of weight
◆ Increasing preoccupation with food
◆ Severe food restriction
◆ Increased physical activity and excessive exercising
◆ Changes in mood; irritability, anxiety, and depression
◆ No known physical or psychological illness that can account for weight loss and other signs

Bulimia

◆ Recurrent episodes of binge eating (rapid consumption of large amounts of food in a relatively short period of time)
◆ Inconspicuous eating during binge
◆ Binge episodes terminated by abdominal pain, sleep, or self-induced vomiting
◆ Feelings of loss of control when bingeing
◆ Vomiting, fasting, exercising, or laxative abuse after bingeing in an effort to prevent weight gain
◆ Repeated attempts to lose weight through food restriction when not bingeing
◆ Fear of not being able to stop eating voluntarily
◆ Frequent weight fluctuations greater than 10 pounds due to the cycle of bingeing and purging
◆ Depressed mood following bingeing

For assistance or further information, contact ANAD (National Association of Anorexia Nervosa and Associated Disorders), Highland Park, Ill., 312-831-3438.

and hospitals. It requires expensive equipment and is time consuming, and thus is not practical for use with large groups of people.

Of the alternative approaches to measurement, the most common is the use of skinfold measurements. Skinfold measurements are taken from several selected sites, such as the triceps, subscapular, or thigh, with skinfold calipers. Formulas are then used to calculate the percentage of body fat. This method is relatively inexpensive, can be used with large groups of people, and produces accurate information when performed by well-trained individuals.

Another approach is the use of the body mass index. *Body mass index* (BMI), a height-to-weight ratio, is calculated by dividing an individual's weight, in kilograms, by the height in meters, squared (BMI = weight/height^2). To calculate the BMI for a male who is 5'8" tall and weighs 170 lb, you would perform the following steps:

◆ Convert weight to kilograms by dividing pounds by 2.2 (170/2.2 = 77.3 kg).
◆ Convert height in inches to meters by multiplying by 0.0254 (68" × 0.0254 = 1.73 m).
◆ Square the height in meters (1.73 × 1.73 = 2.99 m^2).
◆ Divide the weight by the height squared (77.3 kg/2.99 m^2).

The BMI is 25.8. For males, a BMI of 19.0 to 24.9 is considered within the fitness zone.[7] For females, a BMI of 18.0 to 24.4 is considered within the fitness zone.[7] A BMI greater than 27.8 for males and 27.3 for females indicates the individual is heavy for his or her height and may be at increased risk for disease.[7] An excessively low BMI is not desirable and can be associated with health problems such as eating disorders or chronic fatigue.

The BMI allows large populations to be quickly screened for potential health risks to body composition. However, sometimes the results can be misleading when the excess weight is lean as opposed to fat tissue. For example, individuals who engage in a high level of strength training, such as athletes, may have a high BMI. These individuals are not at risk for obesity-related disease because their excess weight is due to lean tissue. For

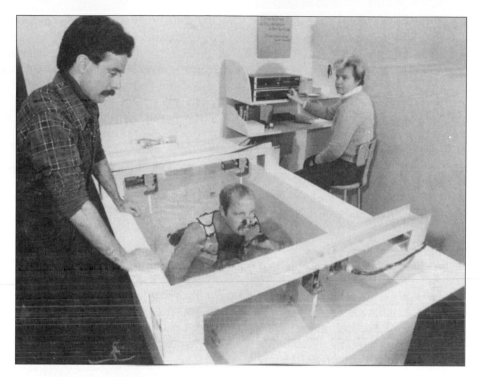

Underwater weighing is a sophisticated, accurate technique used to determine body composition.

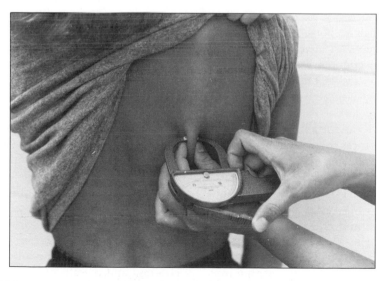

Skinfold measurements can be used to calculate a person's percentage of body fat.

this reason, it is suggested that the BMI be interpreted in conjunction with other measures of body composition.

Muscular Strength and Endurance

Muscular strength is the ability of a muscle or muscle group to exert force against a resistance. Specifically, it is the maximum amount of force that a muscle or muscle group can apply against a resistance in a single effort.

The ability of a muscle or muscle group to exert force repeatedly is known as muscular endurance. Muscular endurance also refers to the capacity of a muscle or muscle group to sustain a contractive state over a period of time.

Muscular strength and endurance are specific to each muscle or muscle group. That is, different muscles in the body can have different levels of strength and endurance. Moreover, muscles used more frequently are stronger and have greater endurance than muscles used less frequently. Maintenance of strength and endurance requires that the muscles be used. When muscles are not used, strength and endurance decrease.

Many people perceive muscular strength and endurance as important only for athletes or those engaged in occupations that require heavy work, for example, construction. While muscular strength and endurance are necessary for these people to perform their responsibilities effectively, these fitness components are also important for all people. Strength and endurance are necessary for performing everyday tasks, maintaining proper posture, and resisting fatigue. As individuals age, maintaining adequate levels of strength and endurance is particularly important, as these fitness components play a critical role in the maintenance of functional independence. Additionally, the development of adequate strength and endurance is an important objective of many rehabilitation programs.

Muscular strength and endurance are important to good health. They contribute to the maintenance of proper posture and the improvement of personal appearance. Because strong muscles provide better protection for body joints, the risk of joint injuries is decreased. Millions of Americans suffer from low-back pain. Weak abdominal muscles and poor flexibility contribute to this problem. Strengthening the appropriate muscles and developing increased flexibility can help alleviate this condition.

High levels of muscular strength and endurance are important for athletes. Many of the advances in athletic performance can be attributed to improvements in training techniques, especially the development of strength. Strength is a critical element of sport performance. Strength training for sport must be specifically related to the particular characteristics required for performance of the sport. Thus the strength training of a sprinter will differ markedly from that of a shot putter, which will be different from that of a gymnast. For effective performance, each athlete requires the development of a high level of strength in specific muscles or muscle groups.

Strength combines with other physical elements to enhance the quality of performance. For example, power, which is strength combined with speed, is an important motor-skill fitness component. Power is the quality that permits a basketball player to jump high and to snare rebounds off the backboard, a golfer to drive a golf ball 250 yards down the fairway, or a gymnast to execute a double-back somersault. Many movements in sport require an explosive effort during execution. When force is generated quickly, the movement is known as a *power movement*. Power is critical to successful performance in many sports today, and proper strength training can enhance this component.

Isometric, isotonic, and isokinetic exercises can be used to develop muscular strength and endurance. Body movements depend on the contraction of muscles. As a muscle contracts, tension is created within the muscle and the muscle shortens, lengthens, or remains the same.

Isometric exercises. A muscle contracts isometrically when it exerts force against an immovable resistance. Although tension develops within the muscle, the length of the muscle remains relatively constant and there is little or no movement of the joint. This is also referred to as a *static contraction*.

When performing isometric exercises, the individual exerts maximum force against an immovable object and tension develops within the muscle. For example, stand in a doorway and place the palms of your hands at shoulder height against the frame. Push with all your might and feel the tension develop in your muscles. Even though you grunt and groan as you contract your muscles to their maximum, it is impossible for you to move the resistance, in this case the door frame. Another approach to performing isometric contractions is to contract one muscle against another muscle, applying an equal and opposite force; in this case, the opposing muscle serves as a resistance. For example, raise your arms to shoulder height and place your palms together. Push against your palms as you contract your muscles. There should be no movement as your muscles work against one another.

When one is performing isometric exercises, it is suggested that the muscle should generate a maximum force for 5 seconds, with the contraction repeated 5 to 10 times each day. Isometrics offer the advantage of not requiring any equipment; any immovable object, or your own body, serves as the resistance. One frequently cited disadvantage of isometric exercise is that strength is developed at only a specific joint angle, not through the entire range of motion. Isometric exercises were most popular in the late 1960s to early 1970s. Isometric exercises now are most often used to develop strength at a specific joint angle to enhance a particular movement or for injury rehabilitation.

Isotonic exercises. Isotonic contractions occur when force is generated while the muscle is changing in length. Movement occurs at the joint, and the muscles involved shorten and lengthen. For example, for one to lift a weight from its starting point when performing a biceps curl, the biceps muscle must contract and shorten in length. This is called a *concentric contraction*. To control the weight as it is lowered back to the starting position, the biceps muscle continues to contract while gradually lengthening. This is referred to as an *eccentric contraction*. When exercising isotonically, it is essential to use both concentric and eccentric contractions for the greatest improvement to occur and also to exercise through the range of motion.

One problem associated with isotonic training is that the force applied to the weight varies throughout the range of motion. This is

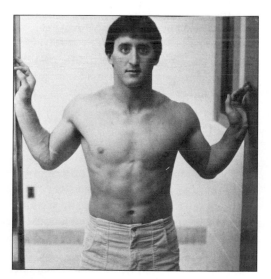
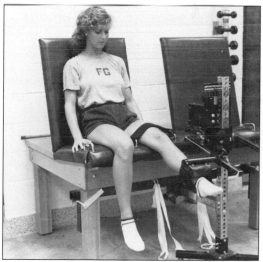

A, Isometric exercise is force exerted against an immovable resistance. **B,** An isokinetic device, such as the Orthotron, provides resistance at a constant velocity.

attributable to the effects of gravity and the system of levers within the body. Once the initial resistance is overcome, lifting the weight can be easy or difficult, depending on the position of the weight relative to the body. Thus the muscles are not working at or near their maximum effort throughout the range of motion.

Common forms of isotonic exercise equipment are free weights, barbells, dumbbells, and various machines such as the Universal gym. Some isotonic exercise machines, such as Nautilus, have been designed specifically to vary the resistance throughout the range of motion. This permits the muscles to exert their maximum effort throughout the entire range of motion.

Isotonic exercises are probably the most popular means of developing strength and endurance. Millions of people use this approach to achieve and maintain desired levels of muscular development.

Isokinetic exercises. When one is performing isokinetic exercises, the length of the muscle changes while the contraction is performed at a constant velocity. Isokinetic devices such as Cybex, Orthotron, and Mini-gym are designed so that the resistance can be moved only at a certain speed, regardless of the amount of force applied. The speed at which the resistance can be moved is the key to this exercise approach. Because isokinetic machines can be expensive, they are most often used in the diagnosis and treatment of various injuries.

The advantages and disadvantages of each exercise approach have been debated in the scientific literature. Many researchers have examined the various types of exercise and training approaches to determine which are safest and most effective for producing a desired gain. Understanding how to design programs using each approach and their advantages and disadvantages probably will be included in your professional preparation coursework.

Muscular strength and endurance can be improved. Many different methods of training can be effective to develop these fitness components. Although weight training is not necessary to realize gains in muscular strength and endurance, this approach is popular with many people. The term *progressive resistance exercise* is commonly used to denote weight-training programs that involve working out against a resistance that is progressively increased as the muscle adapts to the workload or resistance.

Although all principles of training should be incorporated into a weight-training program, the principle of overload is of critical importance. Improvements in strength and endurance occur only when a muscle or muscle group is worked at a higher level than that to which it is accustomed—it must be overloaded. As muscle development increases, the body adapts to the level of resistance. To further improve, the workload must be progressively increased. Once the desired level of fitness is achieved, maintenance of this level requires continued training at the current resistance.

Before discussing the general guidelines for training, it may be helpful to define the following terms:

♦ *Resistance* is the workload or weight being moved.
♦ *Repetition maximum (RM)* is the maximum force that can be exerted or the weight of resistance lifted. One RM is the maximum weight that can be lifted in a single effort. The intensity of the workout can be expressed as a percentage of 1 RM. For example, if a person can bench-press 200 lb, 80% of 1 RM would be 160 lb. Each repetition would be completed using this weight.
♦ *Repetition* is the performance of a designated movement or exercise pattern through the full range of motion.
♦ *Set* is the number of repetitions performed without a rest.

When planning a training program, consideration must be given to the weight used per lift, the number of repetitions per set, the number of sets per workout, and the number of workouts per week. Because there are so many weight-training programs available, only general guidelines with respect to the intensity, duration, and frequency will be presented.

Intensity. The intensity of the workout refers to the extent to which the muscles are overloaded. Overload can be accomplished by any combination of

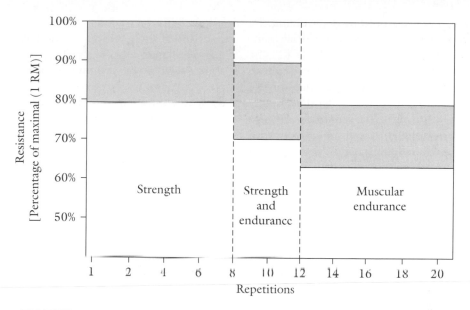

FIGURE 7-2   Guidelines for developing strength and muscular endurance.

the following: increasing the resistance or weight lifted, increasing the number of repetitions per set, increasing the number of sets per workout, increasing the speed at which the repetition is performed, and decreasing the time for rest between sets.

Programs can be designed to develop either strength, endurance, or both. The differences between these programs pertain to the number of repetitions and the amount of resistance. Generally, a strength-training program emphasizes a low number of repetitions (e.g., 8 or less) with a heavy resistance (e.g., 70–80% or greater of 1 RM), whereas endurance-training programs involve performing a high number of repetitions (e.g., 12 to 20) with a low resistance (e.g., 40–70% of 1 RM). For the development of both strength and endurance, a moderate number of repetitions (e.g., 8 to 12) and a moderate resistance are used. Guidelines for strength and endurance training are shown in Figure 7-2. The weight that will create an adequate resistance varies with the individual and the goal of the program.

Time. The duration of the training program depends on the person's level of fitness, fitness goals, equipment available, and time available to work

out. Three sets are often completed of each exercise. The amount of rest between each set varies according to the individual's program.

Frequency. The training program must include time for the muscles to rest and recover from the workout while adapting to a higher physiological level. The same muscle group should not be worked on successive days. It is recommended that exercises be performed 3 or 4 days per week or every other day.

Muscular strength and endurance can be measured. Because muscular strength and endurance are specific to each muscle or muscle group, the level of development can vary among the various muscles or muscle groups. Therefore, the strength and endurance of each muscle or muscle group must be measured.

Strength can be measured isometrically by using a dynamometer. As muscle contraction occurs, the force is transmitted to the instrument and can be recorded (e.g., the hand dynamometer can be used to determine grip strength). Strength can be measured isotonically by determining the maximum amount of weight that can be moved once through the designated range of motion (e.g., bench press); this is 1 repetition maximum or 1 RM.

Endurance can be measured by determining the number of repetitions of a particular movement that can be performed continuously (e.g., the number of repetitions of the bench press that can be performed with a designated resistance) or the number of repetitions performed within a specified period of time (e.g., the number of sit-ups that can be performed in 1 minute). Endurance also can be determined by measuring the time a specific contraction can be sustained (e.g., how long a static push-up can be held).

Measurement of strength and endurance should be specific to the muscle or muscle group. In terms of health fitness, the AAHPERD Physical Best Fitness Program assesses abdominal muscular development and upper body muscular development with the use of modified sit-ups and pull-ups, respectively.

Flexibility

Flexibility can be defined as the maximum range of motion possible at a joint—that is, the extent of movement possible about a joint without undue strain. Although it is one of the most important fitness components, it is often overlooked, and consequently its development is neglected.

Flexibility is not a general quality; it is specific to a particular joint, such as the knee, or to a series of joints, such as the spinal vertebral joints. This means that an individual can have a better range of motion in some joints than in others.

The extent of movement possible at a joint is influenced by the structure of the joint. For example, the elbow and the knee are hinge joints, allowing movement in one direction only; flexion (bending) and extension (straightening) are the only movements possible. In contrast, the shoulder and hip are ball and socket joints; this joint structure allows movement in many directions, usually with a greater range than the hinge joint. Soft tissues such as muscles, tendons, and ligaments greatly influence the range of movement possible at a joint. Flexibility is affected by the length that a muscle can stretch (i.e., its elasticity). When muscles are not used, they tend to become shorter and tighter, thus reducing the joint's range of motion.

Flexibility is essential to performing everyday tasks and is also a critical component in the performance of many sport activities. Activities such as gymnastics, yoga, swimming, karate, and dance place a premium on flexibility. Limited flexibility decreases the efficiency with which everyday and sport activities can be performed. Thus the development of flexibility should be addressed in designing a fitness program.

Flexibility is important to good health. Flexibility is important for maintaining good posture. Poor postural alignment can cause pain and limit one's ability to move freely.

Flexibility can help prevent low-back pain. Nearly 85 million Americans suffer from episodes of low back pain each year. This condition is caused by poor muscle development and poor flexibility. Improving muscle development and flexibility in conjunction with using proper care in sitting, standing, and lifting objects can help alleviate this condition.

Flexibility is also important for preventing muscle injuries. Poor flexibility can contribute to uncoordinated and awkward movements, thus increasing the potential for injury. Muscle soreness and body stiffness following vigorous physical activity can be alleviated by using a good stretching program to develop flexibility both before and after an activity session.

Flexibility is important for the performance of physical activities. Flexibility contributes to the efficient performance of all kinds of physical activities, including everyday tasks and sports. Flexibility helps one perform these tasks to one's fullest potential.

Flexibility is important to the performance of even the simplest everyday activities. Imagine how difficult it would be to get dressed without adequate flexibility. Developing and maintaining flexibility are critical to help elderly persons be functionally independent. Some physical conditions, such as arthritis or cerebral palsy, severely restrict flexibility. Improving flexibility to the greatest degree possible, given one's capabilities, can have a significant impact on one's quality of life—even to the extent of allowing a dependent individual to become functionally independent.

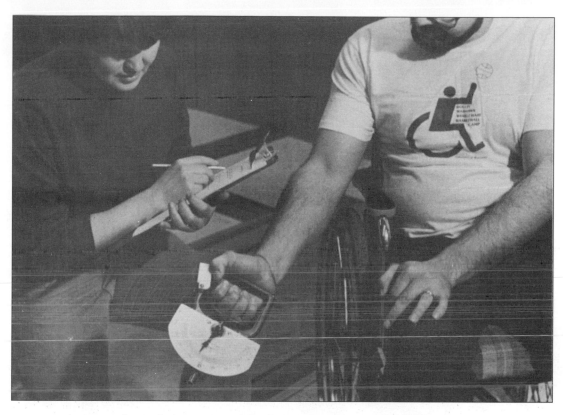

Some devices are specially designed to assess grip strength.

Athletes recognize the importance of flexibility in sport performance. Adequate flexibility can enhance performance capabilities by allowing the athlete to stretch and reach further, to generate more force when kicking or throwing an object, and to change positions more quickly and efficiently. Poor flexibility can adversely affect performance. For example, a sprinter may have a shorter stride length and less speed because tight hamstring muscles can adversely affect his or her ability to flex the hip joint. Because certain sports require an extremely high degree of flexibility for successful performance, stretching exercises to enhance flexibility are typically included as part of an athlete's warm-up and cool-down activities. These activities enhance the elasticity of the muscles and thus help reduce the likelihood of injury and muscle soreness.

Decreased flexibility can be caused by many factors. People who are active tend to have better flexibility than those who are sedentary. When muscles are not used, they tend to become shorter, tighter, and lose elasticity. Consequently, flexibility decreases. Age is another factor that influences the extent of flexibility. It is important to encourage people to remain active as they grow older so that the effects of aging on fitness will be minimized.

Excessive amounts of body fat impede movement and flexibility. Consider the difficulty of severely obese persons when they are trying to tie their shoelaces: the fat deposits serve as a wedge between the parts of the body, thereby restricting movement.

Muscle tension can affect flexibility. Individuals who experience prolonged stress often respond by bracing or tensing the muscles in their neck,

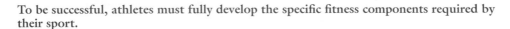

To be successful, athletes must fully develop the specific fitness components required by their sport.

shoulders, and upper back. This tightens the muscles for long periods, thus reducing flexibility. Muscle imbalance also can restrict flexibility. When weight training, for example, if an individual strengthens one group of muscles around a joint while neglecting the development of the opposing group (e.g., the quadriceps muscle group in the front of the thigh is strengthened but the hamstring muscle group in the back of the thigh is not), flexibility will be decreased. Therefore, to ensure maximal flexibility when weight training, it is important to perform each exercise correctly,

through the full range of motion, and develop opposing muscle groups.

Flexibility can be improved. There are several different approaches to developing flexibility. Participating in some physical activities can promote flexibility. Swimming, for example, can improve the flexibility of several joints. Also, because the activity is non-weight-bearing, swimming in a warm pool is often recommended for people with arthritic conditions.

Flexibility also can be improved through a stretching program. Because flexibility is specific

Maintaining flexibility helps elderly people continue to function independently.

The alternate toe touch is an example of a ballistic exercise, which is not recommended by experts. The sitting hamstring stretch is safer and can be performed using static stretching or the contract-relax technique.

to each joint, improvement and maintenance of flexibility requires a program that incorporates specific exercises for the major joints of the body. Flexibility exercises can be performed using ballistic, static, or contract-relax stretching techniques.

Ballistic stretching. This dynamic method uses the momentum generated from repeated bouncing movements to stretch the muscle. Although it is effective, most experts do not recommend this technique because it may overstretch the muscle and cause soreness or injury.

Static stretching. An extremely popular and effective technique, static stretching involves gently and slowly moving into the stretch position and holding it for a certain period of time. Movement should take place through the full range of motion until a little tension or tightness is felt in the muscle or muscle group. As the muscle relaxes, the stretch should be extended and held again. Stretching should not be painful. Care must be taken not to force the joint to move too far, which could cause an injury. Stretches should be held from 10 to 30 seconds and a minimum of five repetitions performed for each exercise. Flexibility exercises should be performed at least three to five times a week. If flexibility at a particular joint is extremely poor, a daily stretching program can be recommended. Flexibility exercises also should be performed at the start and at the end of a workout.

Contract-relax technique. When one is performing stretching exercises, it is important that the muscles involved are relaxed. The contract-relax technique facilitates the relaxation of muscles. Muscles are arranged in pairs; when one contracts, the opposing muscle in the pair relaxes (e.g., when the quadriceps muscles contract, the hamstring muscles relax). When one uses this technique to develop flexibility, the muscle opposite the one to be stretched is contracted for at least 5 seconds. This relaxes the muscle to be stretched. Then the static stretch is performed on the desired muscle. To apply this technique to the development of hamstring flexibility, an individual would contract the quadriceps muscles, thus relaxing the hamstrings. Then a static hamstring stretch is employed. This technique allows the stretch to be performed through a greater range of motion.

A goniometer can be used to measure hip flexion.

Because flexibility is specific, a program for improvement and maintenance of flexibility must include exercises for each movement at the joint for which flexibility is being developed.

Flexibility can be measured. Because flexibility is joint specific, there is no one test that can be used to provide an overall measure of an individual's flexibility. The goniometer, a large protractor with movable arms, provides a measurement of the range of movement in terms of degrees.

There also are a number of tests that have been developed to measure movement at certain joints and require little equipment to perform. The AAHPERD Physical Best Fitness Program, for example, uses the sit-and-reach test to assess the flexibility of the lower back and hamstring muscles.

CONDUCTING FITNESS PROGRAMS

Physical education and sport professionals must follow the principles of exercise when designing a fitness program. The principles of specificity, overload, and progression must be taken into account. Careful consideration must be given to providing for individual differences and for safety. When planning a fitness program to meet individual needs, practitioners must ensure that the participant exercises with sufficient intensity, duration, and frequency to attain desired fitness goals.

Equally important to realizing long-term fitness benefits is the manner in which the program is conducted. Physical education programs in the schools, cardiac rehabilitation programs, and adult fitness programs in community, commercial, and corporate settings should be conducted in a manner that optimizes the chances for maintaining health fitness throughout life.

Fitness programs should include cognitive and affective educational goals as well as physical activity. For fitness to become an integral part of one's life, one must be taught fitness knowledge and an appreciation for the benefits of fitness. Participants should know (1) why fitness is important, (2) the risks associated with being unfit, (3) guidelines for designing a personal exercise program, and (4) how to evaluate and solve their own fitness problems. Program experiences should be structured to develop a positive attitude and a long-term commitment to fitness. These goals can be accomplished by fostering an understanding of the contributions of fitness to one's quality of life. Program participants should have the opportunity to develop proficiency in several physical activities that can be used throughout their lives.

Fitness should be fun. Boring and tedious exercises and calisthenics do little to develop enthusiasm for fitness. Fitness activities should meet the needs and interests of the program participants. Activities selected should be enjoyable to the individual while permitting the attainment of fitness objectives. Not everyone likes to jog; some prefer swimming, bicycling, tennis, or soccer. Practitioners should help each program participant find an activity that is enjoyable yet sufficiently strenuous to contribute to the attainment of fitness goals. When participants engage in activities that are personally satisfying, they are more likely to incorporate those activities into their lifestyle.

Fitness goals should be established and a plan of action to attain them should be developed. Specific fitness goals based on individual needs should be established for program participants. Some individuals may wish to develop an optimal level of cardiorespiratory endurance, others may hope to lose weight, and still others may

GUIDELINES FOR DEVELOPING HEALTH-RELATED FITNESS

Cardiorespiratory Endurance
- ◆ Frequency: 3–5 days/week
- ◆ Intensity: 60–90% MHR*
- ◆ Time: 20–30 minutes
- ◆ Type: Aerobic activity

Muscular Strength and Endurance
- ◆ Frequency: 3 days/week
- ◆ Intensity: Strength requires high resistance, 6–8 repetitions
  Endurance requires low resistance, 12–20 repetitions
- ◆ Time: 3 sets
- ◆ Type: Isotonic or progressive resistance exercises; can also use isometrics and isokinetic exercises

Flexibility
- ◆ Frequency: 3–7 days/week
- ◆ Intensity: Stretch past the normal length until resistance is felt
- ◆ Time: Hold the stretch from 5–10 seconds initially, building to 30–45 seconds
- ◆ Type: Static stretching exercises preferred

Body Composition
- ◆ Maintain present level of physical activity and reduce caloric intake
- ◆ Maintain present level of caloric intake and increase level of physical activity
- ◆ Reduce caloric intake and increase level of physical activity
- ◆ Eat a diet low in fat.

* 50% MHR may be appropriate depending on the health and fitness status of the individual

strive to enhance their flexibility to perform daily living tasks more easily. Such individual objectives must be considered when conducting a program.

Goals provide a direction for participants and help to focus their energy and effort. Goals should be realistic and a reasonable amount of time allotted to attain them. Fitness does not happen overnight—it requires effort, determination, and discipline. Once long-term goals have been established, short-term or weekly goals should be set to help move toward the desired outcome. It is important for program participants to realize that the development of an acceptable level of fitness requires time. It is estimated that 60% or more of the adults who start an exercise program drop out within the first month. Participants should be informed that it will take time for the effects of their efforts to be noticed or felt. It may take as long as 8 weeks to experience many of the major benefits. However, by monitoring their weekly efforts, individuals will be able to see that they are making progress.

Fitness progress should be monitored. Progress should be monitored on a regular basis. This will help individuals to notice their improvement. Each participant should be encouraged to keep a personal fitness log of information, such as the number, time, and intensity of exercise sessions; calories consumed and calories expended; weight changes; and personal feelings pertaining to exercise. Monitoring progress regularly is reinforcing and provides a means of assessing one's improvement.

Fitness requires a maintenance program. Once the desired fitness goals are achieved, a maintenance program is needed. When a person stops exercising, fitness gains are lost in a short time. Just as weight lost is quickly regained if a person reverts to poor eating habits, fitness gains are quickly lost if a person reverts to poor activity habits.

Participants in a fitness program often ask, "How long do I have to keep exercising?" or "Now that I have reached my goal, what do I need to do to keep it?" or "What will happen if I stop exercising?" Fitness gains are easily lost once training stops. Cardiorespiratory gains deteriorate most quickly and can disappear within a few weeks or months of inactivity (5 to 10 weeks).[7,10] Strength gains are longer lasting; some strength gains remain for 6 months to 1 year after cessation of training.[7,10]

Because fitness diminishes when exercising is stopped, an exercise program should be an

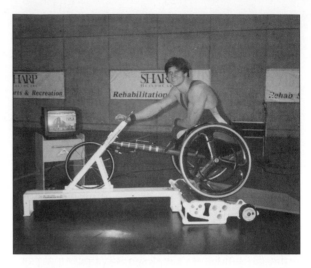

Specialized fitness equipment has been developed to meet the needs of athletes in wheelchairs. This resistance trainer, created by D & J Development, has an interactive computer that simulates road racing conditions.

integral part of one's life. Once the desired fitness goals are achieved, a maintenance program should be incorporated into one's lifestyle. Because it is easier to maintain fitness than to acquire it, modifications can be made in the intensity, duration, or frequency of exercise. However, minimal standards for these components should be followed and exercise must be continued on a regular basis.

Fitness improvements and maintenance are a personal responsibility. Achievement and maintenance of an optimal level of fitness require a personal commitment. Individuals must take personal responsibility for their fitness. Fitness must be valued for the important contributions it makes to one's life. Each person must realize that the benefits accrued from participation in a fitness program are indeed worthy of the effort. All persons must be encouraged to incorporate fitness activities into their lifestyle.

EFFECTS OF TRAINING

The results derived from regular periods of muscular work or exercise are many and varied.

Individuals who participate regularly in exercise adapted to their needs and thereby attain a state of physical fitness may be called *trained*. Individuals who allow their muscles to get soft and flabby and are in poor physical condition can be referred to as *untrained*.

A trained individual is in a better state of physical fitness than a person whose life is sedentary and inactive. When two persons, one trained and one untrained, of approximately the same build are performing the same amount of moderate muscular work, evidence indicates that the trained individual has lower oxygen consumption, lower pulse rate, larger stroke volume per heartbeat, less rise in blood pressure, greater red and white blood cell counts, slower rate of breathing, lower rate of lactic acid formation, and a faster return to normal of blood pressure and heart rate. The heart becomes more efficient and is able to circulate more blood while beating less frequently. Furthermore, in strenuous work that cannot be performed for a long period of time, the trained individual has greater endurance, a capacity for higher oxygen consumption, and a faster return to normal of heart rate and blood pressure. Training results in a more efficient organism. Since improved efficiency of heart action enables a greater flow of blood to reach the muscles and thus ensure an increased supply of fuel and oxygen, more work is performed at less cost; improvements in strength, power, neuromuscular coordination, and endurance occur; coordination and timing of movements is better; and an improved state of physical fitness results.

PHYSICAL ACTIVITY RECOMMENDATIONS FOR GOOD HEALTH

As previously discussed, experts have reached a consensus that cardiovascular health benefits can be achieved by engaging in physical activity below the threshold of training necessary to produce fitness benefits. The Centers for Disease Control and Prevention, the American College of Sports Medicine, and the Surgeon General's report on *Physical Activity and Health*[1] recommends that adults should engage in 30 minutes of physical activity equal to brisk walking on most, preferably all, days of the week. Activity can be accumulated in bouts of 8–10 minutes, but 30-minute sessions are preferred. Activity of greater intensity will yield greater health benefits and is encouraged. Children over the age of 2 should accumulate at least 30 minutes a day of moderate intensity physical activity on most, preferably all, days of the week. Additional physical activity should be encouraged. The National Institutes of Health Consensus Development Conference Statement on Physical Activity and Cardiovascular Health emphasized the importance of children and adults accumulating the minimum of 30 minutes of physical activity on a daily basis. Active lifestyles are encouraged for people of all ages

One way that activity for health benefits can be monitored is through the measurement of caloric expenditure. Caloric expenditure provides an indication of the energy expended. It is recommended that a minimum of 1,000–1,500 calories be expended a week in regular physical activity or no less than 1.35 calories per pound of body weight per day. For optimal health benefits, an expenditure of 2,000–3,500 calories per week is recommended. However, it should be noted that for health benefits to occur, calories must be expended by engaging in activities on most, if not all, days of the week and for long periods of time. Activity must be an integral part of one's lifestyle if these benefits are to be attained.

The important health benefits associated with engaging in resistance training to promote strength led the Centers for Disease Control and Prevention, the American College of Sports Medicine, and the Surgeon General's report on *Physical Activity and Health*[1] to recommend that adults perform strength-developing activities at least twice a week. It was recommended that at least 8–10 strength-developing activities that use the major muscle groups of the legs, trunk, arms, and shoulders be performed at each session, with one or two sets of 8–12 repetitions being performed for each exercise.

These activity recommendations offer people of all ages a multitude of options for including physical activity into their lives. It is hoped that these recommendations will encourage people who were discouraged by the difficulty of adhering to a program of vigorous exercise, such as that associated with health fitness, to include moderate amounts of physical activity into their lives.

SPECIAL CONSIDERATIONS FOR FITNESS

There are many different factors that should be considered in conducting fitness programs. Environmental conditions should be carefully weighed by program leaders. Leaders and program participants should know how to modify their exercise program based on weather conditions. They should also be familiar with the risks associated with exercising in hot and humid weather as well as extreme cold.

Misconceptions about exercise and weight control programs abound. Leaders and program participants should know the truth so that they can make healthy, appropriate decisions about participation.

Program leaders and participants should be cognizant about various contributors and deterrents to fitness. Proper nutrition and stress management can enhance individuals' fitness and overall health and well-being. Deterrents to fitness, such as tobacco, drug abuse, and alcohol, interfere with the attainment and maintenance of fitness and health.

Environmental Conditions and Fitness

Participants' safety should always be the primary concern of professionals conducting fitness programs. Exercising in an exceptionally hot, humid environment or in extreme cold requires both short- and long-term physiological adaptations by the body. Professionals and participants should be aware of the risk these conditions impose and how fitness programs need to be modified for safe participation.

Extreme caution must be used when exercising in hot, humid weather. The body's normal temperature is 98.6°F. During exercise, as the body's temperature rises, several methods are used by the body to cool itself. The main method of cooling is evaporation. As you exercise, you perspire or sweat, and the evaporation of the sweat keeps the body temperature within normal limits. When it is hot and when the relatively humidity reaches 65%, heat loss through evaporation is less effective, and the body's ability to dissipate heat is impaired.[7] Additionally, excessive sweating and lack of fluid replacement can lead to dehydration. A person who is dehydrated stops sweating, and evaporation no longer cools the body. Heat-related problems such as heat cramps, heat exhaustion, and heat stroke can occur under hot and humid conditions.

Heat cramps are muscle cramps, typically in the muscles most used in exercise. Heat exhaustion is characterized by muscle cramps, weakness, dizziness, disorientation, nausea, elevated temperature, profuse sweating, rapid pulse, and collapse. Heat stroke is a life-threatening emergency. The symptoms include a sudden collapse, unconsciousness, rapid pulse, relatively dry skin from lack of sweating, and a core body temperature of 106°F or higher. In heat stroke, the sweating mechanism breaks down and the body is unable to dissipate heat by sweating. If heat stroke occurs, immediate action is necessary to reduce the temperature of the body and access medical care.

To prevent heat-related problems, use caution when exercising in hot, humid weather. Be sure to drink plenty of fluids before, during, and after exercise to replace fluids lost through evaporation. Water and commercial sport drinks such as Gatorade, Powerade, and Thirst Quencher are good for replenishing fluids. Exercise in the coolest part of the day, either early in the morning or in the evening. On extremely hot and humid days, participants should consider decreasing the intensity of their workout to reduce heat stress. Other considerations may involve canceling the workout or exercising indoors in a cool environment. It is also important to take time to acclimatize the body to the hot and humid weather. Acclimatization occurs usually in 5 to 7 days.[7] Exercise should be reduced from the normal level as the body adjusts to the stress of heat.

Cold weather also requires precautions be taken during exercise. Conserving heat is a major concern when exercising in cold weather. Hypothermia, the breakdown of the body's ability to produce heat, can occur when the weather is between 50°F to 60°F and it is damp and windy. Hypothermia occurs when the body temperature drops below 95°F. Shivering and loss of coordination initially occur. As the body's temperature drops further, shivering stops, muscles stiffen, and unconsciousness occurs. This is a medical emergency, and first-aid efforts should focus on raising the body's temperature and seeking immediate medical attention.

Extreme cold can also lead to frostbite. To prevent cold-related problems, participants should be aware of the conditions that contribute to hypothermia. Before exercising, individuals should check both the temperature and wind chill to determine whether it would be dangerous to exercise. Dress properly for exercise in cold weather. Hats should be worn to reduce the loss of body heat through the head. Several light layers of clothing should be worn so that the body temperature can be more easily regulated. Try to avoid getting wet in cold weather, which increases the risk for hypothermia. To prevent frostbite, wear a mask, gloves, and a hat. Be sure to take time to gradually acclimatize to exercising in the cold. In extreme conditions, consider canceling or limiting workouts or moving to an activity that can be performed indoors.

Environmental conditions pose challenges to individuals seeking to work out on a regular basis. It is important to be aware of the current weather conditions, the risks they impose, and the adaptations necessary to exercise safely. Maintaining the core body temperature, taking time to gradually acclimatize to conditions, following safety precautions, and using common sense can help reduce the health risks associated with exercising under conditions of extreme heat, humidity and cold.

Misconceptions about Exercise and Weight Control Programs

Despite the widespread public enthusiasm for fitness, many misconceptions about exercise and weight control still exist. Many people still believe that exercise burns relatively few calories, making its contribution to weight loss insignificant. In reality, exercise can significantly alter the energy or caloric balance, thus facilitating weight loss. It is also erroneously believed that exercise automatically increases appetite; the opposite has been shown to be true. Exercise tends to suppress the appetite and thus contributes to a reduction in caloric intake. Moreover, the increase in the metabolic rate from exercising continues after the workout, thereby burning additional calories.

Another common misconception is that exercise can be used for spot reducing; that is, it can reduce fat from a specific area of the body such as the thighs, upper arms, or abdomen. Research shows that fat loss occurs in proportion to the amount of fat in the body, so that fat loss is greater in those areas with large amounts of fat as compared with those areas where there is less fat. Exercise will, however, increase muscle development in a specific area and may produce a shift in body fluids. While this may enhance one's appearance, it does not significantly reduce the amount of fat in that specific area.

Another fallacy is that passive exercise machines can be used to reduce body weight. Vibrators, rollers, and whirlpools are commonly promoted as means to reduce weight. Electrically powered exercise equipment, such as an exercise bike that only requires the individual to turn it on and sit on it while it does all the work, is increasingly more common. None of these passive approaches to exercise can reduce body fat.

Americans spend billions of dollars a year in a quest to lose excess body fat and weight. Seeking to lose weight and inches quickly, countless people turn to specialized diet plans and pills or enroll in health clubs and fitness programs. Steam baths and saunas are viewed by many people as an effective way to lose weight. Although weight is lost through sweating, such loss is only temporary. The lost fluid is quickly replaced, and the weight is regained. Advertisements promote various gimmicks and gadgets to promote rapid weight loss. These include rubberized or vapor-impermeable suits that purportedly sweat the weight off and mechanical devices that claim to vibrate and shake the fat off. While some approaches to weight loss are based on sound scientific evidence, many approaches fall far short of the fervent claims.

Consumers must learn to discriminate between proper and improper weight-loss approaches and realize that there is no quick and easy method to lose weight. The bottom line is that weight loss requires burning more calories than are consumed. Weight loss and weight maintenance require the integration of sound nutritional practices and regular exercise into one's lifestyle. There is no quick answer to the achievement and maintenance of fitness. Fitness requires dedication, commitment to integrate fitness into one's lifestyle, and use of appropriate training techniques. Physical education and sport professionals must educate the public about the facts pertaining to fitness.

Contributors to Fitness

Proper nutrition and effective stress management contribute to the attainment of a high level of health fitness. Nutrition is important for maintaining a desirable body composition. Physical activity can play an important role in stress management.

Nutrition and Fitness

Nutrition plays an important role in enhancing fitness and health. As a science, nutrition is concerned with the study of foods and their effect on the human body. The central focus of nutrition is the study of food requirements for the production of energy and the regulation of bodily processes.

"You are what you eat" is an adage that captures the critical contribution of nutrition to our health and well-being. What we eat can affect our health, growth and development, and ability to perform various activities that fill our lives. In terms of health fitness, the foods we consume directly affect our body composition and the energy we have available to engage in physical activity. The energy derived from food is measured in kilocalories, which are commonly referred to as calories. Regulating one's energy balance by carefully monitoring caloric consumption and expenditure is important in achieving a desirable level of health

fitness. Individuals must also take care to consume sufficient calories so that they have the energy necessary for work and to lead a physically active lifestyle.

A nutrient is a basic substance that is used by the body to sustain vital processes such as repair and regulation of cellular functions and the production of energy. The six major categories of nutrients are carbohydrates, fats, proteins, vitamins, minerals, and water.

Carbohydrates, proteins, and fats—the three basic foodstuffs—provide the energy required for muscular work. They also have a critical role in the maintenance of body tissues and in the regulation of their functions. Carbohydrates are the major source of energy for the body, and fats are a secondary source.

Vitamins and minerals have no caloric value. Although they are required only in small amounts, they are essential to body functioning. Vitamins are needed for normal growth and development. Vitamins do not provide energy directly, but play a critical role in releasing energy from the foods that are consumed. Minerals are essential to the regulation and performance of such body functions as the maintenance of water balance and skeletal muscle contraction.

Water is the most basic of all the nutrients—it is necessary to sustain life. The most abundant of all the nutrients in the body, water accounts for approximately 60% of the body's weight. Water is necessary for all of the chemical processes performed by the body. It is essential for such functions as energy production, digestion, temperature regulation, and elimination of the by-products of metabolism.

Maintaining a proper water balance is crucial. Insufficient water causes dehydration; severe dehydration can lead to death. People who are physically active should carefully monitor their water intake to ensure that an adequate fluid balance is maintained. This is particularly critical for individuals who exercise in a hot, humid environment. Exercising under these conditions typically causes excessive sweating and subsequently large losses of water. Sufficient water should be drunk to ensure that proper fluid balance is maintained.

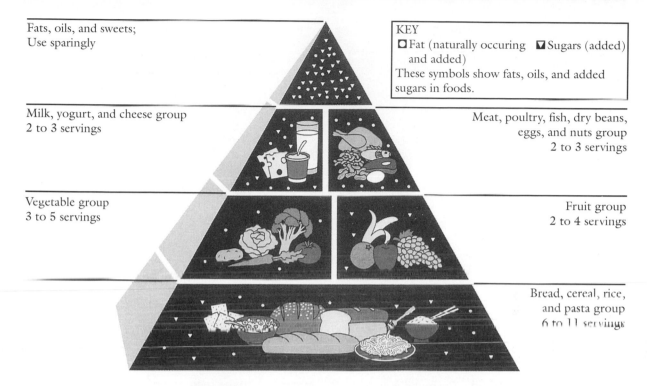

Fats, oils, and sweets;
Use sparingly

KEY
☐ Fat (naturally occuring   ◪ Sugars (added)
   and added)
These symbols show fats, oils, and added
sugars in foods.

Milk, yogurt, and cheese group
2 to 3 servings

Meat, poultry, fish, dry beans,
eggs, and nuts group
2 to 3 servings

Vegetable group
3 to 5 servings

Fruit group
2 to 4 servings

Bread, cereal, rice,
and pasta group
6 to 11 servings

FIGURE 7-3   The USDA Food Guide Pyramid.

A well-balanced diet is necessary to obtain all the nutrients required by the body. The Food Guide Pyramid, shown in Figure 7-3, was designed by the United States Department of Agriculture (USDA) to help people eat a balanced diet that includes sufficient servings from each food group. The base of the food pyramid is the grain group, and the vegetable and fruit group occupy a position above it. Next is the dairy group and the group composed of meat, poultry, fish, dry beans, eggs, and nuts. At the top of the pyramid are fats, oils, and sweets, with an accompanying note advising that these products be used sparingly. All necessary nutrients can be obtained daily by eating a variety of foods from each of the food groups and by following recommendations for servings.

In planning a daily diet, it is also important to carefully monitor caloric intake and the amounts of carbohydrates, fat, and protein consumed. Current dietary practices and recommended dietary goals are shown in Figure 7-4. U.S. health officials have expressed a concern that the current American diet is too high in fat, cholesterol, sugar, and sodium and is lacking in carbohydrates and fiber. Dietary guidelines are shown on page 258.

Dietary planning requires the thoughtful application of nutritional knowledge to ensure that the diet is adequate and balanced. Individual conditions and factors such as age, sex, weight, medical conditions, environment, and level of physical activity must be considered in dietary planning. Because of the significant impact of nutritional practices on health, the production of energy for physical activity, and the regulation of body composition, attaining and maintaining desirable levels of health fitness require careful attention to nutritional practices.

Stress Management and Fitness

Stress is defined as the body's physiological response to demands placed on it. These demands

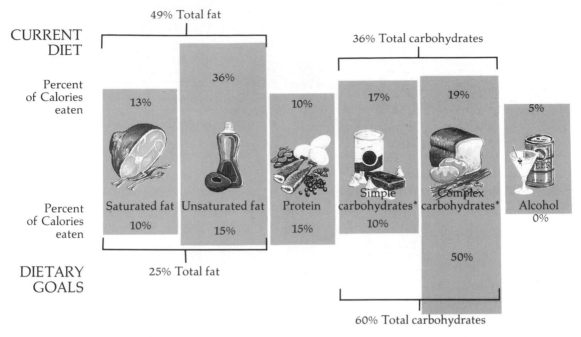

*Estimates based on Senate Select Subcommittee on Nutrition and Health data.

FIGURE 7-4 Current diet in the U.S. compared with the recommended diet.

or stress-producing agents are referred to as stressors.

There are many different types of stressors. Physical stressors are changes in the body's internal or immediate external environment that require the body to adapt. Diet, noise, drugs, exercise, illness, and extremes of temperature are examples of physical stressors.

Many of the stressors that affect our lives today are cognitive in nature. Cognitive stressors occur as a consequence of an individual's perception of an event. Thus whether or not a demand causes stress depends on how the individual chooses to interpret an event and react to it. Events that are interpreted as stressful elicit emotional arousal, which is subsequently manifested in physiological arousal. Some examples of situations that an individual might interpret as stressful are public speaking, taking an exam, value conflicts, and peer pressure.

With respect to cognitive stressors, individuals' perceptions not only determine whether or not an event is stressful but also influence the intensity and

CURRENT DIETARY GUIDELINES FOR AMERICANS (1995)

◆ Eat a variety of foods.
◆ Balance the food you eat with physical activity—maintain or improve your weight.
◆ Choose a diet with plenty of grain products, vegetables, and fruits.
◆ Choose a diet low in fat, saturated fat, and cholesterol.
◆ Choose a diet moderate in sugars.
◆ Choose a diet moderate in salt and sodium.
◆ If you drink alcoholic beverages, do so in moderation.

duration of the stress. Given the same situation, one individual will interpret it as a nonstressor, another individual as a moderate stressor, and yet another individual as a major stressor. Individuals'

Participating in enjoyable activities is an effective means of managing stress. These athletes are competing in archery at the New York State Senior Games.

perceptions and beliefs about their ability to control their lives also influence their handling of the stressor. Some individuals may interpret a demand as a challenge to be overcome, whereas other individuals may interpret the same demand as a threat to their well-being. When perceived as challenges, life's stressors can foster personal growth and development; the same stressors when perceived as a threat can contribute to disease.

Stressors elicit a vast array of changes in the body, resulting in an elevated level of physiological arousal. These changes include increased levels of cardiorespiratory function and skeletal muscle tension. This heightened level of physiological arousal is often referred to as the "fight or flight" response.

When individuals experience stress too frequently, too intensely, or too long, illness can occur. Stress has been found to play a role in coronary heart disease, cancer, hypertension, respiratory disease, gastrointestinal disease, eating disorders, and depression. Stress also impairs the functioning of the immune system. Because of its effect on health and the bodily processes, stress can adversely affect the level of physical fitness.

Managing stress effectively is important to attaining a high level of physical fitness. The goal of stress management is to use stress advantageously, not to eliminate all stress from one's life. An optimal level of stress helps us perform at our best; too little stress or too much stress detracts from our performance. Perhaps the best example is from the realm of athletics. Athletes perform at their best when they are "psyched up"; athletes who are insufficiently or excessively psyched typically experience a decrement in performance.

Management of stress requires that the individual become aware of events that lead to stress, recognize when the stress response is occurring (e.g., become aware of increased heart rate, anxiety, bodily tension), and take steps to reduce stress by either eliminating the stressor or reducing its effects.

A diversity of approaches can be used to manage stress. These include relaxation training, participation in physical activity, cognitive strategies to change an individual's perception of the stressor (i.e., choosing to interpret the event as a challenge rather than a threat), time management, and biofeedback. Unfortunately, some individuals select inappropriate coping techniques, such as alcohol and drug use. Although these techniques may deal with the stress in the short term, over a period of time they can adversely affect one's health and serve as a deterrent to achievement of fitness.

Engaging in regular physical activity and exercise can help individuals effectively manage their stress. Because individuals who are physically fit have a better health status, they are more resistant to the effects of stress than less physically fit individuals. Physical activity has long been recognized as a means of releasing tension and pent-up emotions. Physical activity can also provide a means for the healthful expression of the "fight or flight" response, facilitating the body's return to a normal physiological state. There is recognition of the psychological benefits of regular physical activity.

Relaxation techniques also can be incorporated into many fitness programs. One popular approach is progressive relaxation. This method is based on the premise that individuals are not aware that their muscles are excessively tense. Through planned, progressive movements, individuals tense one muscle group in their body and then relax the muscle group, focusing their attention on the differences they experience between the tense and relaxed states. Individuals apply this approach systematically to their entire body, working with one group of muscles and then moving onto the next. Individuals may begin at the head and work toward their toes or begin at their toes and work toward their head. As individuals become proficient in this technique, they increase their awareness of excessive muscle tension and become able to relax their muscles and release tension at will.

Practitioners should realize the importance of effective stress management in achieving physical fitness. Further, practitioners should recognize the contribution they can make to help individuals learn how to manage stress effectively. Practitioners working in a diversity of settings, ranging from schools to hospitals to various fitness program sites, can help individuals learn how to relax effectively, understand the contribution of physical activity to effective stress management, and learn specific skills to regulate stress.

Deterrents to Fitness

Today's sedentary lifestyle is a major deterrent to fitness. Modern technology has greatly reduced the number of occupational and daily living tasks that require significant physical activity. Tasks such as mowing the lawn are made easier by power mowers. Driving has replaced walking, and elevators have replaced much stair climbing. Many of our leisure activities are sedentary in nature, most notably watching television. Consequently, many Americans do not engage in sufficient physical activity to function at an optimal level. To achieve health benefits, Americans must make a conscious decision and an ongoing commitment to incorporate physical activity into their lives. Individuals can follow a structured exercise program, participate in physical recreational activities, and be more physically active in their everyday routine, for example, by taking the stairs instead of the elevator or parking farther away from a destination and walking the remaining distance.

In addition to inactivity, other lifestyle choices also can serve as deterrents to fitness. Choosing to eat a high-calorie, high-fat diet over a period of time can lead to serious health consequences. Tobacco use is another deterrent to fitness. Smoking cigarettes has been linked to several diseases, most notably lung cancer. Concern has also been raised over the use of smokeless or chewing tobacco, especially the increased use in recent years by young teens and adults. Excessive alcohol consumption and use of drugs such as marijuana and cocaine are also detrimental to achievement of physical fitness.

How we choose to manage the stress we experience can also affect our fitness status and health. Some individuals choose to alleviate stress by using methods that can have an adverse affect on their health in the long run, such as by drinking alcoholic beverages. Persons who desire a healthy lifestyle can manage stress by engaging in appropriate physical activity, seeking the support of friends, and using cognitive strategies that help place stressful experiences in an appropriate perspective.

Individuals who aspire to achieve an optimal level of health and physical fitness must carefully examine their lifestyle choices and behaviors.

Professionals in the realm of physical education, exercise, and sport can make an important contribution to the health of Americans by educating them about the value of leading a positive, physically active lifestyle. However, education alone is not enough. These professionals must provide Americans of all ages and abilities with the skills to be physically active throughout their lifetime.

Tobacco and Fitness

Tobacco use is a major deterrent to achieving health and fitness. The Centers for Disease Control and Prevention estimates that an average of 430,700 premature deaths a year are related to smoking.[11] Approximately 25% of adults smoke. Children and teenagers constitute 90% of all new smokers, with the average youngster starting smoking at age 13. Regular users of tobacco products, especially cigarettes, are more likely to become sick, to suffer from debilitating and extended illnesses, and to die prematurely. The health risk increases with the age at which the individual started smoking, the number of years the individual has smoked, and the number of packs of cigarettes smoked per day. Individuals who start to smoke at an early age (i.e., adolescence) and continue to smoke heavily throughout their life are at greatest health risk and are more likely to die prematurely than their nonsmoking counterparts. The hazardous effects are not limited to users; secondhand smoke is a carcinogen and contributes to the death of 15,000 nonsmokers each year.

Smoking tobacco has been linked to several diseases. Cigarette smoking is a major risk factor in cardiovascular disease, the leading cause of death among all U.S. adults. Tobacco use has been found to play a significant role in all cancers. The American Cancer Society estimates that tobacco use is a factor in approximately 85% of lung cancer cases, and 21% of all coronary heart disease deaths are smoking related.[12] Women who smoke encounter additional health risks. Tobacco use has been found to be associated with problems of infertility, pregnancy, and health status of the newborn child. Smoking is responsible for 20–30% of all low-weight newborns and is linked to Sudden Infant Death Syndrome.[12]

Tobacco use also leads to a host of complex physiological changes that impair physical fitness. Smokers experience shortness of breath and lowered cardiorespiratory endurance. The oxygen-carrying capacity of the blood is reduced, and cardiovascular functioning is impaired. When the body's oxygen-transporting abilities are impaired, it has difficulty responding to the increased demands that physical exertion places on the cardiorespiratory system. The functioning of this system is also impaired as a result of tobacco use. For all these reasons, people who smoke have decreased ability to lead a physically active lifestyle. Not only is smoking harmful to health, but it also impairs the ability to engage in health-promoting behaviors, such as regular physical activity.

The use of smokeless tobacco also presents a serious health risk. Because chewing tobacco and snuff are placed directly in the mouth, users may experience periodontal disease, damage to mouth tissues, and tooth loss from the biochemical changes associated with tobacco use. Smokeless tobacco users are at great risk for oral cancer. They are also at risk for digestive system and urinary tract cancers because users inadvertently swallow saliva that contains carcinogens. In short, smokeless tobacco is associated with severe health risks and should not be considered a safe alternative to cigarette smoking.

Numerous efforts have been made to caution people about the dangers of cigarette smoking. Every cigarette package is imprinted with a message from the U.S. Surgeon General warning the users about health effects; for example, one message reads: "Smoking causes lung cancer, heart disease, emphysema, and may complicate pregnancy." Increasing numbers of schools are including tobacco as part of their drug education curriculum. Government and private restrictions against smoking continue to increase. It is clear that tobacco use is a deterrent to achieving an optimal level of health and fitness.

Drug abuse

The abuse of drugs is another deterrent to fitness. Drug abuse is defined as the use of an illicit drug or the use of a legal drug in a manner that is harmful to health and well-being.[13] Most often abused are psychoactive drugs that can alter one's feelings, behavior, and perceptions. These drugs include stimulants, depressants, hallucinogens, cannabis, opiates, and inhalants. Abusers use these drugs primarily because of their influence on behavior and mood; many substances are used because of the feeling of euphoria or "high" they produce.

Use of these drugs over a period of time can lead to physical and psychological dependence. Physical dependence or addiction occurs when the individual's body needs the drug to maintain its dynamic balance or physiological homeostasis.[13] Continued drug use can lead to tolerance, in which there is diminution of the effects produced by using the drug. To achieve the same effects, the user must consume more of the drug. When an individual is dependent on a drug and does not take it, withdrawal occurs. An individual in the throes of withdrawal may experience such unpleasant symptoms as irritability, depression, nervousness, and digestive difficulties.

Psychological dependence occurs when the user experiences strong emotional cravings or longings to use the drug, despite the health consequences or other problems associated with using the drug.[13] These individuals believe that continued use of the drug is essential to maintaining their sense of well-being.

Many health risks are associated with drug abuse. The degree of risk to the health of an individual depends on the drug abused, the length of time it is used, and the quantity used. Among the related health problems are reduced resistance to infection; damage to the heart, liver, lungs, and kidneys; nutritional difficulties; anxiety; and depression. Additionally, one of the most serious risks associated with the abuse of certain drugs, such as cocaine, is the possibility of death from an overdose or a severe reaction. The adverse physical and psychological effects associated with drug abuse serve as a deterrent to fitness.

Alcohol and fitness

Alcohol is a drug. A strong central nervous depressant, alcohol affects the brain and the spinal cord. Consumption of alcohol can lead to impairment of motor coordination, judgment, and memory. Heavy, rapid consumption of alcohol can lead to serious and life-threatening consequences, including the shutdown of the brain centers that control respiration, heartbeat, and body temperature.

Many individuals choose to drink alcohol because they find it helps them alleviate inhibitions and be more outgoing and confident in social situations. Other people drink alcohol because it helps them relax and relieve anxiety. Social pressures also influence people to use alcohol.

Alcoholism is a serious disease that affects more than 10 million Americans. Individuals who are alcoholics have a pattern of alcohol use characterized by physical and emotional dependence and loss of control over alcohol consumption. Alcoholism not only affects the individual's health but also exerts a negative impact on all aspects of the individual's life, including work, family, and daily activities.

Many serious health problems are associated with chronic alcoholism. Gastrointestinal disorders, liver damage, cardiovascular disease, central nervous system impairment, malnutrition, and some forms of cancer have been linked to heavy alcohol consumption. Additionally, alcohol has been found to play a role in reproductive health problems in women and has been found to impair the health of the unborn child. Heavy drinking can lead to fetal alcohol syndrome (FAS). FAS is characterized by mental retardation, poor growth and development, and a wide range of physical defects, such as cleft palate. This syndrome has long-term implications for the health of the child. Additionally, it has been found that even mild drinking by pregnant women can adversely affect the health of the fetus. Therefore the Surgeon General recommends that women who are considering becoming pregnant or who are pregnant drink no alcoholic beverages.

Because alcohol can adversely affect health, it is a deterrent to fitness. Because alcoholic beverages are high in calories and low in nutrients, regular consumption may negatively affect one's body composition and overall level of fitness. Persons who choose to drink alcohol generally are advised to do so in moderation.

SUMMARY

Exercise physiology is the study of the effects of exercise on the body ranging from the level of the system (e.g., cardiovascular system) to the subcellular (e.g., production of ATP for energy) level. Exercise physiologists are interested in both the acute and chronic adaptations of the body to exercise. Professionals in physical education and sport build on this foundational knowledge in many different ways. Knowledge from exercise physiology is used to design effective fitness programs for people of all ages, to guide the development and implementation of cardiac rehabilitation programs, to plan programs to help children and youths to incorporate physical activity into their life, to conduct training programs for elite athletes, and to structure rehabilitation programs for injured athletes and exercise enthusiasts.

A major concern of the exercise physiologist is fitness development, maintenance, evaluation, and outcomes. Within the profession, interest has increased in health-related fitness as opposed to performance-related fitness. The components of health-related and performance-related fitness are different. And, the extent to which these components are developed depends on individuals' goals. The health-fitness components are cardiovascular function, body composition, muscular strength and endurance, and flexibility. Attainment of desirable levels of these components can enhance one's health and well-being. Individuals who are unfit are at increased risk for disease.

Many health benefits are derived from physical fitness and the incorporation of physical activity into one's lifestyle. Physical education and sport professionals should follow medical guidelines and sound training principles in developing and implementing physical fitness programs. Professionals should be aware of contributors to fitness, such as sound nutritional practices, and deterrents to fitness, such as tobacco and drug abuse. Although the American public's interest in fitness is at an all time high, misconceptions about exercise, diet, and weight control abound. Physical education and sport professionals must take an active role in educating the American public about proper fitness and nutritional practices.

SELF-ASSESSMENT TESTS

These tests are designed to help you determine if you have mastered the material and competencies presented in this chapter.

1. Define exercise physiology and discuss the importance of exercise physiology to the professionals in physical education and sport. Investigate one of the areas of study in exercise physiology and write a short paper on a selected topic of interest to you.

2. Using the information provided in the Getting Connected box, access the *FitnessLink* site. Select two articles to read. Summarize and critique the articles. Share them with your classmates or small discussion group.

3. Using the information provided in the Getting Connected box, access the *PHYS Calculators* site. Calculate your target heart rate, calories expended, body mass index, and health risk. Perform the same calculations for a friend or a parent. Critically review the results. Were they accurate? Discuss the pros and cons of having such information readily available on the World Wide Web.

4. In a short paper, discuss how an individual's lifestyle and habits may be a deterrent to a state of fitness and health. What rationale would you use to persuade a friend or a relative who was tired all the time, feeling overwhelmed by stress, and overweight to start a physical fitness program? What excuses may be offered for not being active? How could you counter these excuses?

REFERENCES

1. US Department of Health and Human Services: Physical activity and health: a report of the Surgeon General, Atlanta, Ga., 1996, US Department of Health and Human Services, Centers for Disease Control and Prevention, National Center for Chronic Disease Prevention and Health Promotion.

2. Siedentop D: Introduction to physical education, fitness, and sport, Mountain View, Calif., 1990, Mayfield.

3. Blair S, Kohl H, and Powell K: Physical activity, physical fitness, exercise, and the public's health, The Academy Papers 21:53–69, 1987.

4. Public Health Service, US Department of Health and Human Services: Promoting health/preventing disease: year 2000 objectives for the nation, Washington, D.C., 1990, US Government Printing Office.

5. Blair S: 1993 C. H. McCloy research lecture: physical activity, physical fitness, and health, Research Quarterly for Exercise and Sport 64:365–376, 1993.

6. Sallis JF, Simons-Morton BG, Stone EJ, Corbin CB, Epstein LH, Faucette N, Iannotti RJ, Killen JD, Klesges RC, Petray CK, Rowland TW, and Taylor WC: Determinants of physical activity and interventions in youth, Medicine and Science in Sports and Exercise 24(6), Supplement: S248–S257, 1992.

7. Prentice W: Fitness for college and life, ed 5, St. Louis, 1997, Mosby.

8. Pollock ML and Blair SN: Exercise prescription, Journal of Physical Education, Recreation, and Dance 52(1): 30–35, 81, 1981.

9. Corbin CB and Lindsey R: Concepts of physical fitness with laboratories, Dubuque, Iowa, 1997, Brown & Benchmark.

10. Hockey RV: Physical fitness: the pathway to healthful living, St. Louis, 1989, Mosby.

11. Centers for Disease Control and Prevention Fact Sheet: Cigarette mortality, September 22, 1997 (www.cdc.gov.).

12. Department of Public Health Alabama: Health department opposes tobacco use, Press Release, April 15, 1997.

13. Payne WA and Hahn DB: Understanding your health, St. Louis, 1992, Mosby.

SUGGESTED READINGS

Corbin CB and Lindsey R: Concepts of physical fitness with laboratories, Dubuque, Iowa, 1997, Brown & Benchmark.

Fitness concepts focusing on health-related fitness are presented, along with laboratory experiences and self-assessment inventories. Topics include physical activity and health, health-related fitness, information on development of fitness components, special considerations for physical activity, and leading a healthy lifestyle.

Corbin CB and Pangrazi RP: How much physical activity is enough? JOPERD 67(4):33–37, 1996.

This article provides clarification of physical activity recommendations in an easy to understand question-and-answer format.

Pangrazi RP, Corbin CB, and Welk GJ: Physical activity for children and youth, JOPERD 67(4): 38–43, 1996.

The authors discuss physical activity recommendations for children and adolescents as well as the appropriateness of the FIT formula for this population group.

Pitetti KH: Clinically relevant symposium: exercise capacities and adaptations of people with chronic disabilities-current research, future directions, and widespread applicability, Medicine and Science in Sports and Exercise 25(4):412–472, 1993.

A series of articles on exercise and special populations, including individuals with paraplegia, quadriplegia, mental retardation, and multiple sclerosis.

Prentice W: Fitness for college and life, ed 5, St. Louis, 1997, Mosby.

Guidelines and activities to promote health-related fitness, including fitness development of all health-related components, nutrition, stress management, and injury prevention and care. Self-assessment tests are included.

Robergs RA and Roberts SO: Exercise physiology: exercise, performance, and clinical applications, St. Louis, 1997, Mosby.

This text begins with an overview of exercise physiology and covers topics related to cellular metabolism, physiological adaptations to exercise, aids to exercise performance, measurement of physiological parameters, and exercise and health.

CHAPTER 8

Sociological Foundations of Physical Education and Sport

Instructional Objectives and Competencies to be Achieved:

After reading this chapter the student should be able to—

◆ Show how sport is a socializing force in the American culture.

◆ Discuss the nature and scope of sport.

◆ Trace the growth of sport in educational institutions in the United States and the attitude of educators toward this growth.

◆ Discuss the sociological implications of educational sport.

◆ Know the dimensions of selected problems with which sport is confronted today such as those concerned with girls and women, children, minorities in sport, violence, and the Olympics.

◆ Formulate a philosophy of sport.

Sport is an important part of this nation's culture and other cultures throughout the world. It captures newspaper headlines, holds television viewers' attention, produces millions of dollars a year in revenue for entrepreneurs, and even impacts international affairs. The Olympic Games is one of the best known international sports events. The Olympic Games are seen by billions of people worldwide. In 1995 NBC paid the International Olympic Committee $3.6 billion for the television rights to the Olympic Games for the years 2000 through 2008. Corporations, eager to capitalize on this large market, pay the International Olympic Committee millions of dollars to be one of many "exclusive" sponsors (e.g., the official credit card, film, sun glasses, etc.). For the 1994 Winter Games and the 1996 Summer Games, each corporate sponsor paid $40 million dollars in cash, goods, and services.

Sport exerts a strong influence on many aspects of the American lifestyle. Millions of Americans are "glued" to their chairs when featured baseball, football, basketball, and golf contests are scheduled to be televised. Advertisers target large percentages of their promotional budgets to buy airtime during sporting events to sell their wares. For example, a 30-second advertisement aired during

GETTING CONNECTED

Gender Equity in Sport—Title IX is the University of Iowa's site on Title IX: overview, history, myths, current research reports, and court actions.

      Site: http://www.lib.uiowa.edu/proj/ge/

National Collegiate Athletic Association site offers an array of information, including information about graduation rates, current news, and statistics.

      Site: http://www.ncaa.org

National Federation of State High School Associations provides information on athletic participation by girls and boys.

      Site: http://www.nfshsa.org

Physical Activity and Sport in the Lives of Girls is an interdisciplinary report on the physical and mental benefits of participation by girls in physical activity and sport.

      Site: http://www.kls.coled.umn.edu/crgws/pcpfs/pcpfs.html#summary

the 1998 football Superbowl sold for $1.3 million. The 1998 rate of $2.6 million a minute is in sharp contrast to the $75,000 charged to advertise during the first Superbowl in 1967. Professional sports teams attract millions of spectators each year. Professional teams spend astronomical sums to obtain the best talent to sustain spectator support and interest and to ensure a profitable year for management. Newspaper coverage devoted to sports occupies more space than all the arts combined, and sports symbols and jargon infiltrate American language, art, and politics.

The big business of sport has also influenced the nature of college and secondary school sport. Schools and colleges, in an effort to field the best teams, may compromise their academic standards. It is not uncommon for academically outstanding colleges to be more widely recognized for the feats of their athletic teams.

Within the last 10 years the number of sport participants in our society has increased dramatically. Millions of people of all ages and abilities participate in a diversity of sport activities. Because of the social, political, legal, and educational influ-

ence of sport on cultures, it is important to examine this phenomenon.

SOCIOLOGY OF SPORT

Sport pervades society to such an extent that it has been described by many experts as a microcosm of society. In other words, sport mirrors the values, structure, and dynamics of our society.[1] As such, sport reflects the characteristics of society. Eitzen and Sage[2] point out that among the characteristics that sport and our society have in common are a spirit of competitiveness, a large concern about materialistic things, the presence of a bureaucracy that dominates individuals, and an inequitable distribution of power. The pervasiveness of sport and its institutional nature have led to the study of sport from a sociological perspective.

Sociology is concerned with the study of people, groups, institutions, human activities in terms of social behavior and social order within society. It is a science interested in such institutions of society as religion, family, government, education, and leisure. Sociologists are also concerned with

The emphasis on being number one is so strong in the U.S. that second-place trophies are often perceived as reminders that someone else was better. Second place is often said to be the "loser's spot."

the influence of social institutions on the individual, the social behavior and human relations that occur within a group or an institution and how they influence the behavior of the individual, and the interrelationships between the various institutions within a society, such as sport and education or religion and government.

As a medium that permeates nearly every important aspect of life, sport has led some physical educators and sociologists to believe that it should receive intensive study, particularly as it affects the behavior of human beings and institutions as they form the total social and cultural context of society. Sport sociology focuses on examining the relationship between sport and society. Coakley[3] lists the major goals of sport sociology to be an understanding of the following:

♦ Factors underlying the creation and the organization of sports

♦ The relationship between sport and other aspects of society, such as family, education, politics, the economy, the media, and religion
♦ The influence of sport and sport participation on individuals' beliefs relative to equity, gender, race, ethnicity, disability, and other societal issues
♦ The social dynamics within the sport setting, such as organizational structure, group actions, and interaction patterns
♦ The influence of cultural, structural, and situational factors on the nature of sport and the sport experience
♦ The social processes associated with sport, including competition, socialization, conflict, and change.

As an area of study, the sociology of sport has grown considerably over the past 30 years. One important event that encouraged the development of sport sociology as a field of study was the initiative of a multinational panel of the International Council of Sport and Physical Education (ICSPE). This group was responsible for the creation of the International Committee of Sport Sociology (ICSS) in Geneva in 1964. In the late 1970s and early 1980s, the North American Society for the Sociology of Sport and the Sport Sociology Academy were established. The North American Society for Sport Sociology holds annual meetings and sponsors the *Sociology of Sport Journal*. The Sport Sociology Academy is one of the academies sponsored by the National Association for Sport and Physical Education (NASPE). It provides an opportunity for dissemination of research and a forum for discussion at the annual meetings of AAHPERD. The ICSS meetings are held in conjunction with those of the International Sociological Association; the ICSS cosponsors the *International Review for the Sociology of Sport* and the ICSS *Bulletin*.

Sport sociologists use sociological research strategies to study the behavior of individuals and groups within the sport milieu. They are concerned with understanding the influence of social relationships, past social experiences, and the social setting of sport activities on the behavior of individuals and groups within sport. Some questions sport sociologists might address are these:

♦ Does participation in sport build character? Does it prepare individuals for life?

♦ Does sport help minorities, including women, become more fully integrated into society? How does participation in sport affect the social and economic status of minorities?

♦ How do the mass media affect sport?

♦ What are the effects of youth sport programs on the lives of participants? the participants' families?

♦ How are politics and sport related? religion and sport? the economic status of the community or the country and sport?

♦ How does interscholastic and intercollegiate sport influence the academic achievement of its participants?

♦ How do coaches influence the lives of their athletes?

♦ What will be the nature of the sport experience in the twenty-first century?

To address these and other questions, sport sociologists may examine historical circumstances, social conditions, economic factors, political climate, and relationships among the people involved.

As a field of study, sociology of sport will likely continue to grow, expanding both in depth and breadth. However, many challenges face the field. For example, Coakley[3] points out that there is a need for further research leading to the development of theories about sport and its relationship to society and social life. Furthermore, Coakley suggests that there is a need to focus additional attention on female participants in sport and on participation in sport throughout one's lifespan (currently only childhood and early adulthood participation are highlighted).

Sport can be viewed as a social institution and examined in relation to its impact on other social institutions such as the economy or the educational system. The effects of sport on participants are also a vital area of study. Before discussing several areas of concern to sport sociologists, it may be helpful to define sport and discuss its nature and scope.

Definition of Sport

In order to study sport in a systematic manner, it is necessary to develop a specific definition of sport. Such a definition may, by its very nature, be limiting and restrictive. Yet it is necessary to provide a focus and a shared perspective by which to understand the relationship of sport to society.

Coakley suggests that sport can be defined as follows:

Sport is an institutionalized competitive activity that involves vigorous physical exertion or the use of relatively complex physical skills by individuals whose participation is motivated by a combination of intrinsic and extrinsic factors.[3]

This definition refers to what is popularly known as organized sport activities. On the basis of this definition, three often asked questions can be addressed: (1) what kinds of activities can be classified as sport? (2) under what circumstances can participation in activities be considered sport? and (3) what characterizes the involvement of participants in sport?

Sport activities

What physical activities can be considered sport? Is jogging a sport? chess? auto racing? weight lifting? Are participants in a pickup baseball game engaged in sport even though their activity is different in nature from the game professionals play?

Sport, as it is defined, requires that participants use relatively complex physical skills and physical prowess or vigorous physical exertion. Because these terms can be conceptualized as part of a continuum, at times it is difficult to make the distinction between physical and nonphysical skills, between complex and simple motor requirements, and between vigorous and nonvigorous activities. Because these terms are not quantified, determining what is complex physical activity and what is not can be a difficult task. Furthermore, not all physical activities involving complex physical skills or vigorous physical exertion are classified as sport. The circumstances and conditions under which these physical activities take place must be considered when classifying a physical activity as sport.

Conditions

The circumstances in which participation in physical activities occurs can be designated as ranging from informal and unstructured to formal and structured. For instance, compare the nature of a playground pickup game of basketball with a scheduled game between two professional teams. The individuals involved in both situations are playing basketball, but the nature and consequences of these games are different. Thus, the question—are both groups of individuals engaged in sport?

When sport sociologists discuss sport, they most often are referring to physical activity that involves competition conducted under formal and organized conditions. Given this perspective, friends engaged in an informal game of basketball are not participating in sport, whereas athletes participating on the professional teams are participating in sport. From the sociological point of view,

Sport is said to be *institutionalized* when there is standardization and enforcement of the rules, emphasis on organization, and a formal approach to skill development.

sport involves competitive physical activity that is institutionalized.

According to sociologists, institutionalization is a standardized pattern or set of behaviors sustained over a period of time and from one situation to another. Thus, competitive physical activity can be considered sport when it becomes institutionalized. Institutionalization occurs when there is standardization and enforcement of the rules governing the activity, emphasis on organization and the technical aspects of the activity (e.g., training, use of strategies, specialization and definition of the roles of players and coaches) and a formalized approach to skill development (e.g., use of experts to provide instruction). Through the process of institutionalization, unstructured and informal physical activities such as throwing a Frisbee become a sport known as *Ultimate Frisbee* where competition and organization are an integral part of the setting in which the activity takes place.

Participation motives

Sport depends on maintaining a balance between intrinsic and extrinsic motivations. When the intrinsic satisfaction of being involved coexists with extrinsic concern for external rewards (e.g., money, medals, approval from parents or a coach), sport occurs. The balance does not have to be 50:50, but when one source of motivation begins to greatly outweigh the other, changes occur in the nature of the activity and the experience of the participants. When participants' intrinsic motives prevail, the organization and structure of physical activity becomes one of play. When participants' extrinsic motives such as medals or money prevail, physical activity changes from sport to what is often referred to as spectacle or work. It should be noted that during the course of a single sport event, participants may shift back and forth from intrinsic to extrinsic sources of motivation. At times participants may be absorbed in the flow of the action and revel in the satisfaction of being involved. Moments later the participants may be motivated by the desire to win a medal or receive the adulation of the crowd; the play spirit becomes replaced with the desire to reap external rewards.

In summary, according to Coakley's definition, three criteria must be met for an activity to be defined as sport. The activity must involve physical skill, prowess, or exertion; it must be institutionalized and competitive in nature; and its participants must be motivated by a combination of intrinsic and extrinsic rewards. These criteria are useful in determining whether or not a physical activity can be classified as sport. Moreover, this definition serves as a focal point for sport sociologists to scientifically examine the role of sport in people's lives and in our society.

WHAT SPORT DOES FOR PEOPLE

Wilkerson and Dodder[4] have conducted research to determine what sport does for people. They found that sport has the following seven functions in society:

1. *Emotional release.* Sport is a way to express emotions and relieve tensions; it acts as a safety valve and a catharsis to relieve aggressive tendencies.
2. *Affirmation of identity.* Sport offers opportunities to be recognized and to express one's individual qualities.
3. *Social control.* Sport provides a means of control over people in a society where deviance is prevalent.
4. *Socialization.* Sport serves as a means of socializing those individuals who identify with it.
5. *Change agent.* Sport results in social change, new behavior patterns, and is a factor that changes the course of history. For example, it allows for interaction of all kinds of people and for upward mobility based on ability.
6. *Collective conscious.* Sport creates a communal spirit that brings people together in a cohesive manner in search of common goals.
7. *Success.* Sport provides a feeling of success both for the participant and the spectator when a player or a team with whom one identifies achieves success. To win in sport also is to win in life.

It is evident that sport, especially in this age of increased participation, holds many meanings for its participants as well as having a significant impact on our society.

SPORT IN THE AMERICAN CULTURE

Sport has had an interesting history in the United States. From the colonial days, when sport for sport's sake was frowned on, until today, when sport has become big business, this phase of the American culture has grown steadily.

Colonial America was concerned with survival. The lifestyle of the early American settlers was concerned with work, not play. Play, in fact, was looked on as a sinful pursuit for adults, particularly in the New England colonies. Only on special occasions did the colonists permit themselves the luxury of engaging in hunts, contests of strength, and competition in wrestling, running, and jumping. However, as years went by and more settlers came to the United States, those activities that were popular in seventeenth-century Europe were introduced. These sports included horseracing, ninepins, hunting, fishing, marksmanship, and dice and card games. Also, the Dutch colonists introduced activities such as bowling, skating, and various types of ball games. With this influx of activities the Puritan opposition to sport gradually gave way to a more liberal and favorable attitude toward participation in games and related activities.

In the postrevolutionary period in the United States interest in sport increased, which continued through the remainder of the eighteenth century and into the nineteenth century. Activities such as rowing and sailing regattas, wrestling and shooting matches, and foot races became popular. In addition, this period saw the introduction of sports into some schools that were modeled after the English educational institutions. The first school to integrate games and sports into the curriculum was the Dummer Grammar School, Byfield, Massachusetts, in 1782. Soccer and baseball were played at Exeter Academy early in the nineteenth century. In college, sports started to be introduced in the middle 1800s, with tennis, baseball, football, rowing, handball, golf, roller skating, ice hockey, and lacrosse becoming popular.

During the last half of the nineteenth century the expansion of sport programs in colleges was slowed to some extent but still steadily increased in popularity. A significant development during this period was the formation of associations of various colleges and universities to have better control of their athletic programs.

In the early 1900s interest was renewed in sport throughout the nation as well as in educational institutions. For example, during the last quarter of the nineteenth century, for the first time in the United States there was a Kentucky Derby, a lawn tennis game, a national baseball league, an Amateur Athletic Union, a sports page in a newspaper, and a Madison Square Garden.

The 1920s saw one of the greatest explosions in sport in the United States. This period produced such outstanding sport figures as Babe Ruth, Bill Tilden, Jack Dempsey, and Ken Strong. The 1920s also saw the beginning of large crowds to attend sport spectaculars. For example, previous to this time boxing had only four $100,000 gates.

However, in the 1920s gates commonly exceeded $1 million and even $2 million.

Since the 1920s a continual expansion of enterprises has occurred in all major areas of sport, such as baseball, basketball, tennis, football, soccer, and golf. Sport has become big business, with billions of dollars being spent on equipment, salaries, stadiums, and supporting supplies. The day of the multimillion-dollar athlete also has arrived. Whereas superstars formerly signed for hundreds and thousands of dollars, many now sign contracts for millions of dollars.

Sport is not just concerned with two teams meeting each other on the playing field. Sport activities are an important part of this nation's culture, and sport sociologists face a challenge in interpreting the role of sport in our way of life. Sport activities in the United States have been found by sociologists to be related to religion, economics, education, and government, to name a few.

Throughout the nation's history sport has been influenced by religious beliefs and economic conditions. During the nation's early developmental years sport activities, especially in New England, were severely hampered because of the religious attitude of the Puritan settlers. Religious attitudes have changed, and some religious institutions are now extremely active in sport. Throughout the nation organizations such as the Catholic Youth Organization and B'nai B'rith provide activities that give youth the opportunity to participate in sport. Schools and colleges under religious control sponsor sport programs.

Sport and the economic conditions of the nation are closely aligned. When the nation was developing, little opportunity was found to participate in sport. However, the rise in industrialization and the resultant increased leisure time have led to an increased awareness of sport. Sport activities have become an important part of American life. Millions of Americans not only take part in sporting events through active participation, but they also spend millions of dollars on sport equipment. They also enjoy sporting events solely as spectators and fans.

Sport has become a part of schools and colleges in the nation. Physical education, intramural, club, and athletic programs have been created by educational institutions to give young people the opportunity to participate in these activities. School sport programs have been associated with improving the fitness of our youth. Within the past decade sport opportunities in colleges and schools have increased tremendously. These programs currently involve millions of youths and young adults in many different sports and at many levels of competition.

SPORT IN EDUCATIONAL INSTITUTIONS

The growth of sport in schools and colleges has been comparatively recent in the United States. The period from 1875 to 1900 saw for the first time a Harvard-Yale football game, a Big Ten Conference, and an All American team. The advent of the radio and "lunar craters," as football coach Alonzo Stagg called the athletic arenas, resulted in an increase in "spectatoritis" and the exploitation of sport for its commercial value.

As sport programs grew, they were extended into the lower educational levels. Athletics started at the college level with a crew race between Harvard and Yale in 1852, followed by the introduction of other sports to the college campus. As higher educational athletic programs gained recognition and popularity, the high schools thought that sports should also be a part of their educational offerings. Next, the junior high schools initiated interschool athletic programs, many of which were carbon copies of those in the senior high schools, which previously had copied the colleges. Today some elementary schools are scheduling games, as competitive sports are pushed further down the educational ladder.

From the beginning, sport was of concern to educators because of its questionable educational worth and the way it can distort a school's or a nation's sense of values. For example, as reported in *Sports Illustrated*, Yale alumni helped raise $180,000 in honor of Walter Camp for the memorial gateway to the Yale Bowl; however, Yale admirers of Josiah Willard Gibbs, one of the greatest physicists the country had produced, were unable to muster $12,000 for a more modest tribute.

Another view of sport in institutions of higher education was advanced by J. Neils Thompson, past president of the National Collegiate Athletic Association (NCAA).[5] Thompson stated, "It seems clear that the image of the institution is clearly influenced by athletic performance. Halfbacks make better copy than philosophers—unfortunate perhaps, but true. Without question, the recruitment of students and the raising of financial support . . . can be favorably impacted by successful athletic programs."

Despite some educators' objections, athletics and sports in the nation's schools, colleges, and universities have continued to grow. Nearly 6.2 million youths participate in sport. In 1996–1997, the National Federation of State High School Associations reported that 3,706,225 boys and 2,472,043 girls participated in interscholastic athletics.[6] Another 16,979 students participated in coeducational sports.[6] Thousands of young men and women participate in collegiate sports. In 1996–1997 the National Collegiate Athletic Association (NCAA), the largest governing body of college athletics, reported that 201,997 males and 129,285 females participated in intercollegiate sports.[7] (This figure includes only those sports in which the NCAA sponsors national championships; thus the overall participation figure is higher.) Title IX and the women's movement have become factors in the participation of an increasing number of girls and women in sports in educational institutions. It is estimated that the number of girls and women participating will gradually approach a figure equal to that of boys and men.

Today school and college athletics are experiencing difficulties beyond those provided by their educational critics. The economy, austerity budgets, student criticism, academic performance of athletes, and concerns for minority and female athletes have caused some educational institutions to curtail, abolish, or reevaluate their sport programs. Since athletics play such an important role in American culture and in physical education

Highly competitive sport opportunities for girls and women have increased during the last decade.

programs, it is interesting to examine some of the sociological implications of sport.

Interscholastic Sports

Interscholastic sports are viewed by many, including the National Federation of State High School Associations, as an integral part of the educational experience for high school students and, increasingly, junior high school students as well. The inclusion of interscholastic sports in the educational curriculum has typically been justified on the basis of sport contributing to educational goals.

While there is widespread support for interscholastic athletics, there has also been much

criticism of these programs. Proponents of interscholastic athletics cite its valuable contributions to the educational mission of the schools. Critics take the position that sport interferes with the attainment of educational goals. Popular arguments for and against interscholastic athletics as presented by Coakley[3] are shown in the box on page 275.

Participation in interscholastic sports can benefit students in several ways. Participation in sport can help students develop a high level of physical fitness and attain a high degree of proficiency in selected sport skills and knowledge of various aspects of the game. Other frequently cited benefits of participation include the development of sportsmanship, cooperation, leadership, and loyalty. Sport can provide opportunities for personal growth, pave the way for the development of friendships, develop decision-making and thinking skills, teach self-discipline and commitment, enhance one's self-esteem and personal status, and promote the acceptance of others regardless of race or ethnic origins.

However, whether participation in sport enhances academic achievement is a very complex and debatable question. When viewed as a group, high school athletes generally have better grade point averages and express more interest in further education than their nonathlete peers.[3] It is important to note, however, that such differences are typically small. Moreover, academic achievement is linked to a number of factors, including academic goals, personal achievement values, and motivation. It is also difficult to isolate the influence of sport participation from other factors known to influence academic achievement such as family background, economic status, support and encouragement from significant others, and individual characteristics.

Interscholastic sport can also heighten school spirit and engender parental support. In many locales across the country, interscholastic athletics provide a focal point for the community.

It appears that interscholastic programs do not use a disproportionate share of budgetary resources when they are maintained in a proper perspective. However, it should be noted that in

POPULAR ARGUMENTS FOR AND AGAINST INTERSCHOLASTIC SPORT

Arguments For

1. Involves students in school activities and increases interest in academic activities
2. Builds the responsibility, achievement orientation, and physical vigor required for adult participation in society
3. Stimulates interest in physical activities among all students in the school
4. Generates the spirit and unity necessary to maintain the school as a viable organization
5. Promotes parental, alumni, and community support for all school programs

Arguments Against

1. Distracts the attention of students away from academic activities
2. Perpetuates dependence and immaturity and focuses the attention of students on a set of values no longer appropriate in industrial society
3. Relegates most students to the role of spectator rather than active participant
4. Creates a superficial, transitory spirit subverting the educational goals of the school
5. Deprives educational programs of resources, facilities, staff, and community support

---

times of austerity they are one of the first extracurricular programs to be threatened with cutbacks.

Whether or not interscholastic sport programs help participants attain desirable educational goals, as well as provide a positive experience for those students involved, depends a great deal on the manner in which the program is conducted. These desired outcomes do not accrue automatically as a result of participation in the program. They can, however, be realized when school administrators and coaches make a concerted and thoughtful effort to structure sport programs to provide experiences that will lead to the attainment of educational goals and fulfillment of students' needs. Suggestions offered by Lumpkin[8] to help promote a positive interscholastic sport experience for participants and the realization of desirable goals are given in the box on page 276.

Interscholastic sport programs are an integral part of the educational experience for millions of U.S. high school students and enjoy widespread support. Nevertheless, in many schools across the country interscholastic sport programs are in serious need of reform. Some programs have little relevancy to the education process. Critics of interscholastic sport also denounce the overemphasis on winning, restriction of opportunities for

students, and eligibility requirements for participation. Concern has also been voiced pertaining to drug abuse, soaring costs, pressures from parents and community supporters, and coaches' behavior.

Overemphasis on winning is one of the most frequently voiced criticisms of interscholastic sport. This disproportionate emphasis is reflected in the increased specialization in one sport by athletes, the participation of injured athletes, the subversion of the educational process, and coaches' jobs depending on their win-loss records.

Compared with just 10 years ago, more high school athletes are foregoing multisport competition and specializing in one sport.[9] Whereas in the past athletes would compete in a fall, a winter, and a spring sport, there is a trend toward competing in only one sport a year. Increasingly, athletes engage in conditioning programs and informal practices for their chosen sport in the off-season and attend specialized sport camps and play in community leagues during the summer. Proponents of sport specialization stress that such an emphasis is needed to develop proficiency in advanced skills and refine strategies, remain competitive with other teams, and increase an athlete's chances of receiving college grants-in-aid. Critics argue that specialization limits athletes' development,

THE INTERSCHOLASTIC PROGRAM

The Interscholastic Sports Program is an outgrowth of the basic instructional program and provides additional physical education experiences in a wide range of sports. The purposes of this program should be to help participants to

Gain a better understanding of their physiological and psychological capabilities, and establish reasonable personal goals

View winning as a means to self-improvement and not as an end in itself

Assume leadership roles in planning and conducting intramural and interscholastic activities

Share in the decision-making process involved in those programs

Participate and/or compete fairly on the factors of age, ability, height, weight, physiological maturity, and strength

Benefit from the expertise of coaches who are certified teachers possessing either a major or a minor in physical education and/or state coaching certification

Receive appropriate medical attention before, during, and after intramural/interscholastic sports programs

1. Medical examinations should be required for all who participate in interscholastic activities.
2. A physician's statement indicating the student's fitness for resuming participation should be required following a serious illness or injury.
3. An athletic trainer or teacher/trainer should be present at all games and practices.

From an administrative standpoint, all secondary school interscholastic contests, including post-season games, should be conducted under the jurisdiction of state high school athletic associations, and the programs should be financed by local Boards of Education.

From AAHPERD.

---

denying them opportunities to develop skills in other activities, participate with other athletes, and learn from other coaches. Athletes who specialize may be exploited by coaches seeking to win, are subjected to overuse injuries, and are at risk for athletic burnout (i.e., are tired and emotionally exhausted from participating) and may drop out of the sport, often near the point of reaching their fullest potential.

In an effort to win, coaches may resort to undesirable behaviors. They may pressure athletes to practice and play when injured. In an effort to maintain player eligibility, coaches may steer athletes toward easier courses, pressure teachers to pass athletes or, in some cases, alter athletes' grades.

Winning is overemphasized when teachers are hired or fired based on their coaching win-loss records rather than their abilities as teachers. Good teachers have been fired because of a poor coaching record, and poor teachers have been retained because of their outstanding coaching accomplishments.

If interscholastic sports are to realize their educational potential, it is important that winning be kept in perspective. The educational goals of learning and development should be emphasized, not the win-loss record.

The restricted number of opportunities for participation is another criticism of interscholastic sports. Interscholastic sports programs usually offer limited opportunities for participation. Schools typically have both a varsity team and a junior varsity team in a variety of sports, although larger schools also may have freshman teams and reserve teams. Thus, when a given school offers both a varsity and a junior varsity basketball team for boys and for girls, perhaps as few as 48 students will have the opportunity to participate. Many students who are less highly skilled are excluded, despite their love of the game, and often no other scholastic sport opportunities are provided for

Title IX legislation stimulated the growth of girls' and women's sports at all levels.

them. Furthermore, in addition to consuming a great deal of the time and energy of physical education teachers, interscholastic sport teams utilize monies, facilities, equipment, and other resources that could be used for general participation. In addition, even though federal legislation has mandated that boys and girls must have equal opportunities, often the informal support and commitment so necessary to develop and maintain quality programs for females is lacking. (This is discussed elsewhere in this chapter.)

Academic requirements for eligibility are also a controversial issue. Most high schools require that students meet certain academic standards to be eligible to participate in extracurricular activities, including sports. These standards often exceed the criteria required to stay in school. Many states have adopted "no pass, no play" policies, setting forth even more stringent requirements for athletes to maintain their eligibility. These requirements vary, but typically the policy bars participation of those individuals who do not pass all of

their courses or who fail to maintain a certain grade-point average during a marking period.

Advocates of this policy believe that establishing stringent standards for participation in sport programs will have a positive effect on athletes' academic performance. In order to maintain their eligibility, athletes will be motivated to pursue their studies. Critics of this policy point out that students who stay in school mainly to play sports now find themselves ineligible and may drop out of school.

The central issue of the no pass, no play controversy is, according to Siedentop,[9] the educational importance of interscholastic sport. Eligibility standards may be appropriate if sport is an extracurricular activity and participation is a privilege to be earned. If, however, sport is an integral part of the educational experience—if it has educational value—then is it appropriate to deny this experience to any student? If participation in interscholastic athletics contributes to educational goals, if the experience can promote learning and foster personal development, why should any student be denied this opportunity? Siedentop[9] also relates this argument to the exclusionary nature of interscholastic sport discussed previously. If participation in sport is an important developmental experience for adolescents, it should be more widely available so that more students, both boys and girls, can benefit.

One of the most serious problems in the schools is drug abuse. Much media attention has been focused on the use of performance-enhancing drugs, such as anabolic steroids, in professional, international, and intercollegiate sports. However, such drug use is a problem in interscholastic sports as well. It is estimated that 4–12% of male adolescents and 0.5–2.9% of female adolescents use anabolic steroids.[10] When taken in amounts far exceeding the recommended dosage (megadoses) and coupled with intense physical workouts, anabolic steroids can produce a significant increase in muscle growth. The side effects associated with such large dosages are serious and lead to irreparable damage. Coaches also must be prepared to address other serious problems, including the use of tobacco, alcohol, and illegal drugs such as marijuana, amphetamines, and cocaine.

Soaring costs are increasingly becoming a concern in interscholastic athletics. Rising costs for injury and liability insurance as well as costs associated with providing programs for girls and for students with disabilities have caused some schools to reduce the scope of their athletic programs and/or require athletes to pay in order to participate. A "pay-to-play" policy requires students who desire to participate in sports to pay for the opportunity. Critics have decried this policy because it discriminates against students who are unable to afford to pay. Some schools and communities, in response, have made provisions so that economically disadvantaged students can participate in the athletic program. However, often few of these students choose to participate.

Many pressures exert an insidious influence on interscholastic sport programs. When school administrators, community members, and parents pressure coaches to win; when the expectations of parents exert too much pressure on their children to excel; and when coaches place undue pressure on their athletes to perform—the quality of the sport experience can deteriorate rapidly. Sport becomes unrewarding and less enjoyable than it should be and harmful to the participants. The educational experience becomes subverted and educational outcomes unrealized.

The quality and nature of the leadership provided is of critical importance in determining whether educational goals will be realized. If learning is to occur and personal development is to be enhanced, then administrators and coaches must structure the program to provide experiences that will lead to the attainment of these goals.

When high school coaches exert undue pressure on athletes to perform, when they excessively control the lives of their athletes, and when they

University of Tennessee coach Pat Summitt gives All-American standout Chamique Holdsclaw sideline instruction during a game. The quality of leadership exhibited by coaches strongly affects the experience of participants.

physically or verbally abuse their athletes to set an example for the rest of the team, then the educational goals of interscholastic sport will go unfulfilled. There are coaches who equate obedience with self-discipline, demand singleminded dedication to sport, and provide no opportunity for athlete involvement in decision making (such as in setting team goals or planning game strategies). These coaches may win games but they are failing to further the aims of education. Coaches who foster personal development of their athletes by guiding them, by allowing them to make decisions and to live with the consequences of those decisions, and by enhancing the worth and dignity of each athlete will help interscholastic sport fulfill its educational mission.

Intercollegiate Sports

The nature of intercollegiate sport in the United States varies greatly. Budgets for athletics may vary from less than $100,000 per year at small private colleges to over $30 million per year at some major universities.[3] The number of sports offered by a school can range from 1 to as many as 25 different activities for men and women.[3] In smaller institutions, the athletic program may be part of the physical education department and be funded from its budget, the coaches have faculty teaching status, and one individual may serve as the coach for two or more teams. In contrast, at larger institutions, separate athletic departments exist; athletics has its own budget and generates substantial revenue from gate receipts and contributions; coaches have no teaching status; and an individual coaches only one sport. Program philosophies vary as well; in some institutions the educational nature of intercollegiate sport is emphasized, while in other institutions sports are seen as big business. Financial assistance for athletes varies and may be directly influenced by the skill of the athlete. Some schools offer no athletic scholarships; financial assistance is based solely on financial need. Other schools offer athletes a full scholarship that covers all expenses for tuition, room, board, fees, and books. Still other schools may offer partial assistance to athletes, such as providing only a tuition waiver. Given the tremendous diversity of intercollegiate sport programs, it is reasonable to believe that the nature of the intercollegiate sport experience for participants varies widely throughout the United States.

Intercollegiate sport is regulated by three primary governing bodies: the National Collegiate Athletic Association (NCAA), the National Association of Intercollegiate Athletics (NAIA), and the National Junior College Athletic Association (NJCAA). These associations attempt to administer intercollegiate athletic programs in accordance with educational principles.

The NCAA is the largest governing body for 4-year colleges and universities. Its nearly 1,000 member institutions are divided into different divisions, based on the characteristics of their athletic program. Division I consists of over 300 institutions and includes those schools that conduct what is generally referred to as "big money," high-profile programs. These big-time programs typically highlight football and/or men's basketball, the best potential moneymakers. Division II and III are composed of approximately 300 and 400 schools, respectively, and conduct programs that place less emphasis on financial gain from their athletic teams.

Many intercollegiate sport programs, excluding the big Division I programs, operate in a manner similar to those found in larger high school programs. These intercollegiate sport programs include some Division I programs and those generally classified as Division II and III by the NCAA as well as those programs governed by the NAIA and the NJCAA. They offer participants similar experiences to those found in high-level interscholastic programs. However, unlike with high schools, college and university coaches need to recruit athletes for these teams. Athletes who choose to attend these schools may be offered some form of financial assistance. This can range from full athletic scholarships to need-based financial assistance.

Athletes who participate in the big Division I programs generally possess a higher level of athletic talent, face a greater time commitment to their sport, receive full athletic scholarships, experience a greater amount of travel, and benefit from

Athletes in well-known programs, particularly in revenue-producing sports, face tremendous pressure to win.

greater media exposure. Pressures to have a winning program are often immense, and the consequences of winning and losing are usually much greater. Economic survival for these programs frequently depends on their ability to generate revenue through gate receipts, contributions, and, increasingly, television contracts. Winning teams generate interest among fans, which increases gate receipts, which provides more money to hire coaches with proven winning records to raise the athletic program to even greater heights. Commercialism and entertainment dominate; educational goals are de-emphasized and often subverted, and athletics is transformed into a business and entertainment venture.

Many of the positive educational outcomes ascribed to participation in interscholastic sport programs can be realized when intercollegiate programs emphasize the attainment of educational goals. Similarly, many of the problems associated with interscholastic programs are evident in intercollegiate programs throughout the country. The overemphasis on winning, concerns about the academic achievements

of athletes and their eligibility for participation, and the use of drugs are some of the problems associated with intercollegiate sports.

As with interscholastic sport, overemphasis on winning can lead to the subordination of educational goals. Such goals as sportsmanship, character development, and social development may be abandoned when winning becomes the most important objective. Desire and pressure to win may lead to the subversion or violation of rules in an effort to recruit the best athletes and maintain their eligibility.

The academic achievement of intercollegiate athletes is a major concern. There are many student-athletes who exemplify the true meaning of the word—they have combined sports and academics successfully. A prominent example is former United States Senator Bill Bradley, who played basketball for Princeton University, was named a Rhodes scholar, and had an outstanding professional basketball career before entering government service. In many colleges and universities, the academic achievements of athletes are comparable to those of their nonathlete peers. Studies have shown that the academic performance of athletes on women's teams, NCAA Division III teams, and other nonrevenue-generating teams is comparable to other college students.

There are, however, many instances in which the term *student-athlete* is truly a misnomer; in these cases athletics is given a much higher priority than academics. This is particularly true of "student-athletes" in the big-time programs. Athletes in these programs, especially those in revenue-generating sports such as football and basketball, face considerable demands on their time and energy that can interfere with their academic work.

Some athletes in big-time programs can successfully balance the time-consuming demands of athletics with the rigorous demands of academics and excel in both areas. However, sometimes the pressures on coaches to win translate into pressure to keep athletes eligible. Focusing attention on eligibility rather than on learning can lead to many abuses. Coaches may recruit athletes who lack the academic preparation needed to succeed at the challenges of college. They counsel athletes into taking easy courses, pressure professors to give them good grades, and encourage athletes to enroll in majors that require little academic effort. Unfortunately, progress toward a degree is not monitored as closely as is the maintenance of athletic eligibility. Additionally, because many black athletes from rural and inner-city schools where quality education programs are often lacking, a higher proportion of black athletes are affected.

In 1990, the U.S. Congress passed a law requiring all colleges and universities to make public the graduation rates of their athletes, starting in 1991. However, even the availability of this information makes it difficult to get a true picture of the graduation rates of athletes. Studies of the graduation rates of athletes yield conflicting results because of the many different methods that can be used to compute them. The 1997 NCAA Division I Graduation Rates Study data is shown in Table 8–1. These graduation rates are based on individuals who received an athletic scholarship and who graduated within six years of their initial college entry. The data show the following:

◆ College athletes with scholarships graduate at a rate similar to other students, about 57% in six years after entering college.

◆ The graduation rate for female athletes is higher than for male athletes, 68% compared with 53%. Female athletes graduated at a rate higher than other female students and at a higher rate than the general student body. (Coakley notes that at institutions where women's sports have become more entertainment-oriented, graduation rates have declined slightly in the 1990s.)

◆ Athletes are graduating at rates slightly higher than students of the same racial and gender group. For example, black male athletes graduated at a rate of 43% compared with 33% for the entire black male student body. Female athletes graduated at a rate of 68%, compared with 58% of all females graduating.

◆ Graduation rates are lowest in the revenue-producing sports of football and basketball. Football players graduate at a rate of 52%, male basketball players at a rate of 45%, and female basketball players at a rate of 67%.

◆ Black athletes graduate at a rate lower than white athletes. For example, the graduation rate for black male basketball players was 39%; that for white males was 58%. Additionally, black athletes are more likely to leave school with a GPA lower than 2.0.[11]

The graduation rates show that athletic administrators need to pay greater attention to fostering, learning and focusing on improving the educational experiences of athletes. Even though athletes are receiving greater educational support (e.g., tutors) than ever before, much more needs to be done. Failure to address these educational needs compromises the academic integrity of the institution and imperils the educational relevance of sports.

The National Consortium for Academics and Sports, under the auspices of Northeastern University's Center for the Study of Sport in Society, works with 140 colleges and universities to design degree-completion programs for former student-athletes. Student-athletes who have left school

TABLE 8-1

Graduation Rates for Division I Student-Athletes and General Student Body Entering College in 1990 and 1984*

Student Group	Percentage of Students Graduating Who Entered in 1990		Percentage of Students Graduating Who Entered in 1984	
	Student-Athletes	General Student Body	Student-Athletes	General Student Body
Student-Athletes	58	56	52	53
Males	53	54	47	51
White Males	57	57	55	54
Black Males	43	33	33	28
Females	68	58	62	54
White Females	70	61	66	57
Black Females	59	42	45	34
Male Basketball Players	45	54	38	51
White Male Basketball Players	58	57	53	54
Black Male Basketball Players	39	33	29	28
Female Basketball Players	67	58	53	54
White Female Basketball Players	74	61	66	57
Black Female Basketball Players	58	42	42	34
Football Players	52	58	47	54
White Football Players	61	59	56	56
Black Football Players	45	39	35	33

* Based on 1997 NCAA Division I Graduation-Rates Summary Data reflect individuals who received an athletic scholarship and who graduated within 6 years of their initial college enrollment. The data from 1984 is before Proposition 48 took effect in 1986.

without completing their degree have the opportunity to continue their education. Since the formation of this program in 1985, about 11,000 former athletes have returned to college and more than 4,600 have received their degree. Almost 7,500 of these athletes never played professional sports. Many had dropped out of college once their eligibility was completed. The NCAA has also started new degree completion grants for athletes who have completed their eligibility and are 30 or fewer credits away from graduation.

In an effort to help remediate the academic abuses associated with big-time, revenue-producing sports and to restore academic integrity, the NCAA in 1983 adopted a rule establishing minimum standards for freshman athletes to be eligible to participate on varsity teams at Division I institutions. Commonly known as Proposition 48, this rule stipulates that in order to be eligible to participate in sports, a first-year athlete must enter college with a 2.0 grade point average (GPA) in 11 specified core high school courses and achieve a minimum score of 700 on the Scholastic Aptitude Test (SAT) or 15 on the American College Test (ACT). Implemented in 1986, this rule permitted students who met only one of the requirements to be accepted at a college and given athletic aid, but they were not permitted to practice with their teams during their first year and had to forfeit one year of eligibility.

The NCAA hoped that Proposition 48 would send a strong message to high schools and their athletes that academic achievement was a prerequisite for students participating in Division I athletics. It was further hoped that this rule would help colleges and universities break the habit of recruiting athletes who had neither the academic background nor the potential to graduate within a 4- or 5-year period. It also provided first-year athletes who needed it a year to strengthen their academic abilities without the added pressures and commitments associated with sports. Since the inception of Proposition 48 in 1986, additional rulings by the NCAA have led to more stringent qualifying criteria. Athletes who fail to qualify no longer can receive athletic financial assistance during their first year. However, they are eligible for institutional financial aid that must come from approved nonathletic sources. In 1993 the NCAA increased the initial eligibility requirements. Starting in 1995, athletes needed a high school GPA of 2.5 in 13 core courses and a minimum score of 68 on the ACT (new scale) or 820 on the SAT (new scale).

In 1996 the NCAA established the NCAA Eligibility Clearinghouse. All high school students wanting to play sports at Division I or II schools must register and be certified by the clearinghouse. The clearinghouse reviews the high school courses taken by the athletes to make sure they fulfill the core course requirements. Grade point averages and ACT/SAT scores are also reviewed to decide if the student meets the eligibility requirements.

Such rulings are controversial. Critics charge that they discriminate against economically disadvantaged students who were not fortunate enough to have received a strong high school preparation for college or those who do not have the resources to retake the standardized tests or pay for commercial test preparation courses. Further concerns are voiced about the cultural bias of the standardized tests, in particular the SAT. When test scores are compared, 14% of whites score lower than 700 on the SAT while 46% of blacks score lower than 700. Moreover, in the 3 years following the implementation of Proposition 48, nearly 90% of the athletes affected by the ruling were black.[3]

Has Proposition 48 been successful in improving the academic performance of athletes? The graduation rates for 1984, the period before the implementation of Proposition 48, are shown in Table 8-1. After Proposition 48 took effect, the graduation rates for athletes rose from 52% to 58%, while the rates for the student body rose from 53% to 56%. The graduation rate for male black basketball players and black football players rose 10%, from 29% to 39% and from 35% to 45%, respectively. Since the enforcement of Proposition 48, approximately 75% of the athletes affected by this ruling have achieved good academic standing in their universities. Having a year to concentrate on academics seems to be beneficial to the athletes. Furthermore, in addition to becoming more concerned about the academic abilities of recruited athletes, some universities have established or expanded academic support services for athletes.

Supporters of this ruling suggest that it has had a favorable impact at the high school level.[13] Young athletes appear to recognize the need to take high school core courses and to regard standardized tests more seriously. Coaches appear to be more encouraging of academic efforts, and academic support services have been developed to help high school athletes strengthen their academic skills.

The long-term effectiveness of Proposition 48 remains to be seen. It is hoped that it will lead to improved educational programs, to an increased emphasis on academic achievement for athletes at both the high school and the collegiate levels, and to restoring much needed academic integrity to intercollegiate athletic programs.

Several other problems beset big-time intercollegiate sports, including the fact that sports have become big business. This commercialism has led to financial concerns receiving a greater priority than the education and personal development of the athletes. Television contracts increase the pressure to have a winning program in order to reap greater financial benefits. Media coverage of sport continues to grow. The recent NCAA $1.7 billion, 7-year contract with CBS reflects the tremendous interest in the commercial value of intercollegiate sports.

The explosive growth of gambling nationwide and the increase in sports waging is viewed by the NCAA as a threat to collegiate athletics. The FBI projected that $2.5 billion was illegally waged on the 1995 NCAA Division I Men's Basketball Championship, second only to money gambled on the National Football League's Superbowl. A survey by the University of Cincinnati of more than 600 Division I football and men's basketball players showed that 25% had gambled money on other college sport events, 4% had bet on a game in which they played, and 5% had received money from a gambler not to play well in a game.[12] The NCAA has taken a strong position on gambling, stating that it has "the potential to undermine the integrity of sports contests, and jeopardizes the welfare of student-athletes and the intercollegiate athletics community."[12]

Many physical education and sport professionals are becoming increasingly concerned about the exploitation of athletes. Some intercollegiate athletes can generate millions of dollars for their institution but the only compensation permitted under NCAA rules is tuition, room, board, books, and fees. Even at the most expensive of institutions, when the total cost of the athletic scholarship is divided by the number of hours athletes are required to devote to their sport, the pay per hour is low.[9] Although critics say it is difficult to place a value on the benefits of a college education, oftentimes athletes are strongly encouraged to focus their energies and efforts on sports instead of academics. Moreover, the educational abuses cited detract from the nature of the educational experience. All too often athletic departments are concerned with athletes' academic status only until their 3 or 4 years of eligibility are used up; after this period, their concern about the academic progress of athletes is minimal. Most adversely affected by this practice are athletes from lower socioeconomic backgrounds and those who have received poor preparation for college from their high schools. These athletes often do not have the financial resources to pay for the extra semesters needed to graduate. Furthermore, because much of their efforts had previously been devoted to sports rather than academics, they may find it difficult to cope with the academic demands without the extra assistance (e.g., tutors) previously available to them as members of sport teams.

Several other issues in intercollegiate sport must be addressed. The media has increased the public's awareness of violations of recruiting regulations. Illegal recruiting practices, such as cash payments to prospective athletes, must be stopped. Drug abuse also is a problem. Athletes, in an effort to enhance their performance, may abuse such drugs as amphetamines and anabolic steroids. Although drug testing policies and procedures have become more stringent, methods to mask the use of drugs have become more clever. The effect of win-loss records on the retention of coaches, the role of coaches within the institutions of higher education, and the role of alumni and other influential supporters in the hiring and firing of coaches must be carefully evaluated and monitored.

The 1980s and the early 1990s have been marked by calls for the reform of intercollegiate athletics. Abuses have become so serious and so widespread that the academic integrity of educational institutions sponsoring these programs is challenged. In 1990 the U.S. Congress called for monitoring athletes' graduation rates. In 1991 the Knight Foundation Commission on Intercollegiate Athletics released a report calling for the reform of intercollegiate athletics. University presidents were called upon to exercise greater control over their sports programs, both in terms of fiscal responsibility and academic integrity.[13] Greater attention must be turned to containing the spiraling costs of intercollegiate athletics. Equally important, careful attention must be given to enhancing the academic performance of student athletes. The NCAA has passed legislation that focuses on providing opportunities and conditions that foster better academic achievements by student-athletes. Among these rulings are the elimination of the athletic dormitories, reductions in the number of hours practiced per week and in the length of the season, and more stringent monitoring of the student-athlete's academic progress toward a degree.

Many other suggestions have been offered by individuals concerned about the abuses associated with intercollegiate athletics. These include elimination of first-year eligibility, further limitations on practice and game schedules, stricter academic standards for eligibility, tying athletes' graduation rates to the number of athletic scholarships that can be offered, and providing coaches with some form of job security to encourage them to more strongly support athletes' academic endeavors and achievements. Other voices have been raised on behalf of athletes' rights, calling for elimination of exploitative, discriminatory, and prejudicial practices directed against minorities, and the reduction of gender inequities.

Like interscholastic sports, intercollegiate sports have the potential to contribute to the educational goals of the institutions that sponsor them. Whether these educational goals are attained depends on the leadership. When winning is overemphasized, commercialism is rampant, and athletes are exploited, the educational relevance of these programs is called into question. When winning is placed in perspective, when academic achievement is strongly supported, and when athletes are encouraged and given opportunities to develop to their fullest potential, then the educational mission of intercollegiate athletics will be fulfilled.

TOWARD AN EDUCATIONAL PHILOSOPHY OF SPORT

The ancient Greeks provided civilization with two disciplines. The first described how sport could be most helpful in the training of a strong and graceful performance and body. The second provided civilization with the basics of philosophical thinking. As the historian Isocrates said:

. . . Certain of our ancestors, long before our time, invented and bequeathed to us two disciplines: physical training for the body, of which gymnastics is a part, and for the mind, philosophy. These twin arts are parallel and complementary, by which their masters prepare the mind to become more intelligent and the body to become more serviceable, nor separating sharply the two kinds of education, but using similar methods of instruction, exercise, and discipline.

Every student of physical education and sport should develop a philosophy of that discipline. A philosophy will represent a guide to decision making, since it will clarify the worth of this field of endeavor in the human experience. Such a philosophy might include how sport should be conducted to make the greatest contribution to humankind. It should help to determine the parameters of educational sport as well as sport outside the formal domains of schools, colleges, and other educational institutions. It should provide an understanding of the history of sport and the contributions it has made over the years, as well as show how it has been misused and has been detrimental to humankind. A philosophy will also help point the way to achieving excellence of performance on the athletic field.

Sport is extremely popular and has a firm foothold in U.S. educational institutions and society. Therefore it is imperative to give direction to athletic programs in a way that will better contribute to the achievement of educational goals. The conduct of sport programs will be more worthwhile if the following four guidelines are used.

Guideline 1—Restructure Athletics to Achieve Cognitive, Psychomotor, and Affective Learnings

Cognitive, psychomotor, and affective learning outcomes are worthy goals for athletics in education. It has been demonstrated that cognitive learning, such as knowledge of rules, player assignments, and the game strategies associated with playing a sport, as well as the phenomena associated with the economic, political, and other interrelationships that exist between sport and society, can be accomplished. It has also been demonstrated that psychomotor learnings in the form of physical skills acquired by the participant as a result of engaging in athletics can be achieved. However, affective learnings may not be accomplished, in light of research that questions the role of sport in bringing about behavioral changes. Therefore, some restructuring may need to take place if sport is to be used as a medium for learning social behavior.

Sport and athletics are an important part of physical education programs in schools and colleges in the United States and have great appeal to young people of all ages, races, colors, and creeds. At the same time society is faced with many social problems, including relations between blacks and whites, the need for cooperative endeavor in achieving goals in a democratic society, and the necessity for constructive rather than destructive competition as people attempt to achieve their personal goals. Therefore, if athletics through a restructuring process can help in bringing about more desirable social attitudes among the many young people who participate in them, in addition to achieving cognitive and psychomotor goals, they would obviously play a much more valuable role in educational programs.

Guideline 2—Provide an Athletic Program Where the Intensity of the Competition Is Developmental in Nature

Physical and motor growth follow a progressive sequence from the time of early childhood to maturity. In other words, they follow a developmental pattern (large muscles develop before fine muscles).

What is true of the physical is also true of the mental and emotional aspects—they are also developmental in nature. Therefore, since the intensity of athletic competition is related to a person's growth and development, it would follow that athletic competition should be of a very low intensity during the early years of childhood and then gradually be increased as the child grows older and becomes more mature.

The intensity of athletic competition is increased when elements are introduced into the athletic experience that provide added motivation for and additional pressure on the participants to excel, and where more is at stake in the competition. For example, when spectators are in the stands, games are scheduled with schools in other communities, awards are offered, admission is charged, sports writers are in attendance, or play-off games for championships are sponsored, the intensity of the competition is increased.

Relating the elements that increase the intensity of the competition to the developmental levels of the student, it is proposed that four levels of intensity of competition for a developmental athletic program exist. These four levels of competition

should be progressively scheduled during the school years in a way that best fits the student and also the administrative grade pattern in the school. The four levels of intensity of athletic competition are as follows:

1. *First developmental level.* Absence of any structured athletic competition.
2. *Second developmental level.* Intramurals, with their low-key competitive involvement of classmates, provide the first structured step-up in the intensity of competition.
3. *Third developmental level.* Extramurals, such as occasional play days, sports days, and invitational meets with schools in other communities, where the stress is on the social and fun aspects of the event rather than the winning, represent an intermediate athletic developmental competitive experience between intramurals and varsity interschool athletics.
4. *Fourth developmental level.* Varsity athletic competition represents a major step-up in the intensity of competition, with elements such as spectators, publicity, leagues, and awards. This type of experience may be provided after each of the previous developmental levels of competition has been utilized for a significant period of time and when the player can successfully cope physically, mentally, emotionally, and socially with such an experience.

Guideline 3—Provide More Athletic Opportunities for Girls, Women, and Athletes with Disabilities

Athletics are a part of the total school program and all students should have the opportunity to take part in them. Changing societal attitudes and federal legislation have promoted the growth of participation by girls, women, and students with disabilities. Participation by girls and women has increased dramatically within the last 25 years, yet many inequities still limit opportunities. Students with disabilities have also been given limited opportunities to participate in athletics. The last decade has seen much progress in providing athletic opportunities for students with disabilities;

however, much more needs to be done. Prejudice and stereotyping have needlessly limited participation. Discrimination against students with disabilities has denied them access to this educational experience.

Increasing opportunities for girls, women, and students with disabilities in athletics should be a professional priority since the benefits of athletic competition should be available to all students. Proper funding, coaching, access to equipment and facilities, and commitment by professionals to equity can help to make this goal a reality. (These issues will be discussed in later chapter sections).

Guideline 4—Institute Changes in the Organization and Administration of Athletic Programs

School administrators play a key role in the development of a sound educational athletic program. They are the persons who are responsible for such programs and should provide the leadership necessary to bring about desirable change. Areas in which changes are needed include the following:

1. Schedule and limit in length practice sessions and number of games played so as not to disrupt the educational process or take a disproportionate amount of the student's time.
2. Conduct sport contests only on school premises. The public arena, where educators are not in control, is a questionable place to conduct athletic contests.
3. Appoint coaches on the basis of their educational qualifications. A knowledge of and an interest in participants, including their physical, mental, emotional, and social makeup, is one of the most important qualifications.
4. Administer athletics as an integral part of the total education program.
5. Sponsor a continuing research program to determine means by which sport can make its greatest contribution to human growth and development.

Sport reflects what the United States is—its people, its character, its values, and its philosophy of life. This country needs more sport and greater participation. Furthermore, Americans need to recognize that regardless of individual ability, sex, race, or economic status, sport opportunities should be available to all people to enrich their lives.

CONCERNS IN SPORT TODAY

Although sports are highly popular and are beneficial for the participants and for the nation, they are also beset by many problems. James A. Michener,[14] the noted novelist, points out the following problems in his book *Sports in America:*

1. Girls and women are discriminated against.
2. Adults who are in charge of children's programs place too much emphasis on winning.
3. Children are engaged in highly competitive sport at too early an age.
4. Money spent by universities to maintain big time sport teams is excessive.
5. The recruitment of high school athletes is often scandalous.
6. Television coverage of sporting events threatens to destroy many of the values that can accrue from sport.
7. Violence in sport is excessive.
8. City politicians use public monies to build large stadiums and then provide them to professional teams at minimal rental rates.

Our views of a few of the major problems facing sport today are discussed in this section. Problems in sport are also discussed in Chapter 14.

Girls and Women in Sport

Prior to the 1970s, opportunities for girls and women to compete in sports were limited. Within the past 25 years, there has been a dramatic increase in girls' and women's participation in sports. This increase is visible at all levels of competition—the Olympics, professional and amateur sports, intercollegiate and interscholastic sports, and youth sports.

The relatively recent increase in participation by girls and women in the United States can be attributed to several factors. These include federal legislation, the women's movement, the fitness movement, and an increased public awareness of female athletes.

Federal legislation, specifically Title IX of the Educational Amendment Act, was one of the most influential factors because it mandated equal treatment for women and men in programs receiving federal assistance. Passed in 1972, Title IX prohibits discrimination on the basis of sex in any educational program or activity receiving federal financial assistance. It states that "no person in the United States shall, on the basis of sex, be excluded from participation in, be denied the benefits of, or be subjected to discrimination under any educational program or activity receiving federal assistance."

Because Title IX is politically controversial and the guidelines complex, implementation and enforcement of this law are difficult. After its implementation, access to sport opportunities for women increased. However, it should be noted that in 1984, in *Grove City College v Bell,* the U.S. Supreme Court ruled in favor of a narrow interpretation of Title IX, stating that it should be regarded as program specific. Thus, only programs directly receiving federal aid are required to comply with Title IX regulations, not the institution as a whole. Because athletic programs typically receive little if any direct federal funding, the threat of losing funding for noncompliance and nonsupport of women's athletics is not a substantial one. Subsequently, the 800 cases of alleged sex discrimination that were being investigated by the U.S. Department of Education's Office for Civil Rights were either narrowed in scope or withdrawn. Four years later, in 1988, the Civil Rights Restoration Act was passed. This law provided for a broad interpretation of Title IX by mandating equal opportunity for both sexes in all programs in any organization that received federal funds. In 1991, the Office of Civil Rights announced that investigation of Title IX athletic complaints would be one of its priorities.

In 1997, 25 years after Title IX, Donna Lopiano, Executive Director of the Women's Sports Foundation, stated that more than 90% of the schools and colleges were not in compliance with Title IX.[15] Is your high school or college in compliance? The Office of Civil Rights has a three-pronged test to determine if an institution is in compliance. A school must meet one of these three tests to be within the law:

1. *Proportionality.* Are the opportunities for males and females substantially proportionate to the school's fulltime undergraduate enrollment? Recent court decisions indicate that being within 5 percentage points is acceptable and within the law. Thus, if 49% of the enrollment is female, between 44% and 54% of the athletes should be female.

2. *History and continued practice.* Even though a school has a disproportionate number of male athletes, as long as the school is adding more women's sports and has added one recently, generally within the last 3 years, the school would probably be considered in compliance.

3. *Accommodation of interests and abilities.* If the school can demonstrate that the women do not have enough ability or interest to sustain additional teams, the school would be considered in compliance. However, if there are club teams playing sports, this could indicate to the court that there is sufficient interest to support another team.

Great strides have been made toward equity. Much more needs to be done to create additional opportunities for participation in sports at all levels.

The impact of Title IX has resulted in noticeable increases in participation of girls and women at both the interscholastic and intercollegiate level. The growth of participation by girls in interscholastic sports following the passage of Title IX can be seen in Figure 8-1. At the intercollegiate level, there was an increase in the number of intercollegiate teams for women, the hiring of qualified coaches, and the offering of athletic scholarships to outstanding high school women athletes. In 1972, 32,000 women competed in intercollegiate sports; in 1996 the NCAA reported that nearly 125,000 women participated in its athletic programs. Spectator interest in women's sports has grown as well. This has resulted in increased attendance at games. For example, in 1996–97, perennial national power Tennessee averaged more than

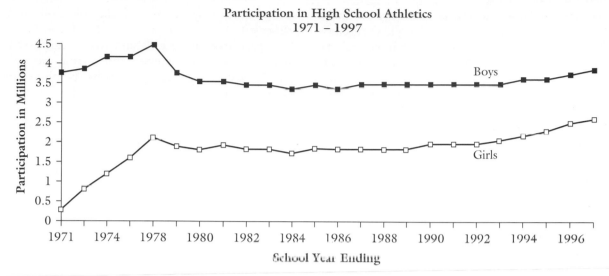

FIGURE 8-1   Boys' and girls' participation in high school athletics.

13,000 fans for its home basketball games. Television coverage of women's sports has increased; the NCAA championships in swimming and diving, basketball, gymnastics, volleyball, and track and field have been televised in recent years. Even coverage of regular season events has expanded.

The women's movement has encouraged increased participation in athletics by women. It has helped redefine societal, occupational, and family roles for women and has given women more control over their lives. The idea that women are enhanced as human beings when they are given opportunities to develop competence has encouraged women of all ages to pursue an increasingly wide array of interests, including sport. Moreover, the changing cultural image of women athletes has contributed to the growth of women's sports. Whereas women athletes were once perceived by many as unfeminine or were stigmatized for engaging in high levels of competition, athletic participation by women is now regarded as acceptable. The extent of the change in attitudes is such that Leonard[16] suggests that athletics can be used by adolescent girls as a means of attaining status in much the same way as it is used for boys. Women athletes have been reported to have lower femininity scores than nonathletes; however, they also

score higher on self-esteem, body image, and psychological well-being. Other research[17] suggests that women athletes may not experience role conflict to the extent previously thought. Women athletes, regardless of their age, sport, or level of experience, are found to experience relatively little dissonance between their roles as women and as athletes. Ideas about what is masculine and what is feminine are based on societal definitions and may be needlessly restrictive, creating barriers to participation.[3] In the future, as society's attitudes continue to change, more people may come to perceive sport not as a masculine activity but rather as a human activity.

Playing sports can be an empowering experience for girls and women by changing their perceptions of themselves. Sports can engender feelings of competence, promote confidence, and help girls and women see themselves as more in control of their lives This is important because, quite often in our society, girls and women are portrayed as weak, dependent, and powerless. The President's Council on Physical Fitness Report, *Physical Activity and Sport in the Lives of Girls,* released in 1997, used an interdisciplinary approach to examine the impact of physical activity and sport on the lives of girls. The report emphasized the contributions physical activity and sport can make to the "complete girl"—her social, physical, emotional, and cultural environment—rather than to just one aspect of the girl's life. Some conclusions follow:

◆ Exercise and sport participation can be used as a therapeutic and preventive intervention to enhance the physical and mental health of adolescent girls.

◆ Exercise and sport participation enhance mental health by offering adolescent girls opportunities to develop positive feelings about their body, improved self-esteem, tangible experiences of competency and success, and enhanced self-confidence.

◆ Sports contribute to educational goals. Compared to their nonathletic peers, high school female athletes have higher grades, lower dropout rates, and are more likely to go to college.

◆ Poverty substantially limits many girls' access to physical activity and sport. This is particularly true for minorities, who are overrepresented in lower socioeconomic groups.

◆ The potential for girls to derive positive experiences from physical activity and sport is limited by lack of opportunity and stereotypes.[18]

The benefits of participation are great. Physical education and sport professionals must create greater opportunities for participation and work to remove barriers that limit participation.

Since the 1970s, the fitness movement has encouraged many women to participate in physical activities, including sport. Many women started engaging in jogging, walking, aerobics, and swimming to realize the associated benefits of fitness, particularly to feel good and look better. While there is still an emphasis on engaging in physical activities to look better and to preserve one's youthfulness, there is also a growing emphasis on the physical development of the body. Additionally, many women have moved from engaging in fitness activities to engaging in competitive athletics; joggers have gone on to participate in road races, marathons, and even triathlons. Interest in fitness has also led to an increase in the number of women participating in community sport programs in such sports as softball, volleyball, and basketball.

As participation by girls and women increases, there will be more women athlete role models. The increased coverage and publicity given to women athletes have allowed girls and women to read about the achievements and watch the performance of women athletes in a wider range of sports than ever before. The accomplishments of the 1996 Olympic gold medal American female athletes in softball, soccer, swimming, track and field, gymnastics, basketball, skiing, and other sports may encourage many girls to participate in sports and pursue their athletic ambitions. Professional opportunities for women are also increasing. In 1996, two professional women's basketball leagues were organized. The American Basketball League and the Women's Basketball League offer elite athletes the opportunity to continue to participate in their sport. Older sisters, mothers, and female friends who are athletes, while not famous, also serve as important role models for these future female athletes.

Legislation, the women's movement, the fitness movement, and increased visibility accorded female athletes have done much to expand opportunities for women in sport. However, while opportunities for girls and women in athletics have increased tremendously over the past two decades, whether participation rates will continue to grow for women depends to a great extent on the expansion of opportunities for involvement and the support and encouragement of female athletic endeavors. Some factors that may limit participation are financial constraints, overt and subtle resistance to comply with government policies and legislation, a decline in women's coaches, and the continued trivialization of women's sports.[3]

Financial considerations may serve to limit opportunities for participation by girls and women. When school, collegiate, and community athletic programs are threatened with cutbacks, programs for girls and women are most at risk for losing financial support. Because these programs are newer and not as established as similar programs for men and boys, they have had less time to gather administrative and community backing and

TABLE 8-2

Ten Most Popular High School Sports for Boys and Girls, 1996–1997*

Boys		Girls	
Sport	Participants	Sport	Participants
1. Football	957,507	1. Basketball	447,687
2. Basketball	544,025	2. Track & Field (Outdoor)	393,946
3. Track & Field (Outdoor)	468,081	3. Volleyball	370,957
4. Baseball	444,248	4. Softball (Fast pitch)	313,607
5. Soccer	296,587	5. Soccer	226,636
6. Wrestling	227,596	6. Tennis	150,346
7. Cross-Country	174,599	7. Cross-Country	145,624
8. Golf	150,578	8. Swimming & Diving	123,886
9. Tennis	136,451	9. Field Hockey	56,502
10. Swimming & Diving	93,523	10. Track & Field (Indoor)	41,024

*Data from 1997 High School Athletics Participation Survey, The National Federation of State High School Associations.

may not be able to elicit sufficient support to survive cutbacks. Participation opportunities for females also may be adversely affected because the establishment and development of new programs generally requires greater financial support and resources than do established programs. Because many programs for females are new or in the process of development, successful growth of these programs requires financial commitment. Yet, despite the need, programs for females tend to be funded at lower levels than programs for males. This lack of funding hampers program growth and adversely affects opportunities for participation and quality competition.

In spite of the passage of Title IX and improvements in opportunities, sex discrimination is still a feature of many athletic programs. New laws are often met with resistance and questions as to how to implement them. Additionally, people tend to be reluctant to change the status quo. Individuals with a vested interest in maintaining the status quo may use their power and control of financial resources to thwart the progress of women's programs. Women across the nation at all levels of competition are still denied fair treatment. Such discrimination can be as blatant as the refusal to

fund a program. But lack of equality often occurs in less noticeable forms, such as the provision of quality equipment, supplies, and uniforms; the assignment of games and practice time; the use of facilities and locker rooms; the allocation of equal funds for travel and the availability of travel opportunities; the access to quality coaches, size of coaching staff, and compensation of coaches; the opportunity to receive support services such as academic tutoring; the administration of medical and training services; and the publicity accorded to individual athletes and the team. Despite prohibitions by Title IX against discrimination, women still do not receive equitable treatment in sport. Furthermore, violations of Title IX are often not prosecuted vigorously. Commitment, time, and effort are needed to ensure compliance with the law and that the spirit of the law becomes an integral part of athletic programs at all levels.

Discrimination is also noticeable in sports outside the school setting. At the international level, for example, where efforts to bring about changes have not been supported by legislation, women typically have fewer events in which to participate and are less likely to be rewarded for their efforts than men. Even though changes have occurred

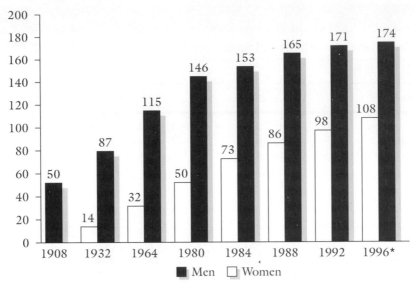

FIGURE 8-2 Number of Summer Olympics events open to women and men. Eleven events in 1996 were mixed (open to both men and women). These eleven events are included in the totals for both men and women.

during the past two decades, women are still underrepresented in international sport. In the Summer Olympic Games, women have fewer events than men and fewer participants. Figure 8-2 shows the number of events open to men and women in the Summer Olympics. In the 1996 Olympic Games in Atlanta, on the U.S. team there were 382 men and 280 women, compared with 342 men and only 96 women in 1972. In the 1996 Games in Atlanta, women made up 36.5% of the athletes compared with only 28.5% of the participants in the 1992 Olympics in Barcelona. Moreover, the male-dominated International Olympic Committee (IOC) is slow to approve additional events for women. The IOC did not approve the 1500 meter run (the metric mile) until the 1972 Games in Munich, the 3000 meter run and the marathon until the 1984 Games in Los Angeles, the 10,000 meter run until the 1988 Games in Seoul, and the 5000 meter run until the 1996 Games in Atlanta. This is difficult to understand since women have been competing in these events internationally for many years.

Today there are fewer female coaches for women's sports than in the years following the passage of Title IX. Despite the fact that women's sport programs have increased, the proportion of women in coaching and athletic administrative positions has declined. For example, at the intercollegiate level, Acosta and Carpenter[19] reported that the percentage of female coaches of women's sport programs decreased from 90% in 1970 to 58% in 1978 to 47.7% in 1996. Reasons for the underrepresentation of women in these positions have been debated widely and the results of the research are confusing. However, one reason that is frequently cited is the lack of well-qualified women coaches and administrators. Recently, several programs have been implemented in the United States in an effort to recruit and train more women coaches. It is also important to note that the lack of visibility of women coaches and administrators within the sport structure provides few role models for females who aspire to careers in these areas.

Although women's participation in sport has increased dramatically during the last 20 years, the accomplishments of female athletes are often trivialized and ridiculed by both men and women. For example, women often have to suffer with team names and mascots that belittle physical competence and minimize the achievement of female athletes. To illustrate, at one university the men's teams are referred to as the Bears and the women's teams as the Teddy Bears; other examples are the Blue Hawks and Blue Chicks, the Rams and Rambelles, and the Tigers and the Tigerettes. Were the men's and women's teams at your high school or college referred to by different nicknames? If so, what messages do these names send to the public about the abilities of the athletes and the seriousness of their endeavors?

The media also tends to downplay the competence of female athletes and reinforces traditional, limiting definitions of gender. Male sport announcers often focus on women's physical attractiveness while directing less attention to their athletic accomplishments.[9] Analysis of the covers of *Sports Illustrated* (the most widely circulated sports magazine in the world) for the last 35 years reveals that only eight women, compared with 173 men, have been featured on three or more covers.[20] Three of these eight women "athletes" were models Cheryl Tiegs, Christie Brinkley, and Elle McPherson—frequently used as part of the magazine's annual swimsuit issue. The five women athletes that appeared were Chris Evert, Martina Navratilova, Mary Decker Slaney, Tracy Austin, and Florence Griffith-Joyner. While the media has increased its coverage of women's athletics at all levels, a greater effort is needed to highlight the accomplishments of women athletes.

Other factors that have contributed to the inequities experienced by women in sport are myths about the consequences of athletic participation and the physical, social, and psychological characteristics of women. Examples of these myths include the belief that strenuous participation in sport can lead to problems in childbearing (it has been shown that athletes who are in excellent physical condition have shorter and easier deliveries and experience fewer problems such as backache after the birth of a child) and the belief that the fragile bone structure of women makes them more likely to experience injuries than men (when both men and women athletes experience similar training regimens and care and practice under the leadership of qualified coaches, injury rates

are similar for both sexes in any given sport). Other myths perpetuate the belief that participating in sports can threaten one's femininity (women athletes typically do not see their involvement as a threat to their image). Although research and education have done much to dispel these myths, they still persist and serve to needlessly limit participation by women.

Events of the past two decades have served to increase opportunities for participation by women in sport at all levels. Federal legislation, the women's movement, the fitness movement, and increased visibility and recognition of the achievements of women athletes have helped females of all ages to benefit from opportunities to participate in sports. However, while progress has been made, continued increases in participation by women will depend on eliminating barriers to involvement such as financial constraints, less than full compliance with Title IX, lack of women coaches and administrators, minimization of women's accomplishments, and unfounded beliefs or myths. Coakley[3] notes that gender equity is a complex issue and suggests that the following guideline from the 1993 NCAA Gender Equity Panel may be helpful in thinking about this issue: "An athletics program is gender equitable when either the men's or women's sports program would be pleased to accept as its own the overall program of the other gender." Qualified and committed leadership is needed to change the structure of sport programs in order to reduce inequities and to further eliminate barriers to participation so that all individuals, regardless of sex, can enjoy the benefits of sport.

Minorities in Sport

Sport is often extolled as an avenue by which to transcend differences in race and cultural backgrounds. It has been said, for example, that "sport is color blind"—that on the playing field a person is recognized for ability alone and rewards are given without regard to race and class. The widely televised performances of black and Hispanic male athletes in such sports as baseball, basketball, track and field, boxing and football suggest to millions of viewers that sport is relatively

As college football teams changed their offensive strategies so that quarterbacks became more like running backs, more African Americans were recruited for the position.

free of the prejudice and the discrimination often found in other areas of society. Despite a commonly held belief that sport allows individuals to accept one another on the basis of their physical competence, close scrutiny of the sport phenomena reveals that sport organizations are typically characterized by the same patterns of prejudice and discrimination found in the surrounding society.

Historically, sport in the United States has been characterized by racism and prejudice. While blacks and other minorities have a rich history of

sport participation, prior to the 1950s minorities were rarely given access to mainstream sport competition in the professional leagues, colleges and universities, and schools. Members of minorities organized their own leagues and competed within them; for example, blacks had their own basketball and baseball leagues. The integration of professional sport did not occur until 1946 when Jackie Robinson "broke the color barrier" by playing for the then Brooklyn Dodgers. Integration of intercollegiate sports occurred later and was particularly slow to occur in the South. The U.S.

Supreme Court's decision in *Brown v Board of Education* in 1954 as well as the civil rights movement of the 1970s slowly led to the integration of schools and the opening of doors to sports for minorities.

In the 1990s, the participation of black athletes is concentrated in a few sports. Black athletes are overrepresented in certain sports such as football, basketball, and baseball. These sports typically require no expensive equipment or training, have coaches readily available through the public schools, and offer visible role models to aspiring athletes. Black athletes are underrepresented in such sports as volleyball, swimming, gymnastics, soccer, golf, and tennis. The expenses increasingly required for many of these sports, such as private lessons and elite coaching, expensive equipment, funds for travel, and club memberships, as well as the virtual lack of role models in these sports, discourages minority participation. Participation by black women has been very limited and accomplishments of black women athletes are typically accorded little attention. Furthermore, black men and women are seriously underrepresented in coaching and managerial positions in all sports. For example, in the National Football League (NFL), approximately 70% of the players are black. However, only 10% of the head coaching jobs are held by blacks. In 1997, 11 NFL teams hired new coaches. None of the teams hired a black head coach even though experts agree that there were several qualified candidates. At the collegiate level, there are 6 black coaches at Division I-A schools out of 112 positions. Percentages are better for college basketball, where 19% of men's coaches and 17% of women's coaches in Division I are black. These patterns of representation reflect forms of discrimination.

Discrimination is also reflected in the pattern of positions played by black athletes in certain team sports. In some sports, such as baseball, football, and women's volleyball, where teams are racially and ethnically mixed, players are stereotyped by position. Players from certain racial or ethnic groups are disproportionately represented at certain positions in a phenomenon known as stacking. For example, in professional baseball, black players are most heavily concentrated in the outfield positions, whereas white players are concentrated at the positions of pitcher, catcher, and the infield, although less so at first base. (See Figure 8-3.) Whites are disproportionately represented in positions requiring leadership, dependability, and decision-making skills, while black players are overrepresented in positions requiring speed, agility, and quick reactions.[3] In women's intercollegiate volleyball, blacks are disproportionately represented at spiker, while whites are overrepresented at setter and bumper.[3] Stacking patterns are widespread and occur in other sports and in countries throughout the world (e.g., in British soccer, black West Indians and Africans are overrepresented in the wide forward position, while white players are overrepresented at the goalie and midfielder position).[3] Stacking reflects stereotypical beliefs about different racial and ethnic groups—for example, that blacks are better jumpers, while whites are better leaders. Although stacking is one of the most studied topics in sociology of sport, there are serious disagreements about why stacking patterns exist. But even though a consensus is lacking about the causes of stacking, it is important to recognize that stacking perpetuates patterns of prejudice and discrimination in sport.

Increased recognition has been given to the problems confronting black and other minority athletes in collegiate sports. Some frequently cited problems are disparity in treatment by coaches, pressures to sacrifice educational goals for athletic goals, difficulty in overcoming an educational background that ill-prepared them for college, social isolation, and prejudicial attitudes held by coaches and teammates. Although desegregation has opened doors, it has not eliminated prejudice and discrimination.

Native Americans have long participated in sports, often uniting physical activities with cultural rituals and ceremonies.[21] Although many Native Americans have achieved success in sports, little recognition has been given to their accomplishments. Public acclaim most often has focused on the few Native Americans, such as Jim Thorpe, who were outstanding athletes on segregated government-sponsored reservation school

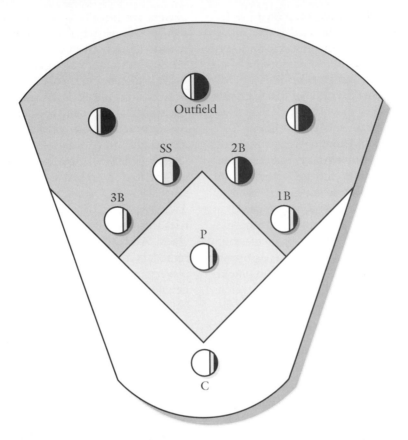

FIGURE 8-3 The percentage of African American players in each position during the 1996 season is depicted by the black areas. The percentage of Hispanics is shown in gray. African Americans remain concentrated in outfield positions, whereas whites are overrepresented in the positions of pitcher and catcher. Hispanics are slightly overrepresented at second base and strongly overrepresented at short stop.

football and baseball teams. On the whole, participation by Native Americans in most sports has been and continues to be limited.

Poverty, poor health, lack of equipment, and a dearth of programs are factors that often serve to limit Native American sport participation. Concern about loss of cultural identity, prejudice, lack of understanding, and insensitivity by others toward Native Americans act in concert with the other factors previously mentioned to curb sport involvement.

One example of this lack of sensitivity is the use of school names and mascots that perpetuate the white stereotypes of Native Americans. Team names such as "Indians" or "Redskins" or a team mascot dressed up as a savage running around waving a tomahawk threatening to behead an opponent reflect distorted beliefs of Native Americans. Such inappropriate or distorted caricatures of Native Americans who, as school mascots, are painted on gymnasium walls and floors, do little to increase student and public awareness of the richness and diversity of Native American culture. It is even more ironic that this occurs in institutions that by definition exist to educate people about the different cultures within the world in which they live. These stereotypes are often accepted as valid depictions of native people and serve to demean the cultural heritage and history of Native Americans.

Concerned American Indian Parents is a group committed to the elimination of Native American stereotypes in advertising and sport. The poster shown on page 298 is one example of this group's efforts to heighten public awareness of the racism experienced by Native Americans that has become an accepted aspect of sport in the United States. As Coakley[3] writes:

The use of the name Redskins cannot be justified under any conditions. To many native Americans, redskin is as derogatory as "nigger" is for black Americans. It is symbolic of such racism that the capitol city of the government that once put bounties on the lives of native peoples has a football team named the Redskins. It symbolizes a continuing lack of understanding of the complex and diverse cultures and the heritage of native peoples and is offensive to anyone aware of the history of native peoples in North America.

Attitudes change slowly. This is particularly true concerning prejudicial beliefs about different race and ethnic groups. Can sport be used to break down prejudices? Although sport can provide a means to break down prejudices, changes in attitudes do not occur automatically nor as often as it is believed. Racial and ethnic prejudices are especially resistant to change. Dedicated and sensitive leadership on behalf of coaches and athletic administrators and thoughtful efforts can help change people's prejudices. Minority athletes—regardless of sex, sport, or level of competition—should be treated fairly and equally.

Sport for Individuals with Disabilities

Individuals with disabilities, like girls and women, had limited opportunities for participation in athletics prior to the 1970s. Changing societal attitudes, the use of sport for rehabilitation, and federal legislation have contributed to the growth of competitive sport opportunities for the disabled. Professional organizations such as AAHPERD advocate participation in physical education and athletics for all individuals, including those with disabilities.

An estimated 28 million people 3 years of age or older have serious limitations affecting their performance of physical activities. About 3.5 million of these persons are school aged. Federal legislation has had a significant impact on the schooling of individuals with disabilities. P.L. 94-142, Education for All Handicapped Children Act, mandated a free and appropriate education in the least restrictive environment for students with disabilities. Provision for instruction in physical education was specifically mentioned in this law. The Rehabilitation Act, specifically Section 504 of P.L. 93-112, stated that students with disabilities must have equal opportunity and access to extracurricular activities including intramurals and athletics. The Amateur Sports Act of 1978, P.L. 95-606, called for the United States Olympic Committee (USOC) to assist amateur athletic programs for individuals with disabilities and, where feasible, to expand the opportunities for meaningful participation by athletes with disabilities in competitions for able-bodied athletes.

Participation also has been encouraged by changing societal attitudes. Changes toward a more humanistic educational philosophy and society's recognition of the rights of individuals with disabilities were seen. Society's acceptance of individual differences and understanding of the capabilities of individuals with disabilities grew. These factors contributed to the integration of individuals with disabilities into society.

Changes occurred slowly. Orr[22] believes that the reluctance of school personnel to provide sport opportunities for disabled persons results from myth, superstition, and sport control. In elaborating on the myth surrounding the handicapped athlete, Orr writes:

The imposed myth is that the handicapped person participating in sports is inferior and different from the so-called 'normal' athlete. The reality is that while the handicapped person usually does not have equal marks in performance of a quantitative nature, the qualitative performance may equal or surpass any other athlete. The effect of the myth has been to obstruct opportunity for the handicapped as time, energy, and funds have been funneled in other directions.

Participation on interscholastic and intercollegiate teams by individuals with disabilities has

A poster used by the Concerned American Indian Parents to increase the public's awareness of racism toward Native Americans.

In the last decade, sport opportunities for athletes with disabilities have increased.

been slow to increase. However, in recent years regional, national, and international competitions for individuals with disabilities have flourished. One of the most visible competitions has been the Special Olympics. The Special Olympics are sponsored by the Joseph P. Kennedy, Jr., Foundation. This foundation has focused more attention on sport for persons with disabilities than any other single organization or legislation.

The Special Olympics were organized in 1968. They were designed to provide youths 8 years of age and over who are mentally impaired with opportunities to participate in a variety of sport and games on local, state, regional, national, and international levels. Thousands of people volunteer to coach youngsters in Special Olympic events such as track and field, swimming, gymnastics, floor hockey, and volleyball. The volunteers include professional athletes in many areas of sport.

As a consequence of the Amateur Sports Act, a Committee of Sports for the Disabled was established as part of the USOC.[23] Some of the committee's responsibilities included promoting sport for disabled individuals; conducting research and disseminating information on various aspects of competition such as sports medicine, equipment design, and performance analysis; and publicizing the accomplishments of athletes with disabilities. Seven major amateur sport organizations for individuals with disabilities were recognized. One of the criteria for recognition as a major sport organization was that the organization had to offer national competition in two or more sports that are included in the program of the Olympic or the Pan American Games. These organizations are The National Association of Sports for Cerebral Palsy, American Athletic Association for the Deaf, National Handicapped Sports and Recreation Association, The National Wheelchair Athletic Association, United States Amputee Association, United States Association for Blind Athletes, and Special Olympics.

The Paralympics are recognized by the International Olympic Committee and provide international competitions for elite athletes with disabilities. Competitors include athletes who are blind, physically disabled, are amputees, and who have cerebral palsy. Competitions are held in the Olympic host country following the Olympic Games. The 1996 Paralympic Games in Atlanta involved more than 3,500 athletes and support staff from 104 countries. The athletes competed in 17 full medal events and 2 exhibition events. The theme "Triumph of the Human Spirit" reflects the importance of focusing on the possibilities and potential of people with disabilities, rather than stigmas surrounding disabilities. Sports are an important vehicle to promote equality, inclusion, accessibility, and awareness about the potential of people with disabilities.

Although sport opportunities are being provided for many youths with disabilities, the need to establish and conduct more sport programs is urgent if the sport needs of all individuals with disabilities are to be met. It is also necessary to encourage athletes with disabilities to participate with able-bodied athletes when feasible.

Sport for Children and Youth

For many Americans, participation in youth sport activities is an integral part of growing up. It is estimated that over 25 million boys and girls participate each year in youth sports, that is, organized sport activities that take place outside the school setting.[23] Furthermore, it is estimated that over 3 million volunteer coaches are involved with these programs. Youth sport ventures are organized around such sports as football, baseball, softball, tennis, ice hockey, golf, gymnastics, soccer, and swimming.[23] An increasing number of opportunities for girls to participate in these programs at all levels is being offered, and it appears that many more children are beginning to compete in these programs at younger ages.

While participation in youth sports has grown tremendously over the past decade, there is widespread concern about the nature and outcomes associated with these programs. Even though these programs are extremely popular, considerable criticism is voiced about the manner in which they are conducted. As you read about the benefits, harmful effects, and criticisms of youth sport programs, it may be helpful to keep in mind your own experiences and those of your friends in youth sport. Consider the following questions:

♦ What did you like most and least about your experiences?
♦ What did you learn from participating in youth sports?
♦ How did your parents influence your participation and what was the extent of their involvement with the program?
♦ How would you characterize the nature and effectiveness of the coaching you received or observed?
♦ How did you, your teammates, parents, and coaches respond to your successes and failures?
♦ At what age did you discontinue your participation in youth sports and what were the reasons for stopping?
♦ What changes would you make in the organization of the program to make the experience a more positive one for all involved?

As with school sports, many benefits have been ascribed to participation in youth sport programs. Proponents of youth sports emphasize that they promote physical fitness, emotional development, social adjustment, a competitive attitude, and self-confidence. In addition, youth sport programs provide opportunities for the development of physical skills, encourage the achievement of a greater level of skill, give children additional opportunities to play, and offer a safer experience than participation in unsupervised programs.

And, as with school sports, one of the greatest criticisms of youth sports is its overemphasis on winning. Critics also voice concerns that children's bodies may be underdeveloped for such vigorous activities, that there is too great an emotional strain and pressure on the participant, and that the players are too psychologically immature to compete in such a setting. Youth sport programs are cited as being too selective and excluding too many children who would like to participate and as promoting specialization at too early an age. Additional criticisms are directed toward overenthusiastic coaches and parents who take winning too seriously, who pressure children to achieve, and who place their needs before the needs of the child.

Overemphasis on winning has led to many of the abuses found within youth sport programs. The desire to win has led coaches to employ such behaviors as conniving to get the best players in the league on their team, holding lengthy practice sessions and endless drills to perfect skills, and berating children for their mistakes. Many physical education and sport professionals decry the overemphasis on winning. They believe that youth sport programs should be developmental in nature—that is, they should be organized and conducted in such a way as to enhance the physical, cognitive, and affective development of each child and youth participant. This development is particularly critical during the child's younger years. The fun of playing (rather than the beating of an opponent) should be stressed, participation opportunities for many children of all abilities should be provided (rather than limiting participation to the gifted few), and the development of skills within the sport and in other sports should be stressed (rather than specialization).

Specialization is another frequently voiced concern. During their early years, children should be given an opportunity to develop proficiency in fundamental motor skills and be exposed to a variety of sports. Some children are guided at an early age into a specific sport such as soccer or into a specific position within a sport such as a pitcher. This early specialization deprives children of an opportunity to develop an interest and skills in a variety of sports.

Concern about specialization has further increased within the last decade. During this time there has been a growth of private sport leagues and clubs that emphasize the development of skills in a particular sport. This often leads to beginning high level sport instruction and competition at an early age; children may begin as early as 3 years of age in such sports as swimming, gymnastics, skating, and soccer.[9] Training is serious and often occurs on a year-round basis. Physically, children may be at risk for the development of overuse injuries because they are often involved in practicing on a daily basis for several hours at a time. Psychologically, these participants may experience burnout from doing the same thing year after year. They may drop out before reaching their optimal level of performance, even after many years of successful participation.

Some professionals in the field of physical education and sport take the position that competitive sport for youth is not inherently bad or good. Instead, they point out that sport is what one makes it. Under sound leadership, if the welfare of the child is the primary consideration, if the environment is warm and supportive, and if the sport is administered in light of the needs and characteristics of the participants, much good can be accomplished. However, if poor leadership is provided, harmful effects will accrue.

Many recommendations have been set forth by professionals to improve youth sports. Professionals suggest that programs be structured so that children can experience success and satisfaction while continuing to develop their abilities. This may mean modification of the rules, equipment, and playing area to promote success and participation rather than failure and elimination. For example, simplified and fewer rules, smaller balls, smaller fields, bigger goals, batting tees rather than pitchers, rule changes to facilitate scoring, and a requirement of equal playing time for all participants are some of the ways that youth sports programs can be changed to make the experiences more positive for all participants.

Programs should be structured to include elements that children find enjoyable within their own informal games. Plenty of action, opportunity for involvement, close scores to keep the game exciting and interesting, and friendship are important to children; these elements should be infused into youth sport programming.[5] Children also should be given opportunities to be involved in decision making, such as deciding what strategies to use or planning a practice session. They can also be given the responsibility for self-enforcement of rules during the game.

As previously mentioned, the quality of leadership can exert a significant influence on the outcomes children derive from participating in youth sports. Coaches within the youth sport programs are typically volunteers, often parents, who have received little if any training on how to coach children. Recognizing this, professionals within the field have directed increased attention toward the development of coaching education programs. These programs emphasize understanding the growth characteristics and developmental needs of children, modifying existing programs to meet these needs, incorporating proper training techniques into the design of the program, and supporting the efforts of children while providing developmentally appropriate opportunities to help them become better players. Enhancing children's self-esteem, recognizing their accomplishments, and praising their efforts are more appropriate than ridiculing, shaming, and belittling their achievements and attempts.

Under qualified leadership, many of the problems associated with youth sport programs can be rectified. Implementation of these recommendations can maximize the positive experiences and minimize the negative experiences of youth sport participants. The key to successful youth sport programs is putting the needs of the child first. Programs should be designed to meet the children's needs, not those of adults. Youth sport programs should be organized on a developmental

Too often, our attention is focused on the game when the important messages are on the bench or in the dugout.

model, not a professional model. Programs should focus on fostering children's physical, cognitive, and affective development. The whole child as a moving, thinking, feeling human being should be considered when designing and conducting youth sport programs.

International Sport: The Olympics

Opportunities for elite nonprofessional athletes to compete in international events are numerous. International championships are contested annually in many sports and special competitions such as the Pan-American Games and the Asian Games that are held every 4 years. College and university students have the opportunity to compete in the World University Games that are conducted every 2 years. The opportunity to compete in these special international competitions is highly regarded, but the most prestigious of the international competitive events is the Olympic Games.

Since the rebirth of the Games in 1896 and the addition of the Winter Games in 1924, competitions for athletes from around the world have been held every 4 years under the direction of the International Olympic Committee (IOC). Many people still ascribe to the beliefs that the Olympics offer athletes an opportunity to extend their limits in a quest to achieve excellence by the accomplishment of personal athletic goals, to establish friendships with other competitors around the world, and to foster international understanding and peace by bringing together the nations of the world.

While these Olympic ideals are highly valued by many people throughout the world, there are many problems that prevent the attainment of these lofty goals. The Olympics have been used by many countries to further political goals. Examples of this include the use of the 1936 Olympic Games by Hitler and the Nazis to highlight Aryan supremacy, the terrorist shootings at the 1972 Munich Games to capture world attention, and the boycotts of the 1976, 1980, and 1984 Olympic Games to make political statements and to influence world opinion. The extent to which the Olympics have been used to promote vested national issues is so widely recognized and accepted that Peter Ueberroth, president of the 1984 Los Angeles Olympic Organizing Committee, said that "we have to accept the reality that the Olympics constitute not only an athletic event but a political event."[5] Worldwide media coverage has intensified the politicization of the Olympics.

Nationalism also undermines the goal of international unity. Athletes march into the arena during the opening ceremonies under their nation's flag, compete as representatives of their nation, and stand proudly during award ceremonies as their national anthem is played. Team sports and national uniforms promote an "us versus them" attitude, judging biases occur in favor of political allies, and up-to-the-minute national medal counts by the media all serve to reinforce nationalism.

Governments recognize the political importance of the Olympics. As the United States traditional dominance of the Games became lessened and the successes of subsidized athletes from other nations such as East Germany and the former U.S.S.R. grew, the U.S. government intervened and amateur sport was restructured. In 1978, Congress passed the Amateur Sports Act. Following its passage, the United States Olympic Committee (USOC) established the United States Olympic Training Center at Colorado Springs, Colorado. The national governing bodies for each Olympic sport were offered the use of training sites and resources to promote the development of athletes. Increasingly, funding is given to athletes by their sport governing bodies to assist them in defraying some of the expenses associated with training. For older athletes, receiving funds to help meet daily living expenses allows them to continue to train without the additional pressures and burdens of holding a full-time job to make ends meet.

The Olympic Games have become increasingly commercialized. In 1968, the Mexico Olympic Games cost $250 million to stage, while the 1980 Moscow Games cost $2.25 billion. Critics have questioned the high cost of the Games, especially in countries where planning and constructing facilities for the Olympic Games places a financial burden on its citizens and deprives them of resources that could be used to enhance their quality of life. The cost of securing television broadcasting rights has also escalated. In 1960 CBS paid $660,000 for broadcast rights; it cost NBC $1.27 billion for the 2000 Games in Sydney and 2002 Games in Salt Lake City, Utah.

The Olympic Games were founded for amateur athletes, those individuals who compete for the love of sport. Defining amateurism and dealing with questions pertaining to participant eligibility have presented a significant problem for the IOC. As we move into the next century, the Olympics are becoming an open competition. Nonprofessional athletes are allowed, under certain conditions, to receive money, and professional athletes in such sports as tennis and basketball are allowed to compete.

Many suggestions have been formulated to restructure the Olympics to attain the goals listed in the Olympic Charter.[5,8] Many people advocate the selection of a permanent neutral site in order to reduce the enormous costs associated with conducting the Games. Others believe that multiple sites should be used for each Olympics and events split between them to ease the economic costs associated with the games, permit more countries to host the Games, and allow participants and spectators to see more countries. Many advocate reducing nationalism and taking steps to promote internationalism. Some suggestions include abolishing national uniforms, revising opening ceremonies to allow athletes to march with athletes of other countries under the Olympic flag, replacing the national anthems and flags featured in award ceremonies with the Olympic anthem and flag, and either eliminating team sports or restructuring them so that players from different countries can play on the same team.

The Olympics offer participants from around the world the opportunity to attain athletic excellence and to develop international understanding. These goals can be accomplished when the Olympics are structured to be conducive to the achievement of these noble goals.

Amateur Sport

An increasing number of individuals are finding challenging and personally satisfying sport experiences through participation in amateur sports. Each year millions of boys and girls participate in sport competitions organized under the auspices of such amateur sport organizations as the Amateur Athletic Union (AAU). For some AAU sport participants, one highlight is the opportunity to compete in the AAU/USA Junior Olympics where Olympic-style competitions are held in 22 sports. Youths who participate in these games have the

The Junior Olympics give amateur athletes opportunities to compete with other athletes throughout the country.

opportunity to travel, make new friends, experience the excitement and thrill of competition, test their skills against a high level of competition, and be recognized for their achievements.

Forty-four states, in response to an interest in amateur sport competition, are holding such Olympic-style state games. New York State's Empire State Games are the oldest, having started in 1977, and their $1.6 million budget is the largest. Other state games include the Badger State Games (Wisconsin), Cornhusker State Games (Nebraska), Garden State Games (New Jersey), the Sunshine State Games (Florida), and Nutmeg Games (Connecticut). Other states are anticipating starting state games in the near future. These state games attract amateur athletes of all ages and abilities. Some states have organized their games into divisions for youths up to college age, open divisions for college-age participants and adults up to age 35, and various masters divisions for those 35 and older, and divisions for athletes with

disabilities. New York state added the Winter Games in 1981. A diversity of sports is offered. For example, the Garden State Games comprises 50 types of sports.

In many state games protocol similar to the Olympics is followed. During the opening ceremonies competitors may march in and participate in a torch lighting ceremony symbolizing the opening of the games. In a manner similar to the Olympic Village, athletes from across the state are housed and fed together in college facilities. Medal ceremonies recognize the achievements of the games' participants. Monetary support for the games may come from state funds or from commercial sponsors. The state game movement has drawn support from the United States Olympic Committee and the President's Council on Physical Fitness and Sports. These games offer athletes within the state the opportunity to compete against each other and it broadens the base of amateur sport. It provides the opportunity for

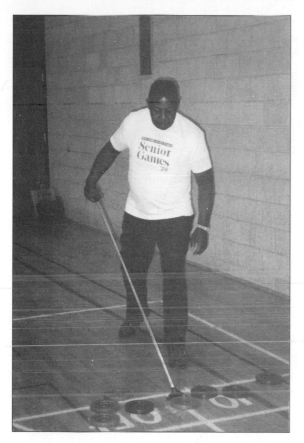

The Senior Games have become more popular throughout the United States. Athletes participate in a variety of activities, including shuffleboard.

thousands of amateur athletes to experience the positive aspects of amateur sport competition.

Another example of the growth of amateur athletics is the National Sports Festival. The sport festival provides opportunities for amateur athletes from across the nation to compete against each other as well as to develop friendships and wholesome rivalries. Several Olympic athletes have participated in both state games and the National Sports Festival. In 1986 the name was changed to the U.S. Olympic Festival.

The amateur athletic movement is not limited to the young, however. The Senior Games and master's competitions in various types of sport such as track and field and swimming promote participation in sport throughout one's lifetime.

Violence

Violence is one of the major problems facing sport today. It is particularly noticeable in professional contact sports such as football and hockey. Physical and psychological intimidation of one's opponent is considered an essential part of professional basketball. Yet, do such forms of intimidation lead to violence? Have coaches gone too far in "psyching" up their teams to go out and "kill" their opponents? In some contact sports, such as hockey, some players are even designated as "enforcers"—charged with protecting their own players and aggressively intimidating their opponents. However, violence is not limited to contact sports; bench-clearing "brawls" occur with greater frequency in even noncontact sports such as baseball. Has violence gotten out of control?

The media has done much to bring incidences of sport violence to the public's attention. Newspapers and sport periodicals give readers glowing, blow-by-blow accounts. Television glamorizes such events, often replaying them in slow motion. Special videos are being produced that show incident after incident of players using violence and force in pursuit of victory.

What impact has violence at the professional level had on other levels of sport? Some experts have expressed concern that the popularity and visibility of professional athletes lead athletes at lower levels of competition to imitate their actions, including their violent behavior. Other athletes, including those at the high school and even the youth sport level, may emulate the playing style of sport professionals. Thus, violence permeates other levels of sport and its impact on the nature of the game grows.

Spectator violence is also a concern, as media coverage of violent behavior at sport events throughout the world verifies. At some events, fans have stampeded the field and, in the process, trampled other fans to death. Outbreaks of fights among fans are reported. Experts have found that spectator violence is related to the actions of the players during the contests. In essence, player violence tends to increase the likelihood of violence by fans during and following the game. The media's promotion of games for their potential for violence tends to encourage spectator violence.

The potential for violence also increases when fans believe that their team was "robbed" of a score or a victory by incompetent or unfair officiating. Crowd dynamics also influence the occurrence of spectator violence, including the amount of alcohol consumed, the importance of the contest, the demographics of the crowd, crowd size, and seating arrangements.

It is important to note that the environment in which the contest takes place contributes to its potential for violence. As Coakley[3] points out, spectators bring the issues and ideologies that are reflective of the events within their communities to sport events. When conflict and violence are an integral part of a community, the likelihood of spectator violence at a local sporting event increases. For example, highly publicized contests between rival high schools where high levels of racial and ethnic tension exist in the communities have led to violence. In some communities, efforts to prevent violence at school sporting events have led to the banning of all spectators from the events or the playing of events at neutral sites.

The question of how to deal with the problem of violence in sport has no single, simple solution. Experts are in agreement, however, that some type of control must be instituted and it must start with persons who love sport and want to protect it from intrusions that will lower its value. They point out that violence is to be abhorred, particularly because it interferes with proper play, detracts from excellent athlete performance, and is barbaric in nature. Most spectators, it is suggested, do not want to see players hurt or crippled. They want to see clean, hard tackles and hard body checks. This is the essence of the game and sport itself.

It has been suggested that to reduce violence stricter penalties should be imposed at all levels of sports. Indeed, athletes in some sports and at some levels of competition are being penalized more severely for violent acts. However, the real and best solution to the problem of violence is a change in attitude on the part of all persons concerned. If subscribed to by professional and amateur players, coaches, spectators, sport entrepreneurs, and the public in general, the ideals of playing within the spirit and the letter of the rules, defeating one's opponent when at one's best, and having respect for other players will reduce the violence marring the playing fields and sport arenas today.

The potential for spectator violence can be reduced when some forethought is given to the factors that contribute to violence and thoughtful planning results in steps to minimize the occurrence of these factors. Reducing violence among contestants, decreasing the media "hype" that portrays the contest as a confrontation among hostile opponents, using competent officials to control the flow of the game, and taking preventive crowd control measures can decrease spectator violence. Violence can also be decreased by formulating better relations between the teams and the community and by athletes taking steps to become actively involved in the community in which they play and live.

SUMMARY

Sport has become an important part of American culture. Sport pervades society to such an extent that it has been described as a microcosm of society. Its pervasiveness has led to the study of sport from a sociological perspective.

Sociology of sport focuses on the study of sport as an institution, the effects of sport on its participants, and the relationship of sport to other societal institutions. Sport may be described or studied from many levels of analysis: sport as a game occurrence, sport as an institutionalized game, sport as an institution, and sport as a social situation.

The growth of sport in schools and colleges in the United States has been comparatively recent. Since athletics play such an important role in educational institutions, it is interesting to examine their influence. Athletics can have positive or harmful effects on its participants.

Several pressing problems exist in American sport today. The opportunities for girls, women, and individuals with disabilities in sport; the minority athlete; amateurism and the Olympics; and youth sport are some of the concerns of professionals.

It is important that every physical education and sport professional have a philosophy of sport. This will help give direction to the sport program and ensure that the desired goals are achieved.

SELF-ASSESSMENT TESTS

These tests are designed to help you determine if you have mastered the materials and competencies presented in this chapter.

1. Discuss how sport is a socializing force in American culture.

2. Discuss the sociological implications of educational sport. What are the benefits and possible disadvantages of participating in educational sport? Reflect carefully on your personal experiences in sport. How did they contribute to your personal development and educational goals?

3. Use the information provided in the Getting Connected box to explore more deeply the extent of participation by girls and women in sport. What are the benefits of participation? How can participation be increased further, especially among underrepresented population groups such as minorities and girls and women from low socioeconomic backgrounds? What can be done to increase the number of women in coaching and athletic administration?

4. Formulate a philosophy of sport that will clarify the worth of athletics and give direction for conducting it so that it will make the greatest contribution to humankind.

REFERENCES

1. Coakley J: Sport in society: issues and controversies, ed 3, St. Louis, 1986, Mosby.

2. Eitzen DS and Sage GH: Sociology of American sport, Dubuque, Iowa, 1982, William C. Brown Co.

3. Coakley J: Sport in society: issues and controversies, ed 6, Dubuque, Iowa, 1998, WCB/McGraw-Hill.

4. Wilkerson M and Dodder RA: What sport does for people, JOPERD 50(2):50–51, 1979.

5. Coakley J: Sport in society: issues and controversies, ed 2, St Louis, 1982, Mosby.

6. National Federation of State High School Associations, January 1997, Personal communication.

7. National Collegiate Athletic Association, January 1994, Personal communication.

8. Lumpkin A: Physical education and sport: a contemporary introduction, ed 2, St. Louis, 1990, Mosby.

9. Siedentop D: Introduction to physical education, fitness, and sport, Mountain View, Calif, 1998, Mayfield.

10. DuRant RH, Middleman AB, Faulkner AH, Emans SJ, and Woods ER: Adolescent anabolic-androgenic steroid use, multiple drug use, and high school sports participation, Pediatric Exercise Science 9:150–158, 1997.

11. National Collegiate Athletic Association: 1997 NCAA Division I Graduation Rates

Summary, Overland Park, Kansas, 1997, National Collegiate Athletic Association.

12. National Collegiate Athletic Association: Sports wagering, Kansas, 1997, National Collegiate Athletic Association.

13. Knight Foundation: Report of the Knight Foundation Commission on Intercollegiate Athletics, 1991. Available from the National Collegiate Athletic Association.

14. Michener JA: Sports in American society, New York, 1986, Random House.

15. Lopiano D: Issues in women's sports: the 1997 story, New York, 1997, The Women's Sports Foundation.

16. Leonard WM: A sociological perspective of sport, Minneapolis, 1984, Burgess.

17. Allison MT and Butler B: Role conflict and the elite female athlete: empirical findings and conceptual dilemmas, International Review of Sociology of Sport 19(2):194–201, 1984.

18. The President's Council on Physical Fitness and Sports: Physical activity and sport in the lives of girls, Washington, D.C., 1997, President's Council on Physical Fitness and Sports.

19. Acosta RV and Carpenter LJ: Women in intercollegiate sport: a longitudinal study—nineteen year update, 1977–1996. Available at http://www.arcade.uiowa.edu/proj/ge/Acosta/womenspt.html#Overview

20. Short Shots, Women & Sport 3(2):2, 1990.

21. Oxedine JB: American Indian sports heritage, Champaign, Ill., 1988, Human Kinetics.

22. Orr RE: Sport, myth, and the handicapped athlete, JOPERD 55(2):34-46, 1979.

23. DePauw KP: Commitment and challenges: sport opportunities for athletes with disabilities, JOPERD 55(20):34–46, 1984.

24. Martens R: Youth sport in the USA. In M Weiss and D Gould, editors: Sport for children and youth, Champaign, Ill., 1986, Human Kinetics.

SUGGESTED READINGS

Acosta RV and Carpenter LJ: Women in intercollegiate sport: a longitudinal study—nineteen year update, 1977–1996. Available at http://www.arcade.uiowa.edu/proj/ge/Acosta/womenspt.html#Overview

Longitudinal data on women's participation, coaching opportunities, and administrative responsibilities are presented in this ongoing study.

Ashe AR, Jr: A hard road to glory: a history of the African American athlete, New York, 1988, Warner Books.

The involvement of African Americans in sports from 1619 to 1988 is chronicled.

Coakley JJ: Sport in society: issues and controversies, ed 6, Dubuque, Iowa, 1998, WCB/McGraw-Hill.

An excellent critical analysis of the many issues within sport today.

Donnelly P: Approaches to social inequality in the sociology of sport, Quest 48:221–242, 1996.

After a discussion of how social inequality in sport can be analyzed, ways in which sport can be used to promote social equality are presented.

Kinkema KM and Harris JC: Sport and mass media, Exercise and Sport Science Reviews 20:127–160, 1992.

The role of the mass media in representing sport to our society is examined.

Landers MA and Fina GA: Learning life's lessons in tee ball: the reinforcement of gender and status in kindergarten and sport, Sociology of Sport Journal 13:87–93, 1996.

This article describes how status and gender roles are reinforced by children's earliest sport experiences: tee-ball.

National Association for Sport and Physical Education: NASPE position statement: exploitation of the interscholastic athlete, Update, AAHPERD, September 1993, NASPE Supplement, p. 1.
Cites abuses of interscholastic athletes, presents examples of exploitation, and has recommendations for redressing the problem.

Oxedine JB: American Indian sports heritage, Champaign, Ill., 1988, Human Kinetics.
Traces the role of sport in Indian societies and the historical and current involvement of Native Americans in sport.

President's Council on Physical Fitness and Sports: Physical activity and sport in the lives of girls, Washington, D C , 1997, President's Council on Physical Fitness and Sports. (This article can also be downloaded from the World Wide Web—see Getting Connected box).

Sperber M: College sports, inc: the athletic department vs the university, New York, 1990, Henry Holt & Company.

A critical analysis of the state of intercollegiate sports.

Thorngren C, editor: Women in sport leadership—the legacy and the challenge, JOPERD 64(3), 1993.
A series of articles examining the historical basis of leadership, current status, and future directions.

Tomlinson A and Yorganci I: Male coach/female athlete relations: power relations in competitive sport, Journal of Sport and Social Issues 21:134–155, 1997.
This article discusses the complex relationship between male coaches and female athletes, including issues related to sexual harassment.

Werner LA, editor: Mascots and team names, Journal of Sport and Social Issues 17(1), 1993.
Three articles focus on the use of Native American names for mascots, logos, and team names, including a discussion of mascot rituals, media coverage, degradation of Native Americans through the use of caricatures. One article focuses on the sexist names and mascots for women's teams.

CHAPTER 9

Psychological Foundations of Physical Education and Sport

Instructional Objectives and Competencies to be Achieved:

After reading this chapter the student should be able to—

♦ Identify and give illustrations of cognitive, affective, and psychomotor types of learning.

♦ Define motor learning and understand the influence of readiness, motor development, motivation, reinforcement, and individual differences in the learning of motor skills.

♦ Understand the information-processing model of motor learning and the stages of learning and be able to draw implications for the teaching of physical education and sport.

♦ Apply to the teaching of physical education and sport basic concepts of motor learning such as feedback, design of practice, and transfer.

♦ Describe the psychological benefits of participation in sport and physical activities.

♦ Discuss the roles of anxiety, arousal, and attention in the performance of motor skills and the application of intervention strategies to enhance performance.

The study of psychology has implications for physical education and sport professionals in such areas as learning theory, motor development, motor control, motor learning, and psychology of sport. The word psychology comes from the Greek words *psyche,* meaning mind or soul, and *logos,* meaning science. Thus, psychology is the science of the mind and the soul. Psychologists study human nature scientifically, and rather than formulate conclusions from casual observations, they sort out and check and recheck human characteristics under reliable conditions. In this manner and through the use of acceptable scientific evaluation, it is possible for psychologists to determine the conditions under which certain human characteristics will operate or learning will occur. These data should theoretically be objective and free from prejudice and bias and should focus attention on impartial and realistic examination of all the evidence.

While the areas of motor development, motor control, motor learning, and sport psychology

GETTING CONNECTED

Coaching Science Abstracts provides abstracts of articles of particular relevance to coaches. Topics include motor learning, psychological training, and sport pedagogy.
　　　Site:　http://www-rohan.sdsu.edu/dept/coachsci/mastable.html

Mind Tools contains information about sport psychology, including goal setting, motivation, self-confidence, imagery and simulation, flow and peak performance, and sport psychology tools.
　　　Site:　http://www.psych-web.com/mtsite/index.html

Neuromuscular Research Center Motor Control Laboratory site has articles pertaining to recent research.
　　　Site:　http://nmrc.bu.edu/MCL/

have their legacy in psychology, in the last 20 years these areas of study have grown tremendously and become increasingly specialized. Although these areas are highly interrelated, researchers in each area have developed their own methods of inquiry and focuses of study. In essence, these are subdisciplines in the realm of physical education and sport. Because of the common psychological foundations inherent in these subdisciplines, however, these areas are all discussed in this chapter.

In this chapter, the terms "teacher" and "learner" are used in their broadest sense to encompass physical education and sport professionals who provide instruction to people of all ages in a diversity of settings.

LEARNING

What is learning? Learning can be defined as a change in the internal state of the learner as a result of instruction, experiences, study, and/or practice. These internal changes are not readily discernible; thus learning must be inferred from behavior or performance. An observer, noting relatively permanent changes in an individual's performance, may assume that learning has taken place. Physical education and sport professionals, whether they are working in a school or non-school setting, should be interested in helping the individuals with whom they work to realize their greatest learning potential. In accomplishing this task, they will benefit from knowing the different kinds of learning, learning theories, key elements of the learning process, and the scientific basis for learning and the control of motor skills.

Learning is typically divided into three areas of study or domains: (1) cognitive, (2) affective, and (3) psychomotor. The physical education and sport professional is concerned with facilitating learning in all three domains.

Cognitive Learning

In teaching for cognitive learning, the teacher is concerned with increasing the individual's knowledge, improving problem-solving abilities, clarifying understanding, and developing and identifying concepts. The development of cognitive learning makes use of the mental process as a primary form of activity. The degree to which time is spent teaching for cognitive development depends on factors such as the information to be imparted and the abilities of the individuals to understand the material being presented. Professionals in the school setting may be concerned with teaching their students rules or strategies pertaining to specific sports or concepts. Professionals working in a community, commercial, or corporate fitness program may be concerned with teaching participants the knowledge necessary to design their own exercise programs or the risk factors associated with coronary heart disease.

Affective Learning

In teaching for affective learning the teacher is concerned with attitudes, appreciations, and values. The primary goal of such teaching is to develop proper and positive attitudes toward physical activity. Teachers may also be concerned about instilling such qualities as sportsmanship, leadership, followership, teamwork, and the need to play according to the rules that govern the game or activity. Fitness leaders may strive to help their clients appreciate how regular participation in physical activities can enhance their lives.

Psychomotor Learning

In teaching for psychomotor learning, the teacher is concerned with the development and improvement of motor skill. This type of learning is the heart of the physical education and sport experience. The focus of psychomotor learning is on the acquisition of motor skills; this includes both fundamental motor skills as well as selective skills in various physical education activities geared to the age, maturation level, and physical condition of each individual. Since motor-skill learning is such an important part of the psychological foundations of physical education and sport, it will be emphasized in this chapter.

MOTOR DEVELOPMENT

Noted psychologist Piaget stated that learning proceeds most rapidly when instructional experiences are geared to individuals' physical and intellectual abilities. For teachers of physical activity to follow this advice and match instructional experiences to the individual's developmental levels, they must understand cognitive, affective, and motor development.

Motor development is the study of the origins of and changes in movement behavior throughout the lifespan. Motor development encompasses the study of the biological and environmental influ-

All aspects of development must be considered when planning for instruction. These students with disabilities are receiving instruction in tennis, a lifetime sport.

ences on motor behavior from infancy to old age.[1] It involves understanding how motor behavior is influenced by the integration of psychological, sociological, cognitive, biological, and mechanical factors.[1]

As an area of study in physical education and sport, motor development traces its roots back to the 1930s. At this time early researchers such as Bayley, Gesell and Thompson, McGraw, and Shirley studied the sequences of motor development in young children, beginning in infancy. Their work led to a better understanding of the sequence of development of mature movement patterns. The researchers found that while the rate at which the children acquired the skills varied, the sequence in which the children learned was relatively invariant; that is, the sequence of learning was the same. Other early leading contributors to the field in the late 1940s were Anna Espenshade, Ruth Glassow, and G. Lawrence Rarick. Among other areas of study, these pioneers attempted to better delineate the relationship of growth and development to human performance. The early work in motor development was largely thought to be closely related to the human maturation process. In other words, motor development occurred in progressive stages as a person grew from childhood to adulthood.

In recent years, however, researchers studying motor development have embraced a more comprehensive approach that is best reflected in two major trends seen in this field. First, there is growing acceptance that motor development is a continuous process and that it should be studied across the lifespan. The traditional approach focused on motor development during the early years of life. Researchers sought to understand the factors that influenced children's acquisition of motor skills as they grew from childhood to adolescence and to understand the processes involved in moving from low to high levels of skill competency.[2] Today, researchers recognize the importance of studying development, including motor development, from infancy to old age.

Second, the study of motor development today emphasizes consideration of the multitude of factors that influence all aspects of development. Development is a highly interrelated process. As Gallahue explains, "Development has been studied in terms of domains (cognitive, affective, psychomotor), age-related behaviors (infancy, childhood, adolescence, adulthood, middle age, old age), and from a biological or environmental bias."[1] When studying motor development, one must consider the interaction of the biological, environmental, cognitive, and affective influences on the individual's motor behavior in a particular age period. Thus professionals must consider the individual's total development in planning instruction in physical activity. As Gallahue points out, unfortunately the convenient separation of behavior into three domains—cognitive, affective, and psychomotor—may lead to the study of each as separate entities of human development and learning.[1] Professionals

must not lose sight of the interrelatedness of human development. As Nichols states in her book on elementary physical education, we must not forget that we are teaching "moving, thinking, and feeling human beings."[3] This advice is applicable to teaching individuals of all ages.

Knowledge of motor development and the ability to accurately assess each individual's level of development are essential in planning appropriate experiences to promote motor skill learning for people of all ages.

MOTOR LEARNING

Motor learning is the study of the acquisition of movement skills as a consequence of practice. Learning of a movement skill is inferred from performance. For example, let us say the goal of instruction is to learn a tennis serve. To assess how well an individual has learned the tennis serve, the instructor would observe the person performing this skill. As the student gains mastery of a skill through practice, his or her performance should improve and become more consistent, that is, less variable. These changes in skill performance would lead the instructor to conclude that learning had occurred. Intimately related to motor learning is the area of motor control. Motor control is the study of the neural mechanisms and processes by which movements are learned and controlled. Understanding these principles is essential to teaching. By understanding the principles that govern motor skill acquisition and the control of movements, the teacher will be better able to design practices to promote learning.

Psychologists have attempted to explain the phenomenon of learning and to answer such questions as how optimal learning takes place and under what laws it operates. Over the years many theories have been advanced to explain the learning process. These theories are applicable to all three learning domains. Typically, professional preparation programs provide undergraduate students with information about these theories as part of psychology, education, and/or teaching methods courses. For the purpose of the brief discussion that follows, the basic theories can be divided into three categories: connectionist theories, cognitive theories, and human machine theories.

Generally, the connectionist or behaviorist theories maintain that learning consists of the learner making a connection or an association between a stimulus and a response or responses. These theorists are concerned with how the bond is formed between an event or stimulus and a behavior. The laws and principles of how this bond is developed have been formulated by such noted researchers as Pavlov, Thorndike, Guthrie, Hull, and Skinner.

The psychologists who support cognitive theories believe that a human being's behavior is determined by his or her various perceptions, beliefs, or attitudes (cognitions or mental images) that concern the environment. The manner in which these cognitions are modified by the human being's experience indicates that learning has taken place. The basic principles underlying the cognitive theories were developed by such Gestalt psychologists as Koffa and Kohler.

Human-machine theories are based on the nature of the makeup of the nervous system. In these theories an analogy is made between the human and machines (computers). These theories hypothesized that the human nervous system performs processes such as input, transmission, processing, output, and feedback. These theorists maintain that learning, including motor learning, is not a result of the strengthening of the stimulus-response process. Instead, they believe that learning results from such factors as more selective input, better processing of information that comes from input, and increased use of feedback. Through such a process the results will be identified more clearly, whether positively or negatively, errors will be more readily discerned and corrected, and more effective learning will take place. Human-machine theories include cybernetical theory, information theory, and feedback theory.

Other approaches have also been used to study motor learning. The contextualist or ecological approach emphasizes the critical role of the environment, specifically the context in which individuals live. Factors such as the family, the school, and the community in which the individual lives are thought to influence development and learning. The developmental biodynamics approach is an interdisciplinary approach to explain the complex, intricate relationship that leads to the control of coordinated movements. Gabbard refers to this approach as trying to understand the relationship between "perception and action" or between the "brain and the body."[4] An applied branch of biodynamics, the dynamical system focuses on understanding how muscles work together collectively, that is, as a coordinated group (e.g., muscles of the hand) as opposed to how each muscle is controlled individually. The context is also considered an influence in development and learning.

Research focusing on the process and mechanisms by which motor skills are controlled and learned is entering an exciting area as we move toward the twenty-first century. Sophisticated technology, advances in research, and interdisciplinary study hold great promise for helping us understand how movements are learned and controlled. One approach used to describe motor-skill acquisition and performance is the information-processing approach.

Information-processing model

In its simplest form the information-processing model comprises four components or processes: input, decision making, output, and feedback. This model is illustrated in Figure 9-1.

Input is the process of obtaining information from the environment. This information is obtained through the senses. Visual, auditory, kinesthetic, and other sensory information is transmitted through the nervous system to the brain where the process of *decision making* occurs. During this procedure the input is processed; that is, it is sifted, evaluated, and interpreted. Relevant

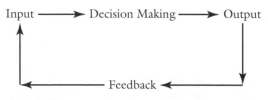

FIGURE 9-1 Information-processing model.

environmental cues are identified. Using this current information and relevant past experiences stored in memory, an appropriate response is selected. A decision is reached about what movement to make. The response is organized; a "motor program" that will control the response is retrieved from memory. The muscles are directed to contract in proper order, with the proper amount of force and with the correct timing to produce the desired movement. The response and its execution are the *output. Feedback* is information about the performance of the movement and its quality, appropriateness, and/or outcome. This information can be used to provide *input* for making ongoing adjustments in performance or to modify the next skill attempt. The knowledge gained from feedback can be used to improve the decision-making process as well as the succeeding output. As an individual becomes more adept at performing the skill, often he or she also becomes more skilled at using the feedback to improve performance.

How the information-processing model works can be illustrated by this simple example. Suppose you are in a soccer game and are in possession of the ball within shooting range of the goal. Should you retain the ball and continue to dribble while maneuvering for a more favorable position? Should you pass to a teammate? Or should you shoot for the goal?

To make this choice, you must first obtain information about your position on the field, the positions of your teammates and the opposing players, and the distance between you and the goalie. This information serves as input. Next, as part of the decision-making process you must analyze and interpret this information with reference to your past experience in the game of soccer and specifically in situations similar to the present one. Within a fraction of a second, based on this analysis and evaluation you must choose the response to make. The decision is influenced by your own and your teammates' past successes in similar situations, the probable actions of the opposing team given their past reactions in similar situations, appropriateness of the various strategies available, and perhaps directions or guidelines from the teacher or coach concerning the desirable course

of action in such situations. You may also consider your own ability as well as your level of confidence in your ability to execute the selected option, be it dribble, pass, or shoot.

After these considerations and deliberations you select an option. Next, you execute the selected movement—you dribble, pass, or shoot. Finally, both during and after execution of the response you receive feedback about your performance. The feedback may focus on whether you executed the movement as intended and/or whether the outcome was successful (e.g., you scored a goal).

Teachers should be familiar with the manner in which individuals learn skills as well as the factors that influence their performance. This understanding will help them design practices that facilitate an individual's opportunity to learn through appropriate structuring of the learning environment. The teacher must give learners appropriate input through the careful selection of teaching methods, materials, and procedures. The teacher must help the learner understand the goal of the movement and then distinguish between relevant and irrelevant information or cues with respect to that goal, drawing the learner's attention to cues essential for the decision-making process and teaching the learner to disregard the irrelevant ones.

The teacher next must help the learner to become a wise decision maker. This can be accomplished by helping the learner evaluate his or her past experiences, by explaining the "why" underlying skills and strategies, by instructing the learner on how to use the available feedback, and by making sure that the learner is attending to the right cues and interpreting the information correctly. The teacher can facilitate the learner's development of the desired skill using proper progressions and by giving the learner appropriate and sufficient practice opportunities.

Finally, the teacher can help the learner by providing feedback about the learner's performance and communicating this information to the learner in an understandable manner. Additionally, the teacher must draw the learner's attention to the feedback available during the execution of the skill as well as the information regarding the outcome of the performance. This information can provide the basis for adjustments in the learner's movements.

As you can see from the information-processing model, the senses play a critical role in motor learning and performance. Vision is one of the most important senses for gathering information or input from the environment to use for decision making. An area of study that is gaining increasing emphasis is sports vision training. *Sports vision training* combines vision science, motor learning, biomechanics, sport psychology, and neuroanatomy to help individuals improve their performance.[5]

An understanding of the manner in which individuals learn skills can help the teacher make the learning process more effective and more enjoyable—that is, less frustrating for the learner. The professional must also be aware that skill learning occurs in stages.

Stages of Learning

As an individual learns motor skills and makes the transition from unskilled to skilled performer, he or she progresses through several stages. Fitts and Posner[6] identified three stages of learning: the cognitive stage, the associative stage, and the autonomous stage. The teacher must be cognizant of the characteristics of the learner at each stage to plan for instruction. Different instructional strategies and techniques are required at each stage to make practice more effective. (See Table 9-1.)

Cognitive stage

The first stage of learning is the cognitive stage. During this stage the learner is endeavoring to understand the nature and/or goal of the activity to be learned. During this stage the learner might be concerned with such questions as "How do I stand?" "How do I hold the tennis racquet?" "How do you score in this game?" "What is the sequence of actions in this swimming stroke?" The learner also needs to pay close attention to the information provided by the instructor; this includes verbal directions as well as visual information, perhaps from demonstration of a skill or a videotape

of a performer executing this skill. After analyzing this information the learner formulates a plan of action based on his or her understanding of the task and the specific directions provided by the instructor. Formulating a plan of action is referred to as establishing a motor plan or an executive plan. A high level of concentration on the task is required as the learner tries to put together the various parts of the skill in the correct sequence.

As the learner makes initial attempts at performing the skill, the performance is characterized by a large number of errors, usually gross in nature, and a great deal of variability. Although the learner may have an idea about what he or she is doing incorrectly, the learner may not know how to correct it. To improve skill performance, the learner needs specific feedback from the instructor, communicated in understandable terms. For example, someone just learning the tennis forehand must concentrate on moving to the correct position on the court, the grip of the racquet, the stance, turning the body, keeping an eye on the ball, making contact with the ball with the head of the racquet so that it goes over the net, shifting the body's weight, following through, and returning to ready position. The beginner at times will hit the ball over the net; the next attempt may see the learner hit the ball into the net or out of the court or miss the ball entirely. The learner's actions, although performed in the correct sequence, may lack the smooth, polished look and the consistency of a highly skilled performer.

Associative stage

The second stage is the associative stage. At this point the basics of the skill have been learned and the learner concentrates on refining the skill. During this stage the learner works on mastering the timing needed for the skill; the learner's performance looks smoother. Fewer errors are committed, and the same type of error tends to recur. The learner is also aware of some of the more obvious errors he or she is making in executing the task and can use this information to adjust subsequent performance. The tennis player learning the forehand may notice more success in getting the ball over the net and inside the boundaries of the

TABLE 9-1

Characteristics Associated with Stages of Learning

Cognitive	Associative	Autonomic
Learners' Focus		
Cognitive understanding of the goal of the skill	Concentration on temporal aspects or timing of movements	Concentration on use of the skill in performance situations, use of strategies
Concentrate on spatial aspects or sequence of skill components		
Performance Characteristics		
Lacks smoothness, inefficient, variable, large number of gross errors	Smoother, less variability, more efficient, reduction of extraneous movements, fewer and reduced range of errors	Smooth, efficient, highly refined and well organized spatially and temporally, adaptable to environmental demands
Teacher's Focus		
Provide overview of nature of skill and goal; feedback on intent of skill; information and demonstration of skill, cognitive understanding	Direct learners' attention to critical cues and feedback available, provide numerous practice opportunities, accommodate individual differences	Focus on refinement of response, consistency for closed skills and flexibility for open skills, use of skill in performance situations, feedback for refinement of movements

court, although he or she cannot place the ball with any assurance. The player may notice a frequent failure to follow through after contacting the ball, but he or she is not aware that the angle of the racquet face needs adjustment. The instructor can provide the learner with additional instruction focusing on specific actions and point out relevant cues.

Autonomous stage

The third stage is the autonomous stage. This stage of learning is reached after much practice. The learner can perform the skill consistently with few errors. The skill is well coordinated and may appear to be performed effortlessly. During this stage the skill has become almost automatic. The learner does not have to pay attention to every aspect of the skill; he or she can perform the skill without consciously thinking about it at all. The tennis player no longer has to concentrate on the

fundamentals of the skill; instead, his or her focus can be directed to placing the ball in the court, varying the speed of the shot, placing spin on the ball, or game tactics. The learner also becomes more skilled at detecting errors and making adjustments, in a sense becoming his or her own teacher.

Individuals do not proceed through these stages at the same rate. It may also be difficult at times to identify what stage an individual is in. To plan practices to promote effective learning, however, the professional must be cognizant of the characteristics and the needs of the learner in the various stages. The professional also needs to be aware of the forces that influence learning.

Forces Influencing Learning

Learning implies a change in a person—a change in the method of both practicing and

Highly skilled performers exemplify the autonomous stage of learning.

performing a skill or a change in an attitude toward a particular thing. Learning implies a progressive change of behavior in an individual, although some changes are rapid, such as when one gains insight into a problem. It implies a change that occurs as a result of experience or practice. It results in the modification of behavior as a consequence of training or environment. It involves such aspects as obtaining knowledge, improving skill in an activity, solving a problem, and making an adjustment to a new situation. It implies that a person has acquired knowledge or skill through instruction or personal study. Learning continues throughout life.

To create an effective learning situation, teachers must be cognizant of the forces influencing

learning. Four of these forces—readiness, motivation, reinforcement, and individual differences—will be discussed.

Readiness and motor learning

Successful acquisition of new information or skills depends on the individual's level of readiness. *Readiness* can be defined in terms of physiological and psychological factors influencing an individual's ability and willingness to learn. Physiological readiness in children is development of the necessary strength, flexibility, and endurance, as well as development of the various organ systems, to such a degree that children can control their bodies in physical activities. Psychological readiness refers to the learner's state of mind. One's feeling or attitude toward learning a particular skill—in other words, the desire and willingness to learn—will affect one's acquisition of that particular skill. To create an effective learning environment the teacher must keep in mind the individual's physiological and psychological readiness.

Teachers planning learning activities must be cognizant of the individual's cognitive, affective, and physical characteristics as well as the individual's past experiences. This knowledge will help the teacher plan an atmosphere conducive to learning. The teacher should structure the learning experience so that the individual experiences success rather than the frustration that may come from trying to learn a task that is too difficult or beyond the individual's ability at that time. The teacher may need to modify the task to make it either easier or more challenging. For example, many Little League baseball teams have started letting the younger children hit the ball off a batting tee rather than hit a pitched ball. This adjustment was made because it was realized that the younger children were having difficulty tracking and successfully hitting a moving object. By allowing children to hit the ball while it was stationary—sitting atop a batting tee—the children were able to practice the skill of striking an object, or batting, and experience success in their endeavors. Certainly hitting the ball from the tee was more satisfying to the children than swinging at the

Learning experience should be appropriate for the participant's abilities.

pitched ball and missing. Adjusting the learning task to the individual's ability requires consideration of the individual's physiological readiness. Planning learning experiences that promote success enhances the individual's psychological readiness to learn.

Motivation and motor learning

Motivation is a basic factor in learning. The term *motivation* refers to a condition within an individual that initiates activity directed toward a goal. The study of motivation focuses on the causes of behavior, specifically those factors that influence the initiation, maintenance, and intensity of behavior.

Needs and drives form the basic framework for motivation. When individuals sense an unfulfilled need, they are moved to do something about it. This desire prompts people to seek a solution to the recognized need through an appropriate line of action. This line of action may require practice,

effort, mastery of knowledge, or other behavior to be successful. For example, an individual who is hungry becomes motivated to seek food, whereas at the cognitive level the individual who wants to pass a certification desires to acquire the necessary knowledge.

Motivation refers to an individual's general arousal to action. It might be thought of as the desire or drive a person must have to achieve a goal to satisfy a particular need. The term *need* refers to an internalized deficiency of the organism. The need might be physiological or psychological. The term *drive* refers to the concept of the stimulus for action. Motivation, for example, might be associated with the drive to exercise to satisfy the need to keep the body healthy. The motivating factor might be internal, resulting from the individual's own desire to be fit, or it might be the result of some outside force, such as peer pressure to be thin.

Although motives are internal in nature, they may be affected by external influences. However, it is common to describe an individual's motives as being either internal or external. Motives such as the desire to develop one's body, to have fun, to test one's limits are examples of internal motives for learning. The desire to win awards, to appease parental pressures for participation, or to win money are examples of external motives for participation. An employee may decide to participate in an employee fitness program because of the desire to enhance his or her health status (internal motivation); on the other hand, the employee may participate because he or she was pressured to do so by the boss (external motivation). Internal motivation is more conducive to positive learning and performance and sustained participation than external motivation. The worth of the activity should be the inducement for learning and participation rather than rewards, punishments, or grades. In physical education and sport programs, motives such as the desire to develop one's body, the desire to learn basic movement skills and eventually develop more advanced skills for specialized games, or the desire to do one's best are all valid and should be encouraged.

Exercise specialists should understand an employee's motivation for participating in a corporate fitness program. These PepsiCo employees are working out at the multimillion-dollar fitness facility in Purchase, New York.

The professional should be aware of the motives for the individual's participation in physical education and sport programs. Individuals' motives for learning and participation may differ considerably, so consideration of individual differences is important. For example, as previously mentioned, some participants in an employee fitness program may be internally motivated to join, while others, whose presence was suggested by their employer, may be externally motivated and perhaps even reluctant to participate in the activities. During the course of the program, however, the externally motivated participants may develop an internal motivation. The change could result because the professional made the program challenging, meaningful, and satisfying to the employee. As a consequence, the once reluctant employee may become an enthusiastic participant in the program.

The actions of the teacher can often have a positive effect on the individual's motivation. In a physical education and sport program not all individuals will be motivated to the same extent to learn new skills; in fact, some individuals may not be motivated to learn at all. The teacher can enhance an individual's motivation for learning through goal setting, that is, establishing challenging, albeit attainable, goals for the individual. Motivation can also be enhanced by structuring the learning environment for success and by making the learning experience positive and enjoyable. An individual's level of motivation may also be enhanced through reinforcement.

Reinforcement and motor learning

Physical education and sport professionals should be alert to the need to reinforce the learning of skills and other behaviors of those under their supervision when the desired performance takes place. *Reinforcement* is using events, actions, and behaviors to increase the likelihood of a certain response (e.g., a skill or a behavior) recurring. Reinforcement may be positive or negative. Reinforcement is considered positive when it is given following the desired response, and it is deemed

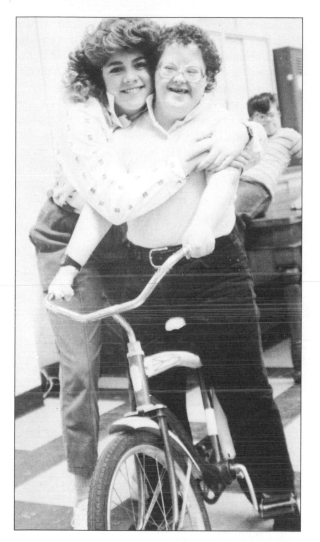

Positive reinforcement is important for learning.

negative when it is withheld following a desired response. Providing encouragement, praise, commendation, or a "pat on the back" following successful execution of a skill is an example of positive reinforcement. Such an acknowledgment of an individual's success not only will serve to reinforce correct skill performance but will also likely motivate the individual to continue in his or her efforts to master the skill. If a teacher belittles an individual's unsuccessful effort to perform a skill and discontinues this behavior when the individual

successfully executes the skill, the teacher is using negative reinforcement.

Two types of reinforcers are tangible and intangible. Tangible reinforcers are material items such as a medal or money. Intangible reinforcers include verbal praise, a "pat on the back," or a nod of approval.

Research suggests that reinforcement is more effective when given immediately after a response than when it is delayed. Random reinforcement tends to be more effective than continual reinforcement. For reinforcement to be effective it must be meaningful to, important to, or desired by the recipient.

Reinforcement, motivation, readiness, and development are important forces in learning. Another important consideration in planning for learning is individual differences.

Individual differences and motor learning

In any learning situation, be it with children or adults, the teacher must provide for individual differences among the learners. The importance of considering individual differences in readiness, motivation, and reinforcement has already been discussed. The teacher also should consider other differences when planning for learning.

Differences in social and economic backgrounds should be considered—some individuals come from middle-class families, while others are economically disadvantaged. These factors can greatly influence the prior experiences these individuals bring to the learning situation. Differences in physical abilities among individuals in the learning situation may be pronounced. Differences in intelligence and preferred learning styles hold implications for the manner in which the skills are to be taught. Personality differences must also be considered. Some individuals are outgoing, whereas others are shy and withdrawn. Some individuals are eager to try new skills, while others are reluctant or intimidated by the prospect of learning something new.

Designing learning experiences to accommodate individual differences requires careful planning and commitment on the part of the teachers. It is not an easy task to design learning experiences for a diversity of abilities, but it is not impossible. Physical education and sport professionals should strive to help each person to be the best he or she can be.

Motor Learning Concepts

In planning for motor learning, the physical educator must consider a learner's level of readiness, development, individual characteristics, motivation, and need for reinforcement. At this point it will be helpful to consider additional concepts, factors, and conditions that promote the learning of motor skills and improve performance.

1. *Practice sessions should be structured to promote optimal conditions for learning.* The manner in which practice sessions are organized can have a critical impact on the amount of learning that occurs. Practices should be organized so that distracting elements are eliminated from the setting. The instructor should ensure that the proper mental set has been established in the mind of the learner, the proper facilities and equipment are available, the learner has the proper background to understand and appreciate the material being presented, and conditions are such that a challenging learning situation exists.

Much research has been done on the organization of practice with reference to the relationship between practice periods and rest periods. (In the literature this is referred to as massed versus distributed practice.) Schmidt,[7] after reviewing the research, stated that "we should recognize that a single, optimal distribution of practice and rest periods does not exist." The design of practice should consider the nature of the task to be learned, the characteristics of the learner, the energy costs of the tasks, and safety. Magill[8] stressed that practice sessions should be structured to maximize the number of opportunities the learner has to try the task. Siedentop[9] emphasizes the need to maximize the amount of time the learner is practicing a task (time-on-task) and the

Physical educators must accommodate individual differences among learners. These elementary school students are working with objects of different shapes as part of a perceptual-motor program.

need for the task to be appropriate for the level of the learner.

2. *Learners must understand the task to be learned.* Helping the learner acquire a cognitive understanding of the nature of the task to be learned is one of the first steps in the learning process. As previously discussed in the stages of learning, the learner must establish an executive or motor plan for action; this involves understanding the nature of the task, analyzing the task demands, and devising techniques to achieve the task goal. This conception of the task or image serves as a guide for the learner's initial attempts.

Typically learners have been helped to establish an image of the task or skill through verbal instructions provided by the teacher. However, the teacher may overuse instructions when faced with the task of describing a complex movement. Too many instructions may overwhelm learners, and in an effort to cope with the avalanche of information about what to do and when to do it, they may disregard much of the information. Instructions should focus on key elements of the task.

Succinct, accurate instructions in conjunction with other techniques such as demonstrations may be more useful than instructions alone in helping the learner understand the task. Demonstrations of the skill allow the learner to form an image of the task. The teacher can use instructions to call the learner's attention to the critical components of the skill. During the learner's initial performances of the task the learner can model the performance exhibited. Children frequently learn skills on their own by imitating or modeling the performance of others. Teachers may also use films or videotapes of skilled performers to provide a model for performance.

3. *The nature of the skill or task to be learned should be considered when designing practice.* Skills can be classified in a variety of ways. To facilitate learning, practices should be appropriate to the type of skill to be learned.

Skills are generally classified on a continuum. One common classification is *open* versus *closed* skills. This classification is based on whether the environment is changing or not changing during the performance of a skill. An open skill is performed in an environment that is changing or variable during the performance of the skill. A closed skill is performed in a stable, unchanging environment. Shooting a goal during a soccer game, hitting a tennis forehand during a match, batting a pitched ball, and dribbling down the basketball court to execute a layup are examples of open skills. Driving a golf ball off the tee, executing a forward $2^{1}/_{2}$ somersault dive from the 3-meter springboard, performing an uneven bars or parallel bars routine in gymnastics, and shooting a foul shot in basketball are examples of closed skills.

The teacher's design of practice should reflect the nature of the skill and the conditions under which the skill will eventually be performed. In practicing closed skills, where the environment remains relatively stable during the performance of the skill, the teacher should emphasize achieving consistency of movement. In performing open skills, the changing environment requires that the performer make alterations in performance to adjust to the changing conditions (e.g., movements of opponents and teammates, speed and direction of the ball, etc.). Thus practice should be variable, with the student exposed to a variety of situations similar to those he or she will actually encounter when performing the skill.

During the initial stages of teaching an open skill, the teacher may structure the environment to be stable (closed) to make learning easier for the beginner. For instance, in learning to bat a pitched ball, the teacher may start the performer out hitting a ball off a batting tee; then the teacher may use a pitching machine set to pitch a ball at a certain speed and height. Finally the performer is given the opportunity to hit balls thrown by a pitcher and must then learn how to adjust his or her swing to the varying speeds and heights of the ball. Thus while open skills may be practiced under closed conditions initially, once the performer is ready, open conditions should prevail. In teaching open skills the teacher must help the performer identify relevant cues in the environment that signify the need to change his or her response. Unlike closed skills in which attainment of response consistency is emphasized, achieving response flexibility and diversity is stressed in open skills. Providing the performer with variable practice conditions is important in learning open skills.

Other motor skill classifications are fine versus gross, discrete versus continuous, and self-paced versus externally paced motor skills. Further information on these skills may be found in the suggested readings at the end of this chapter.

4. *The nature of the task and the background of the learner should be considered in deciding whether to teach the skill by the whole or the part method.* The instructor must decide whether to teach a skill as a whole or to break it down into its component parts. For example, do you teach a skill such as the front crawl stroke as a whole or do you break the stroke down and teach it by parts—arm action, leg action, and breathing? What about teaching the jump shot in basketball? Or the tennis serve? If the learner is highly skilled and has had previous experience in the sport, is the whole or the part method better?

This area has been much researched, but the findings are somewhat confusing. At the risk of generalizing, the instructor should teach a highly complex task as parts. Parts should consist of individual, discrete skills. Tasks in which the skill components are highly interrelated, such as the jump shot in basketball, should be taught as a whole. Highly skilled learners with previous experience in the sport will probably be able to learn effectively if the whole method is used. Low-skilled learners or individuals with short attention spans such as young children may find it easier to learn if taught by the part method. It appears that all learners would benefit from seeing a demonstration of the whole skill; this may enhance the organization of the information provided to the learner and the learner's understanding of the goal of the skill.

If the teacher were to teach the high jump by the part method, the learners would be taught the approach (run to the bar); then they would be taught the jump; next, they would be taught the landing. After all components had been taught, the learners would practice the total skill.

Another option is to use the progressive part method, which consists of initially teaching the first two parts of the skill, combining these two parts into a whole, teaching a third part, then connecting this to the first two parts, and so on. For example, the first two sequences in a dance routine would be taught and practiced, then the third sequence taught; then the third sequence would be added to the first two sequences and all three sequences practiced together. This process of progressively adding parts of a skill is continued until the entire skill is learned.

In summary, the structure of the task, both its complexity and organization, and the characteristics of the learner must be considered in selecting methods of instruction.

5. *Whether speed or accuracy should be emphasized in learning a skill depends on the requirements of the skill.* Teachers are often required to make a judgment as to whether speed or accuracy should be emphasized in the initial stages of learning a skill. For example, a highly skilled tennis player endeavors to serve the ball with as much velocity as possible into the service court. When teaching the

Teachers must decide whether to emphasize speed or accuracy when teaching a skill.

tennis serve, should the teacher emphasize speed, accuracy, or both speed and accuracy? When teaching pitching, should the teacher emphasize throwing the ball as fast as possible, getting the ball into the strike zone all the time, or pitching the ball into the strike zone as fast and as often as possible? This dilemma—whether to emphasize speed or accuracy—is often referred to as a speed-accuracy trade-off. In essence, to perform the skill as accurately as possible means that the performer will have to sacrifice some speed and perform the skill more slowly. Attainment of maximum speed or velocity in performing a skill is at the expense of accuracy. When both speed and accuracy are desired, both qualities will decrease.

Different sport skills have different speed and accuracy requirements. Pitching a ball or performing a tennis serve requires a high degree of both speed and accuracy. In throwing the javelin, speed is more important than accuracy, whereas in the tennis drop shot, accuracy in terms of court placement is more important than speed. The teacher must understand the requirements of the task and design practices accordingly.

The research seems to suggest that skills should be practiced as they are to be performed. This advice is relatively straightforward when the skill emphasizes either speed or accuracy. For example, based on the research findings, speed should be emphasized in teaching the javelin throw and accuracy emphasized in the tennis drop shot. However, what about skills that place a premium on being both fast and accurate, such as pitching a ball or executing a tennis serve? One approach is to have the learner execute the skill as fast as possible and work on accuracy and control after speed has been attained. Another approach is to have the learner focus on being as accurate as possible by reducing the speed of the movements; then, once accuracy is attained, increasing the speed of the movements would be stressed. Emphasizing both speed and accuracy is another approach. The research suggests that when both speed and accuracy are of paramount concern, both variables should receive equal and simultaneous emphasis. The rationale is that mastery is sacrificed when an individual practices a motor skill at slower speed than is needed in the game situation, because the person must readjust to the faster situation. The teacher should understand the speed and accuracy demands of a skill and structure practices so that the learner can practice the skill as it is to be ultimately performed.

6. *Transfer of learning can facilitate the learning of motor skills.* The influence of a previously learned skill on the learning or performance of a new skill is called transfer of learning. The influence exerted may be positive or negative. When a previous experience or skill aids in the learning of a new skill, positive transfer occurs. For example, the student who knows how to play tennis readily learns how to play badminton because both skills require similar strokes and the use of the racquet. Most researchers agree that positive transfer most likely occurs when two tasks have similar part-whole relationships. Again, to use the example of racquet games, since many racquet games such as platform tennis, squash, tennis, racquet ball, and badminton have similar part-whole relationships, it is believed that some transfer takes place. Transfer, however, is not automatic. The more meaningful and purposeful the experience, the greater is the likelihood of transfer. Transfer of training occurs to a greater degree in the following situations: with more intelligent participants, in situations that are similar, where an attitude exists and an effort is made by the learner to effect transfer, when the principles or procedures that are foundational to the initial task are understood, and in situations where one teaches for transfer.

Teachers must also be aware of negative transfer. Negative transfer occurs when a previously learned skill interferes with the learning of a new skill. For example, an individual being introduced to the game of golf for the first time experiences difficulty in swinging the club because of his or her previous experience in another skill such as softball or baseball. In such cases the expression often heard is "You're swinging the golf club like a baseball bat."

Physical educators and coaches have become interested in transferring skills learned in practice sessions to actual game situations. To this end they strive to make their drills as much like a game as possible, or they make an effort in the practice environment to familiarize their team with situations it may encounter in the game. For example, during practice sessions before a basketball game, coaches may have their substitutes imitate the actions of the opponents so that the varsity team is familiar with the opponents' style of play on the night of the game.

Transfer may either facilitate or hinder the acquisition of a skill. Physical educators need to be aware of the principles of transfer so they can use positive transfer to promote skill learning and enhance performance and can readily counteract the effects of negative transfer.

7. Feedback is essential for learning. One of the most critical factors affecting learning is feedback. Feedback is information about an individual's performance. Feedback can serve several functions. It provides the learner with information about his or her performance. Using this information, the learner can make adjustments in the response prior to the next attempt. Second, feedback can serve to reinforce the learner's efforts, strengthening the correct response. Finally, feedback may also serve to motivate the learner by providing information about his or her progress.

Feedback may be classified in many ways. Feedback for error correction may focus on the outcome of the movement or the movement itself. Knowledge of results (KR) provides information about the effects of the movement on the environment, information that tells the learner whether or not the goal of the movement was achieved. Knowledge of performance (KP) provides information about the movement itself. The learner's awareness and feelings about how correctly the movement was executed in relation to the intended movement is knowledge of performance. For example, in shooting a foul shot in basketball the player can readily see if the goal of the movement—putting the ball in the basket—was attained. This is knowledge of results. However, the player may know even before the ball goes in the basket that the shot will be good because the movement "felt right." This is knowledge of performance. Knowledge of performance depends on the learner being sensitive to the "feelings" associated with correct and incorrect performance; in other words the learner becomes aware of what "feels right" and what "feels wrong." Changes in performance occur as the learner compares information about the outcome (KR) with the desired

Videotape feedback is a valuable learning tool. The Omaha Public Schools use video equipment in their physical education classes.

outcome and information about performance (KP) with his or her intended movement. The learner then adjusts his or her performance accordingly until the correct response is achieved.

Feedback may also be classified according to its source or according to when it is presented to the learner. Feedback may be described as intrinsic when the source of the information is the outcome of the task or skill itself.[10] Scoring an ace with a tennis serve, having the shot go slightly wide of the goal in soccer, and scoring on a foul shot in basketball are examples of intrinsic feedback. Information from external sources such as an instructor, friend, or videotape is classified as extrinsic or augmented feedback.[10] When the learner receives information during the performance of the skill, this feedback is referred to as concurrent. Feedback given after the performance is completed is called terminal feedback. Often feedback is a combination of information from various sources. For example, comments from the teacher during the learner's performance provide the learner with extrinsic concurrent feedback. A soccer player seeing the kicked ball go in the goal receives intrinsic terminal feedback.

How can professionals use feedback effectively? Docheff[11] states that the most effective use of feedback includes both general and specific information. One simple method to guide physical education and sport professionals in giving feedback is the use of a "feedback sandwich." The feedback sandwich combines all three functions of feedback: reinforcement, information, and motivation. For example, "Good job, Bob. With your elbow in line, you will always have good alignment when shooting the basketball. Keep up the good work." Physical education and sport professionals should plan for specific feedback. Feedback should be positive and relate to teaching cues. The feedback sandwich offers professionals a guide to increase the meaningfulness and effectiveness of their feedback.

The importance of feedback in the learning of skills is well recognized. Feedback is especially critical during the initial stages of learning a skill. It appears that knowledge of results is more helpful to the individual performing open skills and that knowledge of performance is more valuable to the individual executing a closed skill. With highly skilled performers, whether they are performing a closed or an open skill, knowledge of performance is more helpful. Feedback should be communicated to the learner in a meaningful manner. The teacher should help the learner become aware of the feedback available and teach the learner how to use this information to improve his or her performance.

8. *Learners may experience plateaus in performance.* The extent to which an individual has learned a skill may be inferred from his or her performance. When learning a new skill, an individual may initially demonstrate a sharp improvement in performance. This may be followed by a plateau, or a period in which little or no progress is made. Finally, additional practice results in further improvements in performance.

The plateau may occur for a variety of reasons, such as loss of interest and lack of motivation, failure to grasp a clear concept of the goal to be attained, lack of attention to the proper cues or attention to irrelevant cues, preparation for a transition from fundamental skills to more complex skills in the learning process, or poor learning conditions. Teachers should be cognizant of the plateaus and the conditions under which learners make little or no apparent progress in the activity. They should be especially careful not to introduce certain concepts or skills too rapidly, without allowing sufficient time for their mastery. They should also watch for certain physical deterrents to progress, such as fatigue or lack of strength. Some individuals cannot go beyond a given point because of physiological limits in respect to speed, endurance, or other physical characteristics. Often, however, it is not physiological limits but rather psychological limits that must be overcome. By means of techniques to enhance the learner's interest and enthusiasm, these limits can be overcome.

9. *Self-analysis should be developed.* During the early periods of instruction when the basic techniques of the skill are being learned, learners need frequent instruction and help from the teacher. However, as the skill is mastered, the learner

should rely less on the teacher's help and more on internal resources. A good teacher will help the learner to be his or her own teacher. This involves providing the learner with opportunities for self-criticism and analysis. The learner should be taught how to detect errors and how to correct them. By helping the student become aware of his or her performance and techniques by which it can be improved, the teacher is promoting lifelong learning.

10. *The leadership provided determines to a great degree how much learning will take place.* The teacher should make sure that the learner has a clear idea of the objective to be accomplished. Practices should be designed to maximize the learner's opportunities to perform the skill and minimize unproductive activities such as waiting. The teacher should be continually alert to detect correct and incorrect responses and encourage correct performance. The learner's motivation can be enhanced by providing him or her with opportunities to experience success and by presenting meaningful activities. The teacher should present material appropriate to the learner's level of understanding and be cognizant of individual differences. The teacher should use his or her leadership to promote participants' learning. The box at the right summarizes the guidelines for physical activity instruction.

• • •

This section was designed to provide the reader with a brief overview of some of the concepts and concerns in the realm of motor learning. An understanding of how individuals learn motor skills will help physical education and sport professionals design experiences to promote effective learning. Promoting effective learning is a concern of professionals working in both school and nonschool settings. In the school setting, for example, elementary school physical educators are concerned with helping children master fundamental motor skills, high school teachers focus their efforts on assisting students to acquire skills in a variety of lifetime sports, and coaches spend countless hours helping their athletes refine the skills necessary for high-level performance. In the

GUIDELINES FOR PHYSICAL ACTIVITY INSTRUCTION

1. Use the information-processing model of learning to assist in the planning of learning experiences.

2. Match the type of instruction to the individual's stage of learning.

3. Consider the individual's level of readiness when teaching new skills and information.

4. Plan instructional experiences that take into account the individual's level of development in all three domains—cognitive, affective, and psychomotor.

5. Use the powerful influence of motivation to facilitate learning.

6. Provide positive reinforcement to strengthen desirable responses.

7. Take individual differences into account when teaching by selecting approaches that accommodate a diversity of abilities and needs.

8. Structure practice sessions to promote optimal conditions for learning.

9. Help individuals gain an understanding of the task to be learned and its requirements.

10. Consider the nature of the skill or task when designing practice sessions.

11. Evaluate the task demands and assess the learner's background in deciding whether to use the whole or part method to teach a skill.

12. Study the requirements of the skill to determine whether speed or accuracy should be emphasized in teaching.

13. Facilitate learning by using positive transfer.

14. Incorporate appropriate meaningful feedback to help individuals correct their performance, motivate them, and reinforce their efforts.

15. Be prepared to deal with plateaus in performance.

16. Assist individuals to develop self-analysis skills.

17. Provide strong leadership that contributes to the attainment of the desired objectives.

nonschool setting, athletic trainers may help injured athletes regain efficient motor patterns, while exercise leaders in a corporate or community program may help adults attain proficiency in such lifetime sports as golf or tennis. Thus, understanding how learning occurs and can be facilitated is important foundational knowledge for professionals to possess. The manner in which individuals control their movements (motor control) and the impact of development (motor development) on learning are also important considerations in designing learning experiences.

PSYCHOLOGY OF SPORT AND EXERCISE

Psychology of sport is the application of psychological theories and concepts to aspects of sport such as coaching and teaching. The sport psychologist uses psychological assessment techniques and intervention strategies to help individuals achieve their optimal performance. While sport psychology is concerned with analyzing human behavior in various types of sport settings, it focuses on the mental aspects of performance.

One of the first topics of concern to sport psychologists dealt with personality factors in sports. Today, however, the range of topics is more extensive. Sport psychologists are now concerned with a multitude of subjects such as violence and aggression, arousal, motivation, social reinforcement, and levels of aspiration. Another area of study is the effects of competition on various populations such as youths or elite athletes.

Within the last few years interest has increased in the field of cognitive sport psychology. Cognitive sport psychology focuses on the influence of thoughts and feelings on performance. There is increased recognition that mental skills, like physical skills, can be taught. It now appears that both mental and physical skills are necessary for optimal performance. Areas of study include attentional focus, self-confidence and self-efficacy, self-talk, attributions, and sport intelligence. Cognitive sport psychologists also address the effectiveness of various cognitive intervention strategies such as

hypnosis, cognitive restructuring, thought stopping, mental rehearsal, and self-regulation.

The field of sport psychology is broadening in other ways as well. Initially research efforts focused on elite male athletes. Sport psychologists today are working with both male and female athletes participating at many levels to help them perform at their optimal level. Sport psychologists work with professional sport teams, national sport teams (U.S. Olympic teams in various sports), and intercollegiate teams. Young athletes aspiring to compete at elite levels in such sports as figure skating or gymnastics may engage the services of a sport psychologist to help them attain their lofty goals. Knowledge of sport psychology is also helpful to coaches at all levels, including interscholastic coaches and youth sport coaches. This knowledge can help coaches structure the learning environment to provide a positive experience for their athletes. Coaches can use psychological techniques such as arousal regulation, imagery, and goal setting to help their athletes optimize their performance.

Athletic performance is not the only outcome that can be enhanced through the application of psychological techniques. The improvement of athletes' self-esteem can be achieved more readily through application of appropriate psychological principles. Coaches may also find it beneficial to understand the factors that contribute to athletes' continuing commitment to a sport and the factors that predispose athletes to discontinue sport participation.

The application of sport psychology is not limited to athletics. Physical educators can successfully use this knowledge in a diversity of settings to facilitate the achievement of desired program objectives. Teachers of physical activities in school and nonschool settings can draw on their knowledge of sport psychology to help individuals learn how to direct their attention to relevant cues in the environment and how to optimize their level of arousal to improve performance.

Some sport psychologists today focus their efforts on individuals participating in exercise and rehabilitation programs. Some of their research has sought to identify the psychological determinants of participation in physical activity, the

Paralympians mentally rehearse their performances before the competition begins.

factors that influence the completion of rehabilitation regimens, and the factors that contribute to individuals dropping out of exercise programs. Given the documented evidence supporting the contribution of regular physical activity to health, understanding the psychological dimensions of participation is of critical importance to practitioners working in these areas. Such an understanding can help practitioners design programs and structure experiences to enhance the probability that program participants will engage in physical activity to the extent necessary to achieve concomitant health gains and to incorporate physical activity into their lifestyles.

Sport psychologists can prepare in different ways to work with people. Clinical sport psychologists have extensive training in psychology and are licensed by state boards to treat people with emotional disorders. They enhance their training in psychology with additional training in exercise and sport psychology. Clinical sport psychologists work with athletes who need specialized treatment, such as those who have eating disorders or substance abuse problems. Educational sport psychologists have training in physical education and sport, with extensive training in sport and exercise psychology. They are not licensed psychologists. Educational sport psychologists work with athletes, coaches, and exercisers in the areas of anxiety management, team building, and exercise adherence.

People interested in the psychology of sport had no formal organization to join until 1965, when the North American Society for the Psychology of Sport and Physical Activity (NASPSPA) was formed. A second organization is the Sport Psychology Academy of the National Association of Sport and Physical Education (NASPE); NASPE is a substructure of AAHPERD. The Sport Psychology Academy was founded in 1975. These organizations hold annual meetings that provide a forum for discussion between researchers and practitioners. These meetings provide opportunities for interested professionals to share their needs and concerns, as well as the latest developments and research findings.

The amount of research produced from this field has grown tremendously over the past decade as sport psychologists have sought answers to a diversity of questions. Some of the questions addressed are the following:

- Is the personality profile of the outstanding or elite athlete different from that of the average athlete or of the nonathlete?
- How does participation in physical activities influence one's body image?
- What are the psychological benefits to be derived from participation in physical activities?
- Does one's personality change as a result of participation in sport?
- In what way does anxiety influence performance in various types of sports?
- How can an athlete deal most effectively with the stress of competition? What strategies are

the most helpful for teaching an athlete to use stress to perform at an optimal level?

◆ What factors influence an individual's adherence to an exercise or rehabilitation program?

◆ Is there an optimal attentional focus associated with a specific sport?

◆ How does an individual's self-confidence affect his or her performance? How can self-confidence be developed and then used to maximize performance?

◆ How can self-efficacy in adolescents be increased to promote the establishment of beneficial physical activity patterns?

The next section will provide a brief overview of some of the topics in sport and exercise psychology.

Psychological Benefits of Physical Activity

The role of physical activity in enhancing well-being is receiving increased professional and public recognition. The physiological effects of engaging in physical activity on a regular basis are well documented. There is also a growing body of evidence supporting the psychological benefits of physical activity.[12,13] The psychological benefits of participating in physical activity include the following:

◆ Physical activity improves the health-related quality of life by enhancing both psychological and physical well-being.

◆ Physical activity improves one's mood. Mood states influence our outlook on life, our emotions, thought processes, and behaviors.

◆ Physical activity appears to alleviate symptoms associated with mild depression. Physical activity may be a valuable adjunct to therapy in cases of chronic, severe depression.

◆ Physical activity reduces state anxiety—that is, feelings of tension, apprehension, and fear associated with various situations.

◆ Physical activity can be effective in managing stress. It can serve as a buffer against stress as well as provide a healthful means of stress reduction.

◆ Physical activity contributes to the development of the self. It enhances self-concept and improves self-esteem or feelings of worth. Physical activity promotes greater self-efficacy and self-confidence.

◆ Physical activities offer a means of affiliation with other human beings, an important psychological need.

◆ Physical activities offer participants the opportunity to experience peak moments. Peak moments are characterized by feelings of being "lost" or absorbed in the activity and "flow" or feelings of powerfulness or being able to do no wrong. Participants have reported feelings of euphoria, such as runners' high.

◆ Physical activity provides recreation and a change of pace from long hours of work or study. Individuals return to their daily routine feeling refreshed, both mentally and physically.

◆ Physical activity experiences can present a challenge that, when successfully met, provides a sense of achievement. Some physical activities include certain elements of risk, such as mountain climbing, that provide excitement and opportunities for mastery.

◆ Physical activities offer aesthetic and creative experiences. Activities such as dance allow individuals to express their emotions in a nonverbal manner and provide opportunities for individual interpretation.

The psychological benefits of physical activity are being increasingly understood and offer exciting possibilities for research. The value of physical activity as a therapeutic modality is increasing and new avenues are being explored. Dance therapy and recreation therapy (see Chapter 14) utilize physical activity as part of therapeutic and rehabilitation processes. Their value in alleviating depression and anxiety offer exciting possibilities in treatment and prevention.

Exercise and Adherence

An expanding area of research is investigation of exercise adherence. Researchers have found that patients' adherence to prescribed medical regimens is a great concern. Although figures vary, authorities estimate that half of all patients fail to comply with their medical treatment.[12] The past decade has brought increased recognition of the value of exercise as a therapeutic modality. Exercise is increasingly being prescribed as part of an overall treatment approach to several diseases, including cardiovascular diseases and diabetes. Unfortunately, the compliance rates for participants in exercise programs are similar to those in other medical regimens. Adherence to supervised exercise programs ranges from about 50% to 80% in the first 6 months.[14] Other researchers report that only 30% of individuals who begin an exercise program will be exercising at the end of 3 years.[15]

Knowledge that a particular behavior has either good or harmful influences on our health does not consistently affect our behavior. Most individuals are aware of the factors that detract from wellness—smoking, high-fat diet, sedentary lifestyle, and so on—yet continue to engage in these behaviors despite the health consequences. Why are not more people active? Despite the known benefits, why are there so few participants? And, what can there be done about it?

How do you get people to begin to lead a more active lifestyle? How do you promote behavior change? Many theories and models of human behavior have been used to guide interventions to promote a more physically active lifestyle and encourage health-promoting behaviors. Among the models are the classic learning theories, the health belief model, social cognitive theory, the transtheoretical model, and the ecological perspective.

The classic learning theories emphasize that learning a new complex pattern of behavior, such as moving from a sedentary to an active lifestyle, is achieved by altering many of the small behaviors that compose the overall behavior. This suggests that a targeted behavior, such as walking continuously for 30 minutes a day, is best learned by breaking down this behavior into smaller goals to be achieved, such as walking for 10 minutes daily. Incremental increases, such as adding 5 minutes to daily walking a week, are then made as the behavior—walking–is gradually shaped toward the targeted goal. Rewards and incentives, both immediate and long range, serve as reinforcement and

motivation for the individual to achieve and maintain the targeted behavior. Looking better, receiving a T-shirt for participation, and experiencing a feeling of accomplishment all strengthen and sustain the behavior change.

The health belief model emphasizes that the adoption of a health behavior depends on the person's perception of four factors: the severity of the potential illness, the person's susceptibility to that illness, the benefits of taking action, and the barriers to action. Incorporation of cues to action, such as listing walking on your daily "To Do" list, is important in eliciting and sustaining the desired behavior. Self-efficacy, a person's confidence in his or her capability to perform the desired behavior, is included as an important component of this model.

Social cognitive theory states that behavior change is influenced by environmental factors, personal factors, and attributes of the behavior itself. Self-efficacy is central to this model. A person must believe in his or her ability to perform the behavior (self-efficacy) and must perceive an incentive for changing his or her behavior. The outcomes derived from the behavior must be valued by the person. These benefits can be immediate in nature, such as feelings of satisfaction or enjoyment from engaging in the behavior, or long term, such as improved health from being physically active on a regular basis.

The transtheoretical model of health behavior uses the concept of "stages of change" to integrate the processes and principles of change relating to health behavior.[16] Developed by Prochaska and his colleagues, it was described by Samuelson in 1997 as "one of the most important theoretical health promotion developments of the decade."[17]

The transtheoretical model views behavioral change as a spiraling continuum, moving from a "firm conviction to maintain the status quo by never changing, and proceeds through the conditions of someday, soon, now, and forever."[17] Prochaska's stages of change and a brief description of each are listed below[16,17]:

♦ Precontemplation is when people have no intention to change behavior within the foreseeable future, usually the next 6 months.

People in this stage may be not fully informed about the consequences of their behavior or based on past failures doubt their abilities to change. They may be perceived as resistant or unmotivated.

◆ Contemplation is when people are intending to take action sometime in the next 6 months. In this stage they are aware of and weigh the benefits and drawbacks of changing. This may produce profound ambivalence about change, and people may remain in this stage of "chronic contemplation" or "behavioral procrastination" for some time.

◆ Preparation is when people take small or inconsistent changes toward change, such as developing a plan to change their diet or beginning to exercise.

◆ Action is the point at which individuals have made modifications in their lifestyle. They are engaging in the health-promoting behavior, such as walking briskly for 30 minutes or swimming during their lunch time 3 days a week.

◆ Maintenance is sustaining the change in behavior for at least 6 months. During this time, people become increasingly confident that they can maintain their changes.

◆ Termination is the stage in which the behavior is fully integrated into the lifestyle. People in this stage have a high degree of self-confidence that, despite temptations to relapse, they will continue the behavior.

In this approach, a relapse or discontinuation of the behavior, such as ceasing to exercise, is seen as a return from the action or maintenance stage to an earlier stage. Though relapse occurs often in many behavior changes, only about 15% of the people move all the way back to the precontemplation stage.[16]

Decisional balance and self-efficacy are important aspects of the transtheoretical model. Decisional balance involves weighing the relative pros and cons of the behavioral change, that is, perceived benefits, drawbacks, and barriers to change. The cons outweigh the pros at the precontemplation stage, and the pros outweigh the cons at the action and maintenance stages.[18] The shift in decisional balance appears to occur at the contemplation and preparation stages.[18]

Self-efficacy is a critical feature of this model. Self-efficacy is a person's confidence about his or her competence or abilities in a specific situation. In the context of behavioral change, self-efficacy would be a person's belief that he or she can maintain a healthy behavior, such as exercising, or abstain from an unhealthy behavior, such as smoking. Self-efficacy is typically low at the precontemplation stage and higher in the maintenance and termination stages.

Knowledge of the individual's current stage offers an important guide for intervention programs. The type of intervention should be targeted to the stage. At the precontemplation and contemplation stages, people are not ready for the traditional action-oriented programs, such as beginning an exercise program. Stage-matched interventions, such as education, consciousness raising, and self-reevaluation, are more effective at this point. People at the preparation stage should be recruited into action-oriented programs, such as weight loss or exercise.

The transtheoretical model has most frequently been applied to the cessation of unhealthy, addictive behaviors and more recently to the acquisition of healthy behaviors, such as exercise. Acquisition of a healthy behavior can also be viewed as cessation of an unhealthy behavior; that is, adopting a healthy, active lifestyle can be viewed as ending the unhealthy habit of sedentary living.[18] This model offers physical education and sport professionals great insight into the process of change and guidelines for developing intervention programs.

Another model that has increased in popularity in the last decade is the ecological approach. One criticism of many theories and models for changing health behavior is that they emphasize individual behavior change while paying little attention to the sociocultural and environmental influences on behavior. The ecological approach emphasizes a comprehensive approach to health, including development of individual skills and creating supportive, health-promoting environments. Creating longer-lasting changes and maintenance of health-promoting habits can be enhanced by addressing environmental and societal barriers to change, such as limitations imposed by poverty on access to services or the difficulty in jogging or walking if one lives in an unsafe neighbor. These interventions can take place in the family, school, work sites, community, and health institutions. Societal and environmental influences on health behavior must be considered by physical education and sport professionals.

What are factors that promote adherence, encourage persistence, and prevent dropping out? Researchers have identified several factors that predispose individuals to drop out of exercise programs. In general, the researchers[14,19–20] found that low self-motivation, depression, and low self-efficacy were related to decisions to quit the program, as was denial of the seriousness of one's cardiac condition. Higher dropout rates were found among smokers, blue-collar workers, and individuals who are either obese, exhibit the Type A behavior pattern, perceive that exercise has few health benefits, lead physically inactive lifestyles, or work in sedentary occupations. Lack of social support from significant others, family problems, and job-related responsibilities that interfered with the exercise program were also identified as factors associated with quitting. Social support from other participants was important to individuals who continued in the program. Group exercise programs usually had lower dropout rates than individually designed programs. Programs that were inconvenient to attend and that involved high-intensity exercise were associated with higher dropout rates than programs that were conveniently located and offered exercise of a less intense nature.

Knowing the factors associated with exercise program dropout enables practitioners to target intervention strategies to those individuals at greatest risk of discontinuing their participation. Intervention strategies to improve adherence include educational approaches and behavioral approaches. Educational approaches provide participants with information to increase their knowledge and understanding. Behavioral approaches focus on increasing individual involvement in the program and creating more healthful behavior patterns. These methods use such strategies as reinforcement, contracting, self-monitoring, goal setting, tailoring programs to meet individuals' lifestyles, and enhancement of self-efficacy. Behavioral approaches have been found to be more effective than educational approaches in promoting adherence.

Exercise adherence also can be enhanced through careful program design. One approach is structuring the program to increase the social support available to participants. Successful strategies include forming exercise groups rather than having the individual exercise alone, and involving significant others, such as family members or friends, in encouraging the participant to exercise. Offering programs at times and locations convenient to the participant is important in maintaining involvement. The use of goal setting combined with periodic assessment of progress, use of qualified and enthusiastic leaders, establishment of ongoing leader and participant communication and rapport, and inclusion of a variety of enjoyable activities to meet individual needs are some techniques that can promote exercise adherence and reduce dropout rates.

The issue of adherence to treatment is also beginning to be addressed in the realm of sports medicine. Many of the psychosocial factors that contribute to exercise adherence are also critical to the success of rehabilitation programs. There is increased recognition that sports medicine specialists' and athletic trainers' knowledge of injury mechanisms and treatment protocols is not enough to ensure successful completion of the rehabilitation program. Researchers have found that rehabilitation adherence can be enhanced through the use of such strategies as social support, goal setting, establishment of effective communication, tailoring the program to individual needs, monitoring progress, and building a collaborative relationship to achieve the goals of therapy.[21]

Young professionals aspiring to work in fitness and rehabilitation fields, such as corporate fitness, athletic training, and cardiac rehabilitation, will find knowledge from the subdiscipline of sport and exercise psychology very valuable in their work.

Self-Attitudes and Body Image

Physical education and sport professionals must be concerned with improving the self-attitudes of participants in their programs. Research indicates that physical education and sport can be an important vehicle in the improvement of one's self-image. Physical fitness development may improve an individual's mental health, and motor-skill learning may enhance an individual's inner feelings of self-worth.

Body image is important to individuals of all ages. At a time when society places a great importance on personal appearance, individuals should develop healthy attitudes toward their bodies. People's attitudes and feelings toward their bodies affect personality development. For example, an individual who is obese and unfit may view his or her body as ugly, lack confidence in its performance, experience psychological problems such as low self-esteem as a result of being ridiculed or excluded from a group, and as a consequence may severely limit participation in physical activities. Being sedentary further contributes to being unfit and obese, and further exacerbates one's poor body image—a cycle that tends to be perpetuated. On the other hand, an individual may feel that his or her body is well developed, have confidence that it can meet the challenges of many physical situations, and enjoy participation in physical activities. Feelings about one's body can affect relations with other people and also participation in physical activities.

Body image is particularly important during the adolescent period. For example, some research has shown that when a boy's physique is small, not well developed, and weak over an extended period of time, his behavior is affected. He will become overly shy or aggressive and will reflect internal discord. Individuals who mature late may find their relationships with their peers affected. Often they are excluded from games and sport activities because of the peers' desire to be successful in their game experience. These individuals, excluded from participation because of their lack of physical skills, may consequently develop an unfavorable attitude toward physical activity that may persist to adulthood. The professional may find it difficult to get these individuals to join corporate fitness programs because of their negative adolescent experiences. Individuals who mature early may encounter problems as well. These early maturers may find that although they were always the stars during early game experiences because of their superior physical characteristics in relation to their peers, this status was lost as their friends matured. The loss of star status proves a difficult adjustment for many individuals. Other personality problems have been found in boys with feminine characteristics, girls with masculine characteristics, individuals with narcissistic characteristics, and individuals who possess certain body types and postures.

Adults' attitudes toward physical activity and sport may have been significantly affected by their body image and associated positive and negative physical education experiences in their youth. With the increased emphasis on fitness and weight control in our society today, many adults are enrolling in physical activity and sport programs as a means of achieving these ends. Even adults turned off by physical education programs during their school years may decide to try once again to enjoy physical activity. It is important that the physical education and sport professional who is working with adult participants be cognizant of their previous experiences and put forth a concerted effort to make the present experience positive and personally satisfying.

Since many feelings toward participation are formulated in individuals' youth, it is important that teachers, family members, and other interested persons help each child "be at home in his or her own body." While it may not be possible for every boy or girl to develop the type of body they most admire, within the limitations of body structure each child should be helped to develop a fit and healthy body as well as a positive body image. Following are some suggestions:

♦ Understand the role of body image. This enhances awareness of why some boys and girls have certain attitudes and feelings toward sport and other forms of physical activity.

♦ Use empathy in relations with children who have a poor body image. Help them live comfortably with their own body and physical features.

◆ Help young people understand that it is possible in many instances to improve one's physical appearance. For example, boys and girls can improve their appearance by correcting postural faults and developing a better body build through exercises and activities.

◆ Help each child to achieve and be successful in physical activity experiences. Since success or failure influences self-concept and how one views new tasks and experiences, physical education programs should be planned and organized so that each child who participates achieves success. If a youngster believes he or she is a failure, then the program is also a failure. Note that this refers to personal success rather than success based on a comparison of one's performance with that of other children.

◆ Encourage participation in many different types of physical activities. If properly selected and meaningfully conducted, physical activities can improve self-image, since one will develop strength, endurance, and other desirable qualities.

When physical education and sport professionals understand the role of body image, they are better able to understand why various individuals have certain attitudes and feelings toward physical activity and the contributions physical education and sport can make to these persons.

Personality

Physical education teachers and coaches have long been interested in the positive and negative effects of participation in sport on the development of an individual's personality. Although it has been shown that an individual's personality is formed early in life, some experts believe that personality may be modified by later experiences. Some psychologists theorize that participation in athletics can contribute to personality development. In some cases competitive athletics satisfy basic needs such as recognition, belonging, self-respect, and feelings of achievement, and provide a wholesome outlet for the drive for physical activity

and creativity. These are desirable psychological effects that aid in molding socially accepted personalities. At the same time, however, competitive athletics can produce harmful effects. Two factors that may adversely affect an individual's personality are an overemphasis on winning by coaches, parents, and community members and placing individuals in situations not suited for their physical abilities.

Many sport psychologists have studied the relationship between personality and sport performance. Researchers[22] addressed questions such as "Do athletes differ from nonathletes?" "Can athletes in certain sports be distinguished from athletes in other sports on the basis of their personality?" "Do individuals participate in certain sports because of their personality characteristics?" "Do highly skilled athletes have different personality profiles than less skilled athletes in the same sport?" "Are there certain personality traits that can predict an athlete's success in a sport?"

Sport psychologists' findings have revealed contradictory answers to each of these questions. In many instances problems in research design have contributed to these contradictory results. Cox,[23] after an extensive review of the research on personality and sport, offered the following generalizations about men and women athletes relative to the questions posed above:

◆ Athletes and nonathletes differ with respect to personality characteristics. Various researchers have reported that athletes are more independent, objective, self-confident, competitive, outgoing or extroverted, and less anxious than nonathletes.

◆ Differences in personality traits between athletes and nonathletes are due to a "natural selection" process. This process occurs successfully in the mature individual. However, it has been shown that sport participation has a positive effect on the personality development of young athletes during their formative years. Thus people's youth sport experience can positively or negatively affect the development of their personality.

◆ Athletes in one sport can be differentiated from athletes in another sport based on their personality characteristics. Perhaps the clearest example occurs between individual sport athletes and team sport athletes. It has been shown that individual sport athletes are less extroverted, more independent, and less anxious than team sport participants.

◆ World-class athletes can be correctly differentiated from less skilled athletes by their psychological profile 70% of the time. Personality profiles that include situational measures of psychological states have been shown to be the most accurate in predicting level of athletic performance.

These statements hold several implications for the teacher and the coach. First, while Cox has advanced some generalizations based on an overview of research in the area, much of the research is still inconclusive. As the field of sport psychology grows, it is likely that advances in methodology will yield more definitive answers. Second, each athlete must be treated as an individual. One must recognize that a highly skilled athlete may differ from the "typical" personality; teachers and coaches must understand and respect individual differences in personality. This implies, for example, that different individuals may benefit from different motivational techniques. Third, practitioners who work with young children must be cognizant that participation in sport can have a positive or negative effect on an individual's personality. We can hope that sport psychologists in the future will be able to provide further insight into the relationship between personality and sport.

Anxiety and Arousal

The goal of coaches, teachers, and sport psychologists is to optimize an individual's performance. To achieve this goal they must consider the effect of anxiety and arousal on performance. Anxiety, as defined by Levitt,[24] is a subjective feeling of apprehension accompanied by a heightened level of physiological arousal. Physiological arousal is an autonomic response that results in the excitation of various organs of the body. Examples of this phenomenon seen in athletes are sweaty hands, frequent urge to urinate, increased respiration rate, increased muscle tension, and elevated heart rate.

Anxiety is commonly classified in two ways. Trait anxiety is an integral part of an individual's personality. It refers to the individual's tendency to classify environmental events as either threatening or nonthreatening. State anxiety is an emotional response to a specific situation that results in feelings of fear, tension, or apprehension. The effects of both state and trait anxiety on motor performance have been studied by sport psychologists.

Coaches and teachers consistently attempt to find the optimal level of arousal that allows individuals to perform their best. An arousal level that is too low or too high can have a negative impact on performance. A low level of arousal in an individual is associated with such behaviors as low motivation, inattention, and inappropriate and slow movement choices. A high level of arousal in an individual can cause deterioration in coordination, inappropriate narrowing of attention, distractibility, and a lack of flexibility in movement responses. It is important for each individual to find his or her optimal level of arousal for a given activity. However, no one knows for sure exactly how to consistently reach this ideal state. A variety of approaches have been employed by physical education and sport professionals in pursuit of this goal. These techniques include "pep talks," use of motivational slogans and bulletin boards, relaxation training, imagery, and in some cases the professional services of a sport psychologist.

Sport psychologists and researchers have studied the relationships among anxiety, arousal, and sport performance. Cox,[23] after a review of the research in this area, offered the following ideas:

◆ Athletes who feel threatened by fear of failure experience a high level of anxiety. Fear of failure can be reduced by defining success in individual terms and keeping "winning" in perspective.

◆ Athletes who possess high levels of trait anxiety tend to experience high levels of state anxiety when confronted with competition. Coaches who are aware of their athletes'

Optimal arousal is necessary for superior performance.

levels of trait anxiety can better understand how they are likely to respond in a competitive situation. This knowledge will help coaches select appropriate strategies to adjust athletes' levels of state anxiety and arousal to an optimal level.

◆ Athletes' perceptions of a given situation influence their level of state anxiety. Not all athletes react to the competitive situation in the same manner. Each athlete perceives the same situation in a different way. Coaches must be aware that when placed in the same competitive situation, athletes experience different levels of anxiety. That is why "psych" talks may be an effective means of regulating the arousal level of some athletes and ineffective with other athletes. Techniques must be tailored to the individual athlete and the situation.

◆ An optimal level of arousal is essential for peak performance. The individual characteristics of the athlete, the nature of the skill to be performed, and the competitive situation influence the level of arousal needed.

◆ As the arousal level increases, athletes tend to exhibit the dominant or habitual response. Under the stress of competition they tend to revert to skills they are most comfortable performing. Thus, if a volleyball player has been recently trained to pass the ball in a low trajectory to the setter, under the stress of competition the player may revert to the safer, easier-to-perform, high-trajectory pass.

Research in the area of anxiety, arousal, and motor performance suggests several ways in which coaches can achieve optimal performance from their athletes. Coaches must accept the concept that individuals' perceptions of a situation influence their levels of anxiety and subsequently their levels of arousal. Optimal performance depends on individuals achieving their ideal level of arousal for the situation. Anxiety can affect other factors that influence an individual's level of performance, such as attention.

Attention

An individual's performance is greatly influenced by his or her attention to the task. As previously discussed, an individual must locate, select, and focus on relevant cues to be successful in performing the task (skill or game). Not only must the individual discriminate between relevant and irrelevant cues, but also he or she must maintain the necessary attentional focus for the task. If an individual focuses on the irrelevant cues or fails to maintain the appropriate attentional focus, the performance will be less than optimal.

Nideffer[25] defined attention as the ability to direct senses and thought processes to particular objects, thoughts, and feelings. Attention can be described in terms of two dimensions—width and direction. The width dimension varies from broad to narrow. The direction dimension may be described as external, that is, focusing on environmental cues, or as internal, that is, focusing on thoughts, emotions, and sensations. In any particular situation an individual's attention may be described as broad external, broad internal, narrow external, or narrow internal. An individual who has a broad external focus is directing his or her attention to a wide range of environmental cues; an individual who has a broad internal focus is directing his or her feelings to a multitude of internal thoughts and sensations. In contrast, an individual who has a narrow external focus is concentrating on a few selected environmental cues; an individual who has a narrow internal focus is concerned with selected internal cues and thoughts.

To be successful an individual must match his or her attentional focus to the task demands, which often change as the performance progresses. Thus to be successful, the individual must be able to switch rapidly back and forth between the various attentional styles at will. Let us use batting a pitched ball for an example. As the batter stands outside the batter's box awaiting his or her chance to hit, attention may have a broad internal focus. As the batter waits, he or she is reviewing the coach's directions and the strategies previously favored by the pitcher. The batter internally constructs the current situation, identifying the number of outs and the position of the runners on base. The batter then prepares a strategy. The focus is then narrowed to specific thoughts (narrow internal focus). As the batter stands in the box, he or she may adopt a broad external focus to predict the type of pitch by concentrating on cues from the pitcher. As the ball is released, attention shifts to a narrow external focus as the batter follows the path of the ball.

In an effort to assess individuals' attentional style, Nideffer[25] developed the Test of Attentional and Interpersonal Style (TAIS). The TAIS comprises six scales designed to measure the width and direction dimensions of attention. The broad external scale, the broad internal scale, and the narrow scale (this scale includes both external and internal dimensions) represent effective attentional styles. Three scales reflect ineffective attentional styles. The overloaded external focus assesses the amount of confusion from trying to process too many environmental cues at the same time, while the overload internal focus represents the confusion from trying to think too much. Last, the underinclusive attentional focus reflects an excessive narrowing of attention, often referred to as "tunnel vision."

The TAIS measures attention in general situations. Researchers measuring attention in sport situations have modified Nideffer's TAIS to reflect situations encountered in specific sport environments. Researchers have developed attention tests in the areas of tennis,[26] riflery,[27] volleyball,[28] diving,[28] soccer,[28] baseball,[28] and field hockey.[28] Physical educators need to be cognizant of the attentional requirements of various sports and sport skills, as well as the ability of each individual to attain and sustain the appropriate attentional focus.

An individual's focus of attention may be affected by a variety of factors. One factor that has a critical impact on attention is anxiety. Anxiety tends to narrow and internalize an individual's attentional focus. Physical education and sport professionals need to be aware of the numerous factors that can influence an individual's performance. They must also be aware of the various intervention strategies that can be used to deal effectively with these factors.

Intervention Strategies

In recent years coaches, teachers, and sport psychologists have turned to a variety of intervention strategies to help athletes achieve their optimal performance. As discussed earlier, anxiety and arousal can have harmful effects on athletes' performance. Athletes' performance can also suffer due to lack of motivation, poor level of self-confidence, and, because of the intimate relationship between the mind and the body, negative thoughts and feelings about themselves and their capabilities. With the help of appropriate intervention techniques, athletes learn skills and strategies to regulate their physiological and psychological state to achieve optimum performance.

Sometimes athletes experience excessive anxiety and arousal, which causes a deterioration in their performance. Intervention strategies focusing on reducing this level would benefit these athletes. One way to deal with elevated levels of arousal is through the use of a variety of relaxation techniques. These techniques teach the individual to scan the body for tension (arousal is manifested in increased muscular tension) and, after identifying a higher than optimal level of tension, to reduce the tension to the appropriate level by relaxing. Once specific relaxation techniques are learned, this process should take only a few minutes. Types of relaxation training include progressive relaxation, autogenic training, transcendental meditation, and biofeedback. A note of caution is in order here, however. Athletes should be careful not to relax or reduce their level of arousal too much because this will have a harmful influence on their performance.

In recent years the use of cognitive strategies to facilitate optimum performance has gained increased acceptance. Cognitive strategies teach athletes psychological skills that they can employ in their mental preparation for competition. In addition to focusing on alleviating the harmful effects of anxiety and arousal, these cognitive strategies can also be used to enhance motivation and self-confidence and to improve performance consistency. These approaches include cognitive restructuring, thought stopping, self-talk, hypnosis and self-hypnosis, goal setting, and mental imagery.

Some cognitive intervention techniques focus on changing athletes' thoughts and perceptions. Sport psychologists have realized that athletes' negative thoughts about their abilities, such as the "I can't" attitude, can adversely affect performance. Athletes' internal dialogues—that is, the conversations that athletes in effect carry on with themselves—have also been a focus of cognitive intervention strategies. This dialogue, both prior to and during performance, may reflect athletes' worries about succeeding, their fear of failure, or

Setting goals is the first step toward achievement. Participants in the Tenneco Health and Fitness program record their progress.

Psychological skills can help athletes perform at their peak.

concerns that an undesirable past experience will repeat itself . . . "What if I choke like last time?" . . . "What if I strike out again?" Cognitive restructuring, self-talk, and thought stopping focus on eliminating negative thoughts and replacing them with positive ones such as "I can do it." Cognitive strategies can also be used to alter athletes' perceptions of events, thus reducing anxiety. Affirmation of athletes' ability to succeed in an upcoming competition is another cognitive strategy frequently used to promote optimal performance.

Goal setting can assist athletes by giving them clear, specific objectives to strive to attain. Goal setting involves establishing long-term goals and then identifying specific short-term objectives that lead almost like steps to the achievement of the long-term goals. Goals should be stated in terms of observable behavior so that athletes can readily assess their progress. For example, a volleyball player may have as a goal the improvement of his or her performance. Stated as such this goal is difficult to measure, and the player really has a hard

time determining whether the stated goal has been achieved. This goal could also be stated as "making 90% of my serves and 40% of my spikes as kills." When the goal is presented in this manner, the player can chart progress toward the goal. Goals should be challenging but reachable. Together the coach and the player devise strategies for attaining the goal and frequently evaluate progress.

Imagery is the visualization of a situation. This technique has been used in a variety of ways to enhance performance. It can be used to mentally practice skills or to review outstanding previous performances. By remembering the kinesthetic sensations associated with the ideal performance, the athlete hopes to replicate or improve performance. Imagery has also been used as an anxiety reduction technique. The athlete visualizes anxiety-producing situations and then "sees" himself or herself successfully coping with the experience, thus increasing confidence to perform successfully in similar situations.

Intervention strategies have proved useful in helping athletes maximize their performance.

These strategies are not only for athletes but also have implications for all participants in physical activities and sport. For example, the beginning jogger may derive as much benefit from goal setting as the high-level performer. The practitioner using these strategies must be cognizant of individual differences; otherwise performance may be affected adversely.

The growth of sport psychology has provided physical educators with a clearer understanding of various psychological factors that may affect an individual's performance. Sport psychologists have been able to enhance individual performance through the use of a diversity of intervention strategies. Although much of the work done in the area of sport psychology has been with athletes, many of the findings and techniques are applicable to participants in a variety of physical activity settings such as school, community, and corporate fitness programs. As the field of sport psychology continues to expand, practitioners will gain further insight into how to enhance the performance of all individuals.

SUMMARY

The study of motor development, motor control, motor learning, and sport psychology has its legacy in psychology. These fields of study have expanded tremendously in the past decade and have taken on separate identities.

Motor development is the study of the origins and changes in movement behavior throughout the lifespan. Motor control is the study of the neural mechanisms and processes by which movements are learned and controlled. Motor learning is the acquisition of movement skills as a consequence of practice.

Many theories have been advanced to describe learning. One theory to describe the manner in which individuals learn motor skills is the information-processing theory. According to this theory, learning and performance of skills can be described as a series of information-processing tasks consisting of input, decision making, output, and feedback. Individuals pass through three stages when learning a motor skill: cognitive, associative, and autonomic. Learning is influenced by several forces. Four of these forces are readiness, motivation, reinforcement, and individual differences. To facilitate learning, the professionals should design practices based on sound motor learning concepts.

Sport psychology is concerned with the application of psychological theories and concepts to sport and physical activity. Psychological assessment techniques and intervention strategies are used by the sport psychologist to help individuals attain their optimal level of performance. The physical educator should be aware of the psychological benefits to be derived from participation in physical activity as well as the effect of physical activity on an individual's body image. An individual's personality, anxiety and arousal, and attention can influence his or her performance. Intervention strategies can be used to help individuals to prepare for athletic events. Sport psychology offers the promise of greater insight into the factors that influence performance.

SELF-ASSESSMENT TESTS

These tests are designed to help you determine if you have mastered the materials and competencies presented in this chapter.

1. Give examples in the field of physical education and sport of cognitive, affective, and psychomotor learning.

2. You are a teacher in a school setting, a sport instructor in a community setting working with senior citizens, or fitness leader in a corporate fitness program working with adults. How would you incorporate concepts from each of the following areas in the conduct of your program: readiness, reinforcement, motivation, and individual differences?

3. Select a skill that you are familiar with from your previous physical education experiences. Describe how you would teach this skill to a beginner. In your description include the information-processing model of learning as well as the stages of learning.

4. Justify the claim that participation in physical activity can have positive psychological benefits.

5. Using the information provided in the Getting Connected box, access the *MindTools* site and read about one of the topics in sport psychology, such as goal setting, motivation, or imagery. Choose a topic that interests you. Then write 1 to 2 pages summarizing what you have learned and discussing how you can apply that information in your professional career.

6. In recent years the field of sport psychology has expanded tremendously. As a practitioner, be it as a teacher, coach, adapted physical educator, athletic trainer, or exercise physiologist, you are concerned with optimizing individuals' performance. Discuss the roles of anxiety, arousal, and attention in the performance of motor skills and the use of intervention strategies to enhance performance.

REFERENCES

1. Gallahue DL: Understanding motor development: infants, children, adolescents, Indianapolis, 1989, Benchmark.

2. Haywood KM: Lifespan motor development, Champaign, Ill., 1993, Human Kinetics.

3. Nichols B: Moving and learning: the elementary school physical education experience, ed 3, St. Louis, 1994, Mosby.

4. Gabbard CP: Lifelong motor development, ed 2, Dubuque, Iowa, 1992, Brown & Benchmark.

5. Knudson D and Kluka DA: The impact of vision and vision training on sport performance, JOPERD 68(4):17–24, 1997.

6. Fitts PM and Posner MJ: Human performance, Belmont, Calif., 1967, Brooks/Cole.

7. Schmidt RA: Motor control and learning, Champaign, Ill., 1991, Human Kinetics.

8. Magill RA: Motor learning: concepts and applications, ed 4, Dubuque, Iowa, 1993, Wm. C. Brown.

9. Siedentop D: Developing teaching skills in physical education, Palo Alto, Calif., 1991, Mayfield.

10. Rink JE: Teaching physical education for learning, ed 2, St. Louis, 1994, Mosby.

11. Docheff DM: The feedback sandwich, JOPERD 61(9):17–18, 1990.

12. US Department of Health and Human Services: Physical activity and health: a report of the Surgeon General, Atlanta, Ga., 1996, US Department of Health and Human Services, Centers for Disease Control and Prevention, National Center for Chronic Disease Prevention and Health Promotion.

13. Berger BG: Psychological benefits of an active lifestyle: what we know and what we need to know, Quest 48:330–353, 1996.

14. Brannon L and Feist J: Health psychology: an introduction to behavior and health, ed 2, Belmont, Calif., 1992, Wadsworth.

15. Dishman RK and Sallis JF: Determinants and interventions for physical activity and exercise. In C Brochard, RJ Shephard, and T Stephens,

editors, Physical activity and health, fitness, and health: international proceedings and consensus statement, 214–238, Champaign, Ill., 1994, Human Kinetics.

16. Prochaska JO and Velicer WF: The transtheoretical model of health behavior change, American Journal of Health Promotion 12: 38–48, 1997.

17. Samuelson M: Commentary: changing unhealthy lifestyle: who's ready . . . who's not?: an argument in support of the stages of change component of the transtheoretical model, American Journal of Health Promotion 12:13–14, 1997.

18. Herrick AB, Stone WJ, and Mettler MM: Stages of change, decisional balance, and self-efficacy across four health behaviors in a worksite environment, Journal of Health Promotion 12:49–56, 1997.

19. King AC, Blair SN, Bild DE, Dishman RK, Dubbert PK, Marcus BH, Oldridge NB, Paffenbarge RS, Jr., Powell KE, and Yaeger KK: Determinants of physical activity and intervention in adults, Medicine and Science in Sports and Exercise Supplement 24(6):S221–S236, 1992.

20. Nieman, DC: Fitness and sports medicine: an introduction, Palo Alto, Calif., 1990, Bull.

21. Fisher AC, Scriber KC, Matheny ML, Alderman MH, and Bitting LA: Enhancing athletic injury rehabilitation adherence, Journal of Athletic Training 28(4):312–318, 1993.

22. Vealey RS: Sport personology: A paradigmatic and methodological analysis, Journal of Sport and Exercise Psychology 11:216–235, 1989.

23. Cox RH: Sport psychology concepts and applications, Dubuque, Iowa, 1985, Wm. C. Brown.

24. Levitt EE: The psychology of anxiety, Hillsdale, N.J., 1980, Earlbaum.

25. Nideffer RM: Test of attentional and interpersonal style, Journal of Personality and Social Psychology 34:394–400, 1976.

26. van Schoyck SR and Grasha AF: Attentional style variations and athletic ability: the advantage of a sport specific test, Journal of Sport Psychology 3:149–165, 1981.

27. Etzel EF: Validation of a conceptual model characterizing attention among international rifle shooters, Journal of Sport Psychology 1:281–290, 1979.

28. Fisher AC: Tests of attentional style for volleyball, diving, soccer, baseball, and field hockey, Ithaca College, Ithaca, N.Y.

SUGGESTED READINGS

Berger BG: Psychological benefits of an active lifestyle: what we know and what we need to know, Quest 48:330–353, 1996.

Discusses the four psychological benefits associated with an active lifestyle: enhanced mood, stress reduction, more positive self-concept, and higher quality of life.

Cox RH: Sport psychology: concepts and applications, ed 3, Dubuque, Iowa, 1994, Brown & Benchmark.

In an easy to understand format, Cox discusses key concepts and their application, including personality, attention, anxiety, motivation, self-confidence, and intervention strategies.

Docheff DM: The feedback sandwich, JOPERD 61(9):17–18, 1990.

Docheff offers professionals guidelines to increase the effectiveness of their feedback.

Fisher AC, Scriber KC, Matheny ML, Alderman NH, and Bitting LA: Enhancing athletic injury rehabilitation adherence, Journal of Athletic Training 28(4):312–318, 1993.

Practical strategies to promote athletes' adherence to rehabilitation programs.

Gallahue DL: Understanding motor development: infants, children, adolescents, Indianapolis, 1989, Benchmark.

A comprehensive overview of motor development, including models, factors influencing development, and implications for programming, education, and assessment.

Haywood KM: Lifespan motor development, Champaign, Ill., 1986, Human Kinetics.

A lifespan approach to development, including discussion of related areas such as perceptual motor development, physiological changes and exercise over the lifespan, information processing, and sociocultural influences on development.

King AC, Blair SN, Bild DE, Dishman RK, Dubbert PK, Marcus BH, Oldridge NB, Paffenbarger RS Jr., Powell KE, and Yaeger KK: Determinants of physical activity and intervention in adults, Medicine and Science in Sports and Exercise Supplement 24(6):S221–S236, 1992.

An examination of the factors related to participation in physical activity programs and probability of successful intervention.

Knudson D and Kluka DA: The impact of vision and vision training on sport performance, JOPERD 68(4):17–24, 1997.

The article summarizes important information about vision, shows how vision training can be incorporated into sports, provides practical examples of applying this information to performance, and offers sample vision training exercises.

Peddie BK: What underlies the teaching of motor skills, Physical Educator 52:119–124, 1995.

Practical application of motor learning concepts are presented, as well as guidelines for use by practitioners.

Prochaska JO and Velicer WF: The transtheoretical model of health behavior change, American Journal of Health Promotion 12:38–48, 1997.

The authors clearly present the transtheoretical model of health, including stages of change, decisional balance, interventions, and self-efficacy.

Samuelson M: Commentary: changing unhealthy lifestyle: who's ready . . . who's not?: an argument in support of the stages of change component of the transtheoretical model, American Journal of Health Promotion 12:13–14, 1997.

Weinberg RS and Gould D: Foundations of sport and exercise psychology, Champaign, Ill., 1995, Human Kinetics.

This text introduces the basic principles and applications of sport and exercise psychology, including motivation, goal setting, children in sport and exercise, and team dynamics

Whitall J: The evolution of research on motor development: new approaches bringing new insights, Exercise and Sport Sciences Review 23:243–274, 1995.

The review shows how motor development and research has changed during the past decade and future directions for research endeavors.

PART THREE

Careers and Professional Considerations in Physical Education and Sport

Introduction

In Part Two the historical and scientific foundations of physical education and sport were described. In recent years the expansion of the knowledge base has led to the development of subdisciplines in physical education and sport. This expansion, coupled with the tremendous growth of interest in sports and fitness in our society, has resulted in the development of many career opportunities for qualified physical education and sport professionals.

In Part Three, diverse career opportunities within the field of physical education and sport are described. This section begins with a discussion of career preparation, professional responsibilities, and leadership development in Chapter 10. Chapter 11 discusses traditional career opportunities, such as teaching and coaching in the schools. The expansion of physical education and sport programs to nonschool settings and to people of all ages has resulted in teaching and coaching opportunities outside of the school setting. The tremendous interest in physical fitness and health has stimulated the growth of fitness-, health-, and therapy-related careers. These careers are examined in Chapter 12. Chapter 13 describes career opportunities in media, management, performance, and other related areas. The pervasiveness of sport in our society, combined with the growth of the communications media, has encouraged careers in sport communication, while the development of sport as big business has created a need for professionals trained in sport management. Opportunities for people interested in pursuing careers as performers have also increased during the last decade.

CHAPTER 10

Career and Professional Development in Physical Education and Sport

Instructional Objectives and Competencies to be Achieved:

After reading this chapter the student should be able to—

- Identify career opportunities in physical education and sport.
- Self-assess strengths, interests, goals, and career preferences.
- Understand his or her professional preparation curriculum.
- Discuss the role of practical experience in professional preparation.
- Describe strategies to enhance his or her marketability.
- Identify leadership skills for physical education and sport professionals.
- List professional organizations in physical education and sport.

Traditionally, careers in physical education and sport have focused on teaching and coaching in schools and colleges and universities. Today, teaching and coaching careers in nonschool settings such as community centers (e.g., YMCA or YWCA) and commercial clubs (e.g., gymnastics, tennis, or swimming clubs) are increasingly available. Interest in nonteaching careers is great as well. Many physical education and sport professionals are pursuing careers in the fitness field, working in health clubs or corporate fitness centers. Other professionals are employed in the areas of sport management, sports medicine, and sport media. The increased specialization within the field of physical education and sport has created additional career opportunities. For example,

biomechanists may work for sporting goods companies designing and testing sport equipment and apparel such as running shoes. Exercise physiologists may be employed in a corporate fitness center, hospital cardiac rehabilitation program, or a sports medicine clinic. Career opportunities for a student who has studied physical education and sport have never been greater. Professional preparation for a career in physical education and sport will be discussed in this chapter.

CAREERS IN PHYSICAL EDUCATION AND SPORT

Career opportunities in physical education and sport have expanded tremendously during the past

GETTING CONNECTED

StudentCenter.com About Work offers guidelines for self-assessment, job hunting tips, interview strategies, and allows you to create an on-line resume.

     Site: http://www.aboutwork.com/resume/

Human Kinetics Infokinetics gives descriptions of many different physical activity careers. The site also includes self-assessment and job search strategies. Over 700 professional organizations are also listed on this site. After accessing the site, click on Infokinetics and follow the links to careers and professional organizations.

     Site: http://www.humankinetics.com

The Occcupational Handbook provides descriptions of different occupations, including information about the nature of the work, working conditions, training and other qualifications, job outlook, earnings, and related occupations.

     Site: http://stats.bls.gov/ocohome.htm

AAHPERD, ACSM, and ACSM Web sites include information about the mission of the organization, services, membership, and educational opportunities.

     AAHPER: http://www.aahpcrd.org
     ACSM: http://www.acsm.org
     NATA: http://www.nata.org

20 years. The widening career opportunities are a result of several factors. First, the desire to be fit and an awareness of the concomitant health benefits have stimulated millions of Americans from all segments of our society to embark on fitness programs and engage in a variety of physical activities. This in turn has led to the need for fitness leaders and professionals trained in exercise science. Additionally, people seeking to use their leisure time in an enjoyable manner have sought out physical activities and sports. Specially trained individuals are needed to conduct recreational programs and to teach lifetime sport skills. The increased interest in competitive sports, again by all segments of the population, has served as the impetus for the growth of competitive sport programs, sport clubs, and leagues and the associated career opportunities in coaching, sport management, officiating, and athletic training. Finally, the increase in the depth and breadth of knowledge in physical education and sport has led to the further

development of subdisciplines and expanded career opportunities as biomechanists, sport psychologists, exercise physiologists, and adapted physical activity specialists.

Career opportunities in physical education and sport are limited only by one's imagination. Lambert[1] points out that one's definition of physical education can limit or expand one's horizons. Defining physical education only as "the teaching of sports, dance, and exercise in the public schools" can limit job opportunities to the traditional teaching-coaching career. However, if you define physical education as the "art and science of human movement," "sport education," "fitness education," or "preventive and rehabilitative medicine," many career possibilities become evident. Similarly, defining physical education as the "study of play," the "study of human energy," "perceptual-motor development," or as an "academic discipline that investigates the uses and meanings of physical activities to understand their

Tenneco employees work out on their indoor track.

effects and interrelationships with people and their culture" opens up other avenues of employment. Possible career opportunities are listed in the box on page 351; this list is by no means inclusive but will help readers realize the number and diversity of career opportunities in physical education and sport. These career options will be discussed further in other chapters. Careers involving the teaching and coaching of physical activity skills in a variety of settings are discussed in Chapter 11. Health- and fitness-related careers are described in Chapter 12. Career opportunities in sport management, sport media, and other areas are addressed in Chapter 13.

You also can use your imagination to create new job opportunities suited specifically to your abili-ties and interests. The growth of the knowledge base combined with the expansion of our services to diverse populations has created many new and exciting career opportunities. By combining your abilities within a subdiscipline with your interest in working with a specific population and age group and within a particular setting, you can create a career opportunity uniquely suited to you. The box on page 352 will assist you in exploring these various career options.

The broadening of career opportunities in physical education and sport is an exciting development. Selecting a career from the many available options requires careful consideration of a number of factors.

Choosing a Career

Have you already chosen a career in physical education and sport? Perhaps you decided years ago to pursue a career in teaching, athletic training, or sport broadcasting. On the other hand, you may be like many other students—undecided about a specific career. However, you do know that the field of physical education and sport is of interest, and you have decided to explore the many options in this area. Whether you are committed or undecided about a career, college offers a wonderful opportunity to broaden your base of knowledge about careers in this dynamic field and to explore the growing number of opportunities that are available.

How do you choose a career from the many available? First, it is recommended that you select a career pathway as opposed to a specific job. A career pathway allows you to pursue many different jobs within a specific area, such as sport management. Second, you can remove some of the stress and anxiety associated with choosing a career by realizing that a career decision is not irreversible. Many students change their minds about the career they desire several times during the course of their college education. Third, a career is not a lifelong commitment. Changing careers has become increasingly common. Some people deliberately plan to pursue one career for a while to provide a foundation for a second career. For

PHYSICAL EDUCATION AND SPORT CAREER OPPORTUNITIES

Teaching Opportunities

School Setting	*Nonschool Setting*
Elementary School	Community Recreation/
Junior High School	Sport Programs
High School	Corporate Recreation
Junior/Community	Programs
College	Commercial Sport Clubs
College and University	Youth-Serving Agencies
Basic Instruction	Preschools
Programs	Health Clubs
Professional Preparation	Military Personnel
Programs	Programs
Adapted Physical	Resort Sport Programs
Education	Geriatric Programs
Overseas School	Correctional Institution
Programs	Programs
Military School	
Programs	

Coaching Opportunities

Interscholastic Programs	Commercial Sport Clubs
Intercollegiate Programs	Community Sport
Commercial Sport	Programs
Camps	Military Sport Programs

Sport Media Opportunities

Sport Journalism	Sport Broadcasting
Sport Photography	Sport Art
Sport Writing	

Fitness and Health-Related Opportunities

Cardiac Rehabilitation	Space Fitness Programs
Sports Medicine	Corporate Fitness
Movement Therapy	Programs
Health Clubs	Sports Nutrition
Community Fitness	Athletic Training
Programs	Weight Control Spas
Worksite Health	Military Personnel
Promotion	Programs

Sport Management Opportunities

Athletic Administration	Sport Organization
Sport Facility	Administration
Management	Health Club
Commercial Sport	Management
Club Management	Sports Information
Community Recreation/	Sport Retailing
Sport Management	Corporate Recreation
Intramurals/Campus	Resort Sport
Recreation	Management

Sport-Related Opportunities

Sport Law	Sport Officiating
Professional Athlete	Dancer
Entrepreneur	Sport Statistician
Research	Consulting

example, a student may choose to pursue a career as a teacher and coach for several years before returning to school for training as a sport psychologist. The practical experience gained from coaching enhances the individual's new career as a practicing sport psychologist with a professional team. Additionally, you should periodically evaluate your satisfaction from your chosen career. If you feel little satisfaction from your career, you may choose to pursue opportunities in other career fields.

Choosing a career is a decision-making process. This involves gathering facts, evaluating information, and making a selection from the alternatives available to you. The most important factors influencing your choice of a career are your strengths, interests, goals, and preferences.

Having a realistic perception of your strengths and abilities is important in finding a satisfying and fulfilling career. In selecting a career you should draw on your current strengths and abilities as well as the ones that you have the potential and desire to develop. Identifying your strengths and abilities involves the process of self-assessment.

CREATING CAREER OPPORTUNITIES IN PHYSICAL EDUCATION AND SPORT*

*Explore various career options within the field by combining an area of study with a population group, an age group, or a setting/environment to create a career that matches your individual interests. Add additional items to each column as you think of them. Match items from each column in *any* order. Create your own job title and define responsibilities. For example, combine exercise physiology with disabled youths in a home setting to create a job as a personal fitness trainer to an adolescent with a disability working in the individual's home.

Area of Study	Population	Age	Setting
Adapted physical activity	Athletes	Adolescents	Athletic contests
Biomechanics	Cardiac risks	Adults	Clinic
Exercise physiology	Disabled	Children	College/university
Motor development	Inmates	Elderly	Commercial club
Motor learning	Military	Infants	Community
Sport history	Obese	Youths	Corporation
Sport management	Patients		Correctional institution
Sports medicine	Students		Geriatric center
Sport nutrition			Health/fitness club
Sport pedagogy			Health spa/resort
Sport philosophy			Home
Sport psychology			Hospital
Sport sociology			Media setting
Measurement and evaluation			Park
			Professional/sport organization
			Research laboratory
			Retail establishment
			School
			Space
			Sport facility

Self-assessment should be positive and ongoing. **Ask yourself the following questions about your strengths and abilities:**

◆ What are my strengths?

◆ What are my best personal characteristics?

◆ What personal abilities are reflected in my accomplishments?

◆ What abilities would I like to improve?

◆ What do I like to do?

Reflect on the compliments you have received from your parents, teachers, and peers to gather additional information about your abilities. Have you received frequent compliments on your leadership? on your organizational ability? on your work with very young children?

You must also consider your academic abilities and interests.

◆ What are your academic strengths? math? science? computers? history?

◆ What areas of study do you enjoy? music? language? math? psychology?

◆ What special talents or skills do you possess? Are you an accomplished photographer? golfer? painter? basketball player?

◆ What talents and skills are you interested in developing?

Your decision to pursue a career in the area of physical education and sport reflects your interest in this area. Pursuit of a career in this area also reflects to a great extent an interest in working with people.

In weighing your career options, ask yourself what your personal and professional goals are.

- What are your goals?
- What are you striving to accomplish at this point in your life? What do you wish to accomplish in 5 years, in 10 years, or in 20 years?

Obviously your goals will have a great deal of impact on your selection of a career.

Finally, what are your preferences in terms of your lifestyle and your work?

- Do you want to work in an urban, suburban, or rural setting?
- What kind of environment do you want to live in?
- What ages of people do you prefer to work with?
- Do you prefer to work with people in groups or on an individual basis?
- What kind of facility do you want to work in? school or college gymnasium? hospital? health spa? community center? corporation?
- What are your salary expectations? Would you be comfortable with a salary based on commissions? merit?
- Is salary the most important consideration in your selection of a career, or do you value other rewards associated with the job more? For example, is the personal satisfaction gained from helping a cardiac patient resume a normal activity level more important than your salary?
- What hours and days of the week do you prefer to work?
- How much vacation time would you like each year? Would you be satisfied having two or three weeks off a year, or does two months off appeal to you more?
- How important is job security? career advancement? fringe benefits?

As a result of this self-assessment process, you will become more cognizant of your strengths, interests, goals, and lifestyle and work preferences. If you had difficulty in determining your personal characteristics you may want to take advantage of services offered by the career planning office or the counseling center at your college or university. Trained personnel can help you recognize your assets and articulate your goals. You can take a variety of paper-and-pencil inventories to help identify your abilities and preferences for different types of careers. One test commonly used is the Strong-Campbell Interest Inventory. Computerized inventories, such as DISCOVER, are being used with increased frequency.

Talking and soliciting advice from others may also be helpful in the process. Discuss your self-assessment findings with your family, professors, and your friends. Listen to the advice they have to offer, but remember that ultimately the career decision is yours alone to make. You are the one who has to find the career satisfying and rewarding.

Information about yourself—your abilities, interests, goals, and preferences—should be matched to the characteristics of your prospective career. For example, you can combine your organizational ability with your mathematical ability to pursue a career in sport management. However, before you can accurately match your own assets with a career, you need to obtain further information about your possible vocation.

Matching assets with careers requires an understanding of the nature of the career you are considering. This information is available from a variety of sources. Career planning or counseling center personnel are excellent resources. They can provide you with information about careers and job characteristics as well as prospects for employment in your selected career. College and university libraries are also a good source of information. Ask the reference librarian for assistance if necessary. Two publications that might be helpful are the *Occupational Outlook Handbook*[2] and the *College Placement Annual*.[3] The *Occupational Outlook Handbook* is published annually and provides information about the job market in numerous areas. It is also available on the World Wide Web. The *College Placement Annual* provides information on potential employers in your specific interest area. Another source is the *Encyclopedia of*

Associations;[4] this reference lists professional organizations active in your career area. For example, under fitness the encyclopedia lists the National Athletic Health Institute, Aerobics International Research Society, Association for Worksite Health Promotion, and the National Fitness Association, just to name a few. If you want further information about wellness you can write to the Wellness and Health Activation Networks or the National Wellness Association. Browsing through the athletic section of the encyclopedia, you will discover career opportunities that perhaps you never even realized existed.

Another excellent way to find out about potential careers is to talk to practitioners. Most people will be happy to talk with you about their career and share their perceptions. Ask practitioners the following questions:

◆ What is a typical workday like?

◆ What are the specific responsibilities of the job?

◆ What do you like and dislike about your work?

◆ What are the rewards associated with this career?

◆ What are the negative aspects of this line of work?

◆ What motivated you to seek employment in this area?

◆ How did you prepare yourself professionally for this position?

◆ What is the typical beginning salary associated with this position? What fringe benefits are available?

◆ What opportunities are there for advancement in this field? What are the qualifications for advancement?

◆ To what professional organizations do you belong? What conferences or workshops do you typically attend?

◆ What advice would you give someone seeking to enter this field?

Try to talk to several people in the same career area, because individuals' perceptions will vary as will their experiences.

Still another way to find information about various careers is through your own practical experience. This will be discussed later in the chapter.

Your professional preparation courses will also provide you with information about various career opportunities and their requirements. It is hoped that reading this text and participating in this class will assist you in making a career choice or in solidifying one made previously.

After gathering information about yourself and the characteristics of the career you are choosing, try to make a match between your assets and the requirements and characteristics of your potential career. Although you may already have a career in mind, as you embark on your professional preparation program, be open-minded, flexible, and ready to explore other career opportunities that interest you.

Maximizing Professional Preparation

The process of preparing for a career is referred to as professional preparation. Professional preparation is the attainment of knowledge necessary to be an educated person as well as knowledge essential to understanding the field of physical education and sport. Professional preparation also includes maximizing strengths and developing abilities with reference to one's chosen career. In addition to gaining the knowledge and skills necessary to be a successful practitioner, professional preparation may be thought of as the process of increasing personal marketability. When viewed from this perspective, professional preparation includes not only your coursework and academics but related career experiences as well.

Education

Typically, professional preparation curriculums have been oriented toward preparing individuals for careers in teaching and coaching. This has changed as a result of expanding career opportunities. The growth of the subdiscipline and changing job market has stimulated the development of curriculums to prepare individuals for these expanded opportunities in physical education and sport. While professional preparation curriculums at different institutions may vary, these curriculums do have some commonalities.

Liberal arts. Professional preparation curriculums typically include liberal arts courses. Liberal

Professional curriculums have traditionally focused on preparing students for careers in teaching and coaching.

arts courses provide the opportunity to obtain a broad base of knowledge. These courses are the sciences, math, languages, English, art, and music. Certain liberal arts courses may be required of all students; this can be referred to as the core curriculum. For example, all first-year students may be required to take a writing course and a speech course. Additional liberal arts courses are often mandated, depending on the major area of study. Some courses of study and state accreditation may mandate specific courses, whereas others may allow students to elect the liberal arts courses they wish to take; sometimes a certain number of courses may be required and a certain number deemed elective.

Professional courses. Building on this liberal arts foundation are the professional physical education and sport courses. Professional theory courses focus on conveying knowledge within the discipline of physical education and sport. Professional theory courses required for physical education and sport majors pursuing the same career paths may vary among institutions.

The professional theory courses provide students with knowledge relative to the discipline and are designed to prepare majors for their chosen career. Some courses outside the realm of physical education and sport are required as well. Usually courses and the sequence in which they are to be taken are specified. Thus students preparing for a career in teaching and coaching may take courses in physical education that include curriculum design, teaching methods, activity courses, performance analysis courses, and coaching courses; courses taken outside the area include education courses and psychology courses. Students preparing for a career in exercise science may take professional science courses and outside courses focusing on science (e.g., chemistry and physiology), psychology, and nutrition. In addition to the required professional courses, students may take electives in this area.

Electives. Most curriculums have electives, although the number of electives varies from program to program and from institution to institution. Requirements may be associated with the electives, such as that a certain number must be from the liberal arts and a certain number from the professional area. Some electives may be unrestricted, and students can choose from any area. Electives may be used to pursue a special interest, to broaden your liberal arts background, and/or to enhance your marketability by complementing and strengthening your career preparation. Electives should be chosen carefully to help you achieve your goals. If you anticipate attending graduate school, check carefully to see if you have satisfied all the prerequisites for admission. Students who are planning on pursuing graduate study in another area to complement their degree may have to satisfy several requirements. For example, someone majoring in athletic training who wishes to obtain a Master's degree in physical therapy may have to take additional courses in biology, chemistry, and physics. You can use your electives to take these courses.

Minors. An increasing number of students are taking advantage of their electives to pursue minors and/or concentrations or areas of specialization. (Different institutions define these terms differently, so you should be familiar with how these terms are used at your own institution.) By doing so they broaden their career options and increase their marketability. Some physical education and sport major curriculums require a minor or a concentration. Sport management majors frequently are required to have a minor in business or to take a substantial number of business, economic, accounting, and management courses. Sport communication majors may have a minor in journalism, photography, or speech. Exercise science majors may minor in science or perhaps nutrition and health. Teaching-coaching majors may minor in health, communication, or psychology. In some states, if physical education teaching majors take enough credits in a second specific academic area, they can become certified to teach in that area as well. Often the number of credits required for certification is only a few more than the number required to complete a minor at your institution. Thus physical education teacher majors can become certified to teach math, science, or health. Using credits judiciously can pay big dividends for all students regardless of their course of study.

Practicums. Provision for practical experiences has become a common feature of many physical education and sport curriculums, regardless of the career being pursued. In the teaching-coaching area this practical experience has long been a tradition and is referred to as student teaching. Student teaching typically takes place in the latter part of the student's junior year or during the senior year; this experience may last for a quarter or for a semester. In recent years a concerted effort has been made by professionals to provide their prospective teachers with practical or field-based experiences prior to their student teaching. This allows students to practice the teaching skills learned in their courses and can help them solidify their career decision.

Practical experiences associated with nonteaching physical education and sport programs are commonly referred to as fieldwork or internships.

Fieldwork is typically shorter in duration than an internship; an internship may be similar in length to the student teaching experience. These courses focus on placing students in a practical setting on or off campus. Exercise science majors enrolled in fieldwork may work with clients in a commercial fitness center or health club. As interns, exercise science majors may work in a hospital cardiac rehabilitation program or in a corporate fitness center. Sport management majors may intern with a professional athletic team, whereas sport media majors may gain practical experience with a radio or television station. Athletic trainers usually gain practical experience on campus, putting in hundreds of hours working in the training room and serving as the trainer for various athletic teams. Many professionals view the practical experience gained through fieldwork, internships, and student teaching as vital in career preparation.

Certifications. You can also enhance your professional credentials by taking advantage of various certification programs offered through the college or university and by outside agencies. For example, many students take first aid courses offered by the American Red Cross as part of their curriculum. However, you can also become certified as an instructor in first aid by taking one additional Red Cross course. This instructor certification will allow you to teach first aid and certify your students as meeting the standards of the American Red Cross. The Red Cross offers instructor certification in cardiopulmonary resuscitation (CPR), permitting you to teach and certify people in this important skill. Certification in this area is also offered by the American Heart Association. If you are planning a career in exercise science, such as a corporate fitness center instructor, certification in CPR and first aid will allow you to train employees in these lifesaving areas. These certifications are also helpful if you are pursuing a teaching-coaching career. Even if your institution does not offer these courses, your local American Red Cross can provide you with the necessary training in a short period of time.

If you are interested in a career in athletic training or in exercise science, you may want to

Computer skills are a necessity for physical education and sport professionals. This student is using a computer to complete a biomechanical movement analysis.

consider becoming certified as an Emergency Medical Technician (EMT). The American College of Sports Medicine (ACSM) offers a certification program for individuals interested in fitness and exercise science. ACSM certification is offered for individuals involved in preventive and rehabilitative exercise programs. Certifications include Program Director, Exercise Specialist, Exercise Test Technologist, Health/Fitness Director, Health/Fitness Instructor, and Exercise Leader/Aerobics. Certification as an athletic trainer is given through the National Athletic Trainers Association (NATA).

Certifications also can be obtained in specific sport areas. For example, you can work toward becoming certified as a golf professional or a scuba instructor. Certification by the American Red Cross as a Water Safety Instructor will enable you to teach all levels of swimming. Aerobic dance certification is becoming increasingly popular. Certification and training programs are offered by many

professional organizations, such as the Aerobics and Fitness Association of America (AFAA). Officiating ratings in various sport areas can also be attained from the specific sport officiating governing body.

Some of these certifications may be available through your institution. If not, you can attain these certifications on your own through appropriate agencies and professional organizations. Be sure to check, however, to ensure that the certifying agency is reputable and the certification is highly regarded by professionals in the field. It may be helpful to check with your instructors and practitioners in the field about the appropriate credentials and certifications.

Academic performance. A major determinant of your career opportunities and professional success is your academic performance. Potential employers view academic performance as a strong reflection of a prospective employee's abilities and

Certifications, such as those offered by the American Red Cross in swimming, and practical experience can be assets in preparing for a career.

often as a reliable indicator of one's potential to succeed. You should make a commitment to your academic performance at the start of your college years. Your academic performance may affect your ability to enroll in graduate school.

More students are entering graduate school immediately after completing their undergraduate degree. The increased specialization within the field has made graduate school a necessity for many students and an attractive option for those seeking to increase their knowledge in their area of interest. Attending graduate school for further work in exercise physiology, biomechanics, sport management, sport psychology, sports medicine, adapted physical education, and pedagogy is the choice of many undergraduates. However, this option may not be open to someone who has a poor academic record. Most graduate schools require a minimum grade-point average (GPA) of 3.0 on a 4.0 scale. An even higher GPA may be required to get into the graduate school of your choice. Your undergraduate academic average may influence

whether or not you are awarded a graduate assistantship to defray the expenses of graduate study. Graduate assistantships are also highly prized because of the practical experience they afford the recipient.

Personal development. Development of personal skills and abilities is an important part of the educational process. As part of the self-assessment process, you were able to identify areas of strength and areas needing improvement. Additionally, you should carefully consider how you can develop transferable job skills, skills that can be used in many different positions. Communication skills, leadership skills, and skills in human relations are applicable to working with people in many different settings. The box on page 359 identifies these transferable and highly marketable job skills.

Effective physical education and sport professionals can educate and motivate others to adopt a healthy, active lifestyle. Are you a role model for a healthy lifestyle? Do you incorporate physical activity into your life on a daily basis? Eat a low fat

TRANSFERABLE SKILLS

Transferable skills are those skills that have application to many different careers. They can be developed through course work, related experiences, and personal activities. It is important to use your many experiences to further develop these skills. Identify skills in which further development is needed and make a plan to develop them. Examples of how these skills are important to professionals in different careers in physical education and sport are provided.

Speaking

Develop your skills as a public speaker through class work and leadership experiences. Learn how to prepare remarks, effectively communicate ideas, and motivate people. (Applications: Coach appearing before the school board to justify his/her budgets; sports information director giving an update on the local television station.)

Writing

Write often and learn how to write for different audiences. Shape your skills by writing letters to the editors of the college newspaper and to publications that you read routinely. Write a newsletter for a club or organization to which you belong or for the alumni bulletin. (Applications: Writing a brochure to promote your personal training business; publishing a newsletter for participants in a corporate fitness program.)

Teaching/Instructing

Refine your ability to explain things to people of different ages. Much of the work in the field involves educating individuals with regard to skills, fitness, and healthy lifestyle. Develop your ability to share information and instruct. (Applications: Teaching students in the school setting; instructing an athlete how to rehabilitate an injured knee.)

Interviewing

Learn how to obtain information from people through direct questioning. Pretend you are a reporter and practice interviewing family, friends, and classmates. Learn how to put a person at ease even when talking about difficult subjects. (Applications: Intake interviews for fitness and rehabilitation programs; athletic administrator gathering information to resolve a problem.)

Public Relations

Accept roles where you must meet or relate to the public, such as greeting people, answering the phone and dealing with complaints, fundraising, and making presentations to the public. (Applications: Staff administrator in a professional organization engaging in fundraising.)

Leadership

Assume responsibility for directing an event, supervising the work of others, initiating an activity and directing it to completion. Learn how to advocate on behalf of yourself or others, promote change. (Applications: Advocating for additional community sports opportunities for people with disabilities; directing a corporate fitness program.)

Budget Management

Gain experience in working with a budget, even if it is small. Manage how the funds are dispersed, balance the "books," prepare reports. (Applications: Facility management; ticket sales.)

Negotiating

Work to learn how to bring opposing sides together, help people discuss their differences and resolve difficult situations; learn how to negotiate with those in power. (Applications: Resolving conflicts among employees of a fitness club; negotiating with the publisher of the local paper for more coverage of your events.)

Organizing

Take charge of an event, even a small event, where you bring together people, resources, and events.

Modified from Career Planning and Placement presentation and handout, Ithaca College, Ithaca, N.Y.

Continued.

TRANSFERABLE SKILLS—CONT'D

Manage projects and learn how to delegate and follow through. (Applications: Organize a community health awareness fair or host conference for local teachers to share ideas and activities.)

Computer and Analytical Skills

Develop skills in word processing, spreadsheet, data base, presentation software; data analysis and presentation; Web page construction. (Applications: Construct a database to monitor the progress of your personal training clients; develop a Web page to promote your program.)

---

diet? Deal with stress in a healthy manner? Research conducted by Eastern Washington University showed that although an applicant's fitness level is not normally listed as an official job criterion or even discussed at a job interview, it is an important factor in hiring. In 1990 the university initiated a Fit for Hire program designed to help majors achieve a healthy lifestyle and recognize those who exemplify active living.[5] Three basic components are included in the program: fitness testing, lifestyle or wellness assessment, and individual advising.[5] Students who satisfy program requirements are issued a Fit for Hire certificate. The certificate lets employers know that the students are fit and a role model.

As a student it is important that you become familiar with your curriculum so you can plan your education and strengthen your qualifications for your chosen career. Most institutions assign professors to serve as academic advisors. Work closely with your advisor in planning your program of study. Take advantage of all your education has to offer to become an educated individual and a professional. Create options along your chosen career pathway through judicious selection of courses and commitment to your academics. Your activities and related experiences also can contribute to your professional development.

Related experiences

Your activities and related experiences can significantly enhance your career preparation. Your extracurricular activities can help you develop skills that are relevant to your chosen career. Perhaps it would help to view your extracurricular activities as an unofficial fieldwork or internship of sorts. Certainly, participation on an intercollegiate athletic team as a player, manager, or statistician can enhance your expertise in that sport. Your experience as a sport photographer, sport writer, or editor of the campus newspaper provides you with excellent training for your career in sport media. Being active in the physical education majors club, if your institution has one, contributes to your professional growth. Serving as a member of the student government may develop leadership, planning, and organizational skills applicable to a diversity of careers.

Your work experience can contribute to your professional development as well. Work experience gained through part-time and summer employment can give you valuable on-the-job experience. Although employment opportunities may be difficult to secure, try to find work that relates to your career goals. In the summer, gain experience teaching and organizing activities for people of all ages by working in a community recreational program. Or try to get a job working in a fitness or health club, teaching clients how to use the various pieces of exercise equipment, supervising their workouts, and teaching aerobic dance. To gain practical experience, you may want to consider foregoing a higher paying job in favor of working the career-related job and getting a second job to make ends meet.

Another source of practical experience is on-campus jobs. If you have financial need you may qualify for a work-study job. As a first-year student you may not be able to get the job you want and have to settle for working in the cafeteria, but after your first year you will have a better chance to secure the job you desire. Work-study jobs may be available as an intramural assistant, researcher, tutor, lab assistant, or computer assistant. Of course, you must have the skills to perform the job or the willingness to learn if afforded the opportunity to do so. Another campus employment opportunity open to qualified students is being a resident

Participation in athletics can later prove valuable in securing employment as a coach.

assistant in the dormitories. As a resident assistant you will learn how to work closely with people and develop counseling and programming skills.

Volunteering is another means to gain practical experience. Although volunteering does not pay you any money, try to view it as an investment in your future. Perhaps you would have liked to work for the summer at a corporate fitness center, but have found that the center is unable to hire you due to budgetary constraints. Ask if the center would be willing to accept your services as a volunteer. This means that if you need money for tuition and related costs you may have to work nights and weekends to secure the necessary funds for school. However, volunteering may pay big

dividends when it comes to your career. One word of advice. Even if you are a volunteer, devote as much time and energy to the job as if you were a paid employee. You are being viewed by the management as a potential employee. Perhaps if you do a good job this summer you may be hired on a regular basis for the next summer. Volunteering is a good way to gain entry into your career field. Considering a career in sport broadcasting? Volunteer to be a "go-fer" at a local television station to gain exposure to life behind the scenes. Perhaps this will put you in the right place at the right time to take advantage of any opportunities that may come your way. Volunteering will also allow you to make professional contacts for the future.

As mentioned previously, fieldwork and internships are a good way to gain practical experience. If they are not mandated by your program, find out if you could do one for credit or on a volunteer basis. Many professional organizations are delighted to provide internship experiences for volunteers. AAHPERD, for example, offers internships to interested students. Contact professional organizations within your field of study to see if they would be willing to accept an intern.

Consider volunteering to work with one of your professors on a research project he or she is conducting in your area of interest. If you are attending an institution with a master's or doctorate program in physical education, volunteer to help one of the graduate students collect data for a research project. This research experience will prove enlightening and can be helpful when you are involved in your own graduate education. Again, a reminder. Make a commitment to the research project and let the researcher know you can be counted on to fulfill your responsibilities.

Extracurricular activities, work experiences, and volunteer activities can contribute to your professional development. These practical experiences provide you with the opportunity to work in your chosen career, learn necessary skills, and develop professional contacts. Even though you are just starting your professional preparation for your career, it is not too early to start thinking about being a professional and planning for the future.

Professional involvement

Start early to become a professional. Professional activities are a source of knowledge and growth. One way to start is by becoming active in the physical education, athletic trainers, or exercise science majors club at your institution. If there is not a professional club, try to start one with the help of fellow students and interested faculty.

Join the national association affiliated with your career choice (e.g., AAHPERD, ACSM or NATA). Many professional organizations offer student memberships at reduced rates. Attend the national conventions where you will have the opportunity to meet professionals, make personal contacts, and attend meetings and workshops on research findings and new techniques. If it is not possible to attend the national meetings, many organizations have state or regional associations that hold their own conventions. These may be more convenient to attend and allow you to meet professionals within the same geographical area. Association members, as part of their membership fee, receive professional periodicals. For example, AAHPERD members can select JOPERD, the *Journal of Physical Education, Recreation, and Dance,* or *The Research Quarterly for Exercise and Sport* as one of their publications.

Start to build a professional library. In addition to the professional periodicals to which you subscribe, organize and retain your class notes, handouts, and texts. Many a student who threw out notes for a particular class or sold textbooks found it meant a lot of additional work and money later on when the materials were needed for a job. These materials serve as resources when you are starting out in your career. Undergraduate notes and materials may prove helpful in completing course work in graduate school.

Attaining a Professional Position

Whether you are seeking full-time employment following graduation, part-time or summer employment, an internship, a graduate assistantship, or a position as a volunteer, obtaining the desired position requires a well-planned, concerted effort. Highly desirable positions may attract numerous applicants, and competition may be strong. Therefore it is important to market yourself effectively and prepare thoroughly for this effort.

Preparing yourself to attain a professional position can be viewed as a 4-year ongoing effort. Each year can be viewed as a stepping stone to achieving your long-term goal of employment as a professional or entry into graduate school. A 4-year timeline for achieving your goal is presented in Table 10-1. If you proceed in a systematic manner, you will maximize your professional preparation and enhance your marketability.

Early in your educational career you should begin the process of developing a resume. A resume is a summary of your qualifications and experiences.

To facilitate the writing of your resume, keep a record of all your activities on an ongoing basis throughout your career. People who fail to do so often inadvertently exclude important activities or honors from their resume because they have been forgotten. Some examples of activities that are important to include are honors, athletic participation, employment, professional memberships, and volunteer activities.

One way to keep track of your activities is to use an index card system. Label a file folder "Resume," and each time you participate in a professional activity, engage in an extracurricular activity, or are awarded an honor, make note of it on an index card and put it in the folder. Some students use a computer to effectively keep track of their accomplishments and activities.

Make sure the information you record, be it on an index card or a computer, is accurate and complete. For student teaching, internships, work, and related experiences, be sure that you have the correct title, the correct spelling of the organization, the address, and the name and the title of the person who supervised you. Carefully and accurately portray the responsibilities you performed and give the relevant dates. For example, if you just completed an internship at Xerox Corporation in its corporate fitness program you would write in your resume file:

Internship at Xerox Corporation. Industrial Drive, Rochester, NY, 14859. Supervisor: Dr. Richard Smith, Director of Corporate Fitness. Responsibilities: Assisted with the administration of stress tests; designed individual exercise prescriptions; supervised individual exercise programs; counseled participants in the areas of nutrition, smoking cessation, and stress management. Dates: January–May 1998.

Have you ever been awarded any honors, such as being named to the Dean's List? Make note of it: Dean's List, Fall 1997. Write down extracurricular activities on a yearly basis as well—intramurals, intercollegiate athletics, physical education majors' club member, representative to student government, attendance at the state Association for Health, Physical Education, Recreation, and Dance convention, volunteer for Special Olympics,

and so on. Make note of the dates that you attained certifications as well: for example, "1997: certified by the American Red Cross as a Community CPR Instructor." It is also helpful to make a note of your special skills, such as speaking a foreign language or a high level of competency with computers.

There are many different formats for writing a resume, depending on the purpose for which it is being used. For example, resumes can be used to obtain an interview, as a follow-up to an interview, as a means of highlighting your qualifications for the position, and as a complement to a letter of application. Career planning and counseling centers offer students guidelines for constructing resumes. A sample resume is shown in Figure 10-1. There are computer programs that can be used in writing a resume.

Customize your resume for the particular position that you are pursuing. This may involve developing several different resumes, tailoring your background, strengths, and experience to fit the position being sought. Your index cards or computer records serve as a master list from which to select information and activities to present the best picture of you to the potential employer and enable you to include all relevant information on the resume. Preparing your resume on a computer will allow you to easily edit it and to create different versions.

Resumes should be prepared meticulously and proofread several times to ensure that there are no errors. The resume serves as a writing sample and reflects how well you can communicate. It also reflects your neatness and attention to detail. The resume should be organized in a manner such that the reader's attention is easily drawn to the most important information. It should be printed on high-quality, standard-size bond paper using a high-quality photocopier or laser printer.

As a senior, you should open up a placement file at your institution's placement office. Placement files generally contain demographic information, a resume, and letters of recommendation. Letters of recommendation should be solicited from people who are well acquainted with your abilities. Professors familiar with your work, student teaching

TABLE 10-1

Four-Year Timeline for Professional Preparation

Focus Area	First Year	Second Year	Third Year	Fourth Year
Academic	Learn about requirements of your major, including liberal arts and professional courses; determine how many electives you have to explore areas of interest or to use for a minor.	Begin working on requirements for a minor; carefully monitor your academic performance; remember that many graduate schools require a minimum GPA of 3.0 for admission.	Determine prerequisites for graduate school and plan how to satisfy them. Check to make sure that you are on track to graduate; take advantage of opportunities to join academic honor societies.	Review carefully your requirements for graduation to make sure you have completed them.
Career Goals	Identify short- and long-term career goals.	Identify a unique skill and formulate a plan for its development.	Work on strengthening your transferable skills; reevaluate your short- and long-term career goals.	Solidify career goals for the next 1 year and for the next 5 years.
Campus Activities	Become involved in some capacity in one sport or one fitness-related activity.	Continue involvement in sport and fitness activity; add involvement in another campus organization or other activities.	Undertake some leadership activity in a professional organization, such as chairing a committee or being an officer.	Advance in leadership responsibilities by taking on more challenging and responsible positions.
Professional Activities	Join your majors club; join a local affiliate of a professional organization (e.g., state athletic trainers organization).	Join a national professional organization; attend a professional conference and take advantage of special opportunities for students.	Attend a professional conference and become involved in the organization in a leadership capacity.	Attend a professional conference; take advantage of placement opportunities offered by professional organizations.
Volunteer Activities	Check out opportunities for volunteering in school and hometown communities.	Volunteer for a few hours a week in an organization of interest to you (e.g., Special Olympics, American Heart Association).	Increase volunteer hours or consider volunteering in a different area of interest.	Undertake some leadership responsibilities as a volunteer (e.g., volunteer recruitment).

Related Work	Seek out related work experiences during the school term or summer.	Work in related area during the summer or the school year (e.g., aerobics instructor on campus, fitness trainer in a health club).	Advance in responsibilities you undertake at work; consider a different job to broaden your expertise.	Continue to work and expand responsibilities undertaken; advance to a position of leadership or supervision.
Practicums	Explore practicum opportunities, including both short- and long-term opportunities.	Participate in a short-term practicum, such as fieldwork.	Investigate internship opportunities in your major. Continue to participate in practicum experiences.	Complete full-time internship or student teaching experience lasting at least 10 weeks.
Career Planning	Visit your career planning office. Take advantage of self-assessment and guidance programs to clarify your interests, strengths, and areas needing improvement.	Write a draft of your resume and have it reviewed by a professional or career planning counselor.	Take advantage of career planning seminars on interviewing, writing cover letters, and effective job searches. Update your resume.	Update your resume. Attend on-campus job fairs. Take advantage of alumni networks. Use career planning, the Internet, and other resources to identify potential job openings.
Networking	Get to know faculty and students within your school; interview practitioners about their work.	Take advantage of local professional opportunities, such as conferences, to meet professionals in your field.	Widen your professional contacts and expand your network.	Network with faculty, professionals, friends, and family to identify employment opportunities.
Certifications	Identify certifications that will enhance your professional skills and contribute to your marketability.	Begin to acquire certifications such as CPR, first aid, or water safety.	Add additional certifications as appropriate. Find out the requirements to take major certification exams in your career field—athletic training, fitness, and teaching.	Take certification exams for athletic training, fitness, and teaching.
Application for Employment after Graduation	Become familiar with employment opportunities in the field.	Practice job search skills in securing summer employment, fieldwork, and internship experiences.	Establish a credential file. Secure letters of recommendation for your file.	Apply for jobs.
Application for Graduate School	Become familiar with areas of advanced study within the field.	Explore graduate school options and identify general program prerequisites; develop a plan to satisfy prerequisites.	Write for graduate school applications and determine entrance requirements. Take examinations for entry.	Apply for graduate school and assistantships.

ROBYN LEE WEST

School Address
  221 Eastview Road, Apt. 1
  Ithaca, NY 14856
  Phone: 607-111-5555

Permanent Address
  312 Cherry Lane
  Floral Estates, NY 11003
  Phone: 516-222-555

CAREER OBJECTIVE   To teach physical education in an elementary school, work with children with disabilities to improve their motor performance, and coach soccer and track

EDUCATION   Ithaca College, Ithaca, NY, May 1998
    Bachelor of Science in Physical Education
      Provisional certification K-12
      Minor in Health
      Concentration in Adapted Physical Education

PROFESSIONAL EXPERIENCE   Student teacher, Pine Elementary School (1/3-3/7 1998)
Student teacher, Cayuga High School (3/10-5/14 1998)
Fieldwork in adapted physical education, United Children's Center (1/4-5/2 1997)
Youth Bureau volunteer soccer coach (Fall 1994-1995)
Counselor for children with special needs, Floral Estates Youth Summer Camp
  (Summers 1994-1997)

HONORS AND AWARDS   Dean's List (Fall 1994, 1996, 1997; Spring 1995, 1997)
Who's Who in American Colleges and Universities
Ithaca College HPER Professional Achievement Award

COLLEGE ACTIVITIES   Physical Education Majors' Club (1994-1998; Vice-President 1997-1998)
Intercollegiate Soccer Team (1994-1998; Captain 1997)
Intercollegiate Track and Field Team (1995-1998)
Intramural volleyball and basketball official (1996-1998)
Peer counselor, Health Center (1996-1998)
President's Host Committee for Admissions (1995-1997)

CERTIFICATIONS   American Red Cross Community First Aid Instructor
American Red Cross Water Safety Instructor
American Red Cross Adapted Aquatics Instructor
American College of Sports Medicine Health Fitness Instructor
Rated official in volleyball and basketball

PROFESSIONAL AFFILIATIONS   American Alliance for Health, Physical Education, Recreation, and Dance
New York State Association for Health, Physical Education, Recreation, and Dance
American College of Sports Medicine
Finger Lakes Board of Officials

REFERENCES   Available from the Placement Office, School of Health Sciences and Human
    Performance, Ithaca College

FIGURE 10-1 Sample resume

or internship supervisors, and individuals for whom you worked or volunteered may be able to accurately assess your abilities and qualifications for employment or further study.

Many sources will assist you in locating job openings. College/university placement offices maintain job listings and update these on a continuing basis. Some professional organizations offer placement services to their members and periodically disseminate information about job openings. AAHPERD, the National Athletic Trainers Association (NATA), and the American College of Sports Medicine (ACSM) offer placement services and job listings to their members. Newspapers, state employment offices, and some state education departments have lists of job openings. Job listings are also posted on the World Wide Web.

Networking is one of the most important job search strategies. Contact faculty members, friends, relatives, former employers, and practicum supervisors to see if they know of any jobs anywhere. It is through personal contacts that people learn about jobs before they are even advertised. Attending conferences or participating in professional organizations are great ways to build contacts and expand your network. Be sure to folllow up on all leads in a timely manner.

Once aware of possible vacancies, send a copy of your resume along with a cover letter requesting an interview and/or application. The cover letter is to interest an employer in hiring you. When possible, the letter should be addressed to a specific person by name. It should set forth the purpose of the letter, refer the reader to the resume to note certain qualifications particularly relevant to the position, and relate why you are interested in the position, emphasizing your career goals and potential contributions to the organization. The letter should close with a request for action, either an interview or an application, and should thank the reader for his or her time.

If you are invited for an interview, prepare carefully—in other words, do your homework. Find out as much as possible about the organization, the job responsibilities, and other relevant information. Before the interview, take some time to formulate answers to commonly asked interview questions. The following list contains some common questions.

- What are your career plans and goals?
- When and why did you select your college major?
- How has your education prepared you for this job?
- Which of your experiences and skills are particularly relevant to this job?
- What are your greatest strengths? What are your major weaknesses?
- What is your philosophy of physical education and sport? Can you give an example of how your philosophy has guided your actions?
- What jobs have you held? How did you obtain them, and why did you leave? What would your former supervisors tell us about your job performance?
- What can you tell me about yourself?
- What accomplishments have given you the greatest satisfaction?
- What have you done that shows leadership, initiative, and a willingness to work?
- What salary do you expect to receive? How many hours per week do you expect to work?
- Why should I select you above all other candidates for this position?
- What questions do you have about our organization?

As part of the preparation process, you also should prepare a list of questions to ask the interviewer. Some possible questions follow:

- What are the opportunities for personal growth?
- What are the training programs or educational opportunities offered to employees?
- What are the challenging aspects of this position?
- What are the organization's plans for the future?
- What qualities are you looking for in new employees?
- What characteristics distinguish successful personnel in your company?
- How would you describe the organization's management style?

◆ How would you best use my skills within the organization?

Develop additional questions appropriate to the specific job for which you are interviewing.

First impressions are critical, so create a positive one by your professional appearance, attitude, and personality. Dress appropriately for the interview. So you'll be sure to be on time, plan on arriving ahead of the scheduled appointment time. Greet the interviewer with a firm handshake and be courteous, poised, interested, responsive, and enthusiastic. Be prepared to discuss your accomplishments, skills, interests, personal qualities, and work values in an honest, self-confident manner. Be self-assured, not arrogant or aggressive. Listen to each question carefully and take some time to formulate a thoughtful, concise answer. Remember that you are being evaluated not only on your achievements, but on your ability to think and communicate. At the close of the interview, thank the interviewer for his or her time.

Follow each interview with a thank-you letter. The letter should stress your interest in the position and highlight important topics that you believe went particularly well in the interview. Be sure to thank the interviewer for his or her time and consideration. If you decide after the interview that the position is not for you, thank the interviewer for his or her time and say politely that you are not interested in the position.

When offered a position, again carefully weigh the characteristics of the job with the results of your self-assessment pertaining to your skills, interests, personal and work values, and career goals. If you accept the position, your letter should confirm previously agreed-upon terms of employment and reflect your excitement at meeting the challenges of the position. Should you decide to decline the offer of employment, the letter of rejection should express your regrets as well as thanking the employer for his or her time, effort, and consideration.

Attaining a desired position requires a commitment to marketing yourself effectively. Actively seeking information about position vacancies and diligently pursuing all leads is important for conducting a successful job search. Your resume should truthfully portray your abilities and accomplishments and be tailored to fit the position. Prepare thoroughly for each interview and present yourself as a young professional. Make your final decision thoughtfully and communicate this decision to your potential employer in a professional, timely manner.

LEADERSHIP AND PROFESSIONAL DEVELOPMENT

Developing professionals with strong leadership abilities is critical to the future of the field of physical education and sport. The advancement of knowledge, the growth of programs to reach people of all ages, and the significant contribution to society depend on professional leadership. It is important that professionals entering the field of physical education and sport take an active leadership role in the field.

Leadership is critical to the success of physical education and sport programs. Willis and Campbell describe leadership as a key factor in sustaining participants' involvement in exercise.[6] "No other factor has quite the potential to elicit change in a client as a competent and enthusiastic exercise leader."[6] Mack describes leadership as the distinguishing factor among great coaches. Many coaches are equally good as tacticians with an extensive knowledge of their sports. What separates the great coaches from good coaches is their uniqueness as leaders.[7] Although physical education and sport programs vary considerably, leadership is critical for achieving program success. Although some would say that leaders are born, not made, great leaders themselves would tell you that effective leadership is a skill that can be learned.[7] Smith points out that leaders are people "remarkably like the rest of us, but with a difference that they know the skills and techniques of leadership."[8]

Definition of Leadership

The term *leadership* refers to the art of influencing people to work together harmoniously to achieve set goals that they endorse. According to

Smith, "Leaders have the ability to develop a vision, the skill to articulate that vision in practical terms, and the skill to direct and assist others in executing various aspects of that vision."[8] The leader of a group influences group members' feelings, beliefs, and behavior. A leader can help a group to achieve its goals with a sense of unity, and provide an opportunity for members to achieve self-realization. Leadership involves motivating and vitalizing the members of a group to contribute a maximum effort. It taps vital resources and encourages higher levels of achievement. It eliminates inertia, apathy, and indifference and replaces them with inspiration, enthusiasm, and conviction. It provides for self-fulfillment and satisfying endeavor. It results in power *with* the members, not power of the leader.

The leader should be very conscious of the need for self-realization by each member of an organization or profession. Each individual needs to believe that he or she counts for something, is recognized, and has a sense of worth. At the same time the leader needs to recognize that each individual has different interests, needs, abilities, attitudes, talents, capacities, and creative powers to contribute. The true test of leadership is the number of people's lives it enriches. It is a process of helping people to discover themselves; it is not a process of exploitation.

Many traits, qualities, characteristics, and skills have been used to describe effective leaders. Early research on leadership focused on describing personality traits possessed by effective leaders. Current research suggests that effective leadership is highly interactive. Personal behaviors interface with situational factors to determine the leadership behaviors that will be most effective in a given situation. Thus, a physical education and sport professional possessing certain characteristics may be more effective as a leader in one situation but not as effective in another situation. The characteristics of the group (e.g., class, team, exercise participants) also influence the behaviors necessary for effective leadership. Among the specific characteristics of the group that are important to consider are gender, age, ability level, personality, ethnicity, and experience.[9] The challenge to professionals is to determine which leadership behaviors will be most effective in a specific situation.

Many people believe that leaders are born, not made. However, as you review research on the qualities, traits, and skills of leaders, these are evidently behaviors that can be learned and developed. Smith, in disputing the "born to lead" myth, states, "leadership skills can be described and learned. The key to leadership lies in not having the right stuff from birth, but in getting it."[8] Thus, it is within the power of aspiring professionals in physical education and sport to develop and improve these essential behaviors for strong leadership.

Because of the interactional nature of leadership, not all leadership qualities and skills will be needed in every situation. They will be needed to varying degrees depending on the specific situation and the preferences and needs of the group members. However, professionals who do take the time and put forth the effort to develop these qualities and skills will be effective in a greater variety of situations.

Leadership Qualities

Many qualities have been used to describe effective leaders. Weinberg and Gould note that there is not one distinct set of essential core qualities that assure a person will become a leader.[9] However, they note that leaders seem to have the following qualities in common: intelligence, assertion, empathy, intrinsic motivation, flexibility, ambition, self-confidence, and optimism.[9] These qualities are viewed as necessary, but not sufficient, qualities for leadership. Effective leadership stems from matching the qualities to the situations and the characteristics of the members of the group.

Many other qualities have also been associated with effective leaders. Hard work, determination, and perseverance are frequently cited characteristics. According to Anshel, respected coaches possess these leadership characteristics: genuine concern for people, respect for others, ability to teach, knowledge of the sport, and excellent communication skills.[10] Relationships are based on a long-term commitment to the program and to the attainment of team and individual goals. Fairness in decision making, social support, and positive reinforcement also are important. These characteristics can enhance the effectiveness of all physical education and sport professionals.

Campbell, in a discussion of characteristics of leadership behavior, stated that it is difficult to find any one characteristic that sets leaders apart from nonleaders. Although there is great diversity among leaders, Campbell identifies 14 traits that he views as "tools of the trade."[11] Not all of them are used in every leadership situation, but effective leaders have most of these "tools" well developed and can use them when needed. The 14 traits are these:

◆ **Personality.** Effective people reflect warmth and concern in their interactions with others. They have an outgoing style and enjoy meeting others. Leaders take time to get to know the needs and lives of the people they are leading. A sense of humor is often helpful in dealing with the "ups and downs" of many situations.

◆ **Persuasive.** Communication skills are critical. The ability to speak effectively in public, listen carefully, and write with clarity is important. Leaders must be able to convey their message, communicate their vision, and understand the concerns of the group to be effective. Campbell encourages all students to focus on developing their communication skills, whether through formal courses or informal opportunities, for they are the "bottom line" of leadership.

◆ **Persistence.** Most social changes, whether large or small, occur slowly. Leaders who aspire to improve a situation, chart a new course, or cause change in their organization or community must be prepared to persevere.

◆ **Patience.** Change takes time. Changing people's exercise habits requires patience and ongoing support over a significant period of time. The adage "Rome wasn't built in a day" reminds us that many things, especially if they are worthwhile, do not happen quickly. Both patience and persistence are essential for getting things done.

◆ **Perceptive.** Sensitivity to the wants, needs, moods, and concerns of individuals and the group is critical. Effective leaders appear to have an intuitive sense of what leadership behaviors will be most effective in a given situation. However, this intuition is enhanced through perception.

◆ **Probity.** Honesty and trustworthiness are important. Leaders must represent the facts accurately. Leaders have credibility. Truthworthiness is important, as when dealing with sensitive information about people; issues of confidentiality and professional responsibility are of paramount concern to many people seeking assistance.

◆ **Praise-giving.** Effective leaders offer sincere praise and compliments. They recognize the members of the group for their contributions. Criticism is offered in a constructive manner.

◆ **Positive orientation.** Leaders are optimistic in their outlook. They are positive in their approach, seek to resolve problems through their actions, and view the future as offering new opportunities.

◆ **People-based.** Effective leaders focus their efforts on helping and benefiting people with whom they interact. They are not self-serving in their actions, but committed to meeting the needs of others.

◆ **Possible.** Leaders are realistic in their assessment of what possibly can be accomplished. They carefully consider the desires of the people, the time available, and the resources allocated. Effective leaders determine what ideas for change and solutions to problems are feasible and which are not.

◆ **Practical.** Effective leaders realize that pleasing all of the people all of the time is not realistic or practical. Leaders use the courage of their convictions to stand firm on unpopular decisions and their strength to withstand criticism of their actions.

◆ **Progressive.** Effective leaders create a vision and move the group forward toward its attainment. They are effective in engendering commitment to the vision, mobilizing the

Leaders must have enthusiasm, a strong belief in the value of their endeavors, and the ability to convey these values to others. These physical educators are running with their students at Tilford Middle School, in Vinton, Iowa.

necessary resources, and energizing the group to work toward its attainment.

◆ **Prepared.** Effective leaders have a clear understanding of the steps needed to achieve their goals and the resources required. Knowledgeable and organized, they prepare carefully to achieve their desired outcomes.

◆ **Power-building.** Effective leaders create a shared vision, foster commitment, integrate diverse views, and share leadership by delegating. They network effectively, facilitate involvement, and motivate the group.

When these traits are closely examined, it is evident that they are learned and developed by effective leaders. For many effective leaders, these traits are the result of hard work and the desire to improve. Campbell writes, "I have come to believe that almost any person can with sufficient motivation and work develop to a considerable degree all fourteen of these traits."[11]

Some qualities that students should develop if they wish to be leaders were set forth many years ago by Ordway Tead in his classic book *The Art of Leadership*.[12] Some of these traits that are particularly relevant to leaders in the field of physical education and sport are described below.

◆ **Energy.** Leaders need energy to cope with the many demanding hours of work required and the effort expended in the process. Furthermore, energy is contagious. Leaders set the pace and are examples for others to follow.

◆ **Sense of Purpose and Direction.** Leaders have a strong sense of purpose. The leader's goals are clear and definite, and the road ahead is clearly delineated. This conviction, sense of purpose, and direction requires knowledge and understanding of one's profession and the objectives to be achieved.

◆ **Enthusiasm.** The word *enthusiasm* comes from Greek words that mean "possessed" and "inspired by some divinity." It refers to the quality of having vitality for one's purpose. Leaders not only have a strong belief in professional goals, but also a strong desire to further them. Leaders are excited about these goals and the profession that is trying to accomplish them. This feeling is so intense that it also results in exciting others.

◆ **Integrity.** People must have trust in their leaders. They must know that their leaders are honest and reliable. They want their leaders to keep promises, be honest in their dealings, speak the truth, and say exactly what they mean. Leaders who have integrity act in accordance with the high expectations of their constituency.

◆ **Friendliness and Affection.** Leaders have a passion for people exemplified not by words but by action. Leaders are concerned about the well-being and happiness of other people and are aware of their desires and goals.

◆ **Technical Mastery.** Just as an exercise physiologist must possess technical mastery of the knowledge and skills needed to evaluate an individual's level of fitness or just as a teacher must possess technical mastery of the skills involved in teaching, so must leaders have technical mastery of the organization or profession of which they are striving to be leaders. This means that leaders must know the process by which goals are achieved and must understand how each person's task fits into the total enterprise.

◆ **Decisiveness.** Leaders must get results. The goals of the organization or profession must be achieved. Therefore decisions must be made, courses of action selected, and action taken. This requires courage and soundness of judgment. In fulfilling this responsibility, leaders must follow a sound procedure in arriving at decisions that will enhance the profession.

◆ **Intelligence.** The term *intelligence* as it is used here refers to the ability to appraise situations and then be able to conceptualize the appropriate course of action. Leaders who have this kind of intelligence are able to sense relationships among various aspects of the enterprise, use past experiences when pertinent to solve present problems, and see a line of wise action that needs to be taken. Leaders who have this kind of intelligence have imagination and sound reasoning powers.

◆ **Teaching Skill.** Good leaders are also good teachers in the sense that they set goals, pose problems, guide activities, and create interest. Leaders, like teachers, develop a feeling that the activity being accomplished is important and worthwhile. Leaders, like teachers, start where the member is, with what he or she knows and feels, and proceed from that point to move forward.

◆ **Faith.** Leaders have faith that the effort they expend in accomplishing professional goals is worthwhile and that their faith will inspire others. Leaders have an inner conviction that they are involved in something that will make the world a better place in which to live and that it will enhance the quality of life of people it touches.

As Tead states: "The greatest leaders have been sustained by the belief that they were in some way instruments of destiny, that they tapped hidden resources of power, that they truly lived as they tried to live, in harmony with some greater, more universal purpose or intention in the world."[12]

Leadership Skills

There are many skills essential for leadership. These skills, like the qualities of effective leaders, can be developed with hard work and dedication. McIntyre,[13] in a discussion of leadership skills for administrators in physical education, suggests that leadership skills can be taught through developmental programs. These skills are also appropriate for an individual seeking to become a leader in the profession. Among these skills are peer skills, leadership skills, conflict resolution skills, information-processing skills, decision-making skills, and introspective skills.[13]

Peer skills relate to establishing and fostering effective group and individual peer relationships. Leadership skills include developing a variety of leadership styles, performance evaluation skills, planning skills, and skills to foster positive morale. *Conflict resolution skills* are needed to deal with group conflict in a positive manner. *Information-processing skills* involve the gathering of information, evaluation of information, formulation of action plans based on the information, and dissemination of information to others. *Decision-making skills* typically follow the model of problem identification, generation of alternative solutions, evaluation of the outcomes of possible solutions, and selecting a solution from among the alternatives. Finally, *introspection skills* include sensitivity to one's own behavior and its effects on others. Development of these skills will enhance one's ability to be a leader in the profession.

Mack describes leadership skills as a coach's greatest asset.[7] In a coaching situation, leadership may be the critical factor in determining success. Coaches need to utilize their leadership skills not only in competition but every day in practice. Mack's principles of effective leadership have great relevancy for professionals in physical education and sport. These principles include the following:

◆ *Create a vision and commitment.* Creating a vision is the most critical of all leadership skills. Effective leaders create a shared vision and foster a sense of commitment. They align and motivate the group toward the attainment of the vision.

◆ *Maintain integrity.* Effective leaders have a strong sense of ethics and moral values. They remain firmly committed to their beliefs, and never compromise their values.

◆ *Lead by example.* Effective leaders model the behaviors they seek to develop in their group members. They "practice what they preach"; they "walk the talk." They understand the powerful effects of their actions. They serve as an energizing force.

◆ *Give credit for success and accept responsibility for failure.* Effective leaders recognize the contributions of others to their successes. They acknowledge their failures and learn from their mistakes.

◆ *Praise the contributions of the group.* Effective leaders try to catch group members doing something right. The use of positive reinforcement engenders enthusiasm, builds self-confidence, and fosters commitment.

◆ *Communicate effectively.* Effective leaders display skillful use of a wide array of communication techniques, including listening.

◆ *Delegate.* Effective leaders delegate wisely, giving group members tasks to complete and responsibilities to fulfill. They facilitate the completion of the tasks by giving members the necessary resources, encouraging their efforts, and supporting their actions.

◆ *Practice the Golden Rule.* Treat others as you wish to be treated. Be respectful, considerate, and kind. The age-old Golden Rule, "Do unto others as you would have them do unto you," offers leaders a good standard to follow in their endeavors.

◆ *Create an environment for self-motivation.* Although leaders are often given credit for motivating others, most motivation comes from within the individual. Effective leaders nurture the strengths of the group members, provide meaningful yet challenging opportunities to achieve success, and promote the development of self-confidence and independence.

Many qualities, characteristics, traits, principles, and skills of effective leadership have been discussed.

Professionals in physical education and sport should carefully assess their leadership behaviors and develop a plan to strengthen them further as they continue their career. Mack writes, "Failure to hone leadership skills is an opportunity lost."[7] Physical education and sport professionals should actively seek out experiences and opportunities that allow them to further develop as leaders.

Opportunities for leadership development are plentiful. Smith advises that individuals take the opportunity to practice leadership skills at all levels of responsibility, from working with one person to working at the highest level of an organization.[8] For example, an aspiring professional can learn leadership skills by helping a roommate begin and continue an exercise program, by assisting a friend to learn a new sport, by volunteering to serve as a coach of a youth sport team, or by officiating at intramurals. Taking on progressively more challenging leadership roles in various campus, community, and professional organizations allows a professional to develop further and refine his/her leadership abilities. It is also important to seek to develop leadership skills that are missing from your leadership repertoire.

Smith suggests that while effective leaders have a variety of behaviors and techniques in their repertoire, it may be easier to understand leadership by focusing on the core roles a leader must fulfill at all levels of leadership responsibility, be it in a group or within the profession. These roles include the vision role, the relationship role, the control role, the encouragement role, and the information role.[8] The *vision role* requires that the leader clearly communicate his or her vision to the group. Activities associated with this role are creating a vision statement, setting specific goals contributing to the attainment of the vision, and motivation. In the *encouragement role,* the leader fosters relationships that help move toward achievement of the goal. Fulfilling this role involves nurturing relationships within the group, team building, and networking to gain support. In the *control role,* the leader prioritizes activities to be undertaken and problems to be resolved, as well as determines the resources that will be committed to their solution. This role also encompasses decision making, delegation, and conflict management. In the *encouragement role* the leader recognizes the contributions of members to the group, reinforces efforts through giving incentives and rewards, and supports actions that move the group forward toward its goal. In fulfilling the *information role* the leader maintains the channels of communication within the group and the organization and makes sure that the members of the group have the necessary information to fulfill their responsibilities. Physical education and sport professionals can use Smith's leadership approach to help them work effectively with people under their direction. These roles may be useful to a teacher in helping children to improve their skills, an exercise leader working with program participants, or an administrator seeking to work effectively within a sport organization.

A leader must understand the scientific foundations of his or her field.

Leadership in Physical Education and Sport

Besides the leadership qualities and skills possessed by effective leaders, there are several qualities that each student should possess to become a leader in the field of physical education and sport. These qualities are good health, a pleasant personality, professional competency, articulation, dedication and hard work, respect for other people, desire, accountability, creativity, and an interest in research.

Health and personality

A person wanting to become a leader in the field of physical education and sport will find that good health and a pleasing personality represent assets in achieving this goal. Good health, fitness, vitality, and energy enable professionals to complete their many responsibilities in an effective, efficient manner. Further, physical educators and sport leaders should exhibit the qualities that epitomize good health since they serve as role models for many children and youth. Physical education and sport professionals, by virtue of the nature of their work, are highly visible. Because of this visibility it is important that professionals be role models, that they indeed "practice what they preach." Professionals should exemplify a healthy, fit, active lifestyle.

Personality is also important. Leaders should have positive attitudes; reflect energy, drive, and ambition; have composure, possess poise, a diplomatic approach, and a sense of humor; inspire trust; and be likable. They should exhibit through their actions a genuine interest in people, warmth, and sincerity.

Professional competency

A leader must have an excellent background in physical education and sport. This means possessing the competencies that professors are trying to provide in the various courses that make up the program. A superficial preparation will not do. Leadership requires a mastery of the knowledge, skills, and attitudes related to the biological, sociological, biomechanical, and psychological scientific foundations associated with this area of expertise.

A prospective leader should become a specialist in some area of physical education and sport, such as elementary or secondary school physical education, college physical education, exercise physiology, biomechanics, motor learning, intramurals, or athletic administration. It is important to acquire all the information one can concerning the chosen area of specialization. A prospective leader should try to know more about his or her area of specialization than any other person. The goal should be to become recognized as a person who possesses the "know-how" in regard to the specialty.

However, it must be emphasized that although it is important for professionals to be knowledgeable in their specialized areas, they should have an understanding of the discipline as a whole and of the relationship of their specialized area to this whole.

Various opportunities present themselves for gaining such recognition, including teaching, research, writing articles and books, and serving on professional committees. Other opportunities include attaining certification, serving as a clinician at a workshop, making presentations at conferences, and becoming active in professional organizations.

Articulation

Good articulation is essential for the professional. Leaders must be able to write and speak coherently. They are constantly in front of the public, making speeches and communicating the goals of their profession. As such, they cannot afford to be weak in their written or oral language.

Although specialization is important, one's learning should not stop there. A leader should also be cultured and well-rounded. This means it is important to acquire knowledge in such fields as art, architecture, politics, travel, languages, economics, literature, and music. Since all of this knowledge cannot be gained in college, much of the work will need to be done on one's own. Among other benefits, such learning will help a person converse intelligently with other people. It is important for the student to recognize that as a leader he or she will be associating not only with people in his or her specialty. There also will be meetings with doctors, lawyers, business persons, politicians, and many other people in various occupations. Persons who are intelligent and cultured will make a favorable impression on those with whom they come in contact.

Dedication and hard work

Dedication to the field is a necessity. This does not mean a casual interest that has developed because a student was a star athlete in high school or college. It means a strong conviction that the field of physical education and sport is important because it provides a useful and desirable service to society.

Hard work is also essential to success. The best things in life are not free—one has to work for them. The people who have leadership positions did not arrive in such positions by chance—they worked hard to achieve their status.

Respect for other people

Respect for other people is an essential quality that begins with respect for oneself. Self-respect requires self-awareness, an understanding and acceptance of your personal characteristics and abilities, your goals and your commitment to realize them. It involves acceptance of yourself as an individual of worth and dignity. Respect for others is an extension of respect for yourself.

As a leader, it is important to have respect for the worth and dignity of each individual. This encompasses an appreciation for diversity in cultures, values, and opinions. Leadership involves working with others to bring out the best in each person. An effective leader uses each person's capabilities to the fullest and at the same time helps individuals grow toward realization of their potential. Respecting and caring about the people with whom you work is essential to becoming a leader.

Desire

Students have seen persons who possessed a strong desire and accomplished great things despite many obstacles. These people succeeded because they kept their goals clearly in mind, were not sidetracked, and kept striving for what they wanted out of life. Most young people have a strong desire to be successful. They dream. They commit themselves to being professionals and strive toward the attainment of their goals. They are active role models for what they preach. By doing so, they are becoming all that they are capable of being.

Creativity

Creativity is important in addressing the many challenges facing physical education and sport today. The discovery of something that is truly new or the generation of new solutions to solve perplexing problems is important in the advancement of the field of physical education and sport. The invention of the game of basketball, the origination of movement education, and the emergence of the "new physical education with its emphasis on the development of the entire person" are just a few of the many exciting and creative ideas that have influenced the nature of physical education and sport.

Creative individuals possess imagination, inner maturity, the ability to think, a rich background of knowledge in their field, and flexibility in approaching problems. They are skeptical of accepted ideas and less suspicious of new ones, persistent, and self-confident. Physical education and sport professionals need to think carefully about the present status of the field and the challenges they face. Creativity will help lead to the solutions to these problems, enhance our contributions to society, and further the development of the field as we move toward the twenty-first century.

Interest in research

Professionals are interested in research. Through research the knowledge base of the field is expanded, new applications for knowledge are identified, and solutions to problems are achieved. This interest in research will help us close the gap between research and practice. Although our knowledge base has expanded tremendously, many valid research findings are not being applied in programs across the country. Additionally, more research is needed on many problems confronting professionals today.

Although many professionals are interested in research, they may find it difficult to access current research, interpret the results, and apply the findings to their programs. There has been a greater effort by professionals in the field to disseminate research findings more widely and to ensure that they are communicated to practitioners in an understandable fashion.

Accountability

Accountability in the physical education and sport profession is needed if it is to grow and reach its destiny. There must be accountability to the consumer (i.e., students, clients), society, and oneself. Most important, there must be accountability to the profession. Only through accountability can physical education and sport professionals render a unique and worthwhile service to society in general and to their profession in particular.

To be accountable in the physical education and sport profession, one first must have a sound foundation of knowledge in his or her field of endeavor. The stated goals of the profession must have a scientific basis in such areas as exercise physiology, motor control, motor development, motor learning, biomechanics, and the philosophy, sociology, and psychology of physical education and sport. Therefore each potential leader should have mastered this information.

Accountability is fostered when program goals are clearly stated and activities lead to the attainment of these goals. The use of various assessment techniques enables professionals to determine whether the program's participants have achieved the stated goals. Professionals must be able to show what is actually accomplished in our programs. Accountability enhances the respectability of physical education and sport in the academic world and among the public. There will be recognition that physical education and sport professionals have the proper credentials since they can prove scientifically that the services they render to society can enhance people's quality of life.

Professionalism

Professionalism is a deep commitment to all aspects of the field of physical education and sport. Professionalism means many different things to people and includes several dimensions. Professionalism means exhibiting high levels of professional competence and conduct, possessing required credentials, presenting accurately and truthfully information about the programs and services provided, and exemplifying a commitment to a healthy, active lifestyle. Professionals demonstrate an enthusiasm for their work, an interest in new developments, leadership skills, and involvement in the further advancement of the field.

Professionals exhibit accountability. They fulfill their many professional obligations in an exemplary fashion. Programs are planned, have established goals, are implemented according to current standards of professional practice, are conducted in the best interests of the participants, are monitored for quality on a continuous basis, and are evaluated periodically using accepted assessment techniques. Equally important, the public statements and claims that professionals make about their credentials, programs, and outcomes are accurate and truthful.

Professionals adhere to ethical standards of conduct in their dealings with participants in their programs. These ethical standards serve as guidelines for actions and aid in decision making. Interactions with participants in programs should be appropriate. For example, many codes of conduct and common professional consensus prohibit inappropriate personal relationships between coaches and their athletes, disclosure of confidential information about an employee by a worksite health professional, or discrimination by athletic trainers in their treatment of starting and nonstarting athletes. Actions toward program participants and other professionals in the field reflect honesty, respect, and fairness.[14]

Professionals remember that they are in a position of influence and serve as role models for participants in their programs. Initially, young professionals may want to discount the idea that appearance is important and believe that competence is what matters the most. Yet first impressions and appearances do influence people's perceptions and beliefs. What impression does a sloppily dressed, overweight, out-of-shape, smoking, inarticulate physical education and sport professional make on participants in their program? Compare that impression to the one made by a professional that is nicely groomed, well-spoken, fit, dynamic, enthusiastic, and possesses good health habits. Which professional has more credibility? Effective professionals are exemplary role models; they do "practice what they preach."

The field of physical education and sport is growing rapidly. Professionals are committed to staying up to date with new research findings and changing techniques. They are interested in learning and take advantage of continuing education courses, workshops, conferences, and professional journals to stay abreast of the latest changes. Professionals take an active role in advancing the field through conducting and sharing research, exploring new ideas, and undertaking leadership responsibilities at various levels (e.g., local to regional to national levels). Through networking, professionals exchange ideas and support each other's efforts.

Conventions offer professionals opportunities for communication and fellowship.

Professionalism includes service not only to the profession but to society. Professionals recognize their responsibility to be involved in community service, not only to offer leadership in their area of expertise, but to participate in activities that enrich the community as a whole. Professionals advocate for increased opportunities in physical education and sport for those who have been denied or have limited access to services.

Professionalism is a concept with many different meanings. Professionalism reflects commitment to the field and people whom we serve, respect and consideration for others, and responsibility to oneself, others, and society.

PROFESSIONAL ORGANIZATIONS IN PHYSICAL EDUCATION AND SPORT

Professional organizations play an important role in the growth and development of the field of physical education and sport. Many of the greatest changes in the field have their beginnings in organizational meetings and conferences. Scholarly research, curriculum development, certification requirements, and hundreds of other topics are discussed in detail at conferences and other activities associated with professional organizations. The physical education and sport field, both in the United States and in other countries of the world, has an imposing list of associations concerned with every aspect of the field.

All physical education and sport professionals should belong to the national and state associations in their areas of interest. If all professionals belonged to and worked for their professional organizations, the concerted effort of such a large professional group would result in greater benefits and more prestige for the field.

Why Belong to a Professional Association?

Belonging to a professional organization has many advantages.

1. *It provides opportunity for service.* With the many offices, committee responsibilities, and program functions that professional associations provide, the individual has an opportunity to serve to better this field of work.

2. *It provides an opportunity to shape the future of the profession.* Members can work actively to influence the direction of the field in the future. This can be accomplished through involvement in committees, task forces, and governance. Members can also be active in influencing legislation that will benefit the profession. For example, NASPE, an association of AAHPERD, is actively crusading for daily physical education for all schoolchildren and is using its congressional lobby as one means to achieve this objective.

3. *It provides a channel of communication.* Communication in a field is essential so that members may keep abreast of the latest developments in techniques, of new emphases in program content, and of the many other trends that emerge continually in a growing field. Organizations provide an effective channel of communications by way of publications, meetings, and announcements. The World Wide Web is a growing channel of communication. Many organizations have Web sites and post information for professionals on these sites.

4. *It provides a means for interpreting the field.* The physical education and sport field must be interpreted to the public on national, state, and local levels. This interpretation is essential to achieve public support for the services rendered by the professional practitioner. The professional association provides an opportunity for the best thinking and ideas to be articulately interpreted far and wide. As a result of such endeavors, the profession can achieve recognition, respect, prestige, and cooperation with other areas of education, professions, and the public in general.

5. *It provides a source of help in solving professional and personal problems.* Every physical education and sport professional has problems, both professional and personal. Through their officers, members, conferences, and other activities, professional associations can play an important role in solving these problems. The associations can be of assistance, for example, in solving a professional problem involving the administration of an adapted physical activity program or a personal problem with life insurance.

6. *It provides an opportunity for fellowship.* Through association conferences and meetings physical education and sport professionals get to know others doing similar work, and this common denominator results in friendships and many enjoyable professional and social occasions. The opportunity to build and sustain networks is an important benefit of belonging to a professional organization.

7. *It provides a forum for research.* Professions must continually conduct research to determine the effectiveness of their programs, the validity of their techniques, and the quality of their contributions to society. Professional associations aid in the dissemination of research findings through conferences, workshops, newsletters, and publications. They also support research efforts by promoting collaborative projects and/or by offering grants to help defray costs. Through research, associations also must seek knowledge that will enable the profession to move ahead and expand its services.

8. *It provides a means for distributing costs.* The work undertaken by a professional association is intended to benefit the members. This work requires money. By joining a professional association, professionals rightfully assume their responsibility to share in these costs. If one participates in the benefits, one should also share in the costs of achieving these benefits.

9. *It is valuable in gaining employment.* Through organizations, physical education and sport professionals can develop professional contacts that may prove useful in gaining employment. Through such contacts professionals can learn of prospective employment opportunities or obtain a letter of recommendation for a desired position. Many professional organizations offer placement services for their members. They send their members updates of job openings, have

job openings posted on their Web sites, and have placement services at their national conventions. This is helpful in gaining one's first job as well as in changing jobs.

Numerous professional organizations exist within the realm of physical education and sport to meet the diverse interests and needs of professionals in the field. From the many organizations available, you should select carefully those that best meet your needs and interests. Become involved. Be a committed, active professional willing to work hard to shape the direction and future of this dynamic field.

Professional Organizations

It would be difficult to discuss all the organizations that pertain to the physical education and sport field. The growth of physical education and sport has led to the formation of numerous organizations; it seems that for every specialized area of study as well as for each sport there are organizations for interested professionals.

You can find out about organizations in your areas of interest in several ways. First, talk to other professionals, such as faculty at your undergraduate institution, that may share the same interests. Talk to practitioners in your prospective field of employment and find out the organizations in which they hold membership. Second, you can search the World Wide Web for organizations in your area of interest. Third, a comprehensive listing of all organizations in the United States is given in the *Encyclopedia of Associations*. The listing for each organization includes the purpose of the organization; name, address, and phone number of the person to contact for further information; size of the membership and the association staff; and publications of the association. The *Encyclopedia* is probably available at the reference desk or in the reference section of most college and university libraries.

The American Alliance for Health, Physical Education, Recreation and Dance (AAHPERD), the American College of Sports Medicine (ACSM), and the National Athletic Training Association (NATA) will be described. Examples of associations for

individuals interested in sport psychology, sport sociology, sport philosophy, and sport history are mentioned. Finally, examples for professionals interested in specific sport areas are provided. Since many professional organizations now have Web sites, it is easy to obtain information about professional organizations and even to subscribe on line.

American Alliance for Health, Physical Education, Recreation and Dance (AAHPERD)

AAHPERD was established in 1885 under the title of American Association for Advancement of Physical Education. AAHPERD is committed to developing and maintaining healthy, active lifestyles for all Americans and to enhancing skilled and aesthetic performance. AAHPERD's mission is to "serve as a strong advocate for programs, activities, and policies that contribute toward these endeavors and to provide professional development opportunities for members which lead to enhanced knowledge and professional practice." AAHPERD has over 25,000 members representing many different areas of interest within health, physical education, recreation, and dance. These include administrators, teachers, and coaches at all levels, sports medicine professionals, athletic trainers, dancers, fitness professionals, recreators, and physical activity specialists.

AAHPERD comprises six national organizations.

◆ The American Association for Leisure and Recreation (AALR) is concerned with the promotion of leisure services at the community and national levels and recreation education within the school.

◆ The Association for the Advancement of Health Education (AAHE) is involved with the conduct of health education programs in schools, colleges, and communities as well as being concerned with addressing societal health issues, such as drinking and driving, and promotion of health-oriented legislation.

◆ The American Association for Active Lifestyles and Fitness (AAALF) consists of various special interest groups, such as the Council on Outdoor Education and the Council of Aging and Adult Development, and administrative groups, such as the College and University Administrators Council.

◆ The National Association for Girls and Women in Sport (NAGWS) focuses on improvement of leadership sport opportunities for girls and women at all levels of competition.

◆ The National Association for Sport and Physical Education (NASPE) is concerned with the promotion of physical education and sport at all levels.

◆ The National Dance Association (NDA) seeks to promote dance both within the educational setting and on the community and national levels.

The Research Consortium is also an important part of the Alliance.

Nationally AAHPERD is divided into six district or regional organizations. The Eastern, Southern, Central, Midwestern, Southwestern, and Northwestern districts have a similar purpose to that of AAHPERD, elect officers, and hold district conventions. These district organizations provide leadership opportunities for professionals and allow AAHPERD to present programs specific to regional needs.

State associations provide services to professionals in each state. Membership in the state organization requires a fee; membership in the national organization is optional. State associations provide wonderful opportunities for young practitioners to become involved in their profession. The membership in the state associations total about 30,000, bringing the combined network of national members to over 55,000.

The publications of the Alliance serve to disseminate knowledge about the field to its many members. Among its many publications are *JOPERD* (*Journal of Physical Education, Recreation, and Dance*), the *Research Quarterly for Exercise and Sport, Strategies, Update,* and *Health Education*. In addition, AAHPERD publishes many other materials pertinent to the work of the Alliance, such as the National Content Standards for Physical Education.

The services performed by the Alliance include the following:

◆ Research on a variety of topics and the dissemination of research through conferences, workshops, and published materials.

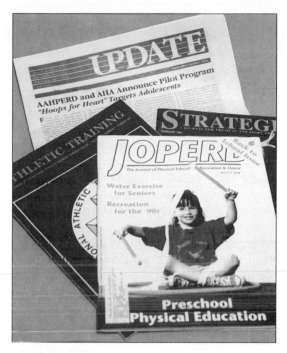

Professional organizations publish periodicals that help disseminate information to members and foster communication among professionals.

◆ Professional development through numerous conferences, workshops, and training sessions.

◆ Advocacy at all levels of government and with other national agencies on behalf of members for such issues as gender equity, coaching certification, and maintenance of educational programs.

◆ Job placement services and professional development services are offered to members.

◆ Recognition of excellence through presentation of numerous awards.

The AAHPERD Student Action Council (SAC) is an organization of students that works for the benefit of its members through student involvement. The group's objectives include (1) greater student involvement in AAHPERD, (2) promotion of professionalism among majors, and (3) promotion of professional interest groups. The Alliance in cooperation with SAC has made available special membership plans for students.

The national office of AAHPERD is located at 1900 Association Drive, Reston, VA 20191 (Phone 800-213-7193, Fax 703-476-8527).

American College of Sports Medicine (ACSM)

ACSM was founded in 1954 and is the largest sports medicine and exercise science organization in the world. The purpose of ACSM is to promote and integrate "scientific research, education, and practical applications of sports medicine and exercise science to maintain and enhance physical performance, fitness, health, and quality of life." From astronauts to athletes to those people chronically diseased or physically challenged, ACSM seeks to find methods that enable people to live longer, work more productively, and enjoy a greater quality of life.

Nationally ACSM is divided into several regional chapters, such as the Mid-Atlantic Chapter of ACSM. Many states have their own chapters as well. The 17,000 members of ACSM include physicians, fitness professionals, cardiac rehabilitation specialists, sports medicine practitioners and athletic trainers, physical education teachers, and coaches. ACSM is affiliated with the International Federation of Sports Medicine (IFSM), an organization that has played an important role for many years in Europe and South America.

ACSM supports many different activities related to health, fitness, exercise, and sports medicine. These activities include the following:

♦ promotion of public awareness and education about the benefits of physical activity and exercise for people of all ages and abilities.

♦ sponsoring certification programs for professionals interested in preventive and rehabilitative exercise.

♦ holding conferences and workshops throughout the year for professionals in the field.

♦ publication of journals including *Medicine and Science in Sports and Exercise, Sports Medicine Bulletin,* and the *Encyclopedia of Sport Sciences and Medicine.*

♦ supporting scientific studies and encouraging research efforts to advance the field.

♦ cooperating with other organizations concerning sports medicine and related areas.

The mailing address of ACSM is P.O. Box 1440, Indianapolis, IN 46206-1440 (Phone: 317-637-9200, Fax: 317-634-7817).

National Athletic Trainers Association (NATA)

The NATA, founded in 1950, is "committed to advancing, encouraging and improving the athletic training profession." There are more than 22,700 members nationwide and over 90% of the membership are certified by the NATA Board of Certification, earning the title *certified athletic trainer* (ATC). In 1990, athletic training was recognized as an allied health profession by the American Medical Association.

The NATA establishes the standards for athletic trainers through its education programs. Nationwide, over 100 colleges and universities offer NATA-approved curricula. Each year, 1,200 to 1,500 athletic trainers earn certification through its program.

The NATA provides a variety of services to their members, including the following:

♦ establishment of professional standards and a code of ethics for athletic trainers.

♦ administration of the certification program.

♦ continuing education opportunities through conventions and workshops.

♦ annual conventions for the benefit of its members.

♦ advocacy efforts to influence legislation beneficial to the field.

♦ promotion of athletic training through public relations efforts.

♦ job placement services for its membership.

♦ publication of journals and newsletters, including the *Journal of Athletic Training,* a quarterly scientific journal, and *NATA News,* a monthly membership magazine.

For further information, contact the NATA at 2952 Stemmons Freeway, Dallas, TX 75247-6103 (Phone: 214-637-6282, Fax: 214-637-2206).

Organizations for the Subdisciplines of Physical Education and Sport

Many of the subdisciplines of physical education also have professional organizations or associations. The number of these specialized organizations continues to grow each year as professionals with specific areas of interest start new organizations in their areas of expertise. Examples of five of these specialized organizations are provided in this section.

North American Society for the Psychology of Sport and Physical Activity (NASPSPA) was founded in 1965. The society is composed of professionals (psychologists, psychiatrists, sport psychologists, and physical educators) whose primary purpose is to promote scientific research and relations within the framework of sport psychology and physical activity by means of meetings, investigations, publications, and other activities. Membership in NASPSPA is open to all people interested in the psychology of sport and physical activity. NASPSPA is affiliated with the International Society for the Psychology of Sports.

The society publishes the *Sport Psychology Bulletin,* a quarterly bulletin, which keeps its members informed about affairs of the society, as well as the field of sport psychology in general. The society also publishes newsletters detailing the activities of the annual convention, which is usually held in the spring. For further information concerning the NASPSPA, write to the society in care of Dr. Kathleen M. Haywood, University of Missouri–St. Louis, Department of Physical Education, St. Louis, MO 63121.

The **Philosophic Society for the Study of Sport (PSSS)** was founded in 1972 at the annual meeting of the American Philosophical Association, Eastern Division. The membership includes persons with varied backgrounds and skills, all having a strong interest in the philosophy of sport. The central thrust of the organization is the scholarly investigation of sport, including implications for practical pursuit. The PSSS publishes newsletters and the *Journal of the Philosophy of Sport.* For further information, contact Professor Janet M. Oussaty, Kean College of New Jersey, Physical Education, Recreation and Health, Union, NJ 07083.

The **North American Society for Sport History (NASSH)** was founded in 1972. The membership comprises individuals interested in sport history, social history, and physical education. The purpose of NASSH is to promote the study, research, and writing of sport history. Another objective is to cooperate with other organizations with similar aims. NASSH publishes the *Journal of Sport History.* Additional information may be obtained from Professor Ronald A. Smith, NASSH, 101 White Building, Pennsylvania State University, University Park, PA 16802.

The **North American Society for the Sociology of Sport (NASSS)** founded in 1980, is concerned with promoting study of the sociology of sport. Dissemination of research in this area is another objective of NASSS. NASSS publishes the *Sociology of Sport Journal.* Further information may be obtained from Dr. Mary Duquin, Department of Physical Education, University of Pittsburgh, Pittsburgh, PA 15261.

The **North American Society for Sport Management (NASSM)** was founded in 1985. The membership includes academics involved or interested in many different aspects of sport management. Membership is open to undergraduate students enrolled in sport management programs of study. The NASSM promotes research, scholarly writing, and development in this growing field. It publishes the *Journal of Sport Management.* For more information, contact Dr. Garth Paton, University of New Brunswick, Faculty of Physical Education and Recreation, Fredericton, NB, Canada E3B 5A3.

Sport Organizations for Coaches and Interested Professionals

Numerous organizations are affiliated with specific sport areas. Many of these organizations sponsor annual conferences and clinics for interested professionals, conduct certification programs, and publish newsletters and journals related to the sport. Professionals who are coaching or teaching in the specific sport are a good source of information about these sport associations. Another source is the *Encyclopedia of Associations.* For example, a professional interested in the sport of swimming would find the following professional organizations listed in the *Encyclopedia:*

◆ American Swimming Coaches Association
◆ Aquatics Exercise Council
◆ College Swimming Coaches Association of America

- ◆ Council for National Cooperation in Aquatics
- ◆ International Amateur Swimming Federation
- ◆ United States Swimming, Inc.
- ◆ United States Diving, Inc.
- ◆ United States Synchronized Swimming, Inc.

A professional interested in the sport of tennis may find membership in one or more of these organizations helpful:

- ◆ Intercollegiate Tennis Coaches Association
- ◆ Professional Tennis Registry
- ◆ United States Professional Tennis Association

- ◆ United States Recreational Tennis Association
- ◆ United States Tennis Association
- ◆ United States Tennis Writers Association
- ◆ Women's Tennis Association

Some professional organizations may have certain requirements for membership, whereas others may be open to any interested individuals. They provide a wonderful means to network with other professionals, learn new skills and techniques, and stay up to date with new advances in the sport.

SUMMARY

Traditionally careers in physical education and sport have focused on teaching and coaching in schools and colleges or universities. Today, teaching and coaching careers have expanded to non-school settings and all segments of the population and have become increasingly popular.

Selecting a career pathway from the many available options requires careful consideration of many factors. To make an informed decision, information must be gathered from the appropriate sources and evaluated. Your personal strengths, interests, goals, and preferences are the most important considerations in choosing a career. In selecting a career you must also consider information about the career itself. This information may be gathered through research and by talking to practitioners in your prospective career.

Professional preparation for a career involves academic studies, related experiences, and professional activities. Planning for a career demands understanding the nature of the work to be performed and the requirements of the job. As you read about different career opportunities in physical education and sport, be flexible and

open-minded and explore career opportunities that interest you.

Professional leadership is needed to ensure the continued growth and vitality of the field of physical education and sport. Leadership is also critical in helping participants in our programs achieve desired goals. Leaders are not born, but made. Leadership qualities and skills can be developed and improved by professionals who desire to enhance their effectiveness.

There are many advantages to belonging to a professional organization. Professional organizations provide opportunities for service, facilitate communication, and provide a means to disseminate research findings and other information to professionals. Membership in a professional organization provides opportunities for networking, a resource for resolution of problems, and may enhance one's employment opportunities.

Numerous professional organizations exist. To find out about a professional organization in one's specific area of interest, one can consult a professional or practitioner in the field, the *Encyclopedia of Associations,* or the World Wide Web.

SELF-ASSESSMENT TESTS

These tests are designed to help you determine if you have mastered the materials and competencies presented in this chapter.

1. Identify 5 career opportunities in physical education and sport. Using the information provided in the Getting Connected box, access the Human

Kinetics site and information about physical activity careers. Find out the skills required, potential employers, and salary associated with each career.

2. Using the questions provided in the text as guidelines, assess your strengths, interests, goals, and preferences. Based on this information, what careers might you choose? If you want, share this information with a fellow student and solicit each other's input regarding possible careers.

3. Develop a multi-year plan to attain your goal. Specifically, in addition to the requirements of your professional preparation program, what other opportunities will you pursue (e.g., certifications,

extracurricular activities, employment) to enhance your professional qualifications?

4. Using the information provided in the Getting Connected box, access StudentCenter.com. Read the information about self-assessment and resume writing. Construct an on-line resume.

5. Through self-reflection, determine what leadership qualities and skills you possess. What qualities do you need to develop?

6. Using the information provided in the Getting Connected box, access the list of associations via the Human Kinetics site. Locate information about two associations in your areas of interest. Access the Web sites for these organizations to obtain further information

REFERENCES

1. Lambert CL: What is physical education? JOPERD 51(5):26–27, 1980.

2. US Department of Labor: Occupational outlook handbook, current edition, Washington, D.C., Department of Labor.

3. College Placement Council: CPC annual, current edition, Bethlehem, Pa, College Placement Council.

4. Akey DS, editor: Encyclopedia of associations, Detroit, Gale Research Co., current edition.

5. Krause JV and Melville DS: Fit for hire—a model for promoting the health and fitness of physical education students. JOPERD 64(4): 61–65, 1993.

6. Willis JD and Campbell LF: Exercise psychology, Champaign, Ill., 1992, Human Kinetics.

7. Mack R: Leadership skills: a coach's greatest asset, Coach 16(4):3–4, 1996.

8. Smith DM: The practical executive and leadership, Lincolnwood, Ill., 1997, NTC Business Books.

9. Weinberg RS and Gould D: Psychology of exercise and sport, Champaign, Ill., 1995, Human Kinetics.

10. Anshel MH: Sport psychology: From theory to practice, ed 3, Scottsdale, Ariz., 1997, Gorsuch Scarisbrick.

11. Campbell R: Leadership, Columbia, Mo., 1997, University of Missouri.

12. Tead O: The art of leadership, New York, 1935, Whittlesey House.

13. McIntrye M: Leadership development, Quest 33(1):33–41, 1981.

14. Stoll SK and Beller JM: Professional responsibility—a lost art, Strategies 9(2):17–19, 1995.

SUGGESTED READINGS

Bolles RN: What color is your parachute? a practical manual for job-hunters and career changers, Berkeley, Calif., current edition, Ten Speed Press.

This book provides practical guidelines for obtaining a job and/or changing careers. The resource section of the book is comprehensive and a valuable guide for obtaining career information.

Cardinal BJ: Cardiorespiratory fitness and physical activity behavior of physical education majors, Physical Educator 52:211–218, 1995.

The article reports on a study of the fitness status and physical activity level of physical education majors and discusses the implications for professional preparation programs.

College Placement Council: CPC annual, current edition, Bethlehem, Pa., College Placement Council.

Available through the career planning office, this annual periodical offers advice on career planning, the job search, and graduate school.

Krause JV and Melville DS: Fit for hire—a model for promoting the health and fitness of physical education students, JOPERD 64(4):61–65, 1993.

Presents a model used by a university to help its students develop healthy lifestyles.

Marston R: Developing professionalism at the undergraduate level, JOPERD 64(7): 36–37, 40, 1993.

Offers suggestions on involving undergraduates in their future profession.

Ruder K, editor: Being professional now, JOPERD 64(7):29–52, 1993.

A series of articles on professionalism and its development through various avenues.

Stoll SK and Beller JM: Professional responsibility—a lost art, Strategies 9(2):17–19, 1995.

Professional responsibility is discussed with reference to personal morality, professional ethics, and social responsibility.

Zakrajsek DL and Pierce W: Academic preparation and the academic consumer, JOPERD 64(5): 20–24, 31, 1993.

Explores the issue of specialization and how a broader professional preparation may be better suited to employers' needs.

CHAPTER 11

Teaching and Coaching Careers in Physical Education and Sport

Instructional Objectives and Competencies to be Achieved:

After reading this chapter the student should be able to—

• Describe the qualities of an effective teacher and his or her responsibilities.

• Describe the advantages and disadvantages of pursuing a teaching career in a school or nonschool setting.

• Describe the similarities and differences between teaching and coaching.

• Discuss the problem of burnout and its effects on teachers and coaches.

• Discuss strategies to maximize opportunities for employment in a teaching or coaching position.

Teaching and coaching opportunities for physical educators have expanded from the school to the nonschool setting and from school-aged populations (i.e., 5 to 18 years) to people of all ages, ranging from preschoolers to senior citizens. Although traditional opportunities in the public school are available, professionals are seeking other avenues of teaching and coaching careers. The national interest in fitness and sport has contributed to the opening of these alternative areas of employment. Moreover, the continued emphasis on fitness, physical activities, and sport opportunities for all age groups presents an encouraging employment picture to potential physical education teachers and coaches. Professionals interested in pursuing a career in these areas will find that attaining a position is possible for those physical educators who possess the appropriate credentials and exhibit perseverance.

The challenge to those who wish to enter the teaching or coaching professions is reflected in the words of Aristotle. He said that those who educate children well are to be honored more than those who produce them, for those who produce children give them only life, but those who educate them give them the art of living well.[1] A physical education teacher or coach has the responsibility to inspire students or athletes with the desire to learn, to have them recognize the need to develop physical skills and be physically active, to see that each one develops to his or her capacity, and to ensure that each one has a successful experience.

GETTING CONNECTED

Clearinghouse on Teacher Education, HPERD presents articles of interest to teachers.
>   Site: http://www.ericsp.org/hprdtoc.html

PE CENTRAL site is a major resource for physical educators. Topics include lesson plans, assessment tools, professional conferences, and how to subscribe to the listserv.
>   Site: http://pe.central.vt.edu

Special Olympics International site offers information about the Special Olympics, programs around the world, and volunteering.
>   Site: http://www.specialolympics.org/

American Sport Education Program site gives information about ASEP and coaching resources.
>   Site: http://www.asep.com/

National Standards for Athletic Coaches lists the coaching domains and the standards associated with each domain.
>   Site: http://aahperd.org/naspe/athstds.html

Sports Media site presents an array of resources for teachers and coaches, including links to lesson plans and drills.
>   Site: http://www.ping.be/sportsmedia/Lesson.htm

National Education Association site contains information about current news and issues in education.
>   Site: http://www.nea.org

National Consortium for Physical Education and Recreation for Individuals with Disabilities site presents information about the Adapted Physical Education National Standards Project, including requirements.
>   Site: http://ncperid.usf.edu/apensp.html

THE TEACHING PROFESSION

Teaching has been the traditional focus of the field of physical education and sport. Even though many types of jobs are now available in the field, many young people still choose to teach and to coach. The school setting remains the most popular setting for teaching, and job opportunities look promising. It is estimated that during the next decade 2 million new teachers (all subjects) will need to be hired to replace the generation of teachers about to retire and to respond to a growing need. The 1990s has seen a surge of interest in teaching.

Teaching in the school and nonschool setting has many benefits as well as some drawbacks. Regardless of the setting, effective teachers hold high expectations for their students, keep them involved in relevant learning activities, and create an atmosphere that promotes learning. Beginning teachers possess competencies in many different areas that enable them to enhance student learning. The use of developmentally appropriate teaching practices helps teachers more effectively address the needs of their learners.

Choosing a Teaching Career

Teaching offers many rewards, regardless of whether it takes place in the traditional school or an alternative nonschool setting. Probably most important is that it offers an opportunity to help shape people's lives and promote a healthy lifestyle. Students select teaching as a career for many reasons. Each prospective teacher should take the time to list his or her reasons for choosing this career.

Many physical educators want to teach because of their love of children and their desire to help others. The conviction that involvement in a sound physical education program can have a significant impact on the quality of life of its participants motivates some individuals to enter the teaching profession. Prospective teachers who have been fortunate to reap the benefits of participation in a sound physical education program often express the desire to share with others the same benefits that they themselves have realized. Other individuals, who had poor experiences while students in physical education, enter the teaching profession because they want to improve physical education programs so that the benefits of quality programs can be attained.

Certainly personal interests, likes, and dislikes influence one's decision to enter the teaching profession. Many choose to teach physical education because of their love for sport and perhaps the desire to transmit this love to others. The opportunity to be outdoors, to work out and stay physically fit, and to have fun are often given as reasons for entering the teaching profession.

The nature of the job attracts many individuals. In the school setting the long vacations, the informality of teaching in the gymnasium as compared with the classroom, and the security offered by tenure are some of the benefits that prompt some people to seek a teaching career. Others may enter teaching because they desire to coach, and in many schools teaching is a prerequisite to coaching. Teaching may also be used as a stepping stone to other careers, such as athletic administration.

Many of these reasons for entering the teaching profession are valid for those seeking to work in nonschool settings. The opportunity to capitalize on one's proficiency in a sport, the desire to share the benefits of participation with others, and the love of working with people may motivate physical educators to prepare for a teaching career in an alternative setting.

The reasons that individuals pursue teaching careers are varied, ranging from a desire and commitment to improve society and the quality of life to a desire to bask in the sun for several months during the vacations. The rewards that accrue from teaching depend to a large degree on the individual and what each person makes of his or her opportunities. The inner rewards, plus the financial and other benefits, can be great for the person who applies himself or herself diligently and sincerely to teaching.

What Are the Benefits and Drawbacks Associated with Teaching?

The teaching profession is considered a service-oriented profession. As with other service-oriented professions, those who enter teaching must often be satisfied with intrinsic rather than extrinsic rewards. Several benefits are associated with teaching physical education in the school setting.

One benefit is salary. At first glance teachers' salaries appear to be very low in comparison with those offered in other professional careers. In 1997 the national average teacher's salary was $38,509.[2] However, remember that teachers typically work 9 months or about 180 school days a year. If the teacher's salary is prorated to the typical 12-month period worked by other professionals, the salary is equivalent to $51,345. Nationally, the average salary ranged from $50,647 in Alaska to $26,764 in South Dakota.[2] When looking at teacher salaries, remember that cost of living varies considerably from place to place. The long vacation periods provide the opportunity to earn additional money, to travel, or to continue one's education. Although teaching is not a lucrative career, the financial picture in many cases is not bleak, as is sometimes thought.

Second, teaching in an educational setting offers job tenure. The primary objective of tenure is to enhance the academic freedom of teachers. However, it can also be perceived as providing teachers with job security. Tenure is typically granted in the public schools after 3 years of satisfactory service to the school district. At the college and university level, tenure is typically granted after 6 years.

Many other benefits associated with teaching attract young people to the field. The intrinsic rewards are great. These include the opportunity to serve as a role model to young people. As many of you know from your own experiences, teachers can exert a great influence on the lives of young students, contributing greatly to their development. Others are attracted to the field because of the chance to teach a diversity of activities. For many young people, one great benefit to teaching physical education is that it offers them the opportunity to coach.

On the other hand, one should be aware that there are several disadvantages to pursuing a teaching career in a school setting. Although the public's confidence in teachers appears to be improving, the lack of wholehearted commitment has resulted in problems of morale, lack of financial support, and pressure to do more with less money and to get by with often inadequate facilities. The teacher is often beset with discipline problems, confronted with overpopulated classes that contain unmotivated students, and required to absorb teaching loads that are too heavy. Teachers often do numerous tasks not related to teaching, such as lunchroom and study hall supervision, hall duty, and playground or bus patrol.

Several benefits are associated with teaching in the nonschool setting. Examples of teaching opportunities in the nonschool setting include working as a tennis or golf professional and teaching in a community recreation program, YMCA/YWCA, or commercial sport club such as a gymnastics club, swim club, or racquetball club. First, since participation in these programs is voluntary, the teacher generally works with individuals and students who are highly motivated and eager to be involved in the activity. In contrast, the teacher in the school setting may have to deal with disinterested students who are mandated to take "gym class." The opportunity to teach physical education without having to deal with problems associated with the schools or other duties required of teachers in the school setting (study hall, etc.) is appealing. Second, many physical educators elect to teach in the nonschool setting because of the opportunity to specialize; many physical educators like the idea of teaching just one activity, such as golf, tennis, or swimming. However, many nonschool settings such as YMCA/YWCA and community recreation programs require the ability to teach a diversity of activities.

There are some drawbacks to teaching in the nonschool setting. Unlike teaching in the schools, there is a lack of job security. The number of participants enrolled in a program may determine whether it continues to be offered and may also determine the teacher's salary. Salaries may vary widely as well. In contrast to school, where the working hours are confined to weekdays (unless one is coaching), working hours at a nonschool setting may be late afternoons and evenings and often weekends. Working hours need to be responsive to the hours the clients have available for leisure time pursuits. Work may also be seasonal, but this depends on the nature of the activity and the location. For example, golf professionals in the Northeast may find work only from May to September, but those pursuing this profession in the South may be able to work year round.

Prospective teachers should identify their reasons for entering the teaching profession as well as evaluate the benefits associated with this career in terms of their personal priorities and goals. Advantages and disadvantages are associated with teaching in both the school and nonschool settings. These must be considered in making a career choice.

What Is Effective Teaching?

Teaching can be defined as those interactions of the teacher and the learner that make learning

Physical education teachers and coaches must be well prepared for working in their field. This prospective teacher is receiving feedback from her instructor about her practice teaching.

more successful.[3] Although it is possible for learning to occur without a teacher's involvement, it is generally accepted that teachers facilitate the acquisition of knowledge, skills, and attitudes. Teachers who are effective use a variety of pedagogical skills and strategies to ensure that their students are appropriately engaged in relevant activities a high percentage of the time, hold positive expectations for their students, and create and maintain a classroom climate that is warm and nurturing.[4]

Salient teacher behaviors can be divided into several broad areas: organization, communication, instruction, motivation, and human relations. These characteristics are common to effective teachers, regardless of the skill to be learned, the age of the students, or the setting in which the teaching occurs.

Organizational skills are very important in establishing the learning environment and facilitating student involvement in activities. The manner in which the teacher structures instruction is of major importance. To be effective the teacher must ensure that the lesson to be presented relates to the stated objectives, meets the needs of the individual learners, and is presented in a logical, systematic manner. Through efficient and thorough planning, effective teachers minimize transition time, that is, the time to move students from place to place, and management time, that is, time used for tasks such as taking attendance. Lessons are planned to ensure that students receive maximum opportunities to practice relevant skills and experience success. Actively supervising and monitoring student performance and providing students with appropriate feedback are characteristics of successful teachers. Skilled teachers bring each lesson to an end by summarizing what has been accomplished and by providing students with an assessment of their progress toward the stated objectives.

Communication skills needed by the teacher include verbal and nonverbal expressive skills, written competencies, and the ability to use the various media. Effective verbal communication skills are essential in the teaching process. The ability to speak clearly and project one's voice in a pleasing manner is essential. Other attributes of a successful teacher are the abilities to give clear, precise directions and explanations and to use terminology and vocabulary that are appropriate to the activity and the level of the learners. The teacher's ability to use questions to elicit student input, to promote student involvement, and to clarify student understanding of the material being presented enhances the effectiveness of the learning process. Effective teachers are also aware of the influence of their nonverbal behavior on the students and learning process. Use of eye contact, smiles, and pats on the back are some of the methods of communicating with students in a nonverbal manner. Through their verbal and nonverbal behaviors, effective teachers model the kinds of behaviors they wish their students to exhibit, such as interest in and enjoyment of the activity and respect for other persons' opinions and needs. Effective teachers communicate enthusiasm, through both their verbal and nonverbal behavior.

Written communication skills are essential, especially in the planning and evaluation phase of teaching. Those teachers who possess effective written communication skills are able to express themselves clearly. The ability to communicate with supervisors, participants, and interested others will help to establish a more successful program.

Expertise in the use of various instructional media techniques is a quality of effective teachers. Use of transparencies, slides, movie projectors, and videotape equipment are skills that should be mastered early in one's career. Appropriate use of media can enhance and accelerate student learning.

Competency in a variety of instructional skills is essential for effective teaching. When planning experiences for students, effective teachers use their knowledge of the content to be taught, in conjunction with instructional objectives and students' needs, to provide appropriate experiences leading to the attainment of stated goals. Effective teaching requires the ability to sequence movement tasks by increasing difficulty and complexity as students progress, and by providing opportunities

for students not only to develop skills but to apply them. Good teachers not only must be able to implement planned experiences effectively but also must be flexible so that they can appropriately modify planned experiences to suit the needs of the students and the situations that arise within the learning environment.

Effective teachers are able to maintain an orderly, productive learning environment, handling discipline problems appropriately while encouraging and providing opportunities for students to learn responsibility and to be accountable for their actions. A wide variety of teaching methods and instructional strategies are judiciously employed to maximize students' active and successful engagement in relevant tasks. The ability to present clear explanations and offer accurate demonstrations contributes to learning. Effective teachers actively monitor their students' performance and are concerned about the quality of their efforts. Teachers are aware of, and capably respond to, the myriad events that occur within the instructional environment; this quality, "with-it-ness," is often described as "having eyes in the back of one's head." Evaluation skills are also important. Teachers must be able to observe and analyze student performance, focusing on the critical elements in relationship to the goal, with feedback reinforcing or modifying responses as necessary.

The communication of high expectations for each student is also important. Teachers should hold high expectations for both student learning and behavior. Positive expectations, including the belief that all students are capable of learning, are important in establishing a warm, nurturing classroom climate and a productive learning environment.[4]

The ability to motivate students to perform to their potential is the goal of every teacher. Skillful teachers use a variety of teaching techniques to stimulate interest in participation and seek creative techniques to involve students in the learning process. They also use appropriate reinforcement techniques to maintain student involvement and promote a high level of student effort. These may include checklists, contracts, award systems, and verbal and nonverbal feedback. Praise is used

BEGINNING PHYSICAL EDUCATION TEACHER STANDARDS: NATIONAL ASSOCIATION FOR SPORT AND PHYSICAL EDUCATION (NASPE) SELECTED STANDARDS

Standard 1. Content Knowledge. The teacher understands physical education content, disciplinary concepts, and tools of inquiry related to the development of a physically educated person.

Disposition 2. The teacher has enthusiasm for the importance of physical education as a means of developing a physically educated person.

Standard 2. Growth and Development. The teacher understands how individuals learn and develop, and can provide opportunities that support their physical, cognitive, social, and emotional development.

Knowledge 3. The teacher has knowledge of expected developmental progressions and ranges of individual variation and can identify levels of readiness.

Standard 6. Planning and Instruction. The teacher plans and implements a variety of developmentally appropriate instructional strategies to develop physically educated individuals.

Performance 10. The teacher creates short- and long-term plans that are linked to learner needs and performance, and adapts plans to ensure learner progress, motivation, and safety.

Standard 8. Reflection. The teacher is a reflective practitioner who evaluates the effects of his/her actions on others and seeks opportunities to grow professionally.

Disposition 1. The teacher is committed to ongoing self reflection, assessment, and learning.

Standard 9. Collaboration. The teacher fosters relationships between colleagues, parents/guardians, and community agencies to support learner's growth and well-being.

Performance 3. The teacher identifies and uses community resources to enhance physical activity opportunities.

NASPE: National standards for beginning physical education teachers, Reston, Va., 1995, AAHPERD.

practices in teaching physical education to young children. Although it was designed for school physical education, many of the guidelines presented are appropriate for physical education programs for all school levels and physical activity programs for people of all ages in community and commercial settings.

Selected guidelines modified to include all people and settings are presented in Table 11-1. As you read each guideline, first reflect on your own experiences in physical education classes and determine whether the practices you experienced were appropriate or inappropriate. Next, reread the guidelines and expand your thinking to conceptualize how these guidelines would apply to leaders (teachers) and participants in a variety of different physical activity programs. For example, what are the implications of these guidelines for the conduct of interscholastic sports? youth sport

programs? programs for the elderly? corporate fitness programs? cardiac rehabilitation programs? preschool motor development programs?

As professionals we can play a significant role in the nation's health by conducting programs to help participants acquire the skills, knowledge, and attitudes to incorporate physical activity into their lives. For us to contribute in a meaningful way, however, we must make sure our programs are of high quality and appropriate to the needs of the participants.

TEACHING RESPONSIBILITIES

Teachers in both school and nonschool settings perform a myriad of tasks every day. Prospective teachers need to be cognizant of their responsibilities. In addition to actually teaching, teachers perform many administrative and professionally thoughtfully; it is contingent on the correct performance, specific in its nature and intent, and sincere. Successful teachers continually update their lessons in an effort to meet students' needs and to make the material presented relevant and challenging to the students.

Effective teachers possess superior human relations skills. They listen to students and accept students as individuals, treating them as such. They strive to instill in each student a sense of self-worth. Effective teachers show concern for the well-being of each student in their classes and endeavor to provide students with opportunities that will enhance their self-confidence. The ability to establish and maintain rapport with students and staff and readiness to acknowledge one's own mistakes are also characteristics that many successful teachers possess. A sense of humor is a welcome attribute as well.

In summary, effective teachers are able to successfully utilize a variety of skills pertaining to organization, communication, instruction, motivation, and human relations. However, effective teaching requires more than these skills; it requires the ability to assess accurately the needs of the moment and to tailor these skills to the specific context and situation. Although many of these skills appear to be innate to certain individuals, all of them can be developed or improved by individuals who desire to become effective teachers.

Competencies for Beginning Physical Education Teachers

What competencies should beginning teachers possess? In 1995, the National Association for Sport and Physical Education (NASPE)[5] developed standards for beginning physical education teachers. The NASPE Content Standards (see Chapter 2) were closely considered in developing these standards. Nine standards were identified. The standards relate to competencies in the following areas:

♦ content knowledge
♦ growth and development
♦ diverse learners
♦ management and motivation
♦ communication

♦ planning and instruction
♦ learner assessment
♦ reflection
♦ collaboration

Associated with each standard are disposition knowledge, and performance competencies. Di positions are fundamental attitudes and belie about teaching that underlie the professional ar ethical basis for practice. Knowledge is the subje matter that a beginning teacher needs to kno and understand. Performance refers to the den onstrated outcomes or teaching skills that th teacher should exhibit or possess. Examples of th standards and sample dispositions, knowledge, an performance competencies are shown in the bo on page 394.

Developmentally appropriate physical activity experiences

Traditionally, the teaching of motor and spor skills has taken place in physical education programs and in athletic programs associated with the schools. However, in the past decade there has been a proliferation of programs to teach movement and sport skills outside of the school setting. Some examples are preschool and day care motor-development programs, community youth sport programs, exercise programs in senior citizen centers, recreational programs in community settings, private sport clubs, and corporate fitness programs. These programs encompass people of all ages and abilities.

Strong leadership and appropriate program design are important if these physical activity programs are to provide a positive experience for the participants and to achieve desired outcomes. How then should these programs be structured to enable the maximum amount of learning to occur and to provide an enjoyable experience for the participants? Perhaps some guidance can be gained from a recent document entitled "Developmentally Appropriate Physical Education Practices for Children," written by the Council on Physical Education for Children (COPEC), a unit of the National Association of Sport and Physical Education (NASPE), an association of AAHPERD.[6] This document outlines appropriate and inappropriate

TABLE 11-1

Developmentally Appropriate Physical Activity Program Practices

Program Component	Appropriate Practice	Inappropriate Practice
Curriculum	The physical activity curriculum has a scope and sequence that is based on goals and objectives that are appropriate for the participants. It includes a balance of activities designed to enhance the cognitive, motor, affective, and physical fitness development of each participant.	The physical activity curriculum lacks developed goals and objectives and is based primarily on the leader's interests, preferences, and background rather than those of the participants.
Development of movement concepts and basic skills	Participants are provided with frequent and meaningful age appropriate practice opportunities that enable individuals to develop a functional understanding of movement concepts (body awareness, space awareness, effort, and relationships), and build competence and confidence in their ability to perform a variety of motor skills (locomotor, nonlocomotor, and manipulative).	Individuals participate in a limited number of activities where the opportunity for them to develop basic concepts and motor skills is restricted.
Cognitive development	Physical activities are designed with both the physical and the cognitive development of participants in mind; leaders provide experiences that encourage individuals to question, integrate, analyze, communicate, apply cognitive concepts, gain a multicultural view of the world, and integrate physical activity experiences with their other life experiences.	Leaders fail to recognize and explore the unique roles of physical activities that allow individuals to learn to move while also moving to learn. Individuals do not receive opportunities to integrate their physical activity experiences with other experiences.
Affective development	Leaders intentionally design and teach activities that allow participants the opportunity to work together to improve their social and cooperation skills. These activities also contribute to the development of a positive self-concept. Leaders help all individuals experience and feel the satisfaction and joy that results from regular participation in physical activity	Leaders fail to intentionally enhance the affective development of individuals when activities are excluded that foster the development of cooperation and social skills. Leaders ignore opportunities to help individuals understand the emotions they feel as a result of participation in physical activity.
Concepts of fitness	Individuals participate in activities that are designed to help them understand and value the important concepts of physical fitness and the contribution they make to a healthy lifestyle.	Individuals are required to participate in physical fitness activities, but are not helped to understand the reasons why.

Adapted from: *Developmentally Appropriate Physical Education Practices for Children,* Council on Physical Education for Children, National Association for Sport and Physical Education, American Alliance for Health, Physical Education, Recreation, and Dance. Modified to reflect developmentally appropriate physical activity programs for people of all ages in a diversity of settings.

Continued.

TABLE 11-1—cont'd

Developmentally Appropriate Physical Activity Program Practices

Program Component	Appropriate Practice	Inappropriate Practice
Physical fitness tests	Ongoing fitness assessment is used as a part of the ongoing process of helping individuals understand, enjoy, improve, and/or maintain their physical health and well-being. Test results are shared privately with individuals as a tool for developing their physical fitness knowledge, understanding, and competence. Individuals are physically prepared for the fitness assessment tests.	Physical fitness tests are given infrequently, solely for the purpose that they are required. Individuals are required to complete a physical fitness test battery without understanding why they are performing the tests or the implications of their individual results as they apply to their future health and well-being. Individuals are required to take physical fitness tests without adequate conditioning.
Calisthenics	Appropriate exercises are taught for the specific purpose of improving the skill, coordination, and/or fitness levels of individuals. Individuals are taught exercises that keep the body in proper alignment, thereby allowing the muscles to lengthen without placing stress and strain on the surrounding joints, ligaments, and tendons (e.g., sitting toe touch).	Individuals perform standardized calisthenics with no specific purpose in mind (e.g., jumping jacks, windmills). Exercises are taught that compromise body alignment and place unnecessary stress on the joints and muscles (e.g., deep knee bends, ballistic or bouncing stretches).
Fitness	Fitness activities are used to help individuals increase personal physical fitness levels in a supportive, motivating, and progressive manner, thereby promoting positive lifetime fitness attitudes.	Physical fitness activities are used by leaders as punishment for individuals' misbehavior (e.g., individuals running laps or doing push-ups, because they are off-task or slow to respond to instruction or the leader wants to teach them a lesson).
Assessment	Leaders' decisions are based primarily on ongoing individual assessments of persons as they participate in physical activities (formative evaluation), and not on the basis of a single test score (summative evaluation). Assessment of individuals' physical progress and achievement is used to personalize instruction, plan the program, identify individuals with special needs, and evaluate program effectiveness.	Individuals are evaluated on the basis of fitness test scores or on a single physical skill test.
Regular involvement	Individuals participate on a regularly scheduled basis because they recognize that it is an important part of their life and essential to their health.	Individuals participate infrequently or fail to recognize the value and contribution of regular participation to their life and health.

TABLE 11-1—cont'd

Developmentally Appropriate Physical Activity Program Practices

Program Component	Appropriate Practice	Inappropriate Practice
Active participation	All individuals are involved in activities that allow them to remain continuously active. Classes are designed to meet an individual's need for active participation in all learning experiences.	Activity time is decreased because of waiting for a turn, insufficient equipment, or organization into large groups. Individuals are eliminated from activities with no chance to reenter the activity.
Activities	Activities are selected, designed, sequenced, and modified by teachers and/or individuals to maximize learning and enjoyment.	Activities are taught with no obvious purpose or goals, other than to keep individuals "busy, happy, and good."
Equity	All individuals have equal access to activities. All individuals are equally encouraged, supported, and socialized toward successful achievement in all realms of physical activities, regardless of race or sex. Statements by leaders support leadership opportunities and provide positive reinforcement in a variety of activities that may be considered equitable.	Individuals' opportunities are limited because of traditional roles (feminine or masculine) and stereotypes. Prejudice and discrimination reduce opportunities for equitable participation.
Success rate	Individuals are given the opportunity to practice their skills at high rates of success adjusted for their individual skill levels.	Individuals are asked to perform activities that are too easy or too hard, causing frustration, boredom, and/or misbehavior. All individuals are expected to perform to the same standard with no allowance for individual abilities and interests.
Time	Individuals are given the opportunity to participate daily at a scheduled time; the length of time is appropriate for the developmental level of the individual.	There is no provision for regular physical activity. Individuals' age and maturational levels are not taken into account when the physical activity program is developed.
Facilities	Individuals are provided an environment in which they have adequate space to move freely and safely.	Classes are held in spaces not free from obstructions where opportunities to move are restricted.
Equipment	Enough equipment is available so that each individual benefits from maximum participation. Equipment is appropriate to each individual's size, skill, and confidence level so that they are motivated to participate.	An insufficient amount of equipment is available for the number of individuals present. Equipment used is inappropriate and may hamper skill development or injure or intimidate individuals.

related tasks. Gensemer[7] groups the activities of teachers into three areas: instructional tasks, managerial tasks, and institutional tasks. Instructional tasks are responsibilities and activities that relate directly to teaching. These tasks include explaining and/or demonstrating how to perform a skill, describing how to execute a particular strategy in a game, evaluating students' performance, motivating students through the use of various techniques, and using questions to check students' comprehension of the material being presented to determine the clarity of the presentation and to elicit student input.

Managerial tasks are activities related to the administration of the class. In the school setting these activities may include taking attendance, dealing with discipline problems, and patrolling the locker room. In a nonschool setting such as a commercial health club or sports center, managerial responsibilities may include setting up and dismantling equipment, equipment repair, handing out towels, distributing workout record sheets, and recording individuals' progress.

Institutional tasks are activities related to the institution in which teaching occurs, that is, the school or organization for which the teacher works. In the school setting teachers may be expected to assume hall duty or lunchroom supervision, attend curriculum or departmental meetings, and conduct parent-teacher conferences. Many physical educators note that counseling students about matters that affect the development of their physical selves and advising students on personal problems occupy a great amount of their time, but the opportunity to be of service to students in this manner is rewarding. In the nonschool setting teachers may also perform institutional duties such as checking membership cards at the front desk, mailing promotional brochures to attract new members, and filling out a variety of reports. In some situations managerial and institutional responsibilities occupy more of a teacher's time than actual teaching.

Teachers have numerous professional responsibilities in addition to the responsibilities previously described. Teachers may conduct research in an

Locker room supervision is one of a teacher's managerial responsibilities.

effort to push back the frontiers of knowledge. Another professional responsibility is to interpret the worth of physical education and sport to the public. This requires that physical educators be well versed in the scientific foundations of the discipline so that they may accurately interpret the worth of physical education and sport to others. Physical educators need to be cognizant that the programs they conduct reflect the aims and the worth of the field. Physical educators symbolize their commitment to the profession by being role models for what they preach; they should exemplify a healthy, active lifestyle. Professionals need to take advantage of opportunities to speak to educators, the community, and civic and other groups about their field of endeavor.

Many physical educators may also have community responsibilities. These are usually engaged in voluntarily. However, the special qualifications and skills of physical educators make them a likely target for requests from community groups to assist with youth and other sport programs such as Little League or adult recreational programs. Physical educators should be interested in providing leadership for such community programs. By exercising a leadership role they can help ensure that such programs are organized and administered in the best interests of youths and adults. By their participation, physical educators are afforded an opportunity to interpret physical education and sport to the public in general. In doing so physical educators become respected and important leaders in the community and gain greater support for their program.

Teachers' responsibilities are not limited to teaching. They perform a wide variety of activities during the course of their workday. Managerial, administrative, institutional, and professional responsibilities are associated with teaching. The exact nature of these tasks may vary from setting to setting. Teaching opportunities in school and nonschool settings and with people of all ages will be discussed in the following section.

TEACHING CAREERS

If teaching is your career goal, there are many different opportunities for work. Traditionally, physical education teachers have worked in the school setting with children and youths. Today, however, there are teaching opportunities available in many other different settings and the wonderful opportunity to work with people of all ages.

Teaching in the School Setting

Teaching positions in the school setting are available in public and private school systems, higher education, and specialized schools. Public and private schools are organized according to various administrative patterns. The traditional grade configuration is elementary school, which is composed of kindergarten and first through eighth grade, and high school, which is composed of grades 9 through 12. Another pattern that is used is the elementary, junior high, and high school configuration (i.e., grades K to 6, 7 to 9, and 10 to 12). An increasingly common pattern incorporates the middle school; here the grade configuration becomes K to 5, 6 to 8, and 9 to 12.

The number of preschool programs in the United States is growing rapidly. Currently 4-year-olds are enrolled in public school programs in more than 30 states. Some schools even enroll 3-year-olds. The National Education Association (NEA) has recommended that states require public schools to offer early childhood education for all 3- and 4-year-olds by the year 2000.[8] The growth of preschool programs has created additional opportunities for physical educators to work with young children to develop motor skills and promote the development of a healthy lifestyle.

In higher education, professional opportunities include teaching in 2-year junior colleges or community colleges and 4-year colleges or universities. There are also teaching positions for those professionals who want to work with persons with disabilities and for those who aspire to instruct in a professional preparation program. Teaching opportunities also exist in specialized schools, such as vocational and technical schools, as well as in developmental centers.

Teaching in an elementary school

Physical education in an elementary school is emerging as the art and science of human

Young children like to test their abilities, such as balance, in a variety of environments.

movement. Quality elementary school programs and teachers seek to instill in children the why of movement, the how of movement, and the outcomes or physiological, psychological, and sociological results of movement. A primary objective of these programs is the sound development of movement skills and motor patterns that make up the movement repertoire of human beings.

Providing a quality physical education program for young children is critical. Participation in a quality program during these formative years will likely instill in the child a love for physical activity that may last a lifetime and a favorable attitude toward physical education. If the experience is less than positive, the youngster may come to hate physical education as well as physical activity, a feeling that could remain with him or her for life. Because of the close relationship between physical activity and health, this could have a significant impact on the quality of the child's life.

Movement experiences are recognized as educationally desirable in the early life of the child. This is the time when a solid movement foundation can

be developed, providing children with a base for future physical development and achievement in various forms of physical activity. Furthermore, it is through movement that children express themselves, are creative, develop self-image, and gain a better understanding of their physical selves. It is through such movement experiences that young children explore, develop, and grow in a meaningful manner.

In the primary grades K to 3, great emphasis is placed on learning fundamental motor skills such as running, jumping, climbing, throwing, catching, kicking, and striking. (See Chapter 4.) Children participate in guided discovery and problem-solving activities focused on movement concepts, including body awareness, spatial awareness, qualities of movement, and relationships. Conceptually based programs further enhance the child's understanding of movement. Perceptual-motor activities help children to develop such necessary skills as eye-hand and eye-foot coordination, laterality and directionality, and tracking of an object. The primary grade curriculum is concerned with developing within each child a positive self-image as a mover. Attention also should be given to developing desirable social skills, such as working with others. Individualized learning, in which students learn at their own pace, is compatible with problem solving, guided discovery, and a creative approach to learning for primary school children.

In the upper elementary school grades, the physical education curriculum focuses on refining fundamental motor skills and applying these skills to the development of sport-related skills. During this time all children should be given the opportunity to participate in a wide range of sport and physical activities rather than be encouraged to specialize in a few selected sports. A school curriculum that offers soccer and football in the fall, basketball and volleyball in the winter, and softball and track in the spring is not providing the diversity of activities necessary to ensure optimum skill acquisition at these grade levels. In addition to being exposed to traditional team sports, students at this level should receive instruction in dance, gymnastics, individual activities (e.g., track and, whenever possible, aquatics). Acquisition of knowledge relative to physical education and the development of qualities of good sportsmanship, leadership, and fellowship should be encouraged.

Specific state requirements should be considered in structuring the elementary school physical education program. Although there is no national curriculum, elementary school physical educators may find the guidelines developed by the Council on Physical Education for Children (COPEC), a substructure of NASPE of AAHPERD, helpful in designing and implementing their programs. COPEC recommends that a quality instructional program provide opportunities for each child to develop motor skills and efficient movement patterns, attain a high level of fitness, learn to communicate through movement, acquire self-understanding, interact socially, and achieve desired psychomotor, cognitive, and affective outcomes. COPEC guidelines also suggest that elementary school children participate in a quality physical education program for a minimum of 150 minutes per week.

Many reasons are given by physical educators for preferring teaching in the elementary schools.

At this level students typically are motivated, eager, enthusiastic, and take pride in their progress. Children at this age enjoy being active and have boundless energy. Many physical educators enjoy the challenge of working with children during their most impressionable and formative years. The rapid, visible skill improvement typical of elementary school students is rewarding and motivating to the teacher.

Teaching in a middle school or junior high school

Teaching students enrolled in a middle school or junior high school presents a unique series of challenges to physical educators. Students are in a period of their development that is fraught with physical, social, and emotional changes. Because of the anatomical and physiological characteristics of this age group, activities must be selected with care. Students at this level are in a period of rapid growth that causes them difficulty in coordinating their actions and often results in awkwardness and excessive fatigue. Students are faced with the task of coping with the myriad changes associated with puberty, including the development of secondary sex characteristics. Social and emotional changes are also experienced. The desire to be independent and the influence of peers are particularly strong. Physical educators need to be aware of and sensitive to the many changes students are experiencing. Students may often seek out the physical education teacher for guidance and support during this time of transition.

At this level physical education programs should include a balance between individual and dual sport activities such as aquatics and tennis and team sport activities such as soccer and basketball. Dance, gymnastics, and fitness activities also should be an integral part of the curriculum. It is important to build on the skills and positive experiences of the elementary school level. Those students who have not progressed as rapidly as their peers in motor development should receive special attention to help them improve their skills. Students' knowledge of physical education should be further expanded and opportunities to apply this knowledge provided. During these school years,

These students at Lyons Township High School, in LaGrange, Illinois, are practicing outdoor survival skills.

students begin to specialize in certain physical activities and actively pursue those interests.

NASPE's Committee on Middle School Physical Education advocates that middle school physical education programs provide opportunities for each student to engage in activities that promote motor skill and fitness development throughout life. Programs at this level should advance knowledge of physical education while enhancing social and emotional development through increased self-responsibility and self-direction. Within the physical education program, students should be grouped by interest and ability, and careful attention should be given to avoiding sex-role discrimination and stereotyping. A minimum of 250 min-

utes of physical education per week, distributed over at least 3 days, is recommended. Additional opportunities for students to participate in physical activity experiences should be provided through intramural programs, club activities, and, when appropriate, interscholastic sports.

Teaching in a high school

At the high school level, students exhibit increased physical, mental, social, and emotional maturity. This is the time of transition from adolescence to adulthood.

One of the primary goals for physical educators teaching at the secondary school level is to socialize students into the role of participants in physical activities suited to their needs and interests. Pangrazi and Darst[9] state that "the most important goal of a secondary physical education program should be to help youngsters incorporate some form of physical activity into their lifestyle." This means that teachers must design and implement physical education programs in such a manner that the students' attitudes, knowledge, and skills are developed with a view to realizing this objective. Pangrazi and Darst[9] contend that the ultimate measure of a successful high school physical education program is the "number of students who incorporate physical activities such as exercise, sport, dance, and outdoor adventure activities into their lifestyles."

The curriculum is generally oriented toward lifetime sports, although team sports also may be popular. It is critical that the physical educator take into consideration the interests and needs of the students in planning the curriculum. During this time students should have the opportunity to develop sufficient skills so that when they leave school they will have the desire and the knowledge to participate in physical activities and sport successfully and enjoyably. Because many students do not continue on to college, it is essential that they acquire the competencies and interest before they leave high school.

NASPE's Secondary School Physical Education Council recommends that programs at the high school level focus on refining skills in a wide range of activities and on developing advanced skills in

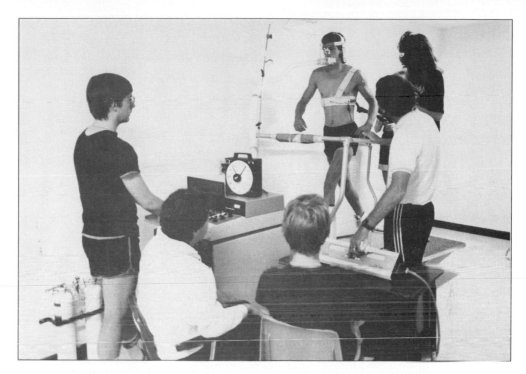

These students at Rock Springs High School, in Wyoming, are conducting an exercise test under their teacher's supervision.

lifetime activities personally selected by the student. Students should learn how to develop personal programs to gain and maintain optimal levels of fitness throughout their lifetime. Knowledge of the scientific principles related to physical education, self-direction in the conduct of individual physical activity programs, and an appreciation of the role of physical activity and sport in society are also outcomes of a quality secondary school physical education program. It is recommended that daily physical education be provided for all students. The length of the class period, the size of the class, and the quality standards used for credit should be comparable with those used for other subject areas within the curriculum.

Many high school physical education programs, while required of the students, offer students the opportunity to select units in which they want to participate. An increasing number of schools have expanded their course offerings by using off-campus community facilities such as a golf course,

ice rink, aquatics center, or ski slope. The trend is toward providing students with increased knowledge and understanding of physical education concepts. This is often accomplished by offering mini-courses on topics of interest, such as fitness or weight management, or by the integration of concepts, such as those presented in Basic Stuff, into regular activity classes. Intramurals, interscholastic sports, and sport clubs offer students additional opportunities to participate in sport, develop expertise, and realize other desirable outcomes.

Teaching physical education in higher education

Prospective physical education teachers may also take advantage of opportunities to teach in higher education. Often a master's degree in an area of physical education is a prerequisite to obtaining a job at this level. In some institutions coaching responsibilities may be associated with teaching

A physical education instructor directs students in an exercise class at Ithaca College.

positions, whereas in other institutions coaches carry no teaching responsibilities.

Opportunities may be found to teach at 2-year community colleges or at 4-year colleges or universities. While typical college students are 18 to 22 years of age, there is a trend toward older individuals returning to college.

Physical educators like to teach at this level for several reasons. The students are more mature, and working on a college campus is enjoyable. Freedom to structure classes is greater, and some individuals believe that more prestige is associated with teaching at the college level.

The status of general or basic instruction physical education programs* in colleges and universities in the United States has changed in recent years. At one time many colleges and universities required all students to take a physical education course each semester—for example, one course a semester for two years. Today physical education at this level is usually voluntary, thus placing responsibility on the physical education department to offer courses that are appealing to students. Because of this need, curriculums at this level tend to be more flexible and to change more often in response to students' interests and needs.

Lifetime sports and recreational activities are emphasized at this level, including such activities as tennis, golf, self-defense, aerobic dance, and personal fitness; outdoor pursuits such as canoeing, camping, and rock climbing; and aquatic activities. Students may have the opportunity to enroll in theory courses in which they study the why of physical education. Class topics may include health concepts, cardiovascular fitness, principles of exercise, biomechanical principles, and development of personalized fitness programs. Some colleges offer courses called "Wellness for Life" or

* These programs are designed to serve all students on campus and are not to be confused with programs designed to educate prospective physical education and sport majors; those programs are referred to as professional preparation programs.

"Fitness for Life." These courses combine theoretical information with laboratory experiences designed to help students acquire the knowledge and skills necessary to lead a healthy lifestyle.

Sport clubs provide interested participants an opportunity for social group experiences and enjoyment of a particular sport activity. Intramurals and intercollegiate sports play an important part in college and university physical education programs. They offer students additional opportunities for participation according to their abilities, needs, and interests.

Teaching physical education and sport in professional preparation programs

Professional preparation programs are designed to prepare students for careers in physical education and sport. Physical educators who aspire to teach at the college and university level and are interested in shaping the direction of their field by preparing future leaders have many opportunities to render this valuable service in the more than 700 institutions that offer such programs.

The qualifications for teaching in professional preparation programs include advanced degrees, an acceptable academic record, an interest in and understanding of college students, a broad view of educational problems, and, many times, previous experience at elementary or secondary school levels. The college teacher must be particularly well versed and highly competent in the field.

A professor in a professional preparation program may teach theory courses in the subdisciplines and related areas such as history and philosophy of physical education, tests and measurements, motor control, motor learning, motor development, biomechanics, exercise physiology, curriculum and methods, organization and administration, sociology of sport, sport psychology, and adapted physical education. These individuals typically possess doctorate degrees in their areas of expertise. Individuals who aspire to teach in professional preparation programs may also teach professional activity and skills courses, as well as courses in coaching methods. These individuals usually possess a high degree of skill in their areas of expertise. Professionals teaching activity and skills courses possess master's degrees, and some individuals may have earned doctorate degrees.

In addition to their teaching responsibilities, teachers are expected to conduct research, participate on department and college or university committees, and advise and counsel students. These teachers are expected to write for professional publications, perform community service, consult, and participate in the work of professional organizations.

The services rendered by physical educators in professional preparation programs can be rewarding. By providing experiences that will help develop desirable qualities, competencies, and attributes in students preparing to become leaders in the field and by doing an outstanding job in this training experience, a teacher's work will live on forever in the lives of students and other leaders of future generations.

Teaching adapted physical activity

Teaching physical education to students with disabilities is another career opportunity. Students with disabilities include those with mental and emotional impairments, physical challenges such as cerebral palsy or amputation, vision and hearing problems, speech disorders, the learning disabled, and other health impairments such as asthma,

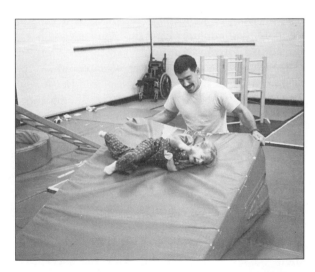

Adapted physical education focuses on modifying activities to meet students' needs.

heart problems, and cancer. Adapted physical activity focuses on adapting or modifying physical activity to meet the needs of students. "Good" physical education is adapted physical education, for the heart of quality physical education and adapted physical activity is education that is developmentally appropriate for the needs of the individual student. With the advent of P.L. 94-142 and other legislation, students with disabilities have the opportunity to participate in physical education.

By law, each identified student with a disability must have an Individualized Education Plan, or IEP. Physical education is mandated by law to be included in each student's educational program. Physical education teachers have the opportunity to participate in the design of the individual plan.

There are several approaches to the inclusion of children with disabilities into the educational setting, including physical education. The Least Restrictive Environment approach places students with disabilities in an educational setting that matches the students' abilities and provides as much freedom as possible. For some students, this may be a placement, with or without an aide, in a "regular" physical education class with peers who are not disabled or it may be placement into a special class or adapted physical education. These classes are generally smaller and contain only children with special needs. The placement of students with disabilities into the regular class is referred to as "mainstreaming."

In the 1990s some educators have advocated that students with disabilities be placed in the regular class setting, including physical education. This inclusive approach insists that all students, regardless of their disability and its severity, be placed in the "regular" classroom in the neighborhood school. Supplemental aids and services are used to help students with disabilities achieve success in the regular class setting. There is considerable debate within many communities about the use of inclusion. Many regular teachers do not feel qualified to include children with special needs in their classes. They feel they lack the specialized training to provide them with a quality educational experience.

Physical education teachers may render many different services to individuals with disabilities. Some schools or school districts have an adapted physical education specialist who provides direct services to individuals with disabilities. In other settings the adapted physical educator serves as a consultant to help other teachers provide needed services.

All physical education teachers should be prepared to work with students with disabilities. Physical educators will be involved in the writing of IEPs. These plans may focus on helping students to correct physical conditions that can be improved with exercise, assisting each student to achieve the highest level of physical fitness within his or her capabilities, aiding the student to identify physical activities and sports suited to his or her abilities and interests, and providing each student with positive experiences conducive to the development of a healthy self-concept.

Prospective physical education teachers interested in working with individuals with disabilities should prepare for this opportunity by taking additional course work in the area of adapted physical activity and special education. Try to obtain practical experience working with individuals with disabilities as part of your preparation for a physical education career.

Physical education teachers can also become certified as adapted physical educators. The Adapted Physical Education National Standards Project was designed to ensure that physical education for students with disabilities is provided by qualified physical educators. As part of this project, national standards were developed and a certification examination was designed to measure knowledge of these standards. The first exam was given in May 1997. More than 200 individuals became Certified Adapted Physical Educators during the first administration.

Physical educators interested in taking the certification examination must demonstrate that they have a bachelors degree in physical education, 200 hours of documented practicum experience in adapted physical education, and have successfully completed at least one 3-credit-hour survey course in adapted physical education. They should also study the Adapted Physical Education National Standards to make sure that they have the broad-based knowledge of physical education required of adapted physical education specialists. Teachers who pass the exam are certified for 7 years and can use the acronym C.A.P.E. (Certified Adapted Physical Educator) after their name. They are listed in the National Registry of Certified Adapted Physical Educators that is distributed to each state education department. They also receive 1 year free membership in the National Consortium for Physical Education and Recreation for Individuals with Disabilities (NCPERID).

Currently there are almost 50 million persons in the United States with disabilities. A majority of those who are school aged are receiving their education in regular educational settings. It is important that all people preparing to teach physical education be able to teach individuals with special needs.

Teaching physical education in special-interest schools

In addition to the students enrolled in public and private schools that serve many children and youth in the United States, there are students enrolled in specialized schools. These include trade and vocational schools, preschools, and schools for men and women who are primarily interested in adult education.

Many schools exist to prepare students for careers in certain trades, crafts, and other vocations. These schools may be affiliated with school districts or may be privately owned and operated. They prepare students for careers in technical fields such as computer repairs or health-service fields such as dental assisting. Some of these schools offer some type of physical education program for their students that is usually similar to those discussed under secondary schools.

As observed earlier, nationwide the number of preschool and early childhood programs is growing at a rapid rate. Many states have 4-year-olds in their public school programs, and some schools are enrolling 3-year-olds. The number of early childhood programs will continue to grow in the future. The importance of providing quality, meaningful experiences to young children is well documented. Health education, play, vigorous physical activity, and opportunities in the arts can make important contributions to the development of these young children. Children who have developmental delays may greatly benefit from perceptual-motor programs. Physical educators who desire to work with very young children can help them to develop motor skills that are the foundation to a lifetime of enjoyable physical activity. Also, through carefully designed movement experiences, children can learn to move and move to learn across a diversity of curricular areas.

Adult education is also thriving throughout the country. Programs are being established in most communities that provide experiences for men and women who desire to enrich their lives. These experiences cover the gamut of educational activities, including English, foreign languages, music, art, and word processing. Courses are also offered in sport skills such as golf and tennis, and recreational sport opportunities are provided. Interest is shown not only in developing fitness but also in learning about the components of fitness and the role of fitness in the attainment of optimal well-being.

● ● ●

A diversity of opportunities exist for individuals interested in teaching in the school setting. These opportunities involve teaching people of all ages. Many opportunities also can be found for the physical educator who is interested in working overseas. Teacher exchange programs and the Peace Corps offer the opportunity to teach in elementary and secondary schools, as well as colleges and universities, in other countries. The United States Armed Forces also operates elementary and secondary schools on overseas bases for students of personnel; it is not necessary to be a member of the military to teach in these schools. Job possibilities are numerous for the prospective physical education teacher who actively seeks a position teaching in the schools.

Teaching in Nonschool Settings

Several options are available for physical educators who desire to teach, but not in the school setting. The growth of interest in sport by people of all ages has stimulated the growth of these other teaching avenues. Teaching opportunities may be found today in commercial sport clubs, community recreational and sport programs, resorts, the Armed Forces, senior citizen and retirement centers, and correctional institutions.

The requirements for employment in these positions, working conditions, salaries, and other benefits vary widely. Some of these teaching positions require a high level of expertise in a particular sport, whereas others require individuals able to teach a diversity of activities. Working hours vary a great deal as well. For some positions, hours are often dictated by the times clients or students are available. If one is working with youths, hours are likely to be after school and on the weekends. If one is working with adults, hours tend to be on the weekends and in the evenings. Daytime work is also available, however. These positions may pay on an hourly basis, have a set salary (which can vary from $10,000 to $25,000 a year or more), or may pay based on the number of students taught. Benefits may vary from none to complete medical, dental, and life insurance plans.

Some teaching positions in nonschool settings require that individuals assume other responsibilities as well. These may include public relations work, soliciting memberships, record keeping, and equipment and facility maintenance.

Some work may be seasonal in nature, depending on the climate and/or type of facility. For example, if you were a teacher and/or director of aquatics at an outdoor facility in the northeastern United States, your employment would probably last from June to September; working at an indoor facility in the Northeast would likely result in a year-round position. In the Southwest, the same job might be year round, regardless of the type of facility.

Because these jobs in essence require teaching skills, many physical educators who desire to teach in the nonschool setting also complete the requirements for teaching certification. By doing so, they increase their range of job opportunities. Other physical educators, having prepared for teaching in the schools, look to these other avenues of employment when they are unable to find a teaching position suited to their needs and interests or as a means of part-time and summer employment. Many employers hiring physical

Physical educators may find teaching and coaching opportunities outside the school setting. This instructor, for example, teaches in a preschool gymnastics program.

educators to fill these positions also view favorably the credentials of those applicants able to list a teaching certificate on their resume. For some positions special certificates may be required, such as certification by the Professional Golfers' Association (PGA) or Ladies Professional Golfers' Association (LPGA) as a golf professional.

The physical educator should also understand why adults and youths seek instruction. Adults seek instruction at these organizations for many reasons. First, they may not have had instruction in the activity or activities during their youth in their physical education classes. Second, they may seek instruction for their own personal growth and pleasure. Instruction may be sought for social reasons, such as the desire to be able to participate in specific activities with friends and family. For example, some adults may seek instruction in golf to be able to successfully participate with business associates in this accepted social activity. The desire to improve and refine one's performance by seeking instruction from a professional is often cited as the reason for enrolling in instructional classes.

Youths enroll in these organizational programs and classes for many of the same reasons as adults. Additionally, youths may enroll in certain activity classes because instruction or interscholastic competition in that activity is not offered in their school. Youths desiring to develop more advanced skills such as in gymnastics or to compete in certain sport activities such as swimming may find these organizations offer experiences that meet their needs. Youths and their parents may seek expert instruction because of aspirations to be a professional player such as in golf and tennis or because of the desire to successfully compete for a college scholarship in certain sport areas; they may find nonschool instructional opportunities essential to the realization of these goals.

Teaching in commercial sport clubs

In recent years the number of commercial sport clubs and facilities has grown tremendously. Tennis and racquetball clubs, gymnastics clubs, swimming clubs, country clubs offering golf and tennis, karate and judo schools, and bowling establishments are examples of commercial sport enterprises.

Since commercial sport clubs usually focus on a particular sport, physical educators who desire to teach in such an organization should possess a high level of expertise in a particular sport. In many instances this expertise can be gained through participation in intercollegiate athletics. Many physical educators also have gained expertise by participating in private clubs such as gymnastic clubs during their youth and continuing their participation throughout their college years. Teaching responsibilities may include private lessons as well as group lessons. There may be the opportunity to coach high-level performers as well. Additional responsibilities may include setting up tournaments such as in a tennis and racquetball club, selling sport equipment and apparel such as in a golf pro shop at a country club, or transporting individuals to competitions such as in a swimming club or a gymnastics club. Many commercial clubs also expect the teachers to assume managerial responsibilities at times.

Employers, in addition to requiring a high level of expertise as a condition of employment, may also require certification. In the aquatics area, certification as a Water Safety Instructor, Lifeguard Instructor, and in pool management may be required. Certification as a golf professional such as through the PGA and LPGA may be necessary. Where not required, certificates may enhance one's employment opportunities.

Teaching in youth and community organizations

The Young Men's Hebrew Association (YMHA), the Young Women's Hebrew Association (YWHA), the YMCA, and the YWCA and similar organizations such as Boys' Clubs, Girls' Clubs, and the 4-H Clubs serve both the youth and adult populations in the community. Religious training was originally the main purpose of many of these organizations. However, sport and fitness are now an important part of their programs. Included in the programs are classes in various physical activities; athletic leagues for industry employees, youth, and adults; and young people's groups. The cost of financing such organizations is usually met through membership dues, community and business contributions, and private contributions.

These organizations are designed to improve participants socially, physically, morally, mentally, and spiritually through their programs of physical activity. Usually these organizations employ physical educators and recreation specialists to teach a wide diversity of activities. In many communities, events are scheduled from early morning to late at night—early bird swim at 6 A.M. for business and professional people before work and late hour racquetball games. Besides instructing clients in sport activities, the physical educator may have the opportunity to serve as a coach of a team. Many youth clubs offer young people and adults the opportunity to compete on athletic teams at the local, state, regional, and national levels. Additional responsibilities include developing health and fitness programs, facility and budget management, and supervising personnel. Many centers, in addition to physical activities, offer programs in exercise and fitness evaluation, cardiac rehabilitation, and health counseling. A background in these areas as well as in teaching would be helpful in seeking employment. Although salaries vary, they are comparable to public school teaching positions.

Although the YMCA, YWCA, YMHA, and YWHA certainly constitute widespread organizations, they are not the only community organizations offering employment opportunities to the physical educator. Other opportunities include working for town and city recreation departments, community centers, youth centers similar in nature to the YMCA/YWCA, and playgrounds. Some of these opportunities may be seasonal, generally available in the summer, but the trend is for more and more programs to operate year round. These programs provide instruction in physical activities for people of all ages, recreational sport leagues, and recreational activities. In addition to teaching and coaching for these organizations, other job possibilities include the supervision of personnel and program development.

Teaching in centers for the elderly

In recent years elderly persons have received considerable attention from the U.S. government and other agencies. The elderly comprise about 11% of the population, and this percentage is increasing yearly. There is also concern for the physical fitness of elderly persons and their need to be physically active to maintain a state of optimum health. In recent years programs for elderly persons offered by recreational agencies, retirement centers, and health care facilities have expanded in the number and types of offerings.

Many of these programs offer instruction in physical activities suited to the abilities and interests of the participants. Exercise is frequently included in these programs. In addition to the physical benefits, physical education programs provide the opportunity for socialization. Physical educators interested in working in such programs may benefit from classes in adapted physical education, sociology, psychology, and gerontology.

Teaching in resorts

The increase in leisure time has stimulated an increase in the travel and tourism industry. The number of resorts has grown, and many resorts offer instruction in various physical activities as part of their programs. Activities offered may include sailing, scuba, tennis, golf, swimming, water skiing, and snow skiing. Expertise in specific sport areas is required for employment in these resorts. Instruction is usually done in small groups or in private lessons. Additionally, responsibilities may include managerial activities and directing social activities. Pay varies, and depending on the location of the resort, work may be seasonal, although many resorts operate year round. Working in a resort offers many desirable side benefits, such as working in an attractive location and usually lush surroundings, and the opportunity to work with changing clientele.

Teaching in the military

The Army, Navy, Marines, Air Force, Coast Guard, and National Guard have extensive physical activity programs that aid in keeping service personnel in good physical and mental condition. In addition to the personnel used to direct the fitness and physical training programs of these organizations, physical educators are needed to instruct service personnel in physical activities and sport for use in their leisure time. The military

Some physical education instructors supervise physical activity for elderly people, such as this resident of the Westwood Home, in Clinton, Missouri.

sponsors extensive recreational programs on its bases, and qualified personnel are needed to direct these programs. Coaches are also needed to assist military athletes in their training for competitions throughout the world. The military also sponsors schools for children of military personnel. Physical educators who desire to teach overseas may wish to consider employment in these schools. For many of these positions physical educators do not have to belong to the military. Physical educators interested in further information about these opportunities should talk to their local military recruiter.

TEACHING CERTIFICATION

Each state has established minimum requirements that must be met by prospective teachers before they become legally certified to teach. The certification of teachers protects schoolchildren by ensuring a high level of teaching competency and the employment of qualified personnel. Many states require that candidates for teaching positions take a standardized test, such as PRAXIS. These standardized tests usually consist of a core battery that tests general knowledge (e.g., knowledge pertaining to art, literature, history, science), communication skills, and professional knowledge. Some states require that students take an additional test in their speciality area, such as physical education. Different states have different passing score requirements for the standardized tests. Some states have their own certification examinations. For example, New York requires teachers take the New York Teacher Certification Examinations.

Since certification procedures and requirements vary from state to state, prospective teachers should obtain the exact requirements from their college or university or by directly contacting the state education department. Because of variations in state requirements, a certificate to teach in one state is not necessarily valid in another state. However, reciprocity among states in a region is increasingly common. Sometimes, where there is not reciprocity, prospective teachers can become certified in another state by merely taking a few additional required courses.

Teaching certificates are required to teach in the public schools. Some private schools may not require their teachers to possess a certificate. Teaching certificates are also an asset to individuals desiring to teach in nonschool settings. Prospective employers may be impressed by candidates who have fulfilled the necessary requirements for certification.

COACHING CAREERS

Many prospective physical educators aspire to a career as a coach. Because a teaching certificate is required by many states to coach, many aspiring coaches enroll in a program of study leading to a teaching certificate in physical education. Some of these prospective coaches seek a dual career as a teacher and a coach, whereas others desire solely to coach and view a teaching career as a means to attain their ultimate ambition.

Within the last decade, coaching opportunities have increased tremendously. The passage of Title IX legislation promoted the growth of interscholastic and intercollegiate competition for girls and women. The increased interest in sport by people of all ages also served as a stimulus to increase opportunities in competitive athletics.

As with teaching, coaching opportunities today exist in both the school and nonschool setting. In the school setting at the interscholastic level, coaches work with middle school, junior high school, and high school athletes. Intercollegiate coaching opportunities are found in 2-year community colleges as well as 4-year colleges and universities.

Outside of the school settings there are many different coaching opportunities. Some young people aspire to coach at the professional level. An increasing number of coaching opportunities are available in commercial or private clubs, such as coaching elite gymnasts or young tennis professionals. Community-based programs offer a multitude of coaching opportunities.

In the past two decades, participation in sport by older adults and people with disabilities have increased. For example, in 1997 more than 10,000 world-class senior athletes participated in the U.S. National Senior Sports Classic IV—the Senior Olympics. This is one of the premier competitions for athletes age 50 and over. The Special Olympics for individuals with mental retardation, the Paralympics, and the Games for the Deaf are attracting record number of participants. Coaching opportunities within these populations are increasing as these athletes strive to be their best.

Teaching responsibilities may be associated with coaching. At the interscholastic level it is expected that coaches will teach classes in the school; often coaches teach physical education. At the collegiate level some coaches are hired solely to coach and have no teaching responsibilities. At other higher education institutions coaches may have teaching

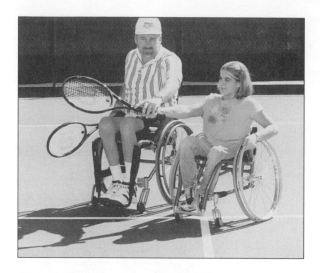

More and more people with disabilities are participating in sports and taking an active role in coaching. Helping to lead the way is Brad Parks, founder of the National Foundation for Wheelchair Tennis.

responsibilities in the general physical education program or in the professional preparation program. Administrative responsibilities also may be associated with coaching.

Choosing a Coaching Career

Individuals aspire to a coaching career for many reasons: their love for the sport, their own previous involvement on athletic teams, and the enjoyment they derived from participation. The desire to continue this involvement and association with athletics, perhaps to share some of what one has learned through athletics, is a strong motivating factor in selecting a coaching career. Individuals may choose to coach because of the profound influence one of their coaches had on their lives. Having a coach who was a positive role model and a desire to emulate this individual can influence one's decision to pursue a coaching career.

Many choose to coach because of their love of children. The opportunity to work with highly skilled and motivated individuals is often cited as a reason for coaching. Many coaches enter the profession because of their belief that participation in athletics can be a positive experience; they are committed to providing opportunities by which young people can develop to their fullest potential, both as athletes and as individuals.

Coaching is a highly visible occupation. Coaches may have a great deal of influence and power within both the institution and the community. The excitement, attention, influence, and recognition associated with coaching make it an attractive career choice.

What Are the Benefits and Drawbacks of Coaching?

Like teaching, a coaching career has both advantages and disadvantages. Many intrinsic rewards are associated with coaching. The opportunity to work with athletes and strive side by side with them to achieve their fullest potential, the excitement of winning and the satisfaction associated with giving the best of oneself, and the respect accorded to a coach are some of the intrinsic benefits of coaching.

There are several drawbacks associated with coaching. The hours are often long and arduous. The practice hours and the hours spent coaching during a competition are the most visible indications of the amount of time involved in coaching. Untold hours may be spent in preparing practices, reviewing the results of games and planning for the next encounter, counseling athletes, performing public relations work, and, at the collegiate level, recruiting.

Salaries vary greatly, depending on the level coached, the sport coached, and the coach's position as head or assistant coach. Salaries at the high school level can range from a small stipend to a few thousand dollars, whereas coaches at the collegiate and professional levels may have contracts worth hundreds of thousands of dollars.

A high turnover rate is associated with coaching. Unlike teaching, coaches are often placed under tremendous pressure to achieve—to have a winning season. Many coaches are fired because of a lackluster win/loss record or for having a poor working relationship with the administration or alumni. Other coaches choose to leave the profession voluntarily, overwhelmed by the pressures and exhausted by the demands, suffering from burnout, disenchanted with the profession, or desirous of a career change.

Teaching and Coaching

Since coaching is in essence teaching, the qualities that exemplify good teachers—organizational, communication, human relations, instructional, and motivational skills—may also be characteristics of effective coaches. Coaches must be able to organize their practices to provide maximum opportunities for all players to learn the skills and strategies essential for play. They must be actively engaged in monitoring the efforts of their athletes. They must be able to communicate what is to be learned in a clear manner and provide athletes with appropriate feedback to improve their performances. Coaches must instill in each athlete a feeling of self-worth and self-confidence, and be able to motivate all players to put forth their utmost effort to achieve their goals.

Many qualities characterize the outstanding coach. First, this person has the ability to teach the fundamentals and strategies of the sport: he or she must be a good teacher. Second, the coach understands the player: how a person functions at a particular level of development, with a full appreciation for skeletal growth, muscular development, and physical and emotional limitations. Third, he or she understands the game coached. Thorough knowledge of techniques, rules, and so on is basic. Fourth, the coach is a model for the players, a person of strong character. Patience, understanding, kindness, honesty, sportsmanship, sense of right and wrong, courage, cheerfulness, affection, humor, energy, and enthusiasm are imperative.

Although coaching is similar in nature to teaching, there are some dissimilarities. Both teachers and coaches are engaged in instructional activities and both must provide opportunities for the learners—students and athletes—to attain the skills and knowledge presented. However, coaches must have the expertise to teach their athletes more advanced skills and are held much more accountable for their athletes' learning than teachers are for their students. The caliber of a coach's instruction is scrutinized by both the administration and the public. If the coach is deemed inadequate in the preparation of the athletes or their learning by the often used standard of the win/loss record, then the coach may be dismissed. Teachers, on the other hand, have less pressure and less accountability for their students' learning, and even if their success rate is not high they will most likely be allowed to retain their position. The coach must work in a pressure-filled arena, whereas the teacher works in a less stressful environment.

Teachers must work with a diversity of skill levels and interests within their classes. Students may be mandated to take "gym" class and may be difficult to motivate. In contrast, coaches work with highly skilled athletes who often possess a high level of commitment to their sport. Their decision to participate is voluntary, and they may be united in their effort toward a common goal. Thus, although there are some similarities between teaching and coaching, there are some striking differences.

Coaching Responsibilities

Many responsibilities are associated with coaching. As in teaching, these responsibilities may be classified as instructional, managerial, and institutional in nature.

The coach's instructional responsibilities include conducting practice and coaching during the game. Although the coach is working with highly skilled athletes, the coach must be a good teacher to instruct the athletes in the more advanced skills and strategies necessary to perform at this level. During practices and games the coach must motivate the athletes to put forth their best effort so that their optimal level of performance can be achieved. In many cases these instructional responsibilities may be the least time consuming of all the coach's responsibilities.

Many coaches spend untold hours in evaluating practices and the results of competitions, and then using this information to plan for forthcoming practices and competitions. For those coaches

Coaches spend countless hours preparing for games and practices.

fortunate enough to have assistant coaches, time must be spent with them reviewing this information and delegating responsibilities for future practices and games. Team managers may relieve the coach of many of the necessary but time-consuming managerial tasks such as dealing with equipment or recording statistics. Additionally, the coach must take care of the necessary public relations functions such as calling in contest results, giving interviews, and speaking in front of groups. Where allowed, recruiting occupies a tremendous amount of time. Phoning prospective athletes, arranging for campus meetings, talking with parents, and scouting contests for potential athletes adds many hours to the day.

The institutional responsibilities are many as well. Interscholastic coaches are expected to take part in many school activities in addition to their teaching responsibilities. Intercollegiate coaches may be expected to attend athletic department meetings or represent the institution on a community committee.

Many other responsibilities and expectations are associated with coaching. Coaches occupy highly visible positions in their institution. In institutions of higher education it is not uncommon for more students to recognize the face of the football or basketball coach than the face of the college president. The coach is expected to reflect a positive image and exemplify the values associated with sport. The actions of the coach as the team wins or loses will influence the public's opinion of the sport program. Establishing and maintaining positive relationships with the community, alumni, and parents is often seen as vital to a coach's success in generating support for the athletic program. Because of their influence and visibility, coaches may be sought after to take an active part in community and civic affairs. They may be called on to train volunteer coaches for community recreational and sport programs or to spearhead a fund-raising drive for United Way.

Many other duties are incumbent on the coach by virtue of his or her position. The coach, because of the close relationship that develops from the many hours of working with his or her athletes toward a common goal, often undertakes the role

of counselor with athletes or assumes the role of a surrogate parent. Athletes turn to their coach for advice about myriad problems. Athletes may have problems associated with their athletic performance or financial, academic, and/or personal concerns. Because of their positions as leaders, coaches are viewed as role models. They are expected to exemplify the highest standards of conduct and are under pressure to live up to these expectations.

Coaches must fulfill many professional responsibilities. Coaches must attend sport and rules clinics so that they are aware of the current trends and latest rule changes in the sport. They are often active in professional organizations related to the sport they coach as well as professional organizations such as AAHPERD. They may be called on to serve as clinicians at some of these groups' meetings or asked to write an article for a professional journal.

The responsibilities and expectations associated with coaching are many. Instructional, managerial, institutional, community, and professional responsibilities compose the work of the coach.

Securing a Coaching Position

Depending on the level you wish to coach, you can take several steps to enhance your chances of securing the coaching position you desire. First, coaching requires a great deal of expertise. Playing experience in the sport you wish to coach may be helpful in this respect. Attending clinics and work shops on advanced techniques and rules may add to your knowledge. Consider becoming a rated official in your sport. Take advantage of coaching certification and licensing programs, such as the one offered for soccer by the United States Soccer Federation. Second, particularly for coaching at the interscholastic level, a teaching certificate may be required. However, this depends on the state in which you wish to coach. Coaching at the intercollegiate level often requires a master's degree.

Prospective coaches should consider developing expertise in a second sport, preferably one that is not in season at the same time as your major sport. For example, if one aspires to coach soccer, a fall sport, one should develop expertise in a spring sport such as lacrosse, baseball, or softball. In many institutions, at both the interscholastic and intercollegiate levels, coaches may be required to coach two sport activities or sometimes be the head coach in one sport and serve as an assistant coach in a second sport. At other institutions, a coach may be involved in one sport throughout the year because of the length of the season.

Practical experience is helpful as well. Volunteering to serve as an assistant coach or working with a youth sport program as a coach during your undergraduate preparation is a step in the right direction and is an invaluable experience. It is important that prospective coaches realize that oftentimes one must be willing to work in other positions in the coaching organization before achieving the head coaching position desired. Serving as a junior varsity coach, working as a graduate assistant coach, or accepting a position as an assistant coach can be helpful in attaining a head coaching position at the desired level.

Certification of Coaches

Criteria for certification of coaches at the interscholastic level vary from state to state. In 1987 only 21 states mandated that interscholastic coaches possess a teaching certificate, although not necessarily in physical education.[10] Furthermore, the increased need for coaches and the lack of teachers available to fulfill these needs has led to the hiring of many nonteacher coaches. In 1997, the number of states allowing nonteacher coaches was 49.[10] As a result, many individuals who hold coaching positions lack the professional preparation and competencies so necessary to conduct educationally sound and safe programs. To address the lack of preparation, 28 states require coach education.[10]

Additionally, concern has been expressed by professionals regarding the qualifications and preparation of youth sport coaches. Millions of children participate in youth sport; millions of adults serve as volunteer coaches. Some of these coaches have excellent credentials and do an outstanding job in keeping winning in perspective and enhancing the development of the young

athletes entrusted to their care. Other coaches lack preparation in safety, skill development, organization, training and conditioning, and the needs of young athletes. To address these concerns, coaching standards and numerous coaching education programs have been established.

The National Association for Sport and Physical Education developed National Standards for Athletic Coaches to provide a national framework for organizations and agencies that provide coaching education and training (see the box on p. 417). Knowledge, skills, and values associated with effective and appropriate coaching of athletes were organized into 37 standards, grouped into 8 domains. The 8 domains are as follows:

◆ Injuries: Prevention, Care, and Management
◆ Risk Management
◆ Growth, Development, and Learning
◆ Training, Conditioning, and Nutrition
◆ Social/Psychological Aspects of Coaching
◆ Skills, Tactics, and Strategies
◆ Teaching and Coaching
◆ Professional Preparation and Development

These standards are not a coaching certification program but a framework for the education of coaches.[11]

There are several coaching certification programs sponsored by private and professional organizations. The American Sport Education Program (ASEP) is the most widely used coaching education program in the United States. ASEP provides education at three levels: volunteer level primarily for youth sport coaches, leader level for leaders of scholastic and club sports, and master level for those who aspire to higher levels of competency. Educational programs are designed for sport parents, sport coaches, and sport directors. ASEP provides training in coaching the young athlete, coaching principles, sports first aid, drugs and sport, teaching sports skills, and a variety of sport sciences. ASEP staff coordinate more than 40 national faculty and more than 2,000 instructors. Over 750,000 people are using ASEP texts and resources. ASEP has been selected by the National Federation of State High School Associations, the YMCA, and thousands of high schools for their coaching education programs.

NATIONAL STANDARDS FOR ATHLETIC COACHES DOMAIN AND SAMPLE STANDARDS

Domain: Injuries: Prevention, Care and Management

Standard 5   Be able to plan, coordinate and implement procedures for appropriate emergency care.

Domain: Risk Management

Standard 9   Understand the scope of legal responsibilities that comes with assuming a coaching position, i.e., proper supervision, planning and instruction, matching participants, safety, first aid and risk management.

Domain: Growth, Development and Learning

Standard 14   Understand the social and emotional development of the athletes being coached, know how to recognize problems related to this development and know where to refer them for appropriate assistance when necessary.

Domain: Training, Conditioning and Nutrition

Standard 25   Demonstrate effective motivational skills and provide positive, appropriate feedback.

Domain: Skills, Tactics and Strategies

Standard 33   Organize, conduct and evaluate practice sessions with regard to established program goals that are appropriate for different stages of the season.

Domain: Teaching and Administration

Standard 34   Know the key elements of sport principles and technical skills as well as the various teaching methods that can be used to introduce and refine them.

Domain: Professional Preparation and Development

Standard 36   Demonstrate organizational and administrative efficiency in implementing sports programs, e.g., event management, budgetary procedures, facility maintenance, participation in public relations activities.

NASPE: National Standards for Athletic Coaches, Reston, Va., 1994, AAHPERD.

The National Youth Sports Coaches Association (NYSCA) has been active in the development of a national training system for volunteer sports youth coaches. Nearly 450,000 coaches have participated in the 3-year, 3-level program to qualify for certification. The first year's training emphasizes the developmental approach to coaching and safety; the second year focuses on physiological and psychological issues; and the third year features sport techniques.

There are other coaching certification programs available, such as PACE (Program for Athletic Coaches Education), a branch of the Institute for the Study of Youth Sports. Specific sports also may have certification programs for their coaches. Coaching certification programs may also be offered at the local level—for example, by the recreation department in charge of youth sports in a community.

Young professionals aspiring to coach should prepare carefully for assumption of this important responsibility. This may be accomplished through your undergraduate professional preparation program or by enrolling in a coaching certification program. Athletic participation and the practical experience of working as an assistant coach or a volunteer youth sport coach in a community program can enhance the professional qualifications of prospective coaches.

BURNOUT

Burnout is increasingly prevalent among teachers and coaches. Burnout is defined as physical, emotional, and attitudinal exhaustion. Because burnout can have a devastating effect on dedicated individuals, young professionals need to be aware of the causes and consequences of burnout and strategies they can use to prevent its occurrence.

There are many causes of teacher burnout: lack of administrative support, lack of input into the curriculum process, and public criticism and the accompanying lack of community support. Inadequate salaries, discipline problems, too little time to do the ever-growing amount of work, large classes, and heavier teaching loads may also contribute to this problem. The lack of challenge, inadequate supervisory feedback, and the absence of

opportunities for personal and professional growth also may lead to burnout.

In the coaching realm, burnout may be caused by seasons that seem to go on without end, administrative and community pressures, and time pressures. Teacher-coach role conflict may also lead to burnout. This role conflict occurs when a disparity exists between the expectations associated with being a teacher and a coach; this results in a multitude of simultaneous, somewhat diverse demands. The teacher-coach, unable to satisfy these demands, experiences role conflict.

In both the teaching and coaching realms, personal problems may interact with professional problems to exacerbate burnout. Personal problems such as family conflicts, money difficulties, or perhaps even divorce or problems with relationships may cause additional stress for the individual. These stresses coupled with professional problems may hasten the onset of burnout.

The consequences of burnout are many and are often quite severe, affecting teachers as well as

Excessive demands can lead to burnout among teacher-coaches

their students. Farber and Miller[12] assert that the most critical impact of burnout may be on instruction. Burned-out teachers may cope with the demands of teaching by sitting on the sidelines, going through the motions of teaching by "throwing out the ball." Infrequent and careless planning of classes, complacency, and behavioral inflexibility may occur as well. Teachers' interactions with their students may also suffer. Burned-out teachers may treat their students in a depersonalized manner, providing them with little encouragement, feedback, and reinforcement of their efforts, and have lower expectations for student performance. Teachers who are burned out may feel dissatisfied with their accomplishments and believe they are wasting the best years of their lives. Burnout can result in deterioration of health. Insomnia, hypertension, ulcers, and other stress-related diseases may manifest themselves in burned-out teachers.

What can be done to cope with burnout? The varied causes and consequences of burnout require a diversity of solutions. Supervisors such as principals and athletic directors can play a crucial role in the prevention and remediation of burnout. Supervisors can provide teachers and coaches with meaningful in-service programs, focusing on developing a variety of teaching and coaching techniques, learning efficient time management, and acquiring effective communication skills. They can also provide teachers and coaches with more feedback about their performance, which can serve as a stimulus for growth. Teachers and coaches can seek out new ideas, professional contacts, and opportunities through participation in professional organizations and conferences. Taking some time off to revitalize oneself during the summer is also a successful strategy. Developing and participating in hobbies or nonwork-related activities are helpful ways to deal with burnout. Establishing and maintaining an appropriate level of fitness, practicing proper nutrition, and getting enough sleep are also positive approaches to dealing with burnout.

Some teachers and coaches seek to cope with the consequences of burnout by adopting inappropriate solutions such as alcohol or drugs. The pervasiveness of burnout and the serious consequences for the teachers, coaches, students, and athletes should make dealing with burnout an important professional priority.

INCREASING YOUR PROFESSIONAL MARKETABILITY

If you are interested in a teaching career in the public schools or in nonschool settings, you can often enhance both your marketability and your ability to teach by building on your assets and interests. Through careful planning of your study program and wise use of your electives and practicum experiences, you can easily improve your chances of gaining the professional position you desire. Many of the same strategies are applicable to coaching as well.

You should enhance your opportunities to teach in the public schools in several ways. One way is to build on talents or skills you already possess. For example, the need is great for bilingual educators. Perhaps you have gained proficiency in a second language because of your family background, the location in which you grew up, or foreign language courses you studied in secondary school. These language skills can be built on with further course work at the college or university level.

Second, additional course work can be beneficial in broadening the abilities of the prospective teacher. Courses in the area of adapted physical education are an asset whether or not one is interested in working only with special needs children. Since adapted physical education emphasizes individualized instruction, the knowledge gained from its study can be applied to all children, including those with special needs mainstreamed into or included in regular physical education classes. Additional courses in health may be helpful because physical educators are often expected to teach one or two health classes. The close relationship between wellness and fitness makes knowledge of health important to the practitioner.

Another possibility, depending on the state in which you plan to teach, is to gain certification to teach in an additional academic area. If you enjoy other areas such as math, science, or health, dual certification would enable you to qualify for additional jobs such as a teaching position that had a teaching load of one-third math and two-thirds physical education or one-third health and two-thirds physical education. Certification in driver education is also a popular choice that enhances one's credentials. To gain dual certification, several courses in your alternate area of study are required. Often the number of courses required for certification may not be many more than are required by your college or university for a minor. The education department in the state in which you plan to teach can provide you with additional information about the requirements for certification.

Individuals interested in teaching in a nonschool setting can enhance their marketability in just the same way as individuals preparing for a teaching position in the public schools. Depending on where one seeks employment, having a bilingual background might be an asset. Experience in adapted physical education will be useful in working with individuals of different abilities and ages. Courses in math and business may be helpful if one is employed by a commercial sport club or fitness center, or community sport program, where the position often involves managerial duties. Because many of these organizations offer some type of health counseling and because the interest of many of the clientele in health, courses in health will be an asset as well. Many employers may view possession of a teaching certificate by someone seeking to teach in these nonschool settings as an asset. Expertise in one or several sport areas may also be a plus, as is possession of specialized certifications.

In the coaching realm, one's previous experience as an athlete in the sport is an asset. Many former athletes have capitalized on their experience to secure coaching positions. Previous work as an assistant or head coach certainly is in one's favor. Professional contacts, official ratings in a sport, and membership in a professional organization are helpful in getting hired or advancing. Many states require that coaches hold teaching certification; holding such certification gives one more flexibility in selecting from job opportunities.

Finally, one can enhance one's credentials by gaining as much practical experience as possible, working with people of all ages and abilities. This holds true whether you are seeking work in a school or nonschool setting or in coaching. This experience can be gained through volunteer work, part-time employment, summer employment, or through supervised field experiences sponsored by your college or university. Being able to cite such practical experiences on your resume may prove invaluable when you are seeking to gain employment. Membership in professional organizations and professional contacts may also be helpful in securing employment.

Teachers and coaches can improve their marketability by acquiring skills in the use of technology. Technology can help teachers and coaches enhance their instructional effectiveness and manage their time more efficiently. Many teachers are now using heart-rate monitors in their classes. These monitors, which attach to the student's wrist, provide immediate and ongoing feedback to students about their heart rate. Some heart-rate monitors store the information so that it can be downloaded to a computer and later analyzed by the teacher. Some teachers use hand-held computers to gather information about a student's performance of different skills during class. Other teachers use computers for a myriad of tasks, such as record keeping, grading, and creating newsletters to promote their programs.

Coaches can use laptop computers and video-editing technology to prepare scouting reports on their opponents. Spreadsheets help coaches quickly calculate statistics and keep track of their budgets. College coaches especially benefit from the use of databases to manage their recruiting activities.

The use of the World Wide Web as a resource for teachers and coaches is growing. There are many Web sites for physical education teachers to use as resources and a means to communicate with other teachers throughout the country. *PE CENTRAL,* established by Dr. George Graham and the doctoral students in the health and physical education program at Virginia Tech, is one of the premier Web sites for physical

• *PE CENTRAL* •

Developed by: **The Virginia Tech Health & Physical Education Program**

Founding Sponsor

Flaghouse, Inc.

March Monthly Equipment Specials (**Discounted** equipment prices for PEC visitors!)

Advertising Rates

Contributors

Senior Editors

Mark Manross
Todd Pennington

Managing Editors

Eloise Elliott
Christopher Hess
Christine Hopple
Reginald Kimball
Bane McCracken
Allen Russell
Steve Sanders
Sandy Smith
Deborah Stevens

PE Central welcomes you to the ultimate Web site for physical education teachers, students, interested parents and adults. Our goal is to provide the latest information about contemporary developmentally appropriate physical education programs for children and youth. We encourage you to submit your own ideas. Site last updated on **3-15-98**. Best viewed with Netscape 3.0+ and/or Internet Explorer 3.0+. Click **RELOAD** button on browser to see latest version of PE Central.

- **Weekly Activities** (Sunday Updates)
  (Cues of the Week, Wellness Tips, Kids Quotes)

- **UPDATED Lesson Ideas** (3/11)
  (PE, Health, Classroom Teacher/Integrated, Preschool, Instant Activities)

- **Assessment Ideas**
  (Paper & Pencil, Alternative (with rubrics), Kids work)

- **Professional Information**
  (PE Journals, Conference Info, Important PE Documents, State/Nat'l Associations)

- **UPDATED Job Center** (3/14)
  (Job Listings, Resumes, Links to other Job Info)

- **PEC Gift Shop**
  (Instant Activity Booklet)

- **Submit Your Ideas**
  (Lesson Ideas, Web Sites, Job Info, Conferences, Criteria for lesson ideas)

- **UPDATED PEC Bookstore** (3/11)
  (Elementary, Secondary, Parents/Kids)
  (In association with **Amazon.com**)

- **UPDATED Top Web Sites** (3/14)
  (Fitness, Health, Dance, & Sport links, PE Programs, Sites featuring PEC)

- **Instructional Resources**
  (Sites with resources to aid in PE/Health Instruction)

- **Equipment Purchasing/School Assemblies**
  (Equipment Co. Web sites, instructional aids, & assemblies)

- **American Master Teacher Program**

  (About AMTP, Calendar, Books, Hosting Info.)
  (**Profs:** Register for Reno Instructor Worshop)

- **USPE E-mail Listserv**
  (Subscribe/Unsubscribe, Set Digest/No Digest, USPE-L Handout)

- **UPDATED About PE Central** (3/10)
  (Editorial Staff, Contributors, Awards, Other Web Sites/Articles featuring PEC, Handouts/Press Releases, Copyright Info)

- **Check the PE Weather**
  (At the **Weather Channel** you can check the current and future weather to see if you can take your PE classes outside!)

FIGURE 11-1 PE Central, established by Dr. George Graham and the doctoral students at Virginia Tech, is one of the premiere websites for physical educators (http://pe.central.vt.edu).

educators. It offers teachers access to lesson plans, instructional resources, assessment ideas, professional information on conferences and workshops, job openings, equipment purchasing, and related Web sites. Through its listserv, physical education teachers can share information and engage in problem solving with other teachers throughout the nation.

Coaches find that the Web offers them the opportunity to share information with coaches throughout the world. A coach may find posted on the Web information about drills, training techniques, and upcoming conferences and clinics. Through several different sites on the Web, college coaches can contact and recruit prospective athletes. Through various sport-specific listservs, coaches can communicate with colleagues worldwide.

Prospective teachers and coaches can enhance their marketability. Building on your skills, taking additional courses, and gaining as much practical experience as possible will increase your options and enhance your opportunities for employment.

SUMMARY

Teaching and coaching opportunities have broadened from the traditional school setting to the nonschool setting and from school-aged populations to people of all ages, ranging from preschoolers to senior citizens. Teaching opportunities in the school setting are available at the elementary level, secondary level, and in higher education. Prospective teachers may also teach physical education in adapted physical education programs and in professional preparation programs. In the nonschool setting, opportunities exist in commercial sport clubs, community and youth agencies, resorts, corporate fitness programs, the Armed Forces, and preschool and day care motor-development programs. Many individuals choose a teaching career because of their strong desire to work with people, because of personal interests, and because of the nature of the job. Individuals desiring to pursue a teaching career, regardless of setting, should be cognizant of the numerous advantages and disadvantages of such a career.

Many prospective physical educators aspire to a career as a coach. Some seek a dual career as a teacher and a coach, whereas others desire solely to coach, and view a teaching career as a means to attain their ultimate ambition. The prospective coach should be knowledgeable of the benefits and drawbacks of this career.

In an effort to improve teaching, researchers have sought to identify characteristics of effective teachers. They determined that effective teachers possess organizational, communication, human relations, instructional, and motivational skills. Teachers have a myriad of responsibilities; their responsibilities may be classified as instructional, managerial, and institutional in nature. Coaching is similar in many respects to teaching. Effective coaches possess many of the characteristics of effective teachers and must assume many of the same responsibilities as well.

One problem that has become increasingly prevalent among teachers and coaches is burnout. Burnout is physical, mental, and attitudinal exhaustion. The causes of burnout are many, and personal problems may interact with professional problems to exacerbate burnout. There are a variety of solutions to this problem.

Many strategies can be used by prospective teachers and coaches to enhance their marketability. They can build on their talents and interests, take additional course work in a supporting area, and gain as much practical experience as possible.

SELF-ASSESSMENT TESTS

These tests are designed to help you determine if you have mastered the materials and the competencies presented in this chapter.

1. In light of the qualities of effective teachers and their responsibilities, assess your own qualifications for this field of endeavor.

2. Discuss the advantages and disadvantages of pursuing a teaching or coaching career in a school and a nonschool setting. If possible, try to interview a physical educator or coach presently working in each setting.

3. Using the information provided in the Getting Connected box, access the *PE CENTRAL* or *Sports Media* sites on the World Wide Web. Explore the information contained within each site. Write a 1 to 2 page paper on the usefulness of the World Wide Web to teachers and coaches.

4. Using the information provided in the Getting Connected box, access the AAHPERD Web site and read the National Standards for Athletic Coaches. Carefully review your own athletic experiences and compare the actions and behaviors of your coaches to the standards. Did your coaches meet these standards? Where did they fall short? Discuss the importance of standards for coaches, especially at the youth sport level.

REFERENCES

1. Bucher CA and Koenig CR: Methods and materials for secondary physical education, St. Louis, 1983, Mosby.

2. National Education Association, Teacher salaries, 1998. (http://www.nea.org)

3. Wuest DA and Lombardo BJ: Curriculum and instruction: the secondary school physical education experience, St. Louis, 1994, Mosby.

4. Siedentop D: Developing teaching skills in physical education, ed 3, Palo Alto, Calif., 1991, Mayfield.

5. National Association for Sport and Physical Education: National standards for beginning physical education teachers, 1995, American Alliance for Health, Physical Education, Recreation and Dance.

6. American Alliance for Health, Physical Education, Recreation and Dance: Developmentally appropriate physical education practices for children, Reston, VA., 1992, AAHPERD.

7. Gensemer RE: Physical education: perspectives, inquiry, and applications, Philadelphia, 1985, W. B. Saunders.

8. Hanson MR: Physical educators must prepare for preschoolers in the public schools, Teaching Elementary Physical Education 3(10):1,7,1992.

9. Pangrazi RP and Darst PW: Dynamic physical education curriculum and instruction for secondary school students, Minneapolis, 1985, Burgess.

10. American Sport Education Program: 1997 national interscholastic coaching requirements report: a shared mission, Champaign, Ill., 1997, Human Kinetics. (http://www.asep.com/)

11. National Association for Sport and Physical Education: National standards for athletic coaches, 1994, American Alliance for Health, Physical Education, Recreation and Dance.

12. Farber BA and Miller J: Teacher burnout: a psycho-educational perspective. Teachers College Record 83(2):235–243, 1981.

SUGGESTED READINGS

Ballinger DA: Becoming an effective physical educator, Physical Educator 50: 13–19, 1993.

Offers suggestions for development as a teacher.

Chelladurai P and Kuga DJ: Teaching and coaching: group and task differences, Quest 48:470–485.

The differences between teaching and coaching are highlighted with implications for role preference, organizational and environmental elements, and resultant job satisfaction.

Graham G, editor: Developmentally appropriate physical education for children, Journal of Physical Education, Recreation, and Dance 63(6), 1992.

Contains articles about various aspects of developmentally appropriate physical education and its implementation.

Graham KC and Stueck P, editors: Critical crossroads—decisions for middle and high school physical education, Journal of Physical Education, Recreation, and Dance 63(7), 1992.

A series of articles addresses the status of physical education in the schools and makes suggestions for improvement.

Kozub FM and Poretta D: Including athletes with disabilities: interscholastic athletic benefits for all, JOPERD 67(3):19–24, 1996.

This article discusses the continuum of opportunities for participation by students with disabilities, benefits for participants, and suggestions for coaches.

Mills BD and Dunlevy SM: Coaching certification: what's out there and what needs to be done?, International Journal of Physical Education 24:17–26, 1997.

An overview of various coaching certification programs is provided, as well as information about their effectiveness.

Rink JE: Teaching physical education for learning, Dubuque, Iowa, 1998, WCB/McGraw-Hill.

Provides information about understanding the teaching/learning process, effective teaching skills, reflective teaching, and observation tools and techniques.

Schempp PG: Constructing professional knowledge: a case study of an experienced high school teacher, Journal of Teaching in Physical Education 13(1): 2–23, 1993.

Offers a vivid portrayal of a teacher and an understanding of his work.

Sherrill C: Adapted physical activity, recreation and sport: crossdisciplinary and lifespan, ed 5, Dubuque, Iowa, 1998, WCB/McGraw-Hill.

A comprehensive textbook on teaching physical education and sports to individuals with disabilities. An excellent resource for physical educators in all settings working with individuals with special needs.

Stoot S, editor: Socialization into physical education, Journal of Teaching in Physical Education 12(4), 1993.

A series on various aspects of and issues related to teacher socialization.

Tsangaridou N and Siedentop D: Reflective teaching: a literature review, Quest 47:212–237, 1995.

Describes theories of reflection, provides an overview of efforts on reflection in the classroom and physical education, addresses issues, and makes recommendations for future research.

Fitness- and Health-Related Careers in Physical Education and Sport

Instructional Objectives and Competencies to be Achieved:

After reading this chapter the student should be able to —

◆ Discuss the responsibilities of a fitness or an exercise specialist.

◆ Describe the various employment opportunities for a fitness or an exercise specialist.

◆ Discuss the responsibilities of an athletic trainer and physical education and sport professionals working in a health-related career.

◆ Describe the opportunities available to an individual desiring to pursue a therapy-related career.

◆ Discuss the various strategies that can be used to enhance one's professional marketability in fitness-, health-, and therapy-related careers.

Within the past decade there has been a dramatic increase in interest in preventive medicine and a greater public awareness of the values of physical activity. Research has substantiated the benefits of exercise and appropriate physical activity in reducing the incidence of cardiovascular disease and in enhancing the rehabilitation of those experiencing this common malady. The increased public awareness of the role of physical activity in health promotion and disease prevention, coupled with the interest in fitness by many segments of society, has stimulated the growth of community, commercial, and worksite health promotion and fitness programs. As a result, employ-

ment opportunities for professionals with preparation as exercise and fitness specialists have grown tremendously. The number of physical education and sport professionals who have found employment opportunities working in preventive and rehabilitative exercise programs has risen sharply, and it appears that this trend will continue in the years ahead.

Another field that has experienced growth is athletic training. Although professional and college athletic teams have typically employed athletic trainers, their employment at the secondary school level is rising. Furthermore, the public's increased participation in a variety of sport activities and the

GETTING CONNECTED

American Heart Association site offers an interactive risk assessment, heart and stroke guide, and exercise guidelines.
> Site: http://www.americanheart.org/

Association for Worksite Health Promotion highlights the benefits of worksite health promotion and contains links to actual worksite programs.
> Site: http://www.awhp.com

Sports medicine and related topics, such as orthopedics, pediatrics, rehabilitation, nutrition, women's health, are found at this site.
> Site: http://www.gen.emory.edu/medweb/medweb.sportsmed.html

American Council on Exercise (ACE) site gives information about ace certification and continuing education courses.
> Site: http://www.acefitness.org

American College of Sports Medicine site provides information on ACSM, including certification exams.
> Site: http://www.acsm.org

National Athletic Training Association site gives information about the National Athletic Training Association, including its certification programs.
> Site: http://www.nata.org

National Strength and Conditioning Association site presents information on certification, professional education, conferences, and publications.
> Site: http://www.nsca-lift.org

medical profession's interest in sport have led to increased employment opportunities for qualified athletic trainers in commercial sports medicine clinics, physical therapy clinics, and hospitals.

Employment opportunities also have become more available for qualified individuals in weight control and health spas and clubs. Qualified individuals may be employed as dance exercise specialists, exercise leaders, exercise test technologists, and weight management counselors.

An increasing number of medical and health care professionals, as well as members of the general public, realize the significant physical and psychological benefits gained by individuals who participate in regular, appropriate physical activity. There is greater recognition of the therapeutic values of movement in helping individuals attain an optimal state of well-being, as well as recover from an illness. Careers in movement therapy, recreation therapy, and dance therapy are available to physical education and sport professionals who desire to work in a therapeutic setting.

FITNESS- AND EXERCISE-RELATED CAREERS

The awareness of the benefits of physical activity by the public, corporate sector, and medical

Members work out at the state-of-the-art Taking Care Center, in Hartford, Connecticut. In addition to the exercise equipment and indoor track, it has a pool and an aerobics studio.

profession has stimulated the growth of preventive and rehabilitative physical activity programs. Students aspiring to pursue careers in this growing area should familiarize themselves with the types of programs typically offered and the nature of responsibilities associated with them, the many career opportunities available, and strategies to prepare themselves for a fitness- and exercise-related career.

Preventive and rehabilitative exercise programs differ in their focus and in the nature of the participants; the setting in which these programs are conducted often is different as well. Preventive exercise program specialists work with healthy adults to increase their level of fitness and realize concomitant gains in health. Rehabilitative exercise

program specialists work primarily with individuals who exhibit the effects of coronary heart disease; they focus on helping these individuals attain a functional state of living and an enhanced quality of life. Preventive exercise programs are commonly found in corporate fitness centers, commercial fitness centers, and community agencies such as the YMCA/YWCA. An increasing number of hospitals are now offering wellness programs. Rehabilitative exercise programs are most often found in hospitals, although some may be found in medical clinics or community agencies or are affiliated with corporate fitness centers.

Preventive and rehabilitative programs often vary in their scope and comprehensiveness. However,

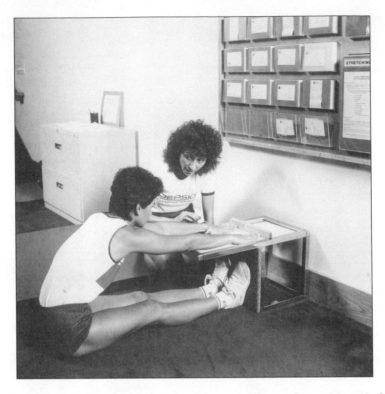

The trained exercise professional must be able to evaluate each participant's fitness level. This PepsiCo staff member is administering the sit-and-reach test to a program participant.

some commonalities may be discerned. Although these programs typically focus on improvement of fitness, they may include other components such as educational programs, health promotion programs, and lifestyle modification. The fitness component of these programs most likely includes some assessment of the individual's current level of fitness, prescription of a program of exercise and activity, opportunities to engage in exercise and activities, and periodic reevaluation of the individual's level of fitness. Educational efforts may focus on instructing individuals on the principles underlying the performance of exercises and physical activity so that they may learn to properly plan their own exercise and activity programs. Health promotion efforts may include health education, such as providing participants with nutritional information, as well as measures focusing on the early detection of disease, such as hypertension screening and cancer detection. Lifestyle

modification may include counseling individuals regarding stress management, weight control, smoking cessation, and alcohol and drug abuse. In addition to these program components, recreational sport opportunities may be offered.

Cooper and Collingwood[1] noted that fitness and wellness programs vary in their structure and offerings. In an effort to maximize the benefits to be realized from participation and to promote adherence to these programs, the Institute for Aerobics Research identified several elements as "generic" services for such programs. Programs should make provisions for medical screening of their participants to ensure that they are safe exercise risks. Program personnel should also evaluate participants' level of fitness and their lifestyle. Exercise programs should focus on individual goal setting; thus exercise and nutritional prescriptions should be developed for each individual. To motivate participants to get started on their programs, supervised group exercise and activity programs should be offered. To sustain changes in fitness and lifestyle, educational classes should be held and provisions should be made for motivation and reinforcement of participants' efforts. Feedback should be ongoing in nature. These generic elements are critical to the success of preventive exercise programs and seem appropriate for rehabilitative programs as well.

The trained exercise and fitness professional working in preventive and rehabilitative exercise programs must be able to perform a wide variety of tasks and be capable of assuming responsibility for numerous aspects of the exercise program. Sol[2] identified the responsibilities of an exercise program specialist as follows:

- ◆ Direct the exercise program, which may be oriented to prevention and/or rehabilitation.
- ◆ Train and supervise staff.
- ◆ Develop and manage the program budget.
- ◆ Design and manage the exercise facility and laboratories.
- ◆ Market the exercise program.
- ◆ Evaluate—in conjunction with a physician— each participant's medical and activity history, a graded exercise test, the pulmonary function tests, and assorted fitness tests.
- ◆ Develop individual exercise prescriptions for participants.
- ◆ Evaluate and/or counsel participants, on request, about nutrition, smoking, weight control, and stress.
- ◆ Accumulate program data for statistical analysis and research.
- ◆ Maintain professional affiliations.
- ◆ Perform other program-specific duties.

The responsibilities that each professional in the program will be asked to assume depend on several factors. These factors include the scope and comprehensiveness of the program, the number of participants, the size of the staff, and qualifications of other staff members. In programs that have a broad range of services, a large number of participants, and several staff members, responsibilities tend to be more specialized. One staff member may direct the program, administer the budget, market the program, and conduct in-service training for other program staff. Some staff members may have as their sole responsibility the conducting of graded exercise tests and the writing of exercise prescriptions. Still other staff members lead the fitness classes and may provide instruction in activities. Providing participants with counseling for lifestyle modification or educating participants about exercise may be the responsibility of other staff members. Finally, another professional may be assigned to accumulate data and conduct statistical analyses. In programs that are narrower in scope or are conducted for fewer participants, the staff tends to be smaller and one professional will perform many more functions.

Opportunities for qualified individuals may be found in a diversity of preventive and rehabilitative exercise programs offered in a variety of settings. These include worksite health promotion and fitness programs, commercial and community programs, and rehabilitation programs. Some individuals are finding employment as personal fitness trainers. Salaries range from $20,000 to over $40,000 a year, depending on the qualifications of the individual, responsibilities assigned, and nature of the job.

Worksite Health Programs

Worksite health promotion programs have grown dramatically over the past decade. Physical activity and fitness programs are typically an integral part of health promotion efforts at the work site. Worksite health promotion programs vary greatly in their scope and the type of health promotion activities offered.

The proportion of work sites offering physical activity and fitness programs has grown from 22% in 1985 to 42% in 1992.[3] The larger the employer's workforce, the more likely it is the employer has a physical activity and fitness program. Thirty-three percent of small corporations (50–99 employees) have worksite programs compared with 83% of large corporations (more than 750 employees).[3]

Worksite physical activity programs are a critical component of the national health promotion and disease prevention program because they have the potential to reach a large percentage of the population. Today's work force comprises 110 million men and women, the majority of whom spend

Many corporations view corporate fitness centers as sound investments.

most the day at the work site. The work site offers an effective way to reach these adults and to provide them with education and access to the means to adopt and maintain a healthy lifestyle. On-site programs are convenient for employees, and offer the peer social support so important for continued participation.

Corporations are willing to invest in worksite programs because it makes economic sense. One payoff from these programs is increased employee productivity and less absenteeism. Healthy employees can work harder and more effectively. Corporations are also investing in programs as a cost containment measure. Corporations are trying to reduce their spiraling health care costs. Businesses lose an estimated $15 billion annually due to health problems and close to $20 billion a year from premature employee deaths. The cost of health insurance premiums continues to rise astronomically. The Wellness Council of America estimates that by the year 2000, the cost of providing medical benefits will be $12,000 for each employee.[4] The short- and long-term benefits to be accrued from employee fitness programs make good sense economically: if employee illness can be curtailed and premature deaths reduced, businesses stand to reap substantial

savings in health care, insurance costs, and disability payments.

Reports show that economic benefits realized from worksite programs varied widely. In 1993 the Centers from Disease Control and Prevention reported that companies saved almost $7 for every $1 invested in an exercise program.[5] Benefit/cost ratios are most widely used to determine the economic benefits. A benefit/cost ratio divides the money saved by the money spent; a ratio of $3.43 means that for every $1 spent, $3.43 was saved. In 1995, Messer and Stone reported positive benefit/cost ratios ranging from 1.15 to 5.52 for a variety of health promotion programs.[3] In 1996, the President's Council on Physical Activity and Sports Physical Activity and Research Digest reported benefit/cost ratios for programs ranging from 0.76 to 3.43. It should be noted, however, that some of these benefit/cost ratios were associated with comprehensive health promotion programs, which included physical activity along with stress management, smoking cessation, and other health promotion efforts.

Corporations may also invest in worksite health promotion programs because of the benefits in terms of human relations and enhancement of morale. Worksite health promotion programs are also important in recruiting and retaining employees. In 1995, the International Society of Certified Employee Benefit Specialists found that wellness and health promotion ranked 10th among 30 top employee benefit health priorities.[7]

Worksite health promotion programs vary widely in comprehensiveness—that is, the number and nature of activities offered. In 1997, the Association for Worksite Health Promotion estimated the percentage of work sites offering different types of health promotion activities.[7] The top 10 activities and the percentage of work sites offering them are listed below:

◆ Job hazard/injury prevention (66%)
◆ Exercise/physical fitness (43%)
◆ Smoking control (42%)
◆ Stress management (39%)
◆ Alcohol/other drugs (38%)
◆ Back care (34%)
◆ Nutrition (32%)
◆ High blood pressure (31%)
◆ AIDS education (30%)
◆ Cholesterol screening (29%)

Physical education and sport professionals aspiring to work in worksite health promotion programs may find themselves working as part of a comprehensive health promotion team.

The Wellness Council of America (WELCOA)[4] offers several suggestions to enhance the success of wellness and health promotion programs. These include the following:

◆ Make the program voluntary.
◆ Continually market the program.
◆ Be sensitive to individual differences with respect to age, culture, and health status.
◆ Evaluate the program often.

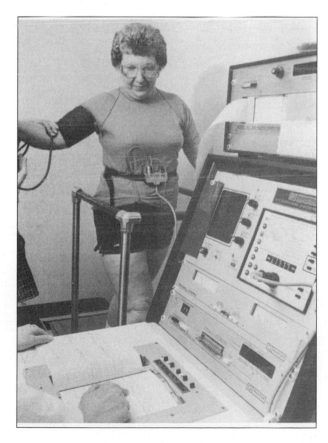

Corporate fitness programs include assessment of current fitness levels. This employee is taking a treadmill test at Sentry World Headquarters, in Stevens Point, Wisconsin.

♦ Make sure that the program staff model healthy behavior.

♦ Recognize and reward people who develop the programs.

♦ Maintain good records in order to properly evaluate the program.

♦ Offer a balance between programs that are fun and those that are clinically significant.

♦ Personalize the programs to the employee's needs.

Worksite health promotion programs offer a great opportunity to improve the health of the nation. However, the effectiveness of this effort must be measured not only in the number of worksite programs but the degree of involvement of employees.

Worksite health promotion programs, especially for physical fitness and activity, are most effective when they can attract at-risk employees, that is, those employees who will benefit the most from the program. At-risk employees are those members of the workforce who are sedentary, obese, possess high cholesterol levels, hypertensive, experience high levels of stress, and smoke.[8] It has

been found, however, that participants in the fitness program tend to already be healthier than nonparticipants.[8] Efforts should be directed at attracting at-risk individuals into the fitness program. Physical education and sport professionals must realize that part of their job responsibilities will be the active and ongoing recruitment of employees to participate in the program. Once employees have begun a program, efforts need to be directed at maintaining involvement so that desirable health benefits can be achieved.

Worksite facilities vary greatly. Some corporations have invested in multimillion dollar facilities—gymnasium, pool, indoor track, aerobics studio, racquetball courts, weight rooms, and playing fields for sport activities. Facilities at other corporations are more modest, perhaps only a weight room and a multipurpose gymnasium.

Within the last 5 years there has been an increase in worksite health promotion and fitness programs for school faculty and staff. These programs vary in nature and scope. Like those found in corporate settings, school programs focus on protecting and improving employees' health

Aerobic dance is a popular offering at health spas, fitness clubs, and corporate fitness centers.

status. These worksite programs are seen by professionals in the health field as an integral part of a comprehensive school health program.[9]

Colleges and universities also are offering programs for their employees. These programs typically emphasize prevention and improvement of health through appropriate lifestyle management. Some institutions offer wellness and fitness programs to their students, on either a credit or non-credit basis. The emphasis is on learning skills and acquiring knowledge to lead a healthy, active life.

Many work sites offer recreational sport programs as well. These recreational programs may include softball and bowling leagues as well as competitive teams. Instruction in physical activities may be offered to employees.

Opportunities for employment in worksite programs are increasing for qualified professionals. In addition to opportunities to work as a fitness and exercise specialist, opportunities are available for individuals to conduct recreational programs and to provide instruction in physical activities and sport skills.

Commercial and Community Fitness Programs

The number of adult fitness programs has increased dramatically. For example, the International Health, Racquet and Sports Club Association reported that between 1987 and 1996 adult memberships at commercial and nonprofit clubs rose 51%, from fewer than 14 million to an all-time high of 20.8 million. Programs offered through community agencies have also increased.

A growing site for community wellness and fitness programs is the hospital setting. These wellness centers integrate recreational and clinical services, incorporating features normally found in health clubs and community centers. These centers are big, multipurpose, with gyms, jogging tracks, state-of-the art exercise equipment, aerobic studios, and sometimes a pool.[10] This growth was stimulated in part by health care reform and the emergence of managed care. This gave hospitals the incentive to focus on prevention to keep people from coming to the hospital in the first place.

Through creation of wellness centers, hospitals could capitalize on changes in health care. These centers offer an array of services, from prevention programs to rehabilitation services, and require professionals that can competently fulfill many different responsibilities.[10]

These programs offer many of the same services as comprehensive employee fitness programs. They may offer graded exercise tests, individualized fitness programs based on the exercise prescription developed from the results of the graded exercise test, educational programs, health promotion programs, and lifestyle modification. Other programs may be less comprehensive in nature; these may focus primarily on the promotion of fitness.

Fitness programs tailored to meet the needs of different age groups are becoming more common. Toddler and preschool programs, as well as programs for the aged, are being offered by both community and commercial agencies and, increasingly, by schools. Professionals working within these programs must be particularly attuned to the developmental characteristics of the age group and adapt programs accordingly.

An increased number of fitness programs are available to address the fitness needs of individuals with disabilities. For example, the Fitness Clinic for Physically Disabled at San Diego State University (SDSU), established in 1983, provides fitness programming to individuals with a wide range of physical disabilities.[11] Fitness programming at the clinic focuses both on improvement of fitness and functional independence. Improvement of functional independence allows participants in the program to assume a greater responsibility for their personal care and other activities of daily living. For individuals with severe limiting conditions, such as quadriplegia and multiple sclerosis, increasing their basic muscular strength, endurance, and balance allows them more independence and greatly enhances the overall quality of their lives. The Fitness Clinic also provides a wonderful practicum experience for SDSU students enrolled in adapted physical education, athletic training, and prephysical therapy programs to apply their fitness and therapeutic skills.

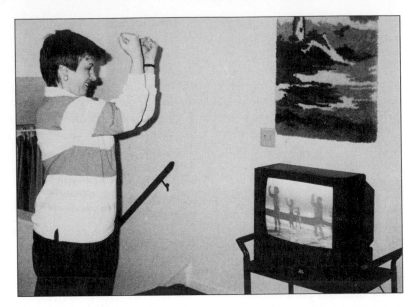

Many people prefer to exercise at home rather than at a club or other facility.

Professional responsibilities within commercial enterprises and community programs are similar to those associated with worksite programs. Employment opportunities within these areas have grown dramatically within the past few years.

One factor that may counter the growth of employment opportunities is the tremendous increase in the sales of home exercise equipment. Many adults who in the past would have paid a membership fee to participate in these programs have chosen to invest the money in home exercise equipment, such as weight machines, bicycle ergometers, cross-country ski machines, and rowing machines. These individuals prefer the convenience of being able to exercise at home. Some professionals have capitalized on this trend by offering one-on-one fitness instruction in the home.

Personal Trainers

A number of physical education and sport professionals have pursued careers as personal fitness trainers. They meet with clients individually in their homes on a regular basis, sometimes as often as 5 or 6 days per week. For each client, the personal trainer conducts a fitness assessment,

develops specific goals and designs a program leading to their attainment, coaches the individual through the workout, and monitors progress. Additional services often include nutritional counseling. Some fitness programs and health clubs are also offering members the services of a personal trainer at an additional cost. Members like the one-on-one attention offered by a personal trainer, believing it enhances their motivation and their effort in performing their program.

Rehabilitation Programs

As the role of exercise in the rehabilitation of individuals with illness, particularly cardiovascular diseases, has become increasingly well documented, the number of rehabilitation programs has grown. Typically, rehabilitation programs are offered at hospitals and clinics, although some programs may be offered through community agencies such as YMCA/YWCAS. Besides the development of fitness, health promotion and lifestyle modification are integral parts of these programs.

Opportunities for employment are similar to those in corporate fitness and adult fitness programs. However, professionals working in these programs tend to work more closely with physicians in monitoring the performance and progress of the programs' participants. To plan rehabilitation programs, the professional needs to be familiar with the medical aspects of each participant's illness, cognizant of the limitations imposed by the illness, and aware of drugs commonly used by the participants and their effects. Professionals working in rehabilitation programs require training to help individuals deal with the psychological aspects of their illness. Professionals must also be ready to deal with participants' fears concerning exercise, such as the often expressed fear that exercise will lead to another heart attack.

Career Preparation

Preparation for a career in this area requires a strong background in the exercise sciences and fitness and practical experience. Students will also benefit from obtaining certification from a recognized organization and becoming involved in professional organizations.

Preparation

Today many colleges and universities offer undergraduate and graduate degrees in health promotion-, fitness-, or exercise-related areas. Undergraduate degree programs are available in exercise science, fitness and cardiac rehabilitation, adult fitness, corporate fitness, and fitness programming. Although the requirements for the degree vary by institution, in the typical program the student takes core courses such as foundations of physical education and sport, anatomy and physiology, kinesiology, biomechanics, exercise physiology, injury prevention and care, sport psychology, sport sociology, tests and measurements, and activity instruction, usually in the area of lifetime sports and aquatics.

In addition to these core courses, more in-depth instruction is provided in exercise science, focusing on assessment of cardiopulmonary function and health status, exercise prescription, exercise leadership, and fitness programming. Certification in cardiopulmonary resuscitation (CPR) is commonly required. Because of the strong relationship of this field to health promotion, students may take courses in nutrition, drug education, pharmacology, and stress management. In completing their preparation, students may find it helpful to take several psychology courses, such as motivation, behavior modification, and individual and group counseling. Computer science courses, statistics, and research methodology will be helpful to students in preparing for the administrative and evaluative responsibilities associated with a position in this field. Finally, business courses will assist the student in dealing with the myriad responsibilities associated with exercise programs, such as budgeting, marketing, and personnel supervision.

To provide students a supervised practical experience where they have the opportunity to apply and further develop their competencies, most programs require an internship. This internship can take place in a diversity of settings, such as a hospital, corporate fitness center, campus fitness program, or commercial enterprise. The internship typically occurs near the end of the program and serves as a capstone experience.

There are also many programs across the country that offer a graduate degree in this area. These programs provide advanced training and an opportunity to specialize. Programs are offered in exercise physiology, fitness programming, cardiac rehabilitation, strength development and conditioning, fitness management, corporate fitness, health fitness, and health promotion. These programs may require that students complete an internship, research project, and/or thesis to graduate.

Certification

Certification programs offered by professional organizations have grown within the last 10 years. These programs try to ensure that individuals who receive certification have the necessary skills and knowledge to competently plan and administer programs.

The American College of Sports Medicine (ACSM) offers one of the most widely recognized certification programs for professionals in this field. Established in 1972, the ACSM certification program encompasses both preventive and rehabilitative exercise programs, offering three levels of certification within each program. For preventive programs, the three levels of certification are (1) Exercise Leader/Aerobics, (2) Health/Fitness Instructor, and (3) Health/Fitness Director. For rehabilitative programs, the three levels of certification are (1) Exercise Test Technologist, (2) Exercise Specialist, and (3) Program Director. Certification within both program areas reflects a progressive level of skills, knowledge, and experience.

ACSM certification requires satisfactory performance on both a written and a practical examination. Prior to the examination, optional workshops and seminars are usually offered that cover the competencies for each level of certification. Information about certification can be obtained via the Web or from ACSM, PO Box 1440, Indianapolis, IN, 46206-1440.

Other organizations have also developed certification programs, including the YMCA, the American Council on Exercise (ACE), the Aerobics and Fitness Association of America (AFAA), and the National Strength and Conditioning Association (NSCA).

The YMCA offers certifications for individuals who work in the many types of health and fitness programs offered by the organization. Three levels of certification are available: (1) Basic Fitness Leader, (2) Fitness Specialist, and (3) Advanced Exercise Specialist. Each level reflects achievement of a greater level of competency. Completion of a workshop is required for each level. Additionally, leadership training is offered to individuals working in the specialized programs of the YMCA, such as the Healthy Back program, the Strength Training Program, and the Seniors program. Information on YMCA certification can be obtained from the YMCA of the USA, 101 North Wacker Dr., Chicago, IL 60606-7386.

ACE offers three types of certifications for fitness professionals. The Personal Trainer certification is for individuals who provide one-on-one fitness training. The Group Fitness Instructor is for fitness instructors who lead group exercise programs. The Lifestyle & Weight Management Consultant Certification is for those individuals who want to offer comprehensive weight-management

consulting that addresses nutrition, behavior modification, and fitness. ACE offers a variety of training workshops and opportunities to gain expertise in speciality fitness areas. ACE can be found on the Web or by contacting ACE, 5820 Oberline Drive, Suite 102, San Diego, CA 92121-3787.

AFAA conducts a certification program, training workshops, and continuing education workshops for fitness professionals. Certification programs include Primary Aerobic Instructor Certification, Personal Trainer/Fitness Counselor Certification, Weight Training Certification, Step Certification, and Emergency Response Certification. Speciality workshops in prenatal fitness, aqua fitness, senior fitness, and resistance training are offered. Certification requires a written and a practical exam. AFAA workshops and home study programs may also be applied toward American College of Sports Medicine continuing certification. AFAA can be contacted via the Web or at AFAA, 15250 Ventura Blvd. Suite 200, Sherman Oaks, CA 91430, phone 800-446-0040.

NSCA's focus is on strength development to improve athletic performance and physical fitness. Membership in the NSCA brings together professionals in the areas of sport science, athletic training, and fitness industries. Two certifications are offered: Certified Strength and Conditioning Specialists (CSCS) and Certified Personal Trainer (NSCA-CPT). Candidates for CSCS certification must hold a Bachelors of Arts or Science degree or be enrolled as a senior at an accredited college or university, be CPR-certified, and pass the exam. The NSCA-CPT is designed for professionals who train clients in a one-on-one situation, such as in a client's home, in a fitness or health clubs, and in organizations such as the YMCA. These professionals often have areas of expertise to accommodate the diverse needs of their clients. They may work with clients who have orthopedic, cardiovascular, and weight problems or who are elderly or have physical disabilities. Both certification programs require practical and written exams. NCSA also sponsors conferences and offers continuing education. NCSA can be contacted via the Web or at 402-476-7141.

As the number of certification programs continues to grow, students are cautioned to check the quality of the program with professors and professionals in the field before pursuing certification. And, as Siedentop points out, "Remember that a 1-week 'intensive' workshop does not provide the level of preparation that a physical education major receives during a 4-year college program."[12]

Professional organizations

Membership in professional organizations and establishment of professional affiliations are important for young professionals. Membership will facilitate the development of professional contacts. It provides the opportunity to update one's skills and knowledge through continuing education programs, workshops, and conventions. Students preparing for a career in this area may find membership in AAHPERD, ACSM, NSCA, and the Association for Worksite Health Promotion to be a valuable professional experience.

HEALTH-RELATED CAREERS

Health-related career opportunities in the realm of physical education have expanded. Careers in athletic training have become increasingly available.

Many employment opportunities are available to men and women at the college and university level.

Career opportunities also exist for physical educators in health and weight control clubs and spas.

In recent years, employment opportunities have increased for professionals with expertise in athletic training. Traditional employment opportunities can be found at the college and professional levels. Employment opportunities at the secondary school level also exist, although fewer than 10% of the nation's high schools currently employ certified athletic trainers. It is likely that employment opportunities at this level will increase in the near future as states and school systems, concerned about the safety of their athletes and their legal liability, mandate the hiring of certified athletic trainers for interscholastic sports.

Another avenue of employment that is available to athletic trainers is in sports medicine clinics. These clinics can be commercial enterprises, affiliated with hospitals, or associated with physical therapy practices. The increase in sport participation by all segments of society has resulted in the need for qualified individuals to evaluate, treat, and rehabilitate injuries.

A new avenue of employment for athletic trainers is in the corporate setting. Companies are realizing that in-house rehabilitation programs, like fitness programs, are cost effective. Some companies are hiring athletic trainers to work in on-site fitness/rehabilitation centers.[13] It is anticipated that employment opportunities within this setting will expand within the next 10 years.

An athletic trainer's responsibilities are numerous and varied in nature, focusing primarily on the prevention of injury and the rehabilitation of injured athletes. In terms of injury prevention and safety, the athletic trainer performs such preventive measures as taping the ankles and knees of athletes prior to practices and competitions. The athletic trainer works closely with coaches in designing and supervising conditioning programs. Advising coaches and athletes regarding the prevention of injuries is an important responsibility of the athletic trainer. Athletic trainers may also assist in preseason physicals. Checking equipment and facilities for safety are tasks often performed by the athletic trainer.

The athletic trainer is often the first person to reach an injured athlete. Thus the athletic trainer must be prepared to deal with a variety of emergencies. The athletic trainer diagnoses injuries and refers athletes to the appropriate medical personnel for treatment. Working closely with the physician, the athletic trainer implements the prescribed rehabilitation program and administers the appropriate therapeutic treatments. The athletic trainer closely monitors the athlete's efforts and progress during the rehabilitation program. Rehabilitation may be a long and arduous process, and the athletic trainer may need to motivate and encourage the athlete during this trying period to put forth the necessary effort to attain complete recovery. Keeping accurate records of athletes' injuries, the treatment program prescribed, and each athlete's progress during the rehabilitation program is part of the athletic trainer's job.

In addition to competencies pertaining to training, an athletic trainer must possess excellent interpersonal skills. The athletic trainer must work closely with the coaches and the team physician. Establishing and maintaining good rapport with these individuals contribute to a harmonious working relationship. Often the athletic trainer is placed in a position of telling a coach that an athlete cannot practice, play in an upcoming game, or return to the competition after an injury. Professional competency and a good rapport help make these difficult tasks a bit easier. The athletic trainer often finds himself or herself serving as a counselor to the athletes. Athletes may talk to the athletic trainer about problems relating to their own performance or that of their teammates or about problems on the team. The athletic trainer must be able to deal with the concerns of injured athletes; injured athletes may be fearful that they may not be able to return to 100% of their ability, that the injury will limit their performance in some way. The athletic trainer must be able to deal with these concerns in a sensitive but truthful manner. The athletic trainer may also be sought out by athletes for advice about their personal and academic problems. The athletic trainer must be able to deal with these numerous problems and concerns in an appropriate and professional manner.

The hours worked by trainers are long. In addition to being in the training room before practice and on the sidelines during practice and

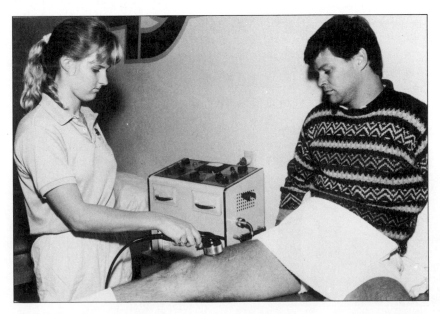

A primary responsibility of athletic trainers is to administer prescribed treatments.

competition, the trainer must often spend several hours in the training room at the conclusion of practices and competitions, dealing with any injuries that may have occurred and giving treatments. Trainers may have to come in on weekends for practice or contests and to give athletes treatments. During the season the athletic trainer travels with the team, and this travel can be quite extensive. Since athletic trainers frequently work several sport activities during the year, the season can go on without end. Less visible responsibilities also consume quite a bit of the athletic trainer's time. Cleaning up the training room, rerolling bandages, sterilizing the whirlpool, and ordering supplies are some of the other responsibilities of the athletic trainer. The long and demanding hours and lack of days off have resulted in some athletic trainers experiencing burnout, just as teachers and coaches do. (See Chapter 11 for a further discussion of burnout and its solutions.) Despite the long hours and other demands, many individuals pursue careers in athletic training because of the opportunity to help athletes attain their fullest potential and their desire to be closely associated with athletics. The intrinsic rewards, such as the satisfaction in helping an injured athlete return to competition quickly and at full potential, are many.

At the professional level, the athletic trainer's responsibilities include injury prevention and the care and rehabilitation of injured athletes. At the collegiate level, the athletic trainer's responsibilities may be expanded to include teaching courses in the physical education or health program. In an institution that offers an approved athletic training curriculum, athletic trainers can teach courses within the curriculum as well as supervise student athletic trainers.

At the secondary level, an athletic trainer may be employed in several different capacities. A school may employ a full-time athletic trainer, or the district may employ a full-time athletic trainer to serve all of the schools within the district. An individual may also be hired as a teacher/athletic trainer. Therefore athletic trainers may find it advantageous to possess a teaching certificate in physical education or another academic area.

Some schools may contract with a sports medicine center for an athletic trainer and for related services.

Athletic trainers affiliated with clinics generally work fewer hours than individuals in a school or professional setting, and their work schedule is often more regular. Trainers who work in these settings typically work on a one-on-one basis with the athlete. However, an increasing number of schools and community sports programs are contracting with these clinics for services. Therefore hours worked and working schedules may be similar to those of trainers employed in a school setting.

Salaries for athletic trainers vary from $20,000 to over $45,000 per year. The work setting, responsibilities, and amount of experience possessed by the individual influence the salary.

The National Athletic Trainers Association (NATA) offers a certification program in athletic training; increasingly this certification is becoming required to obtain a position. Certification can be attained by two routes. An individual can complete an approved athletic training program or can work under the direction of an athletic trainer as an intern or apprentice, so to speak. An approved athletic training curriculum includes courses in biological and physical sciences, psychology, first aid, and specific courses relative to training. Certification requires membership in NATA and passing a written and a practical exam. Information regarding certification procedures can be obtained from an athletic trainer or by writing to NATA, PO Drawer 1865, Greenville, NC 27834.

Some athletic trainers choose to continue their education and attain a master's degree in physical therapy to add to their skills. Prospective athletic trainers interested in pursuing work in physical therapy should check early in their undergraduate career, with institutions offering master's degrees in physical therapy, as to requirements for admission, including course prerequisites. Often courses in physics, chemistry, and math are required for admission to these schools. By knowing the prerequisites early, students may be able to use these courses as electives in their undergraduate professional preparation program. Other athletic trainers choose to continue their education by enrolling in a program leading to a master's degree in athletic training. Being active in professional organizations provides the opportunity to continue one's education through attendance at professional meetings and workshops.

Health and Weight Control Clubs and Spas

The number of health and weight control clubs and spas has increased greatly during the last decade. Many commercial enterprises have been established to capitalize on people's desire to be physically fit, to have a slim figure, and to look one's best. Some of these businesses are independently owned, whereas others are franchises. It is a multibillion dollar industry. As a result some health and weight control clubs and spas are only seeking the public's dollar rather than trying to be of service. However, many spas are reputable, are hiring trained personnel, and have excellent programs. Physical education and sport professionals not only will find a setting for employment in health and weight control clubs and spas, but they also can contribute to upgrading the standards of these businesses.

The activities and services offered by health clubs and spas vary widely. Fitness activities are an integral part of spas. Some spas may even offer graded exercise tests as part of their program. Many spas provide their clients with instruction and the opportunities to practice a variety of sport activities such as tennis, racquetball, volleyball, and swimming. Aerobic dance, swimnastics, weight training, and a diversity of exercise classes are common. Facilities may include pools; racquetball, handball, squash, and tennis courts; and such amenities as whirlpools, saunas, steam rooms, tanning booths, and massages. Health-promotion activities such as diet and nutritional counseling are often offered to the clients.

The cost of membership in these commercial health clubs and spas varies widely, ranging from a few hundred dollars to over a thousand dollars a year. In recent years the number of resort-type spas has grown; individuals desiring to shape up and lose weight check into the spa and stay from one to several weeks.

Another pronounced trend is the growth of commercial diet centers and weight-control spas and clubs. Like health clubs and spas, these may be independently owned or franchises. The focus of these businesses is on weight reduction.

These women are participating in a fitness program at a spa.

Exercise classes and fitness activities, similar to those offered in health clubs and spas, may be part of the weight reduction programs at these commercial enterprises.

The growth of these health and weight-control clubs and spas has led to a diversity of employment opportunities for physical education and sport professionals interested in working in these health-related careers. Responsibilities associated with these positions vary widely. Professionals may gain employment in these commercial enterprises as activity instructors or as exercise leaders. They may be responsible for leading an aerobic dance class or for setting up a weight training program for clients and monitoring their performance. In large clubs professionals may be responsible for training the club's instructors in various exercise techniques and supervising their work with the club's clients. Where weight control and nutritional counseling are primary concerns, professionals may evaluate the clients' dietary habits, design a diet to help them reach their goal, plan individual exercise programs to be followed in conjunction with the diet, and offer nutritional counseling. In many cases the professional will be required to attend in-service workshops on the specific diet approach espoused by the business and will also receive training in nutritional counseling and psychological techniques such as behavior modification.

Physical education and sport professionals may also be employed to manage these facilities. Even if professionals are employed as fitness instructors, they have many other responsibilities that are managerial in nature. These responsibilities may include record keeping, training and supervising employees, developing and implementing social programs, and membership solicitation. The varied responsibilities associated with these jobs suggest that in addition to courses in fitness, students should take courses in health, business, psychology, and recreation. Salaries can range from $23,000 to $40,000. Hours and days worked vary. As the interest in being fit and healthy in our society grows, opportunities for employment in these settings appear to be excellent.

Indoor rowing machines are popular among fitness enthusiasts. Competitions allow participants to test their ability.

THERAPY-RELATED CAREERS

Increasingly, movement in its many forms is being used as a means of therapy. Dance therapy, recreational therapy, and movement therapy are recognized as means of improving the physical, mental, emotional, and social well-being of individuals of all ages.

Dance Therapy

The use of dance has proved very helpful in alleviating physical, emotional, and social problems. It has received wide acceptance as a psychotherapeutic means of physical and emotional expression. Through dance the patient or client has freedom of movement and gains a sense of identity. Dance encourages individuals to recognize their emotions and express them. Through dance, by varying movement qualities, individuals can convey their feelings and ideas to others and perhaps portray emotions that they cannot verbally express. Dance provides a means not only to express one's feelings and emotions to others but also a means of gaining insight into oneself. Dance, by its very nature, can promote sensitivity and awareness.

Dance therapy is one of the fastest-growing professions. It is used in rehabilitation centers, psychiatric centers, geriatric programs, hospitals, and in programs for persons with disabilities. Dance therapy is used with all segments of the population from very young to very old persons. Certification standards for dance therapists have been established by the American Dance Therapy Association (ADTA).

Recreational Therapy

Therapeutic recreation is concerned with problems of physically, emotionally, and socially disabled persons and with elderly persons. Recreation therapists work in community and institutional settings where these individuals are located. Therapists use techniques of play and other recreational activities to help individuals achieve appropriate goals in physical, emotional, mental, and social development. Games, sports, arts and crafts, and social activities are modified to meet the needs of the patients or clients so that the goals of the program can be realized. Job opportunities for recreation therapists exist in nursing homes, senior citizen centers, child and day care centers, recreational programs, YMCA/YWCAS, hospitals, clinics, and private agencies.

Degree programs in therapeutic recreation are available. However, there are employment opportunities for physical education and sport professionals who have the background and desire to work in this area. Physical educators and sport leaders working in a community recreation agency may direct therapeutic recreation programs in addition to teaching physical skills and leading activities. More information about therapeutic recreation is available from the American Association for Leisure and Recreation, 1900 Association Drive, Reston, VA 22091-1599.

Homes for elderly people are a setting for recreation and leisure services. These students from a local middle school, under a teacher's supervision, are helping residents make "popcorn" with several balls on a parachute.

Movement Therapy

Movement therapists use movement to provide individuals an opportunity for expression, as well as to develop movement skills. Movement therapists work with individuals of all ages. In a preschool program a movement therapist may work with children to develop perceptual-motor skills. Another place of employment is the hospital setting or clinic where individuals who have impairments can be helped to learn essential movement skills. Developmental centers or special schools for persons with disabilities may also employ movement therapists.

•   •   •

Individuals interested in pursuing careers in dance, recreational, and movement therapy may benefit from courses in adapted physical education, psychology, health, recreation, and counseling. Many physical education and sport professionals build on their background in physical education, athletic training or exercise science at the undergraduate level to pursue master's degrees in physical, occupational, and corrective therapy. Physical education and sport professionals aspiring to continue their studies and pursue careers in these areas should early in their professional preparation identify courses that are needed as prerequisites for entry into master's degree programs in these areas. Students may then use these prerequisite courses as electives in their undergraduate curriculum.

As recognition of the therapeutic, recreational, and social benefits of movement increases, employment opportunities for physical education and sport professionals in these areas will expand.

INCREASING YOUR PROFESSIONAL MARKETABILITY

Students who are interested in fitness-, health-, or therapy-related careers can do much to increase their professional marketability. Taking additional course work, pursuing certification, building on one's talents and interests, and gaining practical experience will enhance the credentials of individuals seeking a position in these areas.

Additional courses in health will increase one's marketability. Conducting health-promotion programs—nutritional counseling, weight management, substance abuse, smoking cessation, and stress management—is often a responsibility associated with positions in this career area. Thus courses in nutrition, stress management, pharmacology, and drug education will be helpful to students preparing for careers in these areas. Courses in counseling, psychology, and sociology will be helpful as well. Prospective professionals need to develop the skills necessary to help individuals change their fitness and health habits. By understanding various decision-making approaches, motivational techniques, and behavior-modification strategies, physical education and sport professionals can help their clients achieve their goals, whether these goals are increased fitness, weight loss, or learning to manage stress. Since many fitness- and health-related careers include responsibilities such as budgeting, program promotion, membership solicitation, and bookkeeping, courses in business and computer science will help professionals perform these aspects of the job.

Attaining certification may also increase one's marketability. In many exercise specialist and fitness-related jobs, ACSM certification is becoming an increasingly common requirement. Even if such certification is not required for employment, certification as a Health/Fitness Instructor, for example, may be viewed positively by a prospective employer. Although certification in CPR and first aid may be required, it may be helpful to pursue additional certification as a CPR or First Aid Instructor. These certifications enable one to teach CPR or first aid in a corporate fitness center. Professionals interested in working as exercise specialists or athletic trainers may wish to become certified as EMTs. This will provide additional expertise in the area of emergency care. Belonging to professional organizations such as AAHPERD, ACSM, NSCA, NATA, and the National Therapeutic Recreation Society (NTRS) will also allow one to take advantage of workshops and clinics in one's area of interest.

Building on one's interests and strengths through extracurricular and outside experiences can contribute to one's professional expertise. If you are interested in weight training, for example, and work out frequently, take the time to learn about the different approaches to weight training. Expertise in dance is necessary for those seeking a career in dance therapy and can also enhance the skills of individuals seeking to work in corporate and community fitness centers and preschool programs. Aerobic dance has become a very popular approach to fitness and is often used in fitness centers. A background in dance is very helpful to professionals working with preschool children in designing movement experiences and helping children express themselves through movement.

Gaining practical experience through internships, fieldwork, volunteering, or part-time and/or summer employment can enhance one's marketability. There is no substitute for experience. Take advantage of the opportunities to work in potential places of employment to gain insight into the day-to-day work. Working as an assistant to a recreational therapist or physical therapist in a hospital, volunteering as a movement therapist in a preschool, assisting in a sports medicine clinic, supervising clients working out in a health spa, and interning in a corporate fitness center will provide practical experience and the opportunity to put theoretical knowledge gained in your undergraduate preparation into practice, as well as to learn the skills necessary for employment in these positions. Through various practical experiences, professional contacts can be developed as well.

Physical education and sport professionals can increase their opportunities for employment in fitness-, health- and therapy-related careers by several means. Taking additional course work, building on one's interests and strengths, attaining relevant certifications, and gaining practical experience are strategies that will enhance your marketability.

SUMMARY

Within the past decade opportunities for physical education and sport professionals desiring to pursue a career as a fitness or exercise specialist have increased tremendously. Career opportunities exist in preventive and rehabilitative exercise programs. Preventive exercise programs are conducted by corporations, community agencies, and commercial fitness clubs. Rehabilitative exercise programs are typically conducted in a hospital setting, but may be affiliated with corporate fitness programs and community agency programs.

Opportunities for physical education and sport professionals to pursue health-related careers have also grown rapidly. Professionals possessing qualifications in athletic training may find employment working with athletic programs at the professional, collegiate, and, increasingly, the secondary level. Employment opportunities also are available in sports medicine clinics, physical therapy clinics, and hospitals. Physical educators and sport leaders have also been successful in securing employment in health and weight control spas and clubs.

The recognition that participation in movement and physical activities has therapeutic and psychological benefits as well as physical benefits has stimulated the growth of therapy-related careers. These include careers as dance therapists, movement therapists, and recreational therapists.

Physical educators seeking employment in fitness- and health-related careers can increase their marketability by taking additional course work in health, business, and psychology. Gaining as much practical experience as possible will also be an asset in securing employment.

It appears that opportunities for qualified individuals in fitness- and health-related careers will continue to increase in the future.

SELF-ASSESSMENT TESTS

These tests are designed to help you determine if you have mastered materials and competencies presented in this chapter.

1. Describe the responsibilities of a fitness or an exercise specialist. If possible, interview a professional in this career regarding his or her responsibilities and qualifications.

2. Describe the various employment opportunities for a fitness or exercise professional. Review the want ads in several large city papers for three weeks for employment opportunities in this area; describe the positions that you found available.

3. Using the information provided in the Getting Connected box, access the Association for Worksite Health Promotion. Using the links provided, click on three worksite programs. Compare the programs in terms of facilities, program offerings, and other relevant features.

4. Using the information provided in the Getting Connected box, read about one of the certification programs available through the American College of Sports Medicine, American Council on Exercise, National Athletic Training Association, and the National Strength and Conditioning Association. For the association you have selected, investigate the certification programs, benefits offered to members, and opportunities for continuing education. How could this certification be beneficial to you in your chosen career?

REFERENCES

1. Cooper KH and Collingwood TR: Physical fitness: programming issues for total well-being, JOPERD 55(3):35–36, 44, 1984.

2. Sol N: Graduation preparation for exercise program professionals, JOPERD 52(7):76–77, 1981.

3. US Department of Health and Human Services: Physical activity and health: a report of the Surgeon General, Atlanta, Ga., 1996, US Department of Health and Human Services, Centers for Disease Control and Prevention, National Center for Chronic Disease Prevention and Health Promotion.

4. Wellness Councils of America: Health, wealthy and wise—fundamentals of workplace health promotion, Omaha, Nebr. 1993, Wellness Councils of America.

5. Anderson K: Cash rewards are made to a faithful few, USA Today, May 27, 1992, 1–2B.

6. President's Council on Physical Fitness and Sports: Economic benefits of physical activity, Washington, D.C., 1996, The President's Council on Physical Fitness and Sports Physical Activity Research Digest.

7. Association for Worksite Health Promotion: The benefits of worksite health promotion, 1997, Association for Worksite Health Promotion.

8. Lewis RJ, Huebner WW, and Yarborough CM, III: Characteristics of participants and nonparticipants in worksite health promotion, American Journal of Health Promotion 11:99–106, 1996.

9. Drolet JC and Fetro JV: State conferences for school worksite wellness: personal health practices of conference participants, Journal of Health Promotion 24(3):174–178, 1993.

10. Cohon A: Special treatment: hospital wellness centers, Athletic Business 21(7):31–34, 1997.

11. Aufsesser PM and Burke JP: The fitness clinic for physically disabled, Palestra 13:18–20, 1997.

12. Siedentop D: Introduction of physical education, fitness, and sport, Mountain View, Calif. 1990, Mayfield.

13. Zimmerman GR: Industrial medicine and athletic training: cost effectiveness in the nontraditional setting, Journal of Athletic Training 28(2):131–136, 1993

SUGGESTED READINGS

Anderson JJB and Anderson TW: Nutritional guidelines for injury prevention in school athletes, JOPERD 94(4):82, 1993.

Discusses the importance of sound nutrition in prevention of injuries in young athletes and dancers.

Arnheim DD and Prentice WE: Principles of athletic training, St. Louis, 1997, Mosby.

Provides a comprehensive source of information about athletic training, including an overview of the field, prevention strategies, and treatment techniques.

Aufsesser PM and Burke JP: The fitness clinic for physically disabled, Palestra 13:18–20, 1997.

Information about the fitness clinic for the physically disabled is presented, including program goals and the value of the program for young professionals.

Cohon A: Special treatment: hospital wellness centers, Athletic Business 21(7):31–34, 1997.

Hospital wellness centers are growing and offer additional opportunities for professionals in physical education and sport.

Grossman SG, Grieck J, Freedman A, and Fang WL: The athletic prevention programming and leadership education (APPLE) model: developing substance abuse prevention programs, Journal of Athletic Training 28(2):137–144, 1993.

Helps athletic trainers understand their responsibilities in drug and alcohol education and ways to fulfill them.

Hall LK, editor: Developing and managing cardiac rehabilitation programs, Champaign, Ill., 1993, Human Kinetics.

Comprehensive guide for designing and implementing cardiac rehabilitation programs.

Howley ET and Franks BD: Health fitness instructor's handbook, ed 3, Champaign, Ill., 1997, Human Kinetics.

Comprehensive information on planning and implementing fitness programs.

McLeroy KR, Bibeau DL, and McConnell TC: Ethical issues in health education and health promotion: challenges for the profession, Journal of Health Education 24(5):313–318, 1993.

Although this article is written for health educators, physical educators working in health promotion settings may find the examination of basic moral principles and ethical issues relevant to their work.

Walk SR: Peers in pain: the experiences of student athletic trainers, Sociology of Sport Journal 14:22–56, 1997.

This article provides insights about the experiences of student athletic trainers who work with their athlete-peers, including information about their expectations, management of injuries, and risks involved in sport.

Zimmerman GR: Industrial medicine and athletic training: cost effectiveness in the nontraditional setting, Journal of Athletic Training 28(2):131–136, 1993.

Discusses a new avenue of employment for athletic trainers, provides examples of programs, and presents suggestions for professional preparation.

Sport Careers in Management, Media, Performance, and Related Areas

Instructional Objectives and Competencies to be Achieved:

After reading this chapter the student should be able to—

◆ Identify opportunities for professionals in sport management and entry level positions in these careers.

◆ Describe career opportunities in sports media and explain how preparation in physical education and sport can assist individuals in these careers.

◆ Describe career opportunities in performance and other sport related careers.

◆ Discuss how professionals can increase their professional marketability.

Participation in fitness activities and sport at all levels is at an all-time high and it appears that participation will continue to increase in the future. One indication of this growth is the sale of fitness and sports products. In 1997, the Sporting Goods Manufacturer's Association reported that sales of fitness equipment reached $2.9 billion.[1] Sales of sports equipment, sports apparel, and athletic footwear approached $42 billion.[1] Sales of sports licensed products—that is U.S. retail sales of products for the National Basketball Association, National Football League, Major League Baseball, National Hockey League, and colleges/and universities—continue to rise, topping $11.3 billion in 1997.[1] As can be seen from these figures, interest in sports and fitness is tremendous, and the industry has become a big business. As participation and the sporting in-

dustry continue to grow, career opportunities in the various areas of sport management will expand.

Spectator interest in all sports at all levels is rising. Many sports recorded record-high attendance at contests. The NCAA's women's basketball Final Four championships were sold out, as were the men's Final Four championships. The new Women's Basketball League in its inaugural season drew nearly 16,285 fans at its championship game and nearly 50 million more viewed it on television. More than 20 million fans attended regular season NBA games. Major League Baseball, slowly rebounding from its strike, recorded its second highest attendance ever, 63.1 million. The growth of spectator interest in sport at all levels widens the career opportunities for physical education and sport professionals.

The media—television, newspapers, magazines, books, and movies—have come to play an increasingly important role in the realm of sports. Sports coverage by the various media continues to grow and has become big business. Monies paid by television for broadcasting rights to certain sports provide a good example of the magnitude of media involvement in sports. For example, the National Football League will get at least $17.6 billion from four television networks for the rights to broadcast games through 2005. Contrast that to 1960–1961 when the NFL received $600,000 for the television rights. NBC spent $2.6 billion dollars to secure the broadcast rights for the Olympic Games through the year 2008. CBS paid $1 billion dollars to telecast the NCAA men's basketball tournament. Premier sporting events, such as the Olympics, Superbowl, NCAA Basketball, National Basketball League Playoffs, Major League Baseball's World Series, and soccer's World Cup are watched by millions, even billions of people worldwide. For example, the National Basketball Association (NBA) playoffs on NBC were watched by nearly 600 million viewers; NBA programming is seen in nearly 200 countries in 41 languages. Media coverage of women's events is increasing also and is gaining in popularity. As media coverage continues to grow, so will opportunities for qualified professionals seeking a career in this area.

CAREERS IN SPORT MANAGEMENT

The increased growth of competitive athletics, sport participation by all segments of society, and sport-related businesses has created a need for individuals trained in sport management. Many career opportunities exist for qualified individuals in this field.

In recent years the realm of sport management has expanded to include a diversity of opportunities in a variety of settings. Employment opportunities include sport administration, management of sport clubs and facilities, sport and leisure social services, and sport marketing and promotion.

An increasing number of colleges and universities are offering undergraduate and graduate degrees in sport management. In 1992 the National

Association for Sport and Physical Education (NASPE) and the North American Society for Sport Management (NASSM) joint task force on sport management curriculum and accreditation developed a comprehensive set of competencies that should be included in a sport management professional preparation curriculum. The core content for undergraduate programs includes course work in the following areas: behavioral dimensions in sport (e.g., sport sociology), management and organizational skills in sport (e.g., sport management), ethics (e.g., ethics in business), marketing in sport (e.g., advertising), communication in sport (e.g., public relations), economics in sport (e.g., sport enterprise), legal aspects of sport (e.g., risk management), and governance in sport (e.g., sport administration).[2]

Practical experience is an integral part of preparation. An internship is now commonly required; students usually work in a sport management setting for a semester, working at least 40 hours a week and accumulating at least 400 hours. This experience is supervised by a faculty member from the undergraduate institution as well as by a professional at the internship site. Students may gain additional practical experience through fieldwork (short periods of supervised work in a practical setting), by volunteering, or by working in a sport management position during the summer or on a part-time basis during the school year. Practical experiences are also a good way to investigate the growing number of career opportunities in this broad field.

Individuals interested in pursuing a career in this area should understand that they will likely begin their career with employment in an entry level position, often with limited responsibilities. From this position, competent individuals can work their way through middle management and top management positions to assume increased and more broad-ranging responsibilities. Salaries in this field vary widely, ranging from $24,000 to $35,000 per year, although some salaries may be greater than $50,000 per year.

Athletic Administration

There are many job opportunities in the field of athletic administration. One such position is

GETTING CONNECTED

Online Sports Center lists jobs, has a place to post resumes, and has links to sport resources and listservs.
    Site: http://www.onlinesports.com

The Journal of Sport Media offers articles related to all aspects of the media and sport.
    Site: http://infotrain.magill.unisa.edu.au/epub/Special_Editions/ROGEA_WESOD/
         index.htm

The Cyber-Journal of Sport Marketing is a site for researchers, practitioners, and students in sport marketing.
    Site: http://www.cad.gu.edu.au/cjsm/home.htm

Sports Law Materials brings together information related to antitrust, contracts, torts, and federal statutes.
    Site: http://fatty.law.cornell.edu/topics/sports.html

ESPN, USA Today, CNN Sports, NBC Sports and *CBS Sports* sites provide up-to-date information about sports.

ESPN	Site:	http://esnet.sportszone.com
USA Today	Site:	http://www.usatoday.com/sports/sfront.htm
CNN Sports	Site:	http://www.cnn.com/SPORTS/cnnsi/index.html
NBC Sports	Site:	http://www.nbc.com/sports
CBS Sports	Site:	http://www.cbs.com/sports

director of athletics. The director of athletics is responsible for the administration of competitive athletic programs. These positions may be found at high schools, as well as at colleges and universities. Typically, at the high school level the athletic director may be employed as a teacher and, in smaller schools, also as a coach. At the collegiate level as well, athletic directors also may have teaching and coaching responsibilities. In many schools, however, particularly those with large competitive programs, the athletic director may have as his or her sole responsibility the conduct of the competitive program. In many instances athletic directors will have assistant athletic directors to help them in the performance of their work.

The athletic director is responsible for performing a myriad of tasks. The athletic director may delegate these tasks to assistants or perform them himself or herself. The athletic director is responsible

for the administration of men's and women's athletics. This includes both the hiring and ongoing supervision of coaches and assistant coaches. The athletic director must be knowledgeable regarding the rules and regulations governing athletic competition, including rules pertaining to the recruitment and eligibility of athletes. Other tasks are scheduling of athletic contests; arranging for officials; and, for competitions involving travel, planning for transportation, lodging, and meals.

The athletic director is also responsible for the safety of the coaches, athletes, and spectators at home contests. This involves working closely with security personnel and making careful provisions for crowd control. At home contests the athletic director supervises the ticket office and concessions. The athletic director must work closely with other personnel involved in athletics such as the athletic trainers and sport information directors. Establishing a good working relationship with the facilities manager and maintenance staff is important as well.

Development and management of the athletic budget is an important function of the athletic director, who is often expected to work as a fund raiser. Establishing and maintaining good relationships with the community, local support groups such as Booster Clubs, and alumni are seen as vital to the success of the athletic program. The athletic director must also attend professional meetings to keep abreast of changes in rules and governance.

In large athletic programs, such as those at major colleges and universities, there may be a fairly large administrative staff with specific job responsibilities assigned to each person. Many large institutions employ associate and/or assistant athletic directors. A few institutions employ directors of fund raising who are charged with obtaining money to supplement the athletic budget. Some institutions have employees who monitor the institution's compliance with the growing number of rules and regulations of the athletic governing bodies, most notably the National Collegiate Athletic Association (NCAA).

Salaries associated with the various jobs in athletic administration vary widely, depending on the extent of the responsibilities and the size of the program. For individuals who enjoy working with athletics, jobs in athletic administration can be very rewarding.

Director of Intramurals and/or Campus Recreation

College and university intramural programs and campus recreation programs have expanded in recent years. Traditional intramural programs have grown to include a variety of recreational opportunities. Wellness and fitness offerings, such as step aerobics, are also becoming popular. These programs have also expanded to include not only students but faculty, staff, and other campus personnel.

Many titles have been used to describe the individual charged with the administration of these programs. These titles include Director of Intramurals, Director of Recreational Sports, and Director of Campus Recreation. Depending on the institution, the intramural and campus recreation programs may be administered through student services, the physical education department, or the athletic department. In schools with large programs the director may have an assistant or several staff members to help conduct the program.

Responsibilities associated with this position are wide ranging. One of the primary responsibilities is to promote participation. This requires scheduling activities and tournaments that are of interest to students, publicizing programs, and working closely with campus groups such as residential life and student government to promote these programs. Training and supervision of officials are essential if programs are to run smoothly and safely. The director may also be responsible for instructional programs and the supervision of sport and recreation clubs. Often the director is assigned to supervise physical education and athletic facilities and open recreation programs such as recreational swimming. This may entail the training and supervision of numerous students to serve as lifeguards, gymnasium supervisors, or building security guards.

The intramural director may or may not have teaching responsibilities, depending on the size of the program. Programs are usually offered from late afternoon to late at night; frequently in schools with limited facilities, intramurals cannot start until the athletic teams have finished their practices. Programs also may be offered on weekends. Professionals who are interested in promoting educational values through activities and in providing opportunities for others to experience the satisfaction derived from participation will find working in intramural and campus recreation programs an enjoyable career.

Director of Corporate Recreation

More and more companies are providing recreational and sport opportunities for their employees. As the number of programs has increased, so has the need for qualified professionals to direct these activities. The responsibilities associated with this position are similar to those associated with the director of intramurals and/or campus recreation. These responsibilities include establishing a program of activities, setting up athletic teams, scheduling contests, providing for instruction, and supervising personnel. As corporate recreation programs continue to grow, so will opportunities for qualified professionals.

Sport Facilities Management

Facilities manager positions can be found in a diversity of settings. Facilities managers are traditionally employed by colleges and universities. Facilities managers are needed to direct community, municipal, and commercial facilities such as aquatic centers, ice arenas, domed stadiums, sports complexes, and golf courses. The growing number of fitness centers and health clubs has also increased opportunities for individuals interested in facilities management.

Depending on the size of the sport facility, nature of programs, and number of individuals using the facility, the sport facilities manager may perform all the responsibilities by himself or herself or may have an assistant or several staff persons under his or her direction. In some situations the facilities manager may have additional responsibilities; for instance, in a fitness club the facilities manager may also teach exercise classes or monitor individuals' workouts.

The new 70,000-seat Trans World Dome is home to the NFL's St. Louis Rams.

One of the primary concerns of the sport facilities manager is the safety of individuals using the facility. This involves making sure that the facility and equipment are maintained according to accepted standards. Knowledge of building codes, health and sanitation requirements, and law is necessary in this position. In facilities that are used for competitions such as stadiums, the facilities manager must make provisions to ensure the safety and well-being of spectators as well as participants. The manager must be concerned with crowd control and is responsible for security personnel. The facilities manager also is concerned about the business aspects of managing the facility, and he or she can have an impact on the financial success of the facility. The facility must be scheduled for maximum use so as to ensure a profitable financial status. The manager may also supervise other financial aspects of the facility such as ticket sales, concessions, and parking. As the number of facilities continues to grow, opportunities in this area for qualified personnel will expand.

Sport Retailing

Sales of sporting goods—equipment, apparel, and shoes—are at an all-time high. Exercise equipment tops sporting goods sales. It is estimated that adults in half of all U.S. homes own exercise equipment. In 1997, the Sporting Goods Manufacturer's Association reported that fitness equipment sales reached $2.9 billion; it is expected to increase 7% to $3.1 billion in 1998. Treadmills, stair-climbing machines, and free weights are among the most popular purchases. Sports apparel sales were $17.2 billion; sports shirts were the largest category, accounting for over $5 billion in sales. Athletic footwear sales were $8.9 billion. Basketball shoes were the largest shoe category, and accounted for $2.19 billion. Cross-training/fitness shoes, running shoes, and tennis shoes were also popular sellers. Sales of licensed sport apparel topped $11.3 billion in 1997. As can be seen from just a few of these figures, sport is big business. Additionally, the enormous growth of women's sports since the enactment of Title IX has created additional markets for sporting goods.

Manufacturers are now designing equipment and apparel specifically for girls and women, rather than downsizing boys' and men's products. The public's growing interest in sport, fitness, and physical activities has stimulated sales, and the traditional markets such as schools, colleges, and universities, and professional teams have remained strong. Consequently, job opportunities in sport retailing, in both management and sales, have increased and will continue to grow.

The area of sport retailing has several opportunities. Jobs are available as salespersons selling directly to the consumer in sporting goods stores. Job opportunities also are available as manufacturers' representatives. An individual employed in this capacity, perhaps as a representative for Nike Shoes, may sell to buyers for sporting goods stores and to athletic teams in a certain region. Manufacturers' representatives are committed to increasing their company's share of the market. This position entails a great deal of travel. Hours may be spent on the phone setting up appointments with potential buyers and following up on sales calls. Whether a manufacturer's representative is successful depends to a great extent on the quality and reputation of the product he or she is selling and the establishment of personal contacts with buyers for these stores and institutions. Manufacturers' representatives may often submit bids for equipment and goods wanted by stores and institutions. Successful bidding requires that the salesperson be able to meet the buyer's specifications for the equipment and goods at the lowest cost. Manufacturers' representatives may also set up sales booths for their companies at conventions such as the AAHPERD National Convention. Other opportunities in sport sales include positions as a manager or owner of a company.

Salaries for sales positions vary widely. Salespersons may receive a set salary. More often, however, their income is based on commissions and bonuses for the sales they have completed; thus their income may vary widely from month to month. Salespersons who travel may receive a company car or an allowance for the use of their personal car as well as an expense account. Salespersons may receive free equipment and goods or be able to purchase them at substantial discounts.

Being a salesperson requires that an individual be extremely knowledgeable about the products that he or she is selling. The consumer in a sporting goods store often expects the salesperson to be an expert on all types of equipment. Buyers for institutions and stores expect manufacturers' representatives to know all the specifications for the equipment and goods they are selling. A background in physical education and sport is helpful in understanding the demands and nature of various sport areas and the requirements for equipment and goods for these kinds of sports. Courses in business management and accounting are helpful for salespersons. Being a salesperson requires strong interpersonal skills and the ability to identify individuals' needs and to sell them a product that meets their needs. As the interest in sport, physical activities, and fitness continues to grow, opportunities for salespersons will expand as well.

Career Opportunities in Professional Organizations

Qualified physical education and sport professionals may find employment in one of the many professional or specific sport organizations such as AAHPERD, NCAA, National Federation of State High School Associations (NFSHSA), Ladies Professional Golf Association (LPGA), or United States Tennis Association (USTA). Other jobs are available in athletic conferences. The jobs available in professional organizations vary, depending on the nature of the organization and its size. Entry level managerial positions may be available dealing with the day-to-day operations of the organization. Other positions may entail fund raising, handling public relations, conducting membership drives, and directing special projects. If the organization sponsors a national convention, professionals are needed to assist in this endeavor; providing support and guidance to members preparing for local and regional conventions and coordinating meetings of the organization may also be part of one's responsibilities. Writing for the organization's newsletter and editing its periodicals are also jobs performed by individuals working for professional organizations. Professionals are also needed to serve as liaisons with the various committees of the organization. Still other positions in the organization may involve conducting special research projects, gathering data, and performing statistical analyses.

Individuals interested in this kind of career can obtain further information by contacting professional organizations in their area of interest. A complete listing of professional organizations may be found in the *Encyclopedia of Associations;* this book will likely be located at the reference desk of most libraries. Some organizations, AAHPERD, for example, may offer internships to students. Students interested in internships should write to the organization requesting information on these opportunities.

CAREERS IN SPORTS MEDIA

The pervasiveness of interest in sport in our society coupled with the growth of the communication media—television, radio, newspapers, and magazines—has contributed to the growth of career opportunities in sport communication. The last decade has also seen an increase in sport coverage by the media. The growth of media specifically dealing with sport has been phenomenal. For example, the number of sport periodicals has grown, including the number of periodicals dealing with specific sport areas such as running, body building, skiing, swimming, and bowling. Cable television channels such as ESPN provide round-the-clock coverage of sport. This growth has led to a number of career opportunities in sports media.

An individual interested in sports media can pursue one of several careers. These careers include sport broadcasting, sportswriting, sports journalism, sport photography, and sports information.[3]

Sport Broadcasting

Sport broadcasting is one career opportunity that has become increasingly popular. Sport broadcasting opportunities may be found with radio and television stations, including cable television, at local, regional, and national levels. Sport broadcasting requires not only knowledge of the game but also the ability to communicate in a clear, articulate fashion.

Preparation in physical education and sport will be helpful to the sportscaster. Sportscasters need to be knowledgeable about the skills, strategies, tactics, and rules used in sport, including the techniques of officiating. A background in physical education and sport will enable the sportscaster to be cognizant of the sport skills used in the competition and be readily able to detect errors in the athletes' performance. Studying physical education and sport will provide the sportscaster with an understanding of the manner in which athletes train for competition, the physiological effects of performance, and psychological insight into the athlete's actions. Sportscasters must be able to relate this information to the public in easily understood terms, providing the public with insight into the nature of the competition and the essence of the athletes' efforts. Familiarity with the sport enables the sportscaster to fluidly and accurately describe the play-by-play or moment-to-moment action and to present to the listening and watching public a vibrant portrayal of the athletes' actions.

Sportscasters need to have an in-depth knowledge of sport; in the eyes of the public the sportscaster is regarded as an expert on the sport he or she is covering. Therefore it is important that the sportscaster have an extensive preparation in sport. In a physical education and sport preparation program, the potential broadcaster may be exposed to the more common sports areas such as football, basketball, baseball and softball, aquatics, golf, track and field, tennis, and gymnastics. The sportscaster also needs to be familiar with other sports such as auto racing, horse racing, skiing, surfing, boxing, ice hockey, and figure skating.[3] Because instruction in many of these sports areas is typically not provided in professional preparation programs, the sportscaster must seek out experts in these sport areas for instruction, learn through on-the-job experience, or acquire knowledge by research.

Sportscasters' days are often long. Hours spent in front of the camera or the microphone are

Sportscasters must give the audience play-by-play information as well as insight into the game and the athletes' efforts.

most visible. In preparing for a broadcast the sportscaster may put in numerous hours researching the upcoming competition, compiling statistics on athletes' performances, writing scripts, rehearsing certain aspects of his or her performance, arranging and preparing for on-the-air interviews, gathering background information on the athletes, and preparing in numerous other ways. Although many top broadcasters have help with these aspects of the job, individuals just starting their career may have to do all this preparation on their own. In fact, many individuals start out their broadcasting careers by performing just such tasks for the established broadcasters.

Individuals desiring to pursue a career in broadcasting must be able to speak well and not be inhibited by speaking into the microphone or in front of the camera. The ability to think on one's feet is important because the action must be described as it unfolds. Courses or a minor in communication, particularly courses in speaking and interviewing, are critical. Courses or a minor in radio and television are valuable as well.

Practical experience can greatly contribute to one's success in attaining an entry level position in this career field. If your college or university has its own television or radio station, become involved in some aspect of its work. Understand that in many situations to gain a foothold it may be necessary to work on behind-the-scenes chores, such as researching material for the upcoming competition, before being afforded the opportunity to work in front of the microphone. If your college or university does not have a station or you are unable to attain a position at the station, perhaps you can gain experience by volunteering to announce and provide live commentary at college or university sporting events or events at the local high school. Try to gain employment or even serve as a volunteer at a local television or radio station for the summer or on a part-time basis throughout the year. Take advantage of opportunities provided by your college or university for fieldwork or internship at radio and television stations. The prospective sportscaster should also collect samples of his or her work to share with future employers. Audiotapes and videotapes of one's

Media coverage of girls' and women's sports is increasing.

performance as a broadcaster and copies of any reviews received can be an asset in gaining employment in this field.

The hours worked by a sport broadcaster may be varied; they are usually at night and on the weekends. Depending on the position, a lot of travel may be associated with the job. Rewards are great; there are opportunities to meet athletes, watch numerous contests, share one's love of sport with the listening or viewing public, and become intimately involved with the sport. Salaries vary according to one's location (i.e., working for a local station as compared to a national network); one's reputation as a broadcaster (well known or just beginning and without a reputation); and the sport covered. Individuals interested in this career may wish to join professional organizations such as the National Sportscasters and Sportswriters Association (NSSA), PO Drawer 559, Salisbury, NC 28144.

Sportswriting and Journalism

Individuals with a talent for writing may decide to pursue a career as a sport journalist or a sportswriter. The sport journalist may find opportunities for work with newspapers and in sport magazines, the number of which seems to be increasing all the time. Sport magazines may provide coverage of several areas such as *Sports Illustrated* or provide coverage of one specific sport such as *Runner's World*.

Sportswriters and journalists may cover events live or write in-depth or feature articles about athletes or various topics in the sport world. As in sport broadcasting, covering the athletic event and reporting it is the most visible part of this occupation. Researching stories, compiling statistics, and interviewing athletes and coaches are all functions of the sportswriter and journalist. The ability to meet deadlines and to write stories under time pressures is required. The work hours, opportunities to travel, and the rewards associated with this profession are similar to those associated with sport broadcasting.

A background in physical education and sport is helpful to the sportswriter and journalist. A physical education and sport background provides the writer and journalist with a broader understanding of the demands and nature of sport. For example, a sport journalist with course work in sport psychology may be better able to explain to the public why some athletes fail to perform under pressure or "choke," whereas other athletes appear to rise to the occasion. A sportswriter with an understanding of exercise physiology may be better able to explain what happens physiologically to athletes as they endeavor to complete the rigorous marathon. Sportswriters can call on their background in sport philosophy to describe the transcendental experience of an athlete winning an Olympic gold medal.

Prospective sportswriters and journalists can benefit from course work or a minor in writing and journalism. Practical experience, as in all careers, is an asset in gaining employment. Many sportswriters and journalists have gotten their start covering sports for their high school papers and continued this work for their collegiate newspaper. Experience working as an editor of the high school or college paper is an asset as well. These experiences can help prospective sportswriters and journalists gain internships or employment with local newspapers and sport publications. To assist

in gaining employment in this field, individuals should keep a well-organized scrapbook of their work. Individuals interested in pursuing a career in this area should consider joining NSSA.

Some physical education and sport professionals engage in sportswriting as a part-time career. For example, professionals may use their expertise to write textbooks and sport skills books. Another career opportunity in this area is working for a publishing company, editing physical education and sport texts.

Sport Photography

A career as a sport photographer may be attractive to physical education and sport professionals who have a strong interest in photography and the desire to communicate to others the essence and meaning of sport through photographs. Talent as a photographer is a prerequisite to such a career. Opportunities for sport photographers exist with newspapers and sport publications; many sport photographers pursue their careers independently as freelance photographers.

One's background and preparation in physical education and sport can enhance one's career as a sport photographer.[4] Knowing the essentials of sports skills from work completed in biomechanics can help the photographer understand the critical aspects of the skill performance and where to position himself or herself to get the best angle for the photograph. Knowledge gained from exercise physiology of the stress endured by athletes working at their utmost level of effort, understanding gained from the sociology of sport of the significance of sport in our society, and appreciation gained from sport philosophy of the personal meaning that sport holds for its participants can help the sport photographer better capture the true nature and meaning of sport in pictures.

Courses in photography, graphics, and art will be of assistance to the potential sport photographer. Take advantage of opportunities to gain practical experience. Covering sporting events for the campus or local newspapers, taking sport photographs for the yearbook, and contributing photographs to the sports information office to be used in promotional brochures are several ways to gain practical experience and exposure. Sport photographers should maintain a portfolio of their work so that potential employers may readily discern their talent.

Sports Information Director

The sports information director's primary function is to promote athletic events through the various media. Opportunities for employment as a sports information director are found mainly at colleges and universities. At the professional level many of the same responsibilities performed by the sports information director are handled by the director of public relations.

Among many responsibilities, the sports information director must maintain records and compile statistical information on all teams. He or she must design and prepare promotional brochures; this involves writing the copy for the text, obtaining photographs of the athletes, preparing the layout, and making arrangements for printing. Preparation of programs for various contests, including obtaining advertisements for the programs, is another responsibility of the sports information director. The sports information director provides assistance to the media covering home contests, phones in contest results to various media, writes press and television releases, writes commercials, and arranges press conferences and interviews for the media with coaches and athletes. Organization of special promotional events is also the responsibility of the sports information director. In a small school the sports information director may handle all these responsibilities personally, whereas in a larger school the sports information director may have several assistants. The hours are long, as the sports information director may be expected to personally cover many of the athletic events, and quite a bit of travel may be required.

Being a sports information director requires the ability to work closely with the members of the college and university administration as well as the athletic administration, coaches and athletes, and members of the various media. Excellent communication skills—writing, speaking, and interpersonal skills—are essential to this profession. In addition to a background in sport, courses in public relations, advertising, writing, and speech will be helpful. Experience gained in covering high school or college sport as a sportswriter or journalist and/or as a sport broadcaster is valuable. Faced with numerous responsibilities and demands, many college sports information directors would welcome volunteers interested in working in this career field. Volunteers may be assigned to work on promotional brochures, travel with teams to cover the competition, or work with the media covering home events. Volunteers should keep a file of their work. Prospective sports information directors may wish to obtain additional information from the College Sports Information Directors of America (COSIDA).

PERFORMANCE AND OTHER SPORT CAREERS

Dance Careers

Individuals talented in the various forms of dance may aspire to careers as professional dancers. Although college and university programs offer a major or a minor in dance performance, most college-age dancers have developed their talents through many years of private lessons, often commencing at an early age. Opportunities for professional dancers may be found with dance companies, theater companies, and television shows. Resorts and clubs where nightly entertainment is offered to guests are other settings for employment.

Individuals who enjoy dance but do not aspire to careers as professional dancers may decide to transmit their love for dance to others through teaching. Opportunities for dance teachers may be found at schools, colleges, and universities. Many individuals choose to teach dance at private studios; some start their own studios as well. A career as a dance therapist (Chapter 12) is also a viable career choice.

Expanding opportunities for individuals interested in a dance-related career can be found in dance administration. Dance administration may be an attractive choice for young dancers as well as dancers who are ready to retire from their performing careers. Lee[5] states that "dancers should capitalize on their professional strengths of fund raising, promotion, management, and administrative skills while integrating their knowledge of dance in such careers in dance company management as artistic director, managing director, development officer, public relations officer, and booking agent." Further information on dance careers may be obtained from the National Dance Association (NDA).

Professional Athletics

Highly skilled athletes may desire to pursue a career in professional athletics. Although many aspire to a career as a professional athlete, few individuals actually attain this goal. The expansion of men's teams and greater opportunities for women desiring to compete at this level have contributed to increased opportunities for skilled athletes of both sexes to pursue a professional career. Even though the opportunities are greater than in the past, the number of positions for individuals in professional sports is very limited.

The salaries paid to top professional athletes are astronomical and range from hundreds of thousands to millions of dollars. Well-known athletes earn even millions of dollars more in commercial endorsements. Other professionals may not fare as well. Baseball players may spend years in the minor leagues before being sent up to the majors, and golfers may spend years on the professional tour, struggling to make ends meet before attracting a sponsor or winning enough money to break even.[6]

Because of the limited opportunities in professional sports, and because many professional careers can be short-lived, individuals who desire to pursue this career should make every effort to complete their college degree. All aspiring professional athletes should take it upon themselves to ensure that they have the skills to earn a living should they fail to attain the professional ranks or have to leave the professional arena after a few years.

Professional dance requires a great deal of preparation and a high level of skill. These students are participating in a dance class at Florida A & M University, in Tallahassee, Florida.

Officiating Careers

Sports officiating usually starts out as a part-time job, but some individuals elect to pursue it on a full-time basis. The growth of competitive athletics at the high school and collegiate levels has created a need for qualified officials for all sports. Opportunities are also available at the professional level.

Part-time officials can increase their chances for year-round work by becoming certified or rated in two or more sports, each with a different season. Attaining a rating typically requires passing a written exam as well as a practical exam. In some sports, beginning officials must spend a certain period of time working with experienced officials before being able to officiate alone. Individuals interested in information about becoming a rated official should ask an official in the sport, contact the local officials association or board of officials, or write the National Association for Girls and Women in Sports (NAGWS) at AAHPERD.

Individuals interested in officiating should take advantage of opportunities to practice. Officials are needed for high school and college intramurals, summer adult recreational leagues, and youth sport leagues. Volunteering to work at home contests at your college or university as a scorekeeper or in some other capacity is another way to gain experience in this area. In officiating, one must not only know the rules but possess good officiating mechanics. For example, being able to place oneself in the right position at the right time requires an understanding of the flow of the game. Practice will enhance one's officiating skills.

In addition to being knowledgeable about the rules of the sport and skilled at the mechanics of officiating, officials must be able to work under pressure. Officiating also requires good interpersonal skills and communication skills to work with coaches and athletes in highly competitive and stressful situations.

Officials usually work on afternoons, nights, and weekends because this is when most athletic contests are conducted. Some travel is involved. Salaries have improved considerably during the last few years, and officials are often reimbursed for their travel costs. Officiating can be a challenging career on a part-time or full-time basis.

Sport Law

One career opportunity that has attracted the interest of some physical education and sport professionals is sport law. In litigation involving sport, a physical educator's background and practical experience as a teacher and a coach can be an asset.

A career in sport law is not a career that can be prepared for directly through one's undergraduate academic experiences. The practice of sport law requires the completion of law school, which typically involves a 3-year program of study. Admission to law school is very competitive. Admission requires an excellent academic average, and many law schools also have prerequisites or prefer the candidate to have certain areas of undergraduate study. For practitioners with experience seeking to change their career focus, however, sport law may be an attractive area of study. The growth of sport management curriculums has also created a need for individuals with preparation in sport law to teach courses in sport law and liability. Another career opportunity for individuals with expertise in sport law is in working with professional athletes, serving as their agents in contract negotiations.

Entrepreneur

An increasing number of professionals are using their skills and competencies to become entrepreneurs. These individuals develop services and products to meet the public's needs and interests. The broad area of physical education and sport offers many entrepreneurial opportunities to motivated professionals. You may choose to pursue these opportunities on a full- or part-time basis.

Perhaps the most visible of all entrepreneurs in the profession are personal trainers. As discussed in Chapter 12, these professionals work one-on-one with the client, designing and implementing fitness programs tailored specifically to the client's needs. Personal trainers typically visit the client's home to monitor the workout.

Programming in the area of fitness and health promotion offers many entrepreneurial opportunities.[7] Many individuals who are interested in improving their fitness and health are willing to pay professionals for the opportunity to learn the skills necessary to achieve a high level of wellness. Entrepreneurs can design and offer health enhancement programs to meet these needs. Programs can focus on fitness assessment and improvement, nutrition, stress management, or weight reduction. These programs can be presented to interested individuals during the afternoon or evening. These programs also can be marketed to corporations that wish to offer these services to their employees but do not have the expertise to conduct such programs. Creative individuals also can produce and market instructional books and videos focusing on fitness and health.

Some professionals with a strong background in exercise science and administration use their skills to serve as consultants. They visit various fitness sites, such as a health club, assess the current program, make recommendations for improvement, train employees, and organize a system for ongoing program and employee evaluation.

Another opportunity for enterprising individuals with competency in exercise science is the establishment of a mobile fitness and health appraisal business.[8] Using a van filled with appropriate equipment, the professional can travel to different worksites to offer fitness appraisal and health enhancement programs to employees.

Personal coaching is a viable opportunity for individuals with expertise in a specific sport and the ability to coach individuals to achieve a high level of performance.[8] Parents may be interested in obtaining private coaching to help their children further develop sport skills. Many amateur and professional athletes use the services of a personal coach on a regular basis. Opportunities for personal coaching are most commonly found in individual sports such as swimming, diving, golf, tennis, track and field, and ice skating, although participants in team sports (e.g., basketball) may use a personal coach on an intermittent basis to refine selected aspects of their performance.

Professionals with expertise in biomechanics can offer computerized skill analysis services to athletes as well as to coaches interested in furthering their team's performance.[8] The athlete is videotaped and the performance is computer analyzed.

The analysis is reviewed with the athlete and suggestions for improvement are given. Instructional videotapes can be offered to complement this service. Sites for this service typically include golf courses, tennis clubs, sporting goods stores, and various other sport facilities. The professional can also contract for this service with interested individuals, such as a coach desiring an analysis of individual team members' skills or a parent wishing a more detailed assessment of his or her child's skill performance.

Throughout the United States, sport and fitness camps for individuals of all ages are proliferating. Instructional camps are available for virtually every sport, although the most popular sports tend to be soccer, baseball, softball, tennis, golf, and volleyball. The number of instructional sports camps for youths with disabilities also is growing. There are also camp programs that focus on increasing fitness and reducing weight. Although camp programs traditionally have focused on children and youth, there are a growing number of programs that target the adult population, in the areas of both sports and fitness. Directing sports and fitness camps offers many fine entrepreneurial opportunities. Because many of these programs are offered during the summer months or school vacations, teaching and coaching professionals often find employment in such programs and welcome the opportunity to supplement their salary.

There are numerous entrepreneurial opportunities for motivated physical education and sport professionals. Individuals aspiring to such a career must ask themselves two critical questions: (1) Do I have a viable, marketable service or product? and (2) Is there a consumer desire for the service or product? Furthermore, professionals must make sure they have the dedication, enthusiasm, initiative, and self-confidence to pursue this career successfully. The amount of financial resources necessary varies; some services, such as personal fitness instructor, require very little financial investment, whereas other services, such as a mobilized health and fitness business, may require considerable capital to purchase the necessary equipment. Young professionals who are innovative and aspire to be their own bosses will find a host of entrepreneurial

Summer sports camps give children and young adults an opportunity to learn new skills and develop their athleticism. University of Tennessee coach Pat Summitt lectures at a basketball camp with the assistance of her staff and players.

opportunities available to them in the twenty-first century.

INCREASING YOUR PROFESSIONAL MARKETABILITY

Individuals interested in pursuing sport communication and sport management careers can increase their professional marketability in several ways. Taking course work and minors in appropriate areas can enhance one's marketability. For individuals interested in sport media careers, courses or a minor in speech, photography, journalism, and broadcasting will be an asset. Those who are interested in sport management careers can benefit from courses in business, management, law, and communication. Students also need to take courses specifically applying knowledge from other disciplines to sport communication and sport management—for example, courses in sport journalism or sport law.

Individuals interested in pursuing sport media, sport management, performance, and other sport-related careers need to be cognizant that the positions described in this section are often top-level positions. Attaining them requires a willingness to work one's way "up the ladder." Professionals should gain access to these positions through entry-level positions. For example, if you aspire to a career as an athletic director, you may first have to work as an assistant athletic director to gain the necessary experience and skills.

Practical experience is necessary to move up the career ladder. It can be gained from volunteering one's services, summer employment, and collegiate fieldwork and internship opportunities. Practical experience not only allows one to gain and refine the necessary skills but also allows one to develop professional contacts and exposure. These skills and professional contacts will contribute to gaining employment and advancing up the career ladder.

SUMMARY

Sport has developed into a big business. Consequently, individuals trained in sport management are needed. Qualified professionals interested in sport management may pursue careers as athletic directors, directors of intramurals and campus recreation, directors of industrial recreation, and sport facilities managers. Individuals interested in retailing may choose a career in sport business management and sport sales. Managerial opportunities are also available in professional organizations.

The intensity of interest in sport in our society coupled with the growth of the communication media has resulted in the expansion of career opportunities in the field of sport media. Individuals interested in this area can pursue careers in sport broadcasting, sportswriting, sports journalism, sport photography, and sports information.

Talented individuals may elect to pursue careers as performers. Other sport-related careers that may be attractive to qualified individuals are sport officiating and sport law.

Physical education and sport professionals can use many strategies to enhance their professional marketability. Taking course work in supporting areas and gaining practical experience will help individuals attain the position that they desire after graduation.

SELF-ASSESSMENT TESTS

These tests are designed to help you determine if you have mastered the materials and competencies presented in this chapter.

1. Discuss how a background in physical education and sport can be an asset to individuals pursuing a diversity of sport media careers.

2. If possible, interview individuals working in sport management positions. Ask each person to define his or her responsibilities and the skills that are the most helpful in the performance of the job. Determine the entry-level positions in this area. Ask each individual for suggestions about advancing to top-level managerial positions in the field.

3. Discuss the positive and negative aspects of pursuing a performance career. Since performance careers may be of short duration, how can individuals prepare for another career after the culmination of their performance career?

4. Using the information provided in the Getting Connected box, read an article posted on the *Journal of Sport Media* site or on the *Cyber-Journal of Sport Marketing* site. Summarize the article and share what you have learned with your classmates.

REFERENCES

1. National Sporting Goods Manufacturers Association, SGMA Recreation Market Report, 1998.

2. NASPE-NASSM Joint Task Force on Sport Management Curriculum and Accreditation: Standards for curriculum and voluntary accreditation of sport management education programs, Journal of Sport Management 7:159–170, 1993.

3. Lambert C: Sports communications. In WJ Considine, editor: Alternative professional preparation in physical education, Washington, D.C., 1979, National Association of Sport and Physical Education.

4. Clary J: Careers in sports, Chicago, 1982, Contemporary Books.

5. Lee S: Dance administrative opportunities, JOPERD 55(5):74–75, 81, 1984.

6. Heitzman WR: Opportunities in sports and athletics, Lincolnwood, Ill., 1984, National Textbook.

7. Westerfield RC: Entrepreneurial opportunities in health education, JOPERD 58(2):67–70, 1987.

8. Pestolesi RA: Opportunities in physical education: what the entrepreneur can do, JOPERD 58(2):68–70, 1987.

SUGGESTED READINGS

American Alliance for Health, Physical Education, Recreation, and Dance: Entrepreneurial opportunities in health, physical education, recreation, and dance, JOPERD 58(2):64–77, 1987.

A series of six articles discusses entrepreneurship and opportunities available to interested and dedicated individuals.

Chouinard N: Some insights on meaningful internships in sport management: a cooperative education approach, Journal of Sport Management 7:95–100, 1993.

Presents goals and objectives of internships and characteristics of quality internships.

Daddario G: Gendered sports programming: 1992 Summer Olympic coverage and the feminine narrative form, Sociology of Sport Journal 14:103–120, 1997.

The author analyzes the Olympic coverage, suggesting that parallels exist between soap operas and Olympic programming, and that coverage is influenced by the desire to attract a female audience.

Kinkema KM and Harris JC: Sport and the mass media. In JO Holloszy, editor: Exercise and sport science reviews 20:127–160, Baltimore, 1992, Williams & Wilkins.

The various dimensions of the relationship between the mass media and sport are discussed.

Mawson L: Total quality management: perspectives for sport managers, Journal of Sport Management 7:101–106, 1993.

The total quality management technique, which is increasing in popularity in the business realm, is applied to sport management.

NASPE-NASSM Joint Task Force on Sport Management Curriculum and Accreditation: Standards for curriculum and voluntary accreditation of sport management education programs, Journal of Sport Management 7:159–170, 1993.

Presents the approved curricular standards for sport management.

Parkhouse BL: The management of sport: its foundation and application, ed 2, Dubuque, Iowa, 1996, Brown & Benchmark.

Fundamentals of sport management, human resource management, policy, facilities, marketing, economics, and financing are discussed in this text.

Parks JB, Zanger BRK, and Quarterman J: Contemporary sport management, Champaign, Ill., 1998, Human Kinetics.

The scope and opportunities within the realm of sport management, challenges, and professional development are included.

Soucie D and Doherty A: Past endeavors and future perspectives for sport management research, Quest 48:486–500, 1996.

Provides an analysis of research in sport management and presents a conceptual model to guide future research.

Weeks S, editor: Dance careers in the 80s, JOPERD 55(5):73–81, 1984.

Although written for the 80s, presents directions in dance administration and performance that also are applicable for the 90s.

Zakrajsek DB: Sport management: random thoughts of one administrator, Journal of Sport Management 7:1–6, 1993.

Presents an administrative perspective of sport management programs, including the role of sport in society and future directions.

PART FOUR

Issues, Challenges, and the Future of Physical Education and Sport

Introduction

Physical educators and sport leaders need to be aware of the issues and challenges facing the field today. If professionals hope to influence the future direction of physical education and sport in our society, they must lead the way.

Following an overview of issues in physical education and sport today, Chapter 14 examines five of the issues confronting professionals. Four of the challenges to physical education and sport professionals are addressed as well. Chapter 15 discusses trends and the future of physical education and sport.

Issues and Challenges in Physical Education and Sport

Instructional Objectives and Competencies to be Achieved:

After reading this chapter the student should be able to—

♦ Discuss the role of physical education and sport professionals in the consumer education movement relative to physical activity and fitness.

♦ Discuss how physical education and sport professionals can promote the development of values in physical education and sport.

♦ Interpret the role and contribution of physical education and sport professionals in the conduct of youth sport programs.

♦ Identify suggested names for the field currently entitled physical education and sport and discuss the implications of the growth of the field.

♦ Discuss the gap that exists between research and practice, and describe how this gap can be lessened.

♦ Identify and describe strategies physical education and sport professionals could use to promote quality daily physical education throughout the country.

♦ Explain the importance of quality public relations programs in a variety of physical education and sport settings.

♦ Define the role of physical education and sport professionals in attaining the specific fitness and exercise goals delineated in the report *Healthy People 2000*.

♦ Describe specific strategies that could be used to help promote lifespan involvement in physical activity and sport.

Many issues and challenges confront the field of physical education and sport today. As professionals we need to be cognizant of the issues concerning the profession at all levels. As a physical education and sport professional, you will likely be perceived by the public as an expert in matters involving physical education and sport. As such, you need up-to-date information on current issues so that you may give accurate, knowledgeable, and easily understood answers to the public's queries. This requires that you keep abreast of events and developments through newspapers, television, the World Wide Web, professional journals, and professional meetings and conferences.

The field is also facing a great number of challenges. As professionals we must take an active role in meeting these challenges. This requires commitment and professional leadership at all levels. The continued growth of the field, its vitality and its future, depends on professionals' commitment and leadership.

This chapter focuses on some issues and challenges confronting the field. To address all of these issues and challenges would require a separate text. The purpose of this chapter is to introduce some of the issues facing the field today and to discuss five of the issues at greater length. This chapter concludes with a discussion of four of the challenges to the field of physical education and sport and its members.

ISSUES IN PHYSICAL EDUCATION AND SPORT TODAY

Numerous issues confront professionals in physical education and sport today. Some of these issues are presented here, with the goal of creating an awareness of the problems and stimulating further efforts to address them.

Problems within sport exist at all levels, from professional athletics to youth sports. At the professional level, gambling and drug abuse have commanded a great deal of attention, as have astronomical player salaries and striking players and game officials. Increased player violence has raised concern, and growing fan violence has led some teams to curb the sale of alcohol at events. In professional tennis, concern about competitors "burning out" at an early age has led to attempts to curtail the playing schedules of young athletes and to establish minimum age requirements for players to join the tour. Questions also have been raised about the responsibility incumbent on professional athletes to serve as role models to the nation's youth.

Violence is a problem in sports today.

Collegiate athletics have attracted attention as well. The increasing professionalization of collegiate athletics has been decried by many. In many institutions collegiate athletics have become big business, raising the concern that athletics is overemphasized at the expense of academics. Scandals involving the recruitment of athletes, tampering of grades on transcripts to ensure the admission of athletes to schools or their continued eligibility, questions about the academic progress of athletes, and illegal drug use to enhance performance have drawn national attention. Sport governing bodies have sought to rectify these problems by imposing stricter regulations and establishing more stringent academic requirements for student-athletes. However, questions about the place of athletics in educational institutions continue to be raised.

At the high school level questions have been raised about the academic qualifications of athletes as well. The practice of extending favorable treatment to athletes, such as issuing them passing grades when it is not warranted, has resulted in some cases of graduating athletes who are illiterate. Efforts to address this problem have included

GETTING CONNECTED

National Collegiate Athletic Association site offers access to the NCAA news on-line, which contains information on current programs and contemporary issues.

      Site: http://www.ncaa.org

National Federation of State High School Associations site hosts current press releases on high school athletics.

      Site: http://www.nfshsa.org

Sport Information Resource Center is a comprehensive site containing information about sports, fitness and related fields. **SPORTQuest** is the sport information service of *SIRC.*

      Site: http://www.sirc.ca/
                  http://www.SPORTQuest.com/

Women's Sports Foundation site hosts information about girls' and women's participation, publications and reports, and sport and fitness information.

      Site: http://www. lifetimetv.com/WoSport/index.html

the adoption of "no-pass, no-play" rules whereby students must maintain a certain academic average to participate in extracurricular activities. In some school districts, budgetary constraints have led to "pay-to-play" rules where students must pay a fee to participate in extracurricular activities, including athletics. In 1994, the National State High School Association found that 25% of its member schools charged students fees to participate. Many believe that overinvolvement of parents and community members in conjunction with an overemphasis on winning has detracted from the educational value of sport. In recent years concerns have also been expressed about the increase in specialization; athletes are focusing on one sport throughout the entire year instead of participating in two or three sports per year.

Serious concerns have also been raised regarding the conduct of youth sports. One major problem is the overemphasis on winning, especially at the younger levels. This emphasis has led to the abandonment of the developmental approach to sport, which stresses age-appropriate activities and coaching, in favor of the professional approach, which focuses on winning. Youth sport programs could not exist without the thousands of adult volunteers who serve as coaches. Although many of these coaches do an outstanding job, some youth coaches lack the necessary preparation to teach skills, treat injuries, and meet the important developmental needs of children. Communities are offering educational programs for youth sport coaches to help them acquire the necessary skills and understandings to foster a positive sport experience for the young athletes involved. Well-intentioned, but overly involved parents also contribute to problems in this area when they impose pressure on their children to win or use their children to live out their own unfulfilled athletic dreams.

Current issues are by no means limited to sport. The status and nature of school physical education programs, at both the elementary and secondary levels, are being challenged. Physical education programs and teachers face problems similar to those experienced in other academic areas—increased calls for accountability, dwindling economic resources, the need to deal daily with student violence and drug abuse, insufficient parental support, increasingly difficult student discipline, and career burnout. Additionally, physical education faces some unique problems. Class sizes are often larger and more heterogenous than classes in other subject areas. Administrative and teacher support for physical education is often lacking. The many and diverse expectations associated with the multiple roles of teacher and coach may lead to difficulty in meeting these competing demands. There is an ongoing debate among professionals in our field regarding the goals of physical education, desired outcomes and their priority, and the content of the curriculum. Last, physical education is typically undervalued as a school subject, often being perceived as a frill and of little educational value.

Physical education faces tremendous challenges to its integrity as a school subject and increased pressure to fight for its place in the school curriculum. It is ironic that, at a time when the American public's interest in fitness is at an all-time high, support for physical education in the schools is eroding. The public has an increased awareness of the concomitant health benefits to be gained from participation in fitness and physical activities. Yet support is often lacking for physical education, which can provide students with the skills, knowledge, and understanding essential to leading a physically active lifestyle throughout their lifespan.

The growing educational reform movement and its increased emphasis on academics threaten school physical education programs. Time allocated for physical education in the curriculum, which is often less than for other subject areas, may be further reduced as the reform movement takes hold. Only 1 in 4 high school students have physical education daily. Participation in daily physical education declined from 42% in 1991 to 25% in 1995. As we move toward the twenty-first century and increasingly embrace technological approaches to education, children may attend school only 3 days a week and work the remainder of time at home using interactive computers, cable television, and distance learning. Physical education and sport professionals will need to find different settings and use new approaches to reach these students.

The growth of nonschool physical education and sport opportunities is of concern as well. Many of these nonschool programs are conducted by individuals without training in physical education and sport. The growth of commercial sport clubs, fitness centers, and health clubs in response to the public's demand for instruction in sports and fitness development has led to the employment of some individuals without adequate professional preparation in the field. Physical education and sport professionals need to establish leadership in this area.

The growth of interest in competitive sport and fitness has led to the expansion of opportunities available for people of all ages and abilities. Yet, we must give greater attention to meeting the needs of special population groups—the elderly and people of all ages with disabilities. As the growth of commercial programs continues, we must make sure that community programs remain strong so that opportunities are available for those who do not have the ability to pay. The evidence supporting the value of regular physical activity and the contribution of physical activity to health is overwhelming. Although the research shows that the fitness movement involves participants from every population group, individuals who are young, male, white, upper-middle class, suburban, and highly educated are more likely to be involved. Greater efforts must be made to reach all segments of the population—the poor, the elderly, members of minority groups, and individuals with disabilities.

As the emphasis on health promotion and disease prevention continues to increase and the role of physical activity becomes more strongly defined, the schools have the ability to play a more significant role in attaining the nation's public health goals. The schools provide a means to reach millions of children and youth and teach them the skills, knowledge, and positive attitudes necessary for a lifetime of physical activity. Additionally, although the role of personal responsibility is emphasized in health promotion endeavors, it is important not to become insensitive to the impact of social conditions, especially poverty and discrimination, on health status. Providing access to services for all Americans is a pressing need as we approach the twenty-first century.

Equity is another issue that must be addressed by our field. Although it has been over 25 years since the enactment of Title IX, inequal opportunities for males and females in sports still exist. Although sport participation among females increased dramatically during the two preceding decades, inequalities still exist in participation opportunities, budget, facilities, and administrative and coaching positions, as well as in other areas of the sporting enterprise.

Racism is another issue that must be confronted. Desegregation of sports has opened doors for participation of minorities in sports. However, participation has not led to the elimination of prejudice, stereotyping, and exploitative practices. Discrimination and exclusionary practices have limited opportunities for minorities in administrative and coaching positions in sports. Professionals in physical education and sport have spoken strongly about the need to recruit minorities into higher education and prepare them for a multitude of careers in this field.

This section has provided an overview of some of the problems and issues confronting the field of physical education and sport today. Many solutions have been offered for these situations. However, the success of any solution requires the commitment of professionals who are dedicated to the improvement of the field. This past section gave a brief overview of some of the problems and issues facing physical education and sport professionals today. The remainder of the chapter will examine in some detail five of the issues confronting physical education and sport and four of the challenges that need to be met by professionals in the field.

The American Academy of Kinesiology and Physical Education is composed of individuals who have made significant contributions to the profession. In 1981 an Academy poll revealed three of the most urgent issues facing our field. They were (1) the need for physical educators to become active in educating consumers about physical activities, (2) the need for increased emphasis on affective behavior in school physical education programs, and (3) the need for physical educators to assume a more active role in conducting youth sport programs. These issues are still a critical concern today as we move into the next century. These three issues will be discussed briefly in the following section. Additionally, two other issues will be examined—the growing field of physical education and sport, and closing the gap between research and practice.

Many challenges also confront physical education and sport professionals today. Four of these challenges will be addressed in the last section of the chapter. Professionals must become more active in making daily quality physical education programs in the nation's schools become a reality. They also must become more active in public relations efforts to promote physical education programs. Professionals are challenged to attain the national health objectives and to promote lifelong involvement in physical activity and sport for all people.

Leadership in the Consumer Education Movement

Physical education and sport professionals must become active in the consumer education movement relative to physical activities and exercise.[1] The past decade has witnessed dramatic increases in participation in fitness and physical activities by people of all ages. As individuals have sought to become involved in physical activities and fitness, an unprecedented proliferation of products and programs designed to capitalize on these interests has occurred. While many of these programs are sound in nature, others are not as reputable. There is concern about the validity of claims made for some programs and products.

All types of diets, diet pills, and diet and health foods have been advertised as aids to weight reduction, weight management, and healthy living. The marketplace offers the consumer a wide choice of exercise equipment and sport apparel. Books and periodicals concerned with various aspects of fitness and sport occupy conspicuous spaces on the newsstands and bookstore racks. Videotapes of movie stars leading specially designed fitness programs are bestsellers.

Commercial sport clubs, fitness centers, and health spas often advertise their services and programs as leading to quick and dramatic results.

Consequently, the wide range of products and programs relating to physical activities and fitness makes it important that members of the public make an educated choice from among the services and goods available; participation in programs that are unsound or the use of products that are of questionable value can have harmful results. Bearing this in mind, the Academy urges physical education and sport professionals to take a more active role in educating consumers about physical activities and fitness. Professionals must educate both their students and the adult public about physical activities and fitness. This requires that professionals not only be knowledgeable about the various facets of physical activities and fitness, but also that they make the public aware that they are the experts and a resource to which the public can come to seek answers to their questions. Physical education and sport professionals must also provide the public and their students with the necessary skills and knowledge to evaluate their own fitness and physical activity needs and problems. This involves educating the consumer about the "hows" and "whys" of exercising properly. Professionals must also help their students and the public to gain the skills necessary to be lifelong learners and self-educating with regard to physical activity and fitness. The Academy also urged professionals to take increased responsibility to conduct research of a practical and applied nature with respect to fitness and the psychological aspects of physical activity. Professionals need to translate appropriate research findings into practical applications easily understood by the layperson.

Professionals should be leading the fitness movement and exerting a significant influence on its direction. Corbin,[2] in a *Journal of Physical Education, Recreation, and Dance* editorial, asks, "Is the fitness bandwagon passing us by?" Corbin points out that physicians, self-appointed experts, and movie stars are at the vanguard of the fitness movement. Many of these people lack the qualifications, training, and expertise to be directing this movement. Corbin asks, "What is the problem?" He states:

While many physical educators are experts, many are not. Some have no desire to be! I *am not* arguing that we should devote all our efforts to physical fitness or exclude other important educational objectives. I *am* arguing that one of the most important social services we can provide is to teach about fitness and exercise. Like no other profession, we should be knowledgeable in this area.

Corbin suggests that professionals can do several things to "lead the parade!" Physical education and sport professionals should actively seek leadership roles in the fitness movement. First, as experts professionals should be cognizant of current findings in the field. Second, the consumer needs to be made aware that physical education and sport professionals are experts in this field and are a resource for answers as well as advice. Professionals should educate their students and the public to be wise consumers of exercise programs and products. Additionally, professionals should provide their clientele with the knowledge and the skills to solve their own exercise and physical activity problems and to evaluate their own fitness needs.

Ewers[3] echoes Corbin's call for physical education and sport professionals to lead the "exercise parade." He encourages physical education and sport professionals to be "pace setters" by "practicing what you know and believe about the benefits of movement." Physical education and sport professionals must take an active role in the physical activity movement. As professionals we must provide leadership for this movement because it falls within our domain. We must take advantage of this interest in fitness and physical activity to educate people of all ages about fitness and physical activities and to teach them skills necessary for lifetime participation.

Teaching Values in Physical Education and Sport

The development of values, character, and ethical decision-making skills has long been touted as one of the primary purposes of school physical education programs and one of the lasting outcomes of athletic participation. Professionals have promoted our programs as the means to develop such commendable values as cooperation, self-discipline, hard work, fair play, emotional control, and teamwork. The enhancement of self-esteem and self-confidence has also been cited as an outcome of participation in physical education and sport. However, there appears to be a gap between rhetoric and the reality of practice, a discrepancy between the outcomes claimed for physical education and sport and the behaviors practitioners and participants exhibit. While many practitioners believe that ethical and moral development are important, oftentimes they fail to structure their programs to achieve these outcomes or their actions belie their words.

In recent years ethical and moral abuses associated with sport at all levels have gained increased notoriety. Sport has long been extolled as a vehicle for building character and teaching such values as sportsmanship, fair play, honesty, and integrity. Athletes are often placed on a pedestal and viewed as role models for traditional American values. Yet there is a disparity between the educational values

claimed and the behaviors exhibited by athletes and coaches, which can be attributed to the overemphasis on winning at all costs.

Perhaps less obvious are the effects of physical education class on the affective development of students at all levels. If we are committed to the enhancement of self-esteem and the promotion of respect for self and others, why are practices that humiliate, embarrass, or belittle students used or tolerated? Many adults have vivid childhood memories of standing alone in the midst of the gym and being the last chosen for the team, completing a relay race long after all the other students have finished, or predictably being the first student eliminated in a game. Do these practices, and others like them, enhance individual development? How do these practices contribute to the promotion of lifespan involvement in physical activity for all people?

The Academy, concerned about the moral and ethical abuses in physical education and sport, encourages professionals to take action to remedy these abuses. First, although physical education and sport programs offer the opportunity to teach

An overemphasis on winning at all costs can deter the development of values in sport.

values, these outcomes must be actively sought and planned to fulfill the potential of our field to contribute to affective development. The greatest gains in this area will be realized when physical education and sport professionals structure their experiences to promote the development of values and ethical judgments. We can not assume that these outcomes will occur automatically as a result of involvement in physical education and sport. Situations that promote the development of the desired values must be carefully planned for and professionals should take advantage of teachable moments to promote desired behavior. Appropriate behavior should be acknowledged and reinforced.

Achievement of greater moral and ethical growth as a result of participation in physical education and sport also requires that winning be placed in perspective. Wholesome competition should be emphasized. Perhaps our view of competition needs to be modified. How would the nature of the experience and the outcomes achieved be changed if our perspective of competition was changed from that of beating our opponent to challenging our opponent by putting forth our best effort?

Professional preparation programs should help their graduates acquire the competencies necessary not only to teach skills and knowledge but also to promote the development of values and ethical judgments. If we profess to contribute to the development of the whole person, then professionals must be prepared to do so. Just as it is important to plan for the development of values in our programs and not leave development to chance, it is equally important to prepare professionals to undertake this task and not to assume that they know how to do so.

The Academy also urges that the profession establish criteria by which to select appropriate moral and ethical values to be developed. Formal plans for instruction to promote the development of these values should be designed. Additionally, it is recommended that the field develop additional means and methods to assess efforts to promote development in these areas.

Although the Academy directs its comments to school physical education programs and athletics, its collective wisdom holds an important message for professionals in both school- and nonschool-based programs for people of all ages. We must pay close attention to the affective dimension of behavior. If our goal is to promote a physically active lifestyle, we must engender the following affective goals in program participants: (1) confidence in their abilities as movers, (2) a sense of self-worth, and (3) an appreciation of the value of health and the contribution of physical activity to personal well-being. We must empower participants to take responsibility for their lives. Perhaps we must redirect some of our programming efforts to provide more individualized learning that focuses on abilities of people and provides increased opportunities to develop competence in activities that are personally meaningful and satisfying.

Leadership in Youth Sport

Participation in youth sport programs has grown dramatically in the past decade. Most communities now offer youth sport programs, often in several sports and with varying levels of competition. It is estimated that close to 25 million boys and girls participate in these programs. Adult volunteers, without which these programs could not function, number approximately 3 million.

The generally stated purpose of youth sport programs is to promote the healthy physical, psychological, and social development of participants. Although this goal is worthy, youth sport programs have been severely criticized by educators, physical educators, physicians, parents, and the media for the manner in which this goal has been approached and for the failure in many cases to achieve it. The criticism has been directed at the overemphasis on winning and competition, which makes it difficult to attain many of the stated developmental objectives. "Untrained adult volunteers are often the focus of this criticism. The lack of volunteers' knowledge about growth and development factors, psychological processes, training principles, nutrition, equipment use, safety, and injury prevention and treatment has precipitated the criticism."[4]

Because of the controversy surrounding youth sport programs and criticism directed at their endeavors, the American Academy of Kinesiology and Physical Education recommended that professional preparation programs provide prospective teachers and coaches with more information about teaching the young child. The developmental approach to skill acquisition, practical opportunities for students to work with young learners of all skill levels, and remediation techniques for gross motor skills should receive more emphasis in undergraduate professional preparation. The Academy also urged that physical education and sport professionals assume a greater role in the conduct of these programs.[1,5] Physical education and sport professionals have the knowledge and expertise to ensure that all participants have a satisfying and beneficial experience in youth sport. There are several ways that professionals can help make the youth sport experience a more positive one for children and youths. Professionals can work collaboratively with youth sport program administrators and volunteers to develop sound program guidelines. The Bill of Rights for Young Athletes, developed by AAHPERD, offers coaches and parents guidance in structuring the sport experience to achieve more positive outcomes (see box on the right.)

Professionals can serve as a resource for program personnel. Through leading in-service workshops, professionals can share with the adult volunteers information about skill development, psychological development, officiating, and safety and first aid that is essential to the conduct of sound programs. Professionals can also assist in developing minimal competencies in skill and knowledge and possibly establishing certification programs for volunteers. Training volunteers to attain these standards is another way that professionals can contribute to the development of sound programs. The American Sport Education Program,[6] one of the most widely used programs, can assist professionals in this endeavor. This program provides a comprehensive, progressive sequence of objectives and knowledge to be used by program directors and professionals in the training of youth sport volunteers.

YOUNG ATHLETES' BILL OF RIGHTS

1. Right to the opportunity to participate in sports regardless of ability level.
2. Right to participate at a level that is commensurate with each child's developmental level.
3. Right to have qualified adult leadership.
4. Right to participate in safe and healthy environments.
5. Right of each child to share in the leadership and decision-making of their sport participation.
6. Right to play as a child and not as an adult.
7. Right to proper preparation.
8. Right to have an equal opportunity to strive for success.
9. Right to be treated with dignity by all involved.
10. Right to have fun through sport.

From *Youth Sports Guide for Coaches and Parents,* AAHPERD.

Vern Seefeldt, director of the Institute for the Study of Youth Sports, addressed the controversial nature of youth sport. While many adults applaud the benefits of participation in youth sport programs, opponents of youth sport allege that the detrimental effects far outweigh the benefits. Seefeldt suggests that youth sport programs are "neither inherently good nor bad. Like other educational endeavors, their value depends on the quality of adult leadership and the supporting environment."[4]

Seefeldt encourages program volunteers to focus on promoting the continued sport involvement of children rather than emphasizing winning. Coaches must be aware of the reasons children participate in these activities. "Children become involved in sports to have fun, learn specific motor skills, socialize with their friends, and experience the excitement of competition on their own terms. These objectives are so wholesome and compelling that coaches should strive to incorporate them into every practice and contest."[4]

If youth sport is to achieve the desired outcomes, three interdependent changes are necessary according to Seefeldt. First, youth sport program directors must "resist the temptation to maintain the status quo."[4] Changes must be made in youth sport programs to accommodate children of all abilities and interests, not only those children who are highly skilled and competitive. Second, more research must be undertaken. Research is essential if programs are to be based on sound principles. Numerous questions require answers. Areas that need to be addressed include the nature and extent of injuries, optimal ages for learning specific skills, length of practices and duration of playing season, influence of different coaching methods on children's behavior and psychological development, and team selection for greatest equality. Third, sound training programs for youth sport coaches and personnel need to be developed and implemented. These programs should focus on the acquisition of basic competencies in skills, teaching, knowledge, first aid, and psychology that are prerequisites for coaching. In-service workshops are needed to help the millions of adult volunteers acquire these competencies.

Rainer Martens, founder of the American Sport Education Program, also endorses the importance of providing physical activity experiences for children and youth that will "turn kids on to physical activity for a lifetime."[7] According to Martens, to accomplish this objective physical education and sport professionals must take into account several behavioral principles: (1) the Modeling Principle, which states that children model the behavior of significant others in their lives, (2) the Reinforcement Principle, which emphasizes that children are more likely to repeat behaviors for which they are positively rewarded and to avoid behaviors for which they are punished, and (3) the Self-Determination Principle, which recognizes that children typically prefer activities that they select themselves rather than those activities imposed upon them.[7] However, Martens states that the two most fundamental principles influencing participation in physical activity are the Self-Worth Principle and the Fun Principle.

The Self-Worth Principle recognizes that we all need to feel we are competent, have the opportunity to experience success, and believe that we are worthy individuals. Martens explains, "If children initially have positive experiences when being physically active, whether it be in sports or other forms of physical activity, the internal feedback of accomplishment and the external recognition of success deliver a powerful message of achievement and thus greater worthiness."[7] This promotes future participation in physical activity. On the other hand, when children's experiences in physical activity are negative, their feelings of competency are diminished and they become less likely to seek out physical activities. They turn to other activities to engender their feelings of self worth.

Martens views the Self-Worth Principle as the most important principle to increase the participation of children in physical activity, not only in their childhood but throughout the lifespan.[7] Children experience diminished self-worth when participating in physical activities that are too developmentally advanced for them. Additionally, children often are placed in competitive sports programs before they have developed the necessary skills or are psychologically ready to compete with others. Openly criticizing children's performance and belittling their accomplishments rather than applauding their progress contributes to diminished self-worth.

The Fun Principle is integral to promoting involvement in physical activity. Though we know this, we often fail to apply this principle in designing and conducting physical activities for children. Martens asserts, "As we take the fun out of physical activities, we take the kids out of them. They turn their interests elsewhere."[7] How do we take the fun out of physical activity? Martens believes that professionals and adults take the fun out of physical activities and sports by over-organizing the activities, by constantly instructing and evaluating rather than allowing children to play and to apply what they have learned without fearing the consequences of failing or performing poorly. Often there is a discrepancy between the goals of the adults involved in running the activity and the children participating; adults focus on performance while the children focus primarily on having fun. Teaching skills by using boring drills, developing fitness by using calisthenics, using physical activity as a punishment, and placing children in a position of being publicly embarrassed by their performance are some ways in which fun is taken out of physical activity.[7]

How can we promote children's participation in physical activity and improve the quality of their experience? Martens suggests that adults need to keep their long-term objective of encouraging children to be active for a lifetime foremost in their minds. He writes:

When this objective is foremost in the minds of adult leaders, then the emphasis shifts from the outcome of participation to the quality of the experience during participation. If that experience is positive, if that experience enhances children's perceptions of self-worth, or if that experience is fun, then children are far more likely to continue that activity, and to do so for a lifetime.[7]

As professionals, we can take an active role in promoting physical activity programs for children that incorporate these principles and have the vision of lifetime physical activity as the primary objective. This active role extends to making a commitment to provide training for adult volunteers in youth sports so that they understand the importance of these principles and how to apply them to their situation. Furthermore, it is important as professionals to allow children to have some say about the activities in which they participate and to give children the opportunity to experience a wide range of activities so that they can find activities that are enjoyable and satisfying to them.

Youth sport programs have grown dramatically and this growth will likely continue. If children are to benefit from participation in these programs, professionals need to take a more active role in directing the programs. Sound training programs for the millions of volunteers need to be developed and implemented so that the sought-after physical, psychological, and social benefits are realized, and, most importantly, so that millions of children become lifetime participants in physical activity and sports.

Adult volunteers are essential for conducting youth programs.

The Growing Field

Since the early 1960s the body of knowledge about physical education and sport has expanded tremendously. Because of the proliferation of research and scholarship, the theoretical base of physical education and sport is becoming increasingly sophisticated and complex.

The expansion of the depth and breadth of knowledge has led to the development of subdisciplines within the field of physical education and sport that have emerged as areas of study in their own right. These distinct subdisciplines, which once were joined under the umbrella of physical education, have become separate, specialized areas with their own research traditions, professional organizations and publications, and specialized occupations. This specialization is currently increasing. Specialized areas of study are now emerging within the subdisciplines; for example, cardiac rehabilitation is becoming a specialized area within the subdiscipline of exercise physiology.

Many professionals have voiced concern about the increasing fragmentation and specialization of the discipline.[8,9] Lack of communication and co-operation among the increasingly specialized areas is a major concern. Moreover, the increased splintering of physical education and sport into narrow specialties may be harmful to one of the central missions of the physical education and sport professional: helping individuals learn the skills, knowledge, and understandings necessary to move effectively, to enhance health and well-being, and to be physically active throughout their lifespan.

It must be remembered that physical education and sport professionals are concerned with the development of the whole person through the medium of human movement, not just with the development of children's motor skills, physical fitness in adults, or psychological skills enabling elite athletes to perform at an optimum level. It is important not to forget that these specialized areas are actually parts of the greater whole. It is equally important that we not lose sight of our purpose.

Despite the calls for integration by many professionals, it is likely that the specialized areas of study will continue to further develop and become increasingly separate. However, there is a growing realization of the need to help professionals integrate the growing knowledge base to respond better to the needs of the individuals with whom they work.[9] This integration of knowledge would take into account the population being served, the population's needs, and the setting in which the services are provided. Calls also abound for closing the gap between research and practice, with a greater effort being made to link theory and practice.

As the field of physical education and sport continues to grow, many professionals are becoming dissatisfied with the traditional term used to represent the field: *physical education*. Within the past 25 years, our professional emphasis on teacher preparation has changed. Whereas teacher preparation was once the primary focus, it is now only one of many professional programs within the field. Professional preparation programs have become increasingly diversified. The emergence of the exercise and sport sciences has led to many

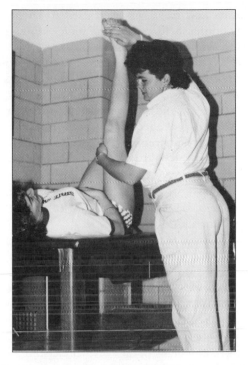

Professionals have adopted titles that more accurately reflect what they do. Athletic trainers, for example, help athletes prevent amd manage injuries.

new professional programs, such as cardiac rehabilitation, adult fitness, sport management, sports medicine, and sport communication. Many professionals feel that the term physical education does not accurately describe the current nature of the field. They believe a new term is needed to represent this field more accurately and to describe what professionals in the field do.

Today, practitioners in the schools continue to refer to themselves as physical educators. However, professionals working with other populations and in other settings have adopted different terms to represent the specialized nature of their work. These professionals may refer to themselves as athletic trainers, sports medicine specialists, adapted physical educators, exercise physiologists, sport psychologists, sport sociologists, fitness instructors, sport specialists, recreation leaders, and so on.

Many terms have been suggested to replace physical education. In this book the term *physical education and sport* has been used to encompass the traditional field of physical education and the growing field of sport sciences.

In 1989 the American Academy of Kinesiology and Physical Education endorsed *kinesiology* as the new umbrella term for the field. Kinesiology, defined as the art and science of human movement, was believed to reflect the true focus of study. Other terms that frequently have been suggested as a name for the field are *sport sciences* and *exercise and sport sciences*. Across the country, many college and university departments of physical education have changed their names to reflect the changing nature of the field.

Regardless of which term is selected, it is important that all professionals realize their responsibility to contribute to the field. Professionals must help physical education and sport establish its identity, its jurisdiction, and its leadership. Whether the field will continue to grow and to realize its potential to enhance the health and well-being of individuals of all ages will depend a great deal on the commitment of professionals.

The Gap between Research and Practice

One of the major problems facing the profession is the need to close the gap between research and practice.[10] A significant time lag is often seen between the conducted physical education and sport research and the utilization of relevant findings. If our programs, regardless of their setting, are to be based on sound principles, then this gap must be narrowed.

Factors responsible for the gap between research and practice are many. Some of these factors may be attributed to the practitioner, while others are associated with the researcher. One factor contributing to this gap is inadequate knowledge of research by the practitioner.[11] Practitioners, in both their undergraduate and graduate preparation, may not have been adequately instructed in research methods and the technical and conceptual skills necessary to conduct and interpret research. Locke writes, "The ordinary teacher, unfamiliar with basic terms and subtle distinctions in the vocabulary of research, is likely to find the usual research report nearly incomprehensible."[12] The lack of preparation hinders communication between researchers and practitioners and the consumption of research reports by practitioners. Practitioners who receive a sound background in research and statistics will be better equipped to communicate with the researcher who conducted the study and to interpret the findings.

Another factor that contributes to the gap is a negative attitude toward research held by practitioners. This negative attitude may deter them from using information revealed through research. Several reasons have been suggested to account for this negative attitude, including the view that research is irrelevant and impractical to the concerns of practitioners,[11,13] an inadequate understanding of research,[12] and failure to answer specific questions practitioners want answered[14] such as those about the teaching-learning process. Whatever the reason for this negative attitude, it militates against the effective use of research findings that may optimize learning.

The lack of time and resources to apply research findings to practical situations also contributes to the gap between research and practice.[15] For example, it is often heard that teachers are too busy to deal with theoretical matters; they must concentrate on daily tasks. In addition to teaching, teachers often are assigned homeroom duty, bus duty, locker room duty, hall duty, or study hall supervision, and may have coaching responsibilities as well. These extra, but required, responsibilities fill up the teacher's day and inhibit the implementation and utilization of research by the teacher. The lack of facilities and equipment with which to implement many of the research findings exacerbates the problem. Other physical education and sport professionals face similar constraints.

Application of research findings to practical settings is also hindered by the limited availability of the research findings. Many researchers publish their results in prestigious professional journals. Many of these journals are not readily available to practitioners. Another source of research is theses and dissertations. While theses and dissertations are available at college and university libraries, these unpublished sources of research are not

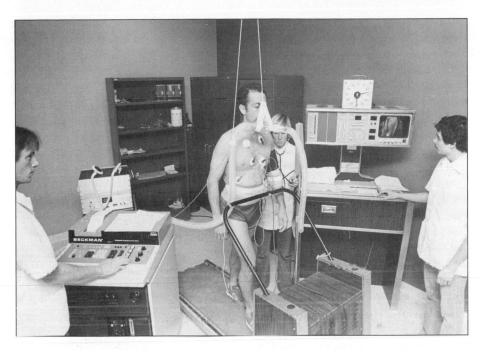

Research augments the knowledge base of physical education and sport.

readily available to practitioners at a distance from these sites. One promising development is the growth of the Internet as a medium for the dissemination of research findings. On-line access to research and significant documents, such as *Physical Activity and Health: The Surgeon General's Report*, will make it easier for practitioners to keep abreast of current developments.

The relatively poor quality of some research and relatively few conclusive research findings contribute to the gap between research and practice. Many research studies suffer from inadequacies, especially with regard to methodological concerns. Locke notes: "Research that is poorly designed, inadequately reported, and seriously misleading constitutes a major impediment to the intelligent guidance of physical education."[12] The fact that different researchers reach disparate conclusions regarding the same research topic makes it difficult for practitioners to apply these findings in a practical setting. The conflicting results of studies present problems for practitioners who wish to use the findings to guide and support their endeavors.

Finally, the unwillingness of researchers to be concerned with the application of their findings contributes to the gap between research and practice. Much of the significant research affecting educational practice in the last 50 years is the result of basic research, that is, research that is concerned with the development of theories or broad generalizations. The failure of investigators engaged in basic research to be concerned with the application of their findings might be a cause of a lag in some cases. Complicated theoretical propositions that are sometimes advanced by researchers engaged in pure or basic research without some explanation of their practical uses are of little value to practitioners. If significant information provided by basic researchers is to be useful, investigators engaged in basic research should devote a portion of their time to development and dissemination.

How can we close the gap between research and practice? We have taken the initial steps by recognizing that the gap does exist. There are several means by which this gap can be reduced. Professional preparation programs can do a better job in preparing physical education and sport professionals to read and interpret research. A thorough background in research and statistics will enable the physical education and sport professional to develop a knowledge of research theory and statistics, locate research reports, and evaluate research studies and interpret their findings. Another approach is for practitioners and researchers to work cooperatively on joint research projects. Researchers too must make a concerted effort to bridge this gap, as well. Researchers should endeavor to address the practical implications of their work when reporting their investigations in journals.

While it is difficult to delineate the size of the chasm between research and practice, it is important that both researchers and practitioners work to narrow this gap. Over the last 10 years the profession has experienced a tremendous growth in knowledge. If this knowledge is to influence the manner in which professionals conduct their programs, a concerted effort must be undertaken to narrow the gap between research and practice.

Finally, individuals are needed to serve as "translators" of research findings. These "translators" would consolidate research findings, identify practical applications, and disseminate this information to practitioners in an easy to understand format. This job needs to be done on a large scale if research findings are to be put to use without the normal "research lag." One step in this direction is the effort by the editorial board of JOPERD. In 1985 the editors instituted a new feature, "Research Works." This feature is designed to present research findings in an applied format, specifically discussing the importance of these findings to the practitioner. In the mid-1990s, the Research Consortium of AAHPERD began publication of *Physical Activity Today,* a research-to-practice newsletter that is distributed to over 25,000 AAHPERD members. The easy-to-read newsletter provides a wonderful way to disseminate research findings to practitioners.

CHALLENGES

The challenges facing physical education and sport professionals will increase as we move into the future. Only four of the many challenges will be discussed in this section: providing daily, high-quality physical education, promoting our programs, working to achieve the nation's health objectives, and encouraging lifespan involvement for all people.

High-Quality Daily Physical Education

The provision of high-quality daily physical education programs in the nation's schools is a challenge to all physical educators. There is evidence that many of the nation's children and youth are inactive and unfit.[16] Inactive lifestyles, sedentary leisure pursuits, and the lack of quality and regular physical education programs in the schools contribute to the poor fitness level of American children and youth.

There is increasingly strong support that regular and appropriate physical activity can contribute to good health and enhance the quality of life for individuals of all ages.[16] There is also increased recognition that to achieve the maximum benefits of exercise an individual must begin to exercise early in life and continue to exercise throughout the lifespan. Daily physical education in school is one of the best means to help individuals learn the skills, knowledge, and values necessary to incorporate physical activity into their lifestyle.

Inadequate time for physical education in the schools is a serious problem. In an effort to address this problem, the United States Congress in 1987 passed the National Physical Education Resolution or House Concurrent Resolution 97. This resolution encourages state governments and local educational agencies to provide high-quality daily physical education programs for all children in grades K through 12. Because the federal government usually recommends educational actions rather than mandating them, this resolution has no force of law. However, it is being used nationally by concerned teachers and parents as a lobbying tool to convince state and local educational policymakers to require daily physical education in all schools.

There is also concern about the quality of the programs offered in schools. Although there are many exemplary programs throughout the United States, many programs are of low quality.

School physical education programs should include aerobic activities to develop cardio vascular fitness.

According to NASPE,[18] a quality physical education program should be sequential and educational in nature. The program should focus on teaching students to do the following:

◆ Understand and participate in vigorous physical activities that can assist in developing and maintaining physical fitness throughout the lifespan
◆ Understand and improve their sports and motor skills
◆ Enjoy using their skills and knowledge as an advantage in establishing a healthy lifestyle
◆ Understand how their bodies work

A variety of activities should make up the physical education program.[17] Activities should include the following:

◆ Aerobic exercises to improve cardiovascular endurance
◆ Exercises to improve flexibility, strength, and muscular endurance
◆ Sport, games, dance, and other activities to develop motor skills
◆ Instruction in how physical activity can contribute to personal health and well-being

NASPE further identifies the components of a quality physical education program.[18] A quality physical education program does the following:

◆ Provides evidence of its effectiveness through the assessment of outcomes that have been achieved
◆ Provides daily opportunities for the development of movement skills and physical fitness
◆ Fosters an understanding of why, when, and how physical activity can be incorporated into a lifestyle
◆ Focuses on the health-related benefits of physical activity and how these benefits can be acquired and maintained
◆ Promotes the development of movement skills for participation beyond grades K through 12
◆ Accommodates the needs and developmental levels of all students regardless of physical and mental ability levels
◆ Teaches students how to apply the concepts of proper exercise in their daily lives

The incorporation of all these activities, the inclusion of these program components, and the realization of the maximum benefits from participation in a high-quality physical education program depend on the program being offered on a daily basis for a sufficient amount of time throughout all the school years. Equally important, physical education should be taught by certified physical education instructors. Just as noncertified and un-qualified teachers are not tolerated in other academic areas, they should not be tolerated in physical education. Qualified and dedicated leadership is needed if the benefits associated with daily high-quality physical education programs are to be achieved.

Each physical education teacher must be willing to take responsibility for promoting the crusade for daily high-quality physical education. Evidence supporting the value of regular and appropriate physical activity continues to mount. Furthermore, there is recognition that health behaviors are formed at an early age and that it is easier to shape positive health behaviors in children than to change unhealthy ones in adults. Moreover, while the current societal interest in wellness and fitness remains strong, now is the time to engender support for daily high-quality physical education programs. Improving the status of physical education in the schools and helping make the dream of daily high-quality physical education a reality for all children and youth are important priorities for all physical education and sport professionals.

Public Relations

Physical education and sport professionals in all careers must take an active role in promoting their programs. Now is the time to capitalize on the widespread public interest in sport, physical fitness, and health. Professionals teaching in the school setting; instructing in community and recreational sport programs; working in commercial sport clubs, fitness centers, and health spas; and directing corporate and community fitness programs must use public relations techniques to market their programs. Professionals must inform the public and prospective clientele of the values that accrue from participation in a sound physical activity and exercise program.

In the school setting where physical education is often regarded as an extra or is cut to make more time for academic subjects, where budgetary cutbacks are becoming increasingly common, and where class sizes are expanding, teachers must be willing to promote their programs to gain the personal and budgetary support of school administrators, politicians, and parents. This requires a commitment to offer an outstanding instructional program and to promote the values of participation in such a program to the public in an understandable manner. Physical education has changed considerably in the 25 years or so since the adult public participated in these programs during their school years. Physical educators must be willing to demonstrate how physical education programs have changed by allowing the adults to observe their programs, conducting demonstrations and other promotional activities, and talking to parents and community groups.

Promotion and marketing of programs is essential in other settings as well. Prospective clientele for community and commercial programs must be aware of the nature of the programs offered and the benefits to be derived from participation in such programs. In the corporate fitness setting physical educators must promote the values and benefits to be derived from participation to management as well as to employees. Corporate management personnel will be reluctant to invest corporate resources, particularly money, to support these programs if they are not aware of their value and/or if the stated benefits are not achieved.

Adults may not have had the opportunity to participate in sound instructional programs during their school years and may not be aware of how physical education programs have changed today. Perhaps they remember physical education classes as a time to perform calisthenics, march, and play the same game over and over again. They may have memories of their lack of success in performing activities in gym class and the ridicule they experienced because they were not skilled athletes. Consequently, some adults may be reluctant to experience failure again and will not enroll in adult fitness programs. Professionals may have to educate men and women about the nature of the program and its benefits. Professionals in all settings must be actively involved in the promotion of their athletic programs, assisting in encouraging and recruiting new participants.

Physical educators must make a concerted effort to actively promote and interpret their programs

Physical education and sport professionals should also be community leaders. These volunteers are helping children warm up before the community's Special Olympics Race for the Gold.

to their clientele and the public. To assist physical educators in this endeavor the *Physical Education Public Information* (PEPI) project was developed by NASPE, an association of the AAHPERD.* Promotional materials have been developed to help the public become aware of the basic values of physical education. Among the values emphasized are the following:

- ◆ Physical education is health insurance.
- ◆ Physical education contributes to academic achievement.
- ◆ Physical education provides skills and experiences that can last a lifetime.
- ◆ Physical education helps in developing a positive self-image and the ability to compete and cooperate with others.

PEPI has focused its efforts on getting these messages across to the public, particularly taxpayers,

students, teachers, administrators, school boards, parents, and funding agencies.

As part of its public relations effort, PEPI promotes National Physical Education and Sport Week, May 1 to 7. Each year a theme is selected for this week as a basis for demonstrating the importance of physical education. Themes include "Fit to Achieve through Quality Daily Physical Education," "Physical Education: Essential for Excellence," and "Physical Education Is for Every Body." Physical education and sport professionals in school settings as well as in community and corporate settings should take advantage of National Physical Education and Sport Week to highlight their program, particularly its contribution to enhancing the quality of life for all people.

Because most young people ages 6 to 16 attend school, the schools offer a nationwide setting for promoting physical activity to young people. The school physical education program can teach children and youth about physical activity, develop behavioral and motor skills to promote

* Information about the PEPI program can be obtained from AAHPERD, 1900 Association Drive, Reston, VA 22091.

This poster was used in the public relations campaign to promote National Physical Education and Sport Week.

lifelong physical activity, foster positive attitudes toward physical activity, and encourage participation in physical activity outside of the school setting. High-quality school physical education programs provide students with the foundation for lifelong participation.

Despite the evidence supporting the value of daily, high-quality physical education, the status of physical education in our nation's schools shows that many students are not receiving physical education throughout their formative years. Only one state, Illinois, requires all students in grades K through 12 to participate in physical education every day. Other research shows that only 25% of all high school students have daily physical education,

and that participation in daily physical education declines as grade in school increases.[16] Physical education is required by 95% of all school districts, but these policies do not require students to take physical education every year.[17] Although 90% of middle, junior high, and senior high schools require at least one physical education course, only half of these middle and junior high schools and only about one-quarter of these senior high schools require the equivalent of at least 3 years of physical education.[17] It should also be noted that only 26% of all states require schools to offer at the senior high level a course in lifetime physical activity.[17]

Other visible efforts to promote physical activity and its value in preventing cardiovascular disease are Jump Rope for Heart and Hoops for Heart, joint projects of the AAHPERD and the American Heart Association. Jump Rope for Heart and Hoops for Heart emphasize the value of physical activity through demonstrations and fund-raising events at local schools. In 1997–1998, nearly 20,000 schools hosted a Jump Rope for Heart event. Over $38 million dollars was raised to benefit research and educational efforts aimed at fighting cardiovascular disease such as high blood pressure, arteriosclerosis, heart attack, and stroke. During the same year, Hoops for Heart raised over $2.4 million and events were hosted at over 3,000 schools. These programs provide a wonderful opportunity for physical educators to promote the value of physical activity and to present a positive image of a professional involved in community service.

Public relations efforts are critical to the success of physical education and sport programs in all settings. Professionals need to become directly involved in public relations programs designed to educate the public about the values and benefits of physical activity and exercise and the contribution of physical education and sport to the quality of life of people of all ages.

Achievement of National Health Goals

Another challenge facing physical education and sport professionals is working collaboratively with other health professionals toward the achievement of the national health goals set forth in the Surgeon General's report *Healthy People 2000*[19] and the forthcoming goals for the year 2010. The *Healthy People 2000* goals reflect a commitment to improve the nation's health through a comprehensive health promotion and disease prevention effort. The goals to be achieved by the year 2000 are to increase the span of healthy life, to reduce disparities in health among population groups, and to achieve access to preventive services for all Americans. The year 2010 goals will build on those of *Healthy People 2000* and reflect a continued effort to increase the span of healthy life for all people.

Healthy People 2000 identified 22 priority areas, one of which was physical activity. For each priority area, specific objectives were identified, the attainment of which would lead to an improvement in the health of the nation's people.

The current fitness status of the American people, the trends set forth by these reports, and the specific objectives are described in Chapter 3. These objectives for the year 2000 were based on the assumption that increases in appropriate physical activity by people of all ages will result in concomitant health gains. The reports also assumed that the primary motive for participation in physical activity will be a personal commitment to improve one's health and enhance the quality of one's life. The objectives for the year 2000 focus on improvement of the health status of all Americans, regardless of age; reduction of risk factors through increased participation in appropriate physical activity; increased knowledge of the public and professionals about the role of exercise in the promotion of health; improvement and expansion of services; and development of improved evaluation systems to assess the public's progress toward these goals.

The specific objectives delineated in *Healthy People 2000* related to physical activity and fitness were outlined in Chapter 3. Briefly, in terms of risk reduction, the objectives focus on increasing the proportion of people age 6 and older who participate in regular and appropriate physical activity

Increasing the amount of time physical educators spend teaching lifetime sports was one of the *Healthy People 2000* objectives.

to enhance health fitness. Priority is also given to reducing the number of people who are overweight. The objectives pertaining to public awareness focus on increasing the proportion of people age 6 and older who are knowledgeable about the benefits associated with regular exercise and who can correctly identify the frequency, intensity, and type of exercises that will contribute to health fitness.

Improving professional education and awareness is another objective. Specifically, the focus is on increasing the number of primary care providers who assess and counsel their patients about physical activity habits as part of a thorough evaluation.

Improved services and protection are also important to the promotion of health. One objective is to increase the percentage of children and youth who receive daily physical education to 50% from a baseline of 36% in the mid-1980s. Increasing the amount of time physical education teachers spend on skills and activities that promote lifetime sport participation is another objective. Expanding the number of employer-sponsored fitness programs and the services offered is yet another objective.

Community physical activity programs can also play an important role in developing and maintaining health fitness. Promoting participation in these programs and expanding the recreational facilities offered are two objectives that need to be achieved.

As you can see, our field can make an important contribution to the improvement of the health status of the American public. Professionals should take an active role in working with other health professionals to attain these objectives. Moreover, our involvement in attaining these objectives will contribute to increased public recognition of the worth and value of our field. Additionally, one benefit that will accrue from our participation in this endeavor is increased employment opportunities.

Employment opportunities for qualified professionals will increase, and new career opportunities will develop. The objective of promoting daily physical education will result in a demand for more teachers. Instructors also will be needed to teach physical activities to adults and the elderly and educate them about the benefits of such activities. The growth of corporate fitness programs will create a need for more professionals qualified in this area.

Can we attain the objectives for 2000 and those for 2010? There has been some progress toward attaining the specific physical activity objectives (see Chapter 3). For example, deaths from coronary heart disease have declined, worksite health promotion programs have increased, and some progress has been made in promoting involvement in moderate and vigorous physical activity. However, the decline in daily physical education is disturbing. Obesity has increased for both children and adults, and much more improvement needs to be made in the physical activity patterns of children and adults. There is much more to be done to achieve our health goals. Professional organizations, such as AAHPERD and ACSM, provide us with strong leadership. However, whether or not we can achieve the stated objectives for physical activity depends on each professional's willingness to commit to attaining these objectives and to

being a role model for a healthy, active lifestyle. Wilmore[20] states:

Each of us in the profession must make a personal commitment to achieve or maintain a good level of physical fitness. How can we be effective in promoting health and fitness if our bodies are not living testimonies of our commitment? What we are communicates so much more than what we say!

As professionals we must practice what we preach. We must work together to educate the American public in a variety of physical activities in which they can participate throughout their lives.

Lifespan Involvement for All People

One of the most heartening changes in the profession within the last 20 years has been the expansion of physical education and sport programs to people of all ages and to a diversity of settings. Traditionally, physical education and sport programs have focused on children and youth and have been conducted in the school and community-recreation settings. However, within the last two decades, the scope of physical education and sport programs has expanded tremendously.

The expanded focus of physical education and sport has led to providing services to new populations. Services have expanded to encompass individuals of all ages. Programs have been developed for infants and toddlers as well as for adults and senior citizens. There has been a greater effort to meet the needs of all people, regardless of their skill level, fitness status, and abilities.

There is an increased recognition that regular and appropriate physical activity can make a vital contribution to the health and lives of all people. It can enhance the quality of one's life as well as its longevity. Additionally, it has become increasingly apparent that our efforts should focus on early childhood education and intervention. Individuals gain the maximum benefits from exercise and physical activity when they begin at an early age and continue their participation throughout the lifespan.

We must begin early to foster active participation throughout the lifespan. The growth of community and commercial sport programs has enabled more children to receive instruction and develop a lifelong interest in sport and fitness activities.

During childhood, fitness and leisure habits are developed; once developed, they become difficult to change. Moreover, it has been shown that such insidious diseases as obesity and coronary heart disease can begin in childhood. Therefore it is important that efforts be made to assist children in acquiring the skills, knowledge, and positive attitudes conducive to good health. Children must be educated to form good health and physical activity habits early in life. Physical educators, parents, and other health professionals should focus their efforts on helping children adopt an active rather than a sedentary lifestyle and on providing them with the skills and knowledge to effectively manage their lifestyles as adults.

It is important to note that the number of programs being provided for preschoolers is growing; it is likely that the number of these programs will increase in the next decade. Motor development programs are being offered to infants and toddlers in hospital and clinical settings. Preschools and day care centers are incorporating physical education programs into their curricula.

In the past decade the fitness and the wellness movements have encouraged an increasing number of adults to incorporate regular physical activity into their lifestyles. Many adults are now engaging in physical activities and exercise of sufficient intensity, duration, and frequency to realize health benefits. Unfortunately, many more adults are not. The majority of adults lead sedentary lives or exercise only moderately. The incidence of physical inactivity increases with age and is influenced by such factors as sex, race, socioeconomic status, educational level, occupation, and geographic location. (See Chapter 3 for further information.) As professionals, we need to help these people change their physical activity and health habits and adopt health-enhancing lifestyles. Creative and educational programs are needed to accomplish this objective.

As we enter the next century, the proportion of elderly in the population will continue to increase. In 1997, people over the age of 65 composed 12.7% of our population. By the year 2025 it is estimated the elderly will compose 18.5%. Furthermore, the elderly will be increasingly healthy and vigorous. Physical education and sport professionals must be prepared to meet the physical activity and leisure needs of this population group. Research shows that people with healthy habits live long, are functionally independent for a great period of time, and experience a higher quality of life. Never has our potential to improve the health and well-being of this population group been greater. We must reach out and involve members of this age group in our programs.

The last decade has also seen an increase in physical education and sport opportunities available to individuals with disabilities. In 1995, 1 in every 5 Americans reported some level of disability. Participation in physical activity and sport makes a significant contribution to the health and fitness of individuals with disabilities. However, the benefits extend further. Dunn and Sherrill[21] state that for some individuals with disabilities, engaging in physical activities contributes to their ability to perform the tasks of daily living, such as dressing, bathing, and preparing for work. Fun, enjoyment, and satisfaction from meeting challenges are other meaningful outcomes of participation. Participation in sport, an important institution of our society, enables individuals with disabilities to become more involved in family and community activities and thus become normalized. For example, children who have a visual impairment can use their proficiency in swimming both to compete and take part in water activities enjoyed by their families. For some individuals with disabilities, participation in sport contributes to self-actualization and feelings of empowerment.

Sport involvement among people of all ages continues to increase. Millions of children throughout the country participate in youth and interscholastic sports. Intercollegiate athletic participation continues to rise. Communities are developing more sport opportunities for adults of all ages. Competitive and recreational leagues offer adults the opportunity to continue their participation in organized sports at a desirable level of intensity. Masters' competitions and competitions for seniors in a variety of sports and at a number of levels—local, state, national, and international—allow many adults and senior citizens across the country to continue their sport involvement. Sport organizations for individuals with disabilities also provide opportunities for competition in a wide range of individual and team sports.

As we continue to expand our focus to meet the needs of new populations, we must also continue to broaden our programs. Because the populations that are served are increasingly heterogeneous, a greater diversity of programs is needed to meet their needs. The minority population is increasing and their needs should not be overlooked. Changes in program content and the manner in which programs are conducted will be necessary to accommodate a wide range of individual differences. Additionally, we must increase our efforts

to recruit minorities into careers in our field; they are presently underrepresented.

Programs have and will continue to expand from the school setting to the community, from the public sector to the private sector. The school setting will be used increasingly as a site for community programs for individuals of all ages. Programs in day care centers, preschools, hospitals, developmental centers, senior centers, nursing homes, community settings, and corporations will continue to expand. Commercial programs in the private sector will continue to increase. Health clubs, fitness centers, private clubs offering sport instruction, and private sport leagues will develop more programs to meet the needs of paying clients. As programs expand to meet the needs of various populations, it is important to ensure that all individuals have access to these programs. Fitness and health opportunities should be available not only to those who have the means to pay. Fitness and health opportunities should be available to all individuals regardless of socioeconomic background.

As the scope of physical education and sport increases and as the focus of the programs offered expands, it is important that professional programs prepare students to capably assume responsibilities within these growing areas. Professional preparation programs have traditionally focused on preparing students to work with children and youth within the school setting. Today, professional preparation programs must provide students with the skills and knowledge necessary to conduct effective programs with different population groups and across the lifespan.

Promoting lifespan involvement in physical activity and sport is a challenge to all physical education and sport professionals. Lifespan involvement can enrich the lives of all people, the young and old, male and female, able-bodied and disabled, rich and poor, fit and unfit, and skilled and unskilled. Making lifespan involvement a reality for many people requires qualified and dedicated physical education and sport professionals willing to work toward attaining this goal.

A

B

A, Winners belong to every age group. B, Participants respond to the square dance call "Take your arms out to the side, like you can hold an ocean wide."

SUMMARY

Many issues and challenges confront professionals in physical education and sport today. The widespread interest in sport by people in our society and the media has made many of these issues highly visible.

Following an overview of the issues in physical education and sport today, three issues identified by the American Academy of Kinesiology and Physical Education as being of great importance to the field were discussed. First, the Academy stressed that professionals need to become more active in the physical activity and fitness consumer movement. Second, professionals must place more emphasis on teaching ethical and moral values through physical education and sport programs. Third, the Academy perceived a need for professionals to become more active in conducting of youth sport programs. Two additional issues were also discussed. As the field of physical education and sport continues to grow, professionals are concerned about the fragmentation of the field and its title. The final issue examined was closing the gap between research and practice.

Many challenges face physical education and sport professionals. Four particularly important challenges were discussed. First, professionals are faced with the challenge of promoting daily high-quality physical education in the schools. The second challenge is to become more actively involved in public relations. Professionals in all settings must market their programs. The third challenge is to attain the goals set forth in the report *Healthy People 2000*. These specific physical activity objectives focus on improving the health status of all Americans. If these objectives are to be achieved, each professional must make a personal commitment to work with professional organizations to accomplish this task and to be a role model exemplifying a healthy, active lifestyle. Last, promoting lifespan involvement in physical activity requires professionals to provide a diversity of services to individuals of all ages. Physical education and sport has the potential to enhance the health and quality of life of people of all ages. Helping individuals to realize this potential is one of our biggest challenges.

The issues and challenges confronting professionals are many. If we are to deal with them, physical education and sport professionals must be knowledgeable about the field of physical education and sport and be willing to assume leadership positions. The manner in which professionals deal with these issues and meet the challenges confronting them will influence the future of physical education and sport.

SELF-ASSESSMENT TESTS

These tests are designed to help you determine if you have mastered the materials and competencies presented in this chapter.

1. Discuss the role of the physical educator and sport leader in the consumer education movement relative to physical activities and fitness.

2. Explain how professionals can promote the development of values in their programs, regardless of the setting.

3. Discuss how professionals can help adult volunteers conduct sound youth sport programs. Discuss the need for physical educators to help in the conduct of youth sport programs in light of your own youth sport experiences.

4. How can the growing disciplinary knowledge be integrated to help practitioners effectively accomplish their responsibilities?

5. Identify strategies to reduce the gap between research and practice.

6. What specific strategies could be employed to encourage the state legislature and the local school boards to mandate daily physical education?

7. Discuss the importance of public relations programs in the physical education and sport setting of your choice.

8. Describe how physical educators through various programming efforts can help individuals attain the fitness and exercise goals set forth in *Healthy People 2000*.

9. Describe various strategies that can be utilized to promote lifespan involvement for people of all ages, abilities, and socioeconomic backgrounds.

REFERENCES

1. Park RJ: Three major issues: the Academy takes a stand, JOPERD 54(1):52–53, 1983.

2. Corbin CB: Is the fitness bandwagon passing us by? JOPERD 55(9):17, 1984.

3. Ewers JR: You must be present to win, Quest 49:238–250, 1997.

4. Seefeldt V: Why are children's sports programs controversial? JOPERD 56(3):16, 1985

5. The American Academy of Physical Education: The Academy papers: reunification, no. 15, Reston, Va., 1981, AAHPERD.

6. American Sport Education Program, Champaign, Ill., current edition, Human Kinetics.

7. Martens R: Turning kids on to physical activity for a lifetime, Quest 46:303–310,1996.

8. Sage GH: The future and the profession. In JD Massengale, editor: Trends toward the future in physical education, Champaign, Ill., 1987, Human Kinetics.

9. Siedentop D: Introduction to physical education, fitness, and sport, Mountain View, Calif., 1990, Mayfield.

10. Bucher CA and Thaxton NA: Physical education and sport: change and challenge, St. Louis, 1981, Mosby.

11. Rothstein AL: Practitioners and the scholarly enterprise, Quest 20:59–60, 1973.

12. Locke LF: Research in physical education, New York, 1969, Teachers College Press.

13. Stadulis RE: Bridging the gap: a lifetime of waiting and doing, Quest 20:48–52, 1973.

14. Barnes FP: Research for the practitioner in education, Washington, D.C., 1963, Department of Elementary School Principles, National Education Association.

15. Broderick FP: Research as viewed by the teacher, Paper presented at the AAHPER National Convention, Detroit, 1971.

16. US Department of Health and Human Services, Physical activity and health: a report of the Surgeon General, Atlanta, Ga., 1996, US Department of Health and Human Services, Centers for Disease Control and Prevention, National Center for Chronic Disease Prevention and Health Promotion.

17. Pate RR, Small ML, Ross JG, Young JC, and Flint CW: School physical education, Journal of School Health 65:312–318, 1995.

18. The National Association for Sport and Physical Education: Fit to achieve educational information, Reston, Va., 1989, AAHPERD.

19. Public Health Service, US Department of Health and Human Services: Healthy people 2000: national health promotion and disease prevention objectives, Washington, D.C., 1991, US Government Printing Office.

20. Wilmore JH: Objectives for the nation: physical fitness and exercise, JOPERD 53:(3), 41–43.

21. Dunn JM and Sherrill C: Movement and its implication for individuals with disabilities, Quest 48:378–391, 1996.

SUGGESTED READINGS

American Sport Education Program, Champaign, Ill., Human Kinetics Publishers.

This multilevel program is designed to help coaches gain a basic understanding of the knowledge necessary to coach athletes at various levels and in a diversity of sports. Further information about this extensive coaching program can be obtained from Human Kinetics, Box 5076, Champaign, Ill. 61820.

Dunn JM and Sherrill C: Movement and its implication for individuals with disabilities, Quest 48:378–391, 1996.

The authors discuss the important contributions physical activity and sport makes to the lives of individuals with disabilities. The benefits of participation for individuals with disabilities include health and fitness, ability to perform tasks of daily living, fun and enjoyment, normalization, empowerment, and opportunity to participate with friends and families in sport.

Ewers JR: You must be present to win, Quest 49:238–250, 1997.

Ewers discusses the importance of our profession directing its energies and resources to meeting the physical activity needs of the growing healthy elderly population.

Harris JC: Using kinesiology: a comparison of applied veins in the subdisciplines, Quest 45:389–412, 1993.

Examines the biophysical sciences, behavioral/sociocultural sciences, and pedagogical sciences with respect to the development of technical and critical/reflective competencies. The importance of promoting the development of critical/reflective competencies in all three areas is discussed, as well as implications for practitioners.

Lawson HA: Why don't practitioners use research? Explanations and selected implications, JOPERD 63(9):36, 53–57, 1992.

Discusses the reasons for research not being used from a multitude of perspectives—the research, the practitioner, the dissemination system, and the standards for certification and accreditation, as well as discusses it as a systemic problem.

McLeroy KR, Bibeau DL, and McConnell TC: Ethical issues in health education and health promotion: challenges for the profession, Journal of Health Education 24(5):313–318, 1993.

Provides some thought-provoking discussion about ethical issues in health promotion and discusses the importance of examining these issues as professionals within this field.

Martens R: Turning kids on to physical activity for a lifetime, Quest 46:303–310, 1996.

Martens emphasizes the importance of self-worth and fun in youth sports and as guiding principles for promoting lifelong physical activity.

Oliver B, editor: Minorities in physical education—African American perspectives on recruitment and retention, JOPERD 64(3): 65-79, 1993.

Presents a series of articles focusing on the recruitment and retention of minorities in the field and the implications of the multicultural society for physical education and sport.

Schneider RE: Don't just promote your profession—market it!, JOPERD 63(5): 70–73, 1992.

Offers a comprehensive marketing approach for school physical education that is also appropriate for other professional programs.

CHAPTER 15

Future of Physical Education and Sport

Instructional Objectives and Competencies to be Achieved:

After reading this chapter the student should be able to—

- Indicate how physical education and sport professionals can capitalize on the increased public interest in health and physical activity.
- Discuss how the changing nature of education and technological advances will influence physical education and sport in the future.
- Show how physical education and sport professionals can establish jurisdiction over their own domain.
- Describe how physical education and sport can improve its delivery system.

What will our world be like in the future? And, what will physical education and sport be like in the twenty-first century? More importantly, what is our vision for physical education and sport in the twenty-first century? To make the most of the future requires a plan for predicting what the future may be like by generating some scenarios, selecting a preferred future, and then prescribing a course of action that will lead to its attainment. Achieving the future of our choice requires strong leadership, a charted course, marshaled efforts and resources to achieve our goals, and the active involvement of professionals at all levels in pursuit of this vision. The future of physical education and sport is *coming*—but only physical educators can decide where it is *going*.[1]

Human beings have always been interested in the future. Today numerous "think tanks" such as the Rand Corporation, the Hudson Institute, and The World Future Society focus on studying the future. Futurists, individuals who study the future, endeavor to unravel the mysteries of the years ahead.

Futurists attempt, using a variety of techniques, to describe the future. They try to predict the course of past and current trends and identify the consequences of selected courses of action. Futurists attempt to define priorities that will lead to a future of our choice. Future studies imply the identification of both desirable and undesirable outcomes. The futurist must assume the responsibility for seeking the alternative that creates a future as close as possible to the desired outcomes.

Some individuals using methods such as expert advice, trend extrapolation, technological forecasting, and scenarios have been very accurate in forecasting the future.

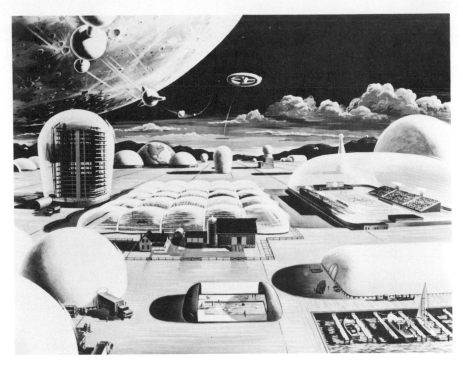

Airshelters in the city of the future.

Dateline 1932: Aldous Huxley[2] wrote in his book *Brave New World,* "The Director [of the school] described the technique for preserving the excised ovary alive . . . showed them how the eggs were inspected . . . immersed in a warm bouillon containing free-swimming spermatozoa. . . ."

Dateline July 25, 1978: Forty-six years later Louise Brown, the first "test-tube baby" (the first child in history to be conceived outside of the womb), was born in England.

Of course, all prognosticators have not been as accurate in their predictions:

Dateline 1943: Thomas Watson, Chairman of IBM, states, "I think there is a world market for maybe five computers."[3]

Although errors are made in forecasting, it is still imperative to try to predict what will happen in the years ahead. Why? Because all of us are going to spend our lives in the future. Why? Because the future to some extent is known and to some extent can be controlled. Why? Because it affects our beliefs and assumptions. We can anticipate

problems. We can plan. Why? Because people shape the future. The space program of the 1960s resulted in a man walking on the surface of the moon, and NASA has the goal of placing a space station in space sometime early in the twenty-first century. One scientist has stated that "An important reason for studying the future is not so we can learn what may happen, but rather to help us decide about what kind of future we want and develop ways to achieve it."

Although forecasting the future of physical education and sport is difficult, it is important that it be undertaken before we are overtaken by future events. One means to plan for the future is to accept the premise of futurist Daniel Bell. Bell indicates that time is not an "overarching leap" from the present to the future. Instead, it has its origins in the past, incorporates the present, and extends into the future. Physical education and sport professionals seeking to forecast the future of the field need knowledge of the past and the present as well as an understanding of what futurists, scientists,

GETTING CONNECTED

Human-Machine Interface Lab provides information about virtual reality projects in medical and rehabilitation training.

Site: http://www.ciap.rutgers.edu/vrlab/

Rehabilitation Sciences Virtual Reality Program focuses on developing and accessing the impact of technology on improving the quality of life for individuals with disabilities.

Site: http://aix1.uottawa.ca/~mlaflamm/

Sporting Goods Manufacturers' Association site provides information on important trends, state of the sport industry, and results of various surveys relating to participation.

Site: http://www.sportlink.com

World Health Organization site offers an annual report on the health of the world as well as fact sheets and press releases on current health problems and initiatives.

Site: http://www.who.org

and experts are predicting about the future. Insight, imagination, creativity, and vision help forecasters predict and describe scenarios for the future.

Planning for the future recognizes that rapid change is a characteristic of our way of life. With each day that passes we live in a different world. Human beings who are age 50 or older have witnessed in their lifetime the start of the atomic age, the space age, and the computer age. They have seen more than 80 new nations appear, the world population double, and the gross world product double and then redouble. As C.P. Snow, the noted British scientist, said, "The rate of change has increased so much that our imagination can't keep up."

Recognizing that change is ever present, certain societal trends and developments can be identified that lend themselves to a better understanding of our future and that of physical education and sport. Examination of trends is one of the simplest forms of studying the future. It is based on the assumption that factors that have shaped the past will continue and be instrumental in forming the future. This approach has serious limitations, such as mistaking fads for real trends or allowing personal biases to cloud professional judgment.[4]

However, careful examination of trends can provide us with a starting point for thinking about the future. Some selected trends and developments that are likely to have an impact on physical education and sport in the future include the health promotion and disease prevention movement, the educational reform movement and the changing nature of education, the growth of technology, changing demographics, and the expanding frontiers of the habitable universe.

SOCIETAL TRENDS AND CURRENT DEVELOPMENTS

As you read about trends and developments and explore the potential implications for the future of physical education and sport, you may find it helpful to contemplate the following questions suggested by Massengale[4]:

◆ If the direction of the trend continues, what will be some positive and/or negative consequences?

◆ If the rate or speed of the trend continues, what will be some positive and/or negative results?

◆ What will occur if the trend levels off or reverses itself?

◆ Which forces are acting to perpetuate this trend? Will these forces continue into the future?

◆ How much is this trend "shapable" by human action?

◆ What type of action would it take to modify the trend?

As you read about each trend and consider each question, try to carefully imagine the implications for professional practice and the influence it may exert on your day-to-day responsibilities as a professional within the field.

Health Promotion and Disease Prevention Movement

The emphasis on the enhancement of health and the prevention of disease is a significant trend in our society. Three related factors in this movement will be discussed: the wellness movement, the physical activity and fitness movement, and the health care reform movement.

Wellness movement

The wellness movement represents one of the most opportune moments in our history. The wellness movement stresses self-help and emphasizes that one's lifestyle—the way in which one lives—influences greatly the attainment and maintenance of personal health. This movement supports efforts directed toward health promotion and disease prevention rather than focusing on the treatment of illness. The wellness doctrine is based on the premise that it is the responsibility of the individual to work toward achieving a healthy lifestyle and an optimal sense of well-being. A healthy lifestyle should reflect the integration of several components, including proper nutrition, regular and appropriate physical activity and exercise, stress management, and the elimination of controllable risk factors (e.g., smoking, excessive alcohol consumption).

Strong support for health promotion and disease prevention efforts was given by three national health reports: *Healthy People*,[5] *Objectives for the Nation*,[6] and *Healthy People 2000*.[7] *Healthy People* identified exercise and fitness as 1 of 15 priority areas that could have a significant impact on the health status of the individual as well as that of the nation. Specific fitness and exercise goals for all segments of the population to be achieved by 1990 were set forth in the *Objectives for the Nation*. Goals for the twenty-first century were delineated in *Healthy People 2000*. Whether or not these goals are achieved depends to a great extent on physical education and sport professionals' willingness to commit to meeting these goals and to work cooperatively with various other professionals and professional organizations to attain them.

The corporate sector has also become interested in the wellness movement. This has led to the development of corporate fitness and wellness programs for the employees. Corporations are willing to invest in these programs because they have found that they result in increased employee productivity, decreased absenteeism, better employee health, and lower insurance costs.

Physical education and sport can make a significant contribution to the wellness movement in many ways. Physical education can provide individuals with the skills and knowledge to exercise properly; help individuals develop abilities in a variety of sport activities that are meaningful and satisfying, thus promoting lifetime participation; and teach individuals a variety of stress management techniques.

Physical activity and fitness movement

Enthusiasm for physical activity and fitness is at an all-time high in the United States today and will continue to increase in the future. Sales of sport equipment, apparel, and home exercise equipment have reached astronomical levels. The number of individuals participating in exercise and sport activities continues to rise, and it appears that physical activity and fitness have become an ingrained way of American life. In 1996 the landmark report *Physical Activity and Health: The Surgeon General's Report* convincingly set forth the contribution of physical activity to health. The positive effects of remaining physically active throughout one's life have motivated many adults to embark on a fitness program and millions of others to continue their participation past the typical stopping point, the end of the school years.

However, when the information about adult participation in physical activity is examined more closely, participation is not as widespread as it seems. Studies conducted in the late 1980s showed only 10% to 20% of adults exercise with sufficient intensity, duration, and frequency to develop and maintain adequate levels of health-related fitness.[7] It is estimated that approximately 40% of the adult population engages in physical activity of moderate intensity often enough to realize some health-related benefits.[7] Given this information, it appears that a large segment of the adult population, nearly 40%, are leading rather sedentary lives.[7] *Physical Activity and Health* reports more recent information on adult activity patterns. These recent studies found that more than 60% of adults are not regularly active, and 25% report participating in no physical activity during their leisure time.[8] Physical activity was more prevalent among men than women, among Caucasians than minorities, among younger than older adults, and among the more affluent than the less affluent.[8] As we move into the future, a greater effort must be directed at involving all segments of the population in regular physical activity.

Although more adults than ever before are engaged in physical activity, there is some concern that the fitness movement is not reaching the children and youth of the country. The National Children and Youth Fitness Studies I[9] and II[10], conducted in the mid-1980s, substantiated this concern. These studies revealed that children and youths have become fatter since 1960. Only about one-third of students participate in daily physical education programs. Secondary school physical education programs tend to focus largely on competitive and team sports rather than on developing individual and lifetime sport skills that can be used by adults throughout their lives. The reports also indicate that the majority of physical activity of the students is performed outside of the school setting, primarily in community settings.

The 1996 Surgeon General's report on *Physical Activity and Health* reached the following conclusions about the physical activity patterns of the nation's youth:[8]

◆ Only about one-half of young people regularly participate in vigorous physical activity. About one-fourth of young people engage in light or moderate physical activity, that is, walking or biking, every day.

◆ About 14% of the young people are inactive, and the prevalence of inactivity is higher among females.

◆ Participation in physical activity declines markedly as grade in school increases.

◆ From 1991 to 1995, the number of students enrolled in daily physical education decreased from 42% to 25%.

In the future, it is important to prevent the decrease in physical activity as youths age and to encourage youths that are active to remain involved. Forming positive activity habits, teaching skills and knowledge, and enhancing youths' self-confidence as movers are important in promoting involvement in regular physical activity throughout the lifespan.

Physical education and sport professionals need to assume a more active role in the leadership of the physical activity and fitness movement. At the vanguard of the movement are physicians, self-appointed experts, and even movie stars.[10] Many of these individuals lack the proper training and qualifications to direct this activity. Professionals also need to make a concerted effort to help the physical activity and fitness movement reach the youth of this country. Physical educators working in the school setting should provide students with the skills and knowledge necessary to assume the responsibility for their own physical activity and fitness needs throughout their lifespan.

Finally, physical education and sport professionals must become more involved in physical activity programs in nonschool settings that are designed to meet the needs of all persons. More physical education and sport programs must be established to meet the needs of the elderly, the very young, and individuals who have disabilities. Also, programs need to be developed to reach individuals who are economically disadvantaged; they lack the financial resources to join health clubs or pay for private sport instruction. Equity in physical activity and fitness is an important professional concern.

Health care reform

The 1990s has been marked by calls for health care reform. Rising health care costs and the growing number of people who are uninsured are two of the primary factors underlying this reform movement. In 1996, health care costs were $1.04 trillion dollars.[12] Health care costs accounted for 13.6% of the GNP, up from 7% in 1970.[12] Health care costs continue to escalate at an astronomical rate. It is estimated that by the year 2000 health care costs will exceed $1.9 trillion unless there is significant reform of our health care system.[8] Despite the fact that the United States spends over a trillion dollars a year on health care, over 40 million Americans are uninsured.

During the last few years numerous health care reform bills have been introduced by Congress. The proposals vary greatly, ranging from coverage for only catastrophic illnesses to comprehensive coverage for nearly all medical services. Other differences include the degree of emphasis placed on health promotion and disease prevention services and activities.

National public health reports, such as *Healthy People 2000,* have emphasized efforts to reduce disease, disability, and death through early intervention and prevention programs. These efforts can lead to improved health status for people of all ages and reduction in health care costs. *Healthy People 2000* identified important ways that physical education professionals can contribute to our national health goals. Conducting quality school physical education programs, promoting community-based physical activity programs, and managing worksite fitness programs are just a few of the many ways that professionals can help provide individuals with the skills, understanding, and encouragement to improve their health by leading a physically active lifestyle.

At this writing, a national health care plan has not been approved. It is envisioned, however, that changes in health care and how health services are delivered could create numerous opportunities for innovative physical activity programs and collaborative partnerships for physical education and sport professionals with other health care specialists.

Education

The last three decades in the United States have been marked by calls for reform of the educational establishment. Advocates for educational reform proclaimed a need to place a greater emphasis on the basic subjects such as English, mathematics, science, social studies, and computer science. Criticism was also directed at teacher competency, school leadership, and professional preparation institutions.

In the early 1990s, school reform proposals focused on providing students with the skills and knowledge to be productive members of the work force in our growing global economy. The *Year 2000 Goals* emphasize school readiness, improved graduation rates, attainment of competency in challenging subject matter, world prominence in math and science, adult literacy, and creation of a safe school environment.[13] These goals further called for increased ongoing opportunities for teacher development and school-parent partnerships to improve student learning.[13]

Education once was considered preparation for life; now it is looked on as a lifelong experience. More than 2 million persons 35 years of age or older are returning to school or beginning their higher education. Alvin Toffler in his book *The Third Wave* stresses that the aging or "graying" of America requires greater public attention to the needs of this population group.[14] Lewis stated that the rapid acceleration and growth of technology, the information era, and the demographic shift to a greater percentage of elderly in our society will have a tremendous impact on the nature of education and our society.[15] He writes that it is of paramount importance that all students acquire the basic skills of reading, writing, and computing. Students must be able to access information, analyze and synthesize it, and apply information in a meaningful way. As technology becomes increasingly sophisticated and our information base grows exponentially, students must have the necessary foundational skills and the opportunities to improve those skills if they are to keep abreast of developments and remain productive in our workforce. The *Year 2000 Goals* stress the importance of schools providing students with the foundation for lifelong learning. Thus, opportunities for adults to return to school to complete their education and receive further training are included in the 1994 Goals 2000: Educate America Act.

School structure is changing as we enter the twenty-first century. More and more states are adding public school pre-kindergarten programs for children ages 3 to 5. Calls for a longer school day and extending the school year to provide increased opportunities for learning are occurring with more frequency. Futurist Marvin Cetron,[16] president of Forecasting International Inc., stated that students may spend only three days a week in school. They would spend the rest of the time at home, learning through the use of computer-facilitated instruction and distance-learning approaches. Textbooks will be supplanted by computers and multimedia learning packages. Distance learning will allow students at several schools within the district or even throughout the nation to receive instruction from a central source. This will help equalize the quality of education provided to all students. Children and youths will not be the only learners; adults will regularly return to school to keep abreast of rapidly growing advances in technology and knowledge in their field.

The schools' use as a community learning center and a service provider will continue to grow. The 21st Century Community Learning Centers program of the Department of Education will lead to the establishment and expansion of the school as a site for community learning. There will be an expansion of before- and after-school, weekend, and summer programs for children and youths. These programs include academic enrichment as well as recreational programs. Greater ties and increased collaboration among public and private agencies, business, institutions of higher education, and cultural and scientific organizations will expand the learning opportunities and services provided not only to children and youth but to adults.

What are the implications of the educational reform movement and the changing structure of the school for physical education? First, to retain physical education as an integral part of the educational curriculum in the future, physical educators must clearly set forth the contribution of physical education to the educational process. To solidify the place of physical education in the educational curriculum in the next decade, physical educators must educate the public and decision makers about the values to be derived from participation in physical education, both in terms of the education and the health of the individual. Physical educators can generate support for physical education in the schools by conducting sound, exemplary programs. Second, as more adults return to school to update their skills, physical educators need to be ready to conduct instructional programs to

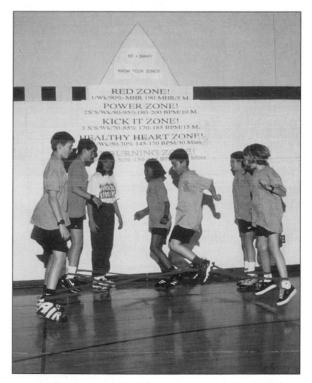

Physical education programs should help students learn the benefits of physical activity and develop skills and habits for lifelong participation in physical activity.

meet adult needs. Third, just as education must teach students to be lifelong learners, so must physical education. Students in physical education class need to have knowledge as well as skills so that they may be self-educative. Fourth, as more and more education takes place outside of the school setting in the home, physical education and sport professionals need to develop new programs to meet the needs of these learners. Finally, as the school continues to grow as a community center for learning for people of all ages, physical education and sport professionals must be prepared to conduct physical activity programs in these settings and to work collaboratively with other professionals in the community to develop comprehensive programs to meet a multitude of needs.

Technology

The past decade has been one of rapid technological advances, many of which have had implications for the future of physical education and sport. Developments in computer technology combined with increasingly sophisticated research techniques have enabled us to widen our knowledge base and will contribute to further growth in the future. The Internet has and will continue to revolutionize education, communication, and many other areas of our professional endeavors in the twenty-first century.

Technology has enabled researchers and practitioners to more clearly understand the impact of physical activity on the body as well as more clearly delineate the relationship among physical activity, exercise, fitness, and health. According to Powers, Ward, and Shanely, the development of more powerful microcomputers has had an "unprecedented effect on research in the field."[17] Other technological advances in the last 30 years that have had a significant impact on the field include the "development of electronic gas analyzers and metabolic measurement carts, blood gas analyzers, computerized muscle ergometers, and the commercially available instruments of molecular biology."[17] These advances have enabled us to explore questions not previously possible, obtain more sophisticated data and perform more complex analyses, and/or reduce the amount of time needed to complete the research process.

Physical education and sport professionals are using computers to perform many essential tasks, such as record keeping, fitness profiling, and database management. Professionals use hand held computers to gather information during various assessment procedures, later uploading the information to their desktop computer, and then using statistical programs to analyze their results. Software programs allow professionals to rapidly construct fitness profiles that are used to provide program participants with feedback about their fitness status. Coaches use laptop computers to input data as they scout their opponents and to quickly access game statistics during the course of the competition.

Computer technology has facilitated improvements in performance. In biomechanics, computer-generated graphical representations of an athlete's performance are compared with a prototypical sport performance, facilitating skill analysis and enhancing corrections. Skiers practice in wind tunnels while coaches and sport scientists study their body position and technique to find ways to reduce resistance from drag and increase speed. Equipment has been designed or reengineered using computer-assisted programs, which has led to improvements in performance. For example, redesigned handlebars for cyclists create a more aerodynamically shaped body position for the racers and lead to decreased time to complete the course. Sport participants at all levels can benefit from many of these improvements.

Developments in biotechnology hold implications for the future of physical education and sport. Experts in tissue engineering estimate that within the next 5 to 10 years, people will routinely have tendons, cartilage, and bones grown, a breakthrough that will benefit injured athletes as well as other individuals whose injuries limit their opportunity to lead a physically active lifestyle. Today muscle fiber typing allows researchers to identify whether an individual has a greater potential to succeed in athletic events requiring strength or endurance. Perhaps in the near future, genetic engineering will be used to program an individual's genes for success in certain sport activities. The first cloning of an adult mammal, Dolly the sheep, was heralded as the greatest scientific breakthrough of 1997. Ethicists and scientists are now engaged in sweeping debates about cloning humans. Genetic engineering can lead to the development of humans with specific traits. Hoberman states that "it is likely that this technology will be used to develop athletes before it is applied to the creation of other kinds of human performers."[18] How will we deal with these complex issues?

There has been a tremendous explosion of high-tech equipment in sports, facilitating better performances by all involved in sport, ranging from elite athletes to the recreational participants. For example, the clap skate has revolutionized the sport of long-track speed skating. Designed by biomechanists from the University of Amsterdam, Netherlands, the clap skate's blade is hinged at the toe allowing the heel to be released; this allows the blade to remain on the ice for a longer period of time when a stride is taken, giving the skater the ability to generate more power and gain greater momentum. At the 1998 Winter Olympics in Nagano, Japan, competitors used the clap skates and set record after record. Gianni Romme, skating in the 10,000 meter speed skate, won in a time of 13 minutes, 15.33 seconds, eclipsing the previous world record by more than 15 seconds.

Changes have been made in both the design of equipment and the materials used to construct the equipment. Titanium golf clubs with enlarged heads, like Big Bertha, have displaced the steel shafts of the old-fashioned woods. Graphite-composite tennis rackets with large racket faces have replaced metal and metal-composite tennis rackets, which replaced wooden rackets years ago. Technology applied to the manufacturing of running shoes has led to increased comfort, while producing fewer injuries for runners of all abilities. Grass fields have been replaced by artificial surfaces, cinder tracks by all-weather tracks, and open stadiums by domed arenas. In the 1998 Sports Super Show, which showcases new products, one of the top five new products was the Radar Ball from Rawlings. The Radar Ball is a baseball with a "built-in" radar that accurately measures the speed at which the ball is thrown and displays it on an LCD on the ball. This provides the pitcher with immediate feedback. This application will probably be extended to other balls and other equipment.

Developments in the field of telecommunication have and will continue to improve our ability to communicate and our delivery systems. The Internet, a web of thousands of computer networks, has dramatically changed how we interact and manage information. E-mail allows rapid, inexpensive communication with colleagues throughout the world. E-mail listservs allow individuals with common interests, such as fitness, to engage in discussions, pose questions, and share ideas.

The World Wide Web (WWW), the multimedia channel of the Internet, is used for many different purposes. Electronic professional journals and documents are posted on the Web, enhancing the dissemination of information. Personalized information services, such as Pointcast, seek out specific information, update it automatically, and send it to the PC user's desktop.[3] For example, using Pointcast, a personal trainer can receive daily updates on training techniques, nutrition, and cardiovascular research. Professionals have easier access to current research and will readily be able to retrieve needed information from virtually anywhere in the world where they have computer access. Research data can be easily shared via the Web or through file transfers.

Internet telephones and videoconferencing enhance communications with professionals throughout the world. The Web and desktop videoconferencing are increasingly being used for distance learning. Courses and even entire degree programs can be completed via the Internet. Continuing education programs offered through distance learning will increase in popularity. For example, a professional in Alaska can "attend" a workshop on fitness hosted by an organization in New York.

Multimedia instruction and interactive tutorials using CD-ROM and/or the Web will allow physical education and sport professionals to tailor learning to the needs of each program participant. Users benefit from enhanced presentations of information. Haggerty writes: "Is it 'better' to read a paper or dissertation about an area, say biomechanics, on a multimedia version with sound, video, graphics, and hypertext rather than on a two-dimensional printed page? What about sport history? Can video clips, sound files, and the actual works be more valuable than a textual description of them?"[3] Participants in a fitness program or schoolchildren accessing various sites on the Web or using a CD-ROM can see a heart pulsating as it beats, follow the course of circulation, and become familiar with the short- and long-term effects of exercise on this vital organ. Multimedia presentations let content be experienced in new ways.

Virtual reality is the use of computers and sensory mechanisms to create simulated, interactive 3-dimensional environments and experiences. Virtual reality can vary in its nature and its sophistication. Head-mounted displays and sensor gloves may be a part of virtual reality. Virtual reality can also be a game or a simulation. It places the body of the user directly inside of the 3-D environment. Virtual reality offers some of the most exciting possibilities for our field and is expected to grow tremendously early in the twenty-first century.

Through virtual reality, real life situations can be recreated, altered, or simulated, allowing the user to react and to rehearse constant or changing scenarios. It provides invaluable training to users and allows them to gain a vast amount of knowledge through their experiences. Bobsledders used virtual reality to train prior to the Albertville Winter Olympics. The athletes were able to rehearse their runs and experience the course in a realistic setting. Haggerty suggests that virtual reality can be used to provide athletes in many sports (e.g., batters, goalies, football players) with a variety of simulated situations to improve their performance.[3] Virtual golf simulators give golfers the opportunity to play many of the great courses while receiving feedback on their shot, distance, and errors. Simulators are being developed for other sports such as baseball. Other possible uses would be in the training of physical education and sport professionals. Preservice teachers could gain experience in organizing a class and managing behavior;

cardiac rehabilitation specialists could gain practice in administering various stress test protocols to patients with varying disease conditions.

Virtual reality is being developed for medical education and training, rehabilitation, and for use by individuals with disabilities. Uses including teaching palpitation, rehabilitation of a hand, and emergency medical training. These virtual reality simulations would be helpful in training athletic trainers and specialists in cardiac rehabilitation. Virtual reality is also being used to help children in wheelchairs learn how to navigate their chair with a joystick and potentially can be used to help people with disabilities participate in "virtual" sports that they can not perform in the "real" world. Although virtual reality is expensive and accessibility is limited, it is expected that this will change as technology becomes more advanced.

Technology offers exciting new possibilities for the field of physical education and sport. Computers help professionals complete their responsibilities more efficiently. Application of technology has led to improvements in sport equipment and performance, benefiting sport participants of all abilities. Biotechnology offers exciting possibilities as well as confronting us with a host of ethical issues that must be addressed. Multimedia technology enhances learning, and distance learning increases access to learning. Telecommunications facilitate interactions with colleagues throughout the world. And, virtual reality offers tremendous possibilities for training, education, and sport participation in the twenty-first century.

Changing Demographics

Demographic trends exert a tremendous influence on the structure of societal institutions and the services they provide to different populations. The age distribution of the population is shifting quite markedly. Longer life expectancies and a declining birthrate have increased the average age of the population. Today, there are more Americans over the age of 65 than under the age of 25 and this aging trend is expected to continue.[19]

America's society is aging. The change is quite dramatic when viewed over the course of the century. In 1900 approximately 4% of the population were 65 or older.[19] In 1997 12.7% of the population fell within this age group, and this is estimated to increase to 18.5% in 2025.[20] Furthermore, there will be an increasing number of very old people, many of whom will be healthy. The number of people 85 years and older is expected to increase from 3.8 million in 1996 to more than 7 million in 2025.[20] Minorities are projected to comprise 25% of the population 65 and older in 2030; this is nearly double the 13% recorded in 1996.[20]

America's population is also becoming more culturally diverse as the number of Asians, Hispanics, African Americans, and Native American citizens increase. It is estimated that by the year 2000, about 33% of school-aged children will be ethnic minorities, and this will rise to over 45% by the year 2020.[21] Because a disproportionate number of minorities are economically disadvantaged, many of these children will be living at or near the poverty level. Further, because socioeconomic status is a significant risk factor in disease, the health status of minorities of all ages is of grave concern.[7]

These forthcoming years will see continued changes in the structure of the family and growing societal problems that must be addressed. The number of single-parent families is rising, including the number of teenage mothers. Single-parent families and dual-career families have led to an increase in "latch-key" children—children who come home at the end of the school day to an empty house. Preschool and day care programs are increasing dramatically. Amidst the changing nature of the family is the problem of a growing array of threats to the health and well-being of our children and youth. Drug and alcohol abuse, violence, child abuse, suicide, and risky sexual behaviors adversely impact the lives of many young people.

What are the implications of these changes for the conduct of physical education and sport programs? We must be prepared to effectively work with the changing population groups. Quality physical activity programs are needed for the growing elderly population both to enhance their health and to provide enjoyable recreational pur-

New technologies can help teachers give students individualized instruction.

suits. Professionals in both school and nonschool settings must be prepared to conduct programs that are sensitive to the needs of an increasingly culturally diverse population.

As physical education and sport shifts to an industry where people pay for desired sport services (e.g., commercial fitness clubs), we must not lose sight of the needs of the economically disadvantaged who cannot afford to pay. One of the major public health goals is to reduce disparities in life expectancy and health between Caucasians and minority groups. Physical activity has been identified as an important element in achieving this goal. Providing access to physical activity programs for children and youth through school physical education programs is only one part of the answer. Professionally, we must explore innovative approaches that will help make physical activity programs available to the population groups that need them as part of a comprehensive health and human service program.

Lawson[22] discusses the interdependence of schools, families, and health and calls for the planning, implementation, and assessment of new intervention strategies for children, youth, and their families that reflect this interrelationship. These strategies would expand the responsibilities assigned to the schools. Preventive and educational health programs for families and children would be established in the schools. These programs would be linked to health and social services within the community. School personnel, health care professionals, and human services providers then would work collaboratively to address the needs of the whole family within the community.

What would physical education's role be in this collaborative venture? Lawson[22] suggests that one approach may be to combine physical education with health education. This integrative approach would focus on health and life enhancement. Through this approach teachers would help individuals acquire the skills, knowledge, and values instrumental to leading healthy, active lifestyles. This integrated program would also contribute to and support community-based family and health services.

As we move toward the twenty-first century and look beyond, as professionals we must be prepared to explore innovative approaches to providing services to people of all ages if the potential of physical education and sport to enhance the quality of life of all people is to be fulfilled.

Expanding Frontiers

The frontiers of the habitable universe are expanding. People in the future may be living as part of a space station colony or on a moon base. The work of the astronauts and the NASA programs has laid the basis for the future in respect to space travel. Space travel may become commonplace in the future. Citizens will be able to purchase a ticket for space travel in the space shuttle much in the same way they purchase a ticket for airline travel.

The July 1976 issue of *National Geographic*[23] visualizes the outcome of a serious proposal that was developed by a group of 30 engineers and social and physical scientists. They describe what a typical colony in space will be like. Ten thousand people, their mission to build more colonies, will live under artificial gravity in an encircling tube called a *torus*. The torus is divided into six separate sections, each of which has supermarket, farming, and residential areas and such facilities as theaters, sport arenas, schools, and libraries. Sunlight is filtered and dispersed by means of mirrors that can be tilted to produce an 8-hour night every 24 hours. Farming is very productive as a result of controlled sunlight, an unfailing water supply, ample fertilizer, equable temperature, and a somewhat higher carbon dioxide content in the air than on Earth. The crop yields are many times of those on Earth.

A second area of the habitable universe that will be an especially exciting place to live in the future is underwater. Since more than two-thirds of the planet is covered with ocean, there will be sufficient room to construct many underwater communities. Futurist Rosen reports on the work of scientist William Backley who has developed a submerged capsule equipped with observation ports that is a model for future underwater communities. A superstructure to the capsule has a helicopter landing pad and docking facilities for surface craft. The capsule is held in place by anchors and is made stable by a concrete mat suspended beneath the unit. An airlock and elevator offer easy access either to the ocean floor or to the surface. Backley's work represents a model for the construction of a future underwater colony that will have residential areas, farming, and other facilities comparable to those that will exist in space.

Physical education and sport professionals need to prepare themselves to help individuals attain their optimal level of fitness while living in these space and underwater environments. Space travelers to distant planets need help in keeping fit while living for long periods of time under conditions of zero gravity. Professionals must conduct research concerning the effects of weightlessness on the body and artificial gravity. Designing exercise programs to deal with differences in the environment falls within the realm of physical education and sport.

PREPARING FOR THE FUTURE

It is tempting to look back on these past two decades, which have been a time of tremendous growth for physical education and sport, and bask in the glow of such accomplishments as the celebration of the one hundredth anniversary of AAHPERD, the growth in professional stature achieved by the various subdisciplines, the tremendous expansion of our knowledge base both in depth and breadth, our efforts to develop programs to meet the needs of people of all ages in a diversity of settings, and the increase in job opportunities within the field. However, if physical education and sport professionals are interested in being involved in the future of their profession, they must also look at areas in which they can improve.

If the potential of our field to enhance the life of people of all ages is to be realized, we must take a more active role in creating our future and shaping our destiny. We must take a proactive rather than reactive stance in dealing with the issues and challenges that confront us. (See Chapter 14.) Furthermore, both individually and collectively, we must reflect more critically upon social issues related to physical education and sport and question long-held assumptions, sacrosanct beliefs, and traditional practices.[24] We must be introspective, engaging ourselves in a thoughtful examination of our actions and values. We also must look outwardly, beyond ourselves, and examine the broader societal issues and their impact on our lives, institutions, programs, and the people with whom we work. But we must move beyond reflection to consider alternatives to the problems that confront us. Personally and professionally, both individually and collectively, we must move toward solutions if the potential of our field is to be fulfilled.

Oberle,[25] in a discussion about the future directions for health, physical education, recreation and leisure, and dance, stressed the importance of exerting quality control within these professions. He suggested each of the disciplines consider the following actions to enhance their effectiveness:

- ◆ Establish minimum standards of competency.
- ◆ Develop programs and services that are flexible to meet changing needs while accomplishing avowed disciplinary objectives.
- ◆ Provide meaningful programs that will meet needs today as well as tomorrow.
- ◆ Reduce ineffective programs.
- ◆ Establish minimum standards for entry into professional preparation programs.
- ◆ Provide high-quality experiences for professionals within the discipline, such as in-service education and graduate education.
- ◆ Develop a system for relicensure for all professionals, not only public school personnel.
- ◆ Establish professional accreditating agencies, as the American Medical Association has done, to ensure quality control.
- ◆ Develop high-quality model programs and build facilities that can serve as the standard for the profession.

As we move into the future, we must establish our professional stature.

A review of the past decade shows two areas—jurisdiction over the physical education and sport domain and the delivery system of physical education and sport—that need the attention of professionals. First, some of the shortcomings of each of the two areas will be described, and then a scenario will be painted for each area in the early twenty-first century.

ESTABLISHMENT OF JURISDICTION OVER OUR DOMAIN

The future of physical education and sport could lie in physical education and sport professionals becoming the publicly recognized leaders in their field of physical activity. Many of the services with which physical education and sport professionals are presently associated lie within the public domain. Unfortunately, physical education and sport professionals are not directing these services. Muscle builders, entrepreneurs, and movie stars associated with health spas, exercise salons, and weight-reducing clinics have invaded our domain, often without proper credentials.[11] Additionally, the public is often not aware of the nature of physical education and sport and the tremendous worth and substance of this field of endeavor

If physical education and sport professionals are to become the publicly recognized leaders in their field, it will be because they have provided themselves with the proper credentials. The credentials necessary to achieve this leadership position are described below:

◆ *Credential 1.* A systematic knowledge base will exist that describes the unique social service rendered by our professionals. This knowledge base will (1) support the art and science of human movement as it relates to sport, dance, play, and exercise; (2) document the fact that physical education and sport foster human growth and development; and (3) convincingly show that a better human being will result by developing the proper relationship of body, mind, and spirit.

◆ *Credential 2.* Physical education and sport will have two program priorities (although there are others) that provide consumers with self-direction in light of the emphasis on self-help medicine and the rising cost of health care. The first priority will be *knowledge*—knowledge that is (1) concerned with the science of movement and the healthful impact that proper physical activity has on the functioning of the human organism and (2) based on scientific findings that are constantly updated and provided to practitioners via retrieval systems in language that can be understood and used.

The second priority will be *skills*—skills taught scientifically, utilizing not only the basic concepts of motor learning, but also advanced technology enabling persons to be taught more effectively and to progress more rapidly.

◆ *Credential 3.* Physical education teaching will become a science as well as an art; it will be governed by rigorous laws enabling professionals to predict with a high degree of certainty the outcome of learning.

Physical education and sport can be a means of fostering human growth and development by teaching people how to help others.

As professionals, we must assume the challenge of leadership for the domain of physical education and sport. We must be accountable for our programs. High-quality programs are essential. We must promote our programs and take steps to ensure that the people who participate in them accrue the stated and personally desired benefits. Physical education and sport programs in the future will become more diverse as we expand our focus to include more populations. Professionals must be sensitive to individual needs when designing programs. Additionally, we must improve our delivery systems to more effectively serve individuals of all ages.

ENHANCEMENT OF OUR DELIVERY SYSTEMS

In the future physical education and sport will need to change the manner in which it provides services, as well as the populations it serves. In other words, physical education and sport needs to change its delivery system.

Some remarks heard from various groups during the past few years suggest that our delivery systems need attention. Here are a few of the comments:

1. Junior high school students at a science fair where models depicting space and underwater living were on display: "How do we get our physical bodies in shape for this existence that we are very likely to experience in the years ahead?"
2. Group of physicians: "You physical and sport educators do a good job making healthy people healthier and skilled people better skilled but a terrible job making unhealthy people healthy and poorly skilled people skilled."
3. Rotary Club: "I look at school physical education and community recreation programs and can't tell the difference between the two. They overlap in the activities they offer and the people they serve. There's also a duplication of facilities and personnel. Why all this waste?"
4. Senior citizen club: "The elderly represent 11% of the population in this country. Is your profession devoting 11% of its total effort to this group?"
5. Student group: "Why don't we have a record system listing information about each person's personal physical education and sport history? We have records pertaining to people's health history. Why not a physical education and sport history record?"

The physical education and sport delivery system requires an overhaul, and new developments in the field of technology and communication, as well as the changing nature of education, will help achieve that overhaul.

The following examples illustrate how trends and developments may shape the future of physical education.

1. The delivery system will be more responsive to individual needs. Use of technology, more personalized instructional approaches, and innovative programming will enable us to better meet the diverse needs of our increasingly heterogenous population. No longer can we rely on one program to meet all needs or, as Lawson[22] states, the "one size fits all" approach. Our delivery system will enable us to better meet the needs of various population groups, including the elderly, the very young, the growing number of ethnic minorities, and those populations historically underserved, such as the economically disadvantaged.
2. The delivery system will render services to the new frontiers of space colonies and underwater communities. Meetings will be held with futurists and scientists. Conditions that simulate space and underwater living will be established in college and university laboratories. Physical education and sport professionals and their students will pursue studies in these areas.
3. The delivery system will provide closer articulation between school physical education and sport programs and community programs. These programs will be combined and centrally administered. This program structure will (1) ensure efficient use of facilities, equipment, and personnel; (2) eliminate

overlapping; and (3) provide for progression throughout life in the program of activities. It will meet the needs of all individuals in the community, including those in their later years who want to become involved in physical activity, sport, and recreational activities.

Also, a computerized record system will exist for each person throughout life wherever he or she goes or lives.

4. The delivery system will make extensive use of distance learning and cable television. Programs will be packaged and syndicated. There will be such features as demonstrations of the step-by-step approach to developing skill in dance, sport, and other activities; lectures relating to such areas as exercise physiology; and demonstrations of methods by which one's physical fitness can be assessed and maintained.

Videotape feedback of one's performance will become increasingly common, and generation of computerized models of ideal performances and actual performances will help individuals learn and improve their motor skills more easily.

5. Computers will play an increasingly important role in our delivery system. Computer information databases and services will be used to disseminate research findings, allowing professionals to more easily keep abreast of current research developments within the fields. Collaborative research endeavors with colleagues at other institutions and with practitioners at various sites throughout the world will be facilitated through telecommunication networking. Additionally, professionals can network with one another to share ideas and programs and to jointly resolve problems confronting them. Computerized resource databases will allow practitioners to more easily individualize programs to meet participants' needs. Computer record-keeping will make it easier for practitioners to identify individuals' needs and to monitor progress toward the attainment of their goals.

As we move into the twenty-first century, we must change our delivery systems to use new technologies to more effectively provide services to an ever increasing clientele. Our delivery systems should encourage participation and maintain involvement in our programs.

THE FUTURE

As they prepare for the future, physical education and sport professionals must do the following:

1. Provide themselves with the proper credentials to establish jurisdiction over their domain.
2. Utilize technological advances to improve the delivery system.
3. Prepare for space and underwater living and for changes in our society.
4. Become a positive role model for a fit and healthy lifestyle, so that others will be favorably influenced to emulate this lifestyle.
5. Help persons to become increasingly responsible for their own health and fitness.
6. Recognize that individuals will live longer and become more fit and active in the years to come.
7. Provide for all persons, regardless of age, skill, disabling condition, and socioeconomic background, throughout their lifespan.
8. Remember that we are involved with the development of the whole person as a thinking, feeling, moving human being.
9. Make a commitment to conduct high-quality programs that are sensitive to individual needs so that physical education and sport's potential to enhance the health and quality of life for all people can be achieved.

Whether or not physical education and sport professionals meet these challenges depends on the members of our field. Remember, the future of physical education and sport is coming, but physical education and sport professionals can determine where it is going. This requires dedicated leadership and the commitment on the part of each professional to be involved in working toward our future. We must take charge of our professional destiny and create a future that allows the full potential of physical education and sport to be fulfilled.

It is likely that all of us, at some time in our lives, will have a significant experience that, as years pass, will come to embody the personal meaning of physical education and sport. Noted physical education leader and author of previous editions of this text, Charles Bucher, related an experience that helped him personally and perhaps will help you to realize anew the tremendous potential of physical education and sport in our society. Bucher wrote the following passage about the New York City marathon, one of the largest marathons in the world:

I was particularly enthralled as I watched the runners, some of whom took as many as five, six, and seven hours to cross the finish lines. Most runners gritted their teeth, gasped for breath, and put on an extra burst of speed as they pounded across. Some runners had given so much of themselves that they were helped onto a stretcher or were carried across.

A runner from Italy, in fourth place, whipped off his sweatband and waved it to the crowd. A runner from California, in second place among the women, clenched her teeth and went the last few strides on sheer will before collapsing across the line. When a long-haired Polish woman, sweat streaming down her face, stumbled slowly toward the line, the crowd cheered and chanted, "Finish it! Finish it!" And *she did.*

A few runners completed the race hand-in-hand. Some went barefoot and some carried their shoes. Each person got a tremendous cheer, but perhaps the loudest cheers of all were for two men who crossed the finish line in wheelchairs.

The runners had done their best—not for acclaim, for a loving cup symbolic of supremacy, or to be a champion—but to prove to themselves that they could do it.

No one could watch the sight without realizing that he or she was witnessing a great moment in America and the world.

No one in physical education and sport could be a part of that experience without feeling the power and potential for our field of endeavor—the power and potential for improving the quality of life for all our citizens.

The marathon perhaps in many ways is symbolic of our society, of America, of physical education and sport, and of the qualities that make our society great, and that we in our field try to develop. It recognizes that the training of the physical is important; but perhaps more important, it shows how the physical *can* and *should* be used as a vehicle that brings into play such desirable qualities as courage, a belief in oneself, a feeling of accomplishment, and, most important, a blending of the mind, body, and spirit in the accomplishment of worthy goals.

Physical education and sport is a dynamic, growing field of endeavor. Its future is very promising. An editorial by the executive directors of AAHPERD published in the *Journal of Physical Education, Recreation, and Dance* expressed a sense of optimism for the 1990s. It stated:[26]

At no time in the history of American Alliance for Health, Physical Education, Recreation, and Dance have we, as executive directors of the national associations, seen more opportunities for professional growth and service within the entire profession. We are highly encouraged by the signs we see for new impact on society, stimulation of teaching and leadership personnel, development of significant projects, and potential for growth in membership. . . . Society wants and needs us. Now is the opportune time!

The vision of lifespan involvement in physical activity for all people is a powerful one, but its achievement requires dedicated and committed professionals. Excellence must be present in all our professional endeavors. After you have read this text, I hope that you, as the reader, have an appreciation for the tremendous substance and worth of this field that you have chosen to study. Physical education and sport has a tremendous potential to enrich and enhance the health and quality of life of all people. Whether this potential is realized depends on each professional's willingness to make a personal commitment to achieving this goal. At the beginning of this text, you were encouraged to take advantage of your educational opportunities and challenged to make a commitment to excellence. At the conclusion of this text, I challenge you, as a young professional, to go forth and be the best you can be.

Competitors at the World Masters Swimming Championship take their marks for the race.

SUMMARY

Planning and knowing what the future will be like is essential if physical education and sport are to take an active part in the direction and shaping of the future. Professionals must start planning for the future now. Such planning requires that professionals recognize that rapid change is characteristic of our way of life.

Several societal trends will influence the future of physical education and sport. The wellness movement and the fitness movement present excellent opportunities for professionals to involve individuals of all ages in appropriate physical activity. The educational reform movement and the changing nature of education indicate that physical education and sport professionals, more than ever before, need to inform the public and decision makers about the contribution of physical education to the educational process. The expanding frontiers of the habitable universe, developments in communications, and other technological developments will influence the future of physical education and sport as well.

Physical education and sport professionals can prepare for the future in several ways. First, professionals need to establish jurisdiction over their domain by obtaining the proper credentials and actively seeking leadership positions. Second, professionals need to improve the delivery systems.

We must provide for people of all ages and utilize technological advances to facilitate learning. We must take an active role in helping individuals prepare for space and underwater living. The future of physical education and sport is *coming*, but only physical education and sport can determine where it is *going*.

SELF-ASSESSMENT TESTS

These tests are designed to help you determine if you have mastered the materials and competencies presented in this chapter.

1. Discuss the implications of the changing nature of education and the impact of technological developments on physical education and sport in the future.

2. Your professor has requested that you supply information to show how physical education and sport can establish jurisdiction over its own domain. Prepare a report on this topic and present it to the class.

3. Develop a plan for the late 1990s that provides specific suggestions for improving physical education and sport's delivery system.

4. Using the information provided in the Getting Connected box, access the *Sporting Goods Manufacturers' Association* site. Using the press releases and the latest state of the industry report, identify upcoming changes and trends in sports participation, fitness, and equipment.

5. Using the information provided in the Getting Connected box, access the *World Health Organization* site. Read the latest report on world health or browse through the press releases to find information on health throughout the world and the United States. Make comparisons on a specific health topic between developing countries and developed countries. Identify trends in disease treatment and prevention and discuss the implications of these trends for the people affected.

REFERENCES

1. Bucher CA and Thaxton NA: Physical education and sport: change and challenge, St. Louis, 1981, Mosby.

2. Huxley A: Brave new world, New York, 1932, Modern Library.

3. Haggerty TR: Influence of information technologies on kinesiology and physical education, Quest 49:254–269, 1997.

4. Massengale JD: The unprepared discipline: selection of alternative futures, Quest 40:107–114, 1988.

5. US Department of Health, Education, and Welfare: Healthy people: the Surgeon General's report on health promotion and disease prevention, Washington, D.C., 1979, US Government Printing Office.

6. US Department of Health and Human Services: Promoting health/preventing disease: objectives for the nation, Washington, D.C., 1980, US Government Printing Office.

7. Public Health Service, US Department of Health and Human Services: Healthy people 2000: national health promotion and disease prevention objectives, Washington, D.C., 1991, US Government Printing Office.

8. US Department of Health and Human Services. Physical activity and health: a report of the Surgeon General, Atlanta, Ga., 1996, US

Department of Health and Human Services, Centers for Disease Control and Prevention, National Center for Chronic Disease Prevention and Health Promotion.

9. Ross JG and Gilbert CG: The national children and youth study: a summary of the findings, JOPERD 56(1):45–50, 1985.

10. Ross JG and Pate RR: The national children and youth fitness study II, JOPERD 58(9):51–56, 1987.

11. Corbin CB: Is the fitness bandwagon passing us by?, JOPERD 55(9):17, 1984.

12. Health Care Financing Administration: Health care spending rise at record low, Press Release, January 13, 1998, Washington, D.C.

13. US Department of Education: Goals 2000, Washington, D.C., 1994, US Government Printing Office.

14. Toffler A: The third wave, New York, 1981, Bantam Books.

15. Lewis AJ: Education for the 21st century, Educational Leadership 41(1):9–10, 1983.

16. Cetron M: Schools of the future. Presented at the Convention of the American Association of School Administrators, Dallas, August 1985.

17. Powers S, Ward K, and Shanely RA: Contemporary exercise physiology research in United States: Influence of technology, Quest 49:296–299, 1997.

18. Hoberman J: Mortal engines: The science of performance and the dehumanization of sport, New York, 1992, Free Press.

19. Jones CJ and Rikli RE: The gerontology movement—is it passing us by? JOPERD 64(1):17-26, 1993.

20. US Administration on Aging and American Association of Retired Persons: A profile of older Americans, 1997, Washington D.C., 1997, US Government Printing Office.

21. Statistical Abstract of the United States, 1993. Lanhan, Maryland, Bernau Press.

22. Lawson HA: School reform, families, and health in the emergent national agenda for economic and social improvement: implications, Quest 45:289–307, 1993.

23. First colony in space, National Geographic 150(1):76–89, 1976.

24. Bain LL: Beginning the journey: agenda for 2001, Quest 40:96–106, 1988.

25. Oberle GH: A future direction plan for our profession, JOPERD 59(1): 76–77, 1988.

26. AAHPERD Executive Directors: In our view, JOPERD 59(8):14, 1988.

SUGGESTED READINGS

American Academy of Physical Education: New possibilities, new paradigms? American Academy of Physical Education Papers No. 24, Champaign, Ill., 1991, Human Kinetics.

A collection of papers that explores potential directions for the future of the discipline, including assessment of past efforts, future research directions, problems, and visions.

Bain LL: Beginning the journey: agenda for 2001, Quest 40:96–106, 1988.

An analysis of societal trends and their implications for physical education programs in higher education is presented.

Cetron MJ, Soriano B, and Gayle M: Schools of the future: education approaches the twenty-first century, Futurist 23(4):18–23, 1985.

Factors affecting the future of schools, characteristics of the students of the future, and changes in the status of teachers and the manner of instruction are described.

Corbin CB: The field of physical education—common goals, not common roles, JOPERD 64(1):79, 84–87, 1993.

Highlights of physical education's changing focus throughout history are presented and developments necessary to make physical education the renaissance field in the next century are described. The importance of professionals working together to achieve common goals is emphasized.

Ellis MJ: The business of physical education: the future of the profession, Champaign, Ill., 1988, Human Kinetics.

A thought-provoking examination of the future of physical education, this book examines major societal trends and their implications for physical education, the activity and leisure industry, the changing nature of the profession, status of physical education in the school setting, and challenges to be faced.

Haskell WL: Physical activity, sport, and health: toward the next century, Research Quarterly for Exercise and Sport 67(Supplement):37–47, 1996.

Haskell discusses how changes in technology have contributed to sloth, lack of leisure time, physical activity in an aging society, and recommendations for enhancing health and physical performance.

Jones CJ and Rikli RE: The gerontology movement—is it passing us by? JOPERD 64(1):17-6, 1993.

The field of gerontology is growing rapidly. We must strengthen our efforts to prepare students for this field and to work effectively with this growing segment of the population.

Lawson HA: Looking back from the year 2082, Journal of Physical Education, Recreation, and Dance 53(1):15–17, 1982.

Three catalysts to change in the nature of physical education as practiced in 2082 are discussed. These are the growth of sport instruction and participation in the community, the self-help movement, and the development of the disciplinary foundation that helped stimulate the growth of alternative careers.

Lidstone JE and Feingold RS, editors: Integration and collaboration: challenge for the future, Quest 43:241–330, 1991.

A special feature comprising 6 articles that examine the issues of integration and collaboration and obstacles facing professionals in the field.

Markley OW and McCuan WR: America beyond 2001: opposing viewpoints, San Diego, Calif., 1995, Greenhaven Press.

Different perspectives on the future are presented, including articles on the aging of America, education, health, and technology.

Martens, R, editor: Technology in kinesiology and physical education, Quest 49, 1997 (entire issue).

This entire issue is devoted to technology and the field of physical education and sport, including articles on sport pedagogy, motor behavior, exercise physiology, and instructional technology.

Massengale JD: Visionary leadership and the physical educator, Physical Educator 52:219–221, 1995.

The characteristics of visionary leaders and their importance to the future of physical education are discussed.

Mohnsen B and Thompson C: Using video technology in physical education, Strategies 10(6):8–11, 1997.

Different uses for video technology are explored, including modeling of performances, concept demonstrations, use of scenarios, and self-analysis.

Naisbitt J and Aburdene P: Megatrends 2000: ten new directions for the 1990s, New York, 1990, William Morrow and Company.

Ten trends that will shape the future including the global economy, the rise of women in leadership, the increased privatization of the welfare state, the increased emphasis on religion, and the growth of the individual are presented, as well as implications for the future.

Rintala J: Sport and technology: human questions in a world of machines, Journal of Sport and Social Issues, 19:62–75, 1995.

A thoughtful discussion of questions professionals in physical education and sport should address as technological advances influence the nature of the field and the experiences of participants.

Toffler A: Future shock, New York, Random House, 1970.

The future and the changes that it will bring are discussed in this classic book.

Photo Credits

Chapter 1 P. 4 Fred Smith, Empire State Games, Albany, NY; p. 5 Matthew Castiglione; p. 7 Senior Citizens Center, Ithaca, NY; p. 9 Linda Buettner; p. 10 From Auxter D, Pyfer, J: Principles and methods of adapted physical education and recreation, ed 6. St. Louis, 1989, Mosby; p. 11 Tom Ward; p. 14 Laura Bitting, Ithaca College; p. 15 Ithaca College Sports Information; p. 16 Fred Smith, Empire State Games, Albany, NY; p. 17 University of Tennessee Sports Information, Nashville, TN; p. 18 University of Nevada at Las Vegas; p. 21 Bill Baun, Tenneco Health and Fitness Program; p. 22 From Bucher, C: Administration of physical education and athletic programs, ed 8, St. Louis, 1983, Mosby; Linda Castiglione; p. 29 Fred Smith, Empire State Games, Albany, NY; p. 31 Patti Nieffer. Figure 1-1 Modified from Anderson DF, Broom EF, Pooley JC, Schrody D and Brown E: Foundations of Canadian Physical Education, Recreation and Sport Studies, Dubuque, IA, 1995, WCB Brown & Benchmark.

Chapter 2 P. 37 Sarah Rich; p. 42 Deborah Wuest, Ithaca College; p. 44 Joan Smith, US Master's Swimming; p. 52 Deborah Wuest, Ithaca College; p. 51, 54, and 57 From Wuest, D, and Lombardo, B: Curriculum and instruction: the secondary school experience, ed 1, St. Louis, 1994, Mosby; p. 53 Rick Heinz, Courtesy Lois Mauch, Agassiz Middle Schools, Fargo, North Dakota; p. 56 Sarah Rich; p. 58 From Nichols, B: Moving and learning: the elementary school physical education experience, ed 3, St. Louis, 1994, Mosby; p. 60 Peter Mainelli, Taking Care, Hartford, CT; p. 66 From Bucher, C: Administration of physical education and athletic programs, ed 8, St. Louis, 1983, Mosby; p. 67 From Safrit, M and Wood, T: Introduction to measurement in sport and exercise science, ed 3, St. Louis, 1995, Mosby. Figure 2-1 Dolly Lambdin, Blanton Elementary School, Austin, Texas and the University of Texas at Austin; Figure 2-2 and 2-3 Courtesy Cooper Institute for Aerobic Research, Dallas, Texas.

Chapter 3 P. 77 Linda Buettner, Deborah Wuest, Ithaca College; p. 78 Deborah Wuest, Ithaca College; p. 80 Deborah Wuest, Ithaca College; p. 86 Linda Castiglione; p. 87 From Nichols, B: Moving and learning: the elementary school physical education experience, ed 3, St. Louis, 1994, Mosby; p. 88 From Bucher, C: Administration of physical education and athletic programs, ed 10, St. Louis, 1993, Mosby; p. 91 Deborah Wuest, Ithaca College; p. 92 Suzi D'Annalto; p. 96 Sarah Rich; p. 97 Deborah Wuest, Ithaca College; p. 104 From Nichols, B: Moving and learning: the elementary school physical education experience, ed 3, St. Louis, 1994, Mosby; p. 105 From Auxter, D, Pyfer, J: Principles and methods of adapted physical education and recreation, ed 6, St. Louis, 1989, Mosby.

Chapter 4 P. 114 Deborah Wuest, Ithaca College; p. 119 From Nichols, B: Moving and learning: the elementary school physical education experience, ed 3, St. Louis, 1994, Mosby; p. 121 Deborah Wuest, Ithaca College; p. 122 Fred Esterbrook; p. 127 Linda Castiglione; p. 132 University of Nevada, Las Vegas; p. 134 Linda Castiglione; p. 134 Fred Smith, Empire State Games, Albany, NY; p. 136 From Nichols, B: Moving and learning: the elementary school physical education experience, ed 2, St. Louis, 1990, Mosby; p. 139 Omaha Public Schools, Omaha, NE. Figure 4-2 From Nichols, B: Moving and learning: the elementary school physical education experience, ed 3, St. Louis, 1994, Mosby.

Chapter 5 P. 148 Smith College Archives, Northampton, MA; p. 149 Sarah Rich; p. 127 University of Nevada, Las Vegas; p. 159 Deborah Wuest, Ithaca College; p. 164 Harold L Ray, Western Michigan University, Kalamazoo, MI; p. 165 Harold L Ray, Western Michigan University, Kalamazoo, MI; p. 166 J. Clarence Davies Collection, Museum of the City of New York; p. 168 Courtesy American Alliance for Health, Physical Education, Recreation and Dance; p. 169 Courtesy American Alliance for Health, Physical Education, Recreation and Dance; p. 170 Smith College Archives, Northampton, MA; p. 171 Aldrich and Aldrich; p. 172 Smith College Archives, Northampton, MA; p. 173 American Alliance for Health, Physical Education, Recreation, and Dance; p. 178 Cynthia Trowbridge, Ithaca College; p. 181 Sarah Rich, p. 183 Scott Cunningham, NBA Photos; p. 186 From Auxter, D, Pyfer, J: Principles and methods of adapted physical education and recreation, ed 6, St. Louis, 1989, Mosby; p. 190 Sarah Rich.

INDEX

Note: Page references in *italics* refer to illustrations; page references followed by *t* refer to tables. The names of World Wide Web sites, when they stand alone, are italicized.